SQL Server 2005
Reporting Services in A

Margaret Co Ralph

NOV-2007

93879

Report Builder

Vista-64bit - Spiron - 1520

SQL Server 2005 Reporting Services in Action

Revised Edition of
Microsoft Reporting Services in Action

BRET UPDEGRAFF

MANNING

Greenwich
(74° w. long.)

For online information and ordering of this and other Manning books, please go to www.manning.com. The publisher offers discounts on this book when ordered in quantity. For more information, please contact:

Specail Sales Department
Manning Publications Co.
Cherokee Station
PO Box 20386
New York, NY 10021

Fax: (609) 877-8256
email: orders@manning.com

Manning Publications Co.
Cherokee Station
PO Box 20386
New York, NY 10021

Copyeditor: Liz Welch
Typesetter: Denis Dalinnik
Cover designer: Leslie Haimes

ISBN 1-932394-76-1

Printed in the United States of America
1 2 3 4 5 6 7 8 9 10 – VHG – 10 09 08 07 06

To Daniel, for your inspiration

brief contents

contents

Part 2 Managing reports 257

foreword

In my foreword to the first edition, I wrote about the process of creating software at Microsoft, specifically the first version of SQL Server Reporting Services. Although the organic style of software development we used for the initial release of the product had proven to be a success, creating the follow-on version would have its own set of challenges.

After launching the product in early 2004, we turned to planning for the new release, which was synchronized with the rest of SQL Server. The release was on track for a delivery in 2005, which meant we had comparatively little time for development of new features. In addition, joining the SQL Server mainline product required the team to adopt new versions of Visual Studio and the .NET Framework, and we had to merge our setup with a new, integrated setup engine. To accommodate this accelerated schedule, our original plan was to provide a small set of incremental improvements over the original version. The broad adoption of the product had already given us a good amount of feedback about what customers felt was missing from the initial release. From an architectural standpoint, we wouldn't change the core of Reporting Services, allowing us to safely add selected features.

At the same time, we also realized that something major was missing from the first version of the product. While developers and IT professionals liked the fact that Report Designer integrated fully into Visual Studio, the most frequent question we received was, "How can nondevelopers build their own reports?" We knew we had to address this need with a tool that was easy to use and that didn't require users to understand a database query language. Fortunately, we didn't have to start from scratch and were able to acquire a small company called ActiveViews to provide the core technology. The result of this acquisition was Report Builder (discussed in chapter 7). As we had in our adoption of the .NET Framework in the first release, we took a gamble again in adoption of the new ClickOnce technology for Report Builder.

The last piece of the puzzle was to continue our investment in a rich platform for reporting. Many customers told us that they wanted to easily embed reporting functionality into their applications. So we separated the report viewing components from the Report Server and provided a rich set of report controls in the release of Visual Studio 2005. These are covered in depth in chapter 11. We actually rebuilt both the

Report Manager web application and the Report Designer to leverage the new controls. The end user of these tools will see little difference in the new release, but building them with the new controls helped us validate their functionality and usability.

Even more than with the first release, books such as Bret Updegraff's *SQL Server 2005 Reporting Services in Action* are critical for helping you get the most out of Reporting Services. As the capabilities of the product have increased, the information and guidance that this book provides will help you leverage the Reporting Services platform to the fullest in your own environment. There are many parts of the product that we weren't fully able to expose or document, and this book will help you unlock some of these hidden gems.

BRIAN WELCKER
Group Program Manager
Microsoft SQL Server Reporting Services

foreword to the first edition

May I let you in on a little secret: creating software at Microsoft is pretty similar to creating software at any other company. I think many people's perception is that Microsoft designs products by having an army of market researchers carefully examine competitive products and survey consumers to determine exactly what features to include in the next release.

The reality is that most of the ideas that go into Microsoft products are the result of small teams of people brainstorming in front of whiteboards or chatting in hallways. I'm not saying we don't know what competitors are doing or what customers are asking for, but the process of translating real-world scenarios to requirements and designs is much more organic than you might think. This flexible approach allows teams to take a fresh look at existing problems, as well as adapt to industry trends and customer demands.

Case in point: when we started building Reporting Services, we didn't set out to copy what other companies had already done. Instead, we asked questions like "What does it mean to build an enterprise reporting product?" "How do we enable people to create powerful data visualizations without writing code?" and, most important of all, "How can we build a platform that people can leverage in their own applications?" The answer to this final question ended up driving a major portion of the product's design.

Building a platform is not something to be taken lightly. It requires that you spend extra time factoring and documenting the interfaces between software components. It means that your components should not use any "back doors" that are not available to other developers using the platform. It also can change the order in which you build the product—you have to focus on the nonvisual parts of the product *before* you work on the user-facing ones. For example, the Reporting Services report processing engine was up and running about a year before the graphical report design tool was ready. During this time, report definition files had to be hand-coded in order to test any new report processing features.

The decision to build a platform also means that you will have to spend time on infrastructure and interfaces at the expense of end-user features. We knew that this trade-off would mean the first version of Reporting Services might look less feature-rich than other more "mature" reporting products. We believed this was the right long-term strategy, as a strong platform would enable others to fill the gaps instead of having to wait for us to add every feature. When asked about this approach, I sometimes pose the question, "Is it better to build a car with a powerful engine and fewer lights on the dashboard, or one with lots of lights that can't go anywhere?"

One decision we made for our new platform was to bet on another new platform: .NET. As we had no legacy code to support, we decided early on to make Reporting Services a 100 percent .NET application. While this may seem like a no-brainer today, when we started building Reporting Services the CLR and the .NET Framework had not yet been released. Although building an enterprise-quality server product on such a new technology stack was a little risky at the time, the decision has paid major dividends in developer productivity and product quality.

Ultimately, the barometer of whether we have succeeded is what our customers and partners are able to build on the platform. Since we released the first version of the product earlier this year, I have seen applications built by customers leveraging the Reporting Services platform in ways I never imagined. But a platform isn't useful if *all* developers don't have the know-how to take advantage of it. Because the product is so new, detailed information and good examples have been sparse and hard to find.

That's where resources like Teo's excellent book come in. This book starts by providing a solid foundation for using the built-in tools included with Reporting Services, but quickly takes you to the next level by focusing on the programmability and extensibility aspects of the product. The focus on these parts of Reporting Services will help you leverage and extend the product feature set in your own applications. Teo's approach is to provide real-world examples and useful scenarios that walk you through the details and give you new ideas to explore. Teo has the ability to take complex topics and break them into smaller sections that can be easily understood. I enjoyed being one of the book's technical reviewers as I was able to see how various parts of the product came to life on the page. I encourage you to use the ideas in this book and take Reporting Services to the next level.

BRIAN WELCKER
Group Program Manager
Microsoft SQL Server Reporting Services

preface

Never say never!

About five years ago, I had the unfortunate task of modifying existing reports for an e-commerce application. I use the word *unfortunate* because I did not enjoy the work. My employer at the time was using a reporting application that required writing Visual Basic 6.0 code to create reports. The idea of programming reports in Visual Basic was strange to me. I felt I could have simply created web pages to generate the reports with less effort. After several weeks of working with this application, I vowed that I would *never* work with a reporting application again.

For a few years, I managed to successfully avoid any sort of report writing. Then, about two years ago as I was preparing for one of my exams for my MSDBA certification, an executive at Crowe Chizek, my current employer, came up to me and said something along the lines of, "Since you are working on your SQL exam, why don't you also spend some time looking into product called Reporting Services?" I admit that I was hesitant to spend any time with this product. But what I found over time was not what I expected: I *really* enjoyed working with Reporting Services—so much, in fact, that over the next year I made presentations to numerous user groups in three states touting my newfound knowledge of Reporting Services. This excitement brought me to TechEd 2005 in Florida, where I met Bill Baker (Microsoft) and his SQL Server Business Intelligence team. I was motivated by what I learned about SQL Server 2005 and the Business Intelligence tools, such as Reporting Services, Integration Services, and Analysis Services.

After returning from TechEd, I helped start a successful SQL Server user group that meets monthly in Indianapolis. I spent the last 12 months at Crowe Chizek working on applications built around Reporting Services. And now, I have coauthored on this second edition of a book on Reporting Services, a reporting application!

Never say never!

BRET UPDEGRAFF

preface to the first edition

In archeology, the Rosetta stone was the key that solved the mysteries of Egyptian hieroglyphics. I believe that with the release of Microsoft SQL Server 2000 Reporting Services, code-named Rosetta, Microsoft gives organizations the key they need to unlock the secrets of enterprise data and unleash the power hidden within.

Looking retrospectively, Microsoft's reporting strategy has been confusing, at least for me. Microsoft Access debuted in the early '90s with a powerful report designer that made desktop reporting child's play.

Enterprise developers, however, have not been that lucky. The lack of comprehensive native reporting capabilities continues even today in the .NET Framework. True, some progress has been made with the advent of print-related controls, such as PrintDocument, PrintPreviewControl, and so on, but still, dealing with the GDI+ (Graphics Device Interface) API is usually the last thing a developer wants to tackle when creating the next line-of-business application. For reasons such as these, report-enabling Microsoft-centric solutions has been traditionally regarded as a tedious chore.

To address this problem, many of us defected to third-party tools. Others chose to fill the void with homegrown, customized solutions. While these solutions address particular needs, they can also be costly, time-consuming, and difficult to implement.

I remember with nostalgia a project that I worked on about five years ago. It called for developing a reporting solution for a major Fortune 100 company. I implemented the solution as a server-based framework, following a design pattern similar to the one discussed in chapter 13. I used Microsoft Access as a reporting tool to generate reports and save them as snapshot files. Once the report was ready, the Report Server would e-mail it back to the user or send the user a link to the snapshot file.

Implementing this solution was a lot of fun, but it took a significant development effort. I wouldn't have had to go through all this if I had had Reporting Services back then. Instead of implementing a homegrown solution, I could have used RS to report-enable the applications.

For this reason, I was very excited when I heard about Reporting Services in late 2003. Finally, there was an easy way to report-enable different types of applications. Subsequently, I was involved in a project where I was able to confirm to myself that, indeed, RS was the reporting platform I had been dreaming about for years.

To share my enthusiasm I decided to write a book about Reporting Services. While I contemplated what the book's scope would be, it dawned on me that I could bring the most value by following my heart and approaching Reporting Services from a developer's point of view. I put myself in a position that many developers could relate to. Here I am, a developer, consultant, and architect, who is tasked with adding reporting features to a given application. How would I go about this?

To answer this question, my book takes a solution-oriented approach, and more than half of it is devoted to integrating different types of applications with RS. As you read this book, you will discover a common pattern. It starts by discussing the requirements and design goals of a given reporting scenario. Then it discusses the implementation choices, and finally it explains how the solution is implemented.

I firmly believe that a technical book should go beyond rehashing the product documentation. I tried my best to follow this path and take up where the RS documentation (which, by the way, is excellent) leaves off. For this reason, my book should be used in conjunction with it. When you read the book, you will notice that sometimes, when I believe I can't explain things any better, I refer you to the product documentation.

Microsoft Reporting Services in Action is written for report authors, administrators, and developers who need a detailed and practical guide to the functionality provided by RS. In the first half, report authors will master the skills they need to create versatile reports. Administrators will learn the ropes of managing and securing the report environment.

The second half of the book is primarily aimed at intermediate-to-advanced .NET developers who are planning to leverage RS to add reporting capabilities to their Windows Forms or web-based applications. However, because of the service-oriented architecture of Reporting Services, the book will also benefit developers who target other platforms but want to integrate their applications with RS.

Microsoft SQL Server 2000 Reporting Services is a great piece of technology. With RS, report authors can create reports as easily as they would in Microsoft Access. Make no mistake, though. RS is a sophisticated server-based platform, and its feature set goes well beyond that of a desktop reporting tool. To use RS effectively, you need to have a solid grasp of how it works and how it can be integrated with different types of client applications. I hope this book makes it easier.

TEO LACHEV

acknowledgments

Writing the second edition of this book has been exciting and yet challenging for me. Many people have helped me meet those challenges.

Most important, I want to thank my wife Jane for sticking with me through the numerous evenings, late nights, and weekends that it took to finish the book. *SQL Server 2005 Reporting Services in Action* could not have been written without her tremendous support. Jane, I love you for what you endured for me.

The Manning team has been amazing throughout the process of writing, editing, and publishing this book. Thanks to publisher Marjan Bace and editor Michael Stephens for finding me and believing in me. Your support has been instrumental. I want to thank my development editor, Lianna Wlasiuk, for her help in converting my disorganized thoughts into organized writing. Lianna, I appreciate your above-and-beyond dedication to this book. As project editor, Mary Piergies has been outstanding in orchestrating the production process. My copyeditor, Liz Welch, did a great job of polishing my manuscript. Special thanks to my technical editor, Monte Holyfield, for verifying that the book is technically correct. Thanks also to Karen Tegtmeyer for managing the review process; the book's publicists, Helen Trimes and Ron Tomich, for getting the word out; and Denis Dalinnik for his deft typesetting and page layout. I am grateful to the rest of the Manning team for their many contributions to this book.

Brian Welcker, Microsoft Group Product Manager for SQL Server Reporting Services, has been phenomenal in helping me with my project on several fronts, including reviewing the book and providing valuable technical feedback, as well as writing the foreword.

I am grateful to the many reviewers of this book. Your comments and reviews helped to shape and tweak the final manuscript. Thanks to Dave Corun, Steve Wright, Aleksey Nudelman, Robbe Morris, Berndt Hamboeck, Andrew Grothe, Nuo Yan, Richard Xin, Dan Hounshell, Vipul Patel, Vinita Paunikar, Arul Kumaravel, and Sergey Koshcheyev.

I would like to thank my parents for always believing in me—and the rest of my family and friends for encouraging and supporting me through the writing of this book.

I would also like to thank my coworkers at Crowe Chizek and Company LLC. I am grateful to Tim Landgrave for introducing me to Manning. Thanks to Paul Thomas,

Mindy Herman, Mark Strawmyer, Caleb Decker, and Derek Bang for creating a fun yet professional environment that has challenged me to be the best person I can be. I am honored to work with such a group of talented and dedicated individuals.

A few others contributed indirectly to the book. Thanks to Steven Gould for his Open Source OpenForecast package that we used in chapter 6 for the report-forecasting example. Thanks to Dino Esposito for his CodeDom sample. Kudos to Peter Bromberg for the ASP.NET menu control, and to Christian Weyer for the dynamic Web services invocation sample.

Finally, thank *you* for purchasing this book! I sincerely hope that you will find it as enjoyable to read as it has been for me to write.

Thanks and happy reporting!

about this book

Following the report lifecycle's logical path, this book explains how you can *author*, *manage*, and *deliver* RS-based reports.

Part 1, "Authoring reports," teaches you the skills that you will need as a report author to create Reporting Services–based reports. Part 1 encompasses chapters 1–7.

Chapter 1 provides a panoramic overview of Reporting Services. The chapter is intended to provide you with a firm grounding in what Reporting Services really is. We look at how RS addresses the reporting problem area, its feature set, and its architecture. To round out the chapter, we jump right in and create our first report. The chapter concludes with discussing RS's strengths and weaknesses.

Chapter 2 focuses on discussing various options for authoring reports. We start by explaining the report-authoring process. We continue by looking at how you can author reports with Visual Studio .NET by using the Report Wizard and the Report Designer, and by importing from Microsoft Access. We also discuss how developers can leverage the open nature of the report definition schema by creating reports programmatically.

Chapter 3 gets to the gist of the report-authoring process by teaching you how to work with report data. It discusses the RS data architecture and shows you how to work with data sources, datasets, and report queries. It emphasizes the role of parameters and walks you through the steps for creating parameterized reports.

Chapter 4 teaches you the practical skills needed for authoring different types of reports with the Report Designer. We create various report samples to complement our discussion, including tabular, freeform, chart, crosstab, subreports, and multicolumn reports.

Chapter 5 shows you how to use expressions and functions to extend your reports programmatically. It starts by emphasizing the role of expressions and how they can be used to manipulate the report item properties. It continues by giving you an in-depth understanding of the RS object model and its collections. Next, we look at the Reporting Services internal functions and how they can be leveraged to add interactive features to our reports, such as reports with navigational features and document maps, as well as localized reports.

Chapter 6 explains how you can supercharge the capabilities of your reports by using embedded Visual Basic .NET code and external code in the form of .NET assemblies.

It presents an end-to-end example that demonstrates how you can leverage custom .NET code to add forecasting features to your reports.

Chapter 7 shows how to enable ad hoc reporting by using the new Report Builder application. This chapter covers how to create report models using Visual Studio as well as how to configure these models. We cover the security around report models and Report Builder. We conclude this chapter by creating both simple and complex ad hoc reports with the Report Builder application.

Part 2, "Managing reports," explains how report administrators can manage and secure the report repository. It includes chapters 8–9.

Chapter 8 discuses different ways of managing the report catalog. It starts by explaining how report administrators can use the Report Manager to perform various management activities. Then it presents other management options, including using the RS Web service, WMI provider, RS script host, SQL Server Management Studio, and other utilities.

Chapter 9 teaches you how to secure the report catalog. It explores the RS role-based security model and the ways it can be leveraged to enforce restricted access to the Report Server.

Part 3, "Delivering reports," discusses how developers can integrate RS with different application scenarios. This part includes chapters 10–12.

Chapter 10 provides an overview of the two application integration options available with RS, URL, and Web services, and how they compare with one another. This chapter teaches you the skills necessary to report-enable WinForm-based applications as well as web-based applications. The chapter walks you through an end-to-end sample, the Report Wizard, that demonstrates various practical techniques you can use to integrate a WinForm application with RS. This chapter also covers various techniques for generating reports on both the client and server sides of a web application. Here we create an enhanced version of the Report Viewer sample control that facilitates server-side web reporting.

Chapter 11 features the ReportViewer controls that are new with Visual Studio 2005. You learn how to use, configure, and program against the different modes of these controls for both Windows and web applications. We show you how to use these controls to help create custom validation for the parameters of your RS reports. We also look into the steps required to deploy these controls into your applications.

Chapter 12 demonstrates how you can distribute reports via subscriptions. It starts by explaining how the RS subscribed-delivery process works. Then, it looks at how you can distribute reports via e-mail and file-share delivery extensions.

Part 4, "Advanced reporting," provides you with advanced techniques so you can make the most out of Reporting Services. It consists of chapters 13–14.

Chapter 13 discusses the implementation details of three custom extensions that can be used to extend the features of RS. It starts by implementing a custom dataset extension to report off ADO.NET datasets. Then, we discuss a custom delivery extension that can be used to distribute reports to an arbitrary Web service. Next, we author a custom security extension. Finally, we show you how to plug in custom HTTP modules to implement preprocessing tasks before the request reaches the Report Server.

Chapter 14 shows you how to conduct a capacity-planning study to evaluate RS in terms of performance and scalability. You learn how to establish performance goals, how to create test scripts with the Application Center Test, and how to stress-test your Report Server installation. You can apply the skills you harvest in this chapter for stress testing not only the Report Server, but any web-based application.

CODE CONVENTIONS

All source code in listings or in text is in a `fixed-width font like this` to separate it from ordinary text. We make use of many languages and markups in this book—C#, Visual Basic .NET, JavaScript, HTML, CSS, XML, and Java—but we try to adopt a consistent approach. Method and function names, object properties, XML elements, and attributes in text are presented using this same font.

In many cases, the original source code has been reformatted: we've added line breaks and reworked indentation to accommodate the available page space in the book. In rare cases even this was not enough, and listings include line-continuation markers. Additionally, many comments have been removed from the listings.

Code annotations accompany many of the listings, highlighting important concepts. In some cases, numbered bullets link to explanations that follow the listing.

AUTHOR ONLINE

Your purchase of *SQL Server 2005 Reporting Services in Action* includes free access to a private web forum run by Manning Publications, where you can make comments about the book, ask technical questions, and receive help from the author and from other users. To access the forum and subscribe to it, point your web browser to `www.manning.com/updegraff`. This page provides information on how to get onto the forum once you are registered, what kind of help is available, and the rules of conduct on the forum.

Manning's commitment to our readers is to provide a venue where a meaningful dialogue among individual readers and between readers and the author can take place. It is not a commitment to any specific amount of participation on the part of the author, whose contribution to the AO remains voluntary (and unpaid). We suggest you try asking the author some challenging questions, lest his interest stray! The Author Online forum and the archives of previous discussions will be accessible from the publisher's website as long as the book is in print.

about the source code

The book's source code can be downloaded from Manning's website at `www.manning.com/updegraff`.

Instead of partitioning the source code on a per-chapter basis, we decided to consolidate most of it in two applications: a WinForm-based AWReporterWin application and a web-based AWReporterWeb application. This approach has several advantages:

- It simplifies the setup—for example, you need only one virtual folder to host the AWReporterWeb web application.
- It allows the reader to launch the samples conveniently from a single application menu.
- It simulates real-world applications—for example, you can encapsulate the code logic in a set of common classes.

SOFTWARE REQUIREMENTS

Table 1 outlines the software requirements needed to run all code samples.

Table 1 Software requirements

Software	Reason	Used in chapters...
Reporting Services 2.0 (Developer or Enterprise edition)	The Standard edition doesn't include custom security extensions and data-driven subscriptions.	All
Microsoft Visual Studio 2005	Required by Reporting Services 2005 for development.	All
Microsoft SQL Server 2005	Required by Reporting Services. You will need to install the AdventureWorks database from the SQL Server media.	All
Microsoft WebService Behavior	For invoking Web services on the client side of a web application. Can be downloaded for free from MSDN.	10
Application Center Test	ACT is included with Visual Studio.	14

continued on next page

Table 1 Software requirements *(continued)*

Software	Reason	Used in chapters...
Analog Web Analyzer	For analyzing IIS logs. Can be downloaded for free from www.analog.cx/.	14
Report Magic	For reporting off analog files. Can be downloaded for free from www.reportmagic.org/.	14

SETTING UP THE SOURCE CODE

Once you download the source code archive, you can extract the zip file to any folder of your hard drive. Once this is accomplished, the folders listed in table 2 will be created.

Table 2 Source code folders

Folder	Purpose	Used in chapters...
AWReporterWeb	An ASP.NET web-based application that demonstrates various web-based reporting techniques. You will need to set up an IIS virtual folder pointing to this folder.	10, 11, 13
AWReporterWin	A WinForm-based application that demonstrates how you can add reporting features to WinForm applications.	2, 8, 10, 11
AWModel	A simple project used for creating Report Models against the AdventureWorks sample database.	7
AWRsLibrary	For report forecasting.	6
Database	A database projects that includes SQL scripts to create stored procedures and views in the AdventureWorks database.	As dictated by the code sample setup instructions
Extensions	Includes the custom data, delivery, and security extensions.	13
OpenForecast	The OpenForecast package, converted to J#.	6
Performance Testing	Includes the test scripts for performance-testing RS.	14
Reports	Includes the sample reports that we author in this book.	All

Most of the code samples include README files with specific step-by-step instructions that you follow to set up the code sample.

Running the sample reports in Visual Studio .NET

Most of you will be eager to run the sample reports immediately. To execute the reports successfully under the Visual Studio .NET Report Designer, follow these steps:

Step 1 Copy `AWC.RS.Library.dll` and `OpenForecast.dll` to the Report Designer binary folder, `C:\Program Files\Microsoft Visual Studio 8\Common7\IDE\PrivateAssemblies`.

Step 2 Open `AWReporter.rptproj` (found under the Reports folder) in Visual Studio .NET 2003.

Step 3 Change the data source credentials of the AW Shared DS data source by double-clicking the `AW Shared DS.rds` file and switching to the Credentials tab. Enter the username and password of a database login that has at least Read permissions to the tables in the AdventureWorks database.

At this point, you should be able to run most of the reports.

Some reports require a more involved setup process. For example, some reports require that additional assemblies, such as `AWC.RS.Extensions.dll` and `AWC.RS.Library.dll`, be configured properly. The README files that accompany the sample code include specific step-by-step instructions on how to configure these assemblies.

Deploying the reports to the Report Server

To run most of the code samples successfully, you need to deploy the sample reports to the Report Server. Assuming that you have Administrator rights to the report catalog, the easiest way to do this is to follow these steps:

Step 1 Copy `AWC.RS.Library.dll` and `OpenForecast.dll` to the Report Server binary folder, `C:\Program Files\Microsoft SQL Server\MSSQL.3\Reporting Services\ReportServer\bin`. This step is needed because some reports reference these assemblies, and the deployment process will fail if these assemblies are not found in the Report Server binary folder.

Step 2 If you haven't done this already, copy `AWC.RS.Library.dll` and `OpenForecast.dll` to the Report Designer binary folder, `C:\Program Files\Microsoft Visual Studio 8\Common7\IDE\PrivateAssemblies`.

Step 3 Open the `AWReporter.rptproj` project (found under the Reports folder) in Visual Studio .NET 2003.

Step 4 Right-click the AWReporter project in the Visual Studio .NET Solution Explorer and choose Properties to open the project's properties.

Step 5 Verify that TargetFolder is set to AWReporter and that TargetServerURL is set to http://<*servername*>/ReportServer, in which <*servername*> is the computer name where the Report Server is installed. If RS is installed locally, the TargetServerURL setting should be http://localhost/ReportServer.

If you installed RS as a named instance the path will be http://*<servername>*/ReportServer$*<instance name>*, where *<instance name>* is the name you provided during installation.

Step 6 Click the Configuration Manager button and verify that both the Build and Deploy check boxes are selected for Debug configuration. Click OK to dismiss the Property Pages dialog box.

Step 7 Right-click the AWReporter project again and choose Deploy. This will build the reports and then deploy them to the report catalog.

Step 8 To verify the setup, open the Report Manager web portal. If RS is installed locally, the default Report Manager URL will be http://localhost/reports (http://localhost/reports$*<instance name>* for nondefault instance installations). Under the Home folder, verify that the AWReporter folder exists. Click its link and run the Sales By Territory report. If everything is OK, the report will render in the browser.

Configuring the AWReporterWeb application

To configure the web-based samples, you need to set up the AWReporterWeb virtual folder by following these steps:

Step 1 Right-click the AWReporterWeb folder in Windows Explorer and choose Properties.

Step 2 Select the Web Sharing tab.

Step 3 Click the Share This Folder radio button.

Step 4 In the Edit Alias dialog box, enter **AWReporterWeb** as an alias.

Step 5 Make sure that the Read Access Permission check box and the Scripts radio button are selected. Click OK to close the Edit Alias dialog box.

Step 6 Open the Internet Information Manager (IIS) console. Right-click the AWReporterWeb folder, choose Properties, and then select the Directory Security tab. Click the Edit button in the Authentication and Access Control panel. Deselect the Enable Anonymous Access check box. Make sure that the Integrated Windows Authentication check box is selected, and click OK.

What's new with SQL Reporting Services 2005?

Reporting Services 2000 was a great product and provided a complete platform for authoring, managing, and distributing reports. However, because it was a first release of the product, it came with common side effects, such as limitations in features that many developers expected to see. The Microsoft RS team did a superb job of listening to the developer audience who used RS 2000, and we saw some exciting additions and enhancements with the RS 2005 release. Table 3 shows some of these additions and enhancements.

Table 3 New features in SQL RS 2005

Feature	Purpose
Direct client printing	Allows you to send a report directly to a printer without having to export to printable format first.
End-user sort	You can provide the ability for an end user to re-sort the data within the report.
Multivalued parameters	Allows you to use multiple values for parameters.
Custom Report Items	Enables ISVs to extend report processing by building custom server controls and embedding them into reports.
Report Designer improvements	There are many improvements to the Designer. We discuss these further in chapter 3.
Analysis Services Query Builder	Lets you easily build complex multidimensional queries using a slick UI.
Web Parts for SharePoint	Lets you easily integrate reports into your SharePoint Portal Server 2003 or Windows SharePoint Services environment.
Report Viewer controls for window forms or ASP.NET	Allows for better integration for .NET web and Windows development.
Report Builder	Allows end users to create ad hoc reports in an easy-to-use Microsoft Office-like environment tool.

about the authors

An experienced software designer and developer, **Bret Updegraff** works as a manager with the Mid Market Microsoft practice of Crowe Chizek and Company LLC. Bret was honored with the MVP status from Microsoft in the category of Windows Server System—SQL Server. He is also a Microsoft Certified Solution Developer, a Microsoft Certified Application Developer, and a Microsoft Certified Database Administrator. Bret, who lives in Fishers, Indiana, is president of the Indianapolis Professional Association of SQL Server (PASS) users group. You can contact him through Manning's Author Online forum or by sending him e-mail at `bretupdegraff@yahoo.com`.

Teo Lachev, the author of the first edition, has many years of experience designing and developing Microsoft-centered solutions. He works as a technology consultant for the Enterprise Application Services practice of Hewlett-Packard. Teo is a Microsoft Certified Solution Developer and Microsoft Certified Trainer. He lives in Atlanta, Georgia.

about the cover illustration

The illustration on the cover of *SQL Server 2005 Reporting Services in Action* is taken from a French travel book, *Encyclopedie des Voyages* by J. G. St. Saveur, published in 1796. Travel for pleasure was a relatively new phenomenon at the time and travel guides such as this one were popular, introducing both the tourist as well as the armchair traveler to the inhabitants of other regions of France and abroad.

The diversity of the drawings in the *Encyclopedie des Voyages* speaks vividly of the uniqueness and individuality of the world's towns and provinces just 200 years ago. This was a time when the dress codes of two regions separated by a few dozen miles identified people uniquely as belonging to one or the other. The travel guide brings to life a sense of isolation and distance of that period and of every other historic period except our own hyperkinetic present.

Dress codes have changed since then and the diversity by region, so rich at the time, has faded away. It is now often hard to tell the inhabitant of one continent from another. Perhaps, trying to view it optimistically, we have traded a cultural and visual diversity for a more varied personal life. Or a more varied and interesting intellectual and technical life.

We at Manning celebrate the inventiveness, the initiative, and the fun of the computer business with book covers based on the rich diversity of regional life two centuries ago brought back to life by the pictures from this travel guide.

CHAPTER 1

Introducing SQL Server 2005 Reporting Services

"So much information, so little time..." the character Poison Ivy would likely say if the Batman saga were taking place in today's enterprise.

Organizations tend to spend much of their IT budgets on streamlining internal processes to gain a competitive advantage. Various data is pulled into Microsoft Excel and passed around departments; mainframe data is exported and loaded into flat files, Excel spreadsheets, and Microsoft Access databases. If users don't have the data they need, they typically have to issue a request for this data to be made available in a new report. In many organizations, these requests consume significant IT and development resources. Too often, Excel spreadsheets are the prevalent reporting tools today, and inaccurate data, and thus wrong decisions, often result from manual data entry, or "pencil pushing." According to Microsoft, today's information workers spend as much as 80 percent of their time gathering information, with only 20 percent left to analyze it and make a decision. Aware of these issues, Microsoft initiated the Microsoft SQL Server 2000 Reporting Services project at the beginning of the new millennium, with a bold vision to "enable employees at all levels of an organization to realize the promise of Business Intelligence to promote better decision making." Now in its second release, Reporting Services 2005 offers you an even more robust feature set.

This chapter provides a panoramic view of Reporting Services (RS). Throughout the rest of this book we use the terms *Reporting Services* and *RS* interchangeably. You will learn:

- Why RS is such a compelling choice for enterprise reporting
- The main parts of the RS architecture
- The report-generation process and report lifecycle
- The steps for creating your first RS report

1.1 WHAT IS REPORTING SERVICES?

Microsoft SQL Reporting Services is a full-featured, server-based, end-to-end reporting application that includes services, tools, and APIs to create, publish, and manage reporting solutions. SQL Reporting Services was originally slated for an initial release with SQL Server 2005. Thanks to the convergence of customer demand and product readiness, RS was introduced as an add-on to SQL Server 2000 at the beginning of 2004. This revised edition book covers the SQL Server 2005 release of Reporting Services, and compares, when relevant, the changes from the SQL Server 2000 release.

Let's consider a typical scenario that Reporting Services can address effectively. Let's say that an organization has built a web portal for submitting orders online. As the business grows, the same organization may need to implement a reporting infrastructure to analyze sales data and understand its business; for example, to identify the top-selling products, customer demographics, and so forth. To accomplish this goal, the organization could leverage RS.

We use the term *report* to refer to the web-based or saved-to-file counterpart of a standard paper-oriented report. For example, an organization may want to give its customers an option to generate various reports online—an Order History report, for instance. Web reporting has traditionally been difficult to implement. Even more difficult has been exporting reports to different file formats. RS solves both problems elegantly by providing an out-of-the-box web-enabled reporting platform, and by providing the ability to manually or programmatically generate exports in the most popular export formats.

Let's get started. In this section we do the following:

- Take a look at the problems that Reporting Services helps us solve
- Learn about the different versions and editions of Reporting Services
- Find out where Reporting Services fits into the SQL Server platform

1.1.1 Solving reporting problems with Reporting Services

Ironically, despite the important role that reporting plays in today's enterprises, creating and distributing reports have traditionally been painstaking and laborious chores. To understand why we need RS, let's analyze the reporting problem space.

Table 1.1 lists some of the most pressing issues surrounding the reporting arena and how RS addresses them.

Table 1.1 How Microsoft RS deals with the reporting problem space

Reporting issue	How RS addresses it
Report authoring can be labor intensive.	By using the powerful Report Designer, you can author reports as easily as you can with Microsoft Access.
There is high demand for centralized report management.	RS enables you to save and manage your reports in a single report repository.
Reports need to be distributed to various destinations.	RS supports both on-demand and subscription-based reporting. Reports can be requested on-demand by WinForm and web-based applications. Alternatively, reports can be distributed to a list of subscribers.
Reports often need to be exported in different electronic formats.	RS supports many popular export formats out of the box. If the format you need is not available out of the box, you can create your own custom format extensions. Report authors have extensive control over the format of the report content.
The proprietary nature of reporting tools doesn't allow you to extend them.	RS has a flexible architecture that allows you to extend RS capabilities by writing custom code.
Reports need to be secured.	RS offers a comprehensive security model that administrators can leverage to enforce secured access to reports by assigning users to roles. When the default Windows-based authentication is not a good fit, it can be replaced with custom security implementations.
Enterprise reporting solutions can be costly.	To minimize cost, RS is bundled and licensed with SQL Server. If you have a licensed copy of SQL Server, you may run RS on the same server for no additional license fee.

Depending on your particular situation you may find other compelling reasons to target RS as your reporting platform of choice. We revisit these RS features throughout this chapter.

Multiple report type support

Your reporting requirements may call for authoring various types of reports that differ in complexity. For example, your users may request that a large report include a document map for easy navigation. RS lets you design a variety of report types, as listed in table 1.2.

Table 1.2 Various report types supported by RS

Report type	Purpose	Example
Tabular	Displays data in a table format with a fixed number of columns.	Excel-type reports
Freeform	Data regions are positioned arbitrarily on the page by the report author.	Invoice details reports
Chart	Presents data graphically.	Employee performance chart
Crosstab (matrix)	The Crosstab (matrix) allows data to be summarized by two or more facts. The columns and rows can be dynamically generated, and/or they can be static and defined by the report author.	A report that shows products in rows and time in columns to summarize sales by product and quarter
Drilldown	Includes expandable sections.	A company performance crosstab report where product can be expanded by category and brand
Drill-through	Link content from one report to another report or website. Clicking the hyperlink executes and displays the linked report.	Customer Order History with hyperlinks on the order identifier to show the order details report
Interactive	Includes interactive features, such as document maps, hyperlinks, visible-on-demand sections, and so forth.	Adobe Acrobat–type reports with document maps on the left side

Although most popular reporting tools support many of the report types shown in table 1.2, RS makes the report-authoring process very simple. For example, report authors can drag and drop items to define the report's appearance.

1.1.2 Choosing a Reporting Services edition

At a very high level, RS can be defined as a server-based platform for authoring, managing, and distributing reports. We discuss the RS architecture in more detail in a moment. For now, note that RS is integrated with and requires several other Microsoft products. Here are the installation requirements for both RS 2000 and RS 2005:

SQL Reporting Services 2000

- Windows 2000 or above as a server operating system
- Microsoft SQL Server 2000 (with Service Pack 3a) and above
- Internet Information Server (IIS) 5.0 or above
- .NET Framework 1.1
- Visual Studio .NET 2003 (any edition) for report authoring and testing

SQL Reporting Services 2005

- Microsoft Windows Installer 3.0
- Windows 2000 SP4 or above as a server operating system

- Microsoft SQL Server 2005 (included)
- Internet Information Server (IIS) 5.0 or above
- .NET Framework 2.0 (included)
- Microsoft Data Access Components (MDAC) 2.8 for systems running Windows 2000

NOTE With RS 2005 you do not need to have a licensed version of Visual Studio installed. If you do not have Visual Studio, RS will install a shell version of Visual Studio 2005, called the Business Intelligence Development Studio (BIDS).

For more information about installing RS, refer to appendix A.

To address different user needs, RS is available in several editions, as you can see by looking at table 1.3. The release of SQL Server 2005 introduces two new editions, called Workgroup and Express. While these new editions offer limited features and functionality of RS, they allow for more flexibility and options across the RS product set.

Table 1.3 RS editions to meet various reporting needs

Edition	Choose when...
Express	You only need basic functionality on a single computer. Express only supports limited rendering formats. Also, you can only use a local and relational database with Express. Security roles are fixed with Express and you cannot use the Management Studio or Report Builder with this edition.
Workgroup	You only need basic functionality on a single computer. Workgroup only supports limited rendering formats. Also, you can only use a local and relational database with Workgroup.
Standard	You need to install RS on a single computer. The Standard edition doesn't support clustered deployment to load-balance multiple RS instances.
Enterprise	You need all RS features, including load balancing, data-driven subscriptions, and Report Builder infinite drill-through.
Developer	You have to integrate RS with client applications or extend its capabilities by writing .NET code. The Developer edition supports the same feature set as the Enterprise edition, but it is for use as a test and development system, not as a production server.
Evaluation	You need to evaluate RS. The Evaluation edition expires after 180 days. This trial edition supports all of the features of the Enterprise edition.

For more information about how the RS editions differ, refer to the product documentation or the "Reporting Services Features Comparison" section in the RS official website at `http://www.microsoft.com/hk/sql/reportingservices/productinfo/features.mspx` (RS 2000) or `www.microsoft.com/sql/2005/productinfo/rsfeatures.mspx` (RS 2005).

For information about RS licensing requirements, visit the Microsoft Reporting Services page at www.microsoft.com/sql/reporting/.

Now that we understand what RS is, let's see how it fits into the Microsoft Business Intelligence vision.

1.1.3 Reporting Services and the Microsoft SQL Server platform

With the release of SQL Server 2005, Microsoft added some feature-rich tools to SQL Server. Many of these new tools fit into the area of Business Intelligence (BI). With this focus, some new tools are available that enable developers to easily build and deploy applications that address the most common data management and analysis challenges facing many organizations every day, such as analysis of vast volumes of data, trend discovery, data management, and of course, comprehensive reporting. Given that, RS is positioned as an integral part of Microsoft's data management and analysis platform. Figure 1.1 shows the placement of RS in the Microsoft SQL Server platform offering.

Table 1.4 outlines the purpose of the major building blocks within the Microsoft SQL Server platform.

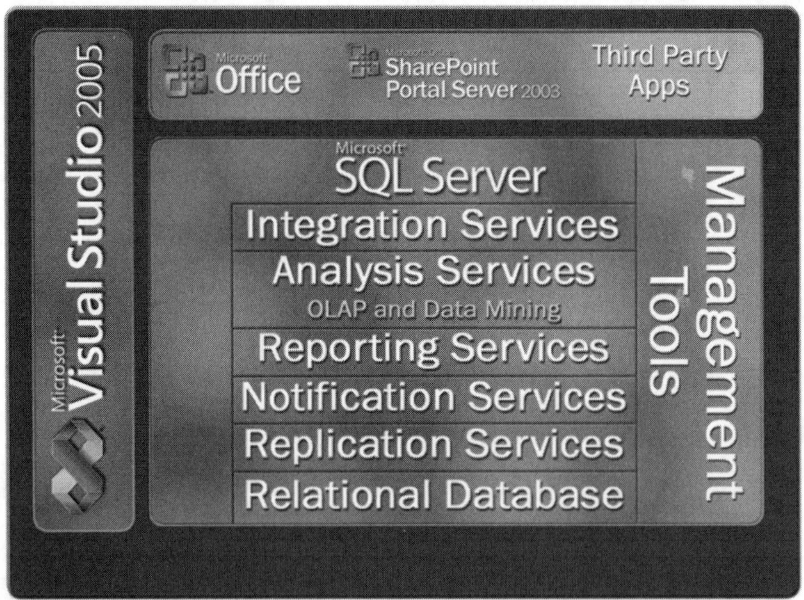

Figure 1.1 The Microsoft SQL Server platform consists of several products layered on top of the SQL Server database engine and addresses various data management and reporting needs.

Table 1.4 The key Microsoft SQL Server platform components

Component	Purpose
Microsoft SQL Server Relational Database Engine	A relational database to store data
Integration Services	Tools for extracting, transforming, and loading data
Analysis Services	An analytical processing (OLAP) and data mining engine
Reporting Services	A full-featured, server-based, end-to-end reporting application that includes services, tools, and APIs to create, publish, and manage reporting solutions
Notification Services	A development platform that lets you build "push" functionality of your applications quickly
Replication Services	Replicates data to heterogeneous data sources
Microsoft Office	Desktop applications for data analysis and reporting
SharePoint Portal Server	Business Intelligence collaboration
Visual Studio 2005	A development tool to create .NET-based applications, including analytical and reporting solutions
Management Tools	Windows and web-based tools for managing and configuring the various services of SQL Server

Most of you have probably used more than one of these products in the past to solve your data management and analysis needs. Some of these products are new with SQL 2005, while some of them have been around for quite some time. What has been missing is a product for authoring, managing, and generating reports that can easily be integrated with all types of applications. RS fills the bill nicely.

Having introduced you to RS, let's take a panoramic view of its features to understand why it can be such a compelling choice for enterprise reporting.

1.2 REPORTING SERVICES AT A GLANCE

Reporting Services offers a broad array of features that can address various reporting needs:

- *Information workers can leverage RS to author both standard ("canned") reports and reports with interactive features*—Here we use the term *standard* to refer to reports that display static data. An interesting aspect of RS is that your reports can include a variety of features that provide interactivity to users. For example, the end user can show or hide items in a report and click links that launch other reports or web pages.
- *Third-party vendors can target RS to package reports as a part of their applications*—With RS 2000 and RS 2005, if customers have RS installed, the vendor setup program can upload the report files to the Report Server. RS 2005 includes stand-alone controls for generating reports directly from report files,

and does not require RS to be installed. Microsoft is partnering with a number of independent software vendors (ISVs) to create add-ons to RS to extend its capabilities. For a full list of the Microsoft partners for RS, visit `www.microsoft.com/sql/reporting/partners/default.asp`.

- *Organizations can use RS to report-enable their business-to-business (B2B) or business-to-consumer (B2C) applications*—For example, an organization can selectively expose some of its data in the form of reports to its business partners.
- *Business workers can use Report Builder, which is bundled with RS 2005, to create ad hoc reports without having to understand the relational or multidimensional data structure that they are reporting against*—Report Builder provides a Microsoft Office–like report-authoring tool that allows end users to create their own reports in a very simple environment.

Let's now take a look at the RS landscape and observe some of RS's most prominent landmarks. Don't worry if you find you are not getting the Big Picture yet. In section 1.3, we take a closer look at the main pieces of the RS architecture.

1.2.1 Authoring features

As a report author, with RS you have several choices for creating reports. We discuss each of these options in detail in chapters 2 and 7. For now, we'd like to introduce you to the Report Designer and the Report Builder application. For advanced report authoring, the Report Designer will likely be your tool of choice. The Report Builder application is an Office-like application that is used to create on-the-fly reports.

Introducing the Report Designer

Using the Report Designer graphical environment, you can create reports of different types, such as drilldown crosstab reports, like the one shown in figure 1.2.

RS doesn't restrict your report-authoring options to static paper-oriented reports. Instead, you can make your reports more versatile and easy to use by adding interactive features, such as expandable sections, hyperlinks, and document maps. Given its tight integration with the Visual Studio integrated development environment (IDE), the Report Designer provides you with access to all report design features as well as team development features, such as source code management.

About the Report Definition Language

At this point, you may be wondering what an RS-based report file looks like and how it is stored. RS saves the report as an Extensible Markup Language (XML) file that is described using the Report Definition Language (RDL) schema.

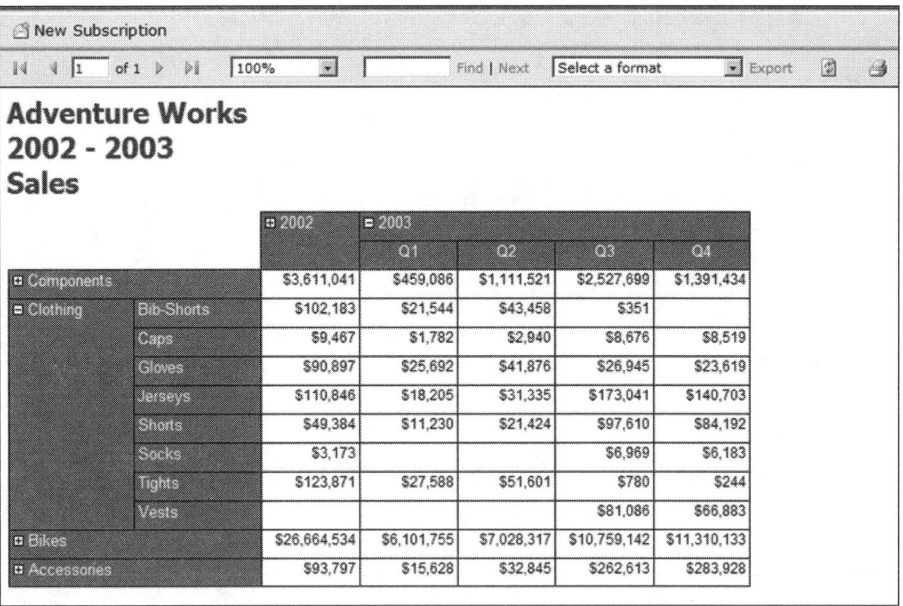

New Subscription

1 of 1 | 100% | Find | Next | Select a format | Export

Adventure Works 2002 - 2003 Sales

		2002	2003			
			Q1	Q2	Q3	Q4
Components		$3,611,041	$459,086	$1,111,521	$2,527,699	$1,391,434
Clothing	Bib-Shorts	$102,183	$21,544	$43,458	$351	
	Caps	$9,467	$1,782	$2,940	$8,676	$8,519
	Gloves	$90,897	$25,692	$41,876	$26,945	$23,619
	Jerseys	$110,846	$18,205	$31,335	$173,041	$140,703
	Shorts	$49,384	$11,230	$21,424	$97,610	$84,192
	Socks	$3,173			$6,969	$6,183
	Tights	$123,871	$27,588	$51,601	$780	$244
	Vests				$81,086	$66,883
Bikes		$26,664,534	$6,101,755	$7,028,317	$10,759,142	$11,310,133
Accessories		$93,797	$15,628	$32,845	$262,613	$283,928

Figure 1.2 With RS you can create various types of reports, including drilldown crosstab reports like this one.

DEFINITION A *report definition* contains report data retrieval and layout information. The report definition is described in an XML schema, called the Report Definition Language (RDL).

Saving reports as XML-based report definition files offers two main advantages:

- *It makes the report format open and extensible*—Using the XML-based RDL format is beneficial for achieving interoperability among applications and vendors. Microsoft is working with other industry leaders to promote RDL as an XML-based standard for report definitions. Visit the RS official website (check "Resources" at the end of this book) to see a list of Microsoft RS partners.
- *It makes the report portable*—For example, you can easily save the report to a file and upload it to another Report Server.

If you use the Report Designer to create your report, its definition will be automatically generated for you. However, just as you don't have to use Visual Studio to write .NET applications, you can write the report definition using an editor of your choice, such as Notepad, or generate it programmatically (as you will see in chapter 2). Of course, the Report Designer makes authoring reports a whole lot easier.

Introducing the Report Builder

The Report Builder is an application that runs on the client machine and provides a user interface for creating ad hoc (on-the-fly) reports. The application is similar in look and feel to the Office suite of products. It is meant to be an easy-to-use application for creating reports and will typically be used by power business users. As you learn in chapter 7, the Report Builder application enables drag-and-drop report building functionality for nondevelopers.

1.2.2 Management features

RS facilitates report management by storing reports and their related items in a central report catalog. To deploy and manage a report, you need to upload it to the report catalog. When this happens, it becomes a *managed* report.

DEFINITIONS Throughout the rest of this book we will use the terms *report catalog* and *report repository* interchangeably to refer to the RS Configuration Database. For more information about this database, refer to section 1.3.2.

A *managed report* is a report that is uploaded to the report catalog.

For .NET developers, the term *managed* here has nothing to do with .NET managed code, although the pattern is the same. While .NET managed code runs under the supervision of the .NET common language runtime (CLR), a managed report is generated under the control of the Report Server.

You may wonder what really happens when a report is uploaded to the report catalog. At publishing time, the Report Server parses the report definition (RDL), generates a .NET assembly, and stores the assembly in the Report Configuration Database for the report. The RDL file is never used again. When the report is processed, the assembly is loaded and executed by the Report Server.

A report can include other items, such as images and data source–related information. These report-related items are also stored in the report catalog. Finally, the report catalog captures additional information, called *metadata*, associated with reports. For example, just as you can organize physical files in folders, RS allows you to organize reports in folders.

DEFINITION The report *metadata* describes additional configuration information associated with a report, such as security permissions, the parent folder, and so forth.

RS offers centralized report management that administrators will appreciate. To simplify the administration of the report catalog, RS comes with a tool called the Report Manager. The Report Manager is implemented as a web-based application, and as such it is easily accessible. This tool empowers you to manage just about any aspect of the report repository, including:

- Report information and metadata, such as the folder structure and report properties
- Data sources from which the report will draw data

- Report parameters (for parameterized reports)
- Security

You learn more about the Report Manager in chapter 8.

1.2.3 Delivery features

Reports hosted under RS can be delivered using on-demand ("pulled") delivery or subscribed ("pushed") delivery. The more common scenario is on-demand delivery, where the user requests the report explicitly. As a report author, you don't have to do anything special to web-enable your report because RS does this for you once it is uploaded to the report catalog.

The "pushed" delivery option alone can justify implementing RS. This option provides end users with the ability to subscribe to reports, so reports will be sent to them when a certain event is triggered—when a timing event triggers, for instance, report subscriptions based on a schedule. As another example, a financial institution could allow its customers to opt in and subscribe to certain reports of interest, such as a monthly bank statement. Then, at the end of the month, the bank statement report could be generated and sent to users via e-mail.

We discuss the report-delivery process in more detail in section 1.5; on-demand delivery is the topic of chapter 10, and subscribed delivery is detailed in chapter 12.

1.2.4 Extensibility features

An important characteristic of every enterprise-oriented product, such as RS, is that it has to be easily extended. Simply put, extensibility relates to the system's ability to accommodate new features that are built out of old ones. One of the things I like most about RS is the extensibility features it includes by virtue of its open and flexible architecture. Developers can easily extend RS by writing .NET code in their preferred .NET language. Specifically, you can extend RS in the following areas:

- *Custom .NET code*—.NET developers can enhance reports programmatically by writing .NET custom code. Chapter 6 demonstrates how you can add forecasting features to your reports by using prepackaged code in the form of .NET assemblies.
- *Data processing extensions*—Out of the box, RS can connect natively to SQL Server, Oracle, or any data source that has an ODBC or OLE DB provider. RS 2005 adds Analysis Services databases, Integration Services projects, XML files, and XML Web services as sources of data. In addition, you can write your own custom data extensions to report off other data structures, as chapter 13 illustrates.
- *Delivery extensions*—Out of the box, subscribed reports can be delivered via e-mail or file share delivery extensions. Developers can write their own delivery extensions to deliver the report to other destinations, such as to web services, as you learn in chapter 13.

- *Security extensions*—By default, RS uses the Windows-based security model to enforce restricted access to the report catalog. If Windows-based security is not an option, you can replace it with custom security models. You see an example of how this may be done in chapter 13, where we implement custom authentication and authorization for Internet-oriented reporting.
- *Rendering extensions*—Generating reports in export formats other than the ones supported natively can be accomplished by writing custom rendering extensions. See section 1.4.2 for more information about the supported export formats.
- *Custom report items*—ISVs can embed custom server controls that provide additional functionality which RS can't provide out of the box. Some examples of custom report items are custom charts, gauges, and maps. These controls are added to the Report Designer Toolbox and have their own set of property pages and dialog boxes.

1.2.5 Scalability features

A *scalable* application responds well under increased loads. RS can scale up and out to address the high-volume reporting requirements of large organizations. It is designed from the ground up to process reports efficiently. For example, it supports several report-caching options, such as report execution caching, snapshots, and report sessions, as we discuss in chapter 8.

Reporting Services Enterprise Edition supports clustered deployment, which you can use to load-balance several RS servers on multiple machines. This allows enterprise organizations with high-scalability requirements to scale out RS and provides fault tolerance. RS performance is the subject of chapter 14.

1.2.6 Security features

RS is designed to provide a secured environment from the ground up. It offers a comprehensive security model for accessing reports that leverages Windows authentication. This model maps the user Windows account or group to a *role*, and the role describes what permissions the user has to access items in the report catalog. Report administrators can add Windows users to predefined roles or create new ones.

Once again, when the default Windows-based security model is not a good fit, you can replace it by plugging in your own custom authentication and authorization implementations in the form of custom security extensions. You learn how to do this in chapter 13.

To promote trustworthy computing, RS leverages the .NET code-based security to "sandbox" custom code based on configurable security policies. We discuss the RS security model in chapter 9.

1.2.7 Deployment features

Because it is server based, RS has zero deployment requirements for integrating with client applications. For this reason, any type of client applications can target RS, not only .NET-based applications. Because you can access RS through the two most popular web protocols, HTTP-GET and Simple Object Access Protocol (SOAP), any web-capable application can be integrated with RS, regardless of the targeted platform and development language. You see both of these protocols in action in chapter 10.

DEFINITIONS The Hypertext Transfer Protocol (HTTP), on which the Internet is based, comes in two flavors: HTTP-GET and HTTP-POST. While HTTP-GET passes request parameters as a part of the URL, HTTP-POST passes them as name/value pairs inside the actual message.

Simple Object Access Protocol (SOAP) is a lightweight XML-based protocol, layered on top of HTTP, for exchanging structured and type information on the Web. In recent years, SOAP has become the industry-standard protocol for communicating with web services.

Integrating your applications with RS requires a good grasp of its architecture. The next section outlines the major RS building blocks.

1.3 RS ARCHITECTURE

An important feature of the RS architecture is that it is *service* oriented as opposed to *object* oriented. Don Box, a prominent Microsoft architect working on the next-generation web services, outlines the following four characteristics of a service-oriented architecture:

- *Boundaries are explicit*—Cross-application communication uses explicit messaging rather than implicit method call invocation.
- *Services are autonomous*—The lifetime of a service-oriented application is not controlled by its clients.
- *Services share schema and contract, not class*—Service-oriented applications advertise their functionality to the outside world using XML-based schemas.
- *Service compatibility is determined based on policies*—By using policies, service-oriented applications indicate which conditions must be true in order for the service to function properly.

You may have used object-oriented reporting tools in the past in which the report consumer instantiates an object instance of the report provider. A characteristic of this model is that both the report consumer and the report provider instances share the same process space. For example, to render an Access report, you need to instantiate an object of type `Access.Application`. Then, you use OLE automation to instruct Access to open the report database and render the report.

You no doubt agree that as useful and widespread as the object-oriented model is, it is subject to some well-known shortcomings. For example, both the consumer and provider are usually installed on the same machine. Consequently, the reports hosted by the report provider are not easily accessible by geographically dispersed clients. For instance, only Component Object Model (COM)-capable clients can interface with Access.

A second shortcoming involves application interdependencies. Object-oriented applications are typically deployed as a unit. All Access clients, for example, need to have the Access type library installed locally to establish a reference to it.

To address these shortcomings, RS departs radically from the object-oriented paradigm. In terms of reporting, the RS service-oriented architecture offers two distinct advantages: (1) Administrators can centralize the report storage and management in one place, and (2) it promotes application interoperability—report consumers can request reports over standard web protocols, such as HTTP-GET and SOAP.

The RS service-oriented architecture can be better explained in the context of a three-tier application deployment view, as shown in figure 1.3.

The RS architecture includes the following main components:

- The Report Server engine, whose main task is to generate reports
- The Report Configuration Database (the report catalog), which serves as a centralized report repository
- The Report Manager, a web-based tool for managing the report catalog and requesting reports.

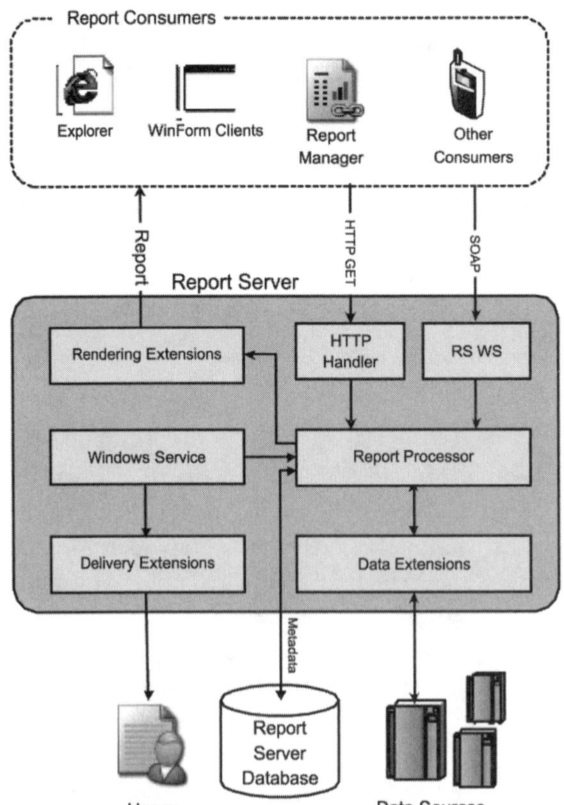

Figure 1.3
Report consumers submit report requests to the Report Server, which queries data sources to retrieve the report data and generate the report.

In the current release of RS we have two complementary tools that are not shown in figure 1.3, but we cover them in detail in chapter 8:

- Reporting Services Configuration Tool, a client configuration tool used to manage virtual directories, service accounts, databases, and e-mail settings
- SQL Server Management Studio, a Windows-based tool for managing SQL Server, including Reporting Services

Let's explain the role of the first three components in more detail, starting with the Report Server. The last two components are covered in detail in chapter 8.

1.3.1 The Report Server engine

At the heart of the RS architecture is the Report Server engine. The Report Server performs the following main tasks:

- Handles the report requests sent by the report consumers. We use the term *report consumer* to describe any client application that requests reports from the Report Server. Once again, this could be *any* application regardless of the language in which it was written or the platform it runs on.
- Performs all chores needed to process the report, including executing and rendering the report, as we discuss in detail shortly.
- Provides additional services, such as snapshots and report caching, authorization and security policy enforcement, session management, scheduling, and subscribed delivery. Do not confuse the Report Server engine with the Report Server database. This is easy to do since the Report Server repository database is named *ReportServer*.

DEFINITION We will use the term *report request* to refer to the set of input arguments that the report consumer has to pass to the Report Server to generate a report successfully. At minimum, the report request must specify the path to the report and the report name. Other arguments can be passed as report parameters, including rendering format, whether the report should include the standard toolbar, and so forth.

Looking at figure 1.3, you can see that the Report Server encompasses several components, including the Report Processor, Windows Service, and extensions. From an implementation standpoint, perhaps the best way to describe the Report Server is to say that it is implemented as a set of .NET assemblies located in the `C:\Program Files\Microsoft SQL Server\MSSQL.3\Reporting Services\ReportServer` folder.

As you know, the Report Server's main role is to generate reports. To accomplish this, the server retrieves the report definition from the report catalog, combines it with data from the data source, and generates the report.

Figure 1.3 and the product documentation indicate that the Report Processor component is responsible for report processing. The implementation details of the processor are not disclosed at the time of this writing, but most likely the majority of its functionality is encapsulated in the Microsoft.ReportingServices.Processing-Core.dll assembly. For the remainder of this book we use the terms *Report Processor* and *Report Server* interchangeably.

Section 1.4 explains the purpose of each of the Report Server components and shows how they relate to report processing.

From an integration standpoint, perhaps the most important observation that you need to draw from figure 1.3 is that the Report Server has two web-based communication façades that expose its functionality to external clients: HTTP Handler, which accepts URL-based report requests submitted via HTTP-GET, and the Web service (shown in figure 1.3 as RS WS), which handles SOAP requests. You will see how these façades impact the report-delivery process in section 1.5.

1.3.2 The Report Server database

When you install RS, the setup program creates the Report Server database structure. This structure is implemented as two physical SQL Server databases: Database #1 is the Report Configuration Database (ReportServer), and it hosts the report catalog and metadata. Database #2, ReportServerTempDB, is used for caching reports. In this section, we'll take a closer look at each.

The Report Configuration Database

The Report Configuration Database, called ReportServer, hosts the report catalog and metadata. As mentioned earlier, in order for a report to be available to the end users, its report definition file must be uploaded (published) to the catalog.

If you open the ReportServer database in the SQL Server Management Studio, you will be able to deduce the purpose of most of its tables. For example, the Report Configuration Database keeps the catalog items in the `Catalog` table, the data source information in the `Data-Source` table, and so forth. Note that Microsoft discourages querying the report catalog directly. Instead, the recommended way to access the report catalog is through the Report Server APIs. Microsoft also discourages you from making data changes directly to the catalog. The reason behind this is that Microsoft may change the catalog schema in the future but will maintain backward compatibility through the Report Server API.

As you may recall, RS can be deployed in a load-balanced cluster environment. In this deployment model, the ReportServer database is shared among all nodes of the cluster.

The Reporting Services Temporary Database

The RS setup program also creates a second SQL Server database named Report-ServerTempDB, which is used by RS for caching purposes. For example, once the report is executed, the Report Server saves a copy of the report in the ReportServer-TempDB database.

DEFINITION *Report caching* describes the Report Server feature of keeping the report intermediate format in the Report Server database for a certain duration.

We return to the topic of report caching in chapter 8.

Let's take a look at the web application used to manage the Report Server.

1.3.3 The Report Manager

Implemented as an ASP.NET web application, the Report Manager performs two main tasks: report management and requests for reports. You can think of the Report Manager as an application façade that communicates with the Report Server via the Report Server APIs. From the Report Server perspective, the Report Manager is no different than any other client application.

Report management

Users familiar with SharePoint Portal Server will find the Report Manager similar to this product both in terms of user interface and purpose. As with SharePoint, you can use the Report Manager to create folders, upload resources, manage subscriptions, and set up security.

For example, figure 1.4 shows that we used the Report Manager to navigate to a folder, `AWReporter`, and retrieved a list of the catalog items under this folder. You can click on a report link to run a report or access and change the report properties.

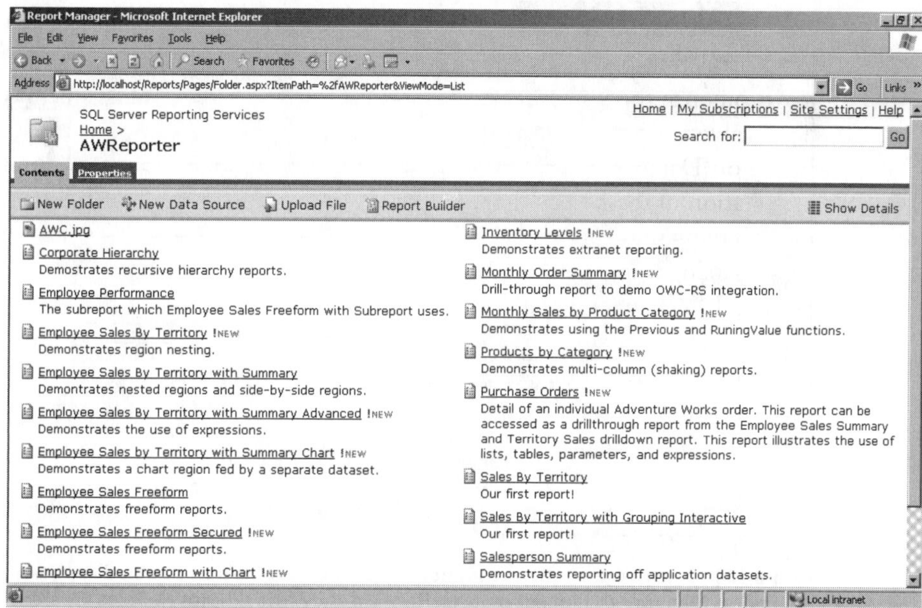

Figure 1.4 Users can use the Report Manager portal to generate or manage reports.

In case you're wondering where the items shown in figure 1.4 come from, we create them in the next few chapters when we discuss the report-authoring process.

Keep in mind that in RS you work with *virtual* folders. Neither the folders nor the report definition files actually exist in a file system. Instead, they exist in the Report Server database as metadata, but they appear as folders and items when you access the Report Server through the Report Manager.

Requesting reports

Sometimes, building a reporting application might be overkill. Small companies might not have the IT resources to do so quickly or simply cannot afford the effort. In such cases, the Report Manager can be used as a reporting tool. Users can navigate to the Report Manager portal and request reports on the spot, as figure 1.5 shows.

Even better, users can use the handy toolbar, which the Report Server generates automatically, to perform various report-related tasks, including specifying parameter values for reports that take parameters (more on this in chapter 3), paging, zooming, searching, and exporting the report to different formats.

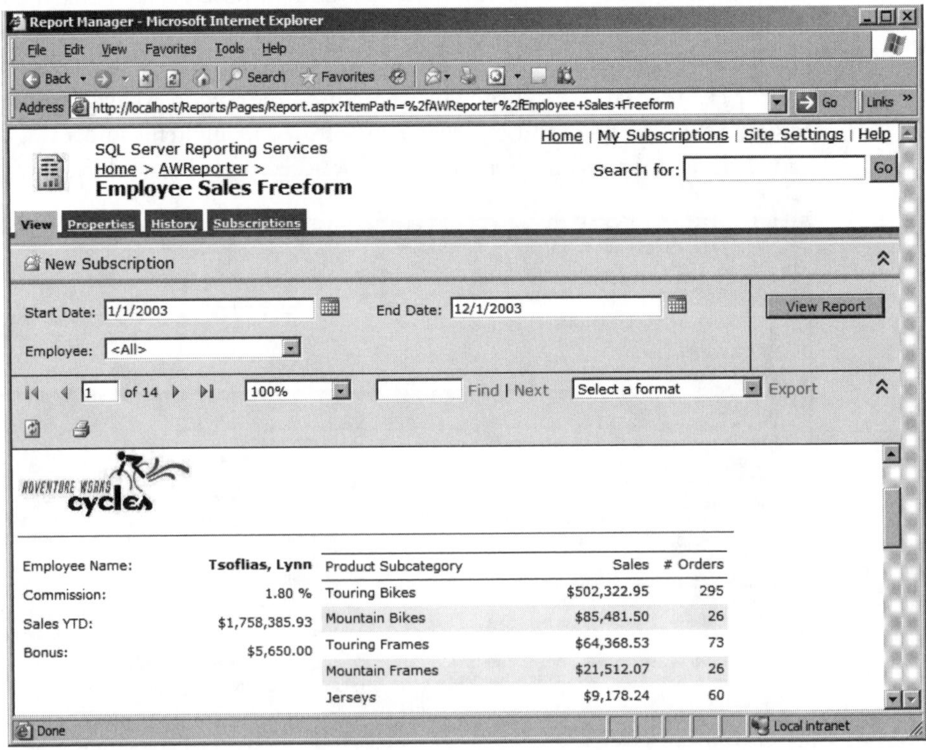

Figure 1.5 Small organizations that don't need to create report-enabled applications can use the Report Manager to request reports. Here we show the Employee Sales Freeform with Chart report generated in HTML.

Now that we've taken a quick tour of the major building blocks of Reporting Services, let's peek under its hood to see how it processes, renders, and delivers reports.

1.4 UNDERSTANDING REPORT PROCESSING

Report processing encompasses all activities performed by the Report Server to generate a report. To understand how the Report Server processes a report, let's see what happens when the report is requested on demand. Figure 1.6 depicts what happens when a report consumer requests a report hosted under the Report Server.

First, the consumer submits ① a report request to the Report Server. Once the report request is intercepted by the Report Server, it is forwarded ② to the Report Processor. The Report Processor parses the request and retrieves ③ the report definition and metadata from the Report Server database. The Report Processor checks whether the user is authorized to access this report. If so, the Report Processor processes the report, which involves three stages: query, execution, and rendering.

Let's get more insight into the execution and rendering stages.

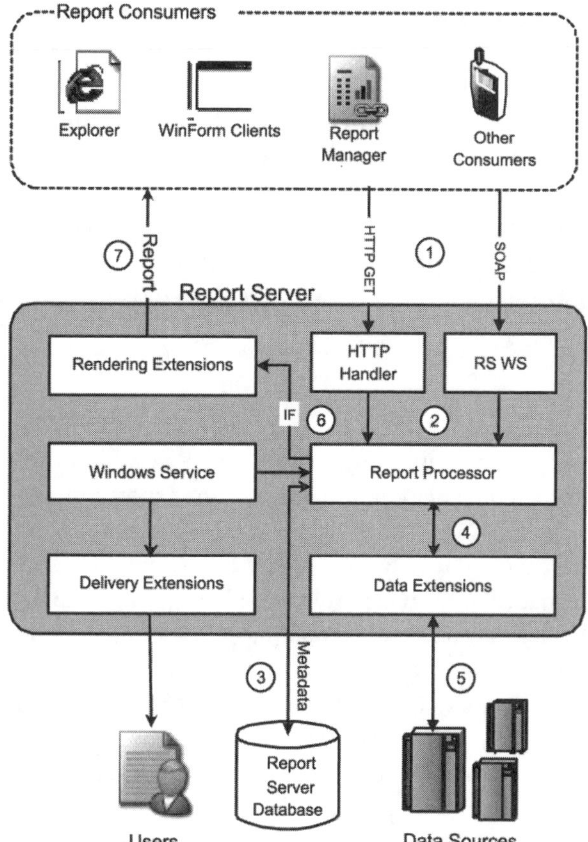

Figure 1.6 Report processing involves querying (5), execution (6), and rendering (7). You can integrate your applications with RS by using the two web communication façades: HTTP Handler and the RS Web service.

1.4.1 Execution stage

The report-execution stage starts when the Report Server begins processing the report and finishes when the report is ready for rendering. For the sake of simplicity, let's assume that the report is requested for the first time.

As we explained earlier, when the report is published, the Report Server parses its report definition (the RDL file), generates a .NET assembly, and saves the assembly in the catalog for the report. During the execution stage, the Report Server loads and executes the assembly. Referring back to figure 1.6, you can see that the Report Server uses a data extension ④ to query ⑤ the data source to retrieve the report data, combines the resulting dataset and report layout information, and produces ⑥ the report in a raw form, called *intermediate format* (IF).

Having the report generated in an IF before it is finally rendered is beneficial in terms of performance. It allows the Report Server to reuse the same IF, regardless of the requested export format. Developers who are familiar with the intermediate language (IL) code execution model in .NET can think of IF in a similar way. IL abstracts the platform on which the code executes, while IF abstracts the rendering format. For example, one report consumer can request the report in an HTML format, while another can request the same report as PDF. In either case, the Report Server already has the raw report; the only thing left is to transform it into its final presentation format. During the rendering stage, the Report Server loads the report IF and renders ⑦ the report in the requested format using a rendering extension.

Once the report IF is generated, it is saved (cached) in the Report Server Temporary Database (ReportServerTempDB). Note that if the report is cached, the report execution stage may be bypassed completely for subsequent requests because the Report Server decides to use the cached IF. We postpone discussing report caching until chapter 7.

1.4.2 Rendering stage

As shown in figure 1.6, the report-rendering stage represents the second (and last) stage in the report-processing pipeline. After the Report Server has the report IF, it renders the report in its final presentation format as per the export format requested by the user. You will be pleasantly surprised to see the plethora of natively supported formats that a report can be exported to. My favorites are HTML and PDF. For example, as figure 1.7 shows, I have loaded a report exported to a PDF file in Adobe Acrobat.

The Report Server delegates the report-rendering process to rendering extensions. RS comes with various rendering extensions that correspond to supported export formats. If the report consumer does not specify the export format explicitly, the report will be rendered in HTML 3.2 or 4.0, depending on the browser capabilities. Table 1.5 lists each out-of-the box RS-supported rendering format.

As we've said before, when the supported formats are not enough, you can write your own rendering extensions.

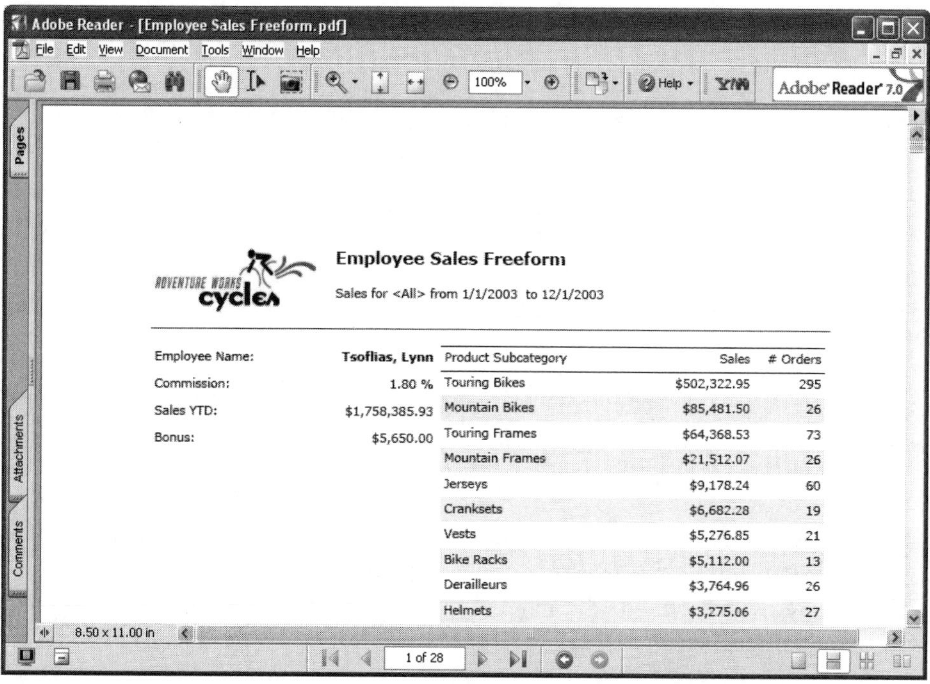

Figure 1.7 With RS you can export your reports to many formats, including Adobe Acrobat PDF. Here, I have exported this report to Adobe PDF and loaded it in Adobe Reader.

Table 1.5 Report-rendering options

Rendering extension	Description
HTML	HTML 4.0 (Internet Explorer 5.0 and above), Netscape (6.2 and above), HTML 3.2 otherwise.
MHTML	MIME encapsulation of the Aggregate HTML Documents standard, which embeds resources such as images, documents, or other binary files as MIME structures within the report. This is a good option to minimize the number of round-trips between the browser and server to fetch resources. MHTML is most useful for sending reports through e-mail, as we see in chapter 14.
PDF	Portable document format (PDF) files viewable using the Acrobat Reader.
Excel	Creates a visual representation of the report in an Excel workbook and translates Excel formulas whenever possible. Users can open the report in Excel to change it.
XML	Creates an XML document containing the data in the report. The schema of the XML document generated is determined by the contents and layout of the report. Users can use the Data Output tab in the Report Designer to control how the XML will be rendered.
CSV	Comma-separated value file, with no formatting.

continued on next page

Table 1.5 Report-rendering options *(continued)*

Rendering extension	Description
Image	Renders reports to bitmaps or metafiles, including any format that GDI+ supports: BMP, EMF, GIF, JPEG, PNG, RIFF, and WMF. By default, the image is rendered in TIFF, which can be displayed with an image viewer. Image rendering ensures the report looks the same on every client. Rendering occurs on the server; all fonts used in the report must be installed on the server.

Once the report is generated it is ready to travel to its final destination: the report user. RS gives you a lot of flexibility to distribute your reports, as you see in the next section.

1.5 DELIVERING REPORTS

As we mentioned earlier, RS supports both on-demand (pull) and subscribed (push) report delivery. To view a report on demand, the user explicitly requests the report from the Report Server. Alternatively, the user can choose to subscribe to a report. With this option, the report is pushed to the subscribers when the report data is refreshed or on a specified schedule.

Let's take a closer look at each delivery option.

1.5.1 On-demand delivery

One of the most important decisions you will make when integrating RS reports in your application is *how* the application will access the Report Server to request reports. Although in some cases the system design may dictate the integration option, occasionally the choice won't be so straightforward and you may have to carefully evaluate the application requirements to determine the best approach. We revisit the on-demand delivery options in more detail in chapter 10. For now, note that reports can be requested on demand in two ways: URL access and the Web service.

URL-based report access

The report consumer requests a report by URL by submitting an HTTP-GET request to the Report Server. The advantages of URL access are its simplicity and better performance. In the simplest case, the consumer can embed the report URL into a hyperlink.

For example, a web-based application can have a drop-down Reports menu, where each link targets an RS report. With the URL access option, the report arguments are passed as query parameters in the report URL. For example, assuming that you have installed the sample reports included with the book source code, the following URL will run the Territory Sales Crosstab sample report with the start date 3/1/2003 and an end date of 4/30/2004.

```
http://localhost/ReportServer?/AWReporter/Territory Sales
 Crosstab&StartDate=3/1/2003&EndDate=4/30/2004
```

Web service

With RS, reports can also be requested by submitting SOAP-based requests to the Report Server Web service. The main advantage of this service is that its feature set goes well beyond just report rendering. It also encompasses an extensive set of methods to manage all aspects of the Report Server, such as uploading reports, retrieving a list of resources from the report catalog, and securing RS.

You can think of the Report Server Web service as a façade to the Report Server that allows RS to be integrated with a broad array of platforms. For example, if you are building an enterprise application integration (EAI) solution, a BizTalk schedule might invoke the Web service `Render()` method, get the XML representation of the report, retrieve some data from it, and pass it on to another application. Or, if your reporting application is B2B oriented and your partner has a Web service, you can send the report results to it in XML.

In some cases, a report consumer will use a combination of both access options to integrate with RS. For example, a report consumer can use the RS Web service to find out what parameters a report takes. Then, the application presentation layer can present the parameters to the user so that the user can enter the parameter values. When the user submits the report request, the application can use URL access to send the request to the Report Server.

Report Viewer controls

If you are building applications with Visual Studio 2005 (.NET Framework 2.0), you will want to take advantage of the Report Viewer controls. These controls take the work out of adding RS reports to your applications. The Report Viewer controls not only help you pull reports from the RS server (remote mode), but also allow you to create reports that work outside of the RS server (local mode). Local mode eliminates the need for your applications to communicate with a report server to take advantage of Reporting Services features. However, using the Report Viewer control outside of a report server has both benefits and limitations. We learn all about the Report Viewer controls in chapter 11.

1.5.2 Subscribed delivery

In the "push" report-delivery scenario, the reports are generated and delivered automatically by the Report Server to a delivery target. Reports can also be delivered at a scheduled time. For example, a financial institution can set up a portfolio balance report to be generated and delivered through e-mail to its customers at the end of each month.

The Report Server Windows service (`ReportingServicesService.exe`) works in tandem with the SQL Server Agent service to generate and deliver subscribed reports.

NOTE SQL Server Agent is a component of Microsoft SQL Server, and it is responsible for running scheduled SQL Server tasks.

For example, if the report is to be generated according to a set schedule, the SQL Server Agent will create a job and move the subscription to the Subscriptions table when the time is up. The RS Windows service periodically polls the Report Configuration Database to find out whether there are any new subscription jobs. If this is the case, the Windows service picks up the job, generates the report, and delivers it to the end users through a delivery extension.

Out of the box, RS comes with two delivery extensions:

- E-mail delivery extension
- File share delivery extension

The e-mail delivery extension delivers the report via e-mail. The report can be delivered to either subscribed users (opt-in subscription) or to a data-driven list of recipients. The file share extension delivers reports to a network share. When these two options are not enough, you can write custom delivery extensions.

Note that the Report Server Windows service doesn't communicate with the Report Server through the HTTP Handler or Web service façades. Instead, because it is installed on the same machine as the Report Server, the Windows service directly loads and calls the Report Server assemblies. This is beneficial for two reasons. The first relates to availability. Even if the IIS server is down, the Windows service will still execute scheduled tasks and deliver reports to subscribers. The other reason is better performance—the web façades are completely bypassed.

Another task that the Report Services Windows service is responsible for is performing background database integrity checks, as well as other administrative tasks.

Before we see RS in action, let's analyze the report lifecycle. A good high-level understanding of the lifecycle is important because the remaining chapters of this book follow an identical flow.

1.6 WHAT IS THE REPORT LIFECYCLE?

By now, you probably realize that the Report Server is a sophisticated reporting platform with a feature set that goes well beyond a desktop reporting tool. To minimize the learning curve, this book follows a logical path based on the *report lifecycle*. The report lifecycle is the process that you typically follow to work with reports, and it involves the three stages as shown in figure 1.8: authoring, management, and delivery.

In the report-authoring stage, you create the RDL file through the use of report-authoring tools. For example, you can use the Visual Studio Report Designer to lay out the report. Recall that both report data retrieval and layout information are described in the RDL file. We'll discuss many more details of the report-authoring stage in chapters 2 through 7.

In the report-management stage, you manage the report catalog. As you recall, the report catalog is stored in the Report Configuration Database. The report catalog keeps the report and all related items. Typical management tasks include organizing

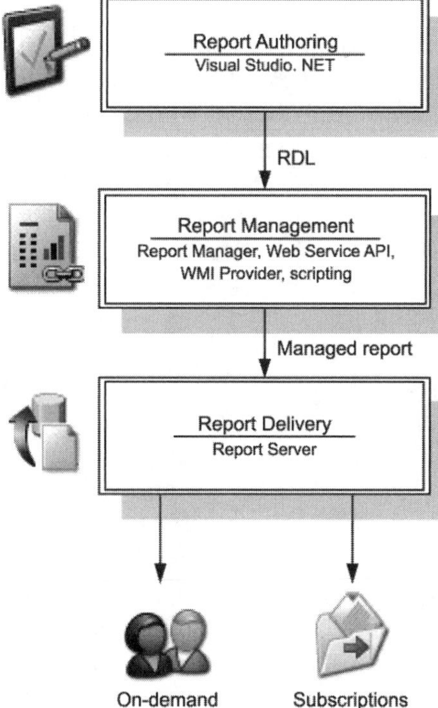

Figure 1.8
Report lifecycle phases include report authoring, management, and delivery. In the report-authoring stage, you lay out the report. In the report-management stage, you deploy and manage the report. Finally, RS provides many ways to distribute your reports to their final destination.

reports in folders, uploading reports, and granting users access to run reports. We take a closer look at report management in chapters 8 and 9.

The report-delivery stage is concerned with distributing the reports to their final destinations, including end users, printers, or archive folders. A managed report can be delivered either on-demand or pushed to the subscribed users. Report delivery is discussed in detail in chapters 10 through 12.

Enough theory! Let's put into practice what we have learned so far and get our hands on RS.

1.7 RS IN ACTION

This section has two main objectives. First, we introduce an imaginary company, Adventure Works Cycles (AWC), which we reference throughout the rest of this book. We discuss various hypothetical reporting challenges that AWC faces and implement solutions to address them.

Second, we get our feet wet and create our first report using the Visual Studio Report Wizard and the AdventureWorks sample database. Granted, this is going to be a simple tabular-style report, but as simple as it is, it showcases all the stages of the report lifecycle. We also use this report in the next three chapters as a practical example to expand our knowledge about RS.

The Adventure Works sample database

Finally, if you install the SQL Server 2005 samples, the setup program installs a sample database called AdventureWorks. This database is also used by other Microsoft products, such as Commerce Server. To install the AdventureWorks, you need to select the advanced options during the installation. See appendix A for more details.

The AdventureWorks database includes a much more "realistic" sales ordering database model than the SQL Server sample databases, Northwind or Pubs. You quickly realize this by surveying the data held in the more than 60 tables. We work with this sample database in this section, and you have a chance to create a report using RS.

1.7.1 About the Adventure Works Reporter

Let's start with a hypothetical problem statement. You are a developer with AWC, which manufactures and sells goods to individuals and retailers. The company has enjoyed tremendous success the last few years. Sales are going up exponentially and the customer base is growing fast. Today, AWC has customers both in the United States and overseas. It has already implemented a web-based ordering online transaction processing (OLTP) system to capture sales orders online.

However, success does not come cheap. Data inaccuracy and slow decision making are among the top complaints by the sales managers. Often, data is captured and consolidated in the form of Excel spreadsheets. A reporting system is needed to present the company with data in a format that's both easy to understand and analyze, and to allow AWC's management to discover trends and see how the company is performing. You have been designated as a lead developer for the new Adventure Works (AW) Reporter system. Fascinated by Microsoft SQL Server 2005 RS, you decide to base your reporting system on it.

NOTE In the real world, you should abstain from reporting off an OLTP database for performance reasons. As the name suggests, OLTP systems must scale to meet large transaction volumes and handle hundreds and even thousands of users. Reporting applications usually submit queries to retrieve and analyze substantial sets of data, which impose data locks on many records in the database. This can severely tax your OLTP system performance. For this reason, reporting and OLTP are usually two mutually exclusive options. A typical solution involves consolidating OLTP data and then uploading it to a data warehouse database that is optimized and designated for reporting purposes only.

1.7.2 Your first report

One crucial piece of information that the AWC management would probably like to know is what the yearly products sales per territory are. With such a report in hand, managers can determine how well AWC is doing in each sales region.

To meet this requirement, let's create the Sales by Territory report. Figure 1.9 shows the final version of the report that we'll create in this section.

Sales By Territory		
Territory	Product Category	Sales
Australia	Accessory	$8,359.74
	Bike	$773,111.46
	Clothing	$18,665.74
	Component	$96,911.11
Canada	Accessory	$32,835.84
	Bike	$2,315,632.98
	Clothing	$86,657.62
	Component	$457,317.56

Figure 1.9 Our first report is Sales by Territory.

This is just one of the many sample reports we design throughout the course of this book. We use the Sales by Territory report in subsequent chapters to demonstrate other RS features.

Table 1.6 shows the list of tasks that we need to accomplish to create the report organized by the report lifecycle stages.

Table 1.6 The task map for creating our first report

Stage	Task	Description
Authoring	Create BI project.	Create a new BI project in Visual Studio.
	Create the report data source.	Use the Report Designer Data tab to configure a database connection to the AdventureWorks database.
	Set the report dataset.	Define a dataset query to retrieve the report data.
	Lay out the report.	Use the Report Wizard and Report Designer to author the report.
	Test the report.	Use the Report Designer Preview tab to preview and test the report.
Management	Deploy the report.	Use Visual Studio to deploy the report to the Report Server catalog.
Delivery	Ensure on-demand report delivery.	Use the Report Manager to navigate and render the report.

As you'll recall, the first stage of the report lifecycle is authoring the report.

Authoring the report

Let's develop our first report using the Report Designer. To do so, we need to create a new Visual Studio Business Intelligence (BI) project.

Task: Create a Business Intelligence Project

To create a project, complete the following steps (see figure 1.10):

Step 1 Open Visual Studio and choose File ➔ New ➔ Project.

Step 2 From Project Types, select Business Intelligence Projects.

Step 3 From Templates, select Report Project.

Step 4 In the Location field, enter **AWReporter**, specify a location, and click OK.

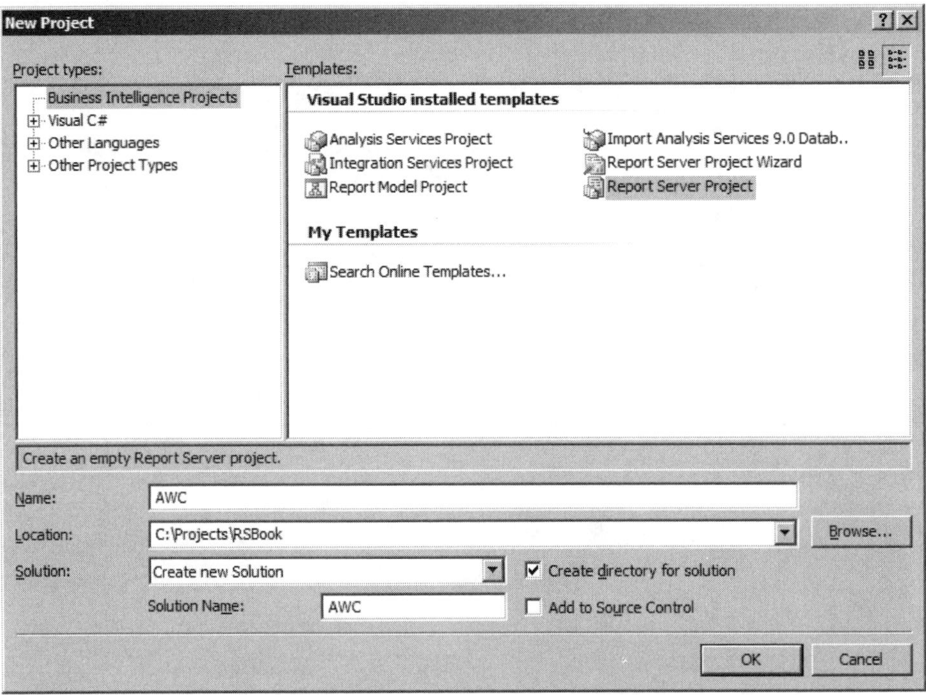

Figure 1.10 Use Visual Studio to create a new BI project.

Step 5 Once the project is created, right-click on the AWReporter project node in the Solution Explorer window and select Properties. The Property Pages dialog box appears, as shown in figure 1.11.

Step 6 Verify that TargetReportFolder is set to AWReporter. This specifies the folder name in the report catalog where all reports defined in the project will be deployed.

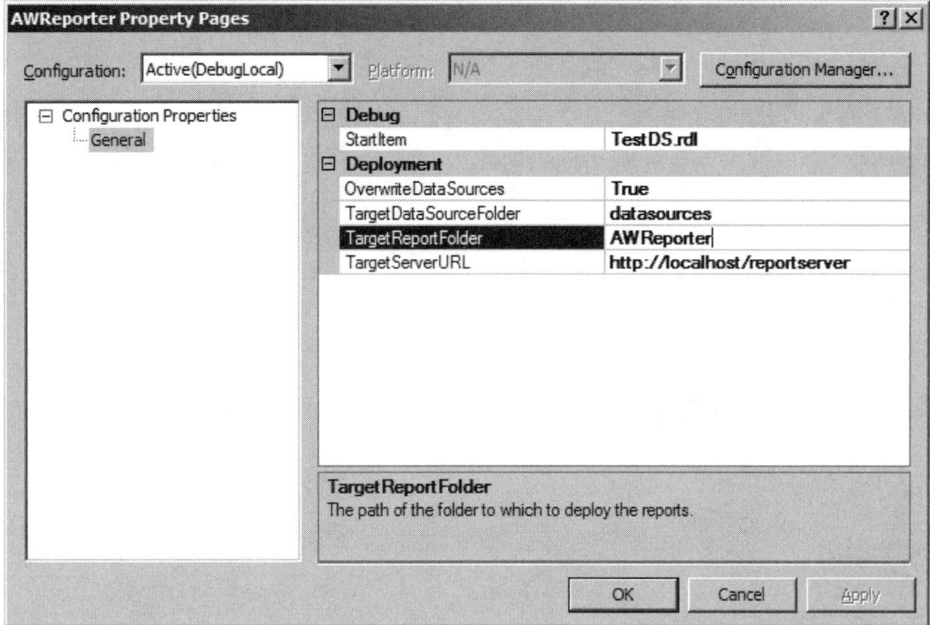

Figure 1.11 Use the report property page to set up the project properties.

Step 7 In the TargetServerURL field, enter the Report Server URL. If RS is installed locally on your machine and you have accepted the defaults during setup, the URL of the Report Server should be `http://localhost/reportserver`. Click OK to close the Property Pages dialog box.

Task: Create the Report Data Source

Next, we create a shared data source pointing to the AdventureWorks sample database. Don't worry if the concept of a shared data source is not immediately clear. When we get to chapter 3 it all begins to make sense.

Step 1 Right-click on the Shared Data Sources node in the Solution Explorer and choose Add New Data Source. The Shared Data Source property window appears, as shown in figure 1.12. By default, RS names the data source with the same name as the database. Since we are going to use this data source for most of the sample reports in this book, let's make the name more descriptive.

Step 2 Enter **AW Shared Datasource** in the Name field. Be sure that Microsoft SQL Server is selected for the Type field, and click the Edit button.

Step 3 When the Connection Properties dialog box appears (see figure 1.13), enter the following information:

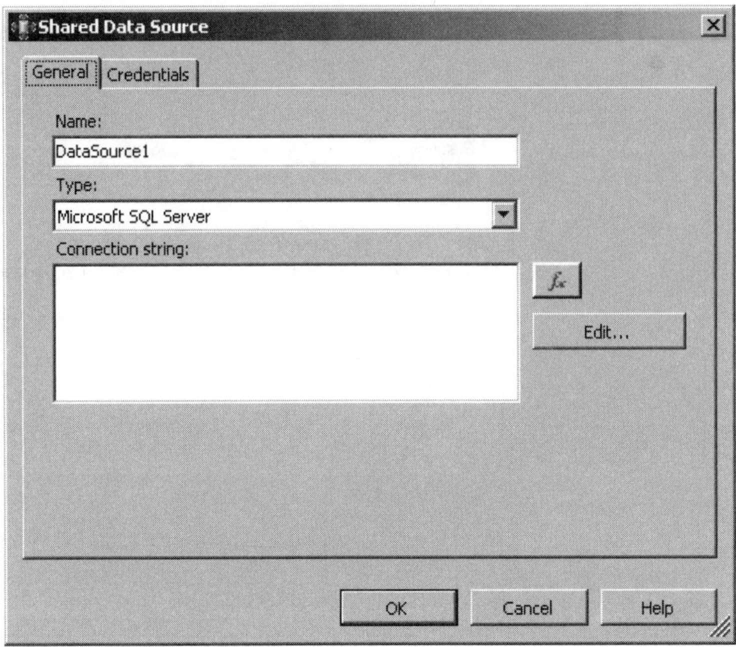

Figure 1.12 The Shared Data Source window allows you to use the same data source for multiple reports.

- *Server Name*—The name of the SQL Server that you use to install RS. In my case, the database is installed locally on a named instance (DEV), which is why the data source name is 16371XP\DEV (16371XP is the name of my computer.).
- *Use SQL Server Authentication*—Enter a valid username and password combination for a SQL Server account that has permissions to query the tables in the AdventureWorks database. Select the Save My Password check box. Note: You can also select Use Windows Authentication for this example (shown in figure 1.13).
- Select the AdventureWorks database from the Select Or Enter a Database Name drop-down list. Test the connection by clicking the Test Connection button. If all is well, click OK.

Now it's time to author the report. We use the handy Visual Studio Report Wizard to save some time.

Task: Set the Report Dataset

Step 1 Right-click on the Reports node in the Solution Explorer and choose Add New Report.

Step 2 On the Report Wizard welcome screen, click Next.

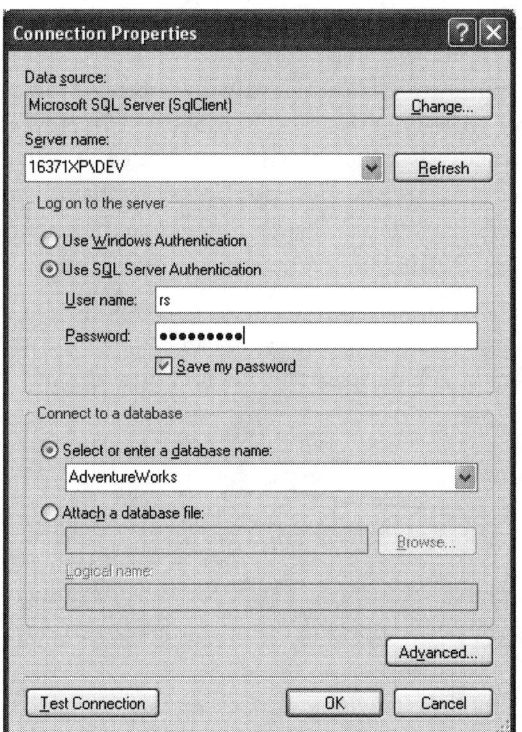

Figure 1.13
The Connection Properties window

Step 3 On the Select the Data Source screen, make sure that AW Shared Datasource is selected under the Shared Data Source section. Click Next.

Step 4 In the Design the Query screen, enter the following SQL statement in the query pane, then click Next:

```
SELECT       ST.Name AS Territory, PC.ProductCategoryID,
             PC.Name AS ProductCategory,
             SUM(SOD.UnitPrice * SOD.OrderQty) AS Sales
FROM         Sales.SalesOrderDetail SOD
INNER JOIN   Production.Product P ON SOD.ProductID = P.ProductID
INNER JOIN   Sales.SalesOrderHeader SOH ON
             SOD.SalesOrderID = SOH.SalesOrderID
INNER JOIN   Sales.SalesTerritory ST ON
             SOH.TerritoryID = ST.TerritoryID
INNER JOIN   Production.ProductSubCategory PSC ON
             P.ProductSubCategoryID = PSC.ProductSubCategoryID
INNER JOIN   Production.ProductCategory PC ON PSC.ProductCategoryID =
             PC.ProductCategoryID
WHERE        DATEPART(YY, SOH.OrderDate) = DATEPART(yy, '1/1/2003')
GROUP BY     ST.Name, PC.Name, PC.ProductCategoryID
ORDER BY     ST.Name, PC.Name
```

This query retrieves the product sales orders grouped by territory and product category. The AW database groups products in subcategories, which are then rolled up to product categories. For the purposes of this report, we summarize the sales data by product categories since this represents the most consolidated level in the product hierarchy, which is exactly what upper management is interested in seeing. The sales amount is retrieved from the `Sales.SalesOrderDetail` table. In addition, the query filters the orders created for 2003. In chapter 3, we make the report parameter driven by allowing the user to pass an arbitrary date.

NOTE We have hardcoded January 1, 2003, in the query. While this query would make sense to use `GetDate()` instead of hardcoding the date for the current year's data, the AW database only has data through 2004.

Task: Lay Out the Report

To lay out the report, perform the following steps:

Step 1 On the Select the Report Type screen, leave the report type set to Tabular. Click Next.

Step 2 On the Design the Table screen, select all fields except ProductCategoryID and click Details so the fields appear in the report details section, as shown in figure 1.14. Click Next.

Step 3 On the Choose the Table Style screen, click Corporate, then click Next.

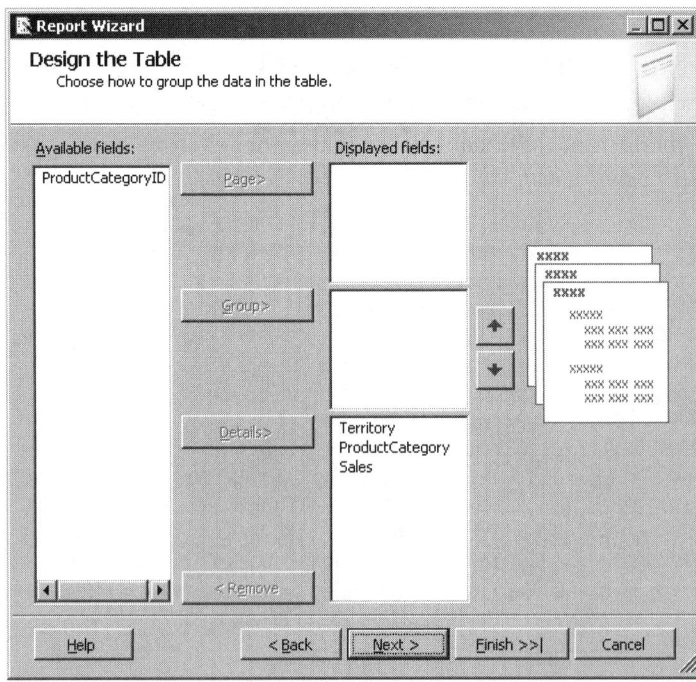

Figure 1.14 Choose which fields will appear on the report and how data will be grouped.

Step 4 Finally, on the Completing the Report Wizard screen, enter **Sales by Territory** as the name of the report. Click Finish, and we're done!

Visual Studio displays the Report Designer with the Layout tab selected, as shown in figure 1.15.

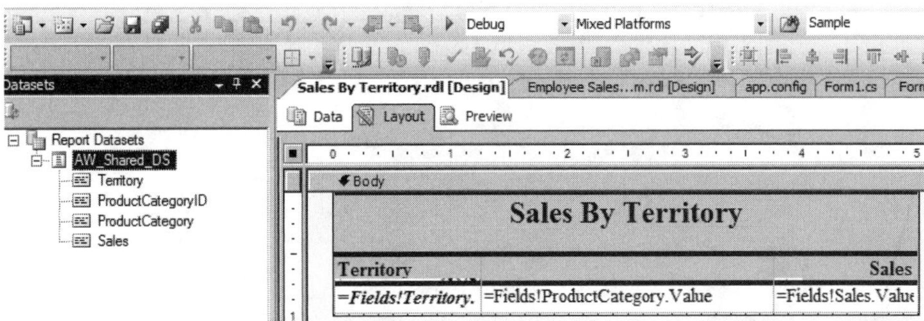

Figure 1.15 Use the Report Designer Layout tab to lay out your report.

The integration with Visual Studio Report Designer allows you to easily preview and test your reports without leaving the Visual Studio IDE.

Task: Test the Report

Let's make some cosmetic changes to enhance our report.

Step 1 Click on the Report Designer Preview tab to see the HTML representation of the report. Notice the report toolbar at the top, which allows you to zoom, print, and save the report in different formats. The Sales field needs some formatting work.

Step 2 Click the Layout tab again to go back to design mode.

Step 3 Right-click on the Sales textbox and choose Properties. Specify the format settings, as shown in figure 1.16. Click OK to close the Textbox Properties dialog box.

Step 4 Increase the width of the Territory and Product Category columns; stretch them out as far as there is space within the report width.

Step 5 Right-click again on the Territory textbox and select Properties.

Step 6 On the Font tab, change the font weight to Bold and the style to Italic. Click OK.

Step 7 Back in the Textbox Properties dialog box, hide the repeating territory names by selecting the Hide Duplicates check box, as shown in figure 1.17.

Step 8 From the report, click on the Sales field. In the properties window enter **c2** as the format property. This will format our Sales field as currency.

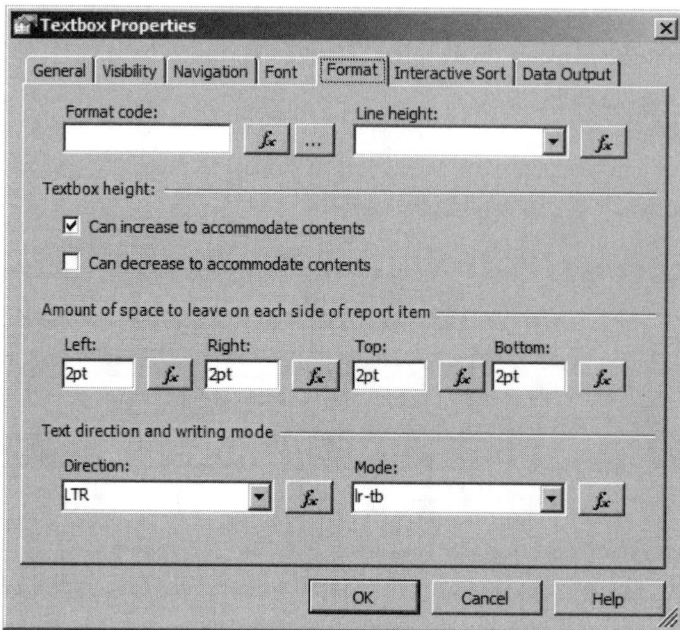

Figure 1.16 Use the Textbox Properties dialog box to set up format settings.

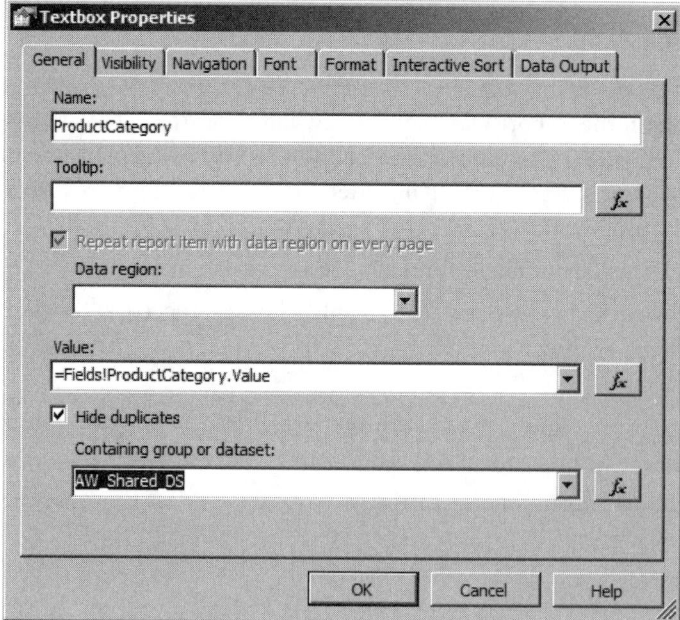

Figure 1.17 Select the Hide Duplicates check box to hide the territory name duplicates.

Preview the report again. Now it should look like the one shown in figure 1.9. Still not very pleasing to the eye, but not bad for a few minutes of work!

Report management

Once you are satisfied with the report, you will need to deploy it to make it available to all users. This is a report-management task that you can accomplish by using the Report Manager. However, if your Windows account has local administrator rights on the computer where the Report Server is installed, you can deploy the report straight from within Visual Studio. Let's do just that.

Task: Deploy the Report

Save your changes.

In the Solution Explorer, right-click on `Sales by Territory.rdl` and choose Deploy. This compiles the report and uploads the report to the report catalog.

> **NOTE** The report RDL includes the report query and layout information. Since we chose to create a shared data source, the data source information is not included in the report RDL. To see this, select the `Sales by Territory.rdl` file from the Solution Explorer, right-click, and select View Code. Visual Studio shows you the report definition of the report.

Report delivery

Once the report has been promoted to a managed report, it can be delivered to your end users. Let's see how users can request the report on-demand by using the Report Manager as a quick-and-easy report-delivery tool.

Task: On-Demand Report Delivery

Open the browser and navigate to the Report Manager URL, which by default is `http://<reportservername>/reports`. Notice that below the Report Manager Home folder there is a new folder, `AWReporter`, and that its name matches the TargetReportFolder setting which you specified in the report project settings.

Step 1 Click on the `AWReporter` folder link to see its contents. You should find the Sales by Territory report link. Under the data sources folder you should see the AW Shared DS data source.

Step 2 Click on the Sales by Territory report link to request the report with the Report Manager.

As you can see, authoring, managing, and delivering reports with RS is straightforward. At this point, you may decide to compare RS at a high level with other reporting tools you've used in the past. The next section discusses how RS stacks up against the competition.

1.8 EVALUATING RS

Throughout my career as a software consultant, I have had the opportunity to turn many clients on to Reporting Services. I am continually impressed by how quickly most developers have learned to effectively build reports and enable end users to get the data they need. Not only is RS easy to use and deploy, it is also surprisingly feature rich. My favorite top ten features, where I believe RS excels, are as follows:

1. *Report Builder*—Adds ad hoc reporting capabilities to your business users. This tool will allow business users to create amazingly complex queries for reports by dragging and dropping fields and selecting filters for the data. In addition, infinite drill-through reporting will change the way you think about ad hoc reports.
2. *Natively exposed as a Web service*—The RS reports are widely accessible, and you don't have to do anything special to publish your reports as web services because they are hosted under the Report Server, which provides a web service façade.
3. *Support of plethora of export formats*—You may be delighted to learn that the ability to export reports to PDF and Excel is provided out of the box. In addition, reports can be delivered in many other popular formats, including web formats (HTML), popular image formats (such as TIFF and JPEG), and data formats (Excel, XML, and CSV).
4. *On-demand and subscribed report delivery*—Another huge plus is the subscribed report delivery option, which allows developers to implement opt-in report features in their applications.
5. *Documented report definition format*—Developers can create reports to be published to the Report Server using Microsoft or third-party design tools that support the RS XML RDL.
6. *.NET Framework integration*—In the extensibility area, you'll appreciate the fact that you are not locked out from a programmability standpoint. As we mentioned earlier, when built-in features are not enough, you can reach out and borrow from the power of the .NET Framework by integrating your reports with .NET code. In addition, the Report Services programming model is 100 percent .NET based.
7. *Extensible architecture*—The RS architecture is fully extensible and allows developers to plug in their own security, data, delivery, and rendering extensions.
8. *Zero deployment*—Thanks to its service-oriented architecture, RS has no client footprint and offers true zero deployment for all application types.
9. *Scalability*—RS can scale better, since it is designed from the ground up to scale in web farm environments.
10. *Cost*—From a cost perspective, it is hard to beat the bundled-with-the-SQL-Server RS pricing model, especially if you compare it with the five-digit price tag of third-party reporting tools.

1.9 SUMMARY

This chapter took you on a whirlwind tour of the RS platform. We discussed its space in the SQL Server platform and addressed how it fits into the Microsoft BI initiative. We also looked at its features and high-level architecture. You even had a chance to use RS and create a simple report based on the AdventureWorks sample database. Now that you have a workable, high-level understanding of its features, you can begin using RS to report-enable your own applications.

By now, you should understand the major components of RS and their role in the report lifecycle. In addition, you should see the advantages that the service-oriented and web-enabled RS architecture has to offer.

Perhaps most important, you should be familiar with the three stages of the report lifecycle: report authoring, management, and delivery. The remaining chapters explore each of these stages in this order. In the next chapter, we discuss different ways to create RS reports.

PART 1

Authoring reports

The report lifecycle starts with the report-authoring phase. Part 1 teaches you the skills that you as a report author will need to master when creating Reporting Services—based reports.

We start by discussing the options Reporting Services offers for creating reports. Since most report authors probably rely on the integrated Visual Studio Report Designer, we explore its report-authoring features in detail.

We explain how to set up the report data source and work with datasets. We also introduce best practices for data management.

The best way to acquire report-authoring skills is by example. For this reason, we author various reports, including tabular, freeform, crosstab, chart, and multicolumn reports, as well as reports with navigational features.

You may often need to enhance your report features programmatically. We show how you can accomplish this by using expressions and functions.

One of the most prominent features of Reporting Services that many developers, including myself, appreciate is its extensible nature. One way you can extend the capabilities of your reports is to integrate them with custom .NET code that you or someone else has written. In this part, you learn how to leverage custom code to supercharge the capabilities of your reports.

Among the many new and exciting features available in Reporting Services 2005 is the Report Builder application. This application allows end users to author their own reports in an ad hoc fashion. We explore the process of setting up the environment for the Report Builder application as well as using this application to create ad hoc reports.

CHAPTER 2

Report authoring basics

In chapter 1 we discussed the report lifecycle and identified the first stage as the report-authoring process. Recall that in this stage, you set up the report data and lay out the report itself. The report data and layout information are described in a report definition file.

You may wonder what options are available to you as report authors with RS. As you will see shortly, RS offers not one but several ways to create reports. In this chapter we discuss:

- The report-authoring process
- Authoring reports using Visual Studio Report Designer
- Generating the report definition language (RDL) report manually

Although you will probably rely most of the time on the Report Designer to author reports, it is important to understand when and how to use the other options. In this chapter, we provide a panoramic view of report-authoring techniques. In chapter 4 we discuss how you can use the Report Designer to lay out different types of reports.

NOTE In chapter 7, you learn how to use the new Report Builder application, which enables users to author reports on the fly.

Before we discuss specific report-authoring options, it may make sense to step back and reflect on the authoring process to learn how you can create reports that meet user requirements.

2.1 THE REPORT-AUTHORING PROCESS: STEP BY STEP

Although there is no magic formula for creating successful reports, I recommend that you follow a process for authoring reports similar to the software development methodology in general. Figure 2.1 shows the four steps you should follow when authoring your reports.

Experienced developers will probably recognize these steps immediately. Just as with software projects, you should resist the temptation to jump into "construction" (report authoring) before you have a good understanding of what your users want. Once the report is ready, it has to be meticulously tested before it is deployed to the report catalog.

Below the name of each step, figure 2.1 lists the typical ways to accomplish that step. For example, you can author a report using VS .NET by generating the report definition programmatically, or using third-party tools.

Let's explain each step in more detail.

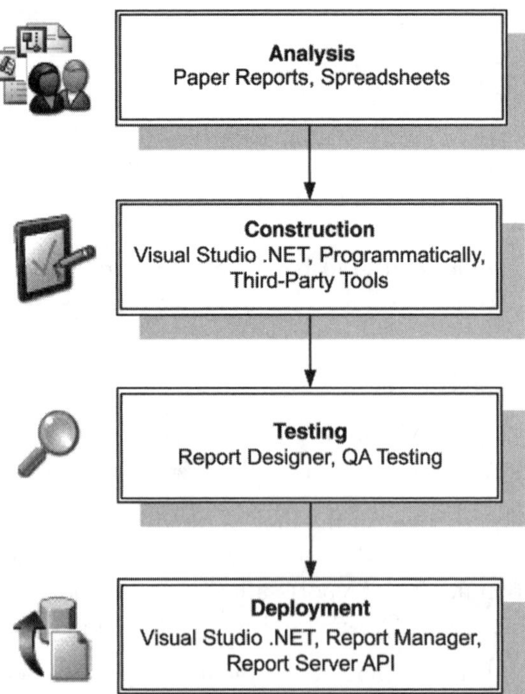

Figure 2.1 The report-authoring process typically consists of analysis, construction, testing, and deployment steps.

2.1.1 Analysis

The objective of the analysis step is to collect the user requirements and prototype the report. In this stage, you typically examine existing report artifacts and other data sources, such as paper reports, spreadsheets, and standard forms, to understand what data is needed and how it is related. In addition, you conduct joint application development (JAD) sessions with your users to clarify the reporting requirements, create throwaway report prototypes, and, in general, do whatever possible to reach a consensus with your users about what the report should look like.

For example, in chapter 1 we created the Sales by Territory report requested by the Adventure Works Cycles (AWC) management. Here, we've assumed that the analysis step has been completed and we know exactly what our users want. If that were not the case, however, we would've started with prototyping the report. First, we could have determined what reporting sources the AWC managers currently use to obtain the same data. Perhaps they use Excel spreadsheets that we can use to see what the report looks like. Once we've determined the report layout, we need to find where the report data originates. In this case, we must find out where the sales data resides—in mainframe, Oracle, SQL Server databases, or XML Web Services.

Sometimes, you find that you don't have all the data you need to satisfy the user requirements. For example, you might discover that some of the information is buried deep within the mainframe abyss and that getting it out to daylight will require another project or two altogether.

A good approach at the end of this stage is to come up with a paper prototype of the report that defines the report look and feel. Next, during the report-design stage, you can use this prototype to flesh out the actual report.

Discussing the Analysis step in any greater detail is outside the scope of this book. However, to emphasize the importance of requirements gathering and analysis, we use a common pattern for the reporting solutions that we build in subsequent chapters. Each reporting solution starts with first, defining the user requirements and second, defining high-level design goals. These issues must be addressed before moving on to the actual implementation.

2.1.2 Construction

If you make it successfully out of the analysis, you graduate to the report-construction phase.

> **NOTE** In an ad hoc tool like the Report Builder, analysis and construction happen at the same time.

The main deliverable of the construction step is the RS-based report. You will generally use one of the report-authoring options described in this chapter to create the report. As we've mentioned, you can use several techniques to create a report, ranging from taking advantage of the integration with VS .NET Report Designer, to generating the report definition programmatically.

If you create your reports interactively by using the reporting tools we discuss in this chapter, report construction is typically a two-stage process: (1) setting up report data, and (2) arranging report items on the report canvas.

With RS, to set up the report data you first specify a data source and define one or more queries, as we discuss in detail in chapter 3. Next, to display the data on the report and add other report items to the layout, you can use data regions (such as tables, matrices, lists, and charts). Chapter 4 shows you how to do just that.

2.1.3 Testing

Just as you test software projects, you should perform unit testing with your reports, as well as quality assurance (QA) testing. With VS .NET you can easily preview the report to ensure that its layout meets the requirements and executes successfully. Once you are satisfied with the layout, inside the VS .NET IDE you can fully simulate the production Report Server environment and determine whether the report will render under given configurations. You see how the Report Designer facilitates the report unit-testing process in section 2.2.2.

Once you have finished unit testing, the report goes to QA for final preproduction testing. If possible, you should designate a separate staging test Report Server for performance and logistics reasons.

2.1.4 Deployment

As we mentioned in chapter 1, to make your report available to end users you have to deploy it to the report catalog. RS provides several options for uploading your reports:

- Upload the report definition (RDL) file manually using the Report Manager. We've already seen how in chapter 1.
- Upload the report from within the VS .NET IDE. We explain this technique in section 2.2.2.
- Upload the report definition programmatically by calling the Report Server Web service (see chapter 8 for more on this approach).

The focus of this chapter is to discuss the available options for authoring RS reports. Let's begin by finding out how we can do that with VS .NET.

2.2 AUTHORING REPORTS IN VS .NET

Reporting Services 2005 includes a VS .NET shell for report authoring. If you already have VS .NET 2005 installed, RS will install a new set of Business Intelligence (BI) projects into VS .NET. If you do not have VS .NET 2005, the installation will install the Business Intelligence Development Studio (BIDS). Throughout the rest of this book we refer to VS .NET and the BIDS interchangeably.

Visual Studio provides several options for authoring RS reports:

- Using the Report Wizard
- Using the development environment to create complex reports
- Importing reports from Microsoft Access

Let's take a closer look at each of these tools, starting with the Report Wizard.

2.2.1 Authoring reports with the Report Wizard

You are already familiar with the Report Wizard because we used it in chapter 1 to create our first report. To start the Report Wizard within VS .NET, right-click on the project node and choose Add New Item. Alternatively, as a shortcut you can right-click on the Reports node and select Add New Report.

As figure 2.2 shows, the Report Wizard supports two report types:

- *Tabular*—The report data is laid out in a tabular format. Optionally, you can define one or more report groups. Grouping allows you to logically organize the data into different sections, as well as provide subtotals or other summary information in the group footer.
- *Matrix (crosstab)*—The report data can be grouped both in rows and columns. With matrix reports, you can define dynamic (expanding) columns to give the user an option to "drill down" for analyzing data further. We discuss this type of report in more detail in chapter 4.

The Report Wizard uses report styles to format the report in one of several predefined styles, including Slate, Forest, Corporate, Bold, Ocean, and Generic. If for some reason

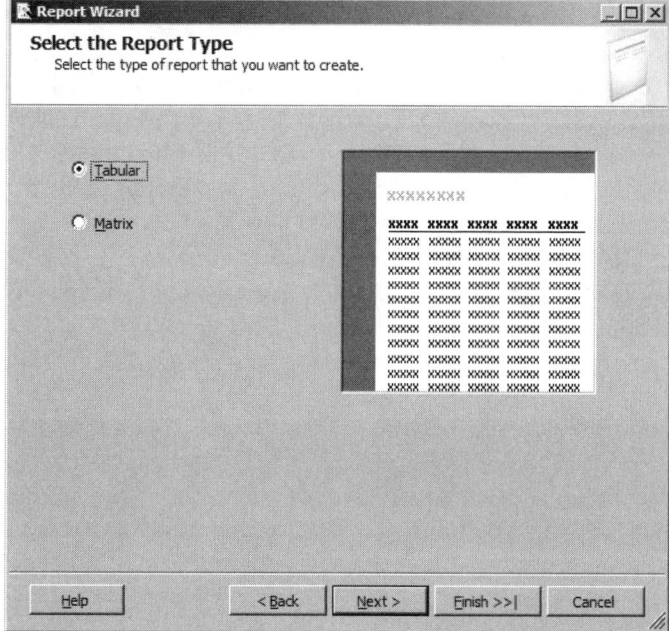

Figure 2.2
The report types supported by the Report Wizard

you want to modify the existing styles or create new ones, you can do so by changing the `StyleTemplates.xml` file, located by default in `C:\Program Files\Microsoft Visual Studio 8\Common7\IDE\PrivateAssemblies\Business Intelligence Wizards\Reports\Styles`. This file enumerates the report styles as XML elements, which you can change using your favorite text editor.

NOTE The styles that the Report Wizard lets you choose from are used only once, during the process of generating the report definition file, to define the report appearance. Currently, RS does not support style templates (or *skins*) that define a common look and feel across reports, similar to the way web developers would use Cascading Style Sheets (CSS) or themes to control the page appearance. This feature has been slated for a future RS version.

Most of you will probably agree that the Report Wizard is a good starting point when you need to generate a report quickly. It saves you time by automating some of the mundane report-authoring tasks, such as laying out the dataset fields. But, as with any wizard, it has its own limitations. For example, the Report Wizard design options are limited to Tabular and Matrix reports only. In addition, the Report Wizard doesn't support multiple regions, region nesting, or multiple datasets. To get the full design feature set supported by RS, you need to switch to the more robust Report Designer.

2.2.2 Authoring reports with the Report Designer

Most of us will rely exclusively on the powerful Report Designer to create and design reports. Therefore, I would like to give you a thorough overview of the essentials. Chapter 3 shows you how to use the Report Designer to set up the report data source and query. In chapters 4 and 5 you'll learn how the Report Designer makes authoring different types of reports a breeze.

If you haven't done this already, start BIDS and open the AWReporter project (`AWReporter.rptproj`) that we created in chapter 1. (If you skipped this step, you can find the AWReporter project included with the book source code.) Then, double-click on the Sales by Territory report in the Solution Explorer pane to open the report in layout mode inside the Report Designer, as shown in figure 2.3.

The Report Designer itself has a tabbed user interface with Data, Layout, and Preview tabs. Their display order corresponds to the sequence of steps you typically follow to author the report:

- *Data tab*—First, you use the Data tab to set up the report data. We discuss this further in chapter 3.
- *Layout tab*—Second, you design the report layout. Chapters 4 and 5 examine designing reports.
- *Preview tab*—Finally, you test report changes using the Preview tab.

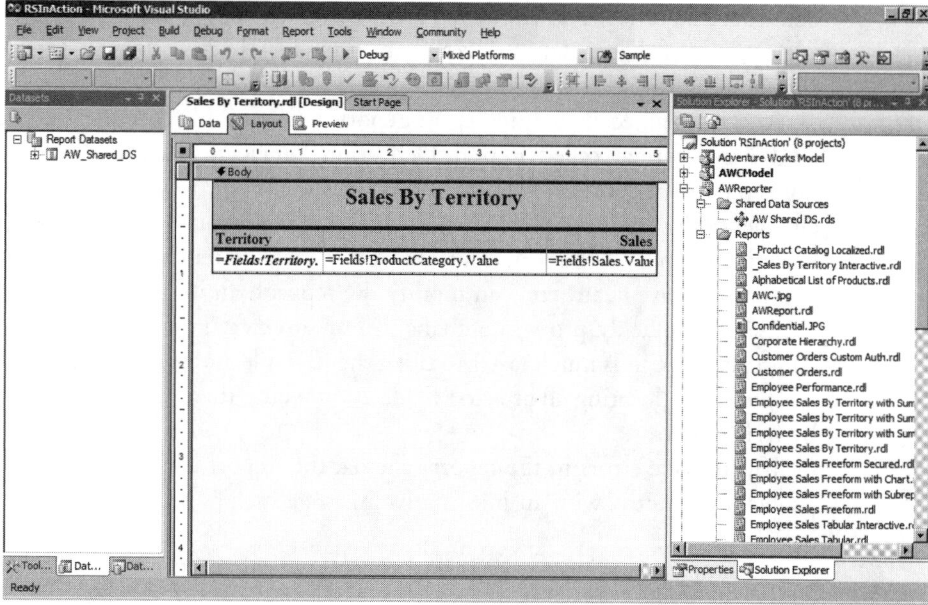

Figure 2.3 The Report Designer's tabbed window allows you to switch easily from one mode to another.

Working with BI projects

You may wonder how business intelligence (BI) projects differ from other types of projects supported by VS .NET. When you open a BI project, the VS IDE changes to accommodate the new project type, as follows:

- Two new menu items (Report and Format) are added to the main menu.
- When the report is in layout mode (the Layout tab is selected), several new toolbars appear to facilitate report formatting, such as Layout, Report Borders, Report Formatting, and Standard.
- A new Datasets toolbox lets you display the report dataset fields. Don't worry if its purpose is not immediately clear—we discuss working with data in chapter 3.
- The Report Items section is added to the toolbox (not shown in figure 2.3). You learn how to work with report items in chapter 4.

As with any other VS .NET solution, you can add more than one project as a part of a single solution. One scenario where this could be useful is when you need to step through custom code executed by a given report, as you see in chapter 6.

You manage the BI project items using the VS .NET Solution Explorer. Each project has two folders: Shared Data Sources and Reports. As its name suggests, the `Shared Data Sources` folder holds the definitions of the data sources—in other words, the connections, which are shared among all reports and projects. The shared data sources are saved in XML files with the extension `.rds`. Again, don't worry if the concept of shared data sources is not immediately clear. It will all make sense in chapter 3.

As we explained in chapter 1, the report definition file describes the report in an XML-based format called Report Definition Language (RDL). The Reports folder holds the report definition (`*.rdl`) files. It is important to note that when you make changes to the report, you are actually changing the report definition file. To view the underlying report definition, right-click on the report item and choose View Code. If you have a brave heart, you can modify the report definition file directly. This could be useful to quickly propagate changes. For instance, if you change the name of a dataset column, it is much faster to open the RDL file and perform search and replace, as opposed to locating all affected fields and making the changes in the layout mode by trial and error.

If you make errors in the report schema, the Report Designer tells you about the problem promptly, with an informative message such as this one:

```
Microsoft Development Environment is unable to load this document.
Deserialization failed: This is an unexpected token. The expected
token is 'NAME'. Line 7, position 9.
```

Besides the report definition files, you can add other external resources to the BI project, such as image files and Extensible Stylesheet Language Transformations (XSLT) transformation files. We talk more about images and exporting reports to XML in chapters 4 and 5, respectively. Although we call them *external*, note that when you upload the report to the report catalog, its associated resources get uploaded to the `Catalog` table in the Report Configuration Database.

Strangely, VS .NET doesn't allow you to create new folders below the `Reports` folder, although the Report Manager does not prevent you from creating nested folders within a project folder. We don't consider this to be a disadvantage because you want to keep the folder structure as flat as possible. We recommend that you either stick with one folder per project or organize the folder structure logically and physically per application. For example, an HR and Payroll application can have separate report folders to hold application-specific reports. We discuss folder management in chapter 8.

Previewing reports

As we mentioned earlier, you can unit-test a report on your development machine by previewing the report. The Report Designer provides two ways to preview a report: the Preview tab and Preview window. Both modes render the report locally. By *locally*, we mean outside the Report Server. In fact, you don't even need the Report Server to preview a report. Being able to work in an offline, "disconnected" mode is useful for several reasons. The report administrator may enforce secured access to the Report Server. All new reports may have to go through a verification and approval process

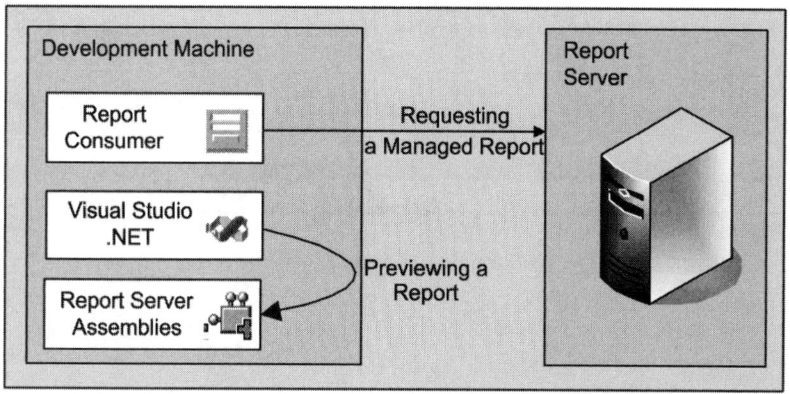

Figure 2.4 When the report is previewed, the Report Designer calls the Report Server binaries directly.

before they are deployed to the production Report Server. For this reason, you could install only the Business Intelligence Development Studio on your development machine. The Report Designer allows you to execute the whole report-authoring process on your computer. Once you are ready, you can ask the report administrator to publish the report.

You might be curious to know how it is possible to preview the report outside the Report Server because we mentioned in chapter 1 that a report is processed by the Report Server. You see, when you install the Report Designer, it installs the report-processing engine used on the Report Server into the Report Designer installation folder. The Report Designer simply delegates the report rendering to the Report Processing binaries, without asking the Report Server explicitly to do so, as shown in figure 2.4.

As figure 2.4 shows, when a report consumer requests a managed report, it asks the Report Server to generate and return the report. However, when the report is previewed with the Report Designer, no request is made to the Report Server. Instead, the Report Designer calls the Report Server binaries that are copied during the RS setup process in the Report Designer folder. For this reason, you can think of the Report Designer as a scaled-down Report Server. Of course, its capabilities are limited to report processing and rendering only.

Previewing reports using the Preview Tab

During the report-design process, you will often find yourself switching to the Preview tab to quickly see what the report looks like in its rendered form. The Preview tab is a mini Report Server by itself, as shown in figure 2.5.

Just as it does when you render a report through the Report Server, the Preview tab adds the standard report toolbar at the top of the report. The standard toolbar automatically generates parameter placeholders for parameterized reports. In addition, it

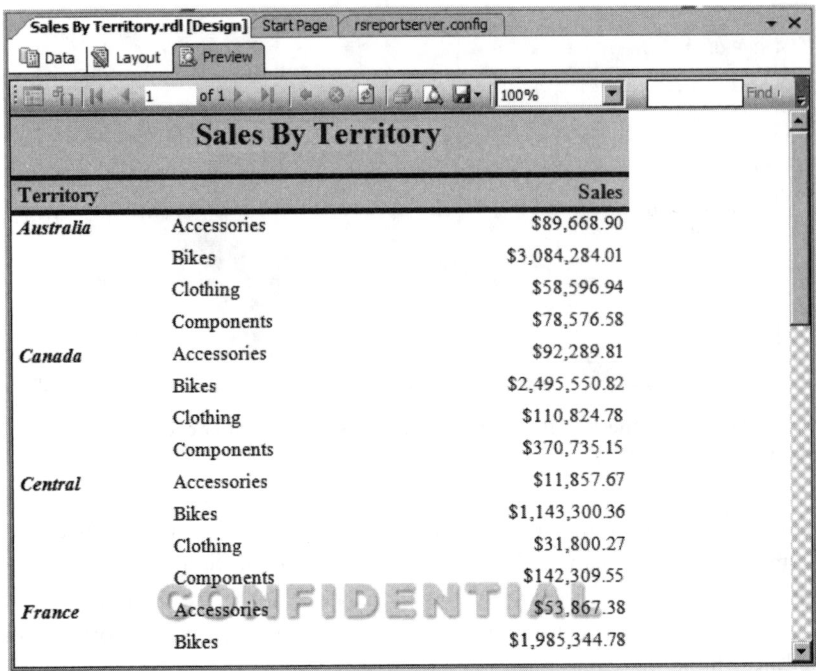

Figure 2.5 The Report Designer Preview tab allows you test the report in the VS .NET IDE.

provides zooming, paging, and printing of the report. Preview mode also allows you to export the report as a file to any supported rendering formats.

Note that previewing a report using the Preview tab bypasses the custom code security policy rules defined in the Report Designer configuration file (`rspreview-policy.config`). As a result, all custom code is granted the FullTrust permission set. If this security jargon doesn't make sense, check out appendix B, where we discuss code access security in detail.

Previewing reports using the Preview window

To preview a report in the Preview window, do one of the following:

- Right-click on the report, then choose Run.

or

- Set the StartItem property in the project settings to the name of the report you want to preview, then press F5.

Why do we need another option for previewing the report? The Preview window offers two additional features that the Preview tab doesn't have:

- It facilitates debugging external code by loading the report in a stand-alone report host process.
- It gives the report author an option to simulate the targeted Report Server environment.

As you see in chapter 6, debugging custom code can be tricky. To facilitate the debugging process, the Preview window loads the report and the custom assembly inside a separate process, called `ReportHost`. This makes debugging a lot easier because developers can add the custom assembly to the BI solution, set the StartItem project setting to the report that uses the custom code, and press F5 to debug the project. When the report calls the custom code, the breakpoints will be hit.

The second reason why the Preview window could be useful is that it can be used to simulate the Report Server environment as closely as possible. The Report Designer settings are stored in a few configuration files, which mirror the Report Server configuration files. For example, the Report Designer code access security policy is stored in the `rspreviewpolicy.config` file, while the Report Server reads its policy from the `rssrvpolicy.config` file.

NOTE The default locations for these files are:

```
C:\Program Files\Microsoft SQL Server\MSSQL.3\
Reporting Services\ReportServer\ rssrvpolicy.config
C:\Program Files\Microsoft Visual Studio 8\ Common7\IDE\
PrivateAssemblies\RSPreviewPolicy.config
```

Unlike the Preview tab, when the report is rendered (or *run*) in the Preview window, the Report Designer applies the settings from these configuration files. If the Report Designer and the Report Server settings are identical, the report will be subject to the same security checks as it would if run on the Report Server. For example, although previewing the Sales by Product Category report (which we create in chapter 6) under the Preview tab succeeds, it fails when run in the Preview window (figure 2.6).

In case you are curious, the reason for the failure is that this report references custom assemblies that require more elevated code security rights than those defined by the default permission set. We discuss code access security in appendix B.

What happens when you press F5 to run the report depends on the Configuration Manager properties, defined for the active project configuration. Figure 2.7 shows these properties for the AWReporter project.

In our case, both the Build and the Deploy check boxes are selected. As a result, when we press F5, VS .NET will build and deploy all reports within our BI project.

TIP If both the Build and the Deploy options are on, VS .NET will build and redeploy all reports inside your BI project before the report is loaded in the Preview window. This could take a substantial amount of time. Once the reports are uploaded to the report catalog, you typically don't want to rebuild and redeploy them each time you press F5. To skip these two steps and get to the Preview window faster, clear the Build and Deploy check boxes.

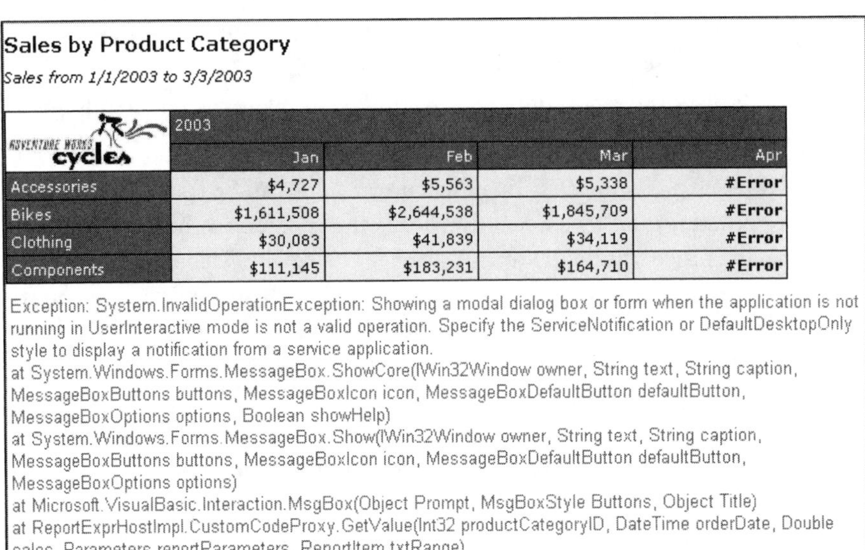

Sales by Product Category

Sales from 1/1/2003 to 3/3/2003

	2003			
	Jan	Feb	Mar	Apr
Accessories	$4,727	$5,563	$5,338	#Error
Bikes	$1,611,508	$2,644,538	$1,845,709	#Error
Clothing	$30,083	$41,839	$34,119	#Error
Components	$111,145	$183,231	$164,710	#Error

Exception: System.InvalidOperationException: Showing a modal dialog box or form when the application is not running in UserInteractive mode is not a valid operation. Specify the ServiceNotification or DefaultDesktopOnly style to display a notification from a service application.
at System.Windows.Forms.MessageBox.ShowCore(IWin32Window owner, String text, String caption, MessageBoxButtons buttons, MessageBoxIcon icon, MessageBoxDefaultButton defaultButton, MessageBoxOptions options, Boolean showHelp)
at System.Windows.Forms.MessageBox.Show(IWin32Window owner, String text, String caption, MessageBoxButtons buttons, MessageBoxIcon icon, MessageBoxDefaultButton defaultButton, MessageBoxOptions options)
at Microsoft.VisualBasic.Interaction.MsgBox(Object Prompt, MsgBoxStyle Buttons, Object Title)
at ReportExprHostImpl.CustomCodeProxy.GetValue(Int32 productCategoryID, DateTime orderDate, Double sales, Parameters reportParameters, ReportItem txtRange)

Figure 2.6 You can use the Report Designer Preview window to find out if the report will render successfully in production.

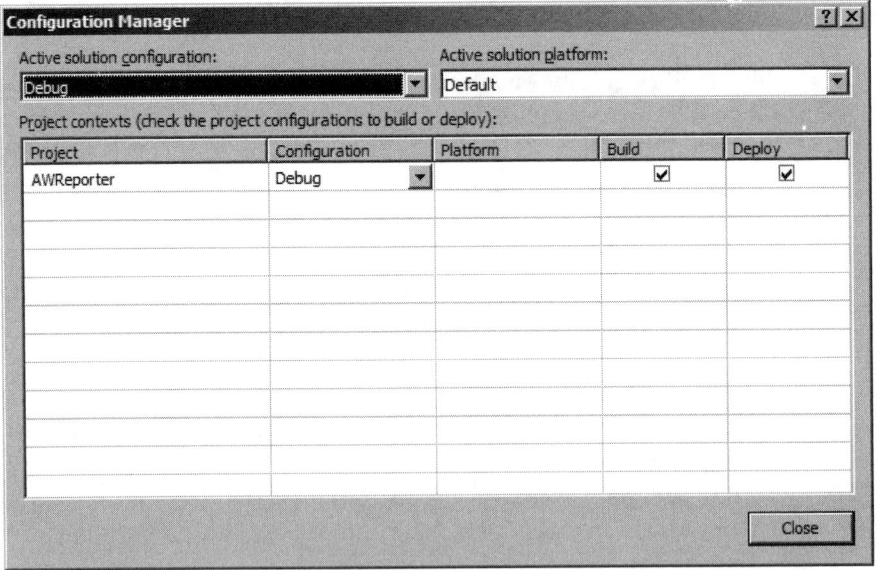

Figure 2.7 Configuration Manager properties determine what happens when you run a BI project. If the Build option is selected, VS .NET will build the project. If the Deploy option is selected, VS .NET will deploy the report items to the report catalog.

Once you've tested the report successfully, you can promote it to a managed report by deploying it to the Report Server.

Building reports

As a part of the testing process, you need to check whether the report can be generated successfully by *building* the report. Using the Report Designer, you can do this in two ways:

- *Explicitly*—To build the whole project, use the Build menu or right-click on the project node in the Solution Explorer and choose Build. To build specific reports, you can select multiple reports by holding the Ctrl key and then build them by right-clicking on the report and selecting Build.
- *Implicitly*—Switching to any of the preview modes or deploying the report causes the Report Designer to build the report automatically.

Building a report doesn't result in a binary, as you would expect when working with .NET development projects. Instead, the build process simply verifies that the report is structured properly and that all field references and expressions are resolvable. If the Report Designer determines that a validation rule is broken, it reports an exception in the Task List. For example, if you misspell a field name, the Report Designer will complain with the following exception:

```
The value expression for the textbox '<textbox name>' refers
to the field '<field name>'.  Report item expressions can only
refer to fields within the current data set scope or, if inside
an aggregate, the specified data set scope.
```

Only a report that compiles successfully can be uploaded to the report catalog. Upon deploying the report, the Report Server enforces this rule by performing the same checks that the Report Designer does when you build the report. For example, you may try to upload a report with syntax errors directly to the report catalog using the Report Manager. However, the attempt will fail with the same error as the one that the Report Designer would report in the Task List if you build the report.

Finally, once the report is tested successfully it is ready to be promoted to a managed report.

Deploying reports

If you have rights to update the report catalog, you can publish the report straight from VS .NET. As a prerequisite for this to happen, you have to set the TargetReportFolder and TargetServerURL settings in the project properties, as shown in figure 2.8.

The TargetReportFolder setting specifies the name of the catalog folder that the report will be uploaded to. If the folder doesn't exist, it will be created. The TargetServerURL setting defines the Report Server URL.

BI projects in VS .NET support separate configurations to address different deployment scenarios. For example, during the QA testing lifecycle, you would typically use a

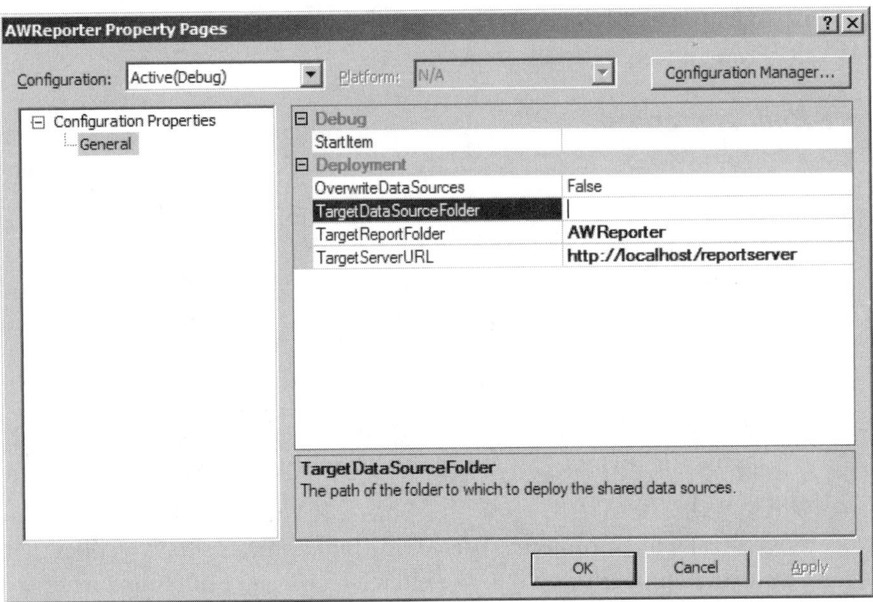

Figure 2.8 Using the project properties, you can specify different configurations to address various deployment needs.

staging Report Server. Once the report is tested, you would deploy to production. To address these deployment needs, the project settings include several predefined configurations, among them Debug, DebugLocal, Release, and Production. Clicking the Configuration Manager button from the project property page will expose this in the Configuration Manager. You can use these configurations any way you want. In fact, you can create your own configurations to meet your needs. For this example let's create a new configuration and name it **staging**. To do this from the Configuration Manager, select New from the Configurations drop-down list. This will open the New Solution Configuration dialog box. Name the new configuration **staging** and select DebugLocal from the Copy Setting From drop-down list. Assuming that you have set up separate staging and production environments, you can set your configurations as shown in table 2.1.

Table 2.1 Using different configurations to address different deployment needs

Configuration	Environment	Purpose
DebugLocal	Local machine	For unit testing with a local instance of Report Server. For example, `TargetServerURL` set to `http://localhost/ReportServer`
Staging	Staging	For QA testing
Production	Production	The production Report Server

You can also define additional configurations if needed by clicking the Configuration Manager button.

To deploy a single report from VS .NET, right-click on its file in the Solution Explorer and choose Deploy. The Deploy command first builds the report. Then, it invokes the Report Server Web service to deploy the report to the Report Server. Similar to building reports, you can deploy multiple reports by selecting them and choosing Deploy from the context menu.

Finally, just as with any other development project, we strongly suggest that you put your BI projects under source control, for example, by using Microsoft Visual SourceSafe or, even better, by using Microsoft Visual Studio Team System. To accomplish this, right-click on the project node and choose Add Solution to Source Control.

You will obtain greater insight into the Report Designer because we use it throughout the next few chapters to author various sample reports.

2.2.3 Importing reports from Microsoft Access

There is a good chance that you may be using Microsoft Access for your reporting needs. Although Access is a great reporting tool and it is becoming more enterprise-oriented with each new release, you may find that moving to Reporting Services could be beneficial for several reasons:

- RS is designed from the ground up for scalability and performance under high loads. As we explained in chapter 1, the Reporting Services architecture is service oriented and facilitates integrating RS with all types of client applications. If you want to integrate Access reports with other applications, you have to rely on legacy technologies, such as OLE Automation, or create your own home-grown solutions, which can entail significant up-front development efforts.
- Some RS features simply do not have Access equivalents, such as report scheduling and delivery, report management, and so forth. For example, with RS you can export reports to many different formats, while Access restricts you to viewing reports with the Access viewer, and exporting is limited to HTML.
- The RS architecture is extensible, while the Access one is proprietary.

There may be other reasons for upgrading from Access to RS, depending on your situation.

Reporting Services supports importing reports from Access 2002 and above only. Microsoft claims that importing from Access preserves 80 percent of the Access report features. For a full list of the supported features, consult the "Importing Reports from Access" topic in the RS documentation. The most noticeable unsupported feature, which will probably cause quite a bit of pain and suffering during the migration process, is Access custom modules and events. Since the report-generation process in RS is not event driven, any custom events that you have defined in your Access report will be lost. As a remedy, you need to find ways to replace your custom code with expressions.

Importing Northwind reports

If you decide to move to RS, you can speed the report-migration process by importing your Access reports. For the time being, Access is the only importing option natively provided by RS.

To demonstrate how this report-authoring option works, let's import reports from the Northwind database that comes with the Access samples.

NOTE The Importing from Access feature is only available if Access 2002 or later is installed.

Step 1 Create a new BI project and name it Northwind.

Step 2 Right-click on the project (or Reports) node in the Solution Explorer, choose Import Reports from the context menu, and then select Microsoft Access.

Step 3 Specify the location of the Northwind database and click OK.

You will see the imported reports added one by one to the Northwind BI project. Because VS .NET doesn't allow you to pick individual reports, all reports will be imported.

Let's open the Alphabetical List of Products report in the Report Designer by double-clicking on its file. The Report Designer opens the report in a layout mode, as shown in figure 2.9.

As you can see, VS .NET has preserved the report layout. Now, try to preview the report. The Preview window complains about compilation errors. A look at the Task List reveals that the culprit is the expression defined in the `FirstLetterOfName` field, which references the ProductName textbox as a report item. Change the expression to

```
=Left(Fields!ProductName.Value,1)
```

Now the report runs fine, as shown in figure 2.10.

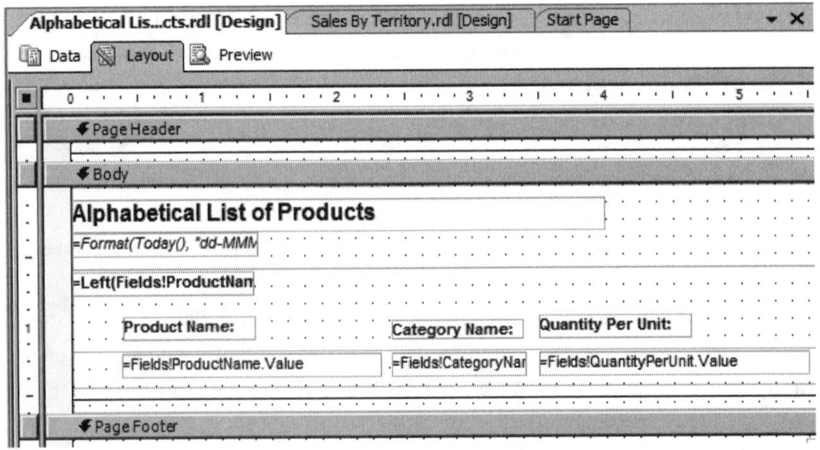

Figure 2.9 The Alphabetical List of Products report (in layout mode) after importing it from Access

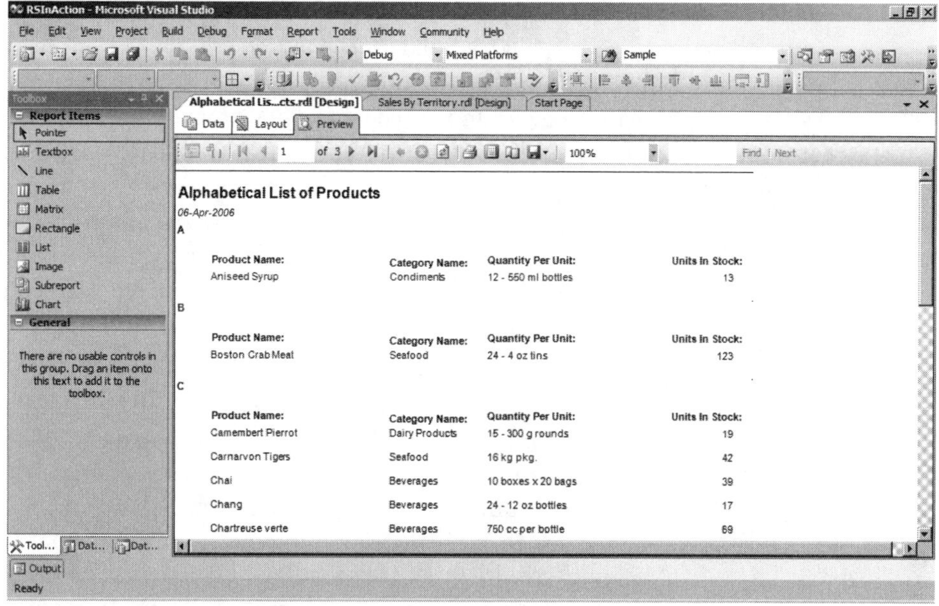

Figure 2.10 The Alphabetical List of Products in Preview mode

Strictly speaking, this report could be rendered more efficiently by using a table region instead of using a rectangle item and a list region, but still, that's not bad for a few minutes of work.

If you are experienced in Access, you can use the import feature not only to facilitate the upgrade process but also to minimize the learning curve and come up to speed quickly with RS. For instance, RS automatically converts Access expressions to their RS VB .NET equivalents; for example, `[Page]` to `Globals.PageNumber`. It is not perfect, but it will save you quite a bit of effort to just lay out the report in the Report Designer.

With RS you are not limited to creating reports interactively. Instead, thanks to the open XML nature of the report definition schema, you can produce reports programmatically.

2.3 CREATING REPORTS PROGRAMMATICALLY

If you need to author reports on the fly, creating reports programmatically by generating the report definition can be a useful technique. Recall that the report definition of an RS-based report is described in a specification called Report Definition Language (RDL).

Imagine that you need to design a multisection report, where each section shows the sales performance of a particular AWC office. A client front-end application could let the user select arbitrary sections to be included in the report. How would you implement this?

One implementation approach could be to filter the report sections at the data source. Then, you can use a data-bound list region to repeat the sections returned by the report query. But what if the database-driven approach is not an option? Ideally, in this case you would want to generate the report sections programmatically, similar to the way you can create dynamic controls in WinForm or web-based .NET applications. Unfortunately, dynamically generating report items is currently not supported by RS.

As a workaround, you can programmatically generate the report definition. Once you get the list of the selected sections by the user, you can load the report RDL in an XML Document Object Model (DOM) and create as many report list items as the number of the selected sections. Next, you can make a call to the report execution SOAP endpoint, which can run a report without publishing.

NOTE See the "Resources" section at the end of this book for a URL to the RDL schema on the Microsoft website. You can also view the RDL XSD through the Report Server by navigating your browser to `http://server-name/reportserver/reportdefinition.xsd`. RDL is composed of XML elements that conform to an XML grammar, which Microsoft created specifically for RS. Microsoft has worked with other industry leaders to promote this grammar as an XML-based standard for report definitions.

Widespread RDL adoption will increase the level of interoperability among report vendors and consumers, just like XML today facilitates interoperability between different platforms. This will open a new world of possibilities. Customers will be able to choose the best-of-breed products without having to worry about vendor lock-in. Vendors can add reporting capabilities to their applications without having to distribute report engines for report rendering. As long as the reports conform to RDL, any RDL-compliant tool can be used as a report generator. For example, a report vendor can create an ad hoc reporting tool which generates RDL files. Once the user is ready with the report, the report definition can be rendered by any reporting tool that understands RDL.

Because the RDL schema is XML based, every developer who is familiar with manipulating XML documents with the XML DOM can generate RS report definitions programmatically. Before you attempt this exercise, though, take some time to review the RDL schema specification, which is described in the RS documentation.

The RDL schema is open and allows developers and vendors to extend it by adding custom elements and namespaces. For example, you might need to develop a custom rendering extension to render a report in a format not supported by RS—for instance, a fixed text format—and you need to pass the name of the output file to it. Microsoft has already thought about this and provided a Custom element defined in the schema, which can be used as a placeholder to pass additional information. You can add your custom extension parameters to the Custom element. This element is ignored by RS, which allows you to add whatever you need to it.

NOTE RS 2000 doesn't support stand-alone reporting from the report definition file. Instead, to generate the report you need to upload the report definition to the report catalog. If you are a third-party vendor, this means that your customers must have RS installed to run your reports. However, RS 2005 does include WinForm and web-based ReportViewer controls for stand-alone reporting. We discuss these controls in detail in chapter 11.

In this section you learn, by example, how to generate RDL in an ad hoc manner. This example highlights the flexibility and extensibility of RS. However, note that the new Report Builder application included with RS 2005 is a full-featured client tool for creating ad hoc reports; we learn more about it in chapter 7.

2.3.1 Generating RDL: The AW Ad Hoc Reporter

A common reporting need for many organizations is to empower its information workers by providing them options to generate reports ad hoc. For this functionality we strongly suggest using the Report Builder application that comes with Reporting Services 2005; however, if the Report Builder application does not meet your needs for ad hoc reporting, you may find you need to create your own ad hoc tool. To demonstrate how this could be done, we've developed the world's poorest ad hoc report generator, the AW Ad Hoc Reporter. The design goals of the AW Ad Hoc Reporter are to:

- Allow the user to report off an arbitrary database table
- Allow the user to define a tabular report ad hoc by dragging and dropping columns
- Generate the report definition programmatically

You can find the AW Ad Hoc Reporter under the chapter 2 menu in the AWReporterWin sample application included in the book's source code. Figure 2.11 shows the AW Ad Hoc Reporter in action.

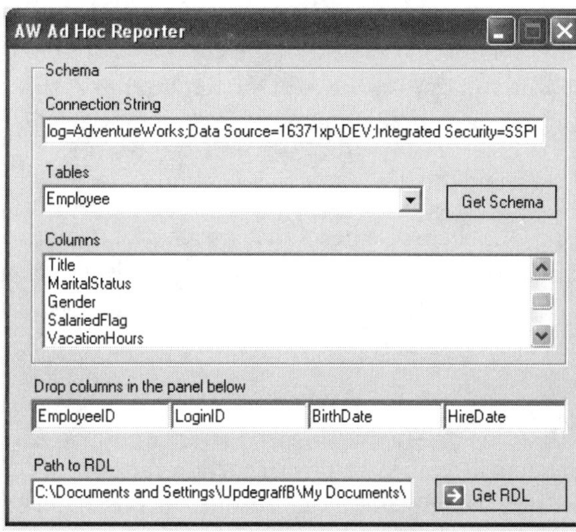

Figure 2.11 The AW Ad Hoc Reporter allows you to create very simple ad hoc reports by generating the report definition file. RS 2005 now comes with its own ad hoc reporting tool, called the Report Builder.

Here we used the Ad Hoc Reporter to author a simple report that has four fields. Once the Get RDL button is clicked, the Ad Hoc Reporter generates the report definition.

Using the Ad Hoc Reporter

The user specifies the connection string and the full path to the output RDL file. Once you change the settings, the application "remembers" by storing them in the .NET isolated storage.

After the connection string is specified, you can list the tables in the requested catalog by clicking the Get Schema button. At this point, a call to the database is made to retrieve the table schema from the requested database.

The list of table names is loaded in the Tables drop-down list. Each time you change the table in the drop-down list, its column schema is fetched from the database and shown in the Columns list.

To specify which columns to include on the report, you drag them from the Columns list and drop them on the panel below. Once a column is dropped, the application creates a textbox to display the column name and adds it to the panel. You can drop as many columns as there is space available in the panel (about four columns). Removing columns from the panel is currently not supported.

Once the report layout is defined, you can generate the report definition by clicking the Get RDL button. Before doing so, make sure that the predefined RDL schema (`Schema.xml`) is located in the application build folder, which by default is `bin\debug`.

Uploading the report definition file

After the report definition file is generated, you can upload the report to the report catalog and make it available to your end users. You can do this manually by using the Report Manager. Alternatively, you can use the Report Server Web service API to upload it programmatically. You see an example of the latter approach in chapter 8.

Now that you've seen how you can use the Ad Hoc Reporter to author report definitions programmatically, let's peek under its hood to find out how it is implemented.

2.3.2 Implementation details

Table 2.2 lists some of the RDL schema elements that we are dealing with for the purposes of this example. It by no means provides full coverage of RDL schema. See the "Resources" section for a link to the RDL section in the RS online documentation.

Let's now see how the Ad Hoc Reporter generates the actual report.

Creating the report table region

To simplify authoring the actual report, we don't generate the report definition file from scratch. Instead, we use a template in the form of a pregenerated RDL file,

Table 2.2 The RDL schema elements used in the Ad Hoc Reporter sample

Element name	XPath	Description
ReportItems	/Report/Body/ReportItems	Contains the report items that define the contents of a report region. The region may have its own ReportItems collection, which lists the report items that belong to this region.
DataSources	/Report/DataSources	Lists the data sources for the report. If the report uses a shared data source, the datasource element will contain a reference to the shared data source. Otherwise, it will contain DataProvider and ConnectionString elements.
DataSets	/Report/DataSets	Contains the datasets defined in this report.

Schema.xml, located in the AWReporterWin/bin/debug folder. This file originated from the report definition of a very basic tabular report that we authored using the Report Designer, as shown in listing 2.1.

Listing 2.1 The predefined tabular report schema

```
  <Table Name="table1">   <— Defines a table with the name "tablel"
    <Height>0.25in</Height>
    <Details>
      <TableRows>
        <TableRow>
          <Height>0.25in</Height>
          <TableCells>      <— Defines the
            <TableCell>        table cells
              <ReportItems>
                <Textbox Name="textbox1">
                  <Style />
                  <Value />
                </Textbox>
              </ReportItems>
            </TableCell>
          </TableCells>
        </TableRow>
      </TableRows>
    </Details>
    <DataSetName>AWReporter</DataSetName>   <— Defines the table dataset
    <Top>0.375in</Top>
    <Width>1.66667in</Width>
    <Style />
    <TableColumns>   <— Defines the table columns
      <TableColumn>
        <Width>1.66667in</Width>
      </TableColumn>
    </TableColumns>
</Table>
```

As you can see, the predefined schema has a table region with one column and one cell only. For the first column that the user drags and drops, we have to update only the name of the cell. For any subsequent columns, we generate a new column and cell in the table region.

Generating RDL

Let's now put on our developers' hats and write some .NET code to generate the report definition. The bulk of the report-generation logic is encapsulated in the `CreateRDL` function, as shown in listing 2.2.

Listing 2.2 Creating the report definition programmatically by loading the report schema in the XML DOM

```
private void CreateRDL()
{
   XmlDocument xmlDoc = new XmlDocument();
   xmlDoc.Load (System.IO.Path.Combine(Application.StartupPath,
             "Schema.xml"));

XmlNamespaceManager xmlnsManager =
   new XmlNamespaceManager(xmlDoc.NameTable);                  <-- Adds the namespaces used in the RDL schema
xmlnsManager.AddNamespace("rs","http://schemas.microsoft.com" _
   & "/sqlserver/reporting/2003/10/reportdefinition");
xmlnsManager.AddNamespace("rd","http://schemas.microsoft.com" _
   & "/sqlserver/reporting/reportdesigner");

   GenerateColumns(xmlDoc, xmlnsManager);      <-- Generates the table region columns
   GenerateCells (xmlDoc, xmlnsManager);      <-- Generates the table region cells
   UpdateDataSource(xmlDoc, xmlnsManager);    <-- Defines the report data source
   xmlDoc.Save(txtRDLPath.Text);
}
```

The application loads the schema using the XML DOM. Because the schema defines XML namespaces, we use the `XmlNamespaceManager` to add the namespaces to the XML document. Then we generate the table region columns and cells. For each cell, we set the field name to be the same as the column name. After that, we embed the data source information into the report definition, which includes the connection string and dataset schema. Finally, we save the RDL file to a location specified by the user in the Path to RDL textbox. Once the report definition is generated, we can test the report by loading the file in a BI project and previewing the report.

2.4 SUMMARY

In this chapter we explored the report-authoring process. This process encompasses several stages: analyzing reporting requirements, authoring, and testing and deploying the report. We emphasized that you should resist the temptation of jumping into report creation without a good understanding of what your users want. After all, the success of reports is measured by how close they match the user requirements.

In this chapter we also discussed different ways to create reports. The options provided by RS are the Report Wizard, the VS .NET Report Designer, and importing reports from Microsoft Access.

Finally, we emphasized the advantages of the RDL schema as an interoperable report storage medium. Thanks to its XML syntax, RDL allows us to generate the report definition programmatically, as we demonstrated with the AW Ad Hoc Reporter sample.

In the next chapter, we continue to explore the report-authoring process by learning how to set up the report data.

CHAPTER 3

Working with data

By now, you know that the report-authoring process involves working with the report data. Specifically, you set up the data in the construction phase of the process.

In this chapter, we provide more in-depth coverage about the Report Designer. You learn how to use the Report Designer Data tab to set up the report data. We cover the following topics:

- Setting up the data source
- Defining report datasets
- Creating dataset queries with the Graphical and Generic Query Designers
- Creating parameter-driven reports

3.1 WORKING WITH DATA SOURCES

In the simplest scenario, you won't need to integrate your report with a database at all. Before ruling out this possibility, consider an e-mail campaign in which you need to send reports to subscribers. For example, Adventure Works Cycles (AWC) may want to notify its customer base about a new product. In this case, the report will not be data driven at all, because it needs only static text and images. If this is the case, you can proceed to laying out the report itself, as discussed in chapter 4.

Most reporting requirements, however, call for data-driven reports. With the proliferation of database standards and providers, reporting off heterogeneous databases has traditionally been difficult, even with the most popular reporting tools. For example, Microsoft Access is limited to supporting only ODBC-compliant databases. One of the most prominent strengths of RS is that it can draw data from any data source that has an ODBC or OLE DB driver. Don't despair if your data source doesn't support ODBC or OLE DB. Developers can extend RS to report off pretty much any data source that exposes data in a tabular format, as you see in chapter 13.

While we aren't excluding the possibility of reporting off less popular data sources, such as flat files or Excel spreadsheets, usually your reports will draw data from designated Online Transaction Processing (OLTP) or Online Analytical Processing (OLAP) databases.

NOTE The RS documentation uses the term *data source* to refer to the definition of a database connection, which may be confusing because the name "data source" is usually associated with the database itself. Perhaps the reason behind this is to differentiate between the connection specification (connection string, credentials, etc.) and the actual physical connection. For the sake of simplicity, we use the terms *data source* and *connection* interchangeably.

In this section, we show you how to define a data source, how to configure an authentication option for it, and how to deploy it. The first step to creating a data-driven report is to set up a connection to the database where the report data resides.

3.1.1 Connecting to the database

Before we show you how to define a database connection, note that with RS your reports are not limited to drawing data from a single data store. Instead, data can originate from multiple heterogeneous databases. For example, let's say you need to create an Employee Sales Summary report that shows salespeople's performance alongside human resources (HR)-related data. You may have the sales data captured in a SQL Server database, whereas the HR data is stored in an Oracle database. One way to consolidate data from these two data sources is to link the Oracle database to the SQL Server. In this case, you need to connect to the SQL Server database only.

NOTE Microsoft SQL Server allows you to attach (link) to OLE DB-compliant data sources called *linked servers*. Once the linked server is set up, you can create stored procedures or statements that span both servers.

When using linked servers is not possible, you can define two database connections that your report will use to draw data from each database, as shown in figure 3.1.

Whether you need to fetch data from one database or several, you have to make some decisions when setting up the database connection. First, you must decide whether the connection will be set up as report specific or shared.

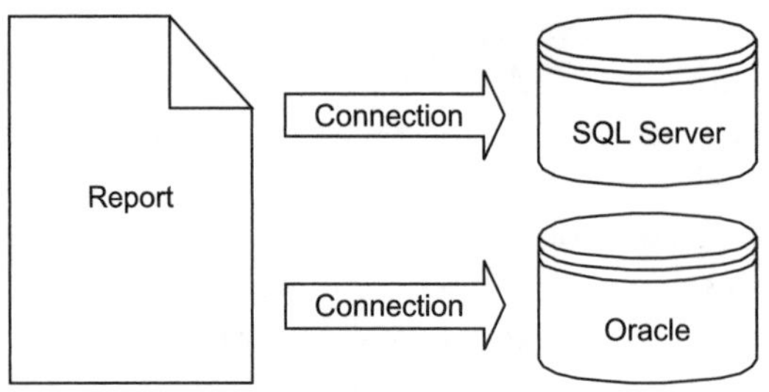

Figure 3.1
With Reporting Services your report can draw data from different databases using multiple database connections (as shown) or by using linked servers.

Report-specific data source

A report-specific connection is embedded into the report definition (RDL) file. Use a report-specific connection when:

- You need to encapsulate the database information inside the RDL file.
- You want to simplify the report distribution and setup.

A report-specific connection makes it possible to distribute both the report layout and connection information in one file. For example, a third-party vendor might choose to store database connection information in the RDL file to simplify the process of distributing the report to its customers. In this case, the connection should be defined as report specific.

You create a report-specific connection as a part of setting up the report dataset (more on this in section 3.2). The process of creating a report-specific connection is similar to setting up a shared connection, as we discuss in the next section. The only difference is that you need to deselect the Make This a Shared Data Source check box in the Select the Data Source page of the Report Wizard, as shown in figure 3.2.

To get to the window shown in figure 3.2, start from the data tab of the Report Designer and select a dataset in the Dataset drop-down list and click the ellipsis (...) button. This opens the Dataset Properties dialog box. On the Query tab, click the ellipsis button located to the right of the Data Source drop-down.

Once you finish configuring the data source, its definition will be embedded in the report, as you can see by inspecting the `DataSources` element in the report definition file. As you'll recall from the Employee Sales Summary example at the beginning of this chapter, one report can draw its data from more than one data source (report specific or shared).

Shared data source

As its name suggests, a shared data source can be used by all reports within the same Visual Studio .NET (VS .NET) Business Intelligence (BI) project. A shared data source offers the following advantages over a report-specific connection:

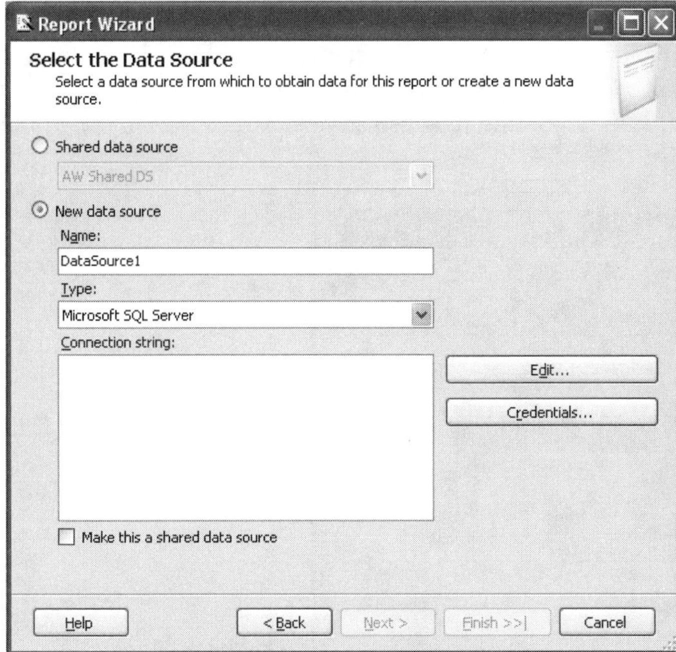

Figure 3.2
To create a report-specific connection, be sure that the Make This A Shared Data Source option is not selected.

- *It ensures that all physical connections that use the same shared data source specification utilize identical connection strings*—This is a prerequisite for connection pooling (more on this in section 3.1.2).
- *It centralizes connection management*—For example, the report administrator can use the Report Manager to change the connection authentication settings, and all reports in the project that share the connection will pick up the new settings.
- *A shared connection is a securable item*—The report administrator can enforce a role-based security policy to control which users can change the connection information.
- *When working with data-driven report subscriptions, a shared connection can be used to retrieve the list of subscribers from the subscriber store*—More on this in chapter 12.

To create a new shared connection, right-click on the project node and choose Add New Item. Then, select Data Source in the Add New Item dialog box. Otherwise, as a shortcut, you can right-click on the `Shared Data Sources` folder and select Add New Data Source.

Setting up the connection properties

To set up a report-specific or shared connection, you use the Connection Properties dialog box, shown in figure 3.3. Depending on which data provider selected, the options will vary in this dialog box. Figure 3.3 shows the options for the ODBC provider.

Figure 3.3
Use the Connection Properties dialog box to set the properties of the data source.

NOTE The ability to create connection strings based on expressions is a new RS 2005 feature that we explore further in chapter 5. If you are still using RS 2000, you may need to change the connection string manually when moving from a development to a production environment. To minimize the migration impact, consider defining data sources as shared.

Regardless of the provider choice you make, the Report Server will use one of the available *data extensions* to talk to the provider.

Working with data extensions

The supported data extensions for the report data source correspond to the .NET data providers included in the .NET Framework. RS 2005 provides several new extensions that you will find very useful and interesting. Figure 3.4 shows the out-of-the-box data extensions. Table 3.1 lists all of the supported extensions with the new RS 2005 extensions in bold type.

Behind the scenes, the Report Server maps your provider choice to one of the supported RS data extensions, as shown in figure 3.5.

The Report Server data extensions are wrappers on top of the .NET data providers. You can think about them as the Report Server Data layer. The data extensions are implemented in the `Microsoft.ReportingServices.DataExtensions` assembly.

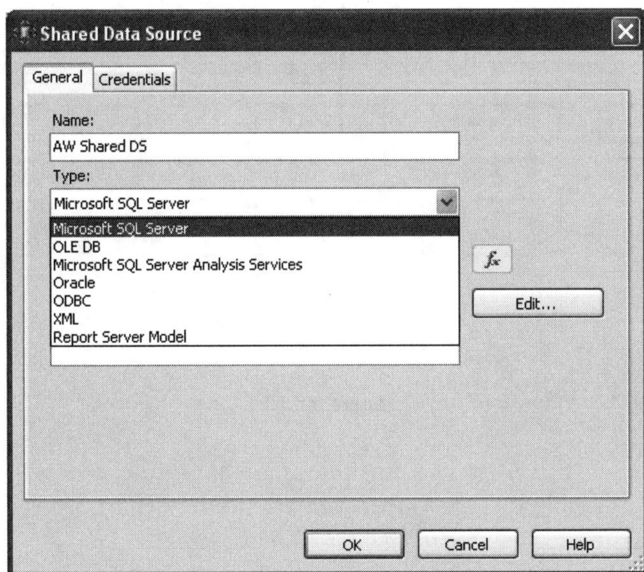

Figure 3.4
The Report Server will use one of these supported data extensions to communicate with the data provider.

Table 3.1 The available .NET data providers

Extension	Description
SQL Server	Data extension for SQL Server
OLE DB	Data extension for OLE DB-compatible data sources
Oracle	Data extension for Oracle
ODBC	Data extension for ODBC
Report Server Model	Data extension using a Report Server Model (see chapter 8)
SQL Server Analysis Services	Data extension for SQL Analysis Services
XML	Data extension for XML (Web Services)
SAP	Data extension for SAP (this is an optional download and not available out of the box)

NOTE We mention the `Microsoft.ReportingServices.DataExtensions` assembly for completeness only. You don't need to reference it explicitly in your BI project.

The extensions supported by the Report Server are enumerated in the Reporting Services configuration files. For example, only the extensions listed under the `<Data>` element in the `RSReportDesigner.config` configuration file will appear in the Report Designer Data Source dialog box.

Similarly, the Report Server will allow only the extensions listed under the `<Data>` element in the `RSReportServer.config` file to execute.

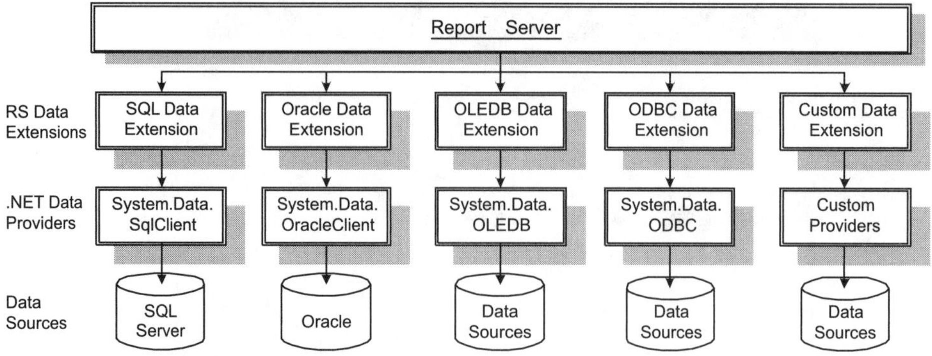

Figure 3.5 The RS Data Extensions are wrappers for .NET Data Providers.

Note that the Report Server data access options are not restricted to the eight data extensions shown in table 3.1. Developers can extend the Report Server by creating custom data extensions, as you see in chapter 13.

Once the data provider is selected, you have to decide how the user will be authenticated against the data source.

3.1.2 Choosing an authentication mechanism

The second decision that you have to make when setting up the report data source is what authentication mechanism RS will use to establish the connection. RS provides four credential options that the Report Server can use to log into the database.

Use the Credentials tab in the Shared Data Source dialog box to specify the authentication settings, as shown in figure 3.6. During design time, the Report Designer will use the credentials settings to authenticate against the data source. Note that for security reasons the credential settings are not saved in the data source definition. Instead, VS .NET caches these settings in memory. If you need to save the credentials in the data source definition, you can manually change the report RDL file (for a report-specific data source) or the report data source (RDS) file (for a shared data source).

The Report Designer Shared Data Source dialog box (shown in figure 3.6) is somewhat inadequate and doesn't display all the authentication options that RS supports. For this reason, let's discuss the full-blown Report Manager Data Source Properties tab, as shown in figure 3.7.

As shown in figure 3.7, you can choose one of the following data source authentication options:

- Credentials Supplied by the User Running the Report
- Credentials Stored Securely in the Report Server
- Windows Integrated Security
- Credentials Are Not Required

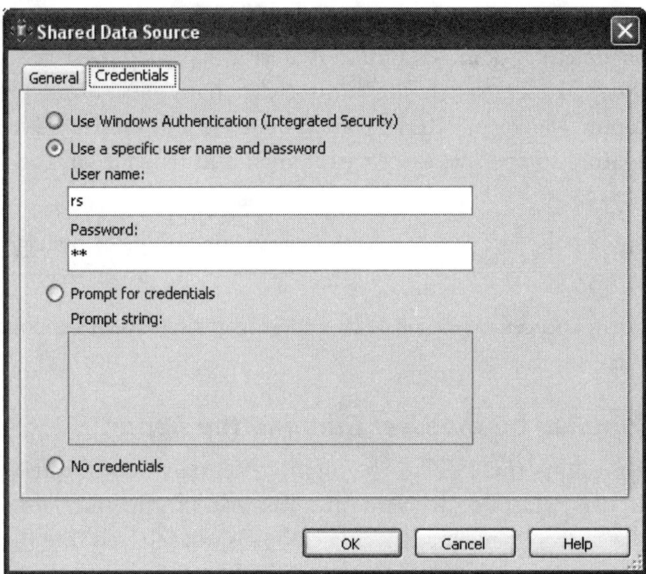

Figure 3.6 Use the Credentials tab to set the connection authentication settings.

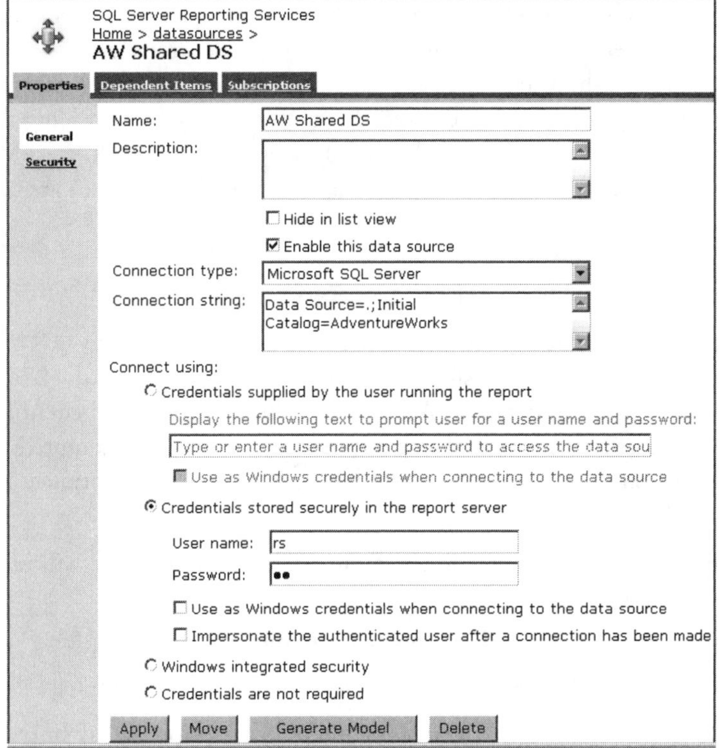

Figure 3.7 Use the Report Manager to specify authentication settings that the Report Server will use to connect to the data source.

To access the screen shown in figure 3.7, use the Report Manager web application or SQL Server Management Studio. Assuming that you have deployed the shared data source to the `AWReporter` folder, you can see the share data source properties by requesting the Report Manager URL in your browser (e.g., `http://localhost/reports`), navigating to the `AWReporter` folder, and clicking on the AW Shared DS link.

NOTE You can also use SQL Server Management Studio to manage the shared data source.

These authentication choices might seem bewildering at first, so let's spend some time exploring each one.

Credentials Supplied by the User Running the Report

This first option prompts the user for the login credentials. It will cause the Report Server to generate two fields, Log In Name and Password, in the standard report toolbar. If the Use as Windows Credentials… check box is not selected, the Report Server will attempt to authenticate the user through standard database authentication. Otherwise, Windows Authentication will be used.

The Credentials Supplied By the User Running the Report option is useful for testing purposes because you can run the report under different login credentials—for example, to troubleshoot end-user authentication issues. However, in a production environment, we recommend you avoid this option. In this case, asking the users to supply the database login credentials may present a security risk. In addition, this option cannot be used with subscribed "pushed" reports because they are generated in an unattended mode.

Credentials Stored Securely in the Report Server

The second option is Credentials Stored Securely in the Report Server. The login credentials you enter here are persisted in an encrypted format inside the `DataSource` table in the ReportServer database. Again, if the Use as Windows Credentials… check box is not selected, standard database authentication will be attempted; otherwise, Windows Integrated Authentication will be used. This second option is most likely your best bet because it:

- Promotes database connection pooling since all connections will use the same connection string.
- Centralizes the credentials maintenance in one place.
- Allows the report to be cached—for more details on caching, refer to chapter 7.

As you can see in figure 3.7, there is an interesting option called Impersonate the Authenticated User after a Connection Has Been Made. This option works only for logins with admin rights and database servers that support user impersonation. In the case of SQL Server, behind the scenes this option executes the `SETUSER` system function to impersonate the database connection, so it runs under the identity of the Windows account of the user requesting the report.

For example, imagine that you log into Windows as `AWDomain\Bob`. The report administrator has chosen the Credentials Stored Securely… option and has entered User Name and Password credentials of an account that belongs to the sysadmin SQL Server role. Now, you request the Sales by Territory report. The Report Server calls `SETUSER AWDomain\bob`. From a database point of view, this is exactly the same as if Integrated Authentication were used.

Windows Integrated Security

Next, we have the Windows Integrated Security option. When you use this option, the Report Server will attempt to establish the connection under the context of the Windows account of the user requesting the report. If you are a .NET developer, this is the exactly the same as if you'd specified the `Integrated Security=SSPI` setting in the connection string. The important thing to remember here is that the Report Server impersonates the call to the database to run under the context of the report user.

For example, in the previous scenario where Bob is requesting a report, the call to the database goes under the `AWDomain\Bob` account. Of course, in order for this to work, the database administrator has to create a database login for this Windows account and grant the right privileges. Using the Windows identity for database authentication is convenient because it allows the database administrator to simplify the database security model by using existing Windows accounts.

However, for performance reasons, we don't recommend you use this option for large reporting applications. Because the connection string for each user will be different (Windows account names and passwords are different), the connections will not be pooled. Actually, to be more accurate, you will end up with as many connection pools as the number of users requesting the report. Not good! This also could open up a security issue in that someone could publish a rogue report with integrated security and trick an administrator into running the report.

Credentials Are Not Required

Finally, the Credentials Are Not Required option allows you to configure a data source connection to use no credentials. This could be useful in the following circumstances:

- *The data source doesn't support authentication*—For example, in chapter 15 we create a custom dataset extension to report off ADO.NET datasets. Because in this case we won't have a database to connect to, we can use the Credentials Are Not Required option.

- *The credentials are specified in the connection string*—As we mentioned at the beginning of this section, you can store the credentials in the connection string by manually changing the data source definition.
- *The report is a subreport that use the credentials of the parent report to connect to its data source*—In this case the subreport will inherit the data source credentials from the parent and there is no reason to set up specific credentials.

When you select the Credentials Are Not Required option, the Report Server uses a special account to make the connection. For more information on how to set up this account, refer to the "Configuring an Account for Unattended Report Processing" section in the product documentation.

Monitoring database connection pooling

If you have experience in writing Microsoft-centric, data-driven applications, you have probably heard about *database connection pooling*. Database connections are expensive resources. Many database providers, such as the .NET SqlClient provider, perform connection pooling behind the scenes to minimize the number of open database connections. When a connection is closed, it is returned to the pool. When the application needs to connect to the database again, the provider checks the pool for available connections. If it finds one, it uses that connection; otherwise, it creates a new one.

So, connection pooling makes your application (in our case, the Report Server) more scalable. The catch is that two connections can share the same pool only if their connection strings are exactly the same, including the login credentials. The Credentials Stored Securely in the Report Server option enforces this rule and enables connection pooling. Therefore, this is our preferred option for better performance results.

To see how each authentication option affects the number of open database connections, open the Performance console from the Administrative Tools program group, as shown in figure 3.8.

Let's first experiment with the Credentials Stored Securely in the Report Server option. Before we start, you may want to change the Report Server session timeout from its default value of 600 to the minimum allowed value of 60 (the `SessionTimeout` column in the `ConfigurationInfo` table in the ReportServer SQL Server database). This causes the report session to expire sooner, which in turn forces the Report Server to query the database when processing the report.

NOTE When you experiment with different authentication options, you might be surprised to find that no connection to the database is created with the new credentials. In the case of SQL Server, you may not see the connection when using the Process Info screen in Enterprise Manager or executing the `sp_who` system procedure. The reason for this is most likely the report session caching that the Report Server does behind the scenes. The default

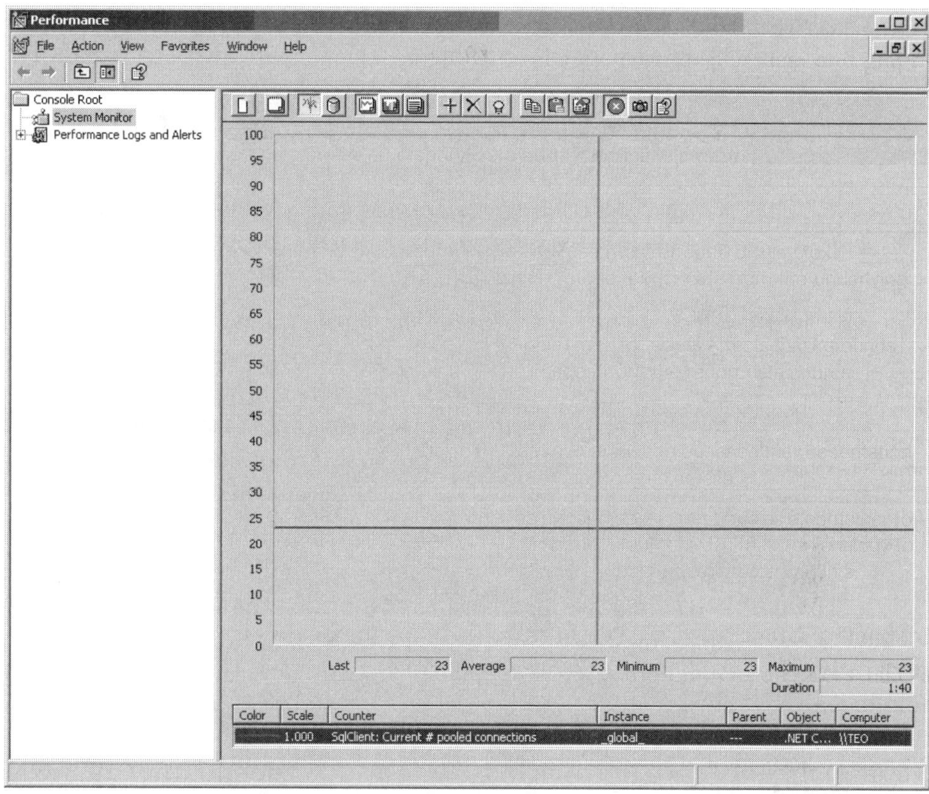

Figure 3.8 Use the SqlClient: Current # Pooled Connections counter found under the .NET CLR DATA category to monitor database connection pooling.

session timeout specified in the `SessionTimeout` field in the `ConfigurationInfo` table (ReportServer database) is 600 seconds. This means that if the Report Server decides to reuse the report intermediate format when the report is requested again, it won't query the data source within that period. Instead, it will use the report IF serialized in the Report Server Temporary Database.

We discuss report caching in detail in chapter 8. For the time being, when you experiment with different authentication connection options, you may want to decrease the `SessionTimeout` value so that the report session expires sooner. Our experiments show that you cannot completely disable the `ReportServer` session caching. The minimum value you can set the `SessionTimeout` field to is 60 seconds. If you decide to change `SessionTimeout`, don't forget to restart IIS. Alternatively, you can manually delete the record in the table `SessionData` (ReportServerTempDb database) or set its Expiration column to a date in the past.

To monitor database connection pooling, follow these steps:

Step 1 Assuming that RS is installed locally on your computer, open the Report Manager by navigating to `http://localhost/reports` in the browser. Navigate to the `AWReporter` folder and click on the AW Shared DS data source.

Step 2 Select the Credentials Stored Securely… option and specify the credentials of a database login that has rights to query the AdventureWorks database.

Step 3 Open the Performance Console and add the SqlClient:Current # Pooled Connections counter found under the .NET CLR Data performance category for the _global_ domain.

Step 4 Open another instance of the browser and request the Sales by Territory report (the encoded report URL should be `http://localhost/Reports/Pages/Report.aspx?ItemPath=%2fAWReporter%2fSales+By+Territory`). Assuming that there is no other connection with the same credentials, you should see the pooled connection counter going up. Wait for one minute or remove the session record from the `SessionData` table in `ReportServerTempDB`.

Step 5 Repeat the process by opening up another instance of the browser and requesting the report again. The pooled connection counter should remain unchanged. This means that the .NET SqlClient provider uses connection pooling behind the scenes and reuses the already existing connection.

Let's now change the authentication options of the data source to Windows Integrated Security. For the new test, you need two Windows user accounts, which are members of the Administrator group. You can use regular user accounts, but you have to specifically give them rights to the database, while members of the Administrator group automatically get admin privileges. Fire up the browser again and request the Sales by Territory report.

Observe the pooled connection performance counter. Now, right-click on the Internet Explorer shortcut and choose Run As. Specify the username and password for the second user account. Run the report again, and you will see the counter going up instead of remaining unchanged. This proves that the Report Server doesn't pool connections.

Let's wrap up our overview of authentication options with some recommendations.

Authentication best practices

To summarize, we recommend that you follow these guidelines for data source authentication:

- Use shared data sources. For example, almost all reports from the AWReporter project use the `AW Shared DS.rds` shared data source.
- Use the Credentials Stored Securely in the Report Server option with standard or Windows-based authentication.

- Don't use an account with admin database privileges! Instead, create a new database login and assign it to a role that has read-only permissions to the database you need to report off.

If you use SQL Server, you can assign the login to the `db_datareader` role, as shown in figure 3.9. In our case, we created a new SQL Server login, named it "rs", and assigned it to the `db_datareader` role. Also, we granted the new login rights to the AdventureWorks database.

As we explained in chapter 2, before end users can run the report, it has to be uploaded to the report catalog. As a part of the deployment process, you must also deploy all data sources that the report uses to the report catalog.

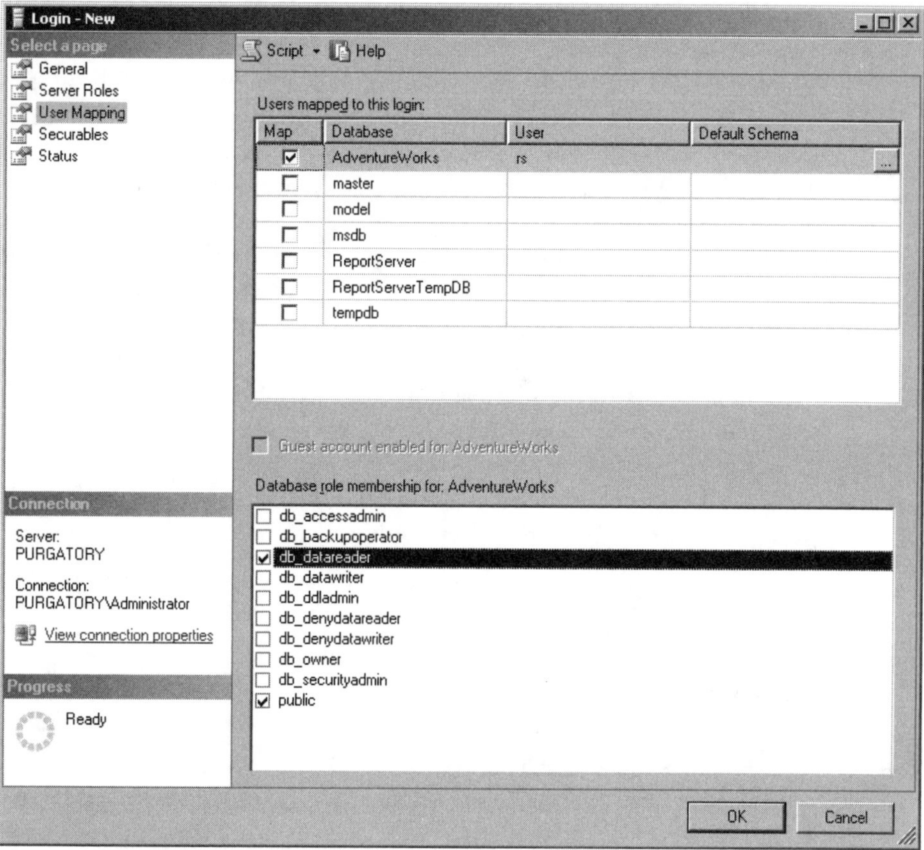

Figure 3.9 With SQL Server you can set up a database login with restricted read-only rights by assigning it to the db-datareader role.

3.1.3 Deploying data sources

Now that we've defined the data source and specified an authentication option, we're ready to deploy it. You don't need to take any extra steps to upload a report-specific data source. As you'll recall, its definition is a part of the report RDL file and travels with it.

Because a shared data source is saved in a separate file, it must be uploaded to the report catalog so it is available to all reports that use it. Assuming that you have Manage Data Sources rights, you can deploy a shared data source straight from VS .NET by right-clicking on its file and choosing the `Deploy` command. Alternatively, the report administrator can upload the file manually using the Report Manager or the SQL Server Management Studio.

What happens when you redeploy the shared data source from the VS .NET IDE depends on the `OverwriteDataSources` project setting (click on the project node in the VS .NET Solution Explorer and choose Properties). If this setting is false (the default), once the new data source has been created, any subsequent changes made to that data source inside the VS .NET project will not be propagated (will not overwrite) to the data source settings in the Report Server database.

Setting `OverwriteDataSources` to false can be both useful and dangerous. It can be useful because during the design phase you can change the data source to point to a local or staging database. You don't have to know the login credentials for the production reporting database. You can use your own set of credentials or use Windows Authentication. It is also dangerous because your development data source may have more rights to that database than the account that will be used in production environment. As a result, when you deploy your report to the production Report Server, it may fail to execute when attempting to retrieve data.

If `OverwriteDataSources` is false, then you will see the following warning when you try to deploy the project within VS .NET:

```
Cannot deploy data source <data source name> to the server
because it already exists and OverwriteDataSources is not specified.
```

Once you have the data source connection all set, it is time to craft the dataset(s) that the report will use.

3.2 WORKING WITH REPORT DATASETS

Just as .NET datasets are used as data carriers in .NET applications, RS datasets are used to expose data to your report. However, the term *dataset* as used by RS has nothing to do with ADO.NET datasets. Instead, it refers to the specification that describes how the data from the database is retrieved, and what that data schema looks like. In this fashion, an RS dataset can be loosely related to a hybrid between a .NET dataset and the data adapter used to fill it in with data. Specifically, in Reporting Services a dataset is made up of:

- The SQL query or statement that will be used to retrieve the report data
- The data source (connection) that the query will use
- The list of database fields (columns) to be used by the report
- Other information that you specify when you set your dataset, such as the options on the Data Options, Parameters, and Filters tabs

You use the Report Designer to set up one or more datasets. As with all report-related elements, the dataset definition is stored in the report definition file.

3.2.1 Understanding the dataset definition

The dataset specification becomes a part of the report definition file and can be found under the <DataSets> element. For example, listing 3.1 shows the abbreviated dataset definition for the Sales by Territory report that we created in chapter 1. To open the report definition, right-click on the Sales by Territory.rdl item in the VS .NET Solution Explorer and choose the View Code command.

Listing 3.1 The <DataSet> element, which contains the report dataset definition

```
  <DataSets>
    <DataSet Name="AW_Shared_DS">
      <Fields>                          <-- Defines the dataset fields
        <Field Name="Territory">
          <DataField>Territory</DataField>
          <rd:TypeName>System.String</rd:TypeName>
        </Field>
        <Field Name="ProductCategoryID">
          <DataField>ProductCategoryID</DataField>
          <rd:TypeName>System.Byte</rd:TypeName>
        </Field>
<!--more dataset fields...-->
      <Query>
        <DataSourceName>AW Shared DS</DataSourceName>   <-- Defines the dataset data source
        <CommandText>                                    <-- Defines the dataset query
SELECT     ST.Name AS Territory, PC.ProductCategoryID, PC.Name AS
<!--the rest of the SQL statement here-->
</CommandText>
      </Query>
    </DataSet>
  </DataSets>
</DataSet>
```

Unfortunately, you can't define a dataset as shared inside a VS .NET BI project. Therefore, the dataset definition is always report specific. It would be nice if you could reuse the dataset definition among reports, similar to the way you can create typed datasets in .NET development projects, but this is not possible with the current versions of Reporting Services.

NOTE Microsoft hints that shared queries, where definitions can be shared among reports, will be supported in a future release of Reporting Services.

Let's now see how to set up a report dataset.

3.2.2 Creating a report dataset

To create a report dataset, you will use the Report Designer Data tab. Select New Dataset from the Dataset drop-down control to bring up the Dataset dialog box, shown in figure 3.10.

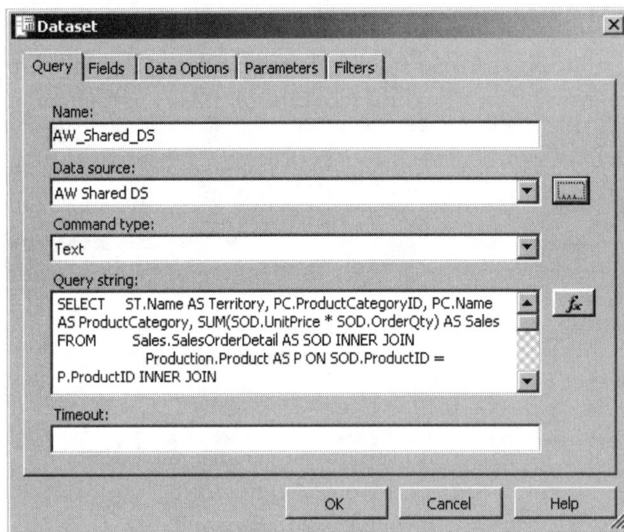

Figure 3.10
Use the Query tab in the Dataset dialog box to specify the dataset name, data source, and query string.

Let's discuss briefly each tab, starting with the Query tab.

The Query tab

The Query tab contains the following fields:

- *Name*—Consider changing the dataset name to something more meaningful, especially if you need more than one dataset for your report.
- *Data source*—Clicking the ellipsis button brings you to the Data Source dialog box (figure 3.11) that you can use to set up a report-specific or shared data source.
- *Command type*—The command type can be Text if the query string you enter is a SQL statement; a stored procedure; or TableDirect, in case you want to specify just the table name and get all data from that table (currently TableDirect is not supported by the .NET SqlClient provider, so this option cannot be used with SQL Server).
- *Query string*—You can type the query text (or stored procedure name) here or copy and paste it from somewhere else. Otherwise, if you prefer to author your

query in a civilized manner, you can leave the Query String text box blank and later use the Graphical Query Designer.

- *Timeout*—You can define a timeout value for the query execution. If you leave it empty, the query doesn't time out.

NOTE Interestingly, when you open a report in the Report Designer and switch to the Data tab, the Report Designer will query the database to retrieve the schema for the underlying datasets. In this way, the Report Designer detects any changes that might have occurred in the database and synchronizes the report dataset(s) accordingly.

The ellipsis button (next to the Data Source field) allows you to create a new data source, or connection, or to use an existing shared data source (figure 3.11).

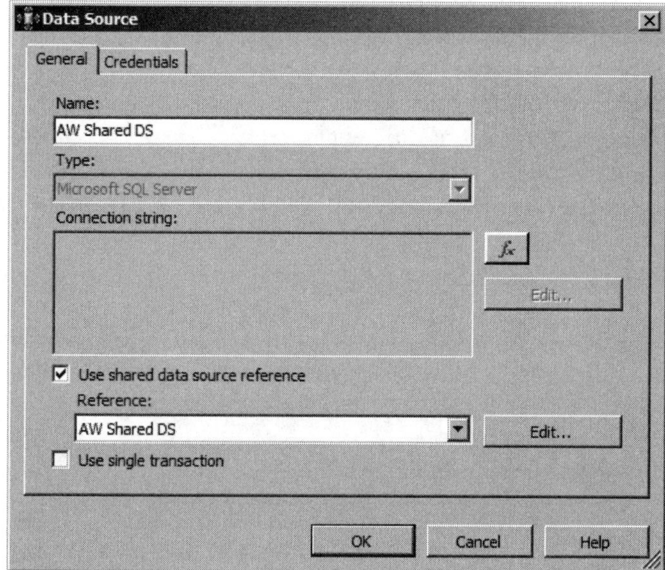

Figure 3.11 You can use a shared data source as a reference.

The interesting setting here is Use Single Transaction, which is not checked by default. If you select it, the Report Server will execute the report queries within a scope of a database transaction. Selecting this option can be useful if you report off an OLTP database and you want to prevent reading uncommitted "dirty" data. To understand how transactions can be useful, consider the following example.

Let's say you have a report with a summary and a details section—for example, a summary section showing the overall company performance and a details section that breaks down sales by territory. To create this report you've decided to use two queries: one for the summary section and another for the report details. By default the Report Server will execute these two report queries in parallel. Let's also assume that you are reporting off an OLTP database and data is volatile. What will happen if the data changes while the report is executing? The numbers in both sections may not match at all, right? To ensure data consistency, you may want to enclose both queries in a single transaction.

There is a good reason for having the Use Single Transaction option disabled by default. Transactions enforce data integrity by means of database locks, and the higher the transaction isolation level, the more locks are imposed. Database locks and performance are mutually exclusive things, so leave that option deselected unless you have a good reason to enable it.

The Fields tab

The Fields tab in the Dataset dialog box shows the dataset fields once the query is executed. Sometimes you may notice that the field list doesn't get refreshed after the underlying query is changed. If this happens, you have to manually synchronize the dataset fields. To synchronize the dataset and database schema, you click the Refresh Fields button. Alternatively, you can use the Datasets toolbox to change the fields manually. The Datasets toolbox and the Fields tab of the Dataset dialog box both offer the same functionality with a different interface. To see the Datasets toolbox, simply press Ctrl-Alt-D on the Data tab or the Layout tab of the Report Designer. (If you've worked with Reporting Services 2000, you should be aware that this Dataset toolbox used to be called the Fields toolbox.)

For example, let's say you add a new field to your SQL statement and the field doesn't appear in the Report Designer. To fix this, right-click on any field in the Fields toolbox and select Add to open the dialog box shown in figure 3.12.

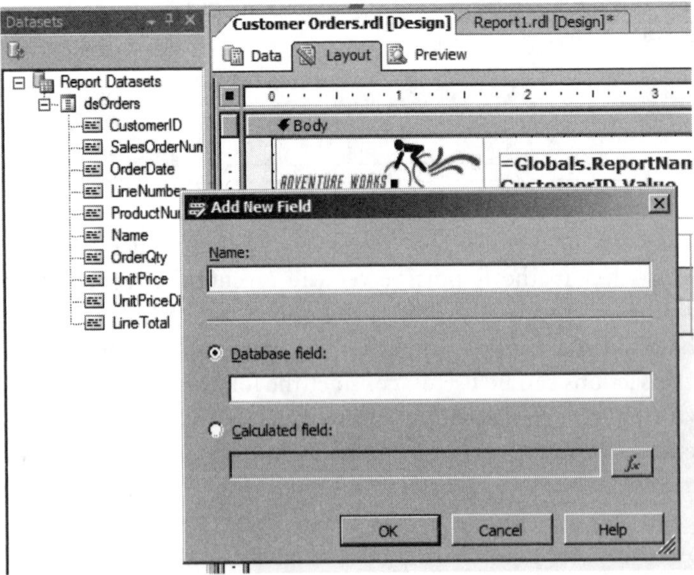

Figure 3.12
Add a new dataset field using the Add New Field dialog box.

You can also create calculated dataset fields. A calculated field is a field based on an expression. Because expressions can reference methods in external .NET assemblies, the sky is the limit as to what the content of a calculated field can be. (We cover expressions in chapter 5.) Of course, if the expression involves only database columns, you are better off using expressions supported by the targeted data source for performance reasons.

If for some reason you want to change the dataset field name to something other than the database column name, you can do this by changing the value of the Field Name property.

The Data Options tab

The Data Options tab allows you to set additional data options for the query, such as case sensitivity, as shown in figure 3.13.

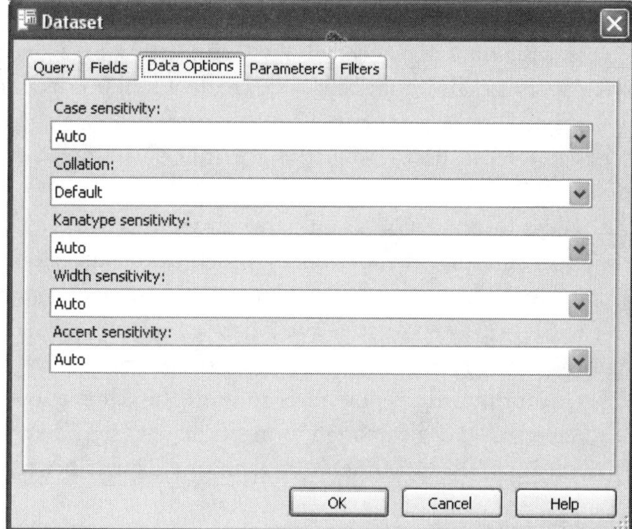

Figure 3.13 You can use the Data Options tab to define additional options for the dataset query.

For example, when you set the Case Sensitivity option to True, the clause `where FirstName = 'john'` will not bring up records where the first names start with capital J.

By default, RS will attempt to derive the values of data options from the data provider when the report runs. For more information about the query data options, see the product documentation.

The Parameters tab

The Parameters tab allows you to define parameters for your query. We discuss working with dataset parameters in section 3.4.

The Filters tab

Use the Filters tab in the Dataset dialog box to limit the data fetched by the query. A dataset filter works like a SQL `WHERE` clause, but an important distinction exists. While you can use a `WHERE` clause in your SQL statement to filter data at a data-source level, a dataset filter limits the data *after* it has been retrieved from the data source.

For example, if you want to filter a Products Sales by Quarter report to show product sales only in 2004, you can do so in one of two ways:

- Use a SQL `WHERE` clause to filter the results at the data source.
- Get the product sales for all years and then eliminate the unwanted records during the report generation using a dataset filter.

As you can imagine, filtering at the data source is much more efficient, so report filters should be used with caution. One possible scenario where filtering can be useful is when you need to enforce security. Let's say that the Sales by Territory report takes a parameter that allows privileged users to request the report for a given territory. However, you want to prevent regional managers who will run the report from requesting a territory they don't supervise. To implement this, create a lookup dataset for available parameter values. Then, set a filter based on an expression, which restricts the parameter choices based on the user's Windows identity. We implement such an example in chapter 9.

Another scenario where filters can be useful is when you need to work with data sources that don't support filtering. If you wonder which data sources don't support filtering, check out chapter 13 where we write a custom dataset data extension. The extension allows you to "bind" a report to a .NET dataset. ADO.NET datasets don't currently support a SQL-like `WHERE` clause, so you cannot easily filter data at the dataset level. However, you can use a report filter to limit the dataset rows.

Sometimes, one dataset may not be enough to meet the data requirements of your report. Fortunately, with RS you can define more than one dataset per report.

3.2.3 Using multiple datasets

To add another dataset to your report, return to the Data tab, expand the Dataset drop-down list, and select New Dataset. This opens the Dataset dialog box shown earlier in figure 3.10.

Having multiple datasets can be useful for two main reasons:

- For parameterized reports you can make the report parameters data driven from a separate dataset. For example, a typical reporting requirement is to restrict the parameter choice to a predefined set of values. To accomplish this with RS, you can use one dataset for the report data and a second one for the parameter lookup values. You'll see an example of this in section 3.4.4.
- Different sections of the report can be driven by different datasets, as you'll see in chapter 4. As we mentioned earlier, multiple datasets don't have to fetch their data from the same data source.

There are a few important points about multiple datasets that we would like to mention. You cannot join datasets as you could join database tables by using relations, even if they have the same fields. As a result, you cannot mix fields from different datasets in a single report region. We look at report regions in chapter 4, but for the time being note that RS supports various report items called regions for different report types, including charts, tables, pivots, and other regions. To display data in a region, you need to associate (bind) it with exactly one dataset.

While the Report Designer allows you to drag fields from one dataset to a region bound to another, you can use only aggregate functions, such as `First()`, `Sum()`, and `Avg()`, when referencing its fields. If you try to reference the field directly (outside an aggregate function), then you will see the following exception during the report-compilation process:

```
Report item expressions can only refer to fields within the
current data set scope or, if inside an aggregate, the
specified data set scope.
```

Chapter 5 details the expression scope rules.

For best performance results, we suggest you minimize the number of the report datasets in your reports. In the best case, you will need only one dataset as an underlying source for the report data. You should carefully evaluate whether you need additional datasets for the available values of report parameters.

One scenario in which you may require an additional dataset is when you have to restrict the parameter choices in the report toolbar for reports requested by URL. With other integration scenarios, the client application may be responsible for collecting and validating parameters. If this is the case, you won't need another dataset to define the parameter lookup values.

To fill in a dataset with data, you need to set up a dataset query. One dataset can be associated with exactly one query. When the report is processed, the Report Server will execute the dataset query statement against the data source and load the dataset. We'll take a closer look at this process next.

3.3 AUTHORING DATASET QUERIES

To help you with setting up the database queries, the Report Designer comes with not one, but two Query Designers: Graphical and Generic. Whereas the main characteristic of the Graphical Query Designer is convenience, the Generic Query Designer excels in flexibility. In this section, you learn how to use both.

3.3.1 Using the Graphical Query Designer

Figure 3.14 shows the Sales by Territory dataset open in the Reporting Services Graphical Query Designer. You may be familiar with the Graphical Query Designer because it is the same one that SQL Server Enterprise Manager, VS .NET, and a plethora of other development tools use. It makes authoring complex SQL statements a

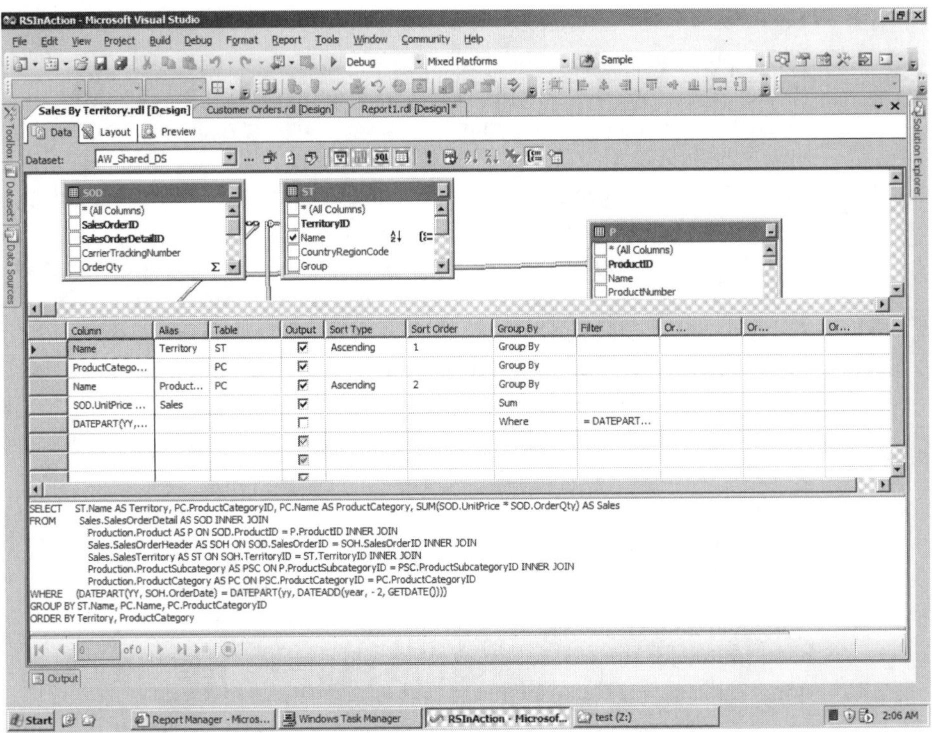

Figure 3.14 Use the Graphical Query Designer to author, test, and run queries.

breeze. Even users unfamiliar with the intricacies of SQL can create sophisticated queries in a matter of minutes.

The Graphical Query Designer also has SQL syntax checking to make sure that any query text you specify makes sense and conforms to the SQL grammar supported by the targeted database. Once you craft your query and execute it, the dataset fields will be shown in the Datasets toolbar on the left, as well as on the Fields tab of the dataset properties.

Authoring a dataset query with the Graphical Query Designer is a matter of completing the following steps:

Step 1 Right-click on the Diagram pane empty area and choose Add Table. Add as many tables from the data source as needed.

Step 2 Select table columns as needed. The Graphical Query Designer shows the resulting SQL statement in the SQL pane.

Step 3 Modify the statement as per your requirements using the SQL pane or the Grid pane.

Step 4 Run the query by clicking the Run button (the one with the exclamation point) to see the results in the Results pane.

3.3.2 Using the Generic Query Designer

Sometimes you will reach the limits of the Graphical Query Designer, as in the following two situations:

- You need to execute multiple SQL statements—for example, to perform some preprocessing at the data source.
- You need to work with SQL statements generated on the fly.

This is where the Generic Query Designer comes in. To learn how to use this Query Designer, let's discuss each of these scenarios in more detail.

Executing multiple SQL statements

Say you need to run an update query to the `SalesOrderDetail` table before the sales order data is retrieved, as shown in listing 3.2.

Listing 3.2 Using batches of statements to update and retrieve data

```
DECLARE @SalesOrderID int
SET     @SalesOrderID = 1

UPDATE  Sales.SalesOrderDetail
SET     UnitPrice = 100
WHERE   (SalesOrderID = @SalesOrderID )

SELECT  *
FROM     Sales.SalesOrderDetail
```

NOTE In the real world, you should avoid retrieving all table columns using the * wildcard in your queries. Instead, for performance reasons you should limit the number of columns to the ones you need.

Granted, using multiple queries could be accomplished by encapsulating both statements inside a stored procedure, but sometimes you may not have this choice.

You may try using the Graphical Query Designer to execute this batch, but you wouldn't get too far. The Graphical Query Designer complains with the following error:

```
The Declare cursor SQL Construct or statement is not supported.
```

Our example doesn't use a SQL cursor at all, but in any case, the Graphical Query Designer refuses to cooperate.

As a workaround, we can switch to the Generic Query Designer (figure 3.15) by clicking on its button (the one to the right of the Refresh Fields button).

If the data source credentials have update rights to the database, the SQL block will execute fine and the dataset fields will be populated based on the columns defined in the select statement (in this case, all columns from the `SalesOrderDetail` table).

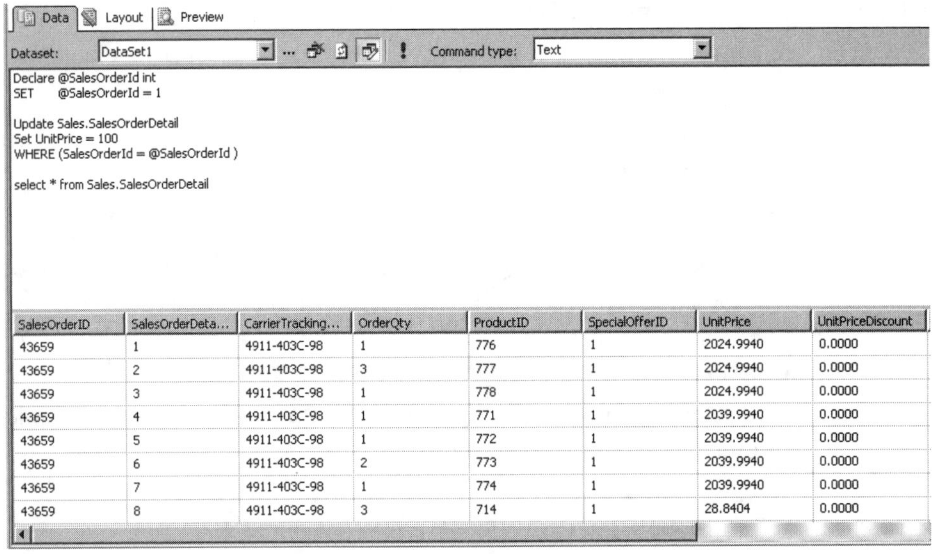

SalesOrderID	SalesOrderDeta...	CarrierTracking...	OrderQty	ProductID	SpecialOfferID	UnitPrice	UnitPriceDiscount
43659	1	4911-403C-98	1	776	1	2024.9940	0.0000
43659	2	4911-403C-98	3	777	1	2024.9940	0.0000
43659	3	4911-403C-98	1	778	1	2024.9940	0.0000
43659	4	4911-403C-98	1	771	1	2039.9940	0.0000
43659	5	4911-403C-98	1	772	1	2039.9940	0.0000
43659	6	4911-403C-98	2	773	1	2039.9940	0.0000
43659	7	4911-403C-98	1	774	1	2039.9940	0.0000
43659	8	4911-403C-98	3	714	1	28.8404	0.0000

Figure 3.15 You can execute multiple SQL statements in the Generic Query Designer.

The Graphical Query Designer is great for creating SQL queries by selecting tables and columns in a graphical manner. The usefulness diminishes if you are creating complex queries that update, use temp tables, or use cursors.

NOTE The previous query requires UPDATE rights to the AdventureWorks database. If the data source account is restricted, the report will fail to execute even if the report doesn't use any of the dataset fields. The reason for this is that when a report is requested, the Report Server executes all report queries to populate the report datasets. For this reason, we recommend that you delete this dataset as soon as you are finished experimenting so that it doesn't interfere with report processing.

Using expression-based queries

A second scenario where you will need to use the Generic Query Designer is when you are working with expression-based queries. Unlike the Graphical Query Designer, the Generic Query Designer doesn't attempt to parse the query text to ensure it is syntactically correct. Instead, it allows you to type whatever you want, and once the query is constructed, it passes the query directly to the data source. For users familiar with Microsoft Access, the Access equivalent is a pass-through query.

We haven't covered expressions yet (see chapter 5), but consider the case in which you want to restrict the results returned from the `SalesOrderDetail` table only if the OrderID is specified. To achieve this, use a Visual Basic .NET (VB .NET) expression, similar to this one:

```
= "select * from Sales.SalesOrderDetail " & _
Iif(Parameters!OrderID.Value Is Nothing, "", _
" where SalesOrderID =" & Parameters!OrderID.Value)
```

NOTE Expression-based queries are susceptible to *SQL injection attacks*. SQL injection happens when some (malicious) SQL code is appended to the legitimate SQL statement contained within the report query. For example, the SQL statement we've just discussed is vulnerable to a SQL injection attack. A hacker could pass another SQL statement to the `OrderID` report parameter—for example, a data modification statement to update, insert, or delete data; or a statement to alter or even drop database objects. As a result, the expression-based statement may look like this:

```
= "select * from Sales.SalesOrderDetail where
SalesOrderID = 1;UPDATE Sales.SalesOrderDetail
(SET // perform data changes here
```

There are a number of strategies for using expression-based statements safely in your reports. One is to filter out the report parameters for valid SQL characters—for example, the semicolon delimiter character in our case.

When the Generic Query Designer determines that expressions are used, it doesn't give you a choice to execute the query by clicking on the exclamation point. As a result, you won't be able to get the dataset fields. Instead, you need to add the fields manually, using either the Fields toolbox or the Fields tab in the dataset properties. Next, drag the fields to the report layout and execute the report. Finally, if the query is based on an expression, as in the above case, don't forget to prefix the text with "=".

We would like to fast-forward a bit and mention that the ability to use an expression to generate the SQL statement on the fly opens a whole new world of opportunities. Your report can call a piece of code defined as an expression or in an external assembly to get the query statement custom-tailored, based on certain conditions. The example that follows is simple but illustrates the expression's flexibility. Say you have a function that returns a SQL statement, like the one shown here:

```
Function GetSQL (ByVal orderID as Integer) as String
   Return "select * from Sales.SalesOrderDetail where " _
   & "SalesOrderID = " _ & orderID
End Function
```

The `GetSQL` function can be defined as an embedded function in the report or located in an external assembly—for example, in the application data layer. We discuss extending RS with custom code in detail in chapter 6.

Once the `GetSQL` function is ready, you can use the Generic Query Designer to set your query text to

```
= Code.GetSQL(Parameters!OrderID.Value)
```

In this case, you are calling the `GetSQL` function and passing the value of the `OrderID` report parameter. Once you manually define the fields that the query returns, you can base our report on the results of this generated on-the-fly query. Talk about flexibility!

Now that you know how to use the Query Designers to create basic dataset queries, let's see how to make them more flexible by using parameters.

3.4 PARAMETER-DRIVEN REPORTS

Your dataset queries won't be very useful if they don't allow users to pass parameters. Report and query parameters allow users to alter the report execution to return a subset of data in the report. For example, you can add a parameter to the Sales by Territory report to enable users to specify the sales year rather than defaulting to the current year. We'll see exactly how to do this in section 3.4.2.

3.4.1 The role of parameters

Recall from chapter 1 that the Report Server enjoys a service-oriented architecture that is entirely server based, and also recall that Reporting Services reports can be requested by both URL and SOAP methods.

The Report Server doesn't offer an object model that can be instantiated and manipulated locally by the report consumer, as you would have probably done in the past with other reporting tools—for example, using OLE Automation to control Microsoft Access. Instead, the only way to control the report-generation process from outside is by using parameters, as shown in figure 3.16.

If you are accustomed to object-oriented programming, this may seem strange at first. But consider the benefits. The service-oriented architecture of the Report Server eliminates tight coupling between the consumer and server. If the Report Server had an object model that could be instantiated locally by the report consumer, then most likely its client base would have been restricted to .NET-based applications only. Instead, thanks to its service-oriented architecture, RS can be integrated with any type

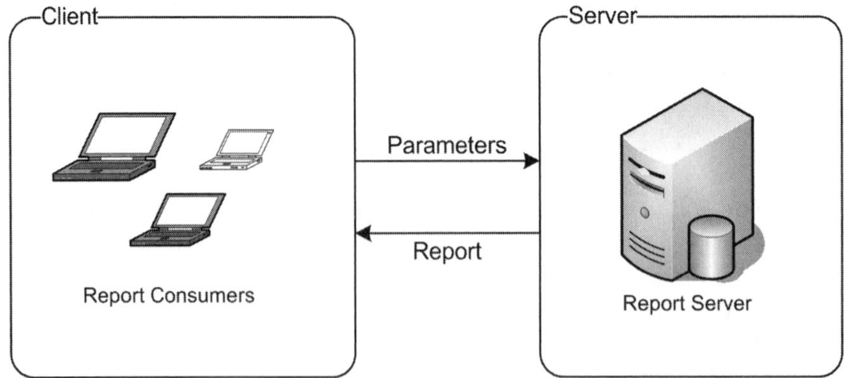

Figure 3.16 From the report consumer perspective, the Report Server can be viewed as a black box that accepts report requests and, optionally, parameters, and also returns reports.

of consumer. Developers familiar with designing stateless web services will find the Report Server programming model similar.

The RS report-processing model is stateless because once the report is generated, the Report Server discards any state associated with the report request. As far as the report-generation process is concerned, you can think of the Report Server as a black box that accepts a report request (optionally parameterized) and returns the generated report. Do you want to sort the report data in a different way? Do you want to filter out the data that the data source returns? Do you want to show or hide certain report items based on runtime conditions?

By using parameters, coupled with custom expressions inside the report, you can achieve just about anything you can otherwise accomplish with an object model. For example, hardcoding criteria in your queries is convenient for the developer, but not very useful for the end users. Often, you will need to make the report interactive by allowing the users to pass report parameters. To accomplish this, a parameter value can be passed to the dataset query or stored procedure to filter out the report data.

Let's see how we can make our Sales by Territory report interactive by allowing users to specify the sales year instead of always defaulting to the current year.

3.4.2 Building parameter-driven queries

We can easily change the Sales by Territory report's dataset query to use a query parameter. Since we are using SQL Server as a database, we need to use named parameters.

NOTE The named parameter syntax is specific to the data extension. In the SQL .NET provider you use named parameters (`@varname`). With the Oracle data extension you use named parameters but with a different prefix (`:varname`). The OLE DB provider doesn't support named parameters, but you can use the question mark (`?`) for parameter placeholders.

To make the query parameter-driven, complete these steps:

Step 1 Start by saving the Sales by Territory report to Sales by Territory Interactive report. The easiest way to accomplish this is to right-click on the Sales by Territory report in the Solution Explorer and choose Copy.

Step 2 Right-click on the project node (AWReporter) and choose Paste. Rename the new report to Sales by Territory Interactive.

Step 3 From the Graphical Query Designer, open the AW_Shared_DS dataset and replace the `DATEPART(yy, DATEADD(year, - 1,'1/1/2003'))` criteria with `@Year`, as shown in listing 3.3 (in bold). In the dataset, we specify a named report parameter called `Year`.

Listing 3.3 Using a query parameter to filter the query data

```
SELECT    ST.Name AS Territory, PC.ProductCategoryID,
  PC.Name AS ProductCategory,
  SUM(SOD.UnitPrice * SOD.OrderQty) AS Sales
```

```
FROM  Sales.SalesOrderDetail AS SOD
  INNER JOIN Production.Product AS P ON
SOD.ProductID = P.ProductID
  INNER JOIN Sales.SalesOrderHeader AS SOH ON
SOD.SalesOrderID = SOH.SalesOrderID
  INNER JOIN Sales.SalesTerritory AS ST ON
SOH.TerritoryID = ST.TerritoryID
  INNER JOIN   Production.ProductSubcategory AS PSC ON
P.ProductSubcategoryID = PSC.ProductSubcategoryID
  INNER JOIN Production.ProductCategory AS PC ON
PSC.ProductCategoryID = PC.ProductCategoryID
WHERE     (DATEPART(YY, SOH.OrderDate) = @Year )
GROUP BY ST.Name, PC.Name, PC.ProductCategoryID
ORDER BY ST.Name, PC.Name
```

Step 4 Now run the query. When the Graphical Query Designer parses the query, it discovers the `Year` parameter and displays the Query Parameters dialog box, as shown in figure 3.17.

Step 5 Enter **2003** in the Parameter Value field and click OK. The query retrieves the sales orders placed in 2003.

Once the Graphical Query Designer parses the parameter, it will add the parameter to the parameter list defined for this query, which can be seen on the Parameters tab of

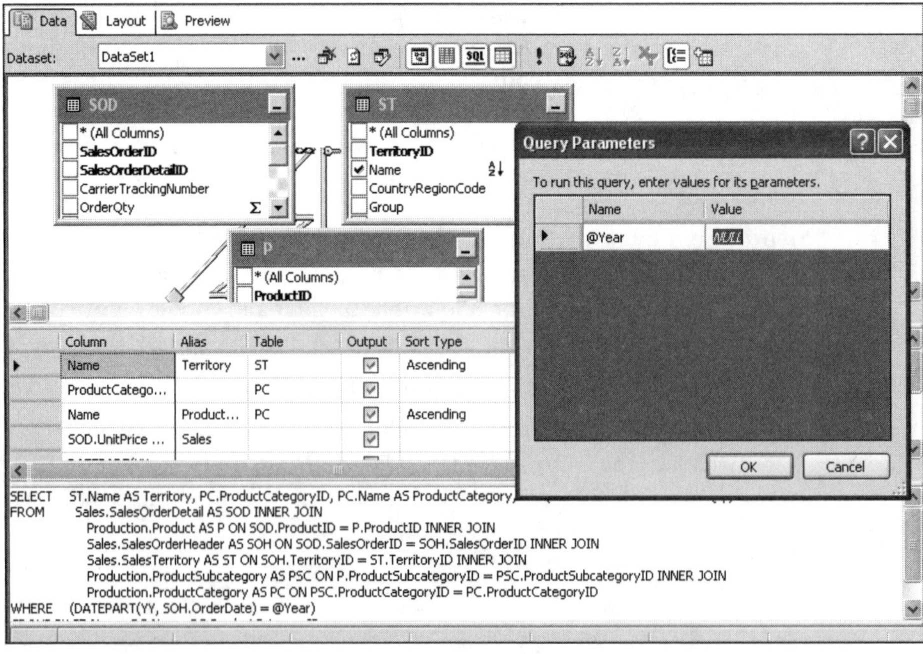

Figure 3.17 To set up a parameter-driven query, specify parameter placeholders.

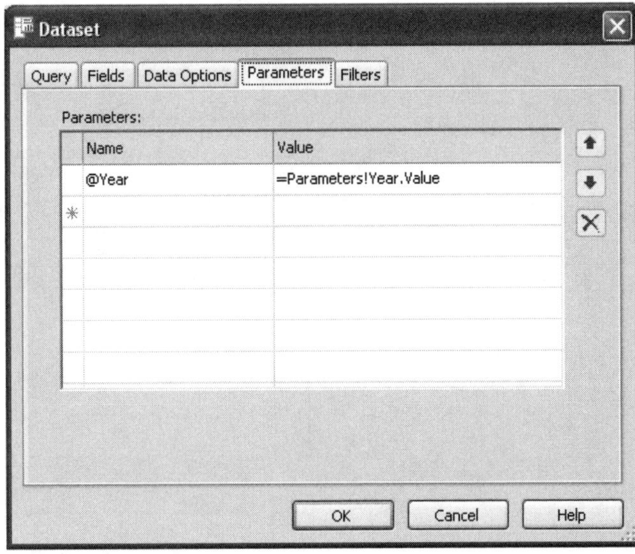

Figure 3.18
Use the Dataset dialog box's Parameters tab to see all parameters defined in the dataset query.

the Dataset dialog box (figure 3.18). To view the dataset properties, select it in the Dataset drop-down list and click on the ellipsis button next to it.

At this point, the `Year` parameter is associated with the dataset query. In addition, the Report Designer automatically creates a report-level parameter with the same name and links the query-level and report-level parameters together. The reason behind this behavior is that the Report Designer assumes that the parameter should be accessible from external callers.

NOTE To pass the parameter value from outside the report—for example, from client applications—you need to create a report-level parameter.

Let's now see how we can work with report-level parameters.

3.4.3 Setting up the report-level parameters

To allow end users to set the value of the query parameter, you need to create a report-level parameter and associate it with the query-level parameter.

If you want to see all report-level parameters defined for a given report, select the Report Parameters submenu item from the VS .NET Report menu. The Report menu is available only in Data or Layout mode (when the Data or Layout Report Designer tabs are active). Figure 3.19 shows the Report Parameters dialog box for the Sales by Territory Interactive report.

As we said earlier, by default the Graphical Query Designer assumes that the report parameter will be publicly accessible and pairs each query-level parameter with a report-level parameter. However, you can manually add or remove report-level parameters if needed.

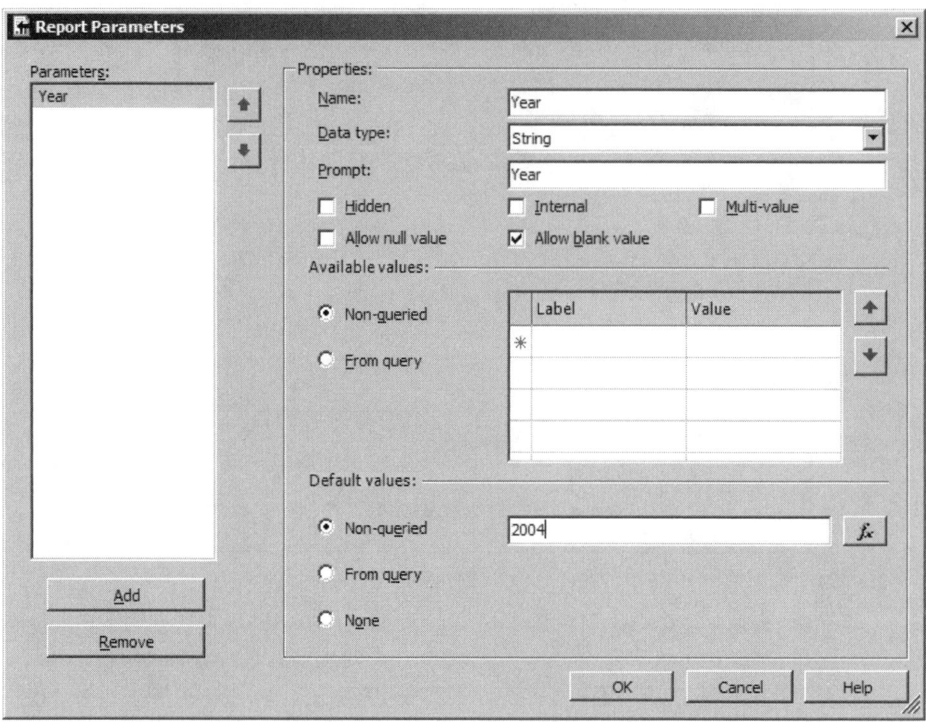

Figure 3.19 Use the Report Parameters dialog box to set up the report parameters.

One scenario that calls for adding parameters manually is when you need more parameters than the report query (or queries) takes. For example, you may need a parameter to pass some value that is used in an expression.

Why would you want to remove a report-level parameter? This can be useful if you don't want the users to pass values to it. For example, the query parameter may be derived internally using an expression and it may not make sense to expose it to the end user. New in RS 2005 is a `hidden` property that you can set to hide the parameter.

NOTE When you remove a query parameter, the Report Designer doesn't assume that you want to remove the report parameter as well. It leaves the report parameter in the report, which may result in an orphaned publicly accessible parameter. To "fix" this, open the Report Parameters dialog box and remove the parameter.

Let's walk through the Report Parameters dialog box.

Specifying a parameter label

The Prompt field allows you to specify a parameter label that will appear on the standard report toolbar. Enter **Year:** for the Year prompt.

Leaving the Prompt field empty results in a read-only parameter that will not show in the standard report toolbar when the report is requested by URL. Moreover, trying to set the parameter explicitly when requesting the report either by URL or SOAP will result in an error. A read-only parameter must have a default value associated with it.

Read-only parameters can be useful for reports that require fixed parameter values. For example, you may have a "Sales by Quarter" report that shows the data for a given quarter that is passed as a parameter value. Let's say that at some point you want to prevent users from running this report for an arbitrary quarter. Instead, you decide to default the parameter value to the current quarter. One way to hide the parameter is to remove it from the report-level parameters. Another option to hide the parameter temporarily is to select the hidden check box.

Specifying the parameter data type

The Data type drop-down list restricts the available choices to Boolean, DateTime, Integer, Float, and String. If you wonder why no other types are available, recall the fact that RS runs in its own isolated process. This requires all parameter values to be serialized between the report consumer and the Report Server. For this reason, the choice of the parameter data types is restricted only to .NET primitive types that can be passed by value.

When you choose a DateTime data type, Reporting Services will place a calendar control next to this parameter for easy selection of dates. This calendar control is much nicer when used by a Windows application rather than applications built for the Web. There is a limitation in selecting past years, however. To go back to a previous year, you need to navigate back one month at a time until you reach the year you would like. We hope that this will be fixed in a future release. We've found that in order to select a data in the past, such as a birth date, it is easiest to choose the data in the calendar for the current year, and then go into the textbox and change the year to the appropriate year. Of course, you can simply ignore the calendar control and type the date into the textbox.

Note that the Report Server automatically casts the parameter values to the data type you specify. For this reason, you can use the methods of the .NET data type structure to retrieve or set the parameter value. For example, if you set the parameter type to DateTime, you can use the `DateTime.Year` property to get to the year because the values of data type in .NET are represented by the DateTime structure.

We see more expression examples in chapter 5.

Specifying parameter attributes

The parameter attributes show up as a set of check boxes in the Report Parameters dialog box. By changing the value of these attributes, we can change the appearance and behavior of each parameter. Table 3.2 defines the parameter attributes. In RS 2005, there are several new attributes (shown in bold).

Table 3.2 The available report parameter attributes

Attribute	Description
Hidden	The user is not prompted for a value, but it can be supplied externally through URL access or the web service API.
Internal	Value cannot be supplied externally. Value can only be set through management API / tools.
Multi-Value	Allows multiple values (e.g., SQL `IN` clause). We cover this in detail in section 3.5.4.
Allow Null Value	Indicates if NULL can be passed as a report value.
Allow Blank Value	Means that an empty string can be passed as a report value. Available only for the String data type.

The Allow Null Value attribute indicates if NULL can be passed as a report value. If a default parameter value is not specified, clearing the check box in effect makes the parameter required. The Allow Blank Value attribute is available only for the String data type and means that an empty string can be passed as a report value.

Let's go back to the Sales by Territory Interactive report and change the data type of the Year parameter to Integer. Finally, to make the parameter required, make sure that the Allow Null Value check box is cleared. Now, let's preview the report (figure 3.20).

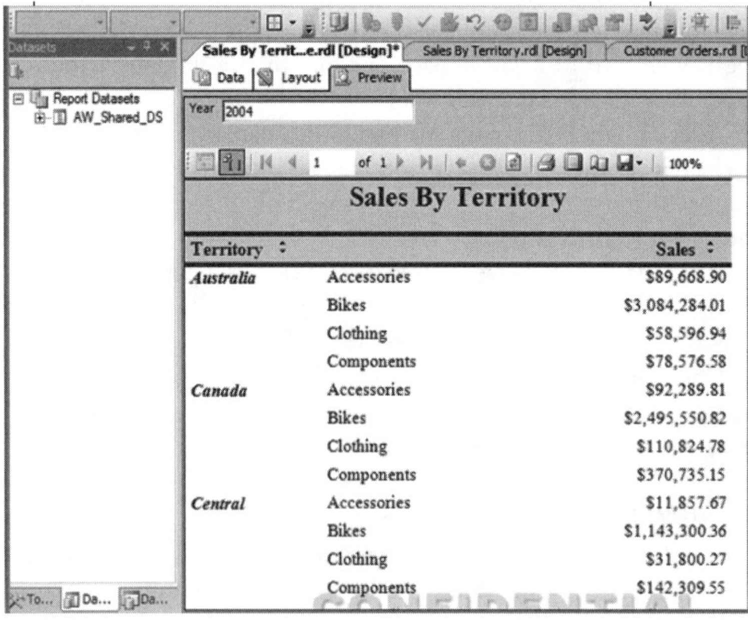

Figure 3.20 The parameterized version of the report takes the year as a parameter.

The report toolbar changes to accommodate the `Year` parameter. Note that if you leave the year field empty, the report is not generated because the year is a required parameter.

So far, so good. But what if you want to restrict the user to select a year from a predefined list of years? For example, it doesn't make sense to allow the user to type 2005 if there are no sales orders placed in that year. To accomplish this, you can define parameter available (lookup) values.

Defining nonqueried lookup parameter values

You're going to provide a drop-down list of valid years from which your users can select. The default value will be 2004.

In the Report Parameters dialog box, make sure that the Non-queried radio button is selected in the Available Values radio group. Then, type the allowed years in the grid, as shown in figure 3.21. Let's also default the `Year` parameter to 2004 by selecting Non-queried under Default Values and entering this value in the accompanying text box.

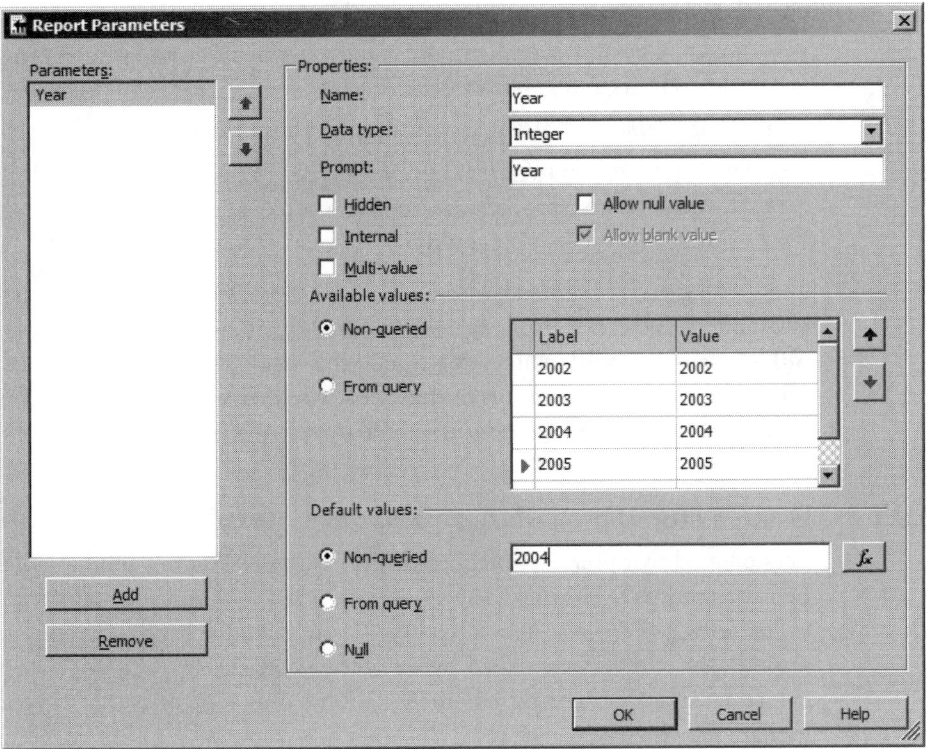

Figure 3.21 Use the Non-queried option to specify a fixed list of report parameter available values.

Preview the report again using the Preview tab and note that the report is generated for the default year of 2004, and the Select Year field is now a drop-down list from which the user can pick one of the available values.

With RS you are not restricted to static available values. You can make the list data driven by basing it on a query or expression. If it is query based, you can specify which dataset column to use for the default value. If the query results in more than one row, the first one is used.

Next, let's see how to implement a data-driven lookup list based on a dataset retrieved from a stored procedure call.

3.5 WORKING WITH STORED PROCEDURES

As you've seen, the Graphical Query Designer makes generating free SQL statements easy. However, the easy way is not always the right way. We highly recommend that in real life you use stored procedures instead of free SQL statements. Stored procedures offer the following advantages:

- *Faster performance*—The database servers parse and compile the stored procedure statements.
- *Reuse*—The SQL statements are located in one place and can be easily reused by other reports and applications.
- *Encapsulation*—As long as you keep the input and output the same, you can change the stored procedure inner implementation as much as you like.
- *Security*—Stored procedures can be secured at a database level. In addition, using stored procedures could help prevent SQL injection attacks.

Using SQL Server, a stored procedure can be used as a substitute for an expression-based query. Instead of using expression-based queries—for example, to generate SQL `WHERE` clauses conditionally—you can do this inside stored procedures. For these reasons, we use stored procedures in this book wherever it makes sense to do so.

In this section, we see how to use a stored procedure to query the values in a lookup list.

3.5.1 Using a stored procedure as a dataset query

Let's pretend that users have requested the ability to filter out product sales for a particular territory. To provide this feature, you add a lookup list of valid sales territories to the Sales by Territory Interactive report. To make the list data driven, you create a second dataset that is generated by a stored procedure. In addition, you synchronize the `Year` and `Territory` parameters so that only territories that have sales in that year are shown.

We wrote a simple stored procedure called `spGetTerritory` that takes an `@Year` input argument. You can find the `spGetTerritory` source code in the `sp.sql` script in the Database.dbp project. For Datasets with the Command Type set to Stored Procedure, you can use the Graphical Query Designer to select a stored procedure and fill your report dataset with data from the stored procedure. Alternatively, you can set the Command Type to Text and call a stored procedure using the following code in the Query String. Using this approach limits you to the Generic Query Designer.

```
Exec spGetTerritory
```

Once you install the `spGetTerritory` stored procedure, be sure to grant EXECUTE permissions to the database login that the AW Shared DS shared data source uses.

The `spGetTerritory` procedure retrieves the list of the sales territories that have orders placed in a given year, as shown here:

```
CREATE PROCEDURE spGetTerritory (@Year int)
AS
SET NOCOUNT ON
SELECT DISTINCT ST.TerritoryID, ST.Name AS Territory
FROM   Sales.SalesTerritory ST INNER JOIN
       Sales.SalesOrderHeader SOH ON ST.TerritoryID = SOH.TerritoryID
WHERE  DATEPART(YY, SOH.OrderDate) = @Year
ORDER BY ST.Name
```

To use this stored procedure as a source for the lookup dataset, follow these steps:

Step 1 Create a new dataset dsTerritory and set the command type to StoredProcedure, as shown in figure 3.22.

Step 2 Enter **spGetTerritory** in the Query String text box or leave the query string blank at this point and click OK to select it later. The Graphical Query Designer shows the Stored Procedure drop-down list, which lists all stored

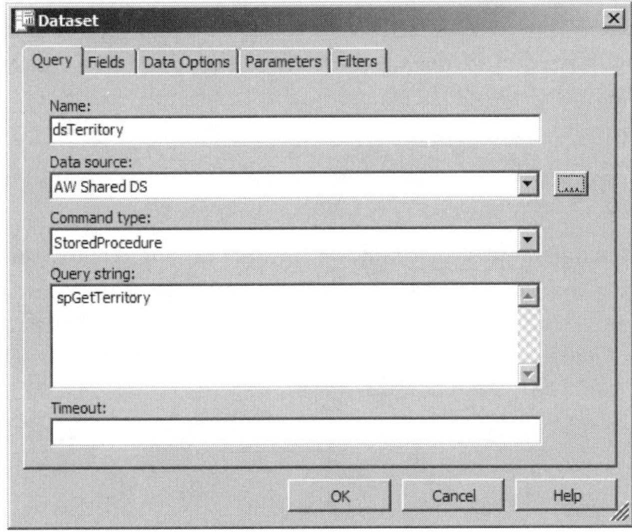

Figure 3.22
To use a stored procedure as a query statement, enter its name in the Query String text box.

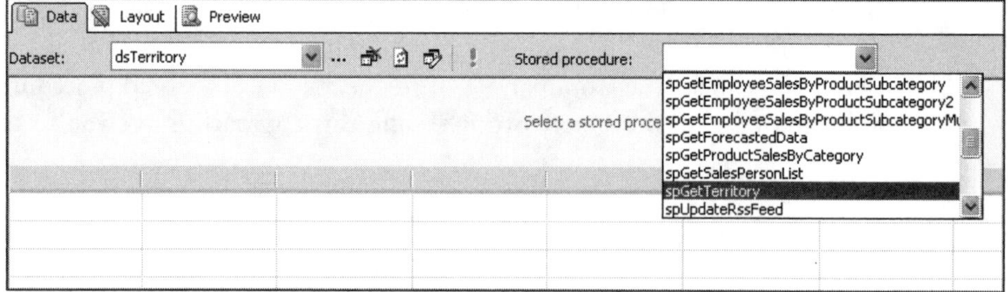

Figure 3.23 When a stored procedure is used as a query text, the Graphical Query Designer shows the list of stored procedures.

procedures that the AW Shared DS database login has permissions to execute. Select spGetTerritory, as shown in figure 3.23, and run the query. The designer displays the familiar Query Parameters dialog box.

Step 3 Enter **2004** and click OK to see the stored procedure call results.

Step 4 Next, open the dataset properties. Switch to the Parameters tab and observe that there is an `@Year` parameter and its value is set to `Parameters!Year.Value`. Because we already have the `Year` report parameter, which we needed for the first dataset, the designer has correctly linked the dsTerritory `Year` parameter to the `Year` report parameter.

Now, it is time to set up the available values for the `Territory` parameter.

3.5.2 Defining query-based lookup parameter values

Open the Report Parameters dialog box from the Reports menu at the top of the Report Designer and specify the settings for the `Territory` parameter, as shown in figure 3.24.

Go back to the Report Designer's Data tab, select the report dataset in the Datasets drop-down list, and in the Query pane of the Graphical Query Designer, change the SQL `WHERE` clause of the dataset query to filter data by the `Territory` parameter, as follows:

```
WHERE (DATEPART(YY, SOH.OrderDate) = @Year) AND
  (ST.TerritoryID = @Territory)
```

Now you have created parameter placeholders for the year and territory in your main dataset. This means that the report will not show any data until you have selected both the `Year` and `Territory` parameters. Let's take a closer look at how your parameters interact with each other.

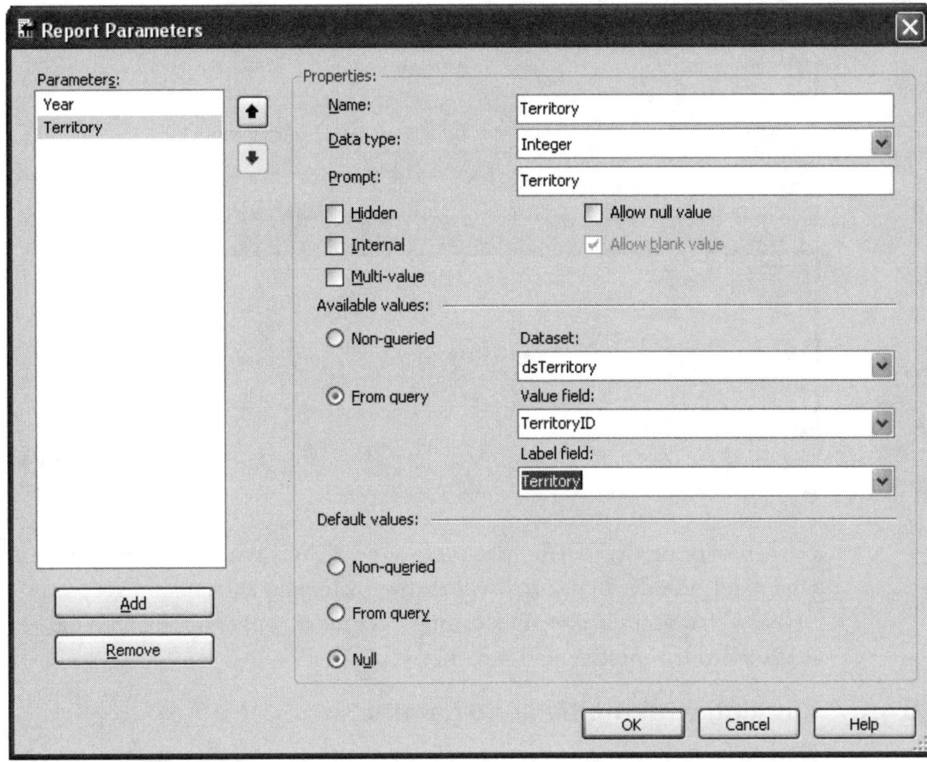

Figure 3.24 Use the From Query settings to define data-driven lookup parameter datasets.

3.5.3 Creating cascading parameters

When creating the dsTerritory dataset, you used the `spGetTerritory` stored procedure. This stored procedure has an input parameter of `@Year`. This matches your report parameter of `Year`, so when the dataset was created, the designer automatically bound your report parameter to your dtTerritory dataset. This means that when you enter a year into the `Year` parameter, your report will call the `spGetTerritory` stored procedure and pass in the year that was entered. This way, your Territory drop-down list will only have valid values available. This is called *cascading* parameters. When you preview the report, you will see that changing the year results in refreshing the Territory drop-down list so that only territories associated with that year are displayed, as shown in figure 3.25.

You may think that the parameter settings (available, default, and null values) that you set using the Report Parameters dialog box are useful only if the report includes the standard report toolbar. Actually, this is not the case. Before the report is processed, the Report Server parses the report request, validates the report parameters, and matches them against the list of available values. For example, if you request the Sales

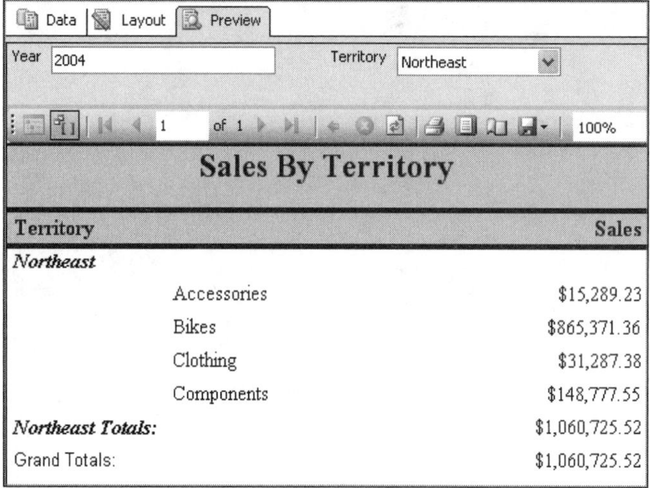

Figure 3.25
The Sales by Territory report contains Year and Territory parameters.

by Territory report via the Report Server Web service and pass 2010 as the `Year` parameter, the Report Server will throw an Invalid Parameter exception.

Now that you have seen cascading parameters in action, let's visit a new feature in RS 2005 called multivalued parameters.

3.5.4 Working with multivalued parameters

New in SQL Reporting Services 2005, multivalued parameters allow you to choose more than one value for a particular parameter and use the results in your SQL query. With RS 2000 you had to work hard to get this functionality to work. As you saw in table 3.2 in section 3.4.3, each report level parameter has five attributes that let you alter a parameter's functionality. The `Multi-Value` attribute will change the way that the parameter field works when the report is rendered. If you are working with a text field, the parameter field will allow you to enter multiple values by entering data and pressing Enter between values. Typically you'll select the `Multi-Value` check box when you are working with a drop-down list of items, such as Territories. We see some examples of how to use multivalued parameters in chapter 4.

3.6 SUMMARY

In this chapter, you learned how to set up report data, which is a prerequisite for creating data-driven reports. We emphasized the fact that with RS you can report off virtually any data store that exposes its data in a tabular format.

We began by showing you how to set up the report data source. Then, we explored how to create one or more datasets to feed the report with data.

You saw how to use the Graphical and Generic Query Designers to author queries, and we examined the role that parameters play in custom-tailoring report queries. Along the way, we showed you how to create parameter-driven reports. We examined the various attributes that affect the functionality and behavior of report parameters. Throughout the rest of this book, the knowledge you have harvested in this chapter will be put into practice to create many interactive parameter-driven reports. In addition, you have probably started seeing the advantages of the RS service-oriented architecture in terms of deployment, such as zero client deployment requirements and interoperability with a wide range of clients.

Now that you have a good grasp of working with report data, it is time to see how you can use the Report Designer to lay out reports. The next chapter demonstrates how to design various kinds of professional-looking reports with the Report Designer.

CHAPTER 4

Designing reports

Once you've set up the report data, you can proceed with laying out the report itself. To accomplish this task with the Report Designer, use the Layout tab. As you learned in chapter 1, Reporting Services supports various report types. In this chapter, you see how the Report Designer can help you design many versatile and professional-looking reports. In the following sections, we:

- Discuss the main parts of the report layout
- Explain how to use data regions and report items
- Create many sample reports to put what you've learned into practice

Because the report design process is very interactive, the best way to present this chapter is by example. After each report type explanation, we create a sample report. At the end, we will have worked through creating tabular, freeform, chart, and matrix reports, as well as subreports, multicolumn reports, and reports with the new interactive sort feature.

Unlike chapter 1, where we used the Report Wizard to quickly create the Sales by Territory report, we create the sample reports in this chapter using the Report Designer.

4.1 ANATOMY OF A REPORT

To be an effective report author, you need to have a good grasp of a report's anatomy. Reporting Services (RS) reports consist of *sections* (also called *bands*) that can contain *report elements*. Report elements include *data regions* and *report items*. Take, for example, the Sales by Territory report, shown in figure 4.1.

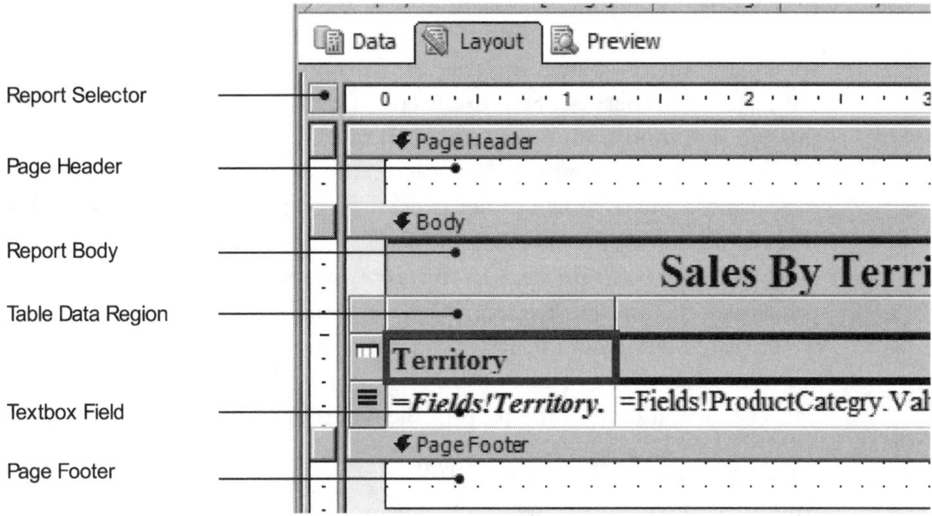

Figure 4.1 A report includes header, body, and footer sections.

The Page Header and Page Footer bands are visible because we've enabled the Page Header and Page Footer options from the Visual Studio .NET (VS .NET) Reports menu.

The report sections are the page header, report body, and page footer. To lay out a report, you drag and drop report elements from the Report Items toolbar (shown in figure 4.2) to the report body section.

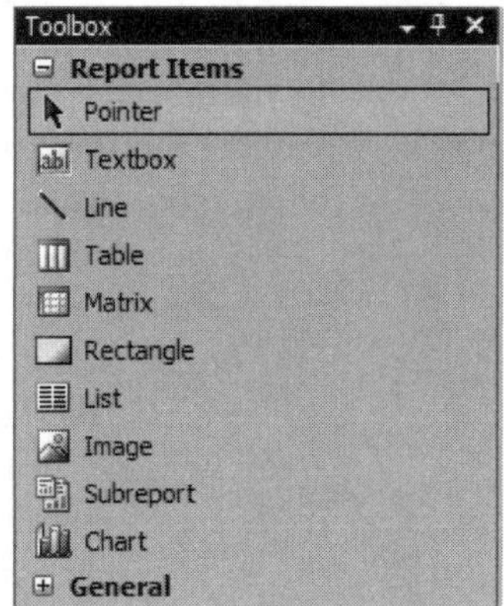

Figure 4.2 You can drag data regions and items from the Report Items toolbar to the report body.

NOTE In our opinion, the Report Items toolbar should have been named Report Elements because it contains not only report items but data regions as well. To avoid confusion, we use the term *report elements* to refer to both report items and data regions.

For example, instead of using the Report Wizard, we could have authored the Sales by Territory tabular report from scratch by dragging the table region from the Report Items toolbar and dropping it into the body section. Then, we could have dragged and dropped the report dataset fields inside the table region. If we had done this, the table region would have created textbox report items behind the scenes to display the dataset data.

4.1.1 Getting started with a new report

Before you start laying out a new report, we suggest that you review the report-level properties and make the appropriate changes right from the beginning. For example, you may want to change the page size and margins settings. Experiment with the GridSpacing properties to set up the layout grid so you can "snap" the report items to the grid as you position them on the report canvas.

To view the report properties, select the report by clicking the Report Selector (the top leftmost square shown in figure 4.1). Then, right-click and choose Properties, or work directly with the VS .NET Properties window. In the VS .NET Properties window, you will recognize some of the report properties, such as the ReportParameters property, which, when selected, opens the familiar Report Parameters dialog box that we discussed in Chapter 3. Leave the rest of the properties alone for now; we discuss them on an as-needed basis.

Let's look at each of the parts of the report anatomy in more detail.

4.1.2 Understanding report sections

An RS-based report consists of three main sections:

- *Page header*—The page header content is displayed at the top of each page.
- *Report body (optional)*—A report always has a body section, which is where most of the report content is located.
- *Page footer (optional)*—The page footer content is displayed at the bottom of each page.

By default, the page header and footer content appear on every report page, including the first and the last. You can suppress the header and footer on the first and last page of the report by changing the PrintOnFirstPage and PrintOnLastPage properties.

RS reports don't have designated report header and footer elements. Instead, you can use the Report Body band to place items that need to appear once at the beginning or end of the report.

Let's now discuss the various building blocks included with the Report Designer and how they can be used to lay out different types of reports. By no means will we try to enumerate each property of every report element. For this, you need to turn to the RS documentation, which provides excellent step-by-step instructions. Instead, after providing a high-level overview of the report structure and elements, we walk you through the process of creating various reports by example.

4.1.3 Understanding report items

With RS you can use the report items shown in table 4.1 to display data and graphical elements.

Table 4.1 Report items you can use to display data and graphical elements

Report Item	Description
Textbox	The textbox is the report item that you will use most often to display text information. Textbox elements can contain static text or data from the underlying data source. You can use expressions for the textbox content.
Image	You use the image item to display binary images for visual effects (backgrounds, logos, etc.) or to display data stored as images from the report data source.
Subreport	The subreport item defines a placeholder that points to another report.
Line	The line item is a graphical element that you can use to enhance the presentation of your report, e.g., to separate a report group from its details.
Rectangle	Rectangles can be used in two ways: as a graphical element and as a container for other report items. Users familiar with .NET development can make an analogy to the panel element. Similar to the panel, you can place report items within a rectangle and you can move them with the rectangle.

Some of the report items shown in table 4.1 deserve more attention. Let's take a closer look.

Working with images

The Report Server supports the following image formats: JPEG, BMP, GIF, and PNG. To display the actual image in the image report item, you set the Source property. The image source can be defined as:

- *Embedded*—In this case, the image data is serialized (MIME-encoded) and embedded in the report definition file. When the report is uploaded to the report catalog, the image is saved in the Report Server database. If you embed the same image in different reports, each report gets its own copy of the image. Similar to working with report-specific data sources, you use the embedded image option when you want to distribute all report-related items in one file.
- *External*—The image refers to an image file that is located in the same project or to a fully qualified URL. If you specify an image that is in the same project, only the name of the image is stored in the report definition file. The actual image is shared across all reports that use it. This simplifies image maintenance because if the image is updated, the change will propagate through all reports that reference the image. You typically use external images for implementing report banners and logos. For example, all the reports inside the AWReporter project use an external image (`AWC.jpg`) to display the company logo. If you specify a fully qualified URL, the image is stored on a server and accessed

through a URL. When you drop an image item from the toolbox, the Image Wizard appears, as shown in figure 4.3. To enter a valid URL path to an image, choose Web. The wizard validates the URL for you so you will know if you typed the path correctly. To select an image that is located in your project, choose Project. Both of these options set the Source property to External.

NOTE When a report is previewed in the Report Designer, external image items are displayed using the credentials of the user. When the report is run on the Report Server, the Report Server uses the unattended execution account. When an unattended execution account is not specified, the Report Server uses the Anonymous user account. If either of these accounts does not have proper rights, the image will not be displayed. For more information on setting up the unattended execution account, see the section "Configuring an Account for Unattended Report Processing" in the RS documentation.

- *Database*—The image is bound to an image column from the report dataset. For example, the Product Catalog report included in the RS samples uses this option to show the product image for each product.

The External option deserves additional attention. We usually shy away from storing images in the database for performance and maintenance reasons. A better approach is to store just the image URL that points to the image file located on a network share or another web server.

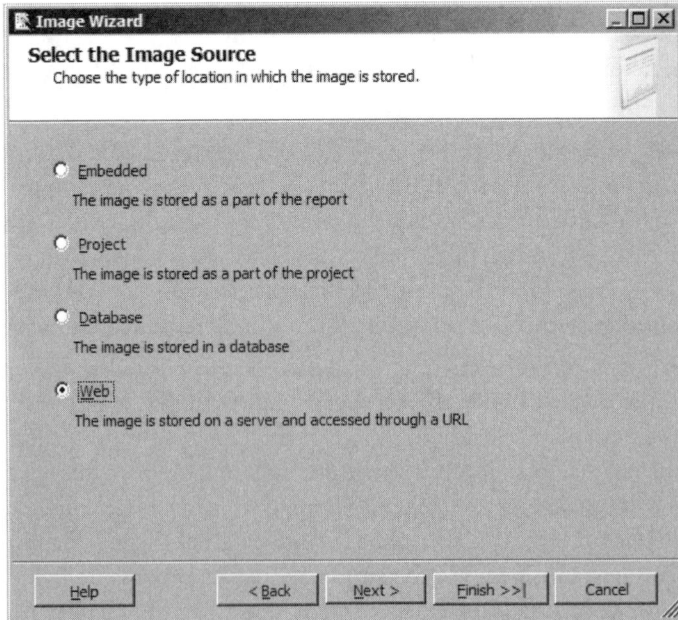

Figure 4.3 The Image Wizard lets you specify how you want to store and retrieve the images used in your reports.

For example, let's say you have an employee table that stores the employees' pictures, among other employee-related data. You have two implementation options:

- You can define that column as an image type and store the employee pictures in binary format.
- Better yet, you can store just the image URL path, for example, `http://www.imageserver.com/images/empid.gif` or `http://imageserver/images/empid.gif`.

Working with subreports

The subreport item defines a placeholder that points to another report. Usually, you opt for subreports when you need to reuse an existing report. Subreports are a popular reporting technique used to display separate groups of data with many reporting tools, such as Microsoft Access.

With RS, you should consider using nested data regions instead of subreports for performance reasons. If you use a subreport within your report, the Report Server has to process both reports separately. This is less efficient than using a single report with two regions. However, sometimes you won't have a choice. For example, nested data regions have a restriction that they must use the same dataset. If you want to use different datasets that need to display correlated data, then the only choice is to create a subreport. We look at subreports in more detail in section 4.6.

NOTE If you do not need to display the report content in a nested fashion, you can use multiple data regions that each use a different data source and dataset.

Working with rectangles

An important (but not so obvious) use for the rectangle item is to group things together so that they move as a unit. In this respect, the rectangle item represents a WinForm panel control that can be used to enclose other controls.

Sometimes, items will get pushed out of alignment with other items on the page. You can group them together with an invisible rectangle and they will be moved together. Section 4.3.1 provides an example of when this could be useful.

NOTE The table region will not allow you to place a line element directly in a column or cell. We have often found the need to place a line under a group heading in order to separate groups of data visually. If you are working with the table or matrix region, you need to use the Rectangle as a holder for this line element. To do this you merge all the cells in a given row and place a rectangle in this cell. You can then place the line in this rectangle. Alternatively, you can accomplish this by setting the border properties of the table or matrix region.

4.1.4 Understanding data regions

Besides report items, the Report Items toolbar includes more sophisticated report elements referred to as *data regions.*

While you can use stand-alone textbox and image report items to display data, they are most useful when they display repeating rows of data from a report dataset. In chapter 3 you saw how RS uses datasets to represent the results of queries returned by data providers. To bind report items to datasets, you use data regions. In this respect, .NET developers may relate RS data regions to ASP.NET data-bound controls, such as the data repeater control.

Table 4.2 lists the data regions that RS supports and describes how they can be used to create different types of reports.

Table 4.2 RS-supported data regions for different types of reports

Region	Report Type	Description
Table	Tabular	The table data region generates as many rows as the number of records in the underlying dataset. You can optionally group or sort data by fields or expressions. For example, for the Sales by Territory report, the Report Wizard automatically generated a table data region to render the report data in tabular format.
List	Freeform	When using the list region, you are not restricted to static columns as with the table region. Instead, you can arrange report items any way you want. Microsoft Access users will find that the list region allows them to place items arbitrarily, similar to how they lay out a report in Access.
Matrix	Matrix (crosstab)	The matrix region can include dynamic columns. Dynamic columns can be configured as hidden. The user can expand a hidden dynamic column to see more data, i.e., drill down into the data.
Chart	Chart	As its name suggests, the chart region displays the report data in chart format. Various kinds of chart types are supported, such as bar, pie, graph, and many more.

To fill in a data region with data, you bind the data region to a dataset by setting its `DataSetName` property.

NOTE If you have already created one or more report datasets, the Report Designer automatically associates a dataset with a data region when you drag and drop a dataset field to the data region. By default, the data region is associated to the first dataset defined.

Data regions are designed to generate repeating sections of data. For example, to display the sales numbers of the Adventure Works Cycles (AWC) sales territories in the Sales by Territory report, you can use a table region. During the report processing stage, the Report Server executes the dataset query, populates the dataset, and passes it to all data regions bound to it so they can render themselves.

All data regions except the chart region can act as containers for other report items. Considering again the Sales by Territory report, you can see that the table data region is a container for the textbox report items that generate the data in the table columns.

At this point, you may ask, "Why do we need data regions at all, when we can place report items directly onto the report?" The short answer is flexibility. The next section should make this clear.

Data region advantages

The advantages of using data regions are as follows:

- They can be used as "supercharged" subreports, as we explain next.
- They can be placed side by side and draw data from separate datasets.

Reports can vary greatly in their layout and complexity. A very simple report might need to display the data in a tabular format only. A more complicated report, however, may include different sections, each of which might be rendered in a different way. Those of you familiar with Access know that complex reports need to be broken into subreports. We discuss subreports in more detail in section 4.6.

With RS, you will find that in most cases you don't need subreports. Instead, you can use individual data regions. This is possible because the data regions can be nested inside other data regions, as you'll see shortly in this chapter. In addition, you can place a data region anywhere you want inside the report body.

You can also position data regions side by side, and each can have its own dataset and be independent from the others. For example, you can place a chart and table region side by side. The chart region can display the company sales per territory in chart format, while the table region can provide a breakdown per product and territory.

Another example where side-by-side data regions could be useful is in a multisection report. For example, imagine that you need to author a sophisticated report that includes a few sections. Based on some business rules, the report may not show certain sections. One way to achieve this requirement would be to break down the report data in sections and implement each section as a separate data region. Then, you could programmatically hide the sections during the report runtime using expressions.

Binding data regions to report datasets

In order for the data regions to display data, they must be associated with a dataset. You don't have to manually bind a data region to a dataset. Once you drag and drop a dataset field to the data region, the Report Designer links that region to the dataset, as you can see by inspecting the `DataSetName` property of the region. You can also manually associate a region to a dataset. This could be useful, for example, if you change the dataset name.

You can customize the message that is displayed inside a data region if the underlying dataset has no rows by using the `NoRows` property, which every data region has. The default setting is an empty string. For example, if the report query results in no rows, you can let the user know by setting the `NoRows` property to No Data to Display.

Setting up paging

As explained in chapter 1, a report can be requested in any RS-supported rendering format. Some formats, such as image and PDF, support page sizes and will repaginate the report based on the page size you specify. Others, such as HTML, will not honor the page size settings and render all data in one page (see the "Working with Multiple Pages" topic in the RS documentation for more information). In such cases, you can use page breaks to improve the report performance; Reporting Services will only have to render the HTML for the page and not for the entire report.

It may seem strange at first that RS doesn't specifically include a page break element that allows you to arbitrarily force a page break at a specific point of the report. Instead, each data region has several page break–related properties that you can use to force a page break before or after the region. You can also enforce page breaks before and after region groups. You see how to use region groups to group related data in section 4.2.1.

Reporting Services doesn't support predefined page layouts and sizes. Instead, you have to explicitly define the page size in units on the Report Properties dialog box.

TIP Sometimes you may need to have control over the number of rows per page for tabular reports. You can accomplish this by using detail groupings (discussed in section 4.2.1) based on expressions. For example, to display 25 rows per page, follow these steps:

1. Add a group to the table and group on the following expression: `=Ceiling(RowNumber(Nothing)/25)`
2. Turn off the group header and footer.
3. Turn on `PageBreakAtEnd` on the group.

If you need web-style paging, you could try using report hyperlinks, the approach we describe in chapter 5.

Now that you've learned about the report layout at a high level, let's see how to put this knowledge into practice by creating different types of reports, starting with tabular reports.

4.2 DESIGNING TABULAR REPORTS

You create tabular reports by using the table data region. You can optionally define report groups by grouping the table region data by fields or expressions, as you see next. In this section, we also look at examples of how to use parameters and interactive features in a tabular report. We round out the discussion by mentioning some limitations of the table region.

4.2.1 Tabular reports with groups

The first report that we created in chapter 1, the Sales by Territory report, is an example of a tabular report. Let's enhance it by grouping data.

If you preview this report, you'll notice that we didn't quite meet the original requirements. The sales management team requested that we group the sales data by territory. However, we've just hidden the duplicated territory names. Let's fix this by using table region groups. The final version of the report is shown in figure 4.4.

Sales By Territory

Territory		Sales
Australia		
	Accessories	$89,668.90
	Bikes	$3,084,284.01
	Clothing	$58,596.94
	Components	$78,576.58
Australia Totals:		$3,311,126.43
Canada		
	Accessories	$92,289.81
	Bikes	$2,495,550.82
	Clothing	$110,824.78
	Components	$370,735.15
Canada Totals:		$3,069,400.57
Central		
	Accessories	$11,857.67
	Bikes	$1,143,300.36

Figure 4.4
This Sales by Territory report is grouped by territory.

Creating a table region group

To group the report data by territory, complete the following steps:

Step 1 Open the Sales by Territory report.

Step 2 Click the table so that the row and column handles appear next to and above the table region.

Step 3 Right-click the handle of any row and select Insert Group. The Grouping and Sorting Properties dialog box appears, as shown in figure 4.5.

Step 4 Change the group name to grpTerritory.

> **NOTE** We highly recommend that you come up with a good naming convention for report item names and use it consistently. It doesn't matter what it is; what does matter is that you have one. You will realize its benefits when you start referencing the report items in expressions. We try to use three-letter prefixes, for example, *txt* for textboxes, *grp* for groups.

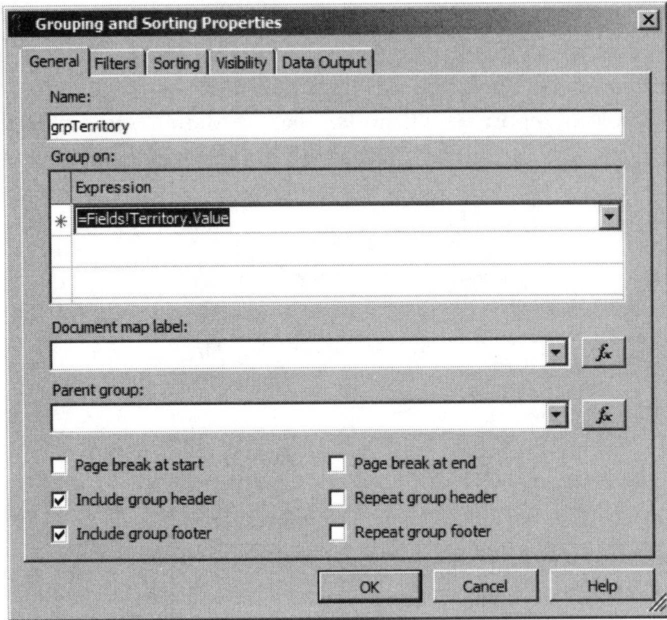

Figure 4.5
The Grouping and Sorting Properties dialog box allows you to set group properties.

Step 5 From the Group On field, select the Fields!Territory.Value field from the drop-down list.

Step 6 Select the Include Group Footer check box to generate group footers after each group to include the sales totals per territory, and then click OK.

Step 7 Next, move the Fields!Territory.Value to the group header by dragging the field (select the field and click on the selection border) from the group detail section to the group header. At this point, your report layout should look like the one shown in figure 4.6. Moving the textbox to the group header displays the territory name only once, at the beginning of each new group.

Sales By Territory		
Territory		Sales
=Fields!Territory.		
	=Fields!ProductCategory.Value	=Fields!Sales.Value

Figure 4.6
Adding the territory name to the group header will display the territory name once at the top of each group.

Creating group subtotals

A common requirement for report groups is to include group subtotals. Let's create a group subtotal that shows the sales per territory.

Step 1 In the group footer cell of the Territory column (see figure 4.7), type the following Visual Basic .NET expression:

```
= Fields!Territory.Value & " Totals:"
```

Step 2 To create a subtotal for the territory group, enter the following expression in the group footer cell of the Sales column:

```
= Sum(Fields!Sales.Value)
```

Now, let's create a grand total footer for the whole table.

Step 3 Select the table. Right-click the handle of any row and choose Table Footer. In the Territory cell, type **Grand Totals:**. In the Sales cell, type the same expression as in the group footer:

```
= Sum(Fields!Sales.Value)
```

At this point, your report layout should look like the one shown in figure 4.7.

Sales By Territory		
Territory		Sales
=Fields!Territory.		
	=Fields!ProductCategory.Value	=Fields!Sales.Valu
=Fields!Territory.\		=Sum(Fields!Sales.
Grand Totals:		=Sum(Fields!Sales.

Figure 4.7
You can also place fields in the footer that will show up once at the end of each group.

Using details grouping

The table region grouping capabilities are not limited to group headers and footers; you can also group the table details data. For example, imagine that the table dataset contains the daily sales data, but you need to consolidate it by quarters. One option is to perform the consolidation at the database by changing your dataset query. This is also the best option in terms of performance.

When this is not possible, you can group the details by using the Details Grouping button on the Groups tab of the table region properties. In our case, to consolidate the data in quarters, we need to add two expressions to the Group On grid: one to group the data by years and one by quarters. If the dataset field that contains the sales date is named Date, then the expressions will be `Fields!Date.Value.Year` and `DatePart("q", Fields!Date.Value)`, respectively.

Using image items

While image items don't have much to do with grouping, we can use the Sales by Territory report to demonstrate how you can use an external image file as a background image. The report uses the `Confidential.jpg` image as a background image of the table region. Once we created the image, we used the table region properties to set the `BackgroundImage Source` property to `External`, `Value` to `Confidential.jpg`, and `BackgroundRepeat` to `NoRepeat`.

Finally, you might want to experiment with borders, fonts, colors, and formatting to make the report more eye-catching.

4.2.2 Parameterized tabular reports

OK, we can almost feel the resentment growing for the now ubiquitous Sales by Territory report. You can relax—we're going to create a new report from scratch to learn more about working with table regions.

Let's say that the AWC management has requested a report that tracks employee performance for a given period of time. To allow users to see the sales data filtered for a given time period and salesperson, the report needs to be designed as parameterized. The employee sales data must be grouped by employee and then by product subcategory and sorted by the employee sales total in descending order.

In its final version, the report will look like the one in figure 4.8.

Because you are already familiar with the table region, we'll highlight a few things worth mentioning, rather than provide step-by-step implementation instructions.

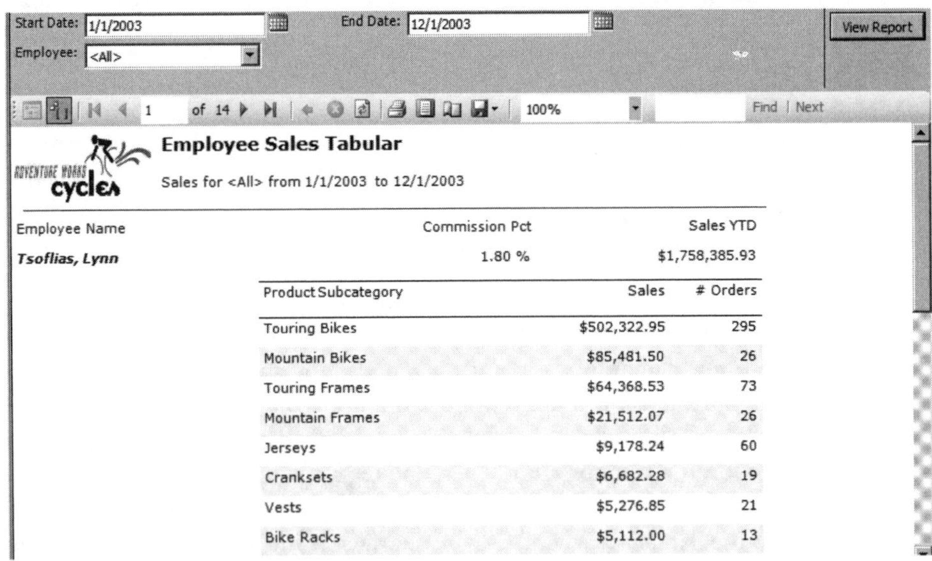

Figure 4.8 The Employee Sales Tabular report showcases how to build reports with query-based Employee parameters

Setting up the report parameter lookup values

Let's start by setting up the report data. For this report, we've defined two datasets.

First, we've set up a dataset (dsEmployeeSales) to retrieve the available parameters for the `Employee` parameter. This dataset gets its results from a SQL query called `dsEmployeeSales.sql` that can be found in the Database project included with the book's source code.

Normally, you would want to use a stored procedure for this dataset; however, RS does not directly support passing multivalued parameter values into stored procedures. For the sake of keeping this demo simple, let's stay focused on how RS supports multivalued parameters with a SQL query. Later in section 4.6 we visit some more advanced techniques for using multivalued parameters with stored procedures.

The `dsEmployeeSales.sql` query has `start date`, `end date`, and `EmployeeID` as parameters. Notice that in the `WHERE` clause we are using the T-SQL `IN` syntax for our `@EmployeeIDs` parameter, as shown here:

```
E.EmployeeID in (@EmployeeIDs)
```

Next we've created the dsSalesPerson dataset to retrieve a list of all employees from the `Employee` table who are also salespeople. This dataset defines the available values for the `Employee` parameter.

Once you've defined the lookup dataset, use the Report Parameters dialog box to configure the report parameters. First, set up the defaults for the date field. Configure the default value of the start date parameter to 1/1/2003 and the end date to 12/1/2003 by placing these dates in the Non-queried default value fields. Also, be sure to set the data type for these date parameters to DateTime. This will enable the date picker control in our report for these parameters. Once the date parameters are set up, set up the `Employee` parameter as shown in figure 4.9.

Notice that we have selected the `Multi-value` property for the `Employee` parameter and that we have selected Integer as the data type.

> **NOTE** One common situation that we have seen developers struggle with is wanting to use stored procedures for the dataset and still use multivalued parameters. Case in point: with this report we have an Integer parameter (`EmployeeId`) that maps to an integer field in the database. When we use a SQL query for our dataset, RS handles the splitting of our `EmployeeId` parameters into a list for the `IN` part of our `WHERE` clause. So, how do we pass a list of integers into a stored procedure? You learn how in section 4.6.

To set up the available values for the `Employee` parameter, select the From Query option and choose the dsSalesPerson dataset from the Dataset drop-down list. We use the `EmployeeID` column from the dataset as a parameter in our `dsEmployee-Sales` query.

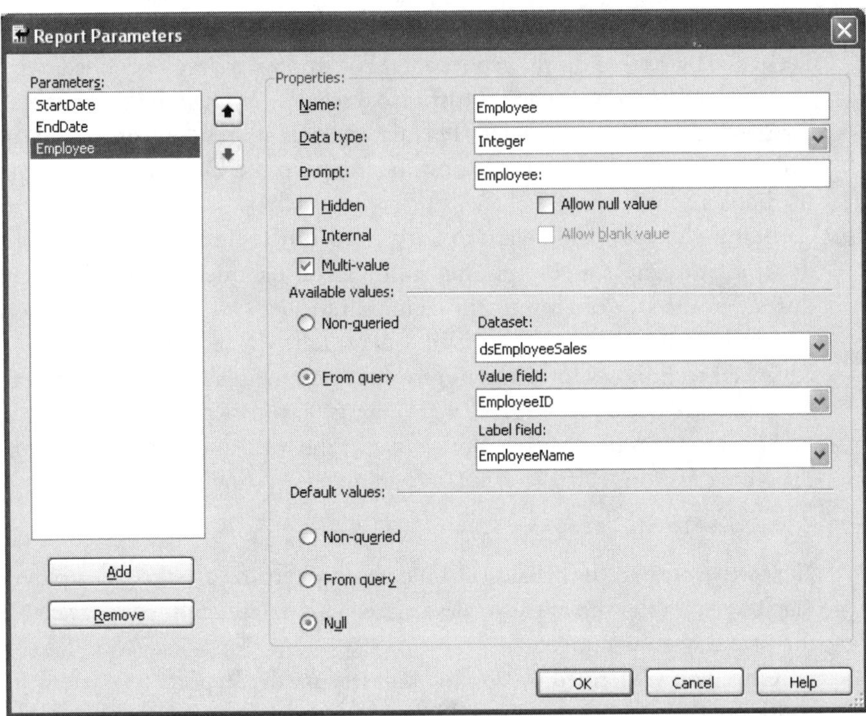

Figure 4.9 You can set up a parameter's available values from a dataset using the Report Parameters dialog box.

Setting up the report header

After we set up the report data, the next step is to design the report as a tabular report.

First, create the report header by adding two textboxes to the report header section: one for the name of the report and another to display the parameter information. The second textbox is based on the following VB .NET expression:

```
="Sales for " & JOIN(Parameters!EmployeeID.Label,",") & " from "
& Parameters!StartDate.Value & " to " & Parameters!EndDate.Value
```

Let's postpone discussing expressions until the next chapter. For now, this is a simple VB .NET expression, which concatenates the label (the visible text) of the `Employee` parameter with the requested date range. Also, note that we use a `JOIN` function to get all of the values from the multivalued parameter.

In addition, we've dragged and dropped the `AWC.jpg` image file, which you can find included in the project. Because this image can potentially be used by all corporate reports, for easier maintenance we've decided to reference the image as an external project image. The easiest way to do that is to add the image file to the project. Then, you drag and drop the image to your report. Another option is to drag and drop the image item from the report toolbox, which starts the Image Wizard. Note that as a part of the report-deployment process, you have to deploy all external images that the report uses.

Laying out the tabular report

Now it's time for the fun part. For the tabular portion of the report, we use a table region called tblEmployeeSales. First, we drag and drop a table region from the toolbox, as shown in figure 4.10. By default, the table region has a table header, details, footer rows, and three columns.

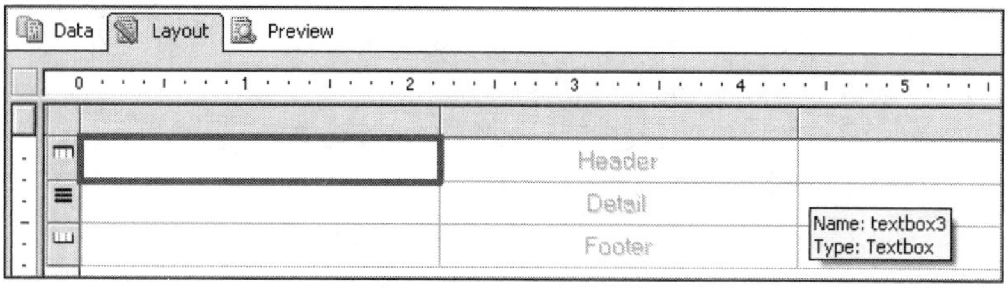

Figure 4.10 The table region initially displays 3 columns of Header, Detail, and footer rows by default.

Once we've dragged and dropped the table region below the header rectangle, let's populate it with the dataset fields, as shown in figure 4.11.

The easiest way to accomplish this is by dragging and dropping the fields from the Datasets window to the appropriate cells. Once you drag the first field and drop it onto the table region, the Report Designer associates the data region and the dataset, as you can see by looking at the `DataSetName` region property.

It may seem a bit odd that the top header row and the details row don't match, but once we add the groups in the next section it will make more sense.

You can manually associate a region with a dataset by expanding the DataSetName drop-down list and specifying a dataset explicitly. Manually associating a region with a dataset is necessary when you rename the region dataset and when you want to replace the dataset with another one. The Report Designer automatically generates a textbox report item once the field is dropped into a cell.

Next, we need to create the appropriate table region groups that will be used to group data by employee and product subcategory.

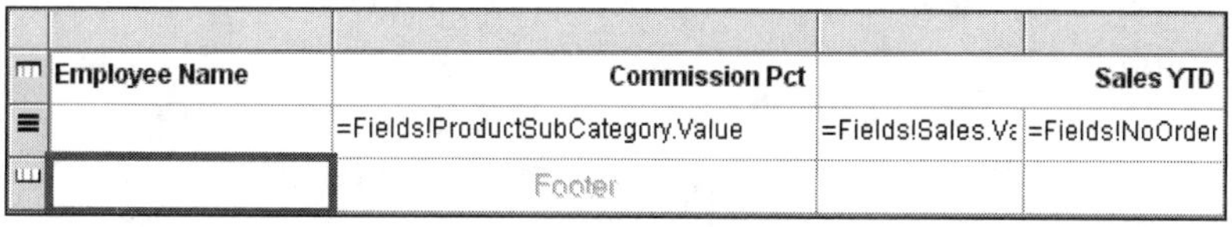

Figure 4.11 To populate a table region, drag and drop these dataset fields.

Grouping the table region data

Let's define two groups: grpEmployee and grpProductSubcategory. If you are looking at the finished report in the source code, you can view the group definitions by clicking anywhere within the table region, selecting the group selector located on the left row handle, and choosing Edit Group from the context menu.

Alternatively, to get to the Group tab of the Table Properties dialog box, follow these steps:

Step 1 Once the table is selected, click on the table selector square (the top leftmost square). At this point, the table selection border changes, as shown in figure 4.12. This puts the table region in Edit mode, so you can resize it or drag it to a new location.

Step 2 Now, you can right-click anywhere on the border and choose Properties to view the table region properties.

Step 3 Select the Group tab in the Table Properties dialog box, as shown in figure 4.13.

When you add the grpEmployee and grpProductSubcategory groups to your report, you'll need to merge some cells together and add fields to your newly created group rows. You'll also want to format your percent and currency fields appropriately. We've added some borders to make the report more pleasing to the eye. When you are done, your report should look similar to figure 4.12.

Employee Name	Commission Pct	Sales YTD	
=Fields!EmployeeName.V	=Sum(Fields!CommissionPct.Value)	=Sum(Fields!SalesYTD.Value)	
	Product Sub Category	Sales	# Orders
	=Fields!ProductSubCategory.Value	=Fields!Sales.V.	=Fields!NoOrc
		=Sum(Fields!Sa	=Sum(Fields!I
	Footer		

Figure 4.12 To put the table region in Edit mode, click the table selector in the upper left corner so that the table border selection changes as shown.

The Groups tab on the Table Properties dialog box shows the defined groups—in our case, the groups shown in figure 4.13.

If you select the grpEmployee group and click the Edit button, you will see that the Group On expression for the first group is set to `Fields!Employee-Name.Value`. This groups the report data by employee. The second group is set to `Fields!ProductSubcategory.Value`; it groups the product data by category and creates the product subcategory header and footer.

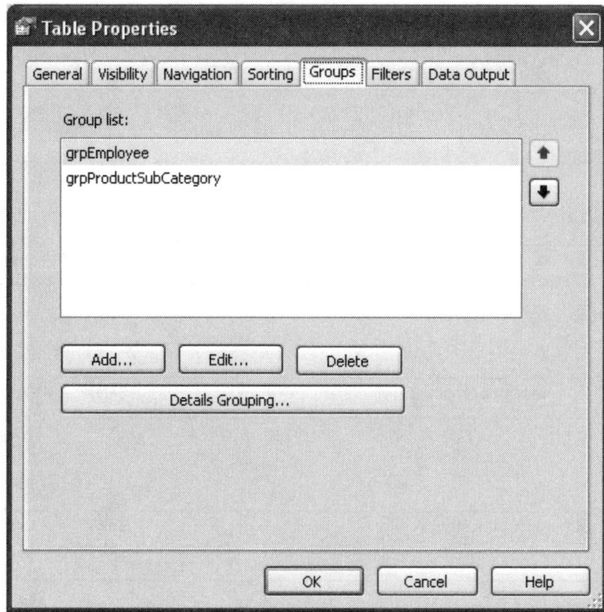

Figure 4.13
For tabular reports, you can view and manage groups from the Table Properties dialog box.

NOTE In general, if you want to achieve better performance, we recommend that you delegate as much data manipulation and massaging as possible to the database. This is what the database is designed for. For example, the Employee Sales Tabular report does all the grouping and sorting in the `spGetEmployeeSalesByProductSubcategory` stored procedure. It sorts the data by employee name in ascending order and then by sales amount in descending order. We use report grouping only to define labels for the columns and totals in the footers.

4.2.3 Tabular reports with interactive features

The *visible-on-demand* group is another interactive feature that you can add to your tabular reports. For example, if the table region has two groups nested one within the other, the parent group can act as a toggle to show or hide the nested group. The table region automatically generates an image that the user can click to expand or collapse the nested group. This visible-on-demand technique can give your tabular reports a "briefing" look. The Employee Sales Tabular Interactive report shown in figure 4.14 demonstrates the visible-on-demand interactive feature.

The new version of the report hides the product subcategory group by default. The user can click the plus indicator to expand the Product Subcategory section and see its details. Users experienced with designing web content will probably agree that designing collapsible sections using JavaScript code and DHTML is not that straightforward. The process usually involves wrapping the section in a `DIV` element and calling client-side JavaScript code to show or hide the section.

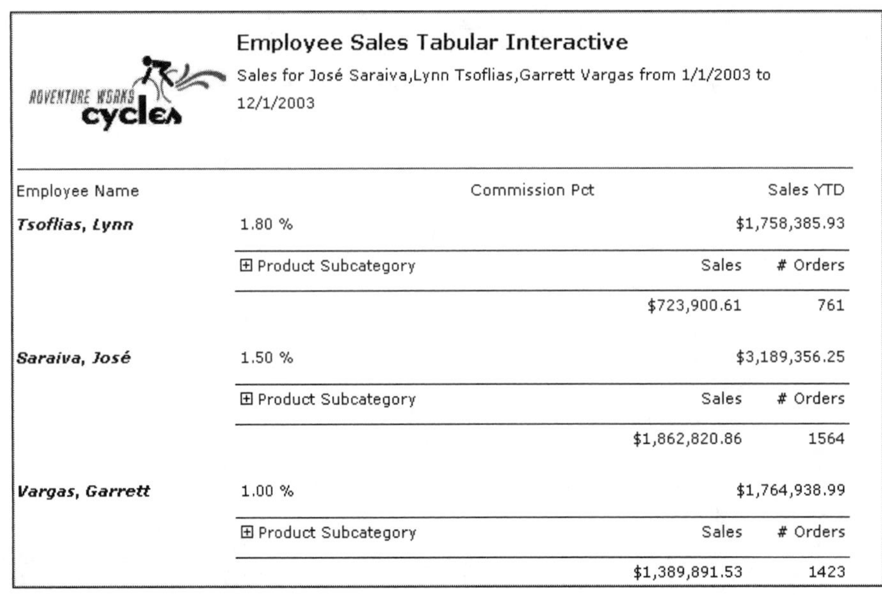

Figure 4.14 This tabular report has visible-on-demand groups that can be expanded by clicking the plus sign next to them.

Using the Report Designer, creating a visible-on-demand section is a matter of setting the nested group visibility to be toggled by the parent group, as shown in figure 4.15.

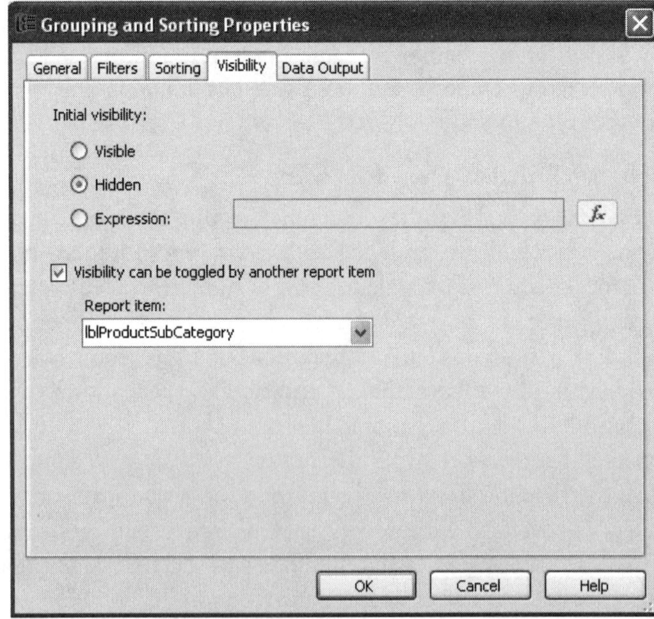

Figure 4.15 Creating visible-on-demand groups can be done from the Grouping and Sorting Properties dialog box.

NOTE To view the appropriate the Grouping and Sorting Properties window, you must start from the Groups tab on the Table Properties window. On this tab select the grpProductSubCategory group and then click the Edit button.

The choice of which textbox item you select in the Report Item drop-down list is important because the expandable plus image will be placed immediately before this item. In this case, in the Report Item drop-down list we select lblProductSubCategory, which is the name of the textbox with a value of Product Subcategory.

4.2.4 Table region limitations

To summarize, the table region works great for simple tabular reports. However, when report complexity increases, you might find the tabular layout restrictive. For example, with the table region, your layout options are restricted to static columns. If the group header and table details have the same number of columns, everything is great. Otherwise, you will find yourself creating new columns and merging existing ones.

For example, the Employee Sales Tabular report sample needs three columns for the Employee group, while it needs four for the Product subcategory group. To solve this, we define four columns at the table level. Then, for the Employee group, we merge the last two columns by selecting both of them, right-clicking, and choosing Merge Cells from the context menu. As you can see, as the complexity of report layout increases, the table region might soon get in the way.

4.3 DESIGNING FREEFORM REPORTS

When the table region is not enough, you can use the list region to create freeform reports. As their name suggests, freeform reports allow you to arrange items arbitrarily inside the list region. In this section, you see examples of how to nest regions, how to nest lists for grouping data, and how to use more than one dataset via side-by-side data regions.

4.3.1 Freeform reports with nested regions

Figure 4.16 shows an enhanced version of the Employee Sales report (Employee Sales Freeform), which now uses list and table regions, with the table region nested inside the list region.

At first glance, the report looks the same. However, the employee information section is now located to the left of the product sales section and its textboxes are arranged in a freeform way, one below the other. Let's see how to author the report.

Working with list regions

First, drag and drop a list region from the toolbox and name it lstEmployeeSales. Then, group the list by employee name, similar to how you grouped the table region earlier. To accomplish this, select the list region, right-click, and choose Properties. Then, click the Edit Details Group button, as shown in figure 4.17.

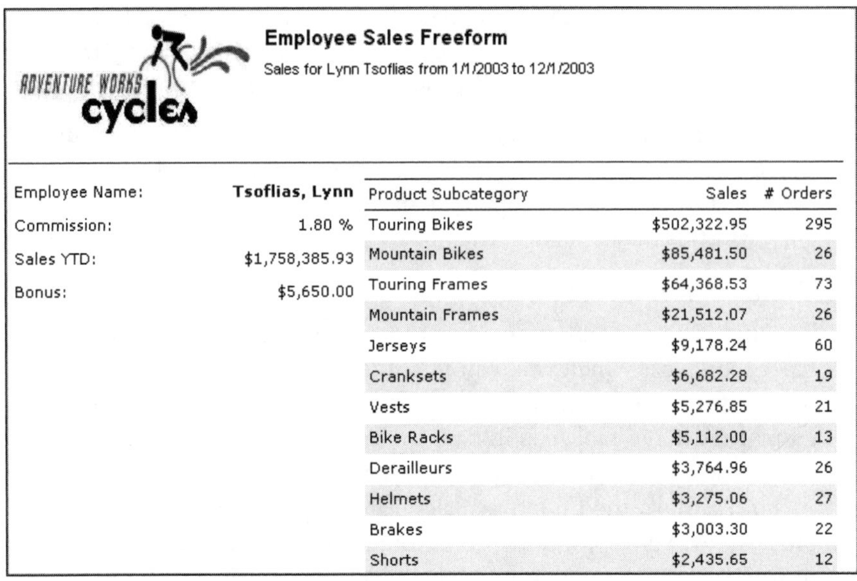

Figure 4.16 Use freeform reports when you need to lay out items arbitrarily on the report canvas.

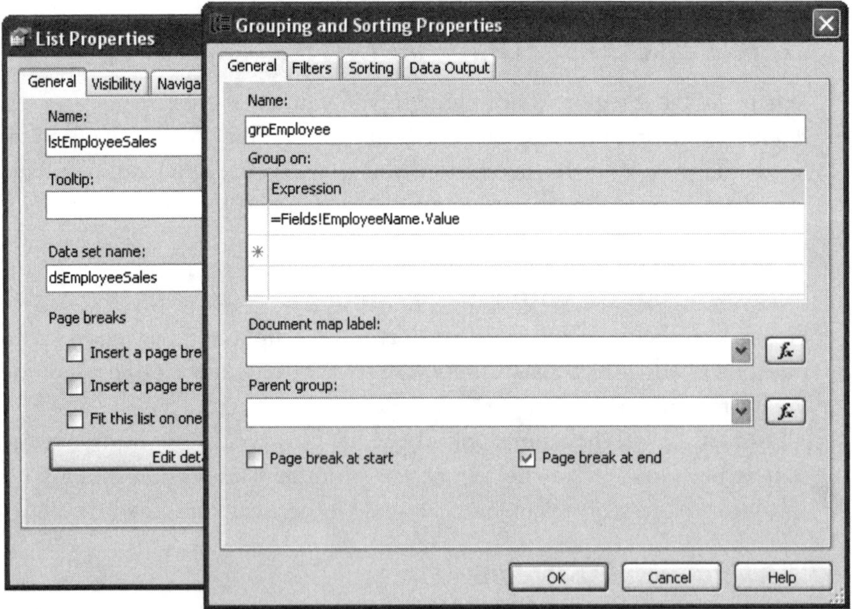

Figure 4.17 The Grouping and Sorting Properties dialog box is also used to view and manage groups for List reports.

This brings us to the familiar Grouping and Sorting Properties dialog box, where you define a new group based on the following grouping expression:

```
=Fields!EmployeeName.Value
```

In the same dialog box, also select the Page Break At End option to generate a page break after the employee group is generated. Then, move the tblEmployeeSales region inside the list region and remove all groups from it. As a result, the table region is now nested inside the list region, so both regions are synchronized.

Laying out the report

Given that we are no longer confined to static columns, we can choose to lay out the employee fields anywhere we want. We can also add as many fields as desired without being restricted to static columns. For instance, we've added the Bonus field from the report dataset. Had the AdventureWorks sample database stored pictures of the employees, we could have added an image report item to display the employee photos as well.

Finally, we enclose all employee fields in a rectangle to prevent some of the fields from being pushed down by the table region. Because the list region now groups the data by employee, the table region needs to show only the product sales in a tabular form. We define a table header and footer to show the table region labels and totals, respectively.

NOTE As we noted earlier, the rectangle report item can serve as a container for other items. When enclosing other items, it prevents the table region from pushing down other items. For example, if we hadn't used a rectangle to enclose the employee fields, the last field would have been pushed down when the report was generated.

4.3.2 Grouping freeform data

While table and matrix regions provide multiple levels of grouping within a single data region, lists can have only one group. This limitation might not be that obvious from the Grouping Properties dialog box because it allows you to define multiple Group On expressions. It is important to note, though, that this will not result in true nested groups because you won't be able to aggregate the results at a group level. Instead, to create two nested groups using lists, you must place a list within another list.

Let's consider an example. What if, for the Employee Sales report, we want to group by territory first and then by salesperson so that we can see the total sales amount per territory? Figure 4.18 shows the Employee Sales by Territory report with this capability implemented.

We now have a new group that breaks down the employee sales data by territory. Although figure 4.18 doesn't show it, before the end of each territory group there is a textbox that totals the sales by that territory.

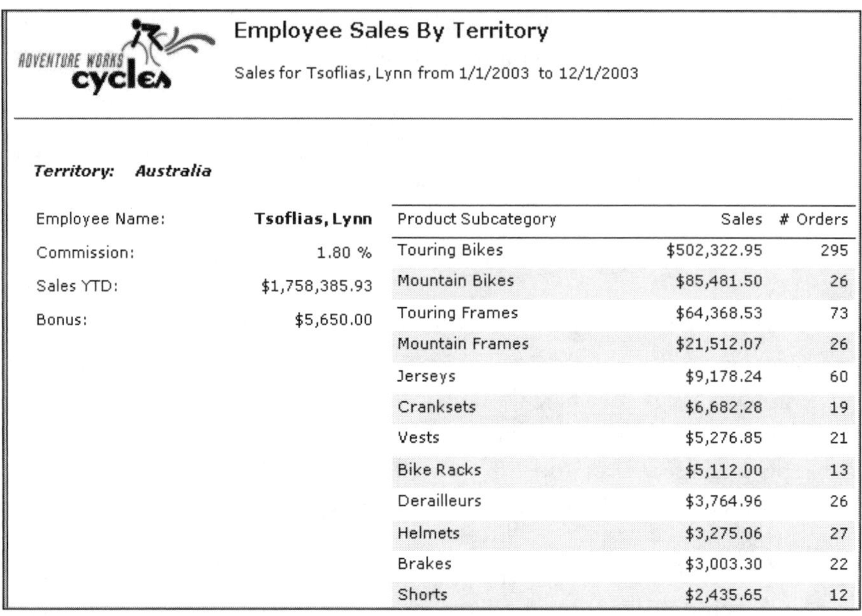

ADVENTURE WORKS cycles

Employee Sales By Territory

Sales for Tsoflias, Lynn from 1/1/2003 to 12/1/2003

Territory: Australia

Employee Name:	**Tsoflias, Lynn**
Commission:	1.80 %
Sales YTD:	$1,758,385.93
Bonus:	$5,650.00

Product Subcategory	Sales	# Orders
Touring Bikes	$502,322.95	295
Mountain Bikes	$85,481.50	26
Touring Frames	$64,368.53	73
Mountain Frames	$21,512.07	26
Jerseys	$9,178.24	60
Cranksets	$6,682.28	19
Vests	$5,276.85	21
Bike Racks	$5,112.00	13
Derailleurs	$3,764.96	26
Helmets	$3,275.06	27
Brakes	$3,003.30	22
Shorts	$2,435.65	12

Figure 4.18 To achieve additional levels of grouping with freeform reports, you can nest data regions within other data regions.

On your first attempt, you might think that to create the new group you could define a new Group On expression using the Grouping Properties dialog box. If you did this, however, you would find out that you couldn't create subtotals on the territory level. Instead, what you need to do is add a new list (lstTerritory) and nest the lstEmployee list within it. The prior list will group the data per territory and the latter per employee. Figure 4.19 shows lstEmployee nested inside lstTerritory.

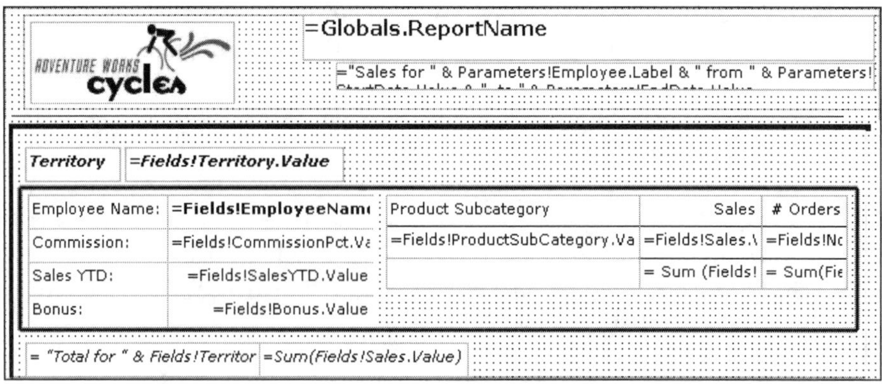

Figure 4.19 Nested lists provide additional levels of grouping.

TIP As you add items to the report, you might find it difficult to select items. For example, it is almost impossible to select an enclosing rectangle by trying to click on its boundaries. You can tab among fields until you select the item you need, but a better way is to use the VS .NET Properties window and select the item from the drop-down list. This will select the item in the Report Designer as well.

Another even faster way to select the item container is to press the Esc key object when the child is selected.

4.3.3 Freeform reports with side-by-side data regions

As we said at the beginning of this chapter, data regions can coexist peacefully next to one another and each of them can be bound to its own dataset. This can be useful when you need to have sections in your report that draw data from separate datasets.

One practical application of using side-by-side regions is creating summary reports. The Employee Sales by Territory with Summary report does exactly this, as shown in figure 4.20.

ADVENTURE WORKS cycles

Employee Sales By Territory with Summary

Sales for <All> from 1/1/2003 to 12/1/2003

Territory	Sales YTD	# Customers
Australia	$1,977,474.81	3631
Canada	$6,917,270.88	1685
Central	$4,677,108.27	71
France	$3,899,045.69	1850
Germany	$2,481,039.18	1820
Northeast	$3,857,163.63	64
Northwest	$5,767,341.98	3433
Southeast	$2,851,419.04	97
Southwest	$8,351,296.74	4581
United Kingdom	$3,514,865.91	1953
Grand Total	**$44,294,026.13**	**19185**

Territory: Australia

Employee Name:	**Tsoflias, Lynn**
Commission:	1.80 %
Sales YTD:	$1,758,385.93
Bonus:	$5,650.00

Product Subcategory	Sales	# Orders
Touring Bikes	$502,322.95	295
Mountain Bikes	$85,481.50	26
Touring Frames	$64,368.53	73
Mountain Frames	$21,512.07	26
Jerseys	$9,178.24	60
Cranksets	$6,682.28	19

Figure 4.20 To work with more than one dataset, use side-by-side data regions.

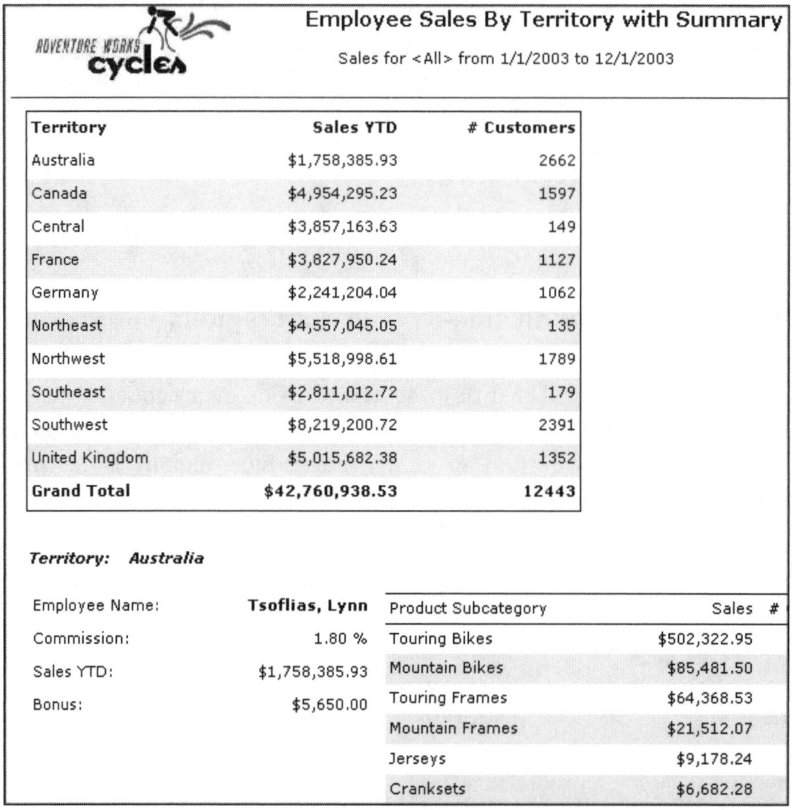

ADVENTURE WORKS cycles

Employee Sales By Territory with Summary

Sales for <All> from 1/1/2003 to 12/1/2003

Territory	Sales YTD	# Customers
Australia	$1,758,385.93	2662
Canada	$4,954,295.23	1597
Central	$3,857,163.63	149
France	$3,827,950.24	1127
Germany	$2,241,204.04	1062
Northeast	$4,557,045.05	135
Northwest	$5,518,998.61	1789
Southeast	$2,811,012.72	179
Southwest	$8,219,200.72	2391
United Kingdom	$5,015,682.38	1352
Grand Total	**$42,760,938.53**	**12443**

Territory: Australia

Employee Name:	**Tsoflias, Lynn**
Commission:	1.80 %
Sales YTD:	$1,758,385.93
Bonus:	$5,650.00

Product Subcategory	Sales	#
Touring Bikes	$502,322.95	
Mountain Bikes	$85,481.50	
Touring Frames	$64,368.53	
Mountain Frames	$21,512.07	
Jerseys	$9,178.24	
Cranksets	$6,682.28	

Figure 4.21 Your reports can have data regions of different types placed side by side.

The report has a summary section at the top to summarize territory sales data. To design the report, we created a new dataset (dsTerritorySummary). Then, we added a new table region (tblSummary) before the lstTerritory region and populated it with the fields from the dataset, as shown in figure 4.21.

With RS, one report can have many regions of different types placed side by side. However, as we mentioned in chapter 3, you should try to limit the number of the report datasets for performance reasons.

Giving only text-oriented reports to users may not be enough. For example, marketing people love charts so that they can spot business trends more easily. The next section teaches you how to design chart reports.

4.4 Designing chart reports

Chart reports display data in an easy-to-understand graphical format. With RS, you can add different types of charts to your reports, including column, bar, area, line, pie, doughnut, scatter, bubble, and stock chart types.

4.4.1 The chart data region

The chart data region is a sophisticated control, and explaining it in detail could easily fill in a whole chapter. Most of you who have experience in authoring chart reports, using other reporting tools such as Microsoft Graph for charting with Access-based reports, will probably find the RS chart region similar. In this section we give you only the essential knowledge for working with the RS chart region. If you need more information, refer to the product documentation.

NOTE If you have experience using the Dundas Software chart control, you'll find yourself in familiar waters, since RS uses this control for charting.

To set up a chart report, you drag and drop the chart data region. Figure 4.22 shows the default appearance of the chart region.

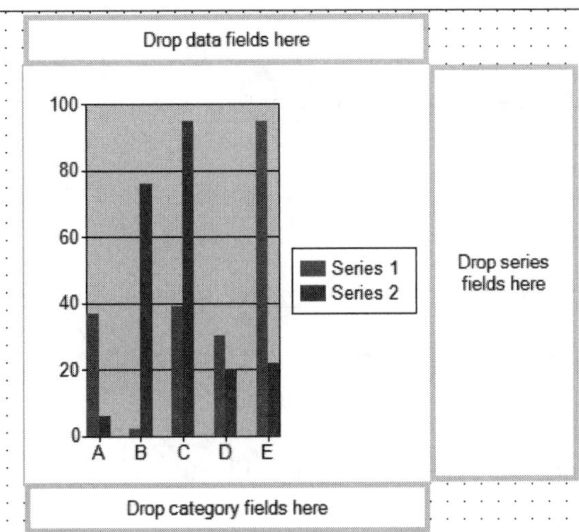

Figure 4.22
The chart region has data, series, and category fields.

Once the chart region is placed on the report canvas, you can change the chart type by right-clicking it and using the context menu or by selecting the General tab in the Chart Properties dialog box, as shown in figure 4.23.

Once you have selected the chart type, you need to set up the chart data by defining the chart values, categories, and series.

4.4.2 Working with charts

To demonstrate a practical example of a chart report, let's assume that the AWC sales management has requested that we change the Employee Sales by Territory with Summary report. Instead of having the report display the territory sales in a tabular fashion, management has requested that the data be presented in a chart format, so they can easily see which countries are performing best.

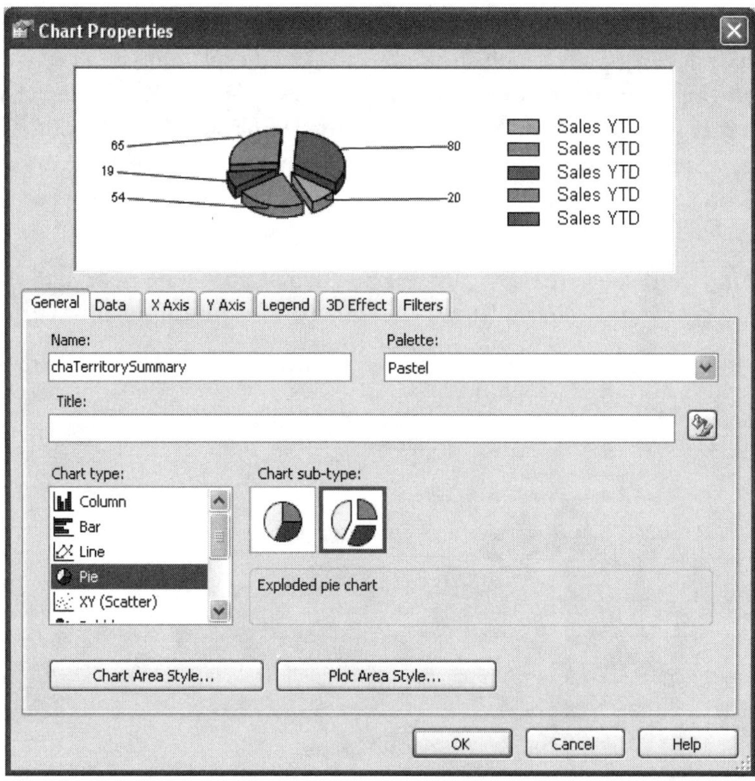

Figure 4.23 Changing the chart type to a pie chart is simple.

Figure 4.24 shows the Employee Sales by Territory with Summary Chart report. This report uses an exploded pie chart. Once we change the chart type, we drag the Territory field from the dsTerritorySummary dataset and drop it into the data fields section. Then, we drag and drop the Sales YTD field into the data fields section, as shown in figure 4.25. As a result, we've configured the chart to display Sales YTD as values and grouped the sales data by territory. Then, using the Category Groups properties, we sort the data by Sales YTD so that the countries will appear on the top of the chart legend.

Next, we enable the chart point labels (the numbers on the slices) by going to the Data tab in the Chart Properties dialog box and clicking the Edit button in the Values section. We define the data labels as shown in figure 4.26.

Because of the limited space on the chart, we use an expression to show the sales value in millions. In addition, we enable the chart legend and set the chart display type to 3D by making changes to the Legend and 3D Effect tabs, respectively.

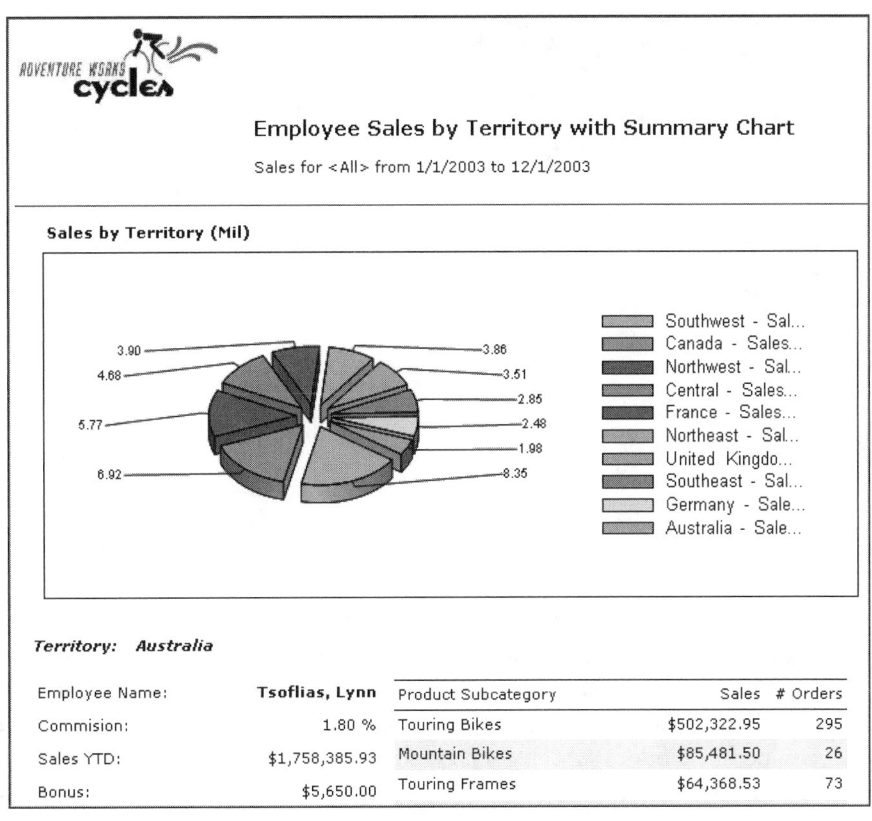

Figure 4.24 You can use a chart report to display the report data in an-easy-to-understand graphical format.

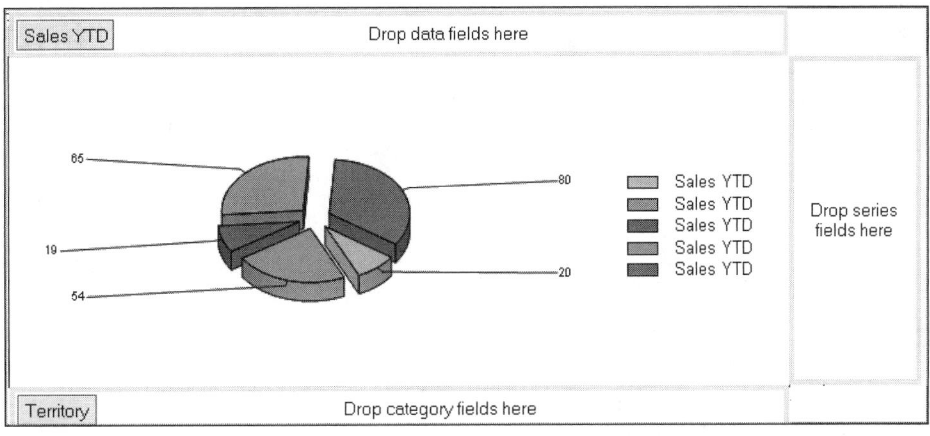

Figure 4.25 Set up the chart data by dragging and dropping fields into the data fields section.

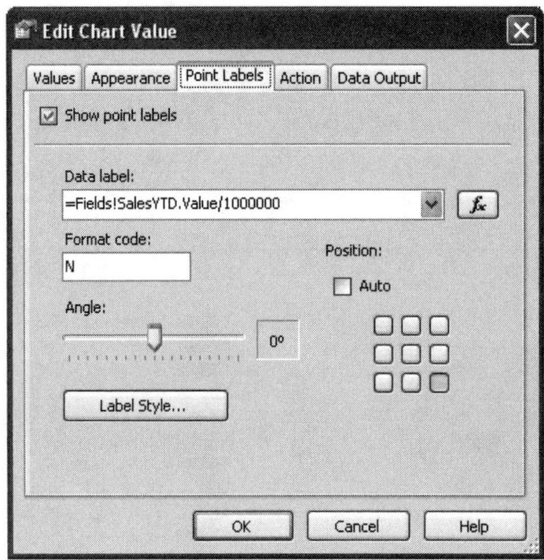

Figure 4.26
Set up the chart point labels to define how the chart displays the data.

4.4.3 Nesting chart regions

Let's look at another example. This time we need to include a chart in each employee section showing the employee performance at a glance. The performance metrics (the chart data fields) will consist of the sales amount and number of orders and will be grouped by product subcategory. Figure 4.27 shows the new Employee Sales Freeform with Chart report.

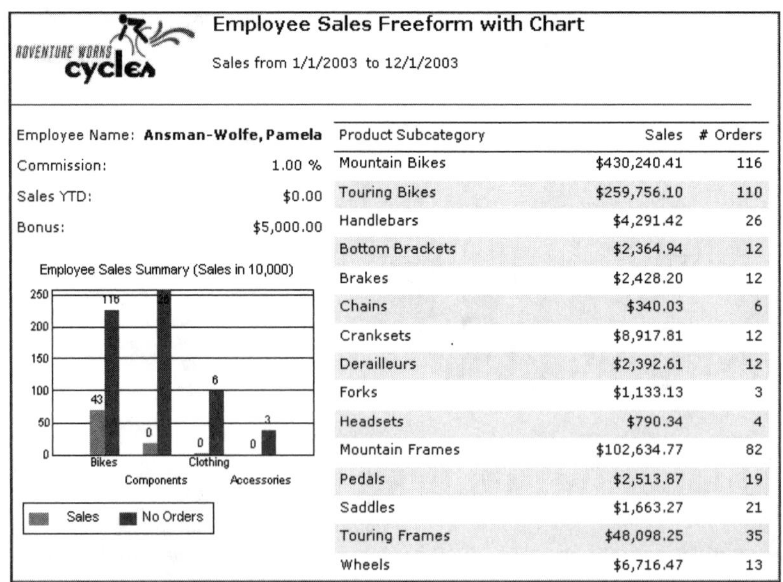

Employee Sales Freeform with Chart

Sales from 1/1/2003 to 12/1/2003

Employee Name:	**Ansman-Wolfe, Pamela**
Commission:	1.00 %
Sales YTD:	$0.00
Bonus:	$5,000.00

Product Subcategory	Sales	# Orders
Mountain Bikes	$430,240.41	116
Touring Bikes	$259,756.10	110
Handlebars	$4,291.42	26
Bottom Brackets	$2,364.94	12
Brakes	$2,428.20	12
Chains	$340.03	6
Cranksets	$8,917.81	12
Derailleurs	$2,392.61	12
Forks	$1,133.13	3
Headsets	$790.34	4
Mountain Frames	$102,634.77	82
Pedals	$2,513.87	19
Saddles	$1,663.27	21
Touring Frames	$48,098.25	35
Wheels	$6,716.47	13

Figure 4.27 You can nest the chart region inside another region.

For the purposes of this report, we change the data source to use a free SQL statement that includes an additional `Group By` clause to group the data by product category. In addition, we simplify the report by removing the employee filter. This reduces the report datasets to one because we've removed the dsEmployee dataset, which was used to define the available values for the Employee parameter.

Next, we add a chart region inside the recEmployee rectangle and change the chart type to Column, Simple Column. Then, we select both the `Sales` and `NoOrders` fields and drop them on the chart data fields section. After that, we drag and drop the `ProductSubCategory` field to the chart category fields section. We also enable the point labels for both values and make a few other minor formatting changes.

Because both the list and chart regions draw their data from the same dataset, they are in sync with each other. If the chart region needs to fetch its data from a different dataset, you have to take an extra step to synchronize both regions, for example, by passing the `EmployeeID` value from the list region to the chart dataset query.

Sometimes it is necessary to rotate results in your reports so that columns are presented horizontally and rows are presented vertically. This is known as creating a *crosstab (pivot) report*, or a *matrix report* according to the RS terminology.

4.5 DESIGNING CROSSTAB (MATRIX) REPORTS

To create crosstab reports with RS, you use the matrix data region. Those of you who are familiar with Microsoft Access will find the matrix region similar to Access crosstab queries. Many of you who have created crosstab reports in the past will probably agree that rotating the data to create this type of report is not easy. The matrix region takes the burden away from developers by allowing even inexperienced users to create crosstab reports in minutes.

4.5.1 Matrix region advantages

This control brings this type of report to a whole new level by:

- Supporting virtual columns to rotate data automatically
- Including interactive features by supporting expanding rows and columns to allow the user to drill down into the data

Rotating data with the matrix region

Retrieving data from the database in a crosstab format is not an easy endeavor. In the case of SQL Server, you have to be well versed in SQL to craft complicated statements using `CASE` expressions. This is what a possible SQL Server query might look like if you want to transpose the sales data from the AdventureWorks sample database in quarters as columns:

```
SELECT  SUM(CASE DATEPART(QQ, OrderDate)
        WHEN 1 THEN UnitPrice*OrderQty ELSE 0 END) AS Q1,
        SUM(CASE DATEPART(QQ, OrderDate)
```

```
        WHEN 2 THEN UnitPrice*OrderQty ELSE 0 END) AS Q2,
        SUM(CASE DATEPART(QQ, OrderDate)
        WHEN 3 THEN UnitPrice*OrderQty ELSE 0 END) AS Q3,
        SUM(CASE DATEPART(QQ, OrderDate)
        WHEN 4 THEN UnitPrice*OrderQty ELSE 0 END) AS Q4
FROM    Sales.SalesOrderDetail  AS SOD INNER JOIN
Sales.SalesOrderHeader AS SOH ON SOH.SalesOrderID = SOD.SalesOrderID
WHERE    DATEPART(YY,OrderDate) = 2003
GROUP BY DATEPART(yy, OrderDate)
```

And this is what the result looks like:

```
Q1              Q2              Q3              Q4
--------------- --------------- --------------- -------------
6682509.7732    8365316.6368    13944911.6542   13315837.1621
```

Now, imagine that you need to display the data in a crosstab report not by quarter but by month, within a user-defined date range. Try creating this report with a SQL statement and you will start appreciating the work that the matrix region does behind the scenes for you! The matrix region makes crafting sophisticated queries to rotate data unnecessary. Instead, once you've defined the virtual columns, the matrix region transposes and aggregates data automatically.

Interactive crosstab reports

Making crosstab reports interactive allows users to drill down through data. For instance, top managers are usually interested in the high-level view of the company performance, such as sales by country. The mid-level management is concerned with a more detailed view of information, specific to their domain, such as sales by stores.

Crosstab reports with expandable groups allow each tier of users to see the level of detail they need. In this respect, developers who have used Microsoft Office Web Components in the past will find the matrix region similar (although less powerful) to the Pivot Table component.

The best way to explain how the matrix region works is by example, as the next section demonstrates.

4.5.2 Working with the matrix region

Going back to our fictitious scenario, the AWC sales management has requested that you create a Territory Sales report, which will be used by the company's top- and mid-level sales managers. The top management wants to see the territory sales consolidated by country on a yearly basis, while the mid-level management needs a breakdown by salesperson per month. Instead of creating two reports, you prudently decide to leverage the power of the matrix region and author only one dynamic report. Figure 4.28 shows the Territory Sales Crosstab report.

The users can expand both rows (territories) and columns (time) to drill down into employees' sales data and months, respectively. For example, the snapshot shows that the user has expanded Canada to see the sales data broken down by all salespersons

Territory Sales Crosstab

Territory Sales from 3/1/2003 to 4/30/2004

ADVENTURE WORKS cycles		2003		2004					
				Jan		Feb		Mar	
		Sales	# Orders	Sales	# Orders	Sales	# Orders	Sales	# Orders
Australia		$723,901	761	$59,444	46	$75,125	59	$200,640	190
Canada	Vargas, Garrett	$1,266,718	1268	$17,272	15	$117,196	136	$111,110	102
	Saraiva, José	$1,704,735	1428	$80,606	114	$110,761	80	$310,933	214
Central		$3,078,358	2832	$165,476	185	$167,581	191	$278,368	220
France		$2,170,158	1630	$40,857	57	$466,573	297	$88,588	76
Germany		$1,003,983	972	$118,754	108	$150,239	147	$81,084	88
Northeast		$3,515,425	2747	$161,920	90	$318,546	228	$248,160	252
Northwest		$3,058,603	2345	$287,556	166	$279,221	199	$403,326	254
Southeast		$1,899,693	1871	$113,563	133	$188,541	170	$181,960	138
Southwest		$5,646,201	4433	$330,316	251	$585,243	361	$427,494	346
United Kingdom		$3,708,164	2974	$219,462	191	$205,603	178	$353,921	273
Total		$27,775,939	23261	$1,595,226	1356	$2,664,627	2046	$2,685,585	2153

Figure 4.28 Creating crosstab reports is easy using the matrix region.

who handle the Canada region. In addition, the user has decided to see the monthly sales data for 2004, while the sales data for 2003 is displayed consolidated.

Let's discuss the essential points of this report design process.

Setting up the report data

First, we set up the dsTerritorySales report dataset with the following SQL statement:

```
SELECT  ST.TerritoryID, ST.Name AS Territory, SP.SalesPersonID,
 C.LastName + N', ' + C.FirstName AS EmployeeName,
 SOH.OrderDate AS Date,SUM(SOD.UnitPrice*SOD.OrderQty)AS
 Sales, COUNT(SOH.SalesOrderID) AS NoOrders
FROMSales.SalesOrderDetail SOD
 INNER JOIN Sales.SalesOrderHeader SOH
  ON SOD.SalesOrderID = SOH.SalesOrderID
 INNER JOIN Sales.SalesPerson SP
  ON SOH.SalesPersonID = SP.SalesPersonID
 INNER JOIN HumanResources.Employee E
  ON SP.SalesPersonID = E.EmployeeID
 INNER JOIN Person.Contact C
  ON C.ContactID = E.EmployeeID
 INNER JOIN Sales.SalesTerritory ST
  ON SP.TerritoryID = ST.TerritoryID
WHERE (SOH.OrderDate BETWEEN @StartDate AND @EndDate)
GROUP BY
 ST.TerritoryID,ST.Name,SOH.OrderDate,
 SP.SalesPersonID, C.LastName + N', ' + C.FirstName
ORDER BY   ST.Name, SOH.OrderDate
```

Since the matrix rows of this report summarize the information in territories and salespersons, the query statement provides these groups. Drilldown per year is achieved with expressions based on the OrderDate field inside the report. The query also takes start and end dates as parameters.

Adding the matrix region

Next, we switch to the layout mode and drag and drop the matrix region into the report, as shown in figure 4.29.

The upper-left cell of the matrix region is the corner cell. You can use it to display a title for the matrix region. In our case, we've used that cell as a container for the AWC logo image.

The matrix data region makes defining the rows and columns in the crosstab easy. To group the data into rows and columns, you must define the row and column dynamic groups.

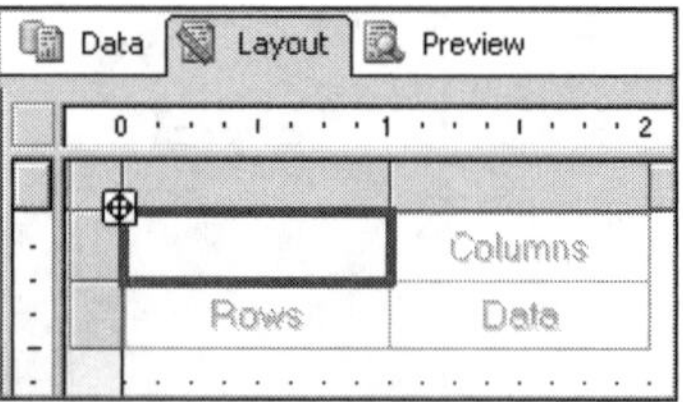

Figure 4.29 You define dynamic and static matrix groups by dragging and dropping dataset fields into the respective areas.

Defining dynamic groups

Dynamic row and column groups can nest within other dynamic row and column groups. You add dynamic groups by dragging and dropping dataset fields to the Rows and Columns areas. The Report Designer displays a helpful bar hint when you drag the field over the row or column headers to show you valid places where you can drop the field to nest the new group inside an existing group.

For example, to drill down by territory and salesperson, we drag and drop the `Territory` and `EmployeeName` fields from the dsTerritorySales dataset into the Rows section. As a result, the matrix region creates two dynamic row groups, which we rename `rowTerritory` and `rowEmployee`, respectively, as shown in figure 4.30.

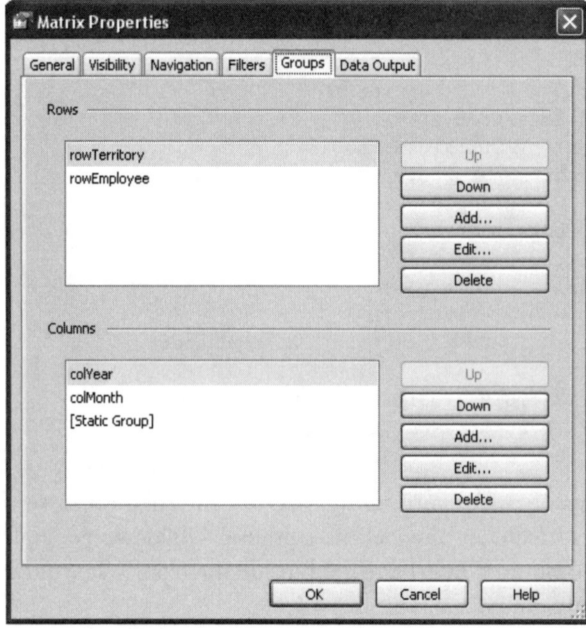

Figure 4.30 You can achieve data drilldown with the matrix region by creating nested column and row dynamic groups.

The Columns section is little bit trickier. Here we need to define dynamic columns for years and months. To achieve this we create two column groups, colYear and colMonth, and set them to be based on the `Fields!Date.Value.Year` and `Format(Fields!Date.Value, "MMM")` expressions, respectively. Because the `Date` field from the report dataset is of type DateTime, you could use the methods and properties of the .NET DateTime structure to retrieve the year and month portions. We also format the month value to show the abbreviated version of the month, for example, *Jan* for January.

Defining static groups

To display the actual data (intersected cells for dynamic row and column groups), you define static rows or column groups. You are not restricted to one static group. When you add more than one static group under a given dynamic column, the dynamic header splits to accommodate the new group. To demonstrate this, let's drag and drop both the Sales and `NoOrders` dataset fields to the matrix region data section, so that users can see the sales dollar amount alongside the number of orders placed per territory segment.

To get the expand/collapse magic working, we have to change the visibility for the rowEmployee and colMonth groups. Figure 4.31 shows the visibility settings for the rowEmployee group.

These settings make the rowEmployee group invisible initially. Only when the user expands the higher-level Territory group does the Employee group become

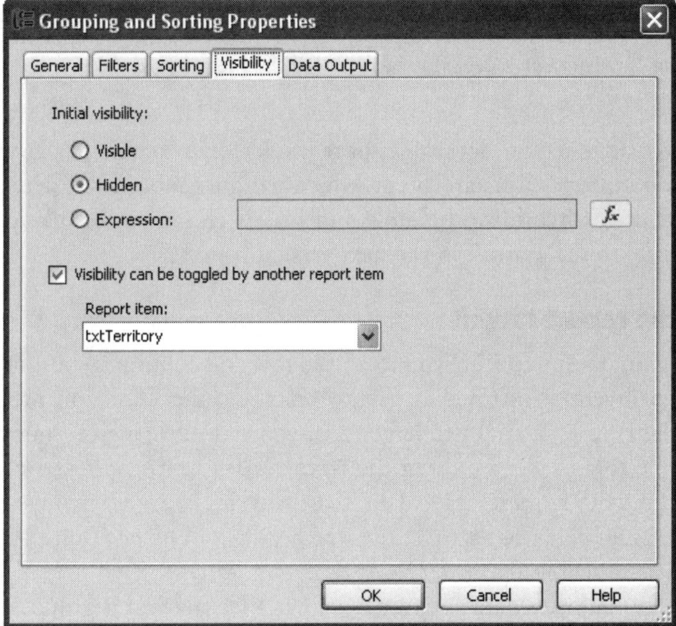

Figure 4.31 You can toggle the group visibility by changing the Visibility settings.

visible. In a similar way, we can set the visibility of `colMonth` to be toggled by the `txtYear` field.

Creating subtotals

With many crosstab reports you may want to sum numeric data horizontally and vertically. The matrix region also allows you to define subtotals to sum the data on row and column groups. The only aggregate operation supported is summing. You create subtotals by right-clicking the header of a row or column dynamic group and selecting Subtotal from the context menu. For the Territory Sales report, let's define subtotals on the Territory and Year levels. Formatting changes, such as setting border styles and background colors, make the report look better, as shown in figure 4.32.

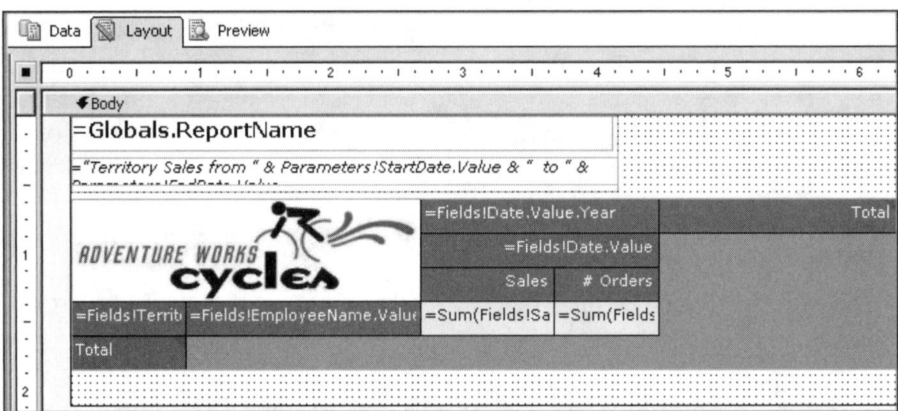

Figure 4.32 The Territory Sales Crosstab report uses the Matrix subtotal.

Currently, the matrix region doesn't support headers and footers per grouping. It is designed for a traditional crosstab layout, which has only subtotals. There are rumors that Microsoft might hybridize the table and matrix regions (most likely by adding table-like features to the matrix) in the next version.

4.5.3 Adjusting the report layout

The matrix region doesn't confine you to a fixed row and column layout. For example, you can get an inverted mirrored layout by changing the Direction property from LTR (left to right) to RTL (right to left). Also, you can move a given number of columns before the row header by using the `GroupsBeforeRowHeaders` property. For example, if you request sales data that falls in between two years and set `GroupsBeforeRowHeaders` to `1`, the row header will be positioned between the year columns, as shown in figure 4.33.

Another feature of the Matrix report type that affects layout is group header locking. Typical implementations of matrix reports tend to show a lot of data. In fact,

Territory Sales Crosstab

Territory Sales from 3/1/2003 to 4/30/2004

2003		ADVENTURE WORKS cycles	2004		Total	
Sales	# Orders		Sales	# Orders	Sales	# Orders
$723,901	761	Australia	$394,023	359	$1,117,924	1120
$2,971,452	2696	Canada	$862,793	818	$3,834,245	3514
$3,078,358	2832	Central	$825,768	844	$3,904,127	3676
$2,170,158	1630	France	$650,714	512	$2,820,873	2142
$1,003,983	972	Germany	$519,188	476	$1,523,171	1448
$3,515,425	2747	Northeast	$925,283	690	$4,440,709	3437
$3,058,603	2345	Northwest	$1,358,373	834	$4,416,975	3179
$1,899,693	1871	Southeast	$595,023	571	$2,494,716	2442
$5,646,201	4433	Southwest	$1,842,561	1290	$7,488,762	5723
$3,708,164	2974	United Kingdom	$1,149,591	901	$4,857,756	3875
$27,775,939	23261	Total	$9,123,318	7295	$36,899,257	30556

Figure 4.33 This shows what happens when you enter 1 in the GroupsBeforeRowHeaders property.

since the number of columns is dynamic, there is no ideal way to enforce a standard width for your report. If you are looking at the column on the far end of the report and you cannot see the row information, your experience may not be very good. This is where group header locking becomes very helpful. We implement group header locking for both the row and column headers in this report by navigating to the Groups tab of the Matrix report properties and then editing the rowTerritory group, as shown in figure 4.34. By selecting the Group Header Should Remain Visible When Scrolling property, we ensure that the group header will not scroll off the screen in our report. We only need to set this value for one of the column groupings since doing this for one column grouping will affect all column groupings.

One interesting performance optimization detail about the matrix region inner workings is that, as we mentioned in chapter 1, it doesn't render all the data at once when the report is rendered in HTML. Instead, you will notice that each time you expand a section, a round-trip (HTTP-GET request) occurs to the Report Server to fetch the data for the expanded section. To be more specific, a matrix report retrieves all data from the data source when the query is executed, produces the report in intermediate format, and serializes it into data chunks in the ReportServerTempDb database. This process is known as *report session caching*, and we discuss this topic in detail in chapter 8.

When a report row or column is expanded, the matrix region posts back to the server to retrieve the report for that section. This improves the report performance because sections are rendered on an as-needed basis. The session management occurs only when the Report Server renders the report in HTML.

You see more of the matrix region in chapter 6 when we discuss how to use expressions in crosstab reports to see forecasted data.

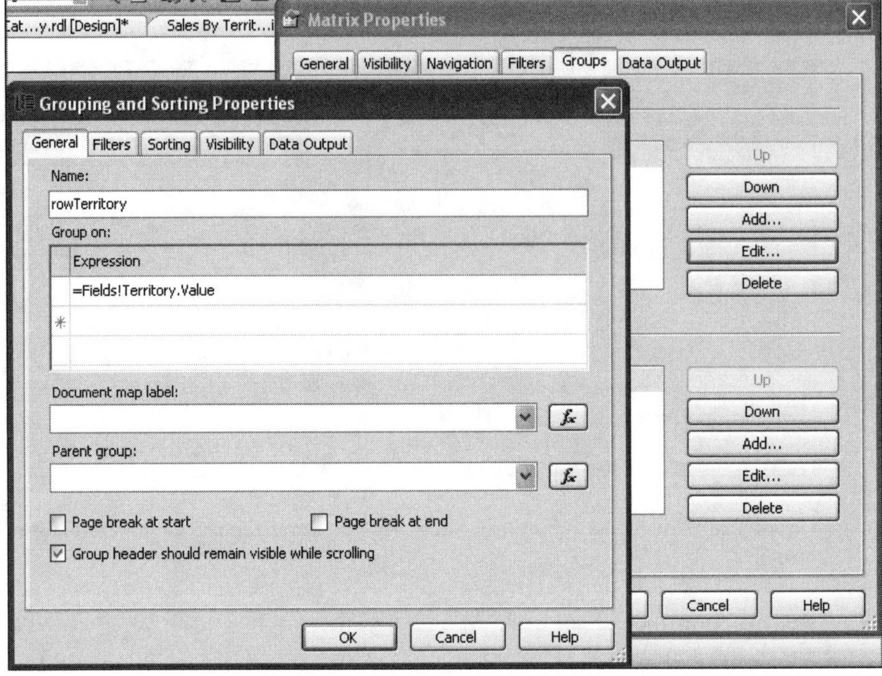

Figure 4.34 You can lock the group headers so that they do not scroll off the page for your matrix reports.

4.6 USING OTHER DESIGN FEATURES IN YOUR REPORTS

As you have seen, you can create several types of reports with RS. Also, several features are available to make your reports more interactive or simply more user friendly. We spend some time in this section checking out some of these features. We take a close look at how to set up multicolumned reports, add interactive sort functionality, pass multivalued parameters into stored procedures, and use subreports.

Let's first see how we can display report data in multiple columns.

4.6.1 Setting up multiple columns

The Report Designer allows you to easily create multicolumn reports. Just like a newspaper, a multicolumn report can conserve space by displaying the report data in more than one column. The Products by Subcategory report demonstrates how you can author such reports, as shown in figure 4.35.

The report shows the product inventory data arranged in three columns to conserve paper space. The trick to creating this report is to make sure that the report data width doesn't exceed the column width, as shown in figure 4.36.

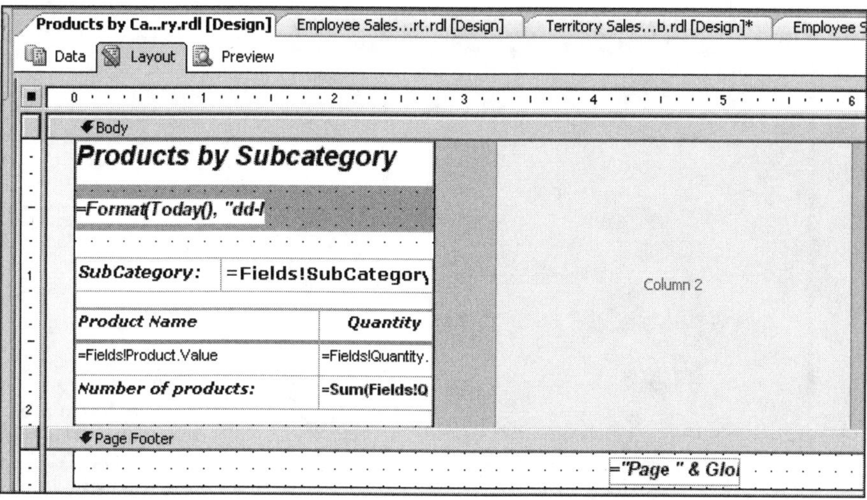

Figure 4.35 Creating multicolumn reports with Reporting Services is easy.

NOTE To see the report rendered correctly in multiple columns, make sure that you preview the report by clicking the Print Preview button. If you just preview the report, you won't see the data flowing in columns because the preview mode doesn't take into consideration the page settings.

To create the report, use a list region for the subcategory section and a nested table region for the product details. Set the body width of the report to 2.75 in. To set up the multicolumn layout, set the number of columns to 3 in the Report Properties dialog box (figure 4.37).

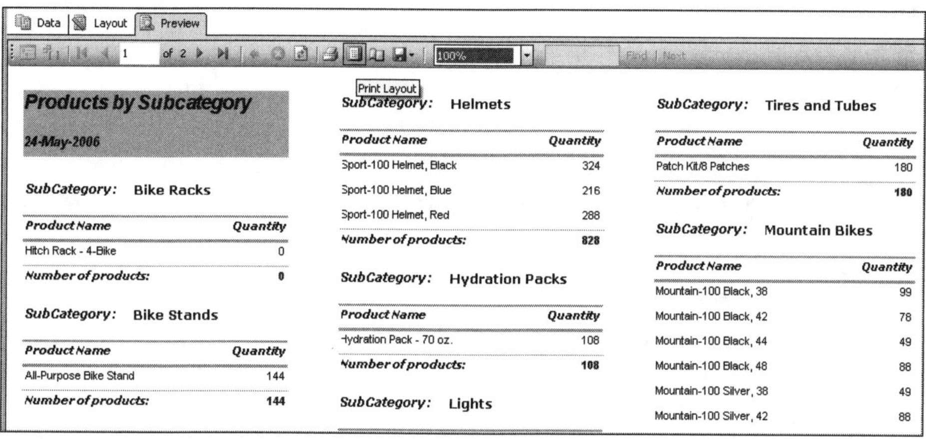

Figure 4.36 The Products by Subcategory report in print mode shows the multiple columns feature.

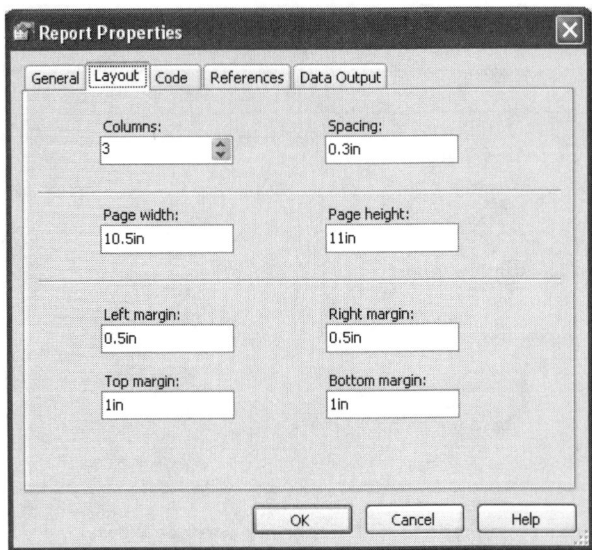

Figure 4.37
Specify the number of columns in the Report Properties dialog box (select the report by clicking the Report Selector, right-click, and choose Properties).

Currently, RS supports defining multiple columns only at the report level. You cannot, for example, define a multicolumn layout per region, for example, a table region.

When setting up the column widths, you must ensure that you have enough page space to accommodate the number of columns, per the following formula:

```
Page width-(left margin + right margin) >= number of columns *
column width + (number of columns - 1) * column spacing
```

The Report Designer eliminates the trial-and-error fitting game by showing you the outline of the columns in layout mode. This allows you to easily see whether the report width exceeds the page width.

4.6.2 Adding interactive sort

Interactive sort is a new feature with the 2005 release of Reporting Services. While you could build in sort functionality in previous versions of Reporting Services, it took quite a bit of customization and coding. Interactive sort enables the end user to re-sort data on the report without going back to the server. Let's take a closer look at this feature.

Interactive sort: providing sort on a single field

Let's create a report that uses the new interactive sort feature. We'll base this report on the Sales By Territory report.

Step 1 To start, copy the Sales By Territory report in the Business Intelligence Designer and rename it to `Sales By Territory Interactive.rdl`.

Step 2 On the Layout tab, right-click on the Territory cell in the header row and select Properties.

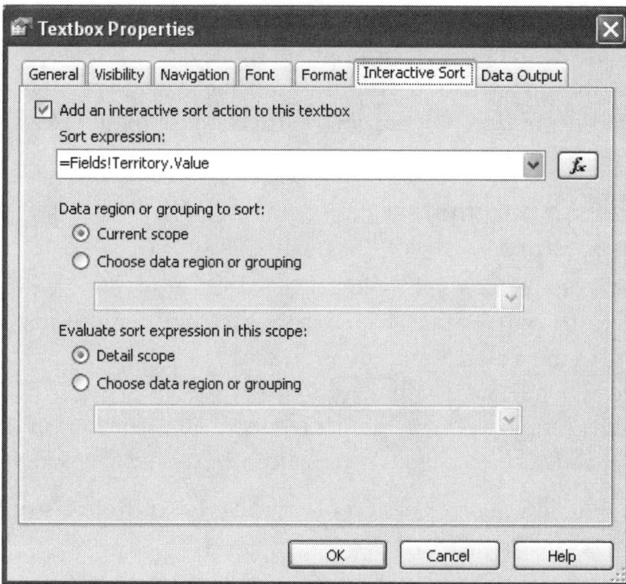

Figure 4.38
The interactive sort features allow you to set up the ability for report users to easily sort the data.

Step 3 In the Textbox Properties dialog box, select the Interactive Sort tab (figure 4.38).

Step 4 Check Add an Interactive Sort Action to this Textbox and select the Territory field from the Sort Expression drop-down list.

Step 5 Click OK and preview the report in the designer.

You will see that RS added an icon to the right of the Territory text in the header. This icon will initialize as a double arrow (one arrow pointing up and one arrow pointing down). This signifies that the data is not yet sorted. Clicking on this icon will sort the data ascending by the Territory field. Note that the icon changes to an image representing this sort. If you click on this image again, it will re-sort descending. This demonstrates the interactive sort in its simplest form. Now let's look at some more advanced sorting.

Interactive sort: providing sorting on multiple fields

Let's add another sort-able field to our Sales By Territory report.

Step 1 From the Layout tab, right-click on the Territory cell in the header row and select Properties.

Step 2 In the Textbox Properties dialog box, select the Interactive Sort tab.

Step 3 Check Add an Interactive Sort Action to this Textbox and select the Sales field from the Sort Expression drop-down list. Then click OK.

Preview the report in the designer. You should now see two sort icons. If you hold down the Shift key and select both icons, you can sort by Facility ascending and Sales (within the Territory) descending.

Notice in figure 4.38 that there are options to choose the data region or grouping to sort by, as well as the data region or grouping that define the scope for the sort expressions. These options will allow you to do advanced interactive sorting so that you can have the sort expression only sort in a particular grouping instead of affecting the entire dataset in the report.

4.6.3 Passing multivalued parameters into a stored procedure

In section 4.2, when we created the Employee Sales Tabular report, we explained that out of the box it is easier to use a free SQL query to accept our multivalued parameter Employee than it is to use a stored procedure. In case you want to use a stored procedure and not a free SQL query, you will need to do a little more work.

Let's start with the Employee Sales Tabular report where we left off in section 4.2.2 (at that point, we'd added interactive functionality). In this section we:

- Write a SQL function to convert a list of `EmployeeIds` from a string to a table returning integer fields.
- Write a stored procedure to accept the `EmployeeIds` and call our function.
- Change the report to use our new stored procedure.

Writing the SQL conversion function

In the `Database` folder in this book's source code you will find a file called `functions.sql`. This script file contains a function called `fn_ParseEmployeeIDsToTable`, which takes one input parameter, `@vc_EmployeeIds`. This parameter is a `varchar(1000)`, which should be plenty big for our needs. Our `Employee` parameter will ultimately fill this function's input parameter based on the user's action. While we won't spend time looking in depth at how this function works, feel free to pull up the code and investigate on your own. For the purposes of this example, it is important to understand that this function accepts the employee information the form of a comma-separated string of IDs. This function returns a T-SQL table with one integer column, `EmployeeId`.

Writing the stored procedure

The `Database` folder in the source code also contains a file called `spGetEmployeeSalesByProductSubcategoryMultiple.sql`. This file contains the script to create the stored procedure that will be used by this report. Here's an abbreviated sample of this script:

```
SELECT    . . .

WHERE (SOH.OrderDate BETWEEN @StartDate AND @EndDate)
   AND E.EmployeeID IN (select * from _
fn_ParseEmployeeIDsToTable( @EmployeeIDs) )
GROUP BY ST.NAME, E.EmployeeID, C.LastName + N', '+ C.FirstName,
```

```
C.FirstName, E.LoginID, SP.SalesYTD, SP.CommissionPct, SP.Bonus,
PSC.ProductSubCategoryID,PSC.Name
ORDER BY  ST.NAME, EmployeeName, Sales DESC
```

Here you can see the three parameters that our report uses in the `WHERE` clause of our query. The part that changed from our original free SQL query appears in the `WHERE` clause on the second line. As you can see, our original parameter variable, `@EmployeeIDs`, has been replaced by a query to our new function.

Modifying the report

Let's now change our report to use our new stored procedure and function. This is as simple as clicking on the Data tab and selecting the dsEmployeeSales dataset. Then delete the query, change the Command type to StoredProcedure, and enter the name of our stored procedure (`spGetEmployeeSalesByProductSubcategoryMultiple`) in the query window.

That's it! Now let's take a look at a way to embed one report into another by using subreports.

4.6.4 Designing subreports

A subreport is a report item that points to another report. As you have seen, RS gives you plenty of design choices, and in many cases you won't need to use subreports at all. There are two main situations, however, that will necessitate using subreports:

- *Reusing existing reports*—You can use the subreport region as a placeholder to host an existing report. For example, you may already have a company sales summary report, like one of the summary reports we created earlier. For easier maintenance, you might want to reuse the report. Each time you change the report, the change propagates to all reports of which this report is part. Also, in some cases you simply have no other choice.
- *Nesting report sections that use different datasets*—This will be the case when you need to nest a data region inside another region and each region uses a different dataset, as in the following example.

Imagine that the AWC management has requested that we change the Employee Sales Freeform with Chart report to show an Employee Performance Summary chart that outlines employee sales for the past 12 months. In other words, the Employee Performance Summary chart needs to ignore the start date parameter and show the sales summary for the previous 12 months relative to the end date parameter.

For example, if the user has requested to see the Employee Sales report from 10/1/2003 to 12/1/2003, the Employee Performance Summary needs to show the monthly breakdown of employee sales starting with 1/1/2003, as shown in figure 4.39.

The report requirements call for creating a new dataset for the Employee Performance Summary chart. Our first impulse might be to base a chart region on the new

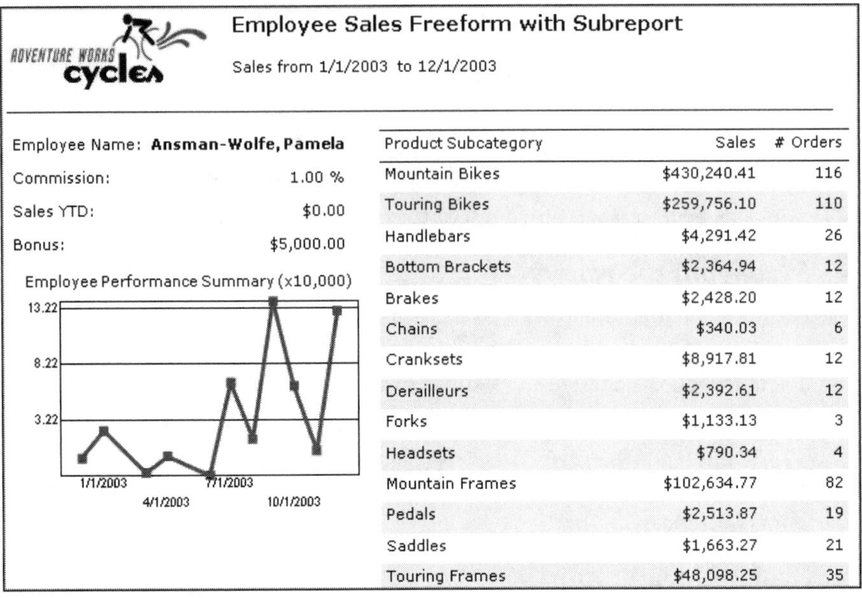

ADVENTURE WORKS cycles

Employee Sales Freeform with Subreport

Sales from 1/1/2003 to 12/1/2003

Employee Name: **Ansman-Wolfe, Pamela**

Commission: 1.00 %

Sales YTD: $0.00

Bonus: $5,000.00

Product Subcategory	Sales	# Orders
Mountain Bikes	$430,240.41	116
Touring Bikes	$259,756.10	110
Handlebars	$4,291.42	26
Bottom Brackets	$2,364.94	12
Brakes	$2,428.20	12
Chains	$340.03	6
Cranksets	$8,917.81	12
Derailleurs	$2,392.61	12
Forks	$1,133.13	3
Headsets	$790.34	4
Mountain Frames	$102,634.77	82
Pedals	$2,513.87	19
Saddles	$1,663.27	21
Touring Frames	$48,098.25	35

Figure 4.39 Use subreports when you need to nest report sections that draw data from separate datasets.

dataset and nest it inside the list region. However, the chart region needs to follow the employee breakdown of the list region. In other words, the chart needs to be synchronized with the employee grouping of the list region. This presents a problem, though, because synchronized nested regions, which use the same groupings, must use the same dataset.

The solution is to create a new subreport for the chart and synchronize the subreport with the main report. Let's create the Employee Performance subreport. There is nothing different about creating a subreport. As you know by now, we'll start by setting up the report data.

Setting up the report data

To create the report dataset, use a free SQL statement as your dataset source, as shown here:

```
SELECT  E.EmployeeID, C.LastName + N', ' + C.FirstName AS EmployeeName,
 SUM(SOD.UnitPrice * SOD.OrderQty) AS Sales,
 COUNT(SOH.SalesOrderID) AS NoOrders,
 DATEPART(yy, SOH.OrderDate) AS Year,
 DATEPART(m, SOH.OrderDate) AS Month
FROM Sales.SalesPerson SP
 INNER JOIN Sales.SalesOrderHeader SOH
  ON SP.SalesPersonID = SOH.SalesPersonID
 INNER JOIN HumanResources.Employee E
  ON SP.SalesPersonID = E.EmployeeID
```

```
  INNER JOIN Person.Contact C
   ON C.ContactID = E.EmployeeID
  INNER JOIN Sales.SalesOrderDetail SOD
   ON SOH.SalesOrderID = SOD.SalesOrderID
WHERE (SOH.OrderDate
   BETWEEN DATEADD(mm, - 12, @Date) AND @Date)
  AND (E.EmployeeID = @EmployeeID)
GROUP BY   E.EmployeeID, C.LastName + N', ' + C.FirstName,
   DATEPART    (m, SOH.OrderDate),
   DATEPART(yy, SOH.OrderDate)
ORDER BY DATEPART(yy, SOH.OrderDate),DATEPART(m, SOH.OrderDate)
```

❶ Specifies parameter placeholders

❷ Groups the data per employee

This statement groups the sales data per employee for the past year relative to the @Date parameter. It defines two parameters: `@EmployeeID` and `@Date` ❶. In addition, the statement breaks down the order date by month and year ❷. This is needed to summarize the sales data per month. To achieve this, create a new calculated dataset field called Date, which is based on the following expression:

```
= new DateTime (Fields!Year.Value, Fields!Month.Value,1)
```

This expression simply converts the month and year back to a date that starts at 12:00 A.M. We could have converted the date in the statement itself using SQL expressions, but we wanted to demonstrate calculated dataset fields.

Configuring the subreport

Next, let's use a chart region to present the data in graphical format. Figure 4.40 shows the subreport in a layout mode. You have already seen how to configure a chart, but this time the chart type is Line.

Once you've created the subreport, you are ready to place it inside a subreport region. The easiest way to do that is to drag the report from the Solution Explorer and drop it

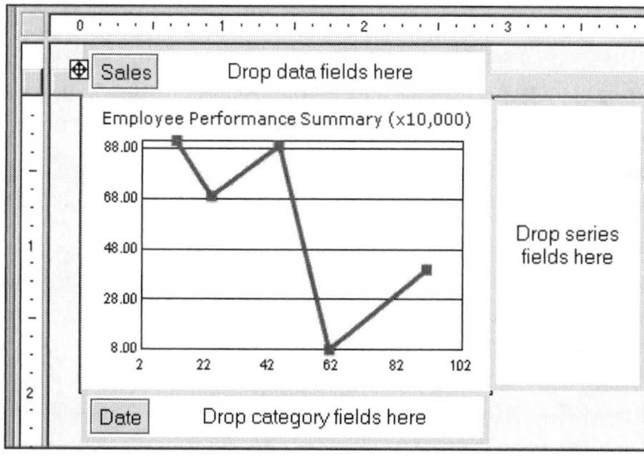

Figure 4.40 Creating a subreport is no different than creating an ordinary report.

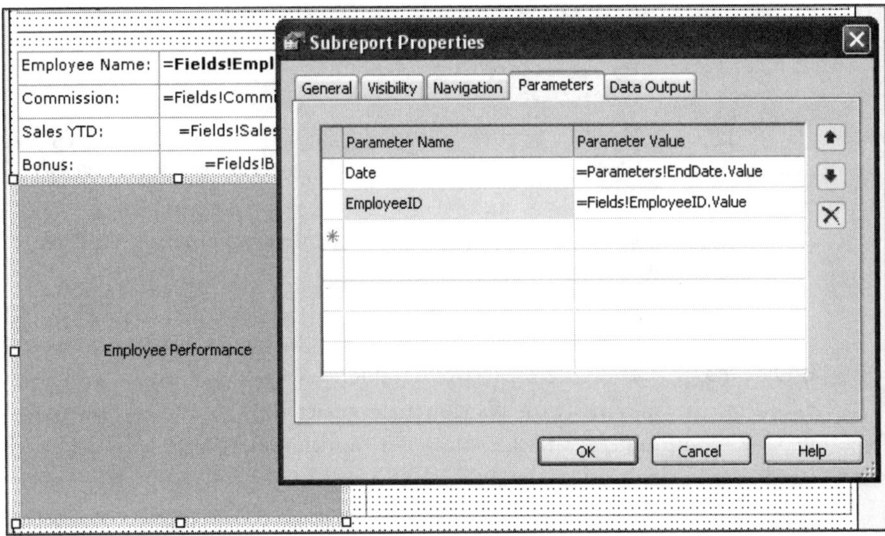

Figure 4.41 Integrate the main report with a subreport.

inside the main report. Because you want to nest the subreport inside the lstEmployee-Sales region, make sure you drop the subreport into the recEmployee rectangle.

Synchronizing the subreport with the master report

Finally, you need to synchronize both reports by passing the required parameters to the subreport. You can set the subreport parameters by using the VS .NET Properties window. Alternatively, you can right-click on the subreport, choose Properties, and select the Parameters tab in the Subreport Properties dialog box, as shown in figure 4.41.

In this example, for the `@Date` parameter of the subreport we pass the `@EndDate` parameter of the main report. We link the `@EmployeeID` subreport parameter to the `EmployeeID` field of the main report dataset. As a result, each time the main report initiates a new Employee group, it passes the `EmployeeID` to the subreport to display the summary data for that employee only.

Set up all required subreport parameters carefully. If you miss some or set them up incorrectly, the subreport will not be shown. Instead, the subreport region will report an exception: "Error: the subreport could not be shown."

4.7 SUMMARY

One of the main strengths of RS is that it gives you the right tools to easily design many different types of reports. The Report Designer enables even novice users to create professional-looking reports in a matter of minutes. As you've seen, the report data regions give you a lot of flexibility for laying out your reports. In this chapter, we discussed the effects of data region nesting and using regions side by side.

We also showed you how to create a variety of reports using regions:

- Tabular reports use the table region.
- Freeform reports use the list region.
- Chart reports use the chart region.
- Crosstab reports use the matrix region.

Finally, we looked at how you can add several features to your reports, such as multiple columns and interactive sort. We also explained how to pass multivalued parameters into stored procedures, and how and when you should create subreports.

Now, it is time to add more advanced report-authoring techniques to your arsenal that will help you create even more sophisticated reports. In the next chapter you learn how to enhance reports with expressions and functions.

CHAPTER 5

Using expressions and functions

Sometimes, reporting requirements may call for advanced techniques that go beyond the scope of the Report Designer. For example, you may need to implement conditional formatting to change the color of report items based on some conditions.

Most modern reporting tools support programming primitives of some sort that developers can use to write expressions and programmatically manipulate report elements. In this chapter, we explore how you can use expressions and functions with Reporting Services to enhance the report capabilities.

Our discussion covers the following topics:

- Writing expressions
- Working with the Report Object Model global collections
- Using functions
- Using expressions to author reports with interactive features
- Examining RS export formats and how formatting can impact the interactive features of a report

To round out this chapter, we show how you can use expressions to add interactive features to your reports, including reports with navigational features and reports with document maps.

5.1 UNDERSTANDING EXPRESSIONS

An RS *expression* is a formula written in Visual Basic .NET syntax that uses a combination of keywords, operators, functions, and constant values to calculate the value of a report item or its properties during runtime. You are already familiar with one of most basic types of inline expressions: the field expression. We used field expressions on many occasions to display the value of a dataset field by referencing the Fields collection; for example:

```
=Fields!Sales.Value
```

Table 5.1 shows some examples of field expressions and describes each.

Table 5.1 Field expressions

Example	Description
`=Fields!Territory.Value`	Returns a dataset field
`=Sum(Fields!Bonus.Value)`	Returns a sum of the values of the specified expression
`=Avg(Fields!Bonus.Value)`	Returns the average of all non-null values from the specified expression
`=Fields!LastName.Value & ", " & Fields!FirstName`	Concatenates multiple fields together
`RunningValue(Fields!Cost.Value, Sum, Nothing)`	Uses a specified function to return a running aggregate of the specified expression
`RowNumber(Nothing)`	Returns a running count of all rows in the specified scope

You have probably used expressions with other reporting tools to achieve some degree of runtime customization, such as implementing calculated fields. For example, say you want to combine the employees' first and last names into one string to set the value of a textbox report item called `txtEmployeeName`. With RS, you can achieve this by using the following inline expression for the `Value` property of the textbox:

```
= Fields!FirstName.Value & " " & Fields!LastName.Value
```

RS allows you to use built-in functions that include your basic standard aggregates as well as some RS-specific functions. `RowNumber` is an example of an RS-specific function.

RS does not limit your use of expressions to setting values of textbox report items. Instead, by using expressions you can manipulate programmatically just about any property of a report item and region. In this section, we cover all aspects of using expressions, starting with the Expression Editor. Next, we look at the syntax of expressions, and then we explore expression order and scope. Lastly, we learn how to deal with expression errors. Memorizing expression syntax can be tedious. To address this, the Report Designer offers you a helping hand with the Expression Editor.

5.1.1 Using the Expression Editor

The Report Designer allows you to write report expressions by typing the expression text manually or using the Expression Editor. You will probably find the first method handy when you want to quickly change the expression text or enter simple expressions. For example, you can click inside a textbox and directly type a field expression to bind the textbox to a dataset field, for example, `=Fields!Sales.Value`.

Alternatively, you can use the Expression Editor. If you used RS 2000 you will find a welcoming change in the Expression Editor. In the previous version of RS it was tough to know whether your expressions contained syntax errors. The Expression Editor in this release will evaluate expressions and check for syntax errors, and it also provides us with IntelliSense.

To open the editor, use one of the following options from within the Report Designer:

- Using the item's VS .NET Properties window, choose the Expression item from the available options for any property that can be manipulated by an expression, for example, the `TextBox.Value` property.
- In the item's Properties dialog box (right-click the item and choose Properties), click the *(fx)* button located to the right of any property that supports expressions.
- As a shortcut when entering an expression for the textbox `Value` property, you can right-click the textbox and choose Expression from the context menu.

Figure 5.1 shows the Expression Editor using the code completion feature. We invoked the Expression Editor by right-clicking one of the textboxes inside the Employee Sales Freeform report and selecting Expression from the context menu.

As shown in figure 5.1, in this case the Expression Editor shows the fields of the dsEmployeeSales dataset using IntelliSense. You can also view the fields by clicking on the Fields label in the tree view on the left.

For your convenience, the three most-used *collections* from the Report Server object model (Globals, Parameters, and Fields) are shown on the left side of the dialog box, so you don't have to memorize the names of their members. We revisit these collections in section 5.2. This dialog box will also provide access to the Datasets collection, Common Functions, Operators, and Constants for easy selection.

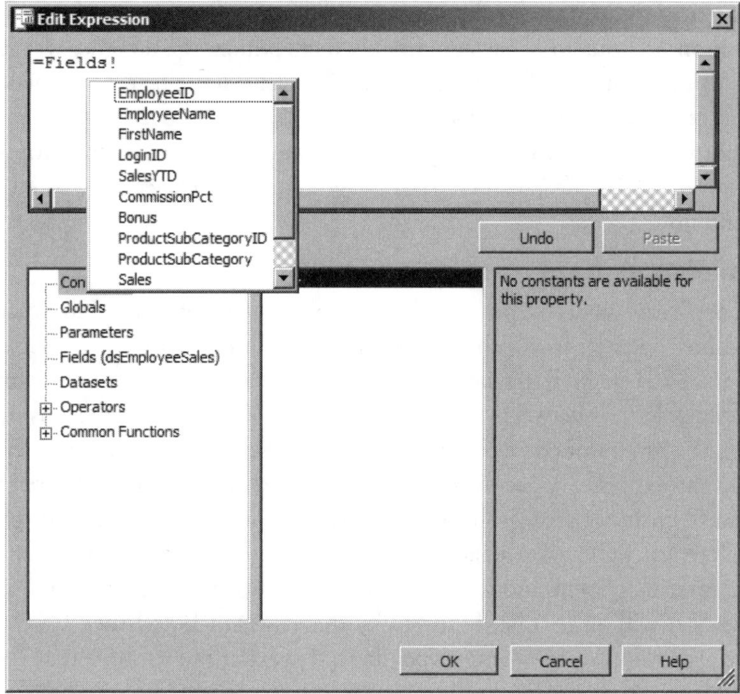

Figure 5.1 Use the Expression Editor to create expressions.

5.1.2 Expression syntax

As we explained in chapter 3, the Report Designer verifies the expression syntax during the report-building process. Just as with any programming environment, you need to learn to play by the compiler's rules. There are a few syntax-related rules about expressions worth mentioning before we see some examples.

First, because you author expressions in VB .NET, the expression syntax is not case-sensitive. For this reason, `fields!Sales.value` and `Fields!Sales.Value` are interchangeable. Be aware, though, that for some reason RS requires that the field names match exactly the dataset field names despite the fact that Visual Basic is not case-sensitive. If they don't, a compilation exception is thrown. For example, if the dataset field is `SalesYTD` but you use `Fields!salesYTD` in your expression, the Report Designer errors out with the following exception:

```
The value expression for the textbox 'txtTerritorySalesYTDTotal'
refers to the field 'salesYTD'.  Report item expressions can only
refer to fields within the current data set scope or, if inside
an aggregate, the specified data set scope.
```

Second, to tell RS that you want to use an expression, you must prefix the expression text with an equal sign (=). The Report Designer reacts in different ways to remind you about this rule. For example, if you type the expression without the equal sign in the Properties window, an invalid property exception dialog box appears. If you type an expression without an equal sign directly in a textbox, the designer won't complain at all. In this case, it will assume that you are entering static text, which will be shown as is when the report is rendered.

In addition to these two rules, your expression syntax needs to comply with the syntax of VB .NET. For a VB .NET language reference, check the VS .NET product documentation.

5.1.3 Determining expression execution order

The Report Server has a rule processor that involves some sophisticated decision making to determine the order in which expressions are executed. For lack of a better term, we refer to it as an *expression sequence processor*. This processor bases its execution decisions on interdependencies between expressions and the location of expressions in a report.

When the processor parses expressions, it discovers any existing interdependencies and ranks the expressions accordingly. For example, say you have three textbox items, A, B, and C, inside a list region. A gets its value from a dataset field. B references A, and C references B. The expression sequence processor will discover that these expressions are interdependent and sort their execution order accordingly. In our example, the value of A will be set first, followed by the values of B and then C.

If the expressions are not interdependent, our experiments show that they are executed sequentially according to their location in the report. For example, expressions that set properties of the Body band are executed before the expressions in items located in the body section.

Is execution order important? Well, knowing the order in which the expression will be executed allows you to write "pseudo" events to do some preprocessing to compensate for the lack of "real" events in RS.

Say you want to initialize some class-level variables in custom code before you call a custom function inside an expression. Also assume that the expression is used to set the value of a textbox item in a table region. Because RS doesn't support events, you may think that you are of out of luck. However, you can use an expression in the Body band, for example, an expression to set the `BorderStyle` property, which will fire before the table region is rendered.

Because there is only one Body band inside the report, this expression will fire once, which, to perform the initialization tasks, is exactly what you want. Inside the expression you can call a method in the custom code, which will set the required state. As you'll see in chapter 9, this is exactly the approach we take to author the Show Security Policy report, so we can initialize the Report Server web service proxy before we call its methods.

5.1.4 Understanding expression scope

One of the things that you need to consider when referencing report items in expressions is the concept of *expression scope*. Simply put, the expression scope defines the boundaries in which the expression can operate. Each dataset, region, and grouping

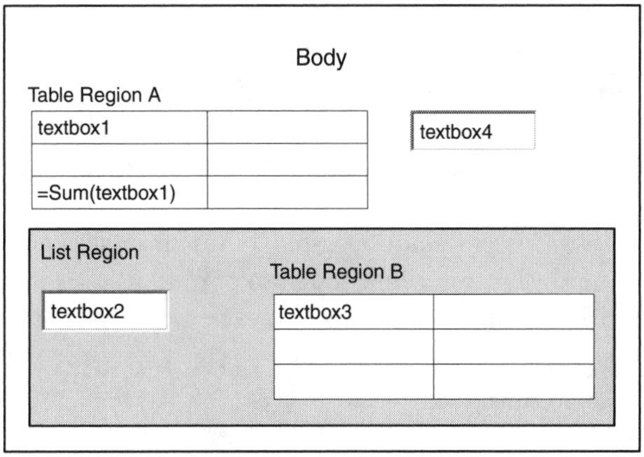

Figure 5.2 Each dataset, region, and grouping defines an expression scope.

defines a scope. The scope rules can get complicated, but the simple rule of thumb is that an expression cannot reference other items outside its current or containing (outer) scope.

The following example should make this clear. Consider the report layout shown in figure 5.2.

You may find this layout similar to that of the Employee Sales by Territory with Summary report we created in chapter 4. Here, we have a table region A placed side by side with a textbox and another table region B nested inside a list. This layout defines several scopes:

- A scope of the report body section
- A scope of table region A
- A scope of the list region
- A scope of table region B

There may be other scopes, such as those for groups defined inside a region. Based on the current or containing scope rule we mentioned earlier, there are some valid and invalid reference combinations, as shown in table 5.2.

Table 5.2 Expression reference examples

Valid references	Invalid references
An expression for the value of textbox3 that references textbox2.	An expression for the value of textbox2 that references textbox3. (Table region B is nested in the list region and it is not in the list's current or containing scope.)
An expression for the value of textbox3 that references textbox4. (Table region B is inside the body region.) However, an expression for the value of textbox4 cannot reference textbox3.	An expression for the value of textbox3 that references textbox1 and vice versa; an expression for the value of textbox1 that references textbox3; neither can it reference textbox2.

How about referencing the `SUM()` aggregate in table region A from either the list region or table region B? At first, you might think that this is not possible because table A is not in the containing scope of both regions. But as with every rule there are exceptions, and the truth is that this combination is allowed. The exception here seems to be a result of the fact that an expression can reference an aggregate value regardless of its scope.

At first, the scope rules may seem mind-boggling, but with some experience it gets easier. Besides, the Report Designer is kind enough to remind us each time we fail to comply with this rule with one of the following two exceptions:

```
The value expression for the textbox '<textboxname>' refers to
the report item '<reportitemname>'.  Report item expressions
can only refer to other report items within the same grouping
scope or a containing grouping scope.
```

Or, if the referenced textbox gets its value from a dataset field:

```
The value expression for the textbox '<textboxname>' refers to the
field '<reportitemname>'.  Report item expressions can only refer
to fields within the current data set scope or, if inside an
aggregate, the specified data set scope.
```

5.1.5 Dealing with expression errors

Similar to programming in other languages, report expression code goes through compilation and execution phases. When you build the report or just request to preview it, the Report Designer parses the report expressions to ensure that the code you entered makes sense and that the code will work with the order of execution. If there are syntax and reference errors, the Report Designer informs you about them by showing an error message in the Preview tab, as shown in figure 5.3.

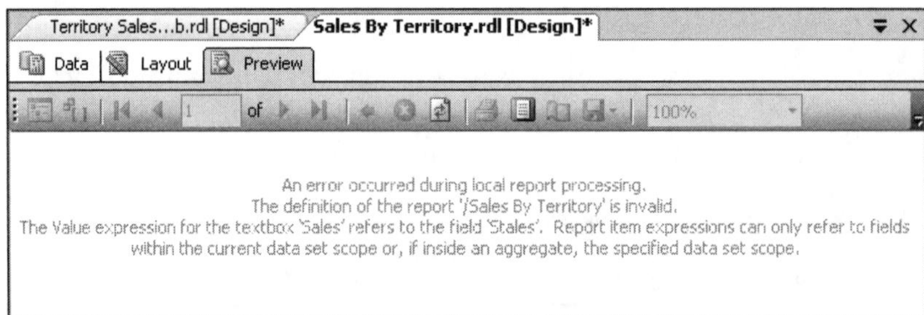

Figure 5.3 If an expression cannot be compiled, an error message is shown in the Preview tab.

The compilation errors are shown in the Task List. The error messages seem to be very descriptive and informative. For example, if we misspell the name of the Sales dataset field as `Sale (Fields!Sale.Value)`, the exception text pinpoints the exact problem:

```
The value expression for the textbox 'txtSales' refers to the
field 'Sale'.  Report item expressions can only refer to fields
within the current data set scope or, if inside an aggregate,
the specified data set scope.
```

When the exception references a report item, you can double-click on the exception text to navigate to the item and inspect it.

Some error conditions are discovered only during runtime. For example, you may have an expression for a calculated field that results in a division-by-zero exception. The way in which runtime errors are reported depends on how the expression is used. If the expression is used to get the value of a textbox, `#Error` is shown in the textbox. Otherwise, the exception is ignored. For example, if you have an expression to conditionally change the color of a line item from black to red, and the expression errors out, it will be ignored and the line will be shown in black.

The most common source of runtime errors, which will probably bite you at the beginning, is omitting the `Value` property when you reference dataset fields, for example, `Fields!Sales` as opposed to `Fields!Sales.Value`. Because `Fields!Sales` references an object of type field, you will get a runtime error with `#Error` as the textbox value without any other complaints from the Report Designer.

Circular references are not allowed even if the expression scope is valid. For example, if textbox A references textbox B and textbox B references textbox A, you won't get a compilation error, but when the report is rendered, the value of B will be set to `#Error`.

To make programming with expressions easier, RS exposes report items as collections referred to as the Report Object Model.

5.2 EXPLORING THE REPORT OBJECT MODEL

To use expressions in your reports, you must have a good grasp of the Report Object Model. RS offers a simplified object model, exposed in the form of global object collections that you can reference in your expressions.

The Report Object Model can be referenced only internally, that is, from code running inside the report. You cannot instantiate a report object externally, as you might have been accustomed to doing with other reporting tools and applications. For example, Microsoft Access exposes its object model as an externally creatable object of type `Access.Application` that external callers can instantiate using OLE Automation.

At first, the inability to create and manipulate the Report Object Model from outside might seem restrictive. However, we view it as a compromise, given the other advantages that the RS architecture has to offer. You may understand this better if you consider the fact that the RS architecture is entirely server based. The RS process lifetime is not controlled by the client application. Instead, Reporting Services runs in its own process and, thanks to its service-oriented architecture, any consumer capable of

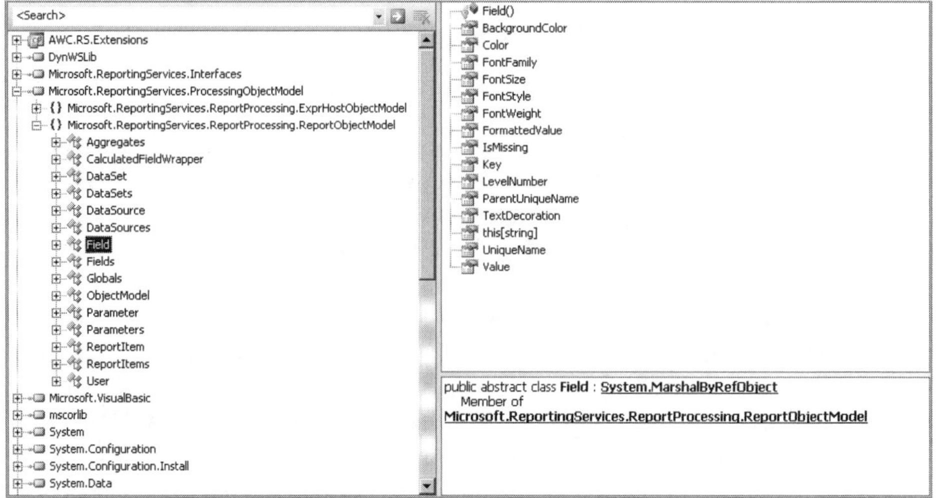

Figure 5.4 The Report Object Model is implemented in the Microsoft.ReportingServices. ProcessingObjectModel assembly. It contains five object collections that you can access programmatically in expressions or custom code.

submitting HTTP GET and SOAP requests can access it. Because RS runs in its own process, it is not possible to instantiate an RS object locally.

The object model is implemented in the `Microsoft.ReportingServices.ProcessingObjectModel` assembly, under the `Microsoft.ReportingServices.ReportProcessing.ReportObjectModel` namespace, as shown in figure 5.4.

You can find the `Microsoft.ReportingServices.ProcessingObjectModel` assembly in the Report Server binary folder (`C:\Program Files\Microsoft SQL Server\MSSQL.3\Reporting Services\ReportServer\bin`) or in the Report Designer folder (`C:\Program Files\Microsoft Visual Studio 8\Common7\IDE\PrivateAssemblies`). To browse the object model using the VS .NET Object Browser, create a new C# or VB .NET project, reference this assembly, and press Ctrl-Alt-J.

NOTE How do we know where the Report Object Model is implemented? When we were experimenting with the object model, we wrote a simple but useful function called `ShowItem`, which you can find in the `AWC.RS.Library` assembly, as shown in the following:

```
public static string ShowItem( object item){
return "Success";
}
```

The idea was to put a breakpoint inside the body of the function, so we could break when we called it from expressions inside the report. For example, to inspect the properties of a dataset field, we could drag and drop a field from the report dataset on the report and use the following expression for the textbox value:

```
=AWC.RS.Library.RsLibrary.ShowItem(Fields!<field name>)
```

Once we break inside the `ShowItem` function, we can explore the item argument in the Watch window. In the case of passing a dataset field, the type of the argument was `Microsoft.ReportingServices.ReportProcessingObjectModel.ReportObjectModel.Field`. Following this hint, we open the `Microsoft.ReportingServices.ProcessingObject` assembly, which reveals the object model shown in figure 5.4. Later in this chapter, we show you how to debug code in an external assembly.

As we said in chapter 3, the only two ways to control the report output are externally by using parameters and internally by using expressions. The Report Object Model exposes five collections that are accessible to you as a developer, as listed in table 5.3.

Table 5.3 Read-only collections exposed by the Report Object Model

Collection	Purpose
ReportItems	Exposes the textbox items in the report
Fields	Wraps the fields of a report dataset
Globals	Encapsulates some global report properties, such as the number of pages
Parameters	Represents the report parameters
User	Includes user-related properties

You can access the items in these collections using all variations of the standard Visual Basic collection syntax:

- `Collection!ItemName`
- `Collection("ItemName")`
- `Collection.Item("ItemName")`

Because the `Collection!ItemName` syntax is the shortest of the three you'll use it the most. The items inside the Globals and User collections are also exposed as properties and can be accessed by `Collection.ItemName`.

Let's now discuss each of these collections and how you can use them.

5.2.1 Using the ReportItems collection

The ReportItems collection contains all textbox report items of the type `Microsoft.ReportingServices.ReportProcessingObjectModel.ReportObjectModel.ReportItem`. It allows the report author to reference the values of other textbox items subject to the scope rules we discussed previously. Note that we said textbox items, because the collection contains nothing else.

NOTE Strictly speaking, the `ReportItem` class serves as a base type, from which the objects inside the ReportItems collection are derived. For example, if you pass a textbox item to the `ShowItem` function, mentioned previously, you will see that its type is `Microsoft.ReportingServices.ReportProcessingObjectModel.ReportObjectModel.TextBox` and it inherits from `ReportItem`. In addition, if you examine the `Microsoft.ReportingServices.ReportProcessingObjectModel.ReportObjectModel` namespace in the Object Browser or .NET Reflector, you will find out that there is a `CheckBox` type defined, which is not currently used. We expect the Report Object Model to evolve in the future and ReportItems collections to include additional report items besides textboxes.

You would expect the ReportItems collection to include all report items placed on the report (not just textboxes), but this is not the case. Why? Because the report item properties can be changed only by expressions and the textbox values are read-only, there is really no good reason to do so. We hope a future version will enhance the object model to expose not only all report items but also their properties (in read-write mode) similar to the WinForm and ASP.NET object models.

Even better, a future RS object model could support creating report items dynamically in code. This would make it possible to generate report sections conditionally. For instance, a `Body_OnLoad` event handler could check some business rules and generate different report regions based on the result, such as a chart or tabular region. For now, the best you can do is to hide a region pragmatically by using an expression.

Implementing conditional formatting

A common requirement is to add conditional formatting features to reports, where the visual appearance of report items (font, color, size, and so on) changes based on some runtime conditions. Consider an example to demonstrate how the ReportItems collection could be used to customize the appearance of textbox report items.

Let's change the Employee Sales by Territory with Summary report to check whether the salesperson has exceeded a certain goal, for example, $2,500,000. If she has exceeded her goal, the report will show an indicator and highlight the person's name in bold. We saved the revised version of the report as Employee Sales by Territory with Summary Advanced.

Figure 5.5 shows what the report looks like when a salesperson has exceeded the goal. When the goal has been exceeded, the text "Exceeded Goal!" shows up in italics. Note that the conditional formatting is based on the Sales total amount (not shown on figure 5.5) and not on the Sales YTD amount.

To implement the new report features, let's add a new textbox called txtExceededGoal inside the recEmployee rectangle and set its value to Exceeded Goal! and its foreground color to red. Then, in the Advanced Textbox Properties dialog box (right-click txtExceededGoal, choose Properties, and in the TextBox Properties dialog box

Territory: ***Central***

Employee Name:	**Caro, Fernando**
Commission:	1.50 %
Sales YTD:	$1,958,815.81
Bonus:	$2,500.00
Exceeded Goal!	

Product Subcategory	Sales
Road Bike	$2,083,024.71
Mountain Bike	$1,114,406.63
Road Frame	$352,405.13
Touring Bike	$302,816.90
Mountain Frame	$255,327.66
Touring Frame	$44,790.62

Figure 5.5 You can use expressions to implement conditional formatting.

click the Advanced button), set its initial visibility to be based on the expression shown in figure 5.6.

To retrieve the employee sales total, we can use the txtSalesTotal textbox, which happens to be the one that holds the sales total amount in the `tblEmployeeSales` table. In terms of performance, this is also the fastest way to get to the aggregate figure, because we don't have to recalculate it. We used the 2,500,000 threshold to toggle the visibility of txtExceededGoal. Strangely, the Boolean logic for the initial visibility is reversed. If the expression evaluates to false, the item is visible; otherwise it is hidden.

Similarly, to change the font of the `txtEmployeeName` field to bold, we implement this expression:

```
=Iif(ReportItems!txtSalesTotal.Value < 2500000, "Normal", "Bold")
```

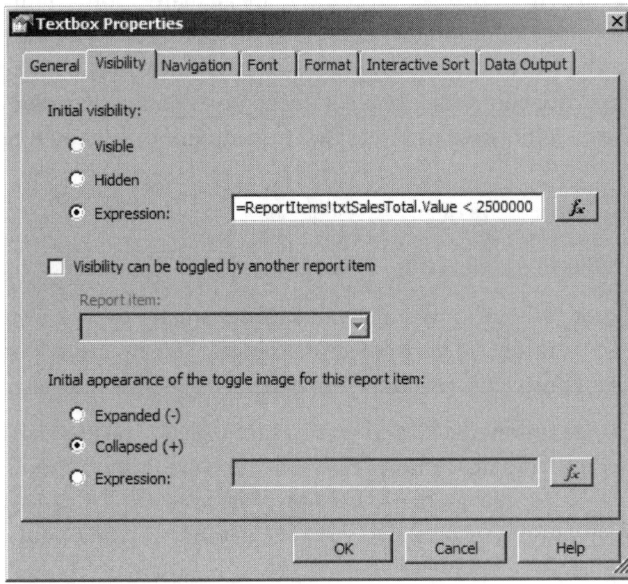

Figure 5.6 Use an expression to conditionally format the visibility of the txtExceededGoal textbox.

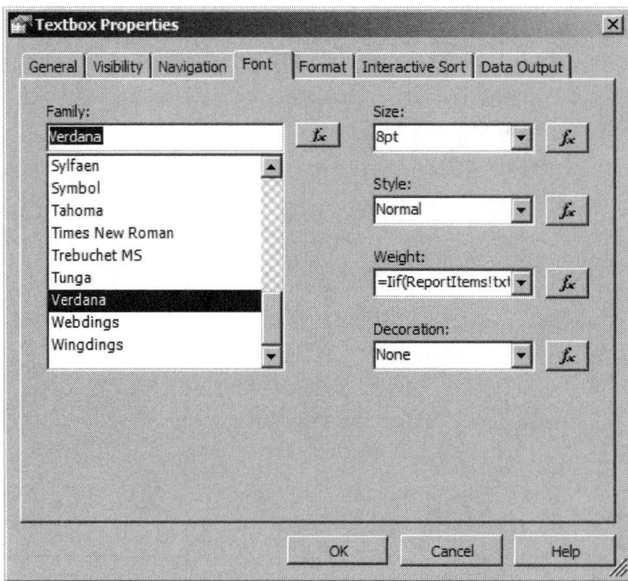

Figure 5.7
Use an expression to set the font weight of the txtEmployeeName textbox.

Figure 5.7 shows this expression in the Weight field of the Font tab of the Textbox Properties dialog box.

The VB .NET `Iif` operator is probably the one you will use most often in your expressions. In this case, if the sales total is less than the targeted amount, the font weight is normal; otherwise it is bold.

The example in figure 5.7 uses what is called a nested `Iif`. This allows us to manage a three-part condition. In theory you could manage many more conditions in one statement. The side effect of nesting `Iif`s is hard-to-read code. When the three-part `Iif` syntax gets in the way, you may find the `Switch` function useful. For example, if we wanted to check for more than one condition and change the color of txtSalesTotal accordingly, we could have used the `Switch` function, as shown here:

```
=Switch(ReportItems!txtSalesTotal.Value < 2500000, "Red",
ReportItems!txtSalesTotal.Value >= 250000 AND
ReportItems!txtSalesTotal.Value < 500000, "Yellow",
ReportItems!txtSalesTotal.Value >= 500000, "Green")
```

The `Switch` function will return the first value that evaluates to true. You need to be careful with the `Switch` function as you can set up cases where it will not return any value. This may cause problems with the report, depending on where you are using it.

NOTE For some reason, the font color is not available on the Font tab in the TextBox Properties dialog box. It is available only on the VS .NET Properties window. To change the font color programmatically, expand the Color property drop-down list and select its first item, <Expression…>.

An interesting note about the `ReportItem.Value` property is that although it references the value in a textbox item, it preserves the underlying data type. For this reason, we were able to reference the sales total amount without any type casting.

Report items limitations

These two expressions get the work done. However, as any seasoned developer will point out, our implementation is not very maintainable for two primary reasons:

- We've hardcoded the threshold figure twice.
- We've coded the same business rule twice.

The first issue could be easily corrected by defining a constant in custom-embedded code for this report. The second issue could be addressed by moving the business logic inside a VB .NET function defined in embedded code or an external assembly, as we discuss in chapter 6. The custom function could then return a Boolean value that we can evaluate in both expressions.

What if we want to get rid of expressions altogether? For instance, can we replace both expressions in our case with a call to a single function or use an internal event to centralize all formatting and data manipulation logic in a single place? We've already said that RS doesn't support events, so the event option is out. What about the first option? Can we write a function and pass the whole ReportItems collection? Unfortunately, the answer is no.

First, the ReportItems collection exposes only the textbox items inside the report, so we don't have access to data regions and other report items. You might say that in our case this is not an issue, because we want to manipulate only textboxes anyway. However, it so happens that the `Value` property is the only property available to us.

Second, to make things even more difficult, the `Value` property is read-only. In other words, if we decide to get innovative and pass the txtExceededGoal and txtEmployeeName items as objects to a custom function, we won't get too far because we cannot change the textbox value inside the function.

So, to recap, the ReportItems collection contains all textbox report items inside the report, and each `ReportItem` object has one read-only, publicly accessible property, `Value`. This means that the only way to change the textbox value programmatically is to attach an expression to the `Value` property inside the Report Designer. By the way, to reference the value of the current textbox item, you can use `Me.Value` or just `Value`.

5.2.2 Using the Fields collection

The Fields collection exposes the fields (columns) from a given row of the report dataset as objects of the type `Microsoft.ReportingServices.ReportProcessingObjectModel.ReportObjectModel.Field`. .NET developers can draw an analogy between the RS `Field` object and `DataColumn` of the ADO.NET `DataTable` class. Unlike the `DataColumn` class, however, each `Field` object inside the Fields collection has only two public read-only properties: `Value` and `IsMissing`.

The `Value` property can return one of the following:

- Nothing (null in C#), in case there is missing data or the data is NULL. To check for Nothing you can use the VB .NET function `IsNothing()` or `<fieldname.Value> Is Nothing`.
- The field value, whose type is cast to one of the standard .NET data types, such as Int32, DateTime, and so on. The type translation that RS performs behind the scenes is really helpful because it allows you to reference the field value directly in strongly typed .NET functions. For example, you might recall that for the Year column in the Territory Sales Crosstab report we used the expression `Fields!Date.Value.Year`. This was possible because the value of the Date field was exposed as a .NET DateTime structure.

Dealing with null and missing values

Unfortunately, the automatic conversion that RS does to translate NULL values and missing data to Nothing may be more trouble than it is worth because sometimes you do need to differentiate between both conditions. For example, in a matrix report you may need to react in a different way when there is no data for a given row and column combination and when the aggregate value is NULL.

One workaround is to replace the NULL values at the data source or in the report query statement with whatever value makes sense, for example, NULL. Then, you can write a simple VB .NET function like the one here to check for both conditions:

```
Function GetValue(value As Object) As Object
        If value is Nothing Then
            Return "N/A"   ' missing data
        Else
            Return value   ' has value or 'NULL'
        End If
End Function
```

Another way to differentiate between missing data and NULL values is to base the textbox on an expression that uses the `CountRows()` function. You see an example of how this could be implemented in chapter 6.

Checking for missing fields

To make dealing with missing values more confusing, the `Field` object exposes a property called `IsMissing`. It is important to note that it doesn't check for missing values. Instead, it returns true if the field is not found in the report dataset. If you are trying to understand the practical use of this, consider the case when the report dataset is returned by a call to a stored procedure.

For example, consider the Employee Sales by Territory report that we developed in the previous chapter to show employee performance. Users belonging to various security roles, such as administrators and clerks, can request this report. In the second case, you might not want to reveal the employee-sensitive information, such as commissions and bonuses.

You can hide these fields using expressions, or you can pass a parameter to the `spGetEmployeeSalesByProductSubcategory` stored procedure to exclude these fields entirely. If you use the latter approach, you can use the `IsMissing` property to exclude these fields from expressions that use them. If you don't check whether they are available, they will show `#Error`.

Finally, the `Field` object also implements an indexer. Currently, its implementation returns NULL. The next version of Reporting Services may include additional properties that data providers, such as the SQL Server .NET provider, could return.

Using the Fields collection in expressions

Here's an example showcasing the Fields collection. We'll change the Employee Sales by Territory with Summary Advanced report and replace the # Orders column with the Percentage of Employee's Total column. The new column will show the sales amount for each product subcategory as a percentage of the sales total, as shown in figure 5.8.

To implement the new requirements, we have to change the expression of the corresponding textbox item to

```
=Fields!Sales.Value/ReportItems!txtSalesTotal.Value
```

To express the data as a percentage, we change the format settings of the textbox properties accordingly.

Another way of implementing Percentage of Employee's Total is to rewrite the previous expression using the txtSales report item, as follows:

```
= ReportItems!txtSales.Value/ReportItems!txtSalesTotal.Value
```

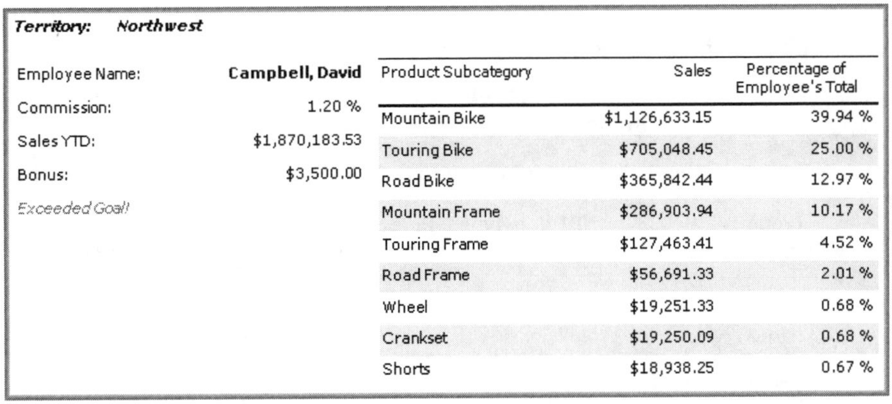

Territory: ***Northwest***

Employee Name:	**Campbell, David**
Commission:	1.20 %
Sales YTD:	$1,870,183.53
Bonus:	$3,500.00
Exceeded Goal!	

Product Subcategory	Sales	Percentage of Employee's Total
Mountain Bike	$1,126,633.15	39.94 %
Touring Bike	$705,048.45	25.00 %
Road Bike	$365,842.44	12.97 %
Mountain Frame	$286,903.94	10.17 %
Touring Frame	$127,463.41	4.52 %
Road Frame	$56,691.33	2.01 %
Wheel	$19,251.33	0.68 %
Crankset	$19,250.09	0.68 %
Shorts	$18,938.25	0.67 %

Figure 5.8 We can use the Fields collection to implement the calculated field Percentage of Employee's Total.

So, should we use the ReportItems or Fields collection? In terms of performance, there is not that much difference, because both are exposed internally as collections. However, if we need to use an aggregate or calculated result that is already available in a textbox, we would reference it using the ReportItems collection. For example, the previous expression will produce the same result, if it is changed to:

```
=Fields!Sales.Value/Sum(Fields!Sales.Value)
```

This expression, however, will calculate the sales total for each row in the `tblEmployeeSales` table, which is less efficient than getting the value from the txtSalesTotal textbox because the work has already been done to calculate the total.

5.2.3 Using the Parameters collection

The Parameters collection exposes the report parameters as objects of the type `Microsoft.ReportingServices.ReportProcessing.ReportObject-Model.Parameter`. Each `Parameter` object has two publicly accessible read-only properties: `Label` and `Value`.

Using parameter labels and values

As we saw in chapter 3, you can define a list of available values for a report parameter, and the list could be explicitly set or dataset driven. Similar to implementing a drop-down control, if you decide to set available values, you can use a pair of values for each report parameter: a label for the visible portion and a value for the actual parameter value.

For example, in the Sales by Territory Interactive report, we used the `TerritoryID` column from the `dsTerritory` dataset as the parameter value, and the `Territory` column as the parameter value. In this case, the `Label` and `Value` parameters map to the parameter `Label` and `Value` properties, respectively. If you don't use available values, the `Label` property returns Nothing, while the `Value` property returns the parameter value.

5.2.4 Using the Globals collection

The Report Server exposes some useful global report properties in the Globals collection, as shown in table 5.4.

Table 5.4 The Globals collection, which includes some common report properties

Property	.NET data type	Purpose
`ExecutionTime`	DateTime	The date and time when the Report Server started processing the report
`PageNumber`	Int32	The current page number
`ReportFolder`	String	The full path to the report, e.g., `/AWReporter` (excluding the ReportServerURL)
`ReportName`	String	The report name, e.g., Territory Sales

continued on next page

Table 5.4 The Globals collection, which includes some common report properties *(continued)*

Property	.NET data type	Purpose
`ReportServerUrl`	String	The Report Server URL, e.g., `http://servername/Reports`
`TotalPages`	Int32	The number of pages

The `ExecutionTime` property can come in handy when you experiment with report caching. We discuss how caching affects the report execution process in chapter 8. When the Report Server determines that it can use the cached report copy, the report is not processed at all. Instead, the cached copy of the report is returned to the user. Hence, the `ExecutionTime` property will not change within the expiration period.

We have already used the `ReportName` property in some of the reports we created so far to display the report name as a report title.

The `PageNumber` and `TotalPages` properties can be used only inside the report page header and footer. For example, the Products by Category multicolumn report displays the current page in the page footer using the following expression:

```
="Page " & Globals.PageNumber
```

5.2.5 Using the User collection

Finally, the User collection contains information about the user who is currently requesting the report. Specifically, the User collection exposes the following two properties:

- *`UserID`*—When Windows authentication is used, `UserID` returns the Windows domain account of the user who runs the report. For example, if Terri has logged in as Terri to the `adventure-works` domain, then `User.UserID` will return `adventure-works\Terri`. If custom authentication is used, then `UserID` will return whatever the extension sets as a user principal. We see an example of how we can use this property to enforce a secured access to report data in the next chapter.
- *`Language`*—The language ID of the user running the report, for example, en-US, if the language is set to English (United States). The `Language` property allows us to localize our reports.

Often, to increase expression power, you will need to call some piece of prepackaged code, exposed as a function, as we discuss next.

5.3 WORKING WITH FUNCTIONS

Reporting Services allows you to reference external and internal (native) functions. You can use external functions located in .NET standard or custom assemblies.

In addition, RS comes with some native functions that encapsulate commonly used programming logic, such as functions that produce aggregate values, count dataset rows, and so forth. We discuss the RS native functions in section 5.3.2.

5.3.1 Referencing external functions

How you reference external functions depends on where the function is located. RS has two commonly used .NET assemblies pre-referenced for you: `Microsoft.VisualBasic` and `mscorlib`. `Microsoft.VisualBasic` contains the types that form the Visual Basic runtime. `mscorlib` is a special .NET assembly that defines the .NET data types, such as `System.String` and `System.Int32`, as well as many frequently used functions and types defined under namespaces starting with System, such as `System.Collections` and `System.Diagnostics`.

The following namespaces from these two assemblies have been already imported by RS, so you can use their types and methods without having to specify namespaces:

- *`Microsoft.VisualBasic`*—This namespace allows you to access many of the common VB runtime functions. For example, in the Territory Sales report, we used the VB.NET `Format` function located in the `Microsoft.VisualBasic` assembly to create a dynamic group, so we can group the report data by month. The expression we used for this purpose was `=Format(Fields!Date.Value, "MMM")`. Or, you can use the `MsgBox` function to help you while debugging your embedded code. As you see in chapter 6, the Report Designer Code Editor has left a lot to be desired and doesn't provide debugging capabilities. Remember, though, to remove the `MsgBox` calls before you deploy your report to the Report Server. If you don't, you will get `#Error` in all textboxes that reference functions with `MsgBox` in your embedded code.
- *`System.Convert`*—Allows you to perform runtime conversion between types, for example, from string to double using `System.Convert.ToDouble()`.
- *`System.Math`*—Provides constants and static methods for trigonometric, logarithmic, and other common mathematical functions.

To reference the rest of the `System` namespaces, you need to specify the fully qualified class name, including the namespace. For example, if you need to use a collection of the type `ArrayList` in an expression, you have to use its fully qualified name, `System.Collections.ArrayList`.

To use functions located in other .NET assemblies, you must reference the assembly first. We discuss working with custom code in detail in chapter 6.

RS comes with a number of native functions that you can use in your expressions. Most of these functions are *aggregate* functions.

5.3.2 Using aggregate functions

Aggregate functions perform a calculation on a set of values from data in datasets, data regions, and groupings and return a single value. Aggregate functions are often used with data region groups to produce data aggregates in the group footer.

We have already seen many examples where we used the most common aggregate function, `Sum()`, to get an aggregated total of the data, such as the Sales Total per employee or product category in the Employee Sales by Territory report.

Another aggregate function that we used to implement conditional formatting was the `RowNumber()` function. The `RowNumber()` function produces a running count of the rows within a specified scope. For example, in the Employee Sales by Territory report, we used `RowNumber()` to alternate the background color for the rows in the `tblEmployeeSales` table region between white and beige. To achieve this effect, we used the following expression for the `BackgroundColor` property of the `tblEmployeeSales` table row to determine whether the row number is odd or even and to format it accordingly:

```
=Iif(RowNumber("tblEmployeeSales") Mod 2, "White", "Beige")
```

Understanding the aggregate scope

When you look at the syntax of the RS aggregate functions, notice that all of them take the argument `Scope`. `Scope` can be set to the name of a group, data region, or dataset. We have already talked about the expression scope, but we want to discuss this concept once again in the context of aggregate functions.

To understand how scopes affect aggregates, recall that a report can have multiple datasets and data regions. The data regions can coexist side by side or be nested one within the other. But how does an aggregate function determine which dataset or region provides the data for the aggregate calculation? For example, if you look at the Employee Sales by Territory Advanced report, we have several expressions that use the `Sum()` function to calculate the total sales amount.

- First, we used it in the expression that defines the txtTerritorySalesYTDTotal textbox value inside the `tblSummary` table region to show the sales total for all sales territories.
- Second, we used it inside `lstTerritory` to get the sales total per territory.
- Finally, we used the same expression inside `tblEmployeeSales` to get the sales total per salesperson.

How does `Sum()` resolve to the right scope?

Obviously, the `Sum()` function has some intelligence built into it to determine the right scope of operation. It so happens that if a scope is not explicitly specified, it defaults to the innermost containing data region or grouping in which the aggregate is defined. So, in our example, the scope of the `Sum()` function defaulted to `tblSummary`, `lstTerritory`, and `tblEmployeeSales`, in that order.

Setting the aggregate scope explicitly

Let's look at one more example. We'll change the Employee Sales by Territory with Summary Advanced report and add another column to `tblEmployeeSales` that

Territory:	*Canada*				
Employee Name:	Saraiva, José	Product Subcategory	Sales	Percentage of Employee's Total	Percentage of Territory's Total
Commission:	1.50 %	Road Bike	$687,096.62	29.85 %	29.85 %
Sales YTD:	$2,153,295.20	Mountain Bike	$641,178.50	27.85 %	27.85 %
Bonus:	$5,000.00	Touring Bike	$487,603.52	21.18 %	21.18 %
		Mountain Frame	$148,812.58	6.46 %	6.46 %
		Road Frame	$108,689.19	4.72 %	4.72 %
		Touring Frame	$87,352.57	3.79 %	3.79 %
		Jersey	$22,922.69	1.00 %	1.00 %
		Shorts	$12,952.62	0.56 %	0.56 %

Figure 5.9 With aggregate functions, you can set the aggregate scope explicitly.

will show the percentage of the salesperson's total relative to the territory total. To achieve this, we can copy and paste the third table column (Percentage of Employee's Total) and use the following expression for the new column:

```
=Fields!Sales.Value/Sum(Fields!Sales.Value, "grpTerritory")
```

Now, we explicitly set the aggregate scope to the `grpTerritory` group scope of the `lstTerritory` list region, which groups the data by territory. In this way, we can get to the territory sales total. Figure 5.9 shows the new version of the Employee Sales by Territory with Summary Advanced report.

Of course, in this particular case, we could have used the value in the txtTerritory-Total textbox, which conveniently displays the territory total, but we wanted to show you how the scope affects the aggregate calculation.

Understanding aggregate scope rules

Rules exist that govern the valid use of scopes. Failure to follow those rules results in the following exception, which you will probably run into quite often at the beginning:

```
The value expression for the textbox 'txtTerritoryGrandTotal'
uses an aggregate expression without a scope.  A scope is required
for all aggregates used outside of a data region unless the report
contains exactly one data set.
```

As the exception text says, one of the rules is that you can specify only an aggregate scope of a containing group, region, or dataset. To demonstrate this, let's change the Employee Sales by Territory with Summary Advanced report to show the grand total for all territories for the given time period. At first attempt, you might think that you can accomplish this by adding a new textbox outside the `lstTerritory` list region and setting its value to `Sum(Fields!Sales.Value)`. However, when you run the report, you will get the "wrong scope" exception that we just discussed. The problem is that because there is no containing scope, the `Sum()` function has no idea how to calculate the expression.

You may try to solve this issue by changing the expression to `Sum(Fields!Sales.Value, "lstTerritory")` so you "tell" the function to use the `lstTerritory` list region. This won't work either, because you can request only a containing scope. In our case, because the textbox is outside any region, there is no containing scope.

The right expression in this scenario is `Sum(Fields!Sales.Value, "dsEmployeeSales")`, so the `Sum()` function calculates the total for the whole dataset, as shown in figure 5.10.

Note that if the report uses only one dataset, you don't have to explicitly specify the dataset name, because the aggregate will default to it if it has no containing scope.

The Report Designer helps you to adopt the scope mentality. When you drag and drop a dataset field from another dataset to a region, it automatically generates an aggregate expression for the textbox value. If the field is numeric, the following expression is generated:

```
=Sum("<field name>", "<dataset name>")
```

As you can see, the Report Designer explicitly sets the scope to the dataset name that the field belongs to. If the field is the numeric `Sum()`, the Report Designer defaults to `Sum()`; otherwise it uses the `First()` aggregate function to retrieve the field value from the first data row.

Implementing running totals

A few other aggregate functions are available with RS that allow you to perform various aggregate calculations, such as counting (`Count()`, `CountDistinct()`, `CountRows()`) and getting the minimum, average, and maximum values, as well as variance and deviation values. Consult the documentation for a full list of all aggregate functions supported by RS. Those of you familiar with SQL will find the RS

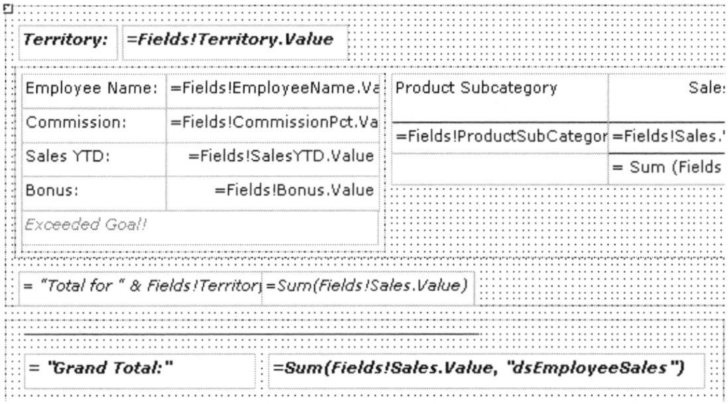

Figure 5.10 You can create a grand total by using aggregate functions and specifying the scope of the calculation.

aggregate functions similar to the ones supported by most databases. The SQL specification defines five aggregate functions that databases must support (`MAX`, `MIN`, `AVG`, `SUM`, and `COUNT`).

An interesting function that we would like to mention is `RunningValue()`. This function allows you to implement running total aggregate calculations, as the Monthly Sales by Product Category report shown in figure 5.11 demonstrates.

The Running Totals column carries over the total from the previous months so the user can see the accumulated-by-month amount. Running totals reports are not easily done using straight SQL. With the helpful `RunningValue()` function, though, authoring this report with RS takes just a matter of minutes. The only thing that you have to do is set the Running Total column expression to:

```
=RunningValue(Fields!Sales.Value, Sum, "dsSales")
```

Of course, if you need aggregate operations other than summing, replace the `Sum` function in `RunningValue` with any other aggregate function with the exception of `RunningValue`, `RowNumber`, or `Aggregate`.

The `Aggregate()` function returns a custom aggregate if the database provider supports user-defined aggregates. SQL Server 2000 does not support custom aggregates. However, with SQL Server 2005 developers can create user-defined aggregate functions. Similar to user-defined functions (UDF), custom aggregates return a single value and they can be written in any of the supported .NET languages.

ADVENTURE WORKS cycles

Monthly Sales by Product Category

Sales for Bike Stands from 5/1/2003 to 5/31/2004

SubCategory	Year	Month	Sales	% Change	Running Totals
Bike Stands	2003	Jul	$636.00	#Error	$636.00
	2003	Aug	$3,339.00	425 %	$3,975.00
	2003	Sep	$3,021.00	-10 %	$6,996.00
	2003	Oct	$4,293.00	42 %	$11,289.00
	2003	Nov	$3,498.00	-19 %	$14,787.00
	2003	Dec	$4,134.00	18 %	$18,921.00
	2004	Jan	$2,544.00	-38 %	$21,465.00
	2004	Feb	$3,021.00	19 %	$24,486.00
	2004	Mar	$2,703.00	-11 %	$27,189.00
	2004	Apr	$4,611.00	71 %	$31,800.00
	2004	May	$3,975.00	-14 %	$35,775.00
Total:			**$35,775.00**		

Figure 5.11 Use the RunningTotal() function to implement running totals.

5.3.3 Using other internal functions

RS provides three other helpful functions that you can use in your expressions: `InScope`, `Level`, and `Previous`.

The `InScope()` function indicates whether the current report item is within the specified scope. This is especially useful with matrix regions, as you see in section 5.4.1 when we discuss reports with navigational features.

Implementing recursive hierarchies

The `Level()` function returns the level offset as an integer value for recursive hierarchy reports. Recursive hierarchy reports are based on self-referential data, which has a parent-child relationship already defined. A typical example is an organizational hierarchy, where each employee record in the database has a `ManagerID` column pointing to the employee supervisor record. RS allows us to quickly generate reports that take advantage of such recursive data relationships.

For example, let's create a report that displays the AWC organizational structure. Figure 5.12 shows the Corporate Hierarchy report.

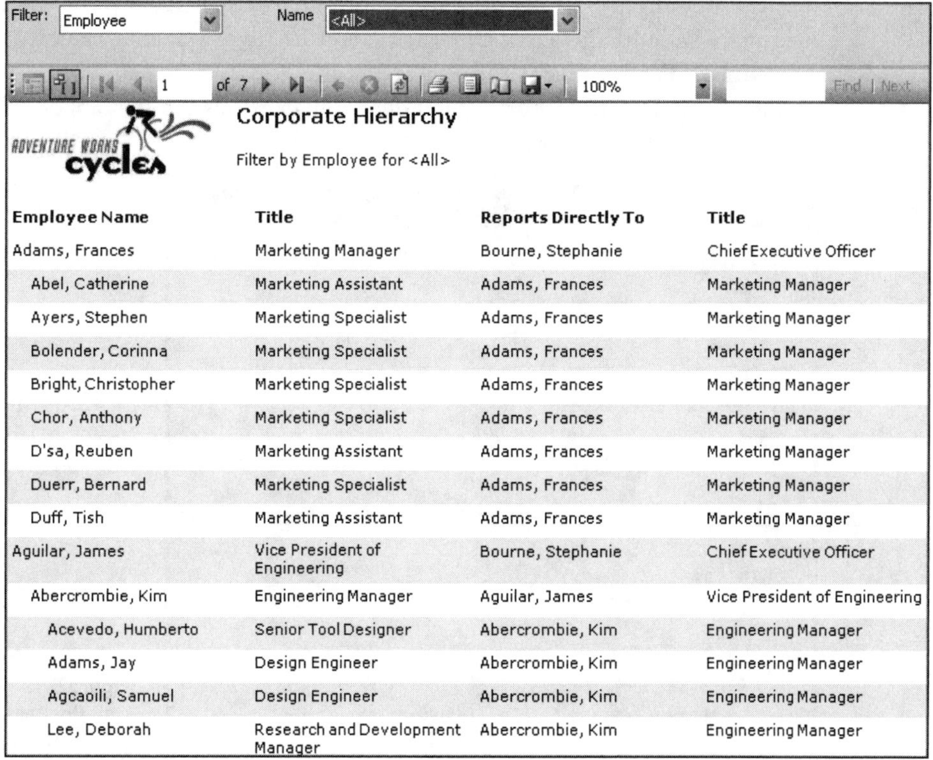
Filter: Employee   Name <All>

1 of 7   100%   Find | Next

ADVENTURE WORKS cycles

Corporate Hierarchy

Filter by Employee for <All>

Employee Name	Title	Reports Directly To	Title
Adams, Frances	Marketing Manager	Bourne, Stephanie	Chief Executive Officer
Abel, Catherine	Marketing Assistant	Adams, Frances	Marketing Manager
Ayers, Stephen	Marketing Specialist	Adams, Frances	Marketing Manager
Bolender, Corinna	Marketing Specialist	Adams, Frances	Marketing Manager
Bright, Christopher	Marketing Specialist	Adams, Frances	Marketing Manager
Chor, Anthony	Marketing Specialist	Adams, Frances	Marketing Manager
D'sa, Reuben	Marketing Assistant	Adams, Frances	Marketing Manager
Duerr, Bernard	Marketing Specialist	Adams, Frances	Marketing Manager
Duff, Tish	Marketing Assistant	Adams, Frances	Marketing Manager
Aguilar, James	Vice President of Engineering	Bourne, Stephanie	Chief Executive Officer
Abercrombie, Kim	Engineering Manager	Aguilar, James	Vice President of Engineering
Acevedo, Humberto	Senior Tool Designer	Abercrombie, Kim	Engineering Manager
Adams, Jay	Design Engineer	Abercrombie, Kim	Engineering Manager
Agcaoili, Samuel	Design Engineer	Abercrombie, Kim	Engineering Manager
Lee, Deborah	Research and Development Manager	Abercrombie, Kim	Engineering Manager

Figure 5.12 Use the Level() function to create recursive hierarchy reports.

The report shows the employee name, his title, and the name and title of his direct supervisor. In addition, the report gives the user two options to filter the report data. First, the user can choose to see whom a given employee reports to, and second, it allows the user to see the employee's subordinates.

The trick to creating a recursive hierarchy report with RS is to configure the Parent Group setting on the region Grouping and Sorting Properties dialog box, as shown in figure 5.13.

In our case, we set the Parent Group to the employee's manager. Once this is done, RS walks recursively through the employee data, starting with the top manager and going all the way down. To offset the table region rows in accordance with the employee hierarchical level, we use the following expression for the left padding setting of the Employee Name textbox (txtName):

```
=Convert.ToString(2 + (Level()*10)) & "pt", 2pt, 2pt, 2pt
```

The `Level()` function returns an integer value indicating the hierarchical level of a row. Thus, for the top manager, `Level()` returns 0; its subordinates have a level of 1, and so on. We simply use the return value from the `Level()` function to offset the text accordingly. To give the user an option to switch between employees and managers, we add the `Filter` parameter with two available values, `Employee` and `Manager`, respectively.

Finally, we base the report dataset query on an expression that appends the appropriate `WHERE` clause accordingly.

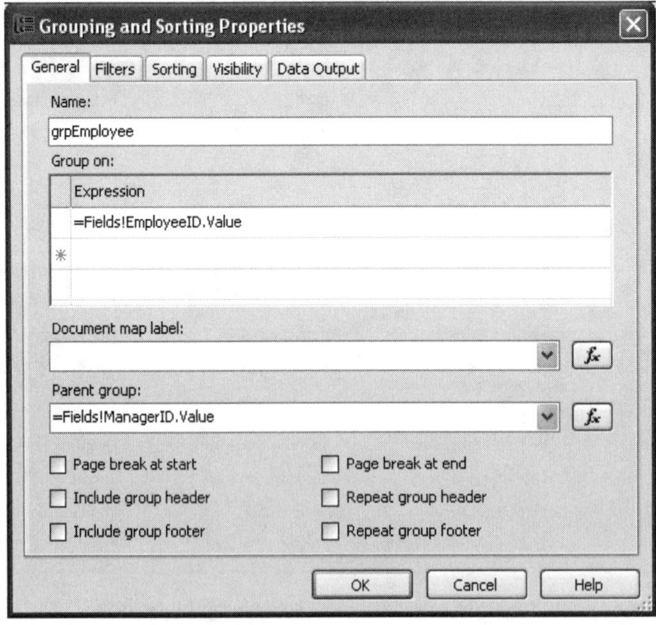

Figure 5.13 Use the Parent Group setting to establish the parent-child relationship.

Implementing data differentials

The `Previous()` function is useful for returning the previous aggregate value from the current or another scope. For example, we can enhance the Monthly Sales by Product Category and add a % Change column to show the change in percentage from one month to the next. Figure 5.14 shows the new version of the report.

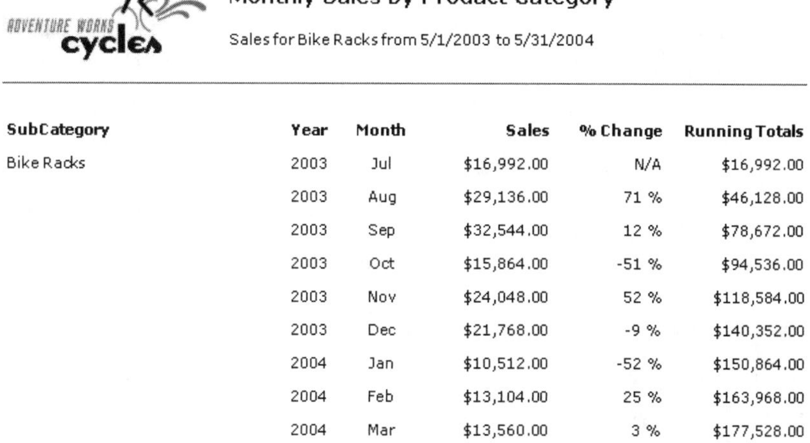

ADVENTURE WORKS cycles

Monthly Sales by Product Category

Sales for Bike Racks from 5/1/2003 to 5/31/2004

SubCategory	Year	Month	Sales	% Change	Running Totals
Bike Racks	2003	Jul	$16,992.00	N/A	$16,992.00
	2003	Aug	$29,136.00	71 %	$46,128.00
	2003	Sep	$32,544.00	12 %	$78,672.00
	2003	Oct	$15,864.00	-51 %	$94,536.00
	2003	Nov	$24,048.00	52 %	$118,584.00
	2003	Dec	$21,768.00	-9 %	$140,352.00
	2004	Jan	$10,512.00	-52 %	$150,864.00
	2004	Feb	$13,104.00	25 %	$163,968.00
	2004	Mar	$13,560.00	3 %	$177,528.00

Figure 5.14 Use the Previous() function to implement the percentage change.

Looking at the report, the user can see that, for example, the sales were up 71 percent from July to August. We use the following expression for the value of the txtPerChange textbox:

```
=Iif(Previous(Fields!Sales.Value)>0, _
(Fields!Sales.Value - Previous(Fields!Sales.Value)) _
/Previous(Fields!Sales.Value), "N/A")
```

First, this expression checks to see whether we have data from the previous month. If not, N/A is displayed. Otherwise, we use the `Previous()` function to get the sales amount for the previous month and calculate the difference.

Now that you know how to use expressions and functions, you can make your reports more interactive by taking advantage of the navigational features that RS provides.

5.4 DESIGNING REPORTS WITH NAVIGATIONAL FEATURES

With Reporting Services you can add navigational features to your reports in the form of hyperlinks and document maps. Document maps enable the report user to jump quickly to a specific area of a large report; hyperlinks allow users to navigate to an external URL-addressable resource.

5.4.1 Reports with hyperlinks

All data regions (including the chart region) support hyperlinks. Hyperlinks in reports can be used to allow the user to navigate to:

- Another report
- A bookmark inside a report, similar to the way you can use bookmarks in Microsoft Word documents
- A URL address; the currently supported options are mailto, http, https, news, and ftp. The URL address can be defined as static text or produced by an expression. For example, in a report that shows a list of vendors, the vendor name hyperlink could navigate the user to the vendor's website.

NOTE Unfortunately, to prevent executing client-side malicious code, Reporting Services doesn't support calling JavaScript functions from hyperlinks.

One common use of hyperlinks is to navigate the user to a URL address.

Using hyperlinks to send e-mail

The Territory Sales Drillthrough report (shown in figure 5.15) demonstrates how you can incorporate navigation capabilities in your reports with hyperlinks.

Now the report displays the salesperson's name as a hyperlink, so the user can conveniently click it to send the salesperson an e-mail message. You can define hyperlinks for textbox and image report items from the Navigation tab of the item's Advanced Properties dialog box, as shown in figure 5.16.

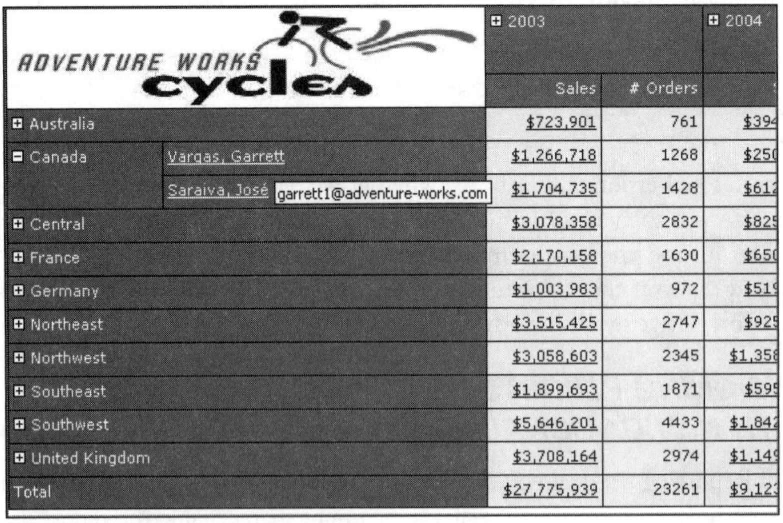

ADVENTURE WORKS cycles		2003		2004
		Sales	# Orders	
Australia		$723,901	761	$394
Canada	Vargas, Garrett	$1,266,718	1268	$250
	Saraiva, José garrett1@adventure-works.com	$1,704,735	1428	$612
Central		$3,078,358	2832	$825
France		$2,170,158	1630	$650
Germany		$1,003,983	972	$519
Northeast		$3,515,425	2747	$925
Northwest		$3,058,603	2345	$1,358
Southeast		$1,899,693	1871	$595
Southwest		$5,646,201	4433	$1,842
United Kingdom		$3,708,164	2974	$1,149
Total		$27,775,939	23261	$9,123

Figure 5.15 Use hyperlinks to navigate the user to a URL address.

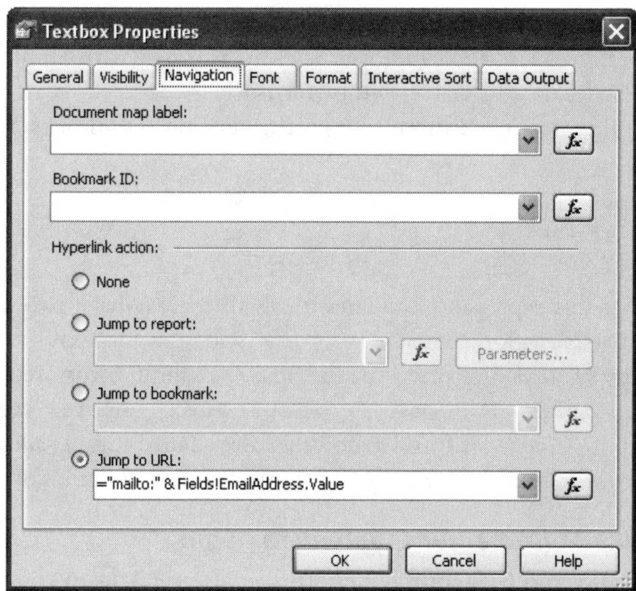

Figure 5.16
To add navigational features to your reports, use the Navigation tab of the report item's Advanced Properties dialog box.

In this example, we've defined the following expression for the Jump to URL hyperlink action property:

```
="mailto:" & Fields!EmailAddress.Value
```

Once you set the hyperlink action, RS automatically changes the mouse cursor to a hand when the user hovers on top of an item with a hyperlink. In addition, we've implemented conditional formatting to underline the person's name only if the `EmailAddress` field is not null.

Finally, we've implemented a tooltip to show the person's e-mail address by setting the `Tooltip` property (VS .NET Properties window) of txtEmployee to the following expression:

```
= Fields!EmailAddress.Value
```

Hyperlinks are frequently used to create drill-through reports.

Creating drill-through reports

The same sample report, Territory Sales Drillthrough, also demonstrates how you can add drill-through features to your reports by setting the hyperlink action to open another report that could show more detailed data for the currently selected item. With RS, you are not restricted to hardcoding the name of the drill-through report. Again, you can use expressions to evaluate a condition and return the report name.

For example, the Territory Sales Drillthrough report evaluates the row grouping scope of the matrix region using the `InScope()` function. If the user has expanded the Employee row group (to drill down and see the salesperson's data), the sales amount hyperlink navigates the user to the Employee Sales Freeform report so the user can see the sales breakdown per product category. If the Employee row group is collapsed, the hyperlink opens the Employee Sales by Territory with Summary Chart report to show the sales data broken down by territory.

To accomplish this we set the Jump to report navigation action of txtSales to

```
=Iif(
InScope("rowEmployee"),
"Employee Sales Freeform",
"Employee Sales By Territory with Summary Chart")
```

To understand what this expression evaluates to, recall that we have two row groups defined in the matrix region: `rowTerritory` and `rowEmployee`. `InScope("rowTerritory")` always returns true, because the sales territory represents the outermost row grouping. `InScope("rowEmployee")` returns false if the Employee row group is collapsed and true otherwise. `InScope()` allows you to determine which row or column group has been expanded and react accordingly.

Using hyperlinks to implement web-style paging

With a bit of creativity and programming effort, you can use links in your reports to implement various custom actions. For example, say you have a large report that takes a very long time to execute and displays hundreds of records. To improve the user experience, you may want to implement custom paging similar to the familiar web-based application-paging concept.

The report could retrieve the report data in chunks, for example, a hundred records at a time. At the end of the report, you can add a textbox with the text "Next page…." You can make the textbox clickable by defining a link that will point to the same report. You can use an expression for the link URL to "remember" the current selection criteria and send it back to the report when a new page is requested.

5.4.2 Reports with document maps

When reports become large, and they often do, it becomes difficult to navigate through them and find the right information easily. For example, suppose that Adventure Works Cycles would like to expose its product catalog report online. This strategy could be beneficial for several reasons:

- Customers and salespersons would be able to access the company product catalog over the Internet.
- The catalog would always contain the up-to-date product information.
- Exposing the product catalog as a report would save substantial time compared with authoring it and maintaining it using web pages, not to mention that the users would be able to export the product catalog to one of the many supported formats.

One potential implementation area of concern is that the product catalog may include hundreds of products and the user may not be able to find the information of interest quickly. RS solves this issue elegantly by allowing report authors to implement *document maps* with links to report areas.

What is a document map?

Similar to a book's table of contents, report document maps present an outline of the report data. In the previous example, the product catalog map could organize the product data in categories, subcategories, and products for faster navigation. By the way, this is exactly what the Product Catalog report, which is included in the Reporting Services samples, does.

Let's look at an example to showcase the advantages of using document maps. We assume that the AWC management would like to see the company sales quarterly performance for a given period broken out by sales territory and store. Because a sales territory could potentially include many stores, the management has requested that we implement some sort of navigational feature that enables users to find a particular store easily. There are at least two possible implementation approaches:

- Pass the store name as a parameter. However, this implementation would require regenerating the report for each store needed.
- Create a document map to organize the sales data in territories and stores.

Figure 5.17 shows the Territory Sales by Store with Map report, which includes a data map for easier navigation.

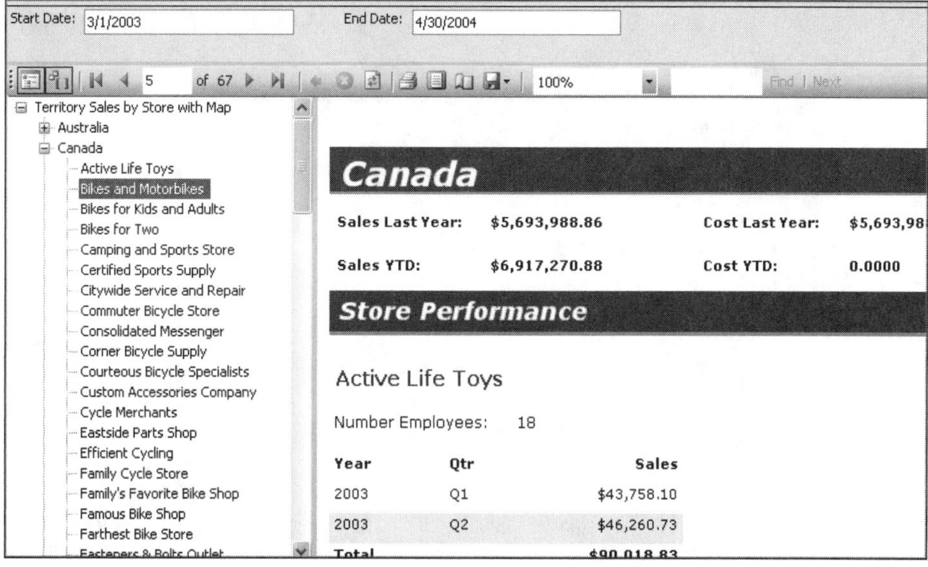

Figure 5.17 Adding a document map to the Territory Sales by Store report makes it easy for users to view and navigate to a store in any given territory.

As you can see, the report displays a hierarchical document map on the left side listing territories and stores alphabetically. The user doesn't have to page through the report to find a particular store. Instead, he can expand the document map and locate the store quickly.

Implementing document maps

Authoring the actual report is nothing we haven't seen so far. We used three regions, one table, and two list regions, to group the data by country, store, and quarter. The table region (`tblStoreSales`) is nested inside the store list (`lstStore`), which in turn is nested inside the territory list (`lstTerritory`).

Now comes the fun part. You may think that implementing a document map might require creating new datasets and expressions. Actually, it really can't be simpler. The only thing that we had to do was to associate the `Label` property of the `lstTerritory` and `lstStore` groups to the corresponding document map label, as shown in figure 5.18.

To achieve the two-level hierarchy of territory and store, for the Territory list we set the document map label to `Fields!Territory.Value`, while for the Store list we set it to the `Fields!Store.Value`. That's all there is to it! RS does the heavy lifting to parse the data recursively and generate the document map when the report is processed.

As you've seen in this section as well as in chapter 4, RS allows you to add a variety of interactive features to your reports, such as a report toolbar, toggled visibility, navigational features, interactive sorting, and document maps. One thing that may not

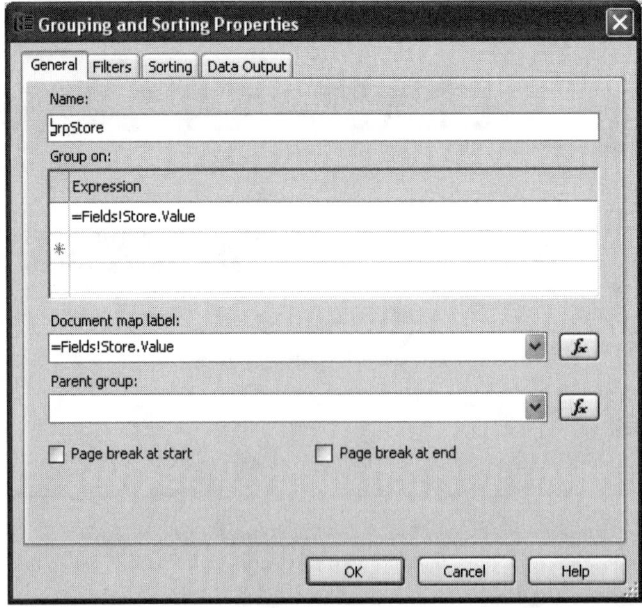

Figure 5.18 Implement a document map in your reports by associating the Label property of the group to a document map label.

be clear is how different export formats impact these features. Let's round out this discussion by looking at some considerations that you need to keep in mind with regard to report rendering.

5.5 REPORT RENDERING CONSIDERATIONS

The area of functionality that is most impacted by exporting is the report interactive features. Table 5.5 shows the interactive features that are supported for each export format.

Table 5.5 Interactive features that are supported for each export format

Feature	HTML	MHTML	Excel	Image	PDF	CSV	XML
Report toolbar	✓						
Toggled visibility	✓						
Navigational features	✓	✓	✓*				
Document maps	✓		✓		✓		

* Hyperlinks to static URLs in rows and column groups only

With Reporting Services, export formats are not securable items. In other words, if the user has rights to render the report, she can export it in any registered format. If you need to limit the export options, the simple solution will be to do this in your client application. The disadvantage is that an adept user can bypass the client application and export the report directly from the Report Server. If this is an issue, you can implement a façade layer between the client application and the Report Server to validate the report requests.

Alternatively, you can also remove the rendering extension elements in the `RSReportServer.config` configuration file (found under the `<Render>` section) to eliminate the possibility that the export format can be used altogether.

5.5.1 Exporting reports to HTML

The Report Server uses the HTML rendering extension to render the report to HTML by default if a rendering format is not specified. HTML 4.0 is used for up-level browsers, such as Internet Explorer 4.0 or above or Netscape 7.0 or above; otherwise, HTML 3.2 is used.

The report-formatting settings, such as fonts, colors, and borders, are encapsulated in an inline stylesheet included in the page. Charts are always saved as image files.

If not already cached by the browser, images are fetched via additional requests to the Report Server. In essence, the browser asks the Report Server to send the image by submitting a URL request to the server, such as the following:

```
http://localhost/ReportServer?/AWReporter/Employee Sales Freeform with
 Chart&rs:Format=HTML4.0&rs:ImageID=0b326371-9aec-4705-87bf-1af02b3d5e78
```

One interesting option that exporting to HTML supports is autorefreshing reports. For example, you can author a company stock performance report that automatically refreshes itself on a set schedule to get the latest stock value. You can set up the report to automatically refresh itself at a certain interval by using the `AutoRefresh` report property. You can find this property both on the General tab of the Report Properties dialog box (select the report by clicking the Report Selector, right-click the report, and choose Properties) and on the report's Properties window. Behind the scenes, this property emits a meta browser tag, for example, `<META HTTP-EQUIV="Refresh" CONTENT="5">` if you set the `AutoRefresh` property to 5 seconds.

In terms of preserving the report fidelity, HTML is your best choice because it supports all interactive features, such as hyperlinks, document maps, and expandable crosstab reports.

There's one performance consideration when exporting reports to HTML. To render an HTML report, the browser loads the report in memory. For large reports, this could result in an "out of memory" exception. To prevent this and display HTML reports faster, you can define page breaks wherever it makes sense. For example, you can place a page break at the beginning or end of region groupings.

To enhance the report performance, the Report Server automatically generates a soft page break after the first page when repaginating HTML reports. Therefore, the first page of report loads quickly even with large reports.

5.5.2 Exporting reports to MHTML

The MHTML (MIME Encapsulation of Aggregate HTML Documents) format, listed as Web Archive in the standard report toolbar, encapsulates the report and its images in a single file. This eliminates the round-tripping to the Report Server to fetch the report images.

Because MHTML is based on MIME, rendering reports in MHTML format will be probably the best export option when you need to push the report to the users via e-mail subscribed delivery, as we discuss in more detail in chapter 12. MHTML is more compact than PDF and TIFF formats. Note, though, that all interactive features except hyperlinks (drill-through reports) will be disabled when you export to MHTML.

5.5.3 Exporting reports to other formats

Here's a quick recap about the rest of the export formats.

Excel

This format could be useful when you want to manipulate the report data offline in Microsoft Excel XP or later versions. Exporting to Excel doesn't require the use of Office Web Components for matrix and charts regions. Consult the documentation about other considerations when exporting reports to Excel.

Image

Exporting a report as an image allows the report to be rendered in BMP, EMF, GIF, JPEG, PNG, TIFF, and WMF image formats. The default option is TIF. Different formats can be requested by passing device settings parameters.

Exporting a report as an image could be useful if you want to show the report easily on a web page or print it consistently regardless of the printer capabilities. On the downside, all interactive report features will be lost. Another disadvantage of exporting to image files is that it substantially increases the report size.

PDF

If the report has a document map, it can be found under the Bookmark tab in Adobe Reader. All other interactive features are lost.

CSV

You can export reports to comma-delimited files. The field delimiter, record delimiter, and text qualifier can be fine-tuned by passing specific switches. See the documentation for all considerations regarding exporting reports to CSV.

XML

As you have just seen, reports can be exported to XML. Only the report data is exported and the report layout information is not preserved.

NOTE Microsoft will probably provide a rendering extension for exporting reports to RTF format with the next release of Reporting Services. If you don't want to wait until then, you have two options. First, you can use third-party rendering extensions, such as the SoftArtisians's OfficeWriter, to export the report to Word format (for more information refer to chapter 14). Or, with the persisting to XML feature available with Office 2003, another option for exporting to Word will be to render the report in XML format, compliant with the Word schema.

5.6 SUMMARY

You can greatly enhance your report features by using expressions coupled with functions. You can write expressions manually or use the Expression Editor. The Reporting Services object model exposes five collections that you can reference in expressions:

- The Fields collection allows you to reference the report's dataset fields.
- The ReportItems collection exposes all textbox items.
- The Parameters collection allows you to reference the parameter values passed to the report.
- The Globals and User collections contain some useful global and user-specific values.

To expand your expression capabilities, you can use native functions that come from RS or external functions from the pre-referenced standard .NET assemblies.

Finally, you can use expressions to add interactive features to your reports, such as links and document maps. You need to be aware of how different export formats impact the report's interactive features. The richest format that offers the most interactive features is HTML.

With RS, you can accomplish much more with expressions than creating calculated fields and calling a limited number of functions. In chapter 6 you learn how to unleash the expression capabilities by integrating them with custom code.

CHAPTER 6

Using custom code

Reporting Services doesn't limit your programming options to using inline expressions and functions. In this chapter, we show you how to supercharge the expression capabilities of your reports by integrating them with custom code. Writing custom code allows you to use advanced programming techniques to meet the most demanding reporting needs.

In this chapter, you:

- See what custom code options RS offers
- Learn how to write embedded code
- Find out how to integrate reports with external .NET assemblies
- Use XSL Transformations (XSLT) to produce XML reports

We show you how to put your custom code knowledge into practice by creating an advanced report that shows forecasted sales data.

With the widespread adoption of XML as an interoperable data exchange format, you also see how you can export reports to XML and custom-tailor the report output by using XSLT.

6.1 UNDERSTANDING CUSTOM CODE

As we mentioned in chapter 1, one of the most prominent features of Reporting Services is its extensible architecture. One way you can extend the RS capabilities is by integrating your reports with custom code that you or somebody else wrote. In general, you have two options for doing so:

- Write embedded (report-specific) code using Visual Basic .NET.
- Use custom code located in an external .NET assembly.

Let's discuss each custom code option in more detail.

6.1.1 Using embedded code

As its name suggests, *embedded* code gets saved inside the Report Definition Language (RDL) file. Before we jump to a code example, here are some limitations that embedded code is subject to:

- You can call embedded code only from within the report that contains the code. Because embedded code is saved in the RDL file, it is always scoped at the report level. For this reason, code embedded in one report cannot be referenced from another report. To create global and reusable functions that could be shared among reports, you have to move them to an external .NET assembly.
- You are restricted to using only Visual Basic .NET as a programming language for writing embedded code.
- As we pointed out in chapter 5, from within custom code you cannot directly reference the report object collections, such as Fields, ReportItems, and so on. Instead, you have to pass them to your embedded methods as arguments.

To call embedded code in your report, you reference its methods using the globally defined `Code` member. For example, if you have authored an embedded code function called `GetValue()`, you can call it from your expressions by using the following syntax:

```
=Code.GetValue()
```

DEFINITION *Shared* (called static in C#) methods can be invoked directly through the class name without first creating an instance of the class. To designate a method as shared, you use the VB .NET Shared modifier. The embedded code option does not support shared methods. On the other hand, *instance* methods are accessed through instances of the class and don't require a special modifier.

With the exception of shared methods, your embedded code can include any VB .NET–compliant code. In fact, if you think of the embedded code as a private class inside your project, you won't be far from the truth. You can declare class-level members and constants, private or public methods, and so on.

Maintaining state

One not-so-obvious aspect of working with embedded code is that you can maintain state in it. For example, you can use class-level members to preserve the values of the variables between calls to embedded code methods from the moment the report processing starts until the report is fully processed. We demonstrate this technique in the forecasting example that we explore in section 6.2.

Note that state can be maintained within the duration of a single report request only. As we explained in chapter 2, the RS report-processing model is stateless. For this reason, the report state gets discarded at the end of the report processing. Reporting Services is a web-based application, and just like any other web application, once the request is handled, its runtime state gets released. For this reason, subsequent requests to the same report cannot share state stored in class-level variables. You need to be careful, though, as all executions share state. This means that in order to do this correctly you need to index your variables by user ID. If you do not manage the state correctly you may start seeing unexpected results that are due to other processes sharing this same state.

Let's now look at a practical example where embedded code can be useful.

Writing embedded code

You can write embedded code to create reusable utility functions that can be called from several expressions in your report. Let's examine an example of how we can do just that.

Suppose that Adventure Works Cycles (AWC) has requested that we change the Territory Sales Crosstab report to display N/A when data is missing, as shown in figure 6.1.

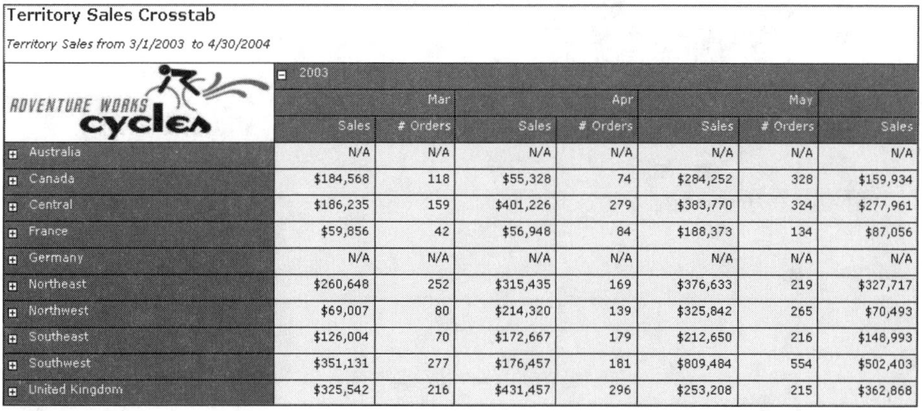

Territory Sales Crosstab

Territory Sales from 3/1/2003 to 4/30/2004

ADVENTURE WORKS cycles	2003						
	Mar		Apr		May		
	Sales	# Orders	Sales	# Orders	Sales	# Orders	Sales
Australia	N/A	N/A	N/A	N/A	N/A	N/A	N/A
Canada	$184,568	118	$55,328	74	$284,252	328	$159,934
Central	$186,235	159	$401,226	279	$383,770	324	$277,961
France	$59,856	42	$56,948	84	$188,373	134	$87,056
Germany	N/A	N/A	N/A	N/A	N/A	N/A	N/A
Northeast	$260,648	252	$315,435	169	$376,633	219	$327,717
Northwest	$69,007	80	$214,320	139	$325,842	265	$70,493
Southeast	$126,004	70	$172,667	179	$212,650	216	$148,993
Southwest	$351,131	277	$176,457	181	$809,484	554	$502,403
United Kingdom	$325,542	216	$431,457	296	$253,208	215	$362,868

Figure 6.1 You can use embedded code to implement useful utility functions scoped at the report level.

Further, let's assume that we need to differentiate between missing data and NULL values. When the underlying value is NULL, we translate it to zero. To meet this requirement, we can write a simple embedded function called `GetValue()`.

Using the Code Editor

To write custom embedded code, you use the Report Designer Code Editor, which you can invoke from the Report Properties dialog box. You can open this dialog box in one of three ways:

- Select the report by right-clicking the Report Selector and choosing Properties.
- Right-click anywhere on the report outside the body area, and choose Properties.
- Select Report Properties from the Report menu.

Then, in the Report Properties dialog box, select the Code tab, as shown in figure 6.2.

The function `GetValue()` can easily be replaced with an `Iif`-based expression; however, encapsulating the logic in an embedded function has two advantages. First, it centralizes the logic of the expression in one place instead of using `Iif` functions for every field in the report. Second, it makes the report more maintainable because if you decide to make a logical change to your function, you do not have to track down and change every `Iif` function in the report.

As you can see, the Code Editor is nothing to brag about. It is implemented as a simple text area control, and its feature set does not go beyond copying and pasting text. For this reason, we highly recommend that you use a standard VB Windows Forms or Console application to write your VB .NET code in a civilized manner and then copy and paste it inside the Code Editor.

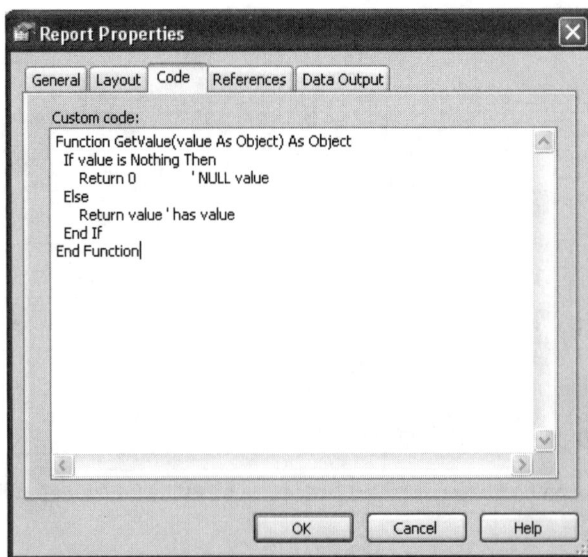

Figure 6.2
Use the Code Editor for writing embedded code. The GetValue() function, shown in the Code Editor, determines whether a value is missing or NULL.

The Report Designer saves embedded code under the <Code> element in the RDL file. When doing so, the Report Designer URL-encodes the text. Be aware of this if you decide to change the <Code> element directly for some reason.

Handling missing data

Once the `GetValue()` function is ready, to differentiate between NULL and missing data in our report, you can base the `txtSales` and `txtNoOrders` values on the following expressions:

```
=Iif(CountRows()=0, "N/A", Code.GetValue(Sum(Fields!Sales.Value)))
```

and

```
=Iif(CountRows()=0, "N/A", Code.GetValue(Sum(Fields!NoOrders.Value)))
```

respectively.

The `CountRows()` function returns the count of rows within a specified scope. If no scope is specified, it defaults to the innermost scope, which in our case resolves to the static group that defines the values in the data cells. Both expressions first check for missing data (no rows) by using `CountRows()` and display N/A if no missing data is found. Otherwise, they call the `GetValue()` embedded function to translate the NULL values.

We recommend that you use embedded code for writing simple report-specific utility-like functions. When your programming logic gets more involved, consider moving your code to external assemblies, as we discuss next.

6.1.2 Using external assemblies

The second way of extending RS programmatically is by using prepackaged logic located in external .NET assemblies that can be written in any .NET-supported language. The ability to integrate reports with custom code in external assemblies increases your programming options dramatically. For example, by using custom code, you can do the following:

- Leverage the rich feature set of the .NET Framework. For example, let's say you need a collection to store crosstab data of a matrix region in order to perform some calculations. You can "borrow" any of the collection classes that come with .NET, such as Array, ArrayList, Hashtable, and so on.
- Integrate your reports with custom .NET assemblies, written by you or third-party vendors. For example, to add forecasting features to the Sales by Product Category report in section 6.2, we leverage the Open Source OpenForecast package.
- More easily write code by leveraging the powerful Visual Studio .NET IDE instead of the primitive Code Editor available in RS.

We hope that at some point in the future, RS will become better integrated with the Visual Studio .NET IDE and support other .NET languages besides VB .NET. Ideally, RS should allow developers to add custom classes to their business intelligence projects and write code using the Visual Studio .NET editor. If this is implemented, enhancing RS programmatically will be no different than writing code in traditional .NET development projects.

Based on preliminary feedback that we received from Microsoft, this seems to be the long-term direction that RS will follow.

Referencing external assemblies

To use types located in an external assembly, you have to first let the Report Designer know about it by using the References tab in the Report Properties dialog box, as shown in figure 6.3.

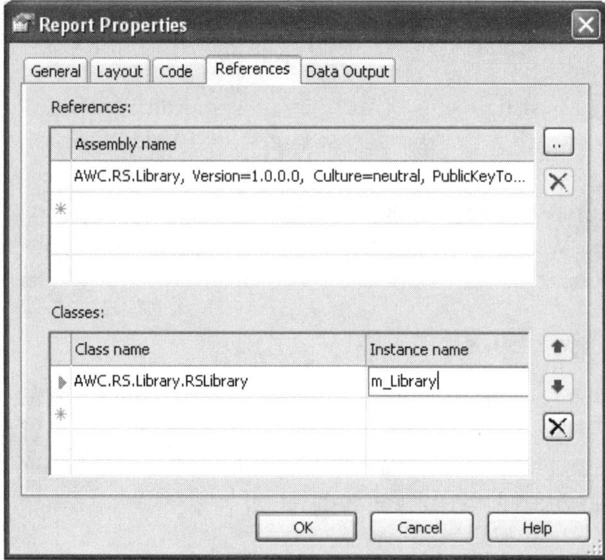

Figure 6.3
Use the Report Properties dialog box to reference an external assembly.

Assuming that our report needs to use the custom `AWC.RS.Library` assembly (included with this book's source code), we must first reference it using the References tab. While this tab allows you to browse and reference an assembly from an arbitrary folder, note that when the report is executed, the .NET common language runtime (CLR) will try to locate the assembly according to CLR probing rules. In a nutshell, these rules give you two options for deploying the custom assembly:

- Deploy the assembly as a private assembly.
- Deploy the assembly as a shared assembly in the .NET Global Assembly Cache (GAC). As a prerequisite, you have to strong-name your assembly. For more information about how to do this, refer to the .NET documentation.

If you choose the first option, you need to deploy the assembly to the Private Assemblies folder so that the assembly is available during the report-testing process. Assuming that you have accepted the default installation settings, to deploy the assembly to the Private Assemblies folder, copy the assembly to `C:\Program Files\Microsoft Visual Studio 8\Common7\IDE\PrivateAssemblies`. Once you have done this, you can build and render the report in preview mode inside VS .NET.

Before the report goes live, you need to deploy the assembly to the Report Server binary folder. Specifically, you need to copy the assembly to the Report Server binary folder, which by default is `C:\Program Files\Microsoft SQL Server\MSSQL.3\Reporting Services\ReportServer\bin`.

Note that deploying the custom assembly to the right location is only half of the deployment story. Depending on what your code does, you may need also to adjust the code access security policy so the assembly code can execute successfully. We discuss the code access security model in chapter 9. If you need more information about deploying custom assemblies, refer to the "Using Custom Assemblies with Reports" section in the RS documentation.

> **NOTE** The default location for RS 2000 Private Assemblies folder is `C:\Program Files\Microsoft SQL Server\80\Toos\Report Designer` and the default directory for the RS 2000 Report Server binary folder is `C:\Program Files\Microsoft SQL Server\MSSQL\Reporting Services\ReportServer\bin`.

Calling shared methods

When using custom code in external assemblies, you can call both instance and shared methods. If you need to call only shared methods (also called static in C#) inside the assembly, you are ready to go because shared methods are available globally within the report.

You can call shared methods by using the fully qualified type name using the following syntax:

```
<Namespace>.<Type>.<Method>(argument1, argument2, …, argumentN)
```

For example, if we need to call the `GetForecastedSet` shared method located in the `RsLibrary` class (`AWC.RS.Library` assembly) from an expression or embedded code, we would use the following syntax:

```
=AWC.RS.Library.RsLibrary.GetForecastedSet(forecastedSet, forecastedMonths)
```

where `AWC.RS.Library` is the namespace, `RsLibrary` is the type, `GetForecastedSet` is the method, and `forecastedSet` and `forecastedMonths` are the arguments.

If the custom assembly is your own, how can you decide whether to define your methods as shared or instance? My short answer is to use shared methods if you don't need instance methods. Shared methods are convenient to call. However, instance methods allow you to maintain state within the duration of the report request. For example, you can preserve the class-level variable values between multiple method invocations of the same type. The state considerations for using code in external .NET assemblies are the same as the ones we discussed in section 6.1.1 for embedded code.

One thing to watch for is using shared class-level fields to maintain state because their values are shared across all instances of the same report. So, depending on how many users are accessing a single report at any one time, the value of a shared field may be changing. In addition, the values of shared fields are not private to a report user, so sensitive user-only data should never be accessed through a shared field or property. Finally, static class-level fields are subject to multithreading locking issues. To avoid these issues, create your classes as stateless classes that do not have class-level shared fields or use instance class-level fields and methods. For more information about shared versus instance methods, see the Visual Studio .NET documentation.

Sometimes, you simply won't have a choice and your applications requirements will dictate the type of method invocation. For example, if the method needs to be invoked remotely via .NET Remoting, it has to be an instance method.

Calling instance methods

To invoke an instance method, you have some extra work left to do. First, you have to enumerate all instance classes (types) that you need to instantiate in the Classes grid (see figure 6.3). For each class, you have to assign an instance name. Behind the scenes, RS will create a variable with that name to hold a reference to the instance of the type.

NOTE When you specify the class name in the Classes grid, make sure that you enter the fully qualified type name (namespace included). In our example (shown previously in figure 6.3), the namespace is `AWC.RS.Library` while the class name is `RsLibrary`. When you are in doubt as to what the fully qualified class name is, use the VS .NET Object Browser or another utility, such as Lutz Roeder's excellent .NET Reflector (see the Resources section at the end of this book for information on this utility), to browse to the class name and find out its namespace.

For example, assuming that we need to call an instance method in the `AWC.RS.Library` assembly, we have to declare an instance variable `m_Library`, as shown in figure 6.3. In our case, this variable will hold a reference to the `RsLibrary` class.

If you declare more than one variable pointing to the same type, each will reference a separate instance of that type. Behind the scenes, when the report is processed, RS will instantiate as many instances of the referenced type as the number of instance variables.

Once you have finished with the reference settings, you are ready to call the instance methods via the instance type name that you specified. Just as with embedded code, you use the `Code` keyword to call an instance method. The difference between a shared and an instance method is that instead of using the class name, you use the variable name to call the method.

For example, if the `RsLibrary` type had an instance method named `DummyMethod()`, we could invoke it from an expression or embedded code like this:

```
Code.m_Library.DummyMethod()
```

Having seen what options we have as developers for programmatically expanding our report features, let's see how we can put them into practice. In the next section, we show you how to use embedded and external code to add advanced features to your reports.

6.2 CUSTOM CODE IN ACTION: IMPLEMENTING REPORT FORECASTING

Here is our fictitious scenario. Imagine that the AWC management has asked to see forecasted monthly sales data grouped by product category. These are the design goals of the sample report that we are going to create:

- Allow the user to generate a crosstab report of sales data for an arbitrary period.
- Allow the user to specify the number of forecasted columns.
- Use data extrapolation to forecast the sales data.

To make these more interesting, let's allow the report users to specify a data range to filter the sales data, as well as the number of forecasted months. To accomplish our requirements, we author a crosstab report, Sales by Product Category, as shown in figure 6.4.

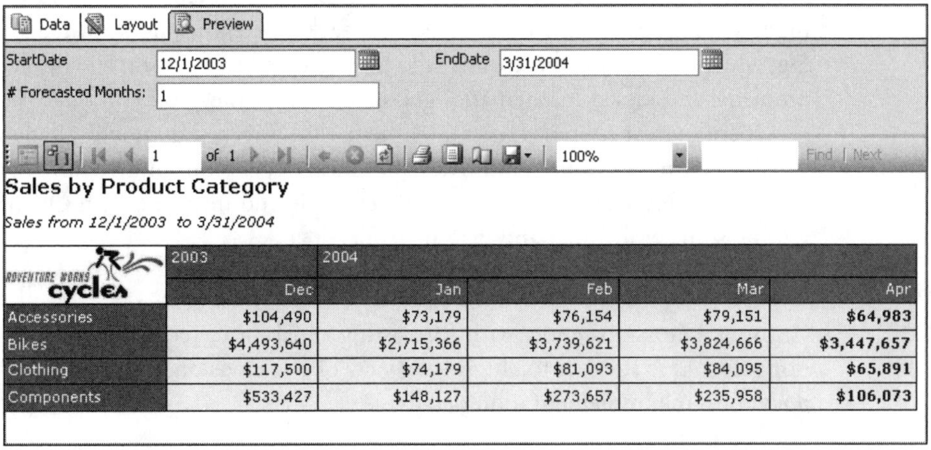

Data | Layout | Preview

StartDate 12/1/2003 EndDate 3/31/2004

Forecasted Months: 1

1 of 1 100% Find | Next

Sales by Product Category

Sales from 12/1/2003 to 3/31/2004

ADVENTURE WORKS cycles	2003	2004			
	Dec	Jan	Feb	Mar	Apr
Accessories	$104,490	$73,179	$76,154	$79,151	**$64,983**
Bikes	$4,493,640	$2,715,366	$3,739,621	$3,824,666	**$3,447,657**
Clothing	$117,500	$74,179	$81,093	$84,095	**$65,891**
Components	$533,427	$148,127	$273,657	$235,958	**$106,073**

Figure 6.4 The Sales by Product Category report uses embedded and external custom code for forecasting.

The user can enter a start date and an end date to filter the sales data. In addition, the user can specify how many months of forecasted data will be shown on the report. The report shows the data in a crosstab fashion, with product categories in rows and time periods in columns. The data portion of the report shows first the actual sales within the requested period, followed by the forecasted sales in bold font.

For example, if the user enters 4/30/2003 as a start date and 3/31/2004 as an end date and requests to see three forecasted months, the report will show the forecasted data for April, May, and June 2004 (to conserve space, figure 6.4 shows only one month of forecasted data).

In this section, we show you how to implement these forecasting features. As you probably agree, implementing forecasting features on your own is not an easy undertaking. But what if we had prepackaged code that does this for us? If this code can run on .NET, our report can access it as custom code. Enter OpenForecast.

6.2.1 Forecasting with OpenForecast

Forecasting is a science in itself. Generally speaking, forecasting is the process used to predict the unknown. Instead of looking at a crystal ball, forecasting practitioners use mathematical models to analyze data, discover trends, and make educated conclusions. In our example, the Sales by Product Category report will predict future sales data by using the data extrapolating method.

There are number of well-known mathematical models for extrapolating a set of data, such as polynomial regression and simple exponential smoothing. Implementing one of those models, though, is not a simple task. Instead, for the purposes of our sales forecasting example, we use the excellent open source OpenForecast package, written by Steven Gould.

OpenForecast is a general-purpose package that includes Java-based forecasting models applicable to any data series. The package requires no knowledge of forecasting, which is great for those of us who have decided to focus on solving pure business problems and kissed mathematics goodbye a long time ago.

OpenForecast supports several mathematical forecasting models, including single-variable linear regression, multivariable linear regression, and so on. Let's now see how we can implement our forecasting example and integrate with OpenForecast by writing some embedded and external code.

6.2.2 Implementing report forecasting features

Creating a crosstab report with forecasting capabilities requires several implementation steps. Let's start with a high-level view of our envisioned approach and then drill down into the implementation details.

Choosing an implementation approach

Figure 6.5 shows the logical architecture view of our solution. Our report uses embedded code to call a shared method in a custom assembly (`AwRsLibrary`) and get the forecasted data. `AwRsLibrary` loads the existing sales data into an OpenForecast dataset and obtains a forecasting model from OpenForecast. Then, it calls down to OpenForecast to get the forecasted values for the requested number of months. `AwRsLibrary` returns the forecasted data to the report, which in turn displays it.

We have at least two implementation options for passing the crosstab sales data to `AwRsLibrary`:

- Fetch the sales data again from the database. To accomplish this, the report could pass the selected product category and month values on a row-by-row basis. Then, `AwRsLibrary` could make a database call to retrieve the matching sales data.
- Load the existing sales data in a structure of some kind using embedded code inside the report and pass the structure to `AwRsLibrary`.

The advantages of the latter approach are as follows:

- *The custom code logic is self-contained*—We don't have to query the database again.
- *It uses the default custom code security policy*—We don't have to elevate the default code access security policy for the `AwRsLibrary` assembly. If we choose the first option, we won't be able to get away with the default code access security setup, because RS only grants our custom assemblies Execution rights, which are not sufficient to make a database call. Actually, in the case of OpenForecast, we had to grant both assemblies FullTrust rights because any J# code requires FullTrust to execute successfully. However, we wouldn't have had to do this if we had chosen C# as a programming language.
- *No data synchronization is required*—We don't have to worry about synchronizing the data containers, the matrix region, and the `AwRsLibrary` dataset.

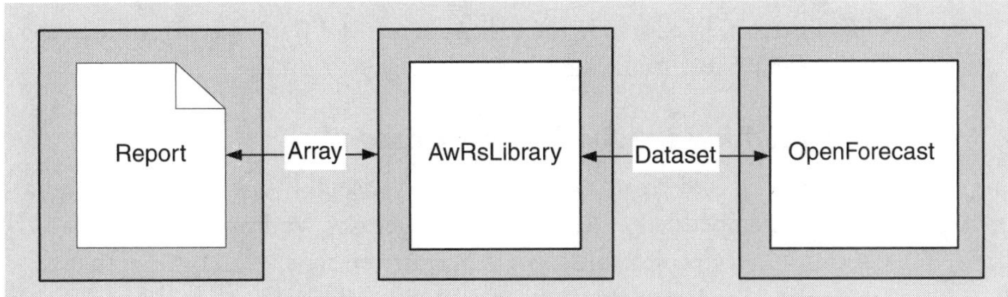

Figure 6.5 The Sales by Product Category report uses embedded code to call the AwRsLibrary assembly, which in turn calls the J# OpenForecast package.

For these reasons, we choose the second approach. To implement it, we use an expression to populate the matrix region data values. The expression calls our embedded code to load an array structure on a row-by-row basis. Once a given row is loaded, we pass the array to `AwRsLibrary` to obtain the forecasted data.

Now, let's discuss the implementation details, starting with converting OpenForecast to .NET.

Migrating OpenForecast to .NET

OpenForecast is written in Java, so one of the first hurdles we have to overcome is to integrate it with .NET. We have two options for doing so:

- *Use a third-party Java-to-.NET gateway to integrate both platforms*—Given the complexities of this approach, we quickly dismiss it.
- *Port OpenForecast to one of the supported .NET languages*—Microsoft provides two options for this. First, we can use the Microsoft Java Language Conversion Assistant (see section 6.5 for more information) to convert Java-language code to C#. Second, we could convert OpenForecast to J#. The latter option preserves the Java syntax, although that code executes under the control of the .NET common language runtime instead of the Java Virtual Machine.

We decide to port OpenForecast to J#. The added benefit to this approach is that the open source developers could maintain only one Java-based version of OpenForecast.

Porting OpenForecast to J# turns out to be easier than we thought. We create a new J# library project, name it **OpenForecast**, and load all `*.java` source files inside it. We include the .NET version of OpenForecast in the source code that comes with this book. Figure 6.6 shows the J# version of OpenForecast open in Visual Studio .NET.

We have to take care of only a few compilation errors inside the `MultipleLinearRegression` class, because several Java hashtable methods are not supported in J#, such as `keySet()`, `entries()`, and hashtable cloning. We also include a WinForm application (TestHarness) that you may use to test the converted OpenForecast. We include the OpenForecast DLL so you can still run the report even if you don't have J# installed.

Implementing the AwRsLibrary assembly

The next step is to create the custom .NET assembly, `AwRsLibrary`, that will bridge the report-embedded code and OpenForecast. We implement `AwRsLibrary` as a C# class library project. Inside it we create the class `RsLibrary` that exposes a static (shared) method, `GetForecastedSet()`. The abbreviated code of this method is shown in listing 6.1.

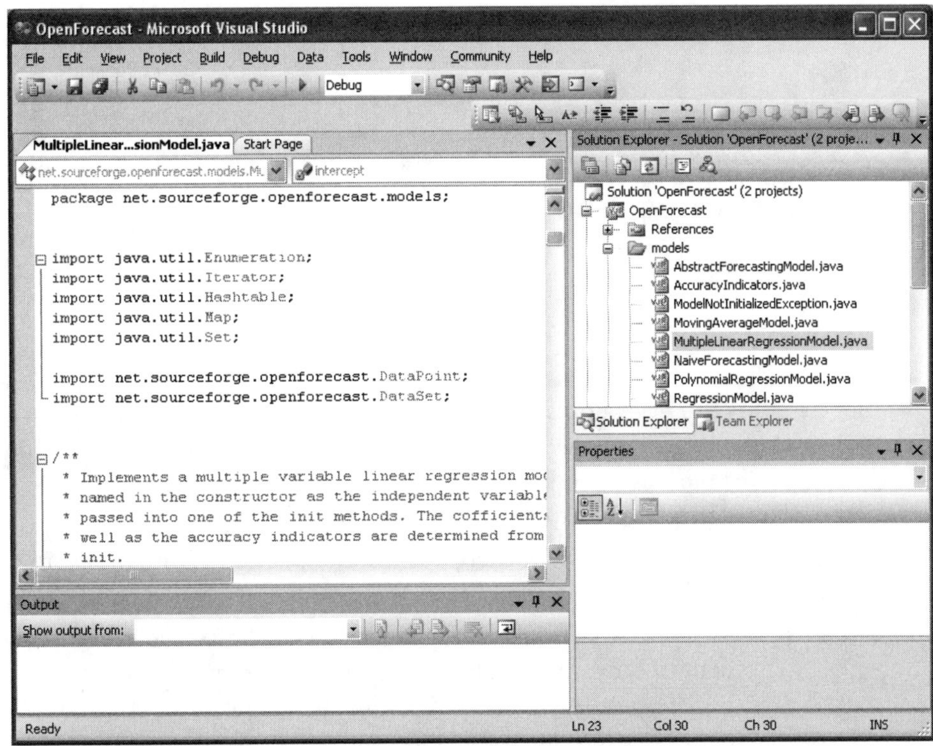

Figure 6.6 To convert Java-based OpenForecast to .NET, we migrate its code to J#.

Listing 6.1 The report-embedded code, which calls the AwRsLibrary GetForecastedSet method, which in turn calls OpenForecast

```
public static void GetForecastedSet(double[] dataSet,
  int numberForecastedPoints ) {
  DataSet observedData = new DataSet();          <-- Defines OpenForecast dataset

  Observation dp;
  for (int i=0;i<dataSet.Length-numberForecastedPoints;i++) {
    dp = new Observation( dataSet[i]);
    dp.setIndependentValue( "x", i);
    observedData.add( dp );                       Obtains a forecasting model from OpenForecast
  }

  ForecastingModel forecaster = new MultipleLinearRegressionModel();  <--
  forecaster.init(observedData);
  DataSet requiredObservations = new DataSet();  <-- Specifies placeholders for the forecasted data
for ( int i=dataSet.Length-numberForecastedPoints;
 i < dataSet.Length; i++ ) {
    dp = new Observation( 0.0 );
    dp.setIndependentValue( "x", i );
```

```
    requiredObservations.add( dp );
  }

  forecaster.forecast( requiredObservations );

  int index =  dataSet.Length - numberForecastedPoints;
  Iterator it = requiredObservations.iterator();
  while ( it.hasNext() ) {
    dataSet[index] = ((DataPoint)it.next()).getDependentValue();
    index++;
  }
}
```

Performs forecasting

Populates the input array

The `GetForecastedSet()` method receives the existing sales data for a given product category in the form of a `dataSet` array, as well as the number of the requested months for forecasted data.

Next, integrating with OpenForecast is a matter of five steps.

Step 1 We create a new OpenForecast dataset and load it with the existing data from the matrix row array.

Step 2 We obtain a given forecasting model. OpenForecast allows developers to get the optimal forecasting mathematical model based on the given data series by calling the `getBestForecast()` method. This method examines the dataset and tries a few forecasting models to select the most optimal. If the returned model is not a good fit, you can request a forecasting model explicitly by instantiating any of the classes found under the model's project folder.

> **NOTE** When testing the report with our sales data, we noticed that `getBestForecast()` returns the PolynomialRegressionModel model, which returns negative values when the sales data varies considerably. For this reason, we explicitly request the MultipleLinearRegressionModel model. We recommend that you try `getBestForecast()` first for your forecasting applications, and only if the returned model doesn't meet your needs should you request a model explicitly.

Step 3 We prepare another dataset to hold the forecasted data and initialize it with as many elements as the number of forecasted months.

Step 4 We call the forecast method to extrapolate the data and return the forecasted results.

Step 5 We load the forecasted data back to the `dataSet` array so we can pass it back to the report's embedded code.

Once we have finished with both the `AwRsLibrary` and `OpenForecast` .NET assemblies, we need to deploy them.

Deploying custom assemblies

As we explained in section 6.1, we need to deploy custom assemblies to both the Private Assemblies and Report Server binary folders. The custom assembly deployment process consists of the following steps:

Step 1 Copy the assemblies to the Report Designer and Report Server binary folders.

Step 2 Adjust the code-based security if the custom code needs an elevated set of code access security permissions.

To make both assemblies, `AwRsLibrary` and `OpenForecast`, available during design time, we have to copy `AWC.RS.Library.dll` and `OpenForecast.dll` to the Report Designer folder, which by default is `C:\Program Files\Microsoft Visual Studio 8\Common7\IDE\PrivateAssemblies`.

Similarly, to successfully render the deployed report under the Report Server, we have to deploy both assemblies to the Report Server binary folder, which by default is `C:\Program Files\Microsoft SQL Server\MSSQL.3\Reporting Services\ReportServer\bin`. In fact, the Report Server will not let you deploy a report from within the VS .NET IDE if all referenced custom assemblies are not already deployed.

The default RS code access security policy grants Execution rights to all custom assemblies by default. However, J# assemblies require FullTrust code access rights. Because the .NET common language runtime walks up the call stack to verify that all callers have the required permission set, we need to elevate the code access security policy for both assemblies to full trust. This will require changes to the Report Designer and Report Server security configuration files.

For more details about how code access security works and how it can be configured, see appendix B. You can also find a copy of our `rssrvpolicy.config` configuration file enclosed with the AwRsLibrary project. Toward the end of the file, you will see two `CodeGroup` XML elements that point to the `AwRsLibrary` and `OpenForecast` files. You will need to copy these elements to the Report Server security configuration file (`rssrvpolicy.config`).

In addition, as we discussed in chapter 2, if you want to preview (run) the report in the Preview window from the Report Designer, you will have to propagate the changes to the Report Designer security configuration file (`rspreviewpolicy.config`) as well.

Once the custom assemblies are deployed, we must write some VB .NET embedded code in our report to call the `AwRsLibrary` assembly, as we discuss next.

Writing report embedded code

To integrate the report with `AwRsLibrary` we add an embedded function called `GetValue()` to the Sales by Product Category report, as shown in listing 6.2.

Listing 6.2 The embedded GetValue() function, which calls the AwRsLibrary assembly

```
Dim forecastedSet() As Double  ' array with sales data
Dim productCategoryID As Integer = -1
Dim bNewSeries As Boolean = False
Public m_ExString = String.Empty

Function GetValue(productCategoryID As Integer, _
  orderDate As DateTime, _
sales As Double, reportParameters as Parameters, _
txtRange as TextBox) As Double

  Dim startDate as DateTime = reportParameters!StartDate.Value
  Dim endDate as DateTime = reportParameters!EndDate.Value
  Dim forecastedMonths as Integer = _
   reportParameters!ForecastedMonths.Value

  If (forecastedSet Is Nothing) Then
    ReDim forecastedSet(DateDiff(DateInterval.Month, _
       startDate, endDate) + forecastedMonths)
  End If

  If Me.productCategoryID <> productCategoryID Then
    Me.productCategoryID = productCategoryID
    bNewSeries = True
    Array.Clear(forecastedSet, 0, forecastedSet.Length - 1)
  End If

  Dim i = DateDiff(DateInterval.Month, startDate , orderDate)
  'Is this a forecasted value?
   If orderDate <= endDate Then
           ' No, just load the value in the array
           forecastedSet(i) = sales
   Else
      If bNewSeries Then
         Try
           AWC.RS.Library.RsLibrary.GetForecastedSet(_
             forecastedSet, _
             forecastedMonths)
           bNewSeries = False
         Catch ex As Exception
           m_ExString  = "Exception: " & ex.Message
           System.Diagnostics.Trace.WriteLine(ex.ToString())
           throw ex
         End Try
     End If
```

Redims the array to hold existing sales data

Holds sales data per product category

Calls AwRsLibrary to get the forecasted set

```
    End If ' is it forecasted value
    Return forecastedSet(i)
End Function
```

Because the matrix region data cells use an expression that references the GetValue() function, this function gets called by each data cell. Table 6.1 lists the input arguments that the GetValue() function takes.

Table 6.1 Input arguments that the GetValue() function takes

Argument	Purpose
productCategoryID	The productCategoryID value from the rowProductCategory row grouping corresponding to the cell.
orderDate	The orderDate value from the colMonth column grouping corresponding to the cell.
sales	The aggregated sales total for this cell.
reportParameters	To calculate the array dimensions, GetValue() needs the values of the report parameters. Instead of passing the parameters individually using Parameters!ParameterName.Value, we pass a reference to the report Parameters collection.
txtRange	A variable that holds the error message in case an exception occurs when getting the forecasted data.

To understand how GetValue() works, note that each data cell inside the matrix region is fed from the forecastedSet array. If the cell doesn't need forecasting (its corresponding date is within the requested date range), we just load the cell value in the array and pass it back to display it in the matrix region. To get this working, we need to initialize the array to have a rank equal to the number of requested months plus the number of forecasted months. Once the matrix region moves to a new row and calls our function, we are ready to forecast the data by calling the AwRsLibrary.GetForecastedSet method.

Implementing the Sales by Product Category crosstab report

The most difficult part of authoring the report itself is setting up its data to ensure that we always have the correct number of columns in the matrix region showing the forecasted columns. By default, the matrix region won't show columns that don't have data. This will interfere with calculating the right offset to feed the cells from the array. Therefore, we must ensure that the database returns records for all months within the requested data range. To implement this, we need to preprocess the sales data at the database. This is exactly what the spGetForecastedData stored procedure does. Inside the stored procedure, we prepopulate a custom table with all monthly periods within the requested date range, as shown in listing 6.3.

Listing 6.3 The spGetForecastedData stored procedure, which ensures that the returned rowset has the correct number of columns

```
CREATE  PROCEDURE [dbo].[spGetForecastedData]
(
    @StartDate smalldatetime,
    @EndDate smalldatetime
)
AS

SET NOCOUNT ON

DECLARE @tempDate smalldatetime

DECLARE @dateSet TABLE                    <-- Defines a custom table to store months
  (
    ProductCategoryID     tinyint,
    OrderDate        smalldatetime
  )

SET     @tempDate = @EndDate


WHIL (@StartDate <= @tempDate)             <-- Inserts the month records
BEGIN
    INSERT INTO @dateSet
    SELECT ProductCategoryID,  @tempDate
    FROM Production.ProductCategory

    SET @tempDate = DATEADD(mm, -1, @tempDate)
END

SELECT        DS.ProductCategoryID, PC.Name as ProductCategory,
  OrderDate AS Date, NULL AS Sales
FROM        @dateSet DS INNER JOIN Production.ProductCategory PC ON
  DS.ProductCategoryID = PC.ProductCategoryID
UNION ALL                                  <-- Returns actual sales data plus dummy records
SELECT      PC.ProductCategoryID,
PC.Name AS ProductCategory,
SOH.OrderDate AS Date,
SUM(SOD.UnitPrice * SOD.OrderQty) AS Sales
FROM        Production.ProductSubCategory PSC
INNER JOIN
            Production.ProductCategory PC ON
PSC.ProductCategoryID = PC.ProductCategoryID
INNER JOIN
            Production.Product P ON
PSC.ProductSubCategoryID = P.ProductSubCategoryID
INNER JOIN
            Sales.SalesOrderHeader SOH INNER JOIN
            Sales.SalesOrderDetail SOD ON
SOH.SalesOrderID = SOD.SalesOrderID ON P.ProductID = SOD.ProductID
```

```
WHERE     (SOH.OrderDate BETWEEN @StartDate AND @EndDate)
GROUP BY SOH.OrderDate, PC.Name, PC.ProductCategoryID
ORDER BY PC.Name, OrderDate
```

Finally, we union all records from the `@dateSet` table (its `Sales` column values are set to NULL) with the actual SQL statement that fetches the sales data.

Once the dataset is set, authoring the rest of the report is easy. We use a matrix region for the crosstab portion of the report. To understand how the matrix region magic works and how it invokes the embedded `GetValue()` function, you may want to replace the expression of the txtSales textbox with the following expression:

```
= Fields!ProductCategoryID.Value & "," & Fields!Date.Value _
  & "," &  Format(Fields!Sales.Value, "C")
```

Figure 6.7 shows what the Sales by Product Category crosstab report looks like when this expression is applied.

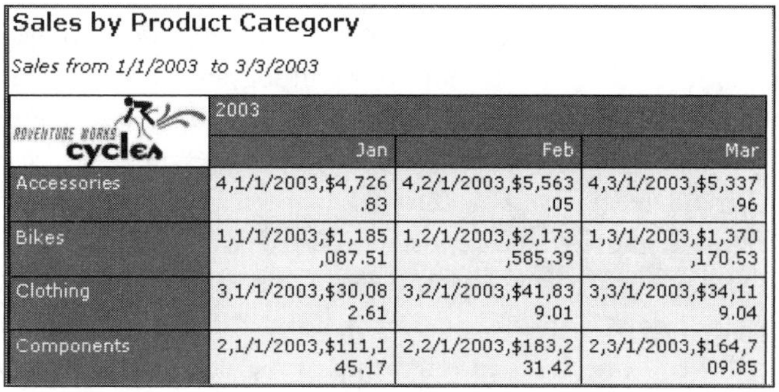

Sales by Product Category

Sales from 1/1/2003 to 3/3/2003

ADVENTURE WORKS cycles	2003		
	Jan	Feb	Mar
Accessories	4,1/1/2003,$4,726.83	4,2/1/2003,$5,563.05	4,3/1/2003,$5,337.96
Bikes	1,1/1/2003,$1,185,087.51	1,2/1/2003,$2,173,585.39	1,3/1/2003,$1,370,170.53
Clothing	3,1/1/2003,$30,082.61	3,2/1/2003,$41,839.01	3,3/1/2003,$34,119.04
Components	2,1/1/2003,$111,145.17	2,2/1/2003,$183,231.42	2,3/1/2003,$164,709.85

Figure 6.7 The Sales by Product Category report with debug data placed in the expression

As you see, we can easily get to the corresponding row and column group values that the matrix region uses to calculate the aggregate values in the region data cells. Now we have a way to identify each data cell. The matrix region is set up as shown in table 6.2.

Table 6.2 Expressions used in the matrix region

Matrix area	Name	Expression
Rows	`rowProductGroup`	`=Fields!ProductCategory.Value`
Columns	`colYear`	`=Fields!Date.Value.Year`
	`colMonth`	`=Fields!Date.Value.Month`
Data	`txtSales`	`=Code.GetValue(Fields!ProductCategoryID.Value, Fields!Date.Value, Sum(Fields!Sales.Value), Parameters, ReportItems!txtRange)`

To implement conditional formatting for the forecasted columns (in this case, to show them in bold), we use the following expression for the font property of the txtSales textbox:

```
=Iif(Code.IsForecasted
(Fields!Date.Value, Parameters!EndDate.Value), "Bold", "Normal")
```

This expression calls the `IsForecasted()` function located in the report-embedded code. The function simply compares the sales monthly date with the requested end date and, if the sales date is before the end date, it returns false.

The only thing left for us to do is to reference the `AwRsLibrary` assembly using the Report Properties dialog box's References tab, as shown earlier in figure 6.3. Note that for the purposes of this report, we don't need to set up an instance name (there's no need to enter anything in the Classes grid), because we don't call any instance methods.

Debugging custom code

You may find debugging custom code challenging. For this reason, we want to share with you a few techniques that we have found useful for custom code debugging.

There aren't many options for debugging embedded code. The only one we have found so far is to use the `MsgBox()` function to output messages and variable values when the report is rendered inside the Report Designer. Be sure to remove the calls to `MsgBox()` before deploying the report to the Report Server. If you don't, all `MsgBox()` calls will result in an exception. For some reason, trace messages using `System.Diagnostics.Trace` (the `OutputDebugString` API) inside embedded code get "swallowed" and don't appear either in the VS .NET Output window or by using an external tracing tool.

When working with external assemblies, you have at least two debugging options:

- Output trace messages.
- Use the VS .NET debugger to step through the custom code.

Tracing

For example, in the `AwRsLibrary.GetForecastedSet` method, we are outputting trace messages using `System.Diagnostics.Trace.WriteLine` to display the observed and forecasted values. To see these messages when running the report inside VS .NET or Report Server, you can use Mark Russinovich's excellent DebugView tool, shown in figure 6.8.

For more information about DebugView, see section 6.5.

Debugging custom code

You can also step through the custom assembly code using the VS .NET debugger by attaching to the Report Designer process, as follows:

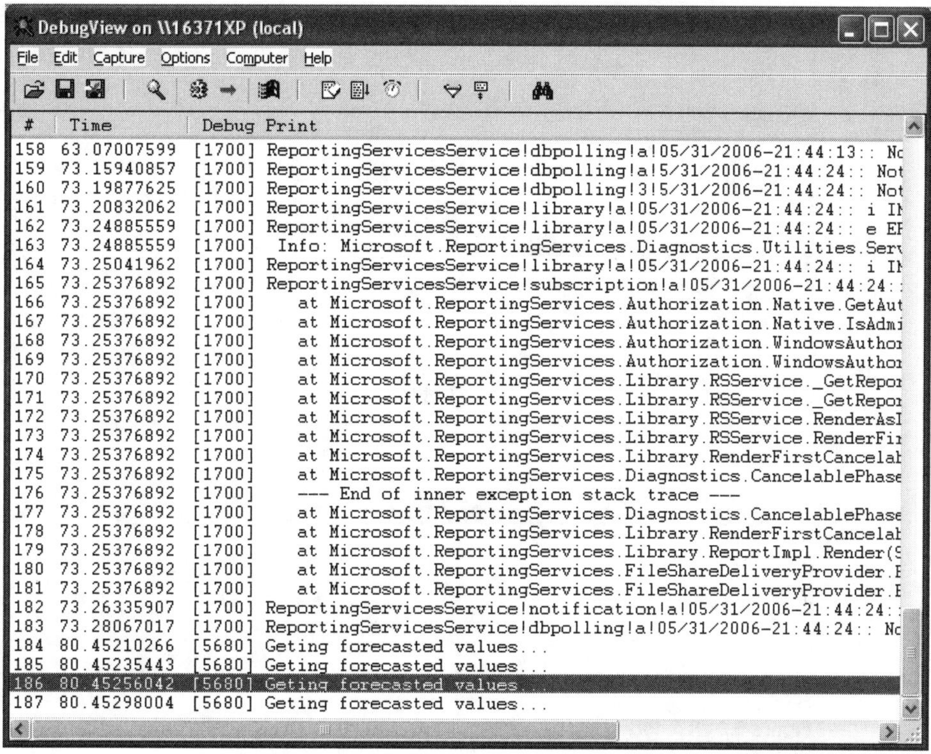

Figure 6.8 You can output trace messages from external assemblies in DebugView.

Step 1 Open the custom assembly that you want to debug in a new instance of VS .NET. Set breakpoints in your code as usual.

Step 2 Open your Business Intelligence project in another instance of VS .NET.

Step 3 Back at the custom assembly project, click on the Debug menu and then choose Attach to Processes. Locate the devenv process that hosts the Business Intelligence project and attach to it. At this point, your Processes dialog box should look like the one shown in figure 6.9. In this case, we want to debug the code in the `AwRsLibrary` assembly when it is invoked by the Sales by Product Category report. For this reason, in the AwRsLibrary project we attach to the RSInAction devenv process. RSInAction is the name of our solution that contains the AWReporter project.

Step 4 In the Business Intelligence project, preview the report that calls the custom assembly. Or, if you have already been previewing the report, click the Refresh Report button on the Preview Tab toolbar. At this point, your breakpoints should be hit by the VS .NET debugger.

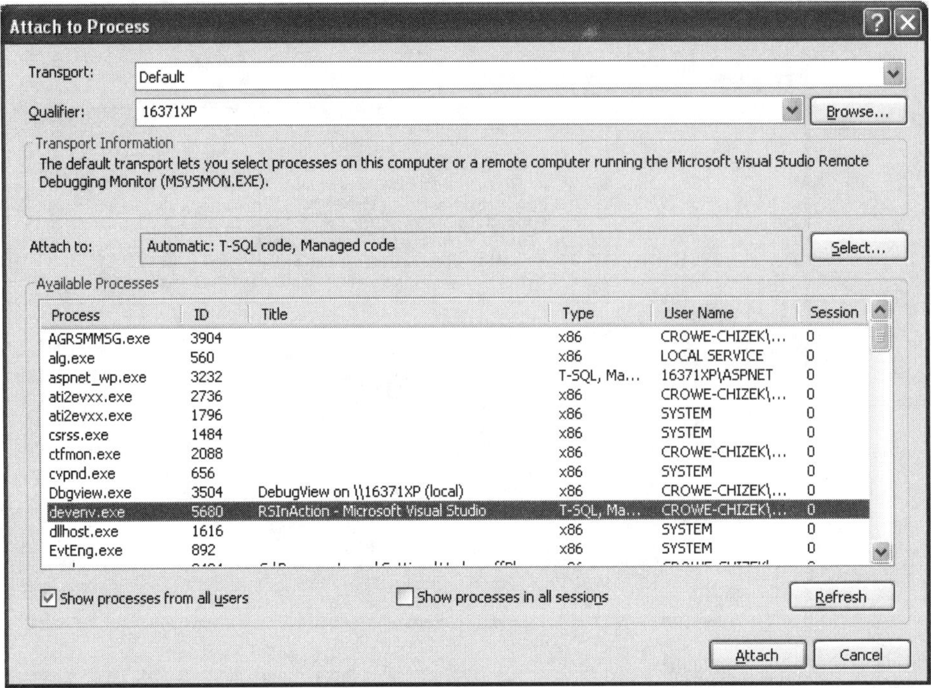

Figure 6.9 To debug custom assemblies, attach to the Visual Studio instance that hosts your BI project.

As you will soon find out, if you need to make code changes and recompile the custom assembly, trying to redeploy it to the Report Designer folder results in the following exception:

```
Cannot copy <assembly name>: It is being used by another person or program.
```

The problem is that the VS .NET IDE holds a reference to the custom assembly. You will need to shut down VS .NET and then redeploy the new assembly. To avoid this situation and make the debugging process even easier, you could debug the custom assembly code by using the Report Host (Preview window). To do this, follow these steps:

Step 1 Add the custom assembly to the VS .NET solution that includes your BI project.

Step 2 Change the BI project start item to the report that calls the custom code, as shown in figure 6.10.

Step 3 Press F5 to run the report in the Preview window. When the report calls the custom code, your breakpoints will be hit.

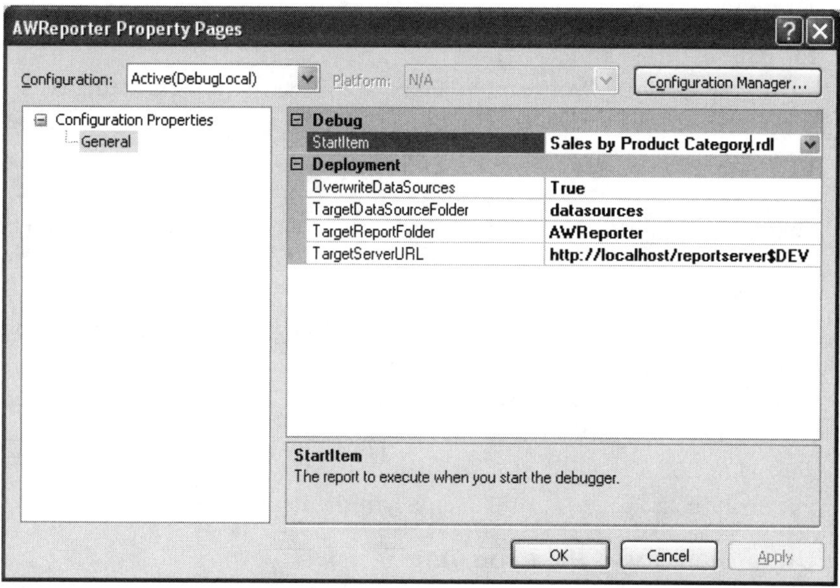

Figure 6.10 Use the Report Host debug option to avoid locking assemblies.

NOTE As explained in chapter 2, what happens when you press F5 to debug a report depends on your project settings. If both the Build and Deploy options are selected in Configuration Manager, VS .NET will build and deploy all reports in your Business Intelligence project before the report is displayed in the Preview window. To avoid this problem and launch your report faster, clear these options or switch to the DebugLocal configuration. This configuration doesn't include the Deploy option by default.

When you're using the Preview window approach, VS .NET doesn't lock the custom assemblies. This allows you to change the build location of your assembly to the Report Designer folder so that it always includes the most recent copy when you rebuild the assembly. As we explained in chapter 2, running your projects in the Preview window is a result of the code access security policy settings specified in the Report Designer configuration file (`rspreviewpolicy.config`).

Let's now look at another way of using custom code in reports in the form of XSL transformations.

6.3 USING XML-BASED REPORTS

You've seen how to use custom code to extend report capabilities programmatically, but, for all its flexibility, custom code has its limitations. For example, besides hiding report items, you cannot control the report output programmatically. However, if you export your reports to XML, you can use custom code in the form of XSL

Transformations (XSLT) to precisely control the XML presentation of the report, as you'll see in this section.

Strictly speaking, from an implementation standpoint, exporting a report to XML is no different than exporting it to any other rendering format, because the actual work is performed by the XML rendering extension (`Microsoft.ReportingServices.XmlRendering.dll`), which happens to be one of the supported RS extensions. However, we decided to devote a section to this export option because this is an extremely useful and important option.

Because the IT industry has embraced XML as the de facto standard for data exchange between heterogeneous platforms, exporting a report to XML opens a whole new world of opportunity. For example, in the business-to-business (B2B) scenario, an organization could expose an inventory report to its vendors. A vendor could request the report in XML to find out the current inventory product levels. The XML document could then be sent to a BizTalk server, which could extract the product information and send it to the manufacturing department.

6.3.1 Understanding XML exporting

The content of the following report elements can be exported to XML: textbox, rectangle, subreport, table region, list region, and matrix region. As a report author, you have full control over the XML presentation of these elements.

To customize the XML-rendered output of the report, you use the Data Output tab of the report element's property pages. Which settings can be customized depends on the type of the element. In general, you can specify the following:

- Whether the report element and its content (for regions, groups, and rectangles) will be exported
- The XML element name
- Whether the report element will be rendered as an XML attribute or element

For example, at a report level, you can specify the root node name and XML schema. At the region level, you can specify whether the region and its items will be rendered at all. At the textbox level, you can tell the Report Server whether the textbox content will be rendered as an XML attribute or element.

When the Data Output settings are not enough, you can further fine-tune the XML output by using custom XSL transformations. For example, while skipping report elements is easy, adding additional XML nodes is not. In cases such as this, you can write an XSL transformation that will be applied by the Report Server after the report is rendered to XML.

Let's now look at a practical example that demonstrates how exporting to XML could be useful.

6.3.2 Exposing the report content as an RSS feed

RSS (which stands for all of the following: RDF Site Summary, Rich Site Summary, or Really Simple Syndication) is an XML-based format that allows information workers to describe and syndicate web content. Many organizations and individuals use RSS for *blogging*. To give our example a touch of reality, let's say that Adventure Works Cycles (AWC) would like to take advantage of the increasing popularity of blogging with RSS feeds. In particular, the company management has requested these requirements:

- Future promotional campaigns must be exposed as an RSS feed. The AWC customers could subscribe to the feed using their favorite RSS newsreader and be notified about future product promotions.
- Each promotional item must include a hyperlink that will show more details about the campaign, such as discounted products and their sale prices.

Implementation options

How can we implement these requirements? One approach is to add the promotional information as static or dynamic web content to the company's web portal. For example, the products page could include a section that lists the current promotions. As far as exporting the promotional data as XML for the purposes of the RSS feed, we could create a Web service that would query the AdventureWorks database, retrieve the promotion details in XML, and write them into an RSS blog file.

Another implementation option could be to author an RS report that would supply both the HTML and XML content. The RSS Web service could then request the report as XML and append the promotional information to the RSS blog file. The RSS item hyperlink could bring the customer to the HTML version of same report. Of course, the latter option assumes that you are willing to allow web users to access your Report Server directly by URL. This is not as bad as it sounds. If Windows authentication is an issue, you can replace it with a custom security extension to authenticate and authorize your web users, as we discuss in chapter 13.

Which approach will work better for you depends on your particular needs and limitations. In our case, let's go for the latter to demonstrate the exporting-to-XML feature. To recap, our design goals for the new report sample are as follows:

- Export the report to RSS-compliant XML format.
- Append the report XML to an RSS feed (we postpone the actual implementation until chapter 8).

Implementing the report

Let's start by creating a new report called Sales Promotion. The report gets the promotional data from the `SpecialOffer` and `SpecialOfferProduct` tables. In addition, it takes one parameter, `Campaign` ID, which the user can use to request a specific campaign.

Volume Discount 11 to 14!!!

Discount: 2.0000% **From:** Sunday, July 01, 2001 **To:** Wednesday, June 30, 2004

Product No.	Product	Color	Size	Weight	Dealer	Old Price
CA-1098	AWC Logo Cap	Multi			$6.92	$8.99
CL-9009	Bike Wash - Dissolver				$2.97	$7.95
LO-C100	Cable Lock				$10.31	$25.00
CH-0234	Chain	Silver			$8.99	$20.24
VE-C304-M	Classic Vest, M	Blue	M		$23.75	$63.50
VE-C304-S	Classic Vest, S	Blue	S		$23.75	$63.50
FB-9873	Front Brakes	Silver		317	$47.29	$106.50
FD-2342	Front Derailleur	Silver		88	$40.62	$91.49
GL-F110-L	Full-Finger Gloves, L	Black	L		$15.67	$37.99
GL-F110-M	Full-Finger Gloves, M	Black	M		$15.67	$37.99
GL-H102-L	Half-Finger Gloves, L	Black	L		$9.16	$24.49
GL-H102-M	Half-Finger Gloves, M	Black	M		$9.16	$24.49
GL-H102-S	Half-Finger Gloves, S	Black	S		$9.16	$24.49

Figure 6.11 The Sales Promotion report serves as both the RSS feed source and the HTML campaign details page.

For example, figure 6.11 shows the second page of the Sales Promotion report when the user requests a campaign with an ID of 2.

As you can see, this report is very similar to the RS Product Catalog report sample, so we won't spend much time discussing its implementation details. Instead, let's focus on explaining how to export the report's content to XML.

Understanding the RSS schema

What the report's XML output needs to be depends on which version of the RSS specification you have to support. For example, listing 6.4 shows what the sales promotion RSS feed should look like if it conforms to RSS version 2.0.

Listing 6.4 The Sales Promotion RSS feed for notifying AWC subscribers about promotions

```
<rss version="2.0">          General feed-
<channel>                 <- related header
  <title>AWC Promotions</title>
  <link>http://www.adventure-works.com/</link>
  <description>Great discounted deals!</description>
  <language>en-us</language>
  <ttl>1440</ttl>
  <item xmlns:n1="http://www.awc.com/sales" xmlns:xs="http://www.w3.org/
2001/XMLSchema">   <- Feed item
```

```
    <title>LL Road Frame Sale!!!</title>
    <link>http://localhost/reportserver?/AWReporter/Sales
Promotion&SpecialOfferID=2&rs:Command=Render&rs:Format=XML
    </link>
    <description>Great LL Road Frame Sale!!!</description>
    <pubDate>Saturday, January 10, 2004</pubDate>
  </item>
  <item xmlns:n1="http://www.awc.com/sales"
  ➥  xmlns:xs="http://www.w3.org/2001/XMLSchema">
    <!-Another item information here-
  </item>
</channel>
</rss>
```

Given the feed in listing 6.4, figure 6.12 shows how it is rendered in the IntraVNews RSS Reader, which is integrated with Outlook:

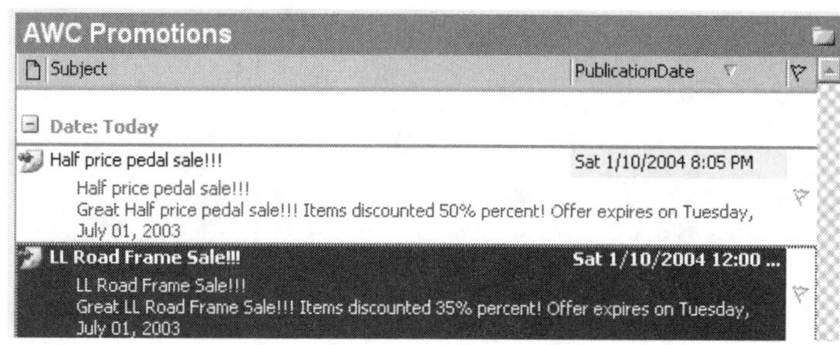

Figure 6.12 The AWC Promotions feed is rendered in IntraVNews.

Let's now examine what needs to be done to massage the report output to make it compliant with the RSS schema.

Defining the report XML output

The first step required to export the report to an RSS-compliant format is to fine-tune its XML output. We've made a few changes using the Data Output tab for various elements, so the report renders to the abbreviated XML schema shown in listing 6.5.

Listing 6.5 The Sales Promotion report rendered in XML

```
<SalesPromotion xmlns=http://www.awc.com/sales xmlns:xsi="http://
www.w3.org/2001/XMLSchema-instance" xsi:schemaLocation="..."
Name="Sales Promotion" Date="2004-01-10T00:00:00.0000000-05:00">
  <Promotions>
    <Promotion Description="LL Road Frame Sale!!!">     <-- Represents an item
      <ProductInfo>                                         in the RSS feed
        <Products>
          <Product ProductNumber="FR-T98U-44"
             Product="HL Touring Frame - Blue, 44" Color="Blue"
             Size="44" Weight="2.92" ListPrice="1003.9100"/>
```

```
            <Product ProductNumber="FR-T98R-44"
            ➥ Product="HL Touring Frame - Red, 44" Color="Red"
              Size="44" Weight="2.92" ListPrice="1003.9100"/>
          </Products>
        </ProductInfo>
      </Promotion>
    </Promotions>
</SalesPromotion>
```

The most important change you have to make is to explicitly set the XML Schema setting at the report level, as shown in figure 6.13. If the Data Schema setting is not specified, the Report Server will autogenerate the XML document global namespace to include the date when the report is processed. This will interfere with referencing the document elements from an XSL transformation, so make sure you explicitly set the schema namespace.

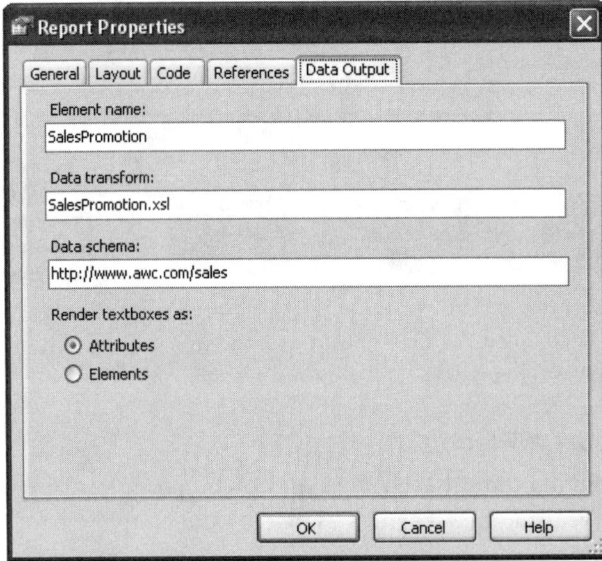

Figure 6.13 Use the Data Output report settings to define the report XML root element name and namespace.

Writing the XSL transformation

Once you have finished making adjustments to the XML schema, the next step will be to write an XSL transformation to transform the XML output to an RSS-compliant format. To fit the Sales Promotion output to the RSS schema, we wrote the simple XSL transformation, as an XSLT file, shown in listing 6.6.

Listing 6.6 Using XSL transformations to fine-tune the report's XML output

```
<?xml version="1.0" encoding="UTF-8"?>
<xsl:stylesheet version="1.0"
```

```
xmlns:n1="http://www.awc.com/sales"
xmlns:xs="http://www.w3.org/2001/XMLSchema">
  <xsl:template match="/">
   <xsl:for-each select="n1:SalesPromotion/n1:Promotions/
     n1:Promotion">
    <item>
     <title><xsl:value-of select="./@Description"/></title>
     <link>http://www.adventure-workds.com/promotions</link>
     <description>Great <xsl:value-of select="./@Description"/>
       Items discounted
       <xsl:value-of select="./@DiscountPct"/> percent! Offer
          expires on
        <xsl:value-of select="./@StartDate"/>
      </description>
     <pubDate><xsl:value-of select="./@StartDate"/></pubDate>
    </item>
   </xsl:for-each>
  </xsl:template>
</xsl:stylesheet>
```

Loops through all promotion elements

Generates an RSS item

The XSL transformation simply loops through all sales promotions and outputs them in XML according to the RSS item specification. Strictly speaking, in our case there is always going to be only one XML sales promotion node, because we use a report parameter to select a single campaign. Finally, we need to add the XSLT file to our project. Similar to working with images, we have to add the XSLT file to the same report project and subsequently upload it to the report catalog when the report is deployed. The Report Server cannot reference external XSLT files.

The last implementation step is to take care of appending the current sales promotion item to the RSS blog file. The easiest way to accomplish this is to manually update the RSS feed XML file on the web server when there is a new promotional campaign. RSS newsreaders could reference this file directly, for example, by going to `www.adventure-works.com/promotions.rss`. Of course, if the requirements call for it, the process could also be fully automated. We see how this could be accomplished in chapter 10, where we implement a table trigger that invokes a custom web service when a new sales promotion record is added to the database.

To subscribe to the RSS feed, AWC customers can configure their favorite RSS readers to point to the blog file. Once they do so, they are notified each time the blog file is updated.

6.4 SUMMARY

In this chapter we learned how to integrate our reports with custom code that we or someone else wrote.

For simple report-specific programming logic, you can use embedded VB .NET code. When the code complexity increases or you prefer to use programming languages other than VB .NET, you can move your code to external assemblies.

For interoperability with different platforms and languages, you can export your reports to XML. You can control precisely the report output by using the Data Output tab coupled with custom XSL transformations.

By now, you should have enough knowledge to be able to author reports with Reporting Services. We'll now move on to one of our favorite features of Reporting Services 2005: the ad hoc reporting tool Report Builder.

CHAPTER 7

Ad hoc reporting with the Report Builder application

Mary in accounting is looking at some of her end-of-month reports and finds something out of the ordinary with a particular transaction type. Because her aggregated report shows very little detail, Mary is unable to resolve the problem with this particular transaction grouping.

Bob works as a sales manager and has access to reports that show his monthly sales activity. He is interested in locating a list of customers who purchased bikes two years ago and also purchased accessories for their bike last year, and who have not made any accessory purchases this year. Unfortunately, Bob does not have a tool that enables him to filter his data in this manner.

Information workers like Mary and Bob may often need information that does not show up in any of their "canned" reports. As developers, it is unlikely that we could design a set of reports to cover every situation and every business need. Information workers often need to make effective and timely decisions based on the business data. A common problem is that the data they need can only be found by mixing and matching multiple reports, or simply that the data cannot be found at all in any available reports. What do information workers do in this case? Where will they get the answers they need? Will they have to wait for this data to be made available through a new report? And, if so, how long before this report is made available?

In our experience in the consulting world, and especially working with Reporting Services, these questions are asked frequently. Historically, the solution to these problems has not been simple, and in fact, has created more problems. One problem is that information workers usually do not have Visual Studio available to them (even if they did, they probably would not feel very comfortable using this tool). A second problem is that while information workers probably understand the business model for their company, they would likely struggle to understand the data model where the data resides.

The real solution is to provide information workers with a simple-to-use tool that hides the complexity of the underlying data source. This tool must also provide them with the ability to create their own reports to explore corporate data whenever they need the information. This is known as *ad hoc* or *self-service* reporting. With ad hoc reporting, Mary can track down that troublesome transaction by requesting, on the fly, a report that shows all account activity for that transaction type that falls within a particular time range. She can also specify that the report show customer information which is tied to this account. Bob can also benefit from ad hoc reporting by creating a report with a simple means of doing advanced filtering. We see this in action in section 7.3.4. This capability is now possible with the Report Builder application that comes with RS 2005.

In this chapter we'll introduce you to the Report Builder, show you how to set it up, how to manage it, and how to create both simple and complex reports in an ad hoc fashion. After reading this chapter, you'll understand the architecture of the Report Builder and know how to expose your SQL Server data to privileged end users who can then build secure, ad hoc reports. You'll also be able to teach and train end users in creating their own reports. You'll be the star of the show when you introduce infinite drill-through reporting, which we cover in section 7.3.3.

7.1 About the Report Builder application

The Report Builder is by far the biggest addition to Reporting Services since its original release in 2004. The Report Builder is an application that runs on the client machine and provides the user interface for creating ad hoc reports. This application is similar in look and feel to the Microsoft Office suite of products. It is meant to be an easy-to-use application for creating reports and is typically used by so-called power business users.

The Report Builder is a "ClickOnce" application. This is a new technology from Microsoft that allows you to manage the application at the server level. ClickOnce technology is a Windows Forms application that is deployed through a website. The application is installed and loaded on the client but it can only be opened by requesting it first from the server. This allows you to manage future releases on the server, and it means that the clients will automatically get the new release when they launch the Report Builder.

In this section, we'll show you the Report Builder UI, describe the process for setting up the Report Builder environment and requesting ad hoc reports, and discuss the tools available for completing this process.

7.1.1 A quick tour of the Report Builder

Later in this chapter you'll see how business users can easily create complex reports without having to build queries in code. The Report Builder is not a replacement for using the Visual Studio design tools; it can create complex *queries* but not complex *reports*. The Report Builder derives its power from being easy for nondevelopers to use. As shown in figure 7.1, the UI lets users build and filter reports in an ad hoc fashion by dragging and dropping data fields (shown on the left) directly onto the report design area (shown on the right).

The Report Builder application provides the UI for designing and viewing reports, saving them to the Report Server, and opening existing Report Builder–created reports.

Throughout this chapter, you'll get a good jump-start on creating ad hoc reports and understanding the Report Builder environment. As the examples demonstrate, Microsoft created the Report Builder with ease of use in mind since they expected *nondevelopers* would be the ones using the application. However, the main focus of this

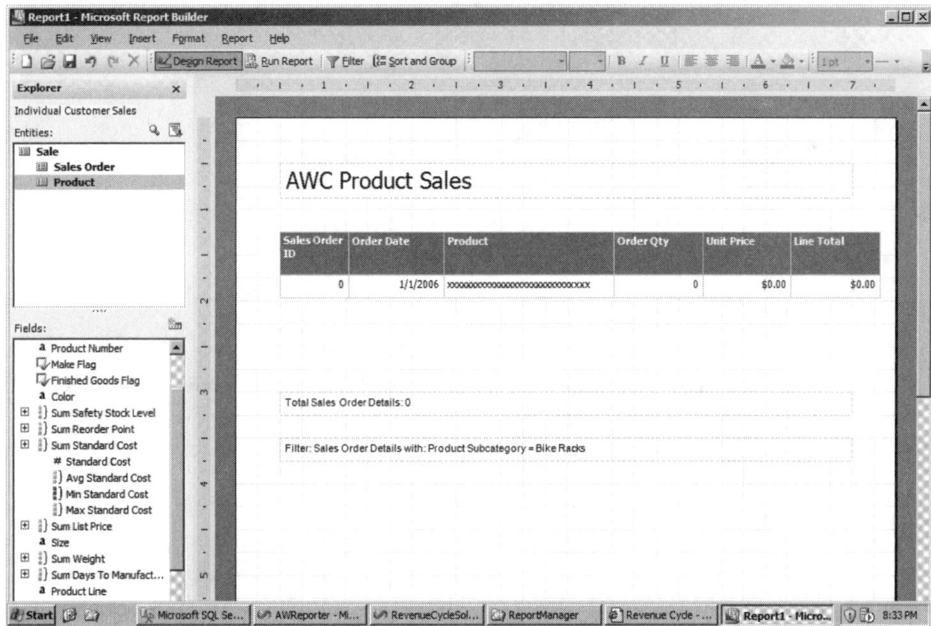

Figure 7.1 The Report Builder application provides a simple environment for creating ad hoc reports.

chapter is not learning to use the Report Builder. We spend more time showing you how to set up and prepare the Reporting Services environment for ad hoc capabilities. While the Report Builder is likely the only tool covered in this chapter that most *business users* will see, the application by itself is not sufficient enough to create ad hoc reports. Developers or database administrators must do the up-front work of establishing the Reporting Services environment before any ad hoc reports can be created.

NOTE The Report Builder is not intended to be used as a new tool for *developers* to create reports as it certainly has its limitations, specifically in the area of creating complex reports.

7.1.2 Setting up for ad hoc reporting

Building simple ad hoc reports against business data without the use of complex report-creation tools is not a new concept. It is, however, new to Reporting Services, and in our opinion it is by far the best addition in this release. In this section, we explore the steps you need to complete before end users can create ad hoc reports using the Report Builder. Table 7.1 summarizes the six-step process for creating ad hoc reports.

Table 7.1 Steps for creating ad hoc reports with Reporting Services

Step	Description	See Section
Developer Steps		
1	Choose a source database for building ad hoc reports.	7.2
2	Build a report model.	7.2
3	Deploy the report model.	7.2.5
End-User Steps		
4	Launch the Report Builder.	7.3.1
5	Use the Report Builder to select the model and build a report.	7.3.2
6	Run or save the report.	7.3.2

The first three steps will be taken by you, the developer, to set up the environment; the last three steps can be repeated and completed as needed by your end users. These high-level steps may seem pretty simple, but as developers we spend quite a bit of time in step 2.

Step 1 Choose a source database for building ad hoc reports. The first thing you need to do is choose a database that you want to expose to your end users for ad hoc reporting. With the current release of Reporting Services, you must choose a SQL Server database or a SQL 2005 Analysis Services database. This is more limiting than what is available for creating and designing reports using the Business Intelligence Development Studio (BIDS).

NOTE Using only SQL Server is a limitation of the report model designer within BIDS. We expect that future releases will support ad hoc reporting against other data sources.

Step 2 Build a report model. The second and most involved step is building a *report model.* A report model is a business description of the underlying data source. The model will abstract the complexities of the database from the end user, thus making it easier for business users to create their own reports. The model describes the source database in terms of entities, attributes, and relationships, and exposes them to the end user within the Report Builder. Report models are typically built by developers who have a good understanding of the source database and are usually built using the BIDS environment. As you see in section 7.2, this is a very detailed process with a number of configurable parts and is the heart and soul of building ad hoc reports.

Step 3 Deploy the report model. Once you have built the model, you need to deploy it to the Report Server. This process is similar to the process we use to deploy reports (see chapter 1). We cover report model deployment in section 7.2.5. As developers, our work is typically completed after this step, though you may play a role in training the end users how to use the Report Builder. In steps 4 through 6, we finally get to see the Report Builder in action.

Step 4 Launch the Report Builder. The most common way to launch the Report Builder application is to navigate to the Report Manager portal (`http://[servername]/reports/`) and click the Report Builder button, shown in figure 7.2. In section 7.3.1 you learn some other options for launching the Report Builder application.

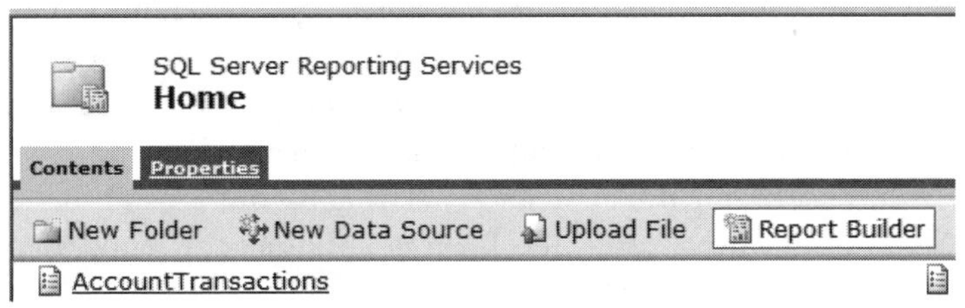

Figure 7.2 You can launch the Report Builder application from the Report Manager.

The Report Builder is the application that our business users will use to create and manage ad hoc reports. As we mentioned in section 7.1.1, the Report Builder is a ClickOnce application, so the installation will occur if needed when they click the button.

Step 5 Select the model and build a report. When you click the Report Builder button, the application opens and presents you with options to choose a report model and type. Once you make your selections and click OK, you see the design window of the Report Builder (see figure 7.1 earlier in this chapter). As you can see, the report model exposes entities and fields on the left that you can drag onto the design surface. You learn all about entities and fields in section 7.2.

Step 6 Run or save the report. Once you've created a report, you can run it, save it, or both. Running the report will render the report inside the Report Builder, and toggling between preview and design is very clean. Saved reports are saved to the Report Server and can be managed in the same way as other non–ad hoc reports that are stored in the Report Server. Reports that are saved to the Report Server can later be opened from the Report Builder application as well.

We went through these six steps pretty quickly and in little detail, but don't worry—we cover many of the details throughout the rest of the chapter. Before you can build your model and construct your first report, you need to understand the tools available to you.

7.1.3 The Developer toolset for ad hoc reporting

To complete the first four steps outlined in the previous section, you have three tool options for setting up the environment and creating and managing report models. In this section, we'll take a look at these tools; all are included with SQL Server 2005:

- Business Intelligence Development Studio (BIDS)
- Report Manager
- SQL Server Management Studio

Business Intelligence Development Studio (BIDS)

BIDS is the design environment that developers use when creating Business Intelligence (BI) applications. This includes such applications as SQL Server Integration Services (SSIS) applications for extracting, transforming, and loading data; SQL Server Analysis Services (SSAS) applications for building data warehouses; Reporting Services applications for complex "canned" reports; and report model applications for building and managing report models. As developers and architects, the BIDS environment is where we spend most of our time and energy setting up our environment for ad hoc reporting. Section 7.2 covers using the BIDS environment to build Report Model projects detail.

Report Manager

As you learned back in chapter 1 (section 1.3.3), the Report Manager is an ASP.NET web portal application that performs two main tasks: report management and requests for reports. You can think of the Report Manager as an application façade that communicates with the Report Server via the Report Server APIs. You learn more about using and interacting with the Report Manager in chapter 8, but for now just understand that you can use this environment to build and deploy report models.

The Report Manager environment is very limited compared with the BIDS environment. With the Report Manager you can create a data model by simply choosing a data source and instructing the Report Manager to build a model from that data source. This technique creates a model based on the data source without offering you any opportunity to tweak and configure that model. In other words, if you use the Report Manager to build a report model, you are stuck with all of the defaults that are created during this process. You can, however, open this model in the BIDS environment and make any changes to it as if you'd created it in the BIDS environment.

SQL Server Management Studio

The SQL Server Management Studio is an integrated environment used both by developers and database administrators for accessing, configuring, managing, administering, and developing all things SQL Server. If you've worked with SQL Server in the past, you're already familiar with the SQL Server Enterprise Manager. The Management Studio replaces the previous versions of the SQL Server Enterprise Manager. In fact, you can use the new Management Studio to manage older versions of SQL Server as well.

To say that the Management Studio is simply the next version of the Enterprise Manager does not do it justice. The new Management Studio allows developers and administrators to manage relational databases (like our AdventureWorks database), SSIS, SSAS, SQL Mobile databases, and Reporting Services.

Similar to the Report Manager, you use the Management Studio to build report models in two steps: 1) select a data source and 2) instruct the tool to create a report model. This builds a very basic model with all configurations set to defaults. To modify these defaults, you need to open the model in the BIDS environment. This tool provides you with an easy way to build and deploy simple report models in a short amount of time.

Building simple models using the Report Manager or the SQL Server Management Studio is pretty straightforward. For more information on this topic, see the SQL Server Books Online documentation. To build models that are more complex (and, therefore, more useful to the end user), you can use the BIDS environment. In fact, let's take a look at how to build report models next.

7.2 BUILDING THE REPORT MODEL USING BIDS

Report models are the heart and soul of ad hoc reporting with RS. In section 7.1.1 you learned about the tools available for building report models. You saw how to build basic report models using the Report Manager and SQL Server Management Studio. You also learned that if you want full control of the creation and maintenance of your report models, you need to use BIDS. In this section, you learn how to take full control of your report models and all the steps involved by using the BIDS environment. Of the six steps that we outlined earlier, the first three belong to the developer, and what better tool to use than BIDS? The first step is simple: choose a database that you want to model. This step also involves understanding how your end users want to use this database, what information they need from it, and planning the model. Since in this chapter we're living in a hypothetical world, we work for AWC and have to model our favorite database, AdventureWorks! Well, step 1 is complete and now comes the fun part: steps 2 and 3. We spend the rest of this section executing these steps. Put your developer hat on and let's get to work.

7.2.1 Building a report model project

To get started building a report model, we need to first create a *report model project*. This is a new Visual Studio BI project type available with SQL Server 2005 and BIDS, the main tools used to build and edit report models. Once created, the report model project environment breaks the report model into three layers:

- Data Sources
- Data Source Views
- Report Models

Throughout the rest of this section we explore these three layers in detail so that you will fully understand how to best configure report models against your unique data sources. To understand the report model project, let's walk through an example.

To begin, start a new project in the VS .NET BIDS environment by selecting the Report Model Project template, as shown in figure 7.3.

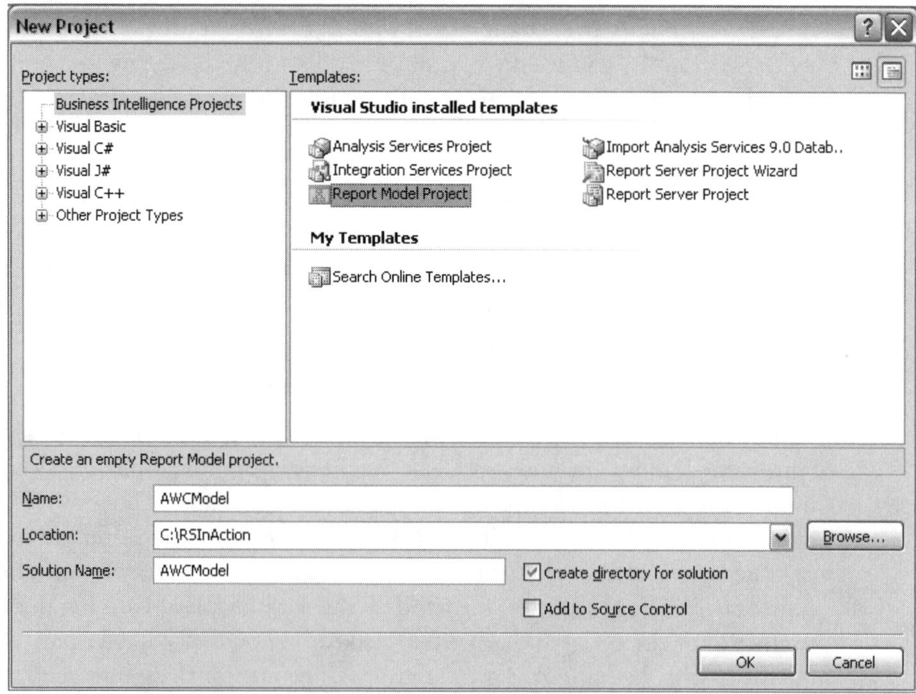

Figure 7.3 Report Model Project is a new template found under the Business Intelligence Projects in Visual Studio.

The source code for this walkthrough can be found in the AWCModel project in the solution available with this book. Once you create the project, you see a folder that represents each of the three main layers of a report model in the Solution Explorer (figure 7.4).

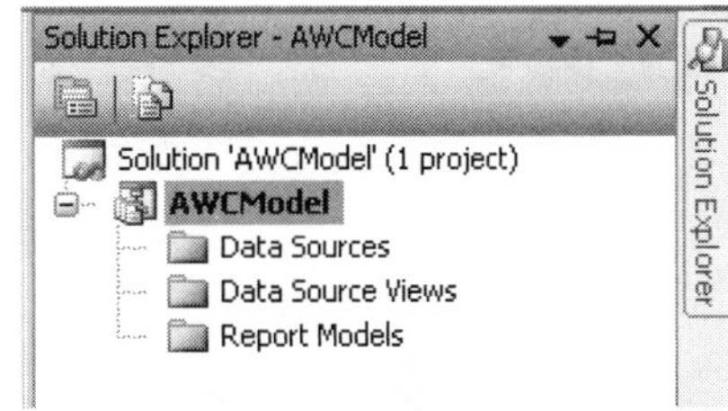

Figure 7.4 The three layers of a report model project are Data Sources, Data Source Views, and Report Models.

In the next sections you gain a better understanding of each of these layers. If you've worked with SSIS or SSAS, then you should see a pattern here. The first two layers of these projects also consist of Data Sources and Data Source Views. This is certainly not a coincidence. In fact, as BI developers, we appreciate the ability to share and reuse these layers among the various project types.

7.2.2 Setting up the data source

The first layer of the report model represents setting up the data source. A report model data source is a file with a `.ds` extension that contains connection information in an XML format. While the file extension and XML schema are unlike the data sources used in RS Report projects, it is exactly the same file and schema used in other BI projects such as SSAS and SSIS. In fact, later in this section we explore how you can use these other data sources in your report model projects. Unlike the data sources in our RS report projects, the report model data sources can only reference SQL Server 2000 and above, or Analysis Services 2005.

Now that you have an understanding of report model data sources, let's get our feet wet and explore the details.

Creating a data source

To create a data source in our project, right-click on the Data Sources folder and select Add New Data Source, or you could select Add New Item from the Project menu (or press Ctrl-Shift-A). This launches the Data Source Wizard. This wizard is shared by SSAS, SSIS, and Report Model Projects. It's a little different from the wizard we used in chapter 3 to create our Report Server data sources, and presents us with some additional options.

The first screen is a splash screen telling us that we've launched a wizard and describes a little bit about the process. The second screen is where we define our database connection for this project.

Define the database connection

At this point, the Data Source Wizard screen displays database connections that we've already created, even connections from the other BI projects (figure 7.5).

In figure 7.5 you can see that there are three options for creating our database connection. You can click the New button to create a connection from scratch, or you can choose one of these options:

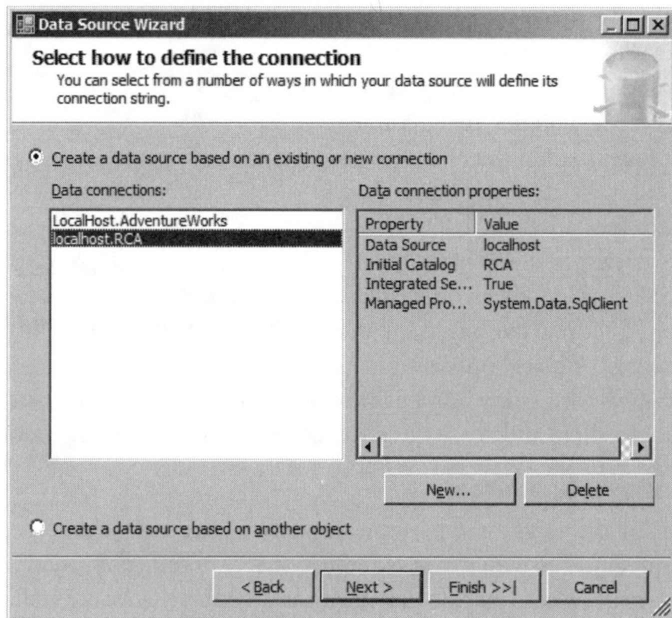

Figure 7.5
Create a data source based on an existing connection, from scratch, or based on another object.

- Create a Data Source Based on an Existing or New Connection
- Create a Data Source Based on Another Object

Let's examine each option.

If you've already created a database connection in an SSAS, SSIS, or report model project and this is the same connection that you want to use for this wizard, then you can leave the Create a Data Source Based on an Existing or New Connection option selected, select the available connection, and click Next. The final screen will show you what you've entered and prompt you to name this data source.

To create a new connection from scratch, simply click the New button. This opens the Connection Manager, shown in figure 7.6.

This window is similar to the Connection Properties window in report projects, with some minor differences. The first and most important difference is the inability to select a non-SqlClient provider. In this version of the Report Builder, you can only build models on SQL Server databases. Although you are limited to SQL Server databases, thankfully you are not forced to use SQL Server 2005.

The second difference is merely cosmetic. The Connection Manager includes an All button. This is the same as the Advanced button in the Connection Properties window in report projects. Clicking the All button exposes all of the properties for the connection. This allows you to modify some of the advanced options, from connection pooling to packet size to timeout values.

The third option is to create a data source based on another object. If you select this option and click Next, you are presented with the two choices shown in figure 7.7.

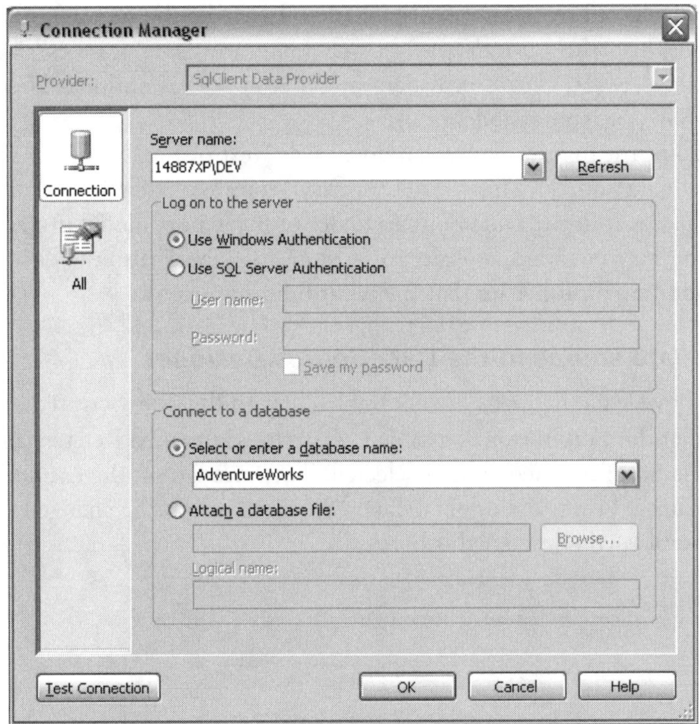

Figure 7.6
The Connection Manager window is similar to the Connection Properties window in report projects.

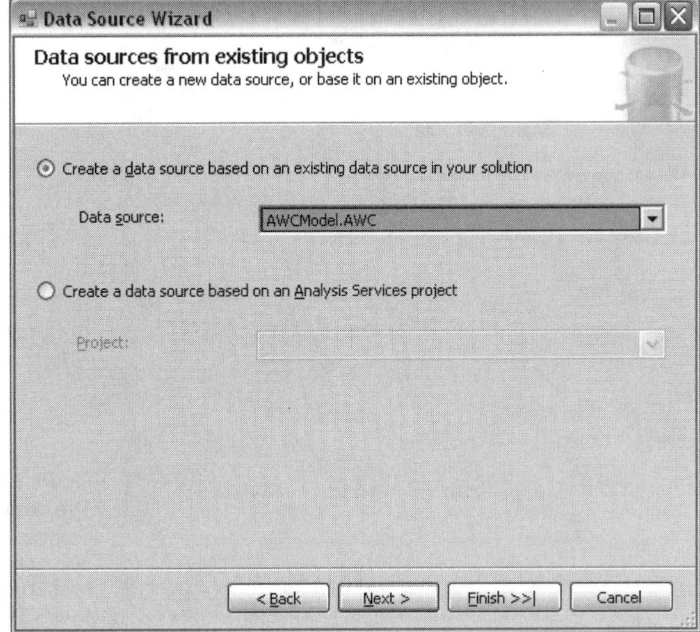

Figure 7.7
You can create data sources based on existing data sources in the current solution or based on an Analysis Services project.

Here we have selected an already existing data source from the current project. If your solution (not just the current project) contains any data sources that use the `System.Data.SqlClient` provider, then they appear as options. These could be from SSAS, SSIS, or report model projects.

At this point the only thing we can do is click Next or Finish and provide a name for this new data source. This creates an exact copy with ties to the original data source and places it in the Data Sources folder of our report model project.

While you may not want an exact copy, you can go back into the data source and edit some additional properties that the wizard did not expose.

View the data source in the Data Source Designer

Figure 7.8 shows what happens if you double-click on the newly created data source.

Notice that the Edit button is disabled when the Maintain a Reference to Another Object in the Solution check box is selected. This means that the connection information is managed from the original data source and cannot be changed for the new data source unless you deselect this box.

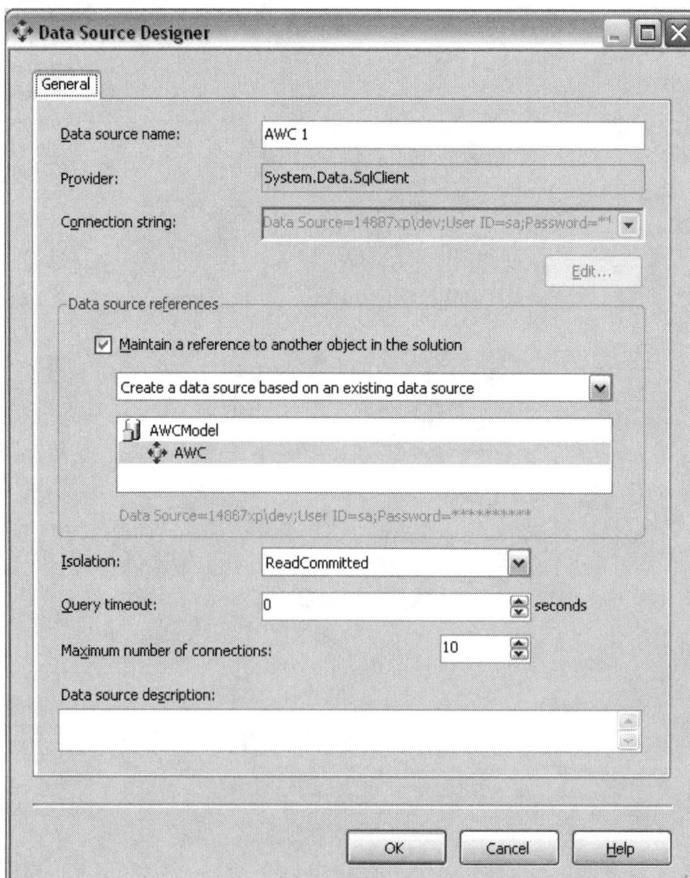

Figure 7.8 The Data Source Designer allows you to manage properties such as Query Timeout and Maximum Number of Connections.

The other interesting options in the Data Source Designer are Isolation, Query Timeout, and Maximum Number of Connections.

- You can change the Isolation setting from ReadCommitted to Snapshot. For more information, see "Working with Snapshot Isolation" in the "Resources" section at the end of this book.
- The Query Timeout setting allows you to manage your resources in the case of a long-running query. The default is 0, which tells the data source not to time out.
- You can also limit the number of connections that use this data source.

Congratulations, you have made it through creating and configuring data sources for report models. For the purpose of this walkthrough, be sure to create a data source that uses the AdventureWorks database. Although this may seem like a lot of work, it really isn't. With an understanding of the Data Sources layer of report models, you are now ready for a new concept: the data source view.

7.2.3 Creating a data source view

The second layer of a report model is called Data Source View, and is a representation of tables and views in the underlying database defined by a data source. The data source view shows the tables not as they are in the database, but more as we would like them to appear. Creating a data source is a prerequisite for creating a data source view.

Let's get started by right-clicking on the Data Source Views folder in our report model project and selecting Add New Data Source View. This fires up the Data Source View Wizard. The first step in this wizard after the splash screen prompts you to select a data source. This screen, shown in figure 7.9, lists the data sources that exist in your current project. In case you were anxious and skipped the previous section, you can create a data source on the fly using the same method that we mentioned earlier by clicking the New Data Source button.

Clicking the Advanced button displays some additional options, as shown in figure 7.10. We discuss these options in the next section, but for this walkthrough be sure that you leave the advanced options in the default state.

Using the advanced options

The advanced options provide you with a couple of settings for managing the way that the wizard will configure your data source view. While in most cases you won't have to change the defaults, you may find yourself in a situation where it's necessary.

The first advanced property is the Restrict to Schema(s) option. One of the many exciting changes to SQL Server 2005 is the separation of user and schema: there is no implicit connection between the database users and the schema. For more information on this change, see "User-Schema Separation" in the "Resources" section at the end of this book. If you want to limit the objects that are retrieved in the next step, you can limit them by schema by entering a comma-delimited list of schemas. The example in figure 7.10 will limit the results to tables and views in the Sales and Production schemas.

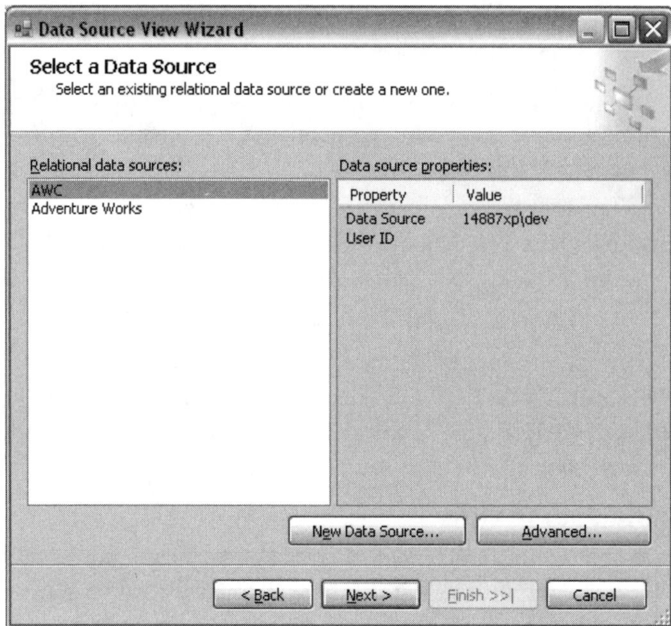

Figure 7.9
You can select an existing data source or create one on the fly on the Select a Data Source page of the wizard.

The other advanced property is the Retrieve Relationships option, which is selected by default. To understand why you would want to use this option, it is important to see how and why the wizard uses relationships in creating the data source view. Relationships are critical in the design of a report model. Without relationships a model would not add much value. As you see later, the relationships drive the functionality and features of creating ad hoc reports in an easy fashion. If the database you are referencing has foreign keys, the wizard uses these keys to manage relationships in the data source view. If you don't have keys set up, you have a couple additional options that allow you to specify the necessary relationships.

Select tables and views

Once you have selected a data source and optionally filled out the advanced options, click the Next button. At this point the wizard retrieves a list of tables and views for the data source that you specified and applies any filters indicated by the Restrict to

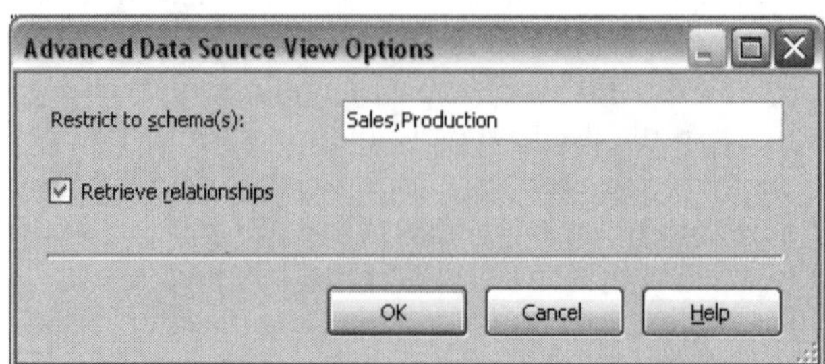

Figure 7.10
You can limit data source view tables by schema in the Advanced Data Source View Options dialog box.

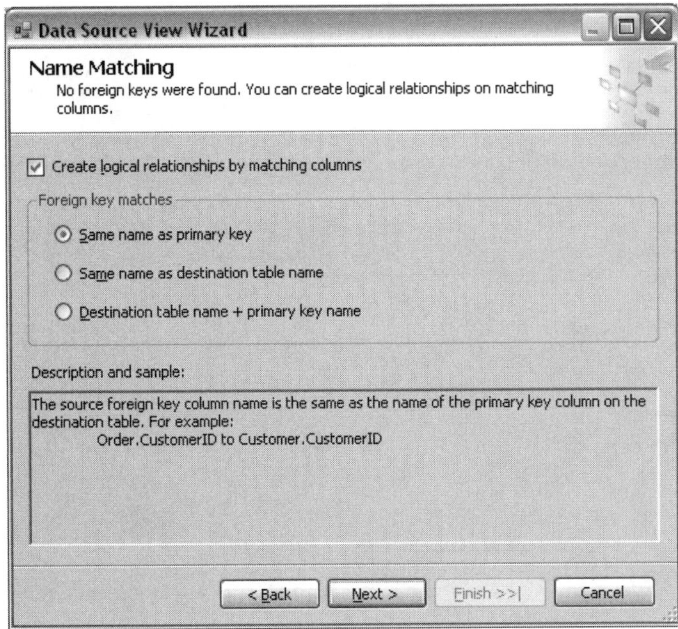

Figure 7.11 This screen allows you to configure the wizard to detect relationships if your tables don't have foreign keys.

Schema(s) advanced option. Second, the wizard looks at the foreign keys for the tables that are returned. If the tables don't have foreign keys, you see the Name Matching page, shown in figure 7.11. This page provides options that instruct the wizard to create relationships based on the names of our database objects.

NOTE The Name Matching screen is only available in the Enterprise Edition of SQL Server 2005. If you are using the Standard or Workgroup Edition, you have to define the relationships outside the wizard.

Since we're using the AdventureWorks database, whose relationships are managed through the use of foreign keys, we don't see this screen. Instead we see a screen displaying all tables and views in the AdventureWorks database. At this step in the wizard we can select the tables and views that we want to use in our report model. If we had limited the schema in the advanced section, the wizard would have used this information to limit the tables and views returned to the Available Objects area.

Find the `Sales.SalesOrderDetail` table and move it to the Included Objects area either by double-clicking on the table name or by selecting the table name and clicking the > button. Do the same for the `Sales.SalesOrderHeader` table. You should see a screen similar to figure 7.12.

Press and hold the Ctrl key and select both of the tables in the Included Objects area. With both tables selected, click the Add Related Tables button. This adds ten tables to this list that have a relationship to the originally selected tables. The relationships are defined either by foreign keys or by logical relationships that were detected from selections in the Name Matching step of the wizard. After you've moved over the tables that

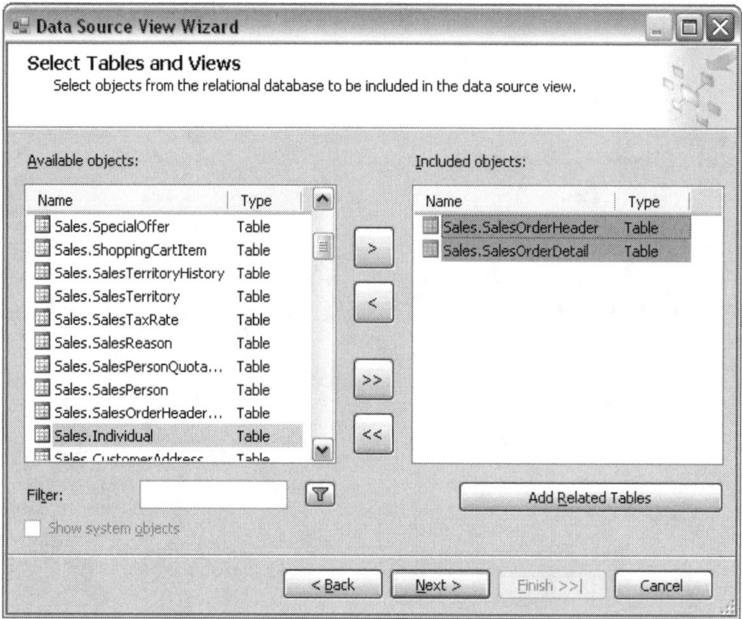

Figure 7.12 The wizard allows you to select the tables that you want to represent in the data source view.

you want to use in your model, click Next. The wizard shows you all the objects you've selected and prompts you for a name. Name this data source view **Sales Order**, and click the Finish button. This is as far as the wizard will take you, but there is a lot more that you can do to modify your data source view from within the designer.

NOTE The Add related Tables button is not enabled when using Views, nor is it enabled when using MSDE as a data source.

After the wizard finishes, double-click on `AWC.dsv` in the Data Source Views, folder to see a diagram listing your tables in the designer. This is the design view of the data source view that we created.

Viewing the data source view diagram

As mentioned earlier, the `.dsv` file is simply an XML file describing the data source view. To view the XML, you can right-click on the `.dsv` file and choose View Code.

If you've completed the previous steps correctly, you should see a diagram representing all of the tables and their relationships. From the data source view diagram, you can modify the tables and views.

The wizard did a pretty good job of adding the tables that we wanted, but after further investigation we realize that we are missing a very important table, the `Production.Product` table. To add this table, follow these steps:

Step 1 Right-click anywhere in the open space of the Data Source View Designer and choose Add/Remove Table. This opens the same screen we saw in the wizard.

Step 2 Choose the `Production.Product` table and the `Production.ProductCategory` table and add it to the list of included objects by clicking the > button.

Step 3 Click OK. This adds the `Product` and `ProductCategory` tables to our data source view.

> **NOTE** This table wasn't added by the wizard because the AdventureWorks database doesn't have a physical key representing the relationship between our starting table, `Sales.SalesOrderDetail`, and the `Production.Product` table. However, this missing relationship will provide a great opportunity for you to learn how to manually add physical keys later.

Let's explore some of the options in the Data Source View Designer. By clicking on tables and columns and viewing the properties window, you can see that they all have an attribute named `FriendlyName`. Modifying this attribute allows the Report Builder to interpret the column and table names so that they are more useful to the end user. Figure 7.13 shows the options available by right-clicking on the `Production.Product` table.

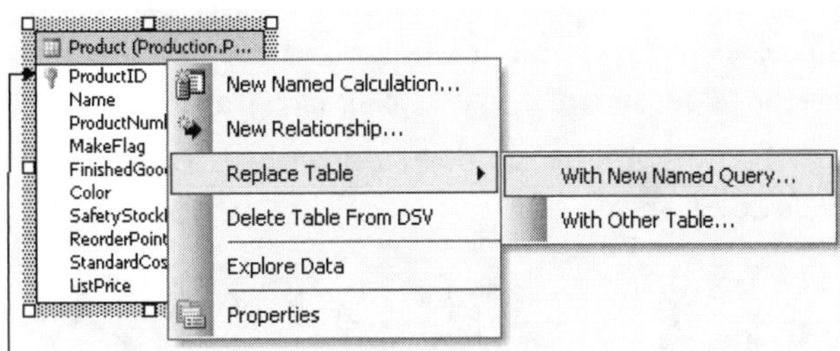

Figure 7.13 You can create named calculations and logical relationships, explore data, and more from the Data Source View Designer.

Named calculations are logical columns added to data source view tables that are built using expressions. Suppose you need to show reports with the profit margin of products. Simply right-click on the header of the `Production.Product` table, select New Named Calculation, and enter the information as shown in figure 7.14. Named calculations show up in the diagram as the last column in the table with a calculator icon to the left of the column name.

During the wizard phase of this walkthrough, we mentioned that the wizard creates your data source view relationships based on physical keys in the database. We also mentioned that in cases where you don't have physical keys, you can create them manually. Let's add a missing relationship from the `Product` table to the `Sales.SalesOrderDetail` table.

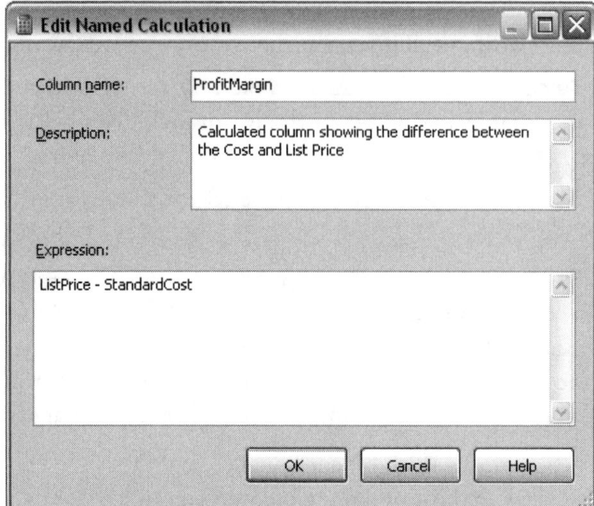

Figure 7.14 Named calculations are added to data source view tables using expressions.

Step 1 Right-click on the `Sales.SalesOrderDetail` table and select New Relationship. This opens the Create Relationship window.

Step 2 Specify the Source and Destination tables for your relationships. The Source table is your foreign key table, or your "many" table in a many-to-one relationship. The Destination table is the table that typically contains the primary key, or the "one" side of a many-to-one relationship.

Step 3 As shown in figure 7.15, select the `ProductID` column from both the `Sales.SalesOrderDetail` and `Product` tables. For those of us who

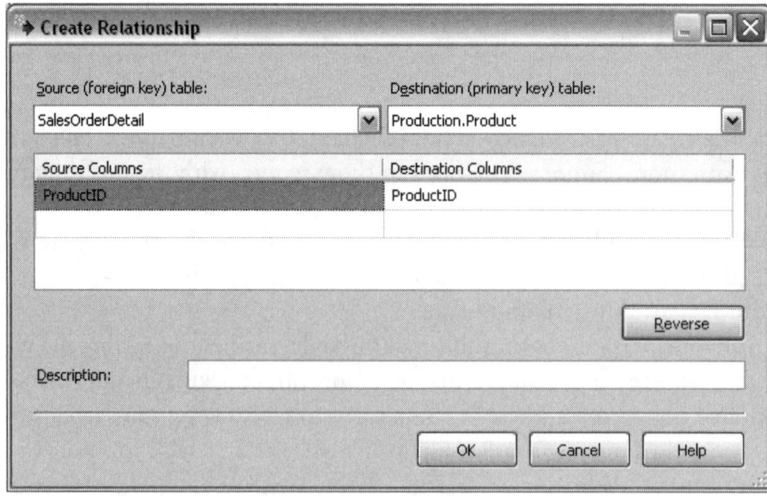

Figure 7.15 The Create Relationship window allows you to create logical relationships without changing physical database objects.

struggle with remembering which table to start with in order to specify the relationship, the Create Relationship window provides a Reverse button that flips the source and destination for you.

The Replace Table option shown in figure 7.13 lets you change the table view to derive from a SQL query instead of directly from a database table. This allows you to join tables or even perform custom calculations within your query. Let's add `ProductName` to our `Sales.SalesOrderHeader` table.

Step 1 Right-click the `Sales.SalesOrderDetail` table, select Replace Table, and then select With New Named Query.

Step 2 Enter the following query in the SQL pane:

```
SELECT     Sales.SalesOrderDetail.SalesOrderID,
           Sales.SalesOrderDetail.SalesOrderDetailID,
           Sales.SalesOrderDetail.CarrierTrackingNumber,
           Sales.SalesOrderDetail.OrderQty,
           Sales.SalesOrderDetail.ProductID,
           Sales.SalesOrderDetail.SpecialOfferID,
           Sales.SalesOrderDetail.UnitPrice,
           Sales.SalesOrderDetail.UnitPriceDiscount,
           Sales.SalesOrderDetail.LineTotal,
           Sales.SalesOrderDetail.rowguid,
           Sales.SalesOrderDetail.ModifiedDate,
           Production.Product.Name AS ProductName
FROM         Sales.SalesOrderDetail INNER JOIN
   Production.Product ON
           Production.Product.ProductID = Sales.SalesOrderDetail.ProductID
```

This query joins the `SalesOrderDetail` with the `Product` table and adds the `ProductName` to the result set. It is important to note that by converting this table to a named query, you lose the ability to add any calculated columns. This should not be a problem because you can simply add any expressions using T-SQL in your query.

Finally, you can explore the data from the data source view diagrams by right-clicking on the table and selecting Explore Data. This allows you to see the data in four views: Standard Table, Pivot Table, Chart, and Pivot Chart.

This section covered a lot of information, and while we probably could have devoted an entire chapter to data source views, this should provide you with enough information to build some pretty complex and detailed views. The knowledge you gained from this section will prepare you for building data source views for Analysis Services as well as Integration Services projects. It is now time to focus on the final layer that we will deploy out to the Report Server.

7.2.4 Building the report model

Report Models is the final and main layer of a report model project. End users (non-developers) don't necessarily understand the relationships between related tables in the underlying database. However, we as developers understand these relationships and can abstract the complexities by building report models.

When you build a model, it derives its information from the data source view. The Report Models layer is also referred to as the *semantic* layer. The Semantic Model Definition Language (SMDL) is the language that defines a report model. When you build a model using any of the tools we discussed in section 7.1.1, you create an XML file with the `.smdl` file extension—the report model. Rather than forcing you to understand and memorize this definition language, the BIDS environment allows you to manipulate the XML in a graphical design environment. The Report Models layer can be broken up into three main components:

- Entities
- Attributes
- Roles

Let's build our first model using the Report Model Wizard and then discuss how you can edit and configure this model using the designer.

The five steps in creating a report model using the wizard are:

1. Start the Report Model Wizard.
2. Choose a data source.
3. Select report model generation rules.
4. Update statistics.
5. Choose a model name and run the wizard.

Similar to creating the data source and data source view, we begin by right-clicking on the Report Models folder and selecting Add New Report Model from the context menu.

The first screen after the splash screen prompts you to choose a data source view. The view we created in the earlier section should show up here. Also notice that there is a New Data Source View button. Clicking this button launches the Data Source Wizard we covered earlier. For this example, choose the AWC data source view that we created and click Next. You should see the Select Report Model Generation Rules screen, shown in figure 7.16. This step allows you to select the rules used in building your report model. The rules are listed and described in figure 7.16. Accept the default values and click Next.

Next you see the Model Statistics screen, which lets you choose whether or not the wizard will update the model statistics. For those of you familiar with database statistics, you may be concerned that this will update them. However, model statistics and database statistics are not the same and the database statistics will not be modified in any way by choosing this option. The wizard uses these statistics to determine the unique count of values for particular attributes, to determine the cardinality of the data structure, and to help generate settings that you see later. Since this is the first time

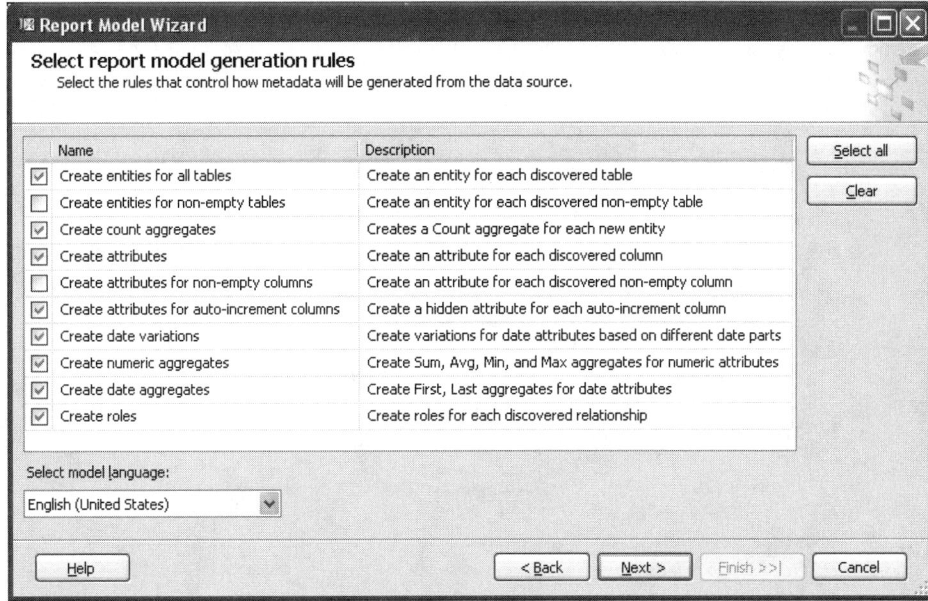

Figure 7.16 Report model generation rules allow you to control the rules that the Report Model Wizard follows when building a report model.

you're seeing this screen, leave the default setting of Update Model Statistics Before Generating checked.

The next step in the wizard prompts you for a model name. Let's call this model AWC. Click on Run to start the Report Model wizard engine. It begins by checking the column uniqueness and width, and then starts processing the rules on the tables and columns in our data source view.

As figure 7.17 shows, the wizard makes two passes in building the model. The first pass creates your entities, attributes, and roles. The second pass takes information collected in the first pass and applies it to the newly created items. This second step applies formatting, modifies properties of your entities and attributes, chooses and creates drop-down lists for attributes, and identifies large groups of data. Figure 7.18 shows what the model looks like in the BIDS environment.

Now that you've built your first model, let's dive in and see what you have.

Entities

The Report Model Wizard automatically creates a set of entities for you based on the data source view that you selected. Entities are logical collections of model items and are most easily matched to the tables in your database. It is important to understand that entities can be derived from one table or many tables in the database. An *entity* is an object that contains attributes or roles that further describe the entity. An example would be a Customer entity, which may contain attributes such as CustomerName or

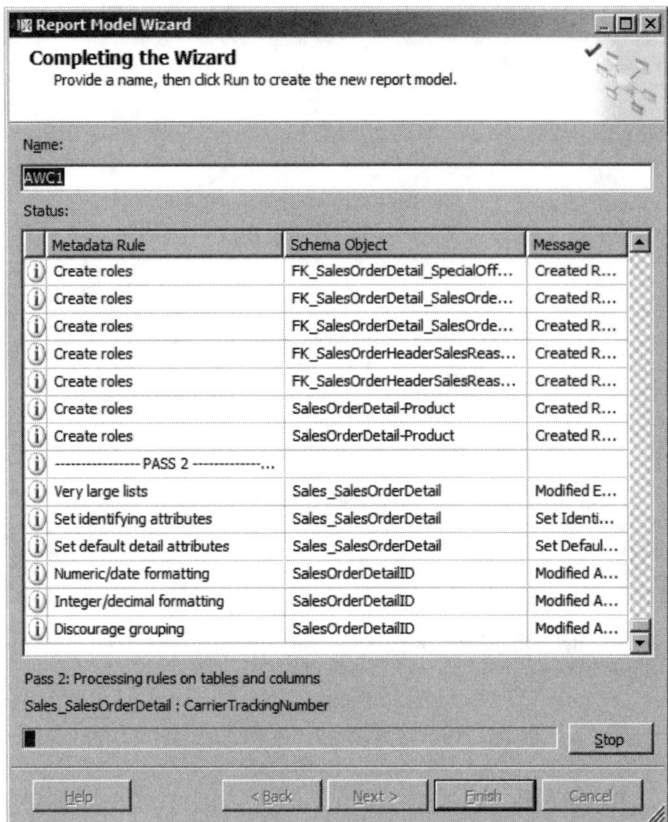

Figure 7.17 The Report Model Wizard makes two passes against our data source view to process rules for the model.

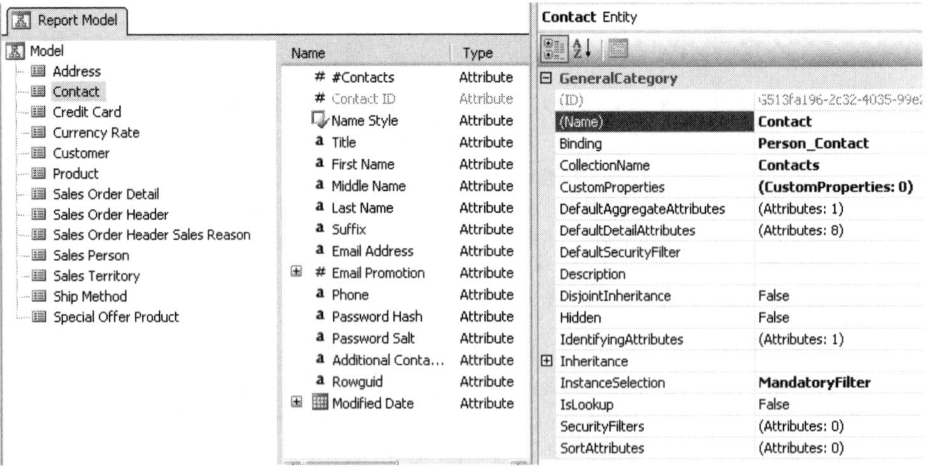

Figure 7.18 Editing the report model in the designer is as simple as modifying properties.

CustomerType. This same entity might also have roles, such as Address or Sales Orders. We discuss roles later, but for now just keep in mind that roles are contained within an entity. Entities will be the starting point for creating ad hoc reports with the Report Builder. Typically an ad hoc report creator will want to see customers, orders, and employees, and then filter the results by attributes of the entities. Although the wizard creates entities and sets the entity properties, we are not limited to keeping the default settings that the wizard creates. In this section you learn about some of the properties that you can modify which affect the entity in the resulting report model. You can find each of these properties by selecting the entity on the left side of the BIDS designer and modifying the properties in the properties window. Figure 7.18 shows the report model in the BIDS environment.

Table 7.2 shows some properties of the Entity object. This is not a comprehensive list, but it does include the most commonly modified properties. For example, you may want to modify the `DefaultDetailAttributes` property to contain a different set of fields. The Report Model Wizard takes a best guess at the fields that you want to have as default attributes. As you learn later on in our examples, you can select and drag an entire entity or simply select and drag attributes of an entity onto the design surface of the Report Builder. If you drag the entire entity, the attributes that will show up on the design surface are those defined in the `DefaultDetailAttributes` property.

Table 7.2 Comment entity properties

Property	Description
`IdentifyingAttributes`	Specifies the attribute(s) that uniquely identify the entity.
`DefaultDetailAttributes`	This is a collection of attributes that will be placed in the Report Builder when the entity is dragged to the design area.
`SortAttributes`	Specifies the attribute(s) by which this entity will be sorted.
`IsLookup`	This property indicates that the Report Builder should treat this entity as a lookup table instead of a full-fledged entity. In some cases you may have an entity that has only one attribute of value to the end users who are building reports. A good example of this is the Product SubCategory entity. If you set the `IsLookup` property of the Product SubCategory entity to true and then set the `IdentifyingAttribuites` property to the name field (this is the subcategory name), this will allow the product subcategory to appear as an attribute of the product entity. This makes it possible for the users to easily select a product subcategory without having to navigate to a related entity in the designer. It is important to note that if you change this value to true, you can only specify one field in the `IdentifyingAttributes` property.
`Hidden`	If you do not want to expose a certain entity in your model, you can set this property to true and it will not be available to your ad hoc report builders.

continued on next page

Table 7.2 Comment entity properties *(continued)*

Property	Description
`InstanceSelection`	This specifies the type of selection control that is used in the Report Builder when the entity is selected in the Report Builder. The Report Model Wizard will set this value based on the number of available options for the entity. Four choices are available for this property. We see examples of how this affects the Report Builder application in section 7.3. The four available options are: **Dropdown**: This value should only be used for small lists. If the number of instances of this entity is more than 25 or so, you may want to use a list instead. **List**: This value is best used when the number of instances is too large for a drop-down and when the list does not require filtering. **FilteredList**: This value should be used when you are working with a large number of instances and you want the users to be able to filter the list in the Report Builder application. **MandatoryFilter**: This property will force users to provide additional filters if they are using this entity in a report. This value is used when the number of instances is very large and is used to keep the end users from creating reports that will return too much data that will take a long time to query.

If you do not want an entity to show up in the model, you can use the `Hidden` property. Now that you've seen what you can do to modify the properties of the `Entity` object, let's dig a little further down the tree and check out your options for modifying the attribute properties.

Attributes

Attributes are simply fields of an entity that you want to expose in your model. These may be directly mapped to database fields or based on expressions or calculated data. If Customer is an entity, then `CustomerName` might be an attribute of that entity. Table 7.3 shows some of the common properties of the `Attribute` object that you may want to modify in creating your report model. Once again, this is not a comprehensive list but simply some of the most commonly modified properties. For a complete list, look in the SQL Server Books Online documentation that comes with SQL Server.

Table 7.3 Comment attribute properties

Property	Description
`Binding`	Specifies which underlying table column this attribute is bound to (not applicable for expression-based attributes).
`Expression`	Specifies the expression for expression-based attributes. SMDL defines various aggregate (SUM, COUNT, etc.), conditional (IF), conversion, date (YEAR, DAY, etc.), logical (AND, OR), mathematical (MOD), and text functions.

continued on next page

Table 7.3 Comment attribute properties *(continued)*

Property	Description
`IsAggregate`	Informs the client application if this attribute can be aggregated. For example, you would typically set this property to false for attributes such as phone numbers or names.
`Hidden`	A hidden attribute is not directly displayed to the end user, but you could use the field in expressions when building your model.
`EnableDrillthrough`	Lets end users see entity details.
`DiscourageGrouping`	This is a Boolean field that if set to true will discourage end users from grouping on this field. You will want to set this to true for fields that are typically unique, such as phone numbers, Social Security numbers, or fields holding dollar values.
`Format`	This uses the .NET format strings to instruct the Report Builder how to format the field. There are additional format strings besides the standard .NET formats that can be used for Booleans and dates. For more information see the "Attribute Object (Report Model)" section in the SQL Server Books Online documentation.
`ValueSelection`	This determines the behavior of the Report Builder for selecting values of this attribute. The possible values are none, list, and dropdown. If none is selected, the user will have to specify a value by typing it; dropdown and list provide a user interface for the users to select values. It is important to note that if the `IsAggregate` property is set to true for this attribute, then the value of this property is ignored.

Just like with the `Entity` object, the `Attribute` object has a `Hidden` property that is used to hide an attribute from the ad hoc report builder. The `DiscourageGrouping` property is used to keep ad hoc report builders from using this field for grouping. Another important property is the `Format` property. The Report Model Wizard examines the data in your database in addition to looking at the data type that you have provided, and defaults this property to a "best guess" as to how you'd like this field to be formatted. If the wizard's best guess doesn't meet your requirements, you can modify this property to properly format the attribute. The properties of the `Attribute` object give you a powerful level of control. Let's now examine the `Roles` object and see how you can modify the default properties when building your report model.

Roles

What are roles and how do they fit into your report models? Roles are objects that describe how one entity is related to another. Roles can define one-to-one, one-to-many, or many-to-many relationships. Roles are how the report model defines the relationships between entities. You could say that a role is the glue that holds the model together. Table 7.4 shows some of the most common properties that you will find yourself working with.

Table 7.4 Common role properties

Property	Description
`Binding`	This is the database object that represents this role.
`Cardinality`	Choices are One, Many, OptionalOne, and OptionalMany.
`ExpandInline`	Indicates that the client application should not show the role to the user and that the fields of the related entity should be displayed instead as if they were part of this entity.
`Hidden`	Similar to the `Hidden` property of the `Entity` or `Attribute` object, this property determines whether this role is visible in the Report Builder.
`HiddenFields`	This property allows you to specify fields that you do not want to be available for this role. This means that by setting fields as hidden through this property, you could allow attributes to be available from the entity level but not available when viewed through a role
`Linguistics`	The `Linguistics` properties of the role contain properties for `SingularName` and `PluralName`. This element is not allowed if `Name` is omitted. In this case, `SingularName` and `PluralName` default to the `Name` and `Collection` of the related entity, respectively.

The `HiddenFields` property is very interesting. It allows you to take attributes that are exposed through an entity and hide them from being exposed through a role. Let's look at an example with our AdventureWorks model. Let's say that you have an Account entity and an AccountTransaction entity. The AccountTransaction would likely be specified as a role to the Account entity. The AccountTransaction entity has an attribute called `TransactionCode`. If you set the `HiddenFields` property to false, then when you are viewing the AccountTransaction as a role (or subentity) of the account, you won't see the `TransactionCode` field. If you were to look at the top-level entity of AccountTransaction, you would see this field.

Now that you've seen the power of modifying properties of the `Entity`, `Attribute`, and `Roles` objects, let's see how you can use folders to help you organize your model.

Using folders to organize entities

You can create folders in your model to better organize your model entities. These folders show up in the Report Builder just as they do here in the BIDS designer. Once you've added a folder to your model, you'll be able to drag entities into the folder. This can be a useful way to put similar entities together for better organization of your model, especially when you have a large number of entities. Adding folders is as simple as right-clicking the root node (Model) in your report model and choosing New > Folder, as shown in figure 7.19.

You see an example of how folders can be used in report models in section 7.3.4. You have now created your first report model and are ready to make it available to your end users.

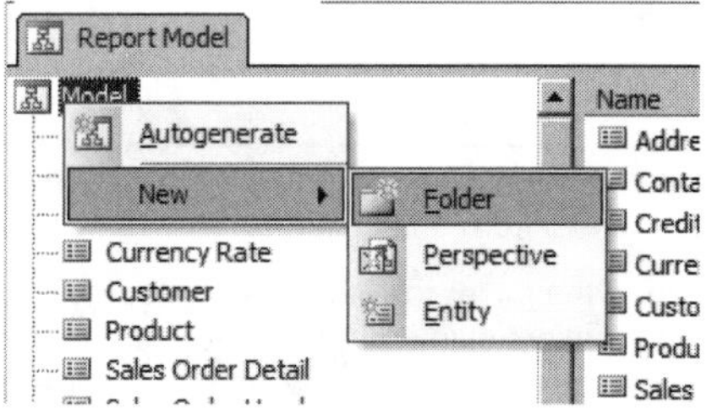

Figure 7.19
You can add folders to help organize your entities in your model.

7.2.5 Deploying report models

Once you've built and configured your models, you need to deploy them to the Report Server so that the Report Builder can use it. This is as simple as deploying your Report Server reports. The first step in deploying report models is ensuring that the project properties are configured properly. Figure 7.20 shows the properties window for our report model project.

To understand the options, refer to table 7.5. Once you've configured your report model project properties, deploy the model by simply right-clicking on the model and choosing Deploy. If you make changes to your model, you need to deploy the model before end users can see these changes.

If you make changes to your data source view and you need these changes to be reflected to your model, you have to autogenerate your model by selecting Autogenerate

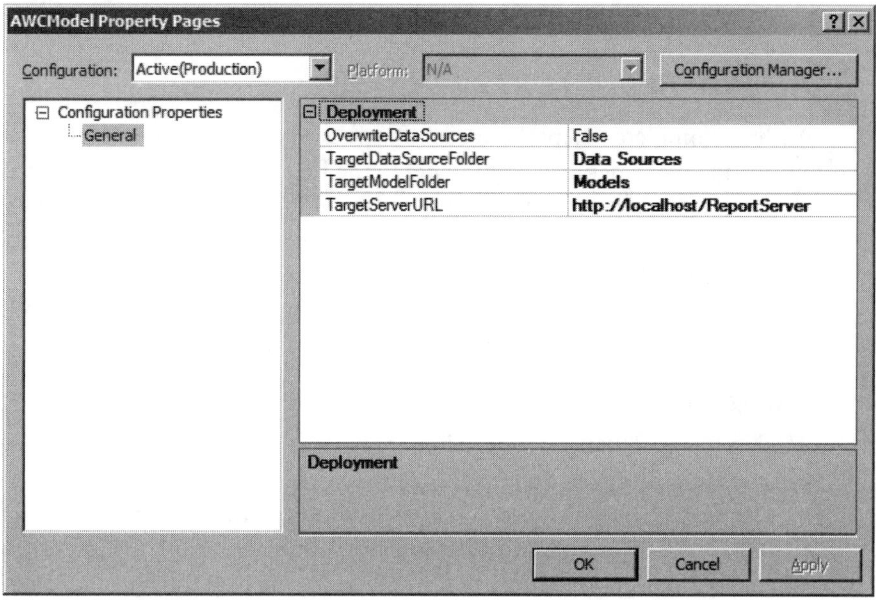

Figure 7.20 The report model properties allow you to set up the Report Server and folder to which the model will be deployed.

Table 7.5 Deployment properties for the report model project

Property	Description
`OverwriteDataSources`	If this is true, the data source will be overwritten every time you deploy a report model from this project.
`TargetDataSourceFolder`	This is the path to the folder to which the data sources will be deployed for this project starting from the root of the Report Manager. If you enter a folder that does not currently exist, when you deploy the process will create the folder for you.
`TargetModelFolder`	This is the path to the folder to which the models will be deployed for this project starting from the root of the Report Manager. If you enter a folder that does not currently exist, when you deploy the process will create the folder for you.
`TargetServerURL`	This is the URL to the Report Server that you want to deploy to. By default this path is `http://[servername]/reportserver`. In the case of a nondefault instance of SQL Server, the path is `http://[servername]$[instance]/reportserver`. An example of a nondefault instance is `http://DEVSERVER$SQL1/reportserver`.

from the Reporting Model menu in the BIDS report model project. Doing this overwrites your existing model, so you should be careful.

As you can see, deployment of report models is pretty straightforward. Now that you've completed the first three steps for setting up the Report Builder, it is now time to see how you can use this new model.

7.3 AD HOC REPORTING IN ACTION

We have completed steps 1 through 3. We have our database selected, we've built a model, and we've deployed our model to the Report Server. We have now done everything needed to allow business users to start building reports. We can now take off our database developer hat and put on a different *developer* hat: the ad hoc report builder hat—which looks a lot like the one on the cover of this book.

Prepare yourself! In this section we walk through the entire process of creating an ad hoc report from the business user's perspective.

7.3.1 Launching the Report Builder

We first looked at launching the Report Builder in section 7.1.2; in this section, you also see some advanced options for launching this application.

The first thing you need to do is navigate to the Report Manager (`http://[servername]/reports`). If you have permission to use the Report Builder, you should see the Report Builder button on the home page. (If this button is not showing up, see section 7.4 to enable the Report Builder.) Clicking this button launches the Report Builder application. The Report Builder is different from most client applications your end users will be used to. When you click the Report Builder button

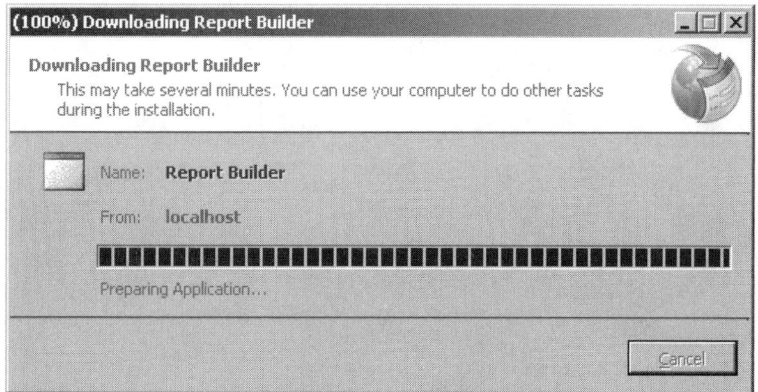

Figure 7.21 As long as the client has the .NET Framework 2.0 installed, the Report Builder will automatically install onto their computer.

for the first time, it prompts you to install the Report Builder. Figure 7.21 shows the installation dialog box.

The next time you click the button, the system will check your version and if it is the same as the version on the Report Server, then the application will simply open. If the server has been updated, the system will install this new version and then run it.

Once the Report Builder is launched, you should see a screen similar to the one shown in figure 7.22. Here you can see a list of the report models that have been deployed to the Report Server.

You have now seen how simple it is to launch the Report Builder from the Report Manager. This is not the only way to launch this application. Alternatively, you can launch the Report Builder by navigating to the following URL:

```
http://<localhost>/reportserver/reportbuilder/reportbuilder.application
```

Any application that can communicate with your Report Server can provide a link or button that points to this URL. Let's examine the Report Builder application as it appears when it is first launched.

As shown in figure 7.21, when the Report Builder opens you see the Getting Started pane to the right of some empty gray space. This pane provides a user interface for opening saved reports and creating new ones.

The New section displays a list of all of reports from the Report Server models that you have access to. The Report Layout section allows you to choose one of three report types: Table, Matrix, or Chart. You should recognize these from chapter 4.

For now, select the AWC report model, then choose Table (columnar) as the Report Type, and click OK. You're now ready to create your first table report.

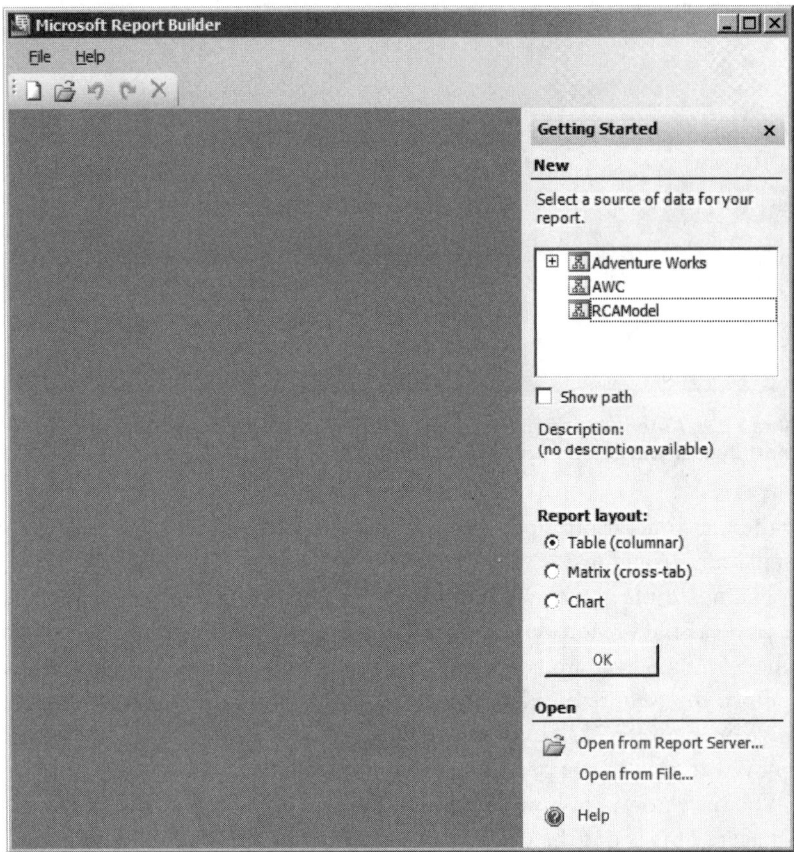

Figure 7.22 The starting screen for the Report Builder allows you to choose your report model and type of report.

7.3.2 Creating the Product Profit Margin report

Once you choose your model, select a report type, and click OK, the Report Builder opens in design mode. You can make the following selections:

- Click in the title bar and name this report **Product Profit Margin**.
- Select the Product entity from the Entities list box (on the left side of the designer). This selection populates the Fields list box with Product-related fields.
- Drag and drop these fields onto the designer, as shown in figure 7.23: Name, Product Number, Finished Goods Flag, and Total Profit Margin.

Once you've added fields from an entity, the Entities list box will only show entities that are related to the one in use on the design surface. This keeps users from creating reports that don't work by only allowing related fields to be added to the design surface.

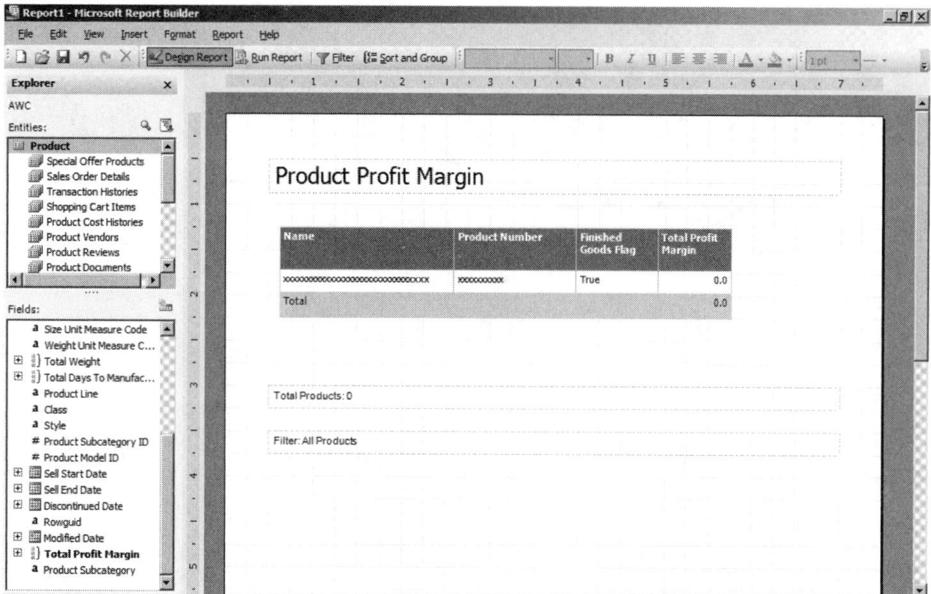

Figure 7.23 The Report Builder designer allows us to drag entities and fields onto the design surface.

You have now created your first ad hoc report. You can run this report by clicking the Run Report button. This creates a report with about 12 pages listing products and their profit margin.

Modifying the report

Let's make the following modifications to our report:

- The Profit Margin field does not make sense for products that are not finished goods. So let's filter this report to show only finished goods.
- If we are limiting this to only finished goods, then the Finished Goods Flag field is not necessary on this report. This provides us an opportunity to learn how to remove fields and filter reports.
- Finally, we want to format the Profit Margin field as currency.

If you are still viewing the report after running it, click the Design Report button to return to the design mode. To remove the Finished Goods Flag field, right-click on the field and select Delete. To format the Profit Margin field, select both the detail and total cells for the field by holding the shift key while selecting both cells, right-click the selected cells, and click Format. Select the currency format, as shown in figure 7.24. The default options for formats vary based on the type of field selected.

To add a filter to your report, simply click the Filter button in the BIDS designer. This opens the Filter Data window. Just like the main design window, the

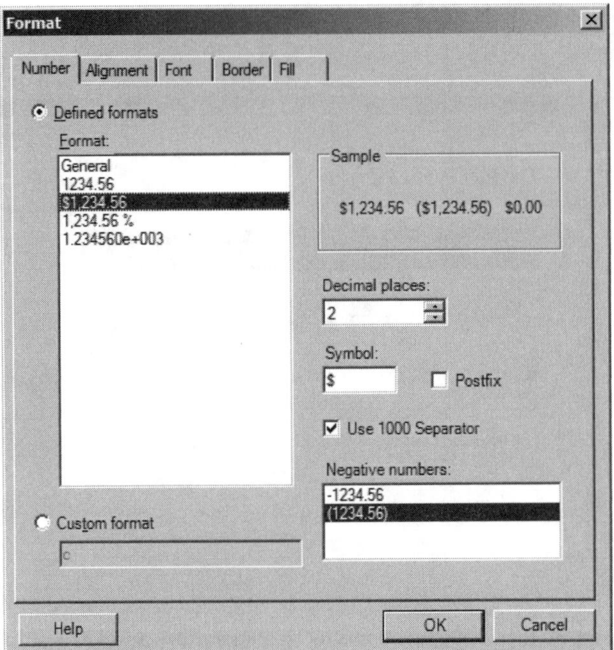

Figure 7.24
You can format fields in the Report Builder by right-clicking on the cells and choosing Format.

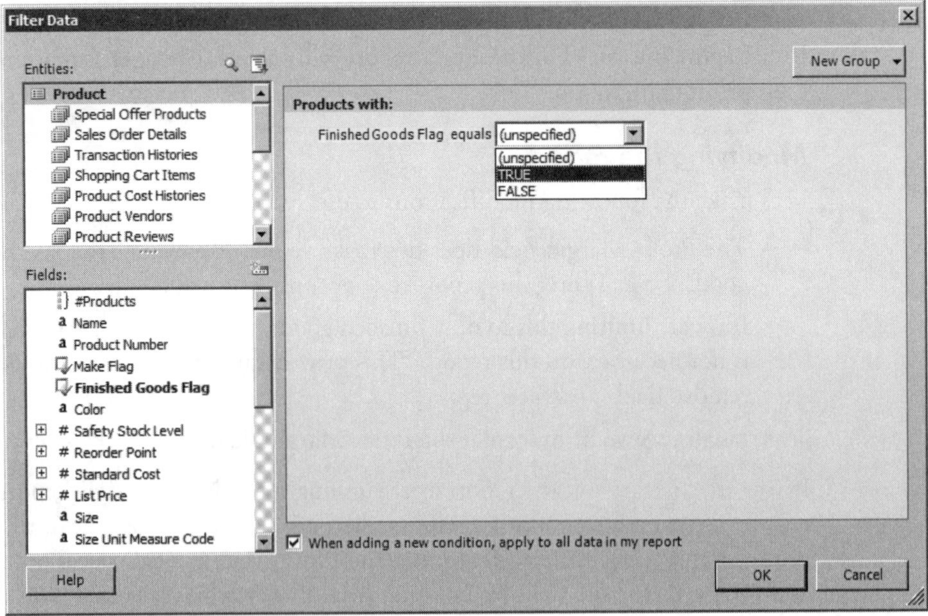

Figure 7.25 The report model provides the filter box with a list of possible values to filter by.

Filter Data window shows the entities and fields on the left and allows you to drag and drop fields to the right side. With the Product entity selected, drag the Finished Goods Flag field from the Fields list box onto the filter area at the right. Figure 7.25 shows that our model is smart enough to know what the possible options are for filtering.

By clicking on the field in the filter area, you see three options: Edit as Formula, Prompt, and Remove Condition. Edit as Formula allows you to make more advanced calculations for formatting when the available options are not enough. The Prompt option lets you to select this filter item as a prompt field. That way, this field becomes a parameter in the resulting report. The Remove Condition option lets you delete filters that you don't want. Filters default to the Equals comparison. If you click on the Equals entry, you're presented with a list of options. Since Finished Goods Flag is a Boolean field, we only see Not or Equals. Figure 7.26 shows the options that are available for numeric and string fields.

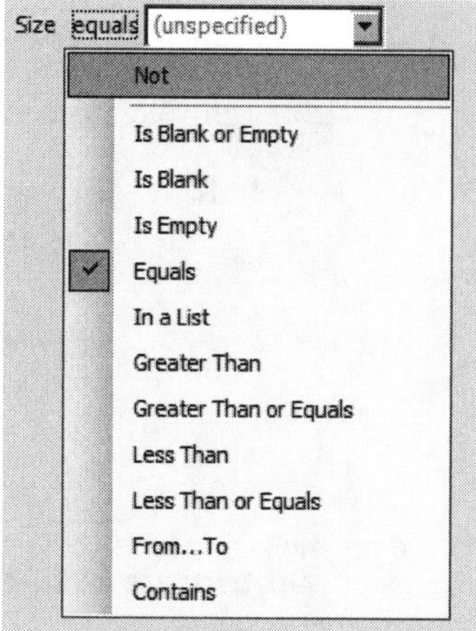

Figure 7.26 There are a number of options for filtering data in the Report Builder

Select TRUE from the drop-down list and click OK. You now have a report showing only the finished goods. If you run the report, you should see that the number of pages went from 12 to 7.

7.3.3 Getting more with infinite drill-through reporting

With infinite drill-through reporting, the report you create in the Report Builder is simply a starting point for further inquiry. Reports authored with the Report Builder automatically provide end users with infinite drill-through functionality.

Infinite drill-through reporting is the ability to start with the results of a report and continue to "drill through" to a new layer of the data. This can be done continuously until there are no other logical paths to follow. These paths are directly linked to the roles (relationships) in the data model. In many situations, the data model will create a circular path of information; thus the term *infinite drill-through*.

But what does this mean exactly?

Suppose we create a report, using the Report Builder, that shows all of the sales from a particular region, and that also shows the order number. If the model is set up correctly, when we run this report we can click on the order number and it will load up a new report showing the details of that order. If those details include a product, we can then click on the product and see the details of that product. If the product details report shows us a product category, this category can link us to a list of all products in that category; this report can then take us to another report. You get the idea. Imagine the power your business users will feel when they spend 5 minutes creating a report that gives them access to this type of drill-through.

Notice that earlier we warned you that this will work *only* if the model is set up correctly; that is, the model must understand the relationships between entities. As you learned in section 7.2, relationship management operates through roles. A model isn't of much value without roles, so as long as you relate your entities to one another through roles, you won't need to do anything else to enable infinite drill-through.

NOTE Be warned that infinite drill-through is only available with the Enterprise version of SQL Server 2005. After receiving a free copy of SQL Server Standard Edition at the Chicago SQL Launch, it didn't take long for me to install it and start building report models. Imagine my surprise when I created my first Report Builder report and the infinite drill-through didn't work. I looked for ways to make it work by exploring my model project. Finally, I remembered that I was using the Standard Edition.

Temporary drill-through reports

Temporary drill-through reports are automatic with the Enterprise edition of SQL Server. When a user creates a report by using the Report Builder, the infinite drill-through features are built in. These reports are called *temporary* reports because they are automatically created by the Report Server when they are requested and aren't saved like traditional reports.

When a user clicks on a data item, the Report Server determines the entity that belongs to the item that was clicked on and creates a report on the fly. The server uses the report model information to build these reports based on one of two templates:

- *Single Instance Data*—For a single instance of an entity such as information on a customer
- *Multi Instance Data*—For a list of entity items such as a list of products in a particular category

These templates are very basic and therefore the reports will not be particularly nice looking. Because the templates can't be modified, you are stuck with the layout and color of these temporary reports. This might seem like a real downer, especially if you create a nice-looking report in the Report Builder and then the drill-through reports don't match this look and feel. But what if you could create your own detailed reports, complete with your own branding look and feel, and then assign them to particular entities in your model? Well, you can—with static drill-through reports.

Static drill-through reports

Static drill-through reports are simply predefined, published reports that you can map to specific parts of a report model. You must create static drill-through reports in the Report Builder and save them to the Report Server. Once you've done this, you can go into SQL Server Management Studio and assign the reports to specific parts of your model. These reports will replace the temporary drill-through reports. For more information on assigning published Report Builder reports to specific entities, search for "How to Map a Predefined Report in a Report Model" in the SQL Server Books Online documentation.

Keep in mind that access to these static drill-through reports is managed through the role security. If you map a static drill-through report to a particular entity and the user who selects this entity does not have access to your report, they will see a temporary drill-through report instead.

7.3.4 Advanced filtering with the Report Builder

Remember Bob from the introduction of this chapter? Bob is a sales manager who is interested in creating an ad hoc report that shows a list of names and emails addresses for his customers who

- Purchased bikes two years ago
- Purchased accessories for their bike last year
- Have not purchased any accessories this year

For this example, let's use the completed Adventure Works report model (included with the source code for this book) and use 2004 as the current year. Be sure to open and deploy this project before starting the Report Builder. Once the project has been deployed, launch the Report Builder from the Report Manager. When the Report Builder opens, select the Adventure Works report model, choose the Table (Columnar) option, and click the Open button.

Let's start by placing on the design surface the data fields that we want displayed on the report. Select the Customer entity on the left. This ensures that the Customer Attributes appear in the Fields section at the bottom left of the Report Builder. Move the Customer Name and Email Address fields onto the report. Notice that the fields in use by the report are shown in bold in the Fields selection list.

Once you have the fields on the main design surface, click the Filter button. This displays the Filter Data window. Table 7.6 lists the steps for specifying our advanced filter.

Once you've completed the steps in table 7.6, your screen should look similar to figure 7.27. The current report will now show Bob all customers who purchased bikes in 2002 and accessories in 2003. This is close to meeting his requirements—but not quite.

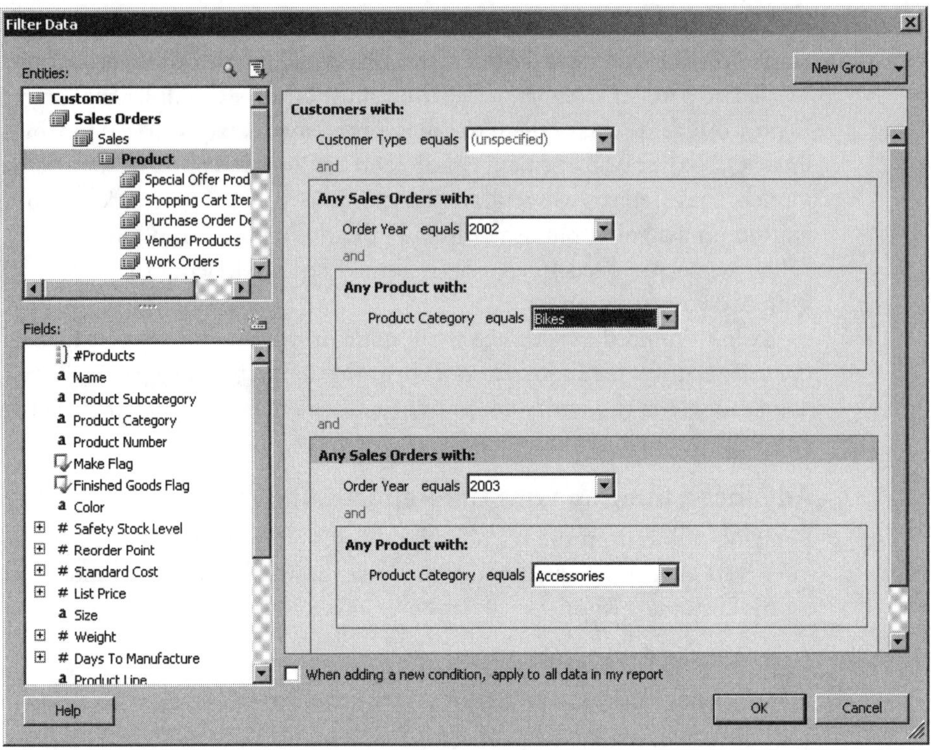

Figure 7.27 Advanced filtering can be very simple.

Table 7.6 Advanced filter steps

Step	Advanced filter setting	Details
1	Deselect the When Adding A New Condition, Apply To All Data In My Report check box.	In our previous example, the product profit margin report, we kept the When Adding A New Condition, Apply To All Data In My Report checkbox selected. For this example be sure that this check box is not selected. This allows us to create distinct grouping within our filter.
2	Filter by Customer Type.	With the Customer entity selected, drag Customer Type from the Fields section onto the filter design surface. Choose I from the drop-down list. In the AdventureWorks database two customer types are defined: Individual (I) and Store (S).
3	Filter by Order State/ Province.	Select the Sales Order entity and then the Bill To Address entity. From the Fields list drag the State Province field under the Customer Type filter. Bob's territory is the state of Washington, so choose Washington from the drop-down list.

continued on next page

Table 7.6 Advanced filter steps *(continued)*

Step	Advanced filter setting	Details
4	Create the Order Year 2002 grouping.	With the Sales Order entity selected, expand the Order Date attribute and drag the # Order Year field onto the surface. Notice that the Report Builder put an "and" separator and adds our new selection in its own filter grouping called Any Sales Order With. The filter grouping functionality was enabled during the first step when we deselected the check box at the bottom of the Filter Data window. Choose 2002 from the # Order Year field drop-down list.
5	Add Product Category to the Order Year 2002 grouping.	Choose the Sales entity and then the Product entity. From the Fields list drag the Product Category into the new grouping that we created. To add this field to the 2002 Order Year grouping, you need to drop the field inside the 2002 grouping box. Choose Bikes for this field.
6	Create the Order Year 2003 grouping.	Create another grouping by selecting the Sales Order entity and drag the # Order Year just like we did earlier and choose 2003 as the Order Year. Be sure to place this field under our 2002 grouping and not inside it. Also similar to our previous step, choose the Product Category and place it in the 2003 grouping box, and then select Accessories from the drop-down list.

Bob wants to see all of his customers who purchased bikes in 2002, accessories in 2003, and nothing in 2004. To complete this, we must create a new grouping for the Order Year 2004 and alter the default way it filters. So there are two more steps, as table 7.7 shows.

Table 7.7 The steps continued...

Step	Advanced filter setting	Details
7	Create the Order Year 2004 grouping.	In the Filter Data window, select the # Order Year from the Sales Order entity as we did twice previously and create a new grouping box. Select 2004 for this # Order Year.
8	Alter the group's default filtering.	Now, when you click on the header that currently says Any Sales Orders With, you will see that you have other options. Choose No Sales Orders With from the drop-down list. This will fulfill our requirements.

You've just seen how easy it is to create complex filtering when creating ad hoc reports in the Report Builder. While knowing how to create filters for ad hoc reports is important, understanding the security model around these reports and around the Report Builder is equally necessary. In the next section, we turn our focus toward Report Builder security.

7.4 IMPLEMENTING REPORT BUILDER SECURITY

The security for the Report Builder can be done in a variety of ways at different levels in the architecture. In this section, you'll get a strong understanding of how to set up security for the Report Builder application. We cover the various ways that you can implement security when using the Report Builder application.

7.4.1 Securing the Report Builder with roles

To use the Report Builder, you need the following:

- *A system role assignment with the task Execute Report Definitions*—When you install Reporting Services there will be two system roles: System User and System Administrator, and, by default, these role assignments have this task selected.
- *Item-level role assignments for the report model itself*—A new role, Report Builder, will provide viewing and navigation permissions on report models. This permission may be inherited from a parent folder.

Roles for accessing and using the Report Builder

Let's start with the first layer of securing the Report Builder: access to the application itself. As you learned in step 4 of section 7.1.1, there are only two ways to launch the Report Builder: through the Report Manager or through a URL path. If your user or group is not assigned to a system role with the task Execute Report Definitions, then you will not see the Report Builder button in the Report Manager.

A good way to check for this assignment is to create a Windows user on your machine and place him in a group that is not specified in the System User or System Administrator roles. If you log in as this user and navigate to the Report Manager, you should not see the Report Builder button.

To add a user or group to one of the system roles, open the SQL Management Studio and connect to your Report Server.

> **NOTE** For more information on how to connect to your Report Server using the SQL Server Management Studio, see chapter 8.

From the main node for your server, right-click and select Properties, as shown in figure 7.28.

In the Properties window select the Permissions page, which lets you add users or groups and select the system role that you want to place them in. This can be a very important step. We have run into many situations where clients have set up Reporting Services but can't figure out how to get the Report Builder button to show up. We hope reading this will save you some precious time.

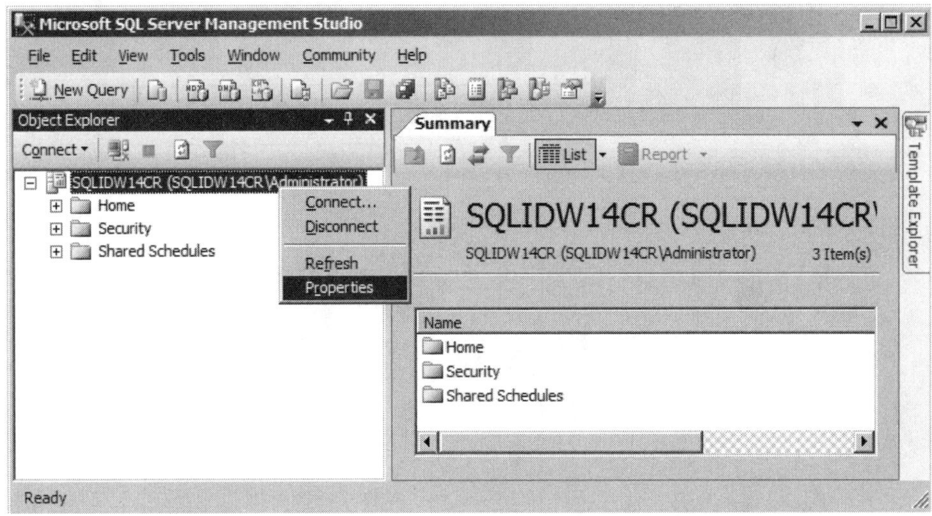

Figure 7.28 You can manage the system roles from the SQL Server Management Studio.

Roles for accessing and using report models

You can also manage security for the models you've created by assigning item-level roles. The Report Builder role provided out of the box in Reporting Services offers permissions that let users view and work with models. The Publisher role allows users to upload both reports and models to a Report Server. This is done with the Publisher-specified tasks Manage Reports and Manage Models.

We cover roles and tasks more thoroughly in chapter 9. You can specify permission for models at the folder level in the Report Manager or at the model level itself. After you've read chapter 9 you'll realize that this is similar to managing permissions for reports and data sources. Although this level of security is nice, it is interesting to see that you can get more granular with your permissions by securing items in a model.

7.4.2 Securing report model items

Securing items in a model allows you to control the access to specific parts of your model. You need to use the SQL Server Management Studio to get to this level of security. When you open the SQL Server Management Studio you will be prompted for connection information by the *Connect to Server* window. In order to connect to the Report Server be sure to select "Reporting Services" from the *Server type* drop-down. To do this, navigate to the models in Management Studio and right-click on the name of the AWC model in the Models folder. In the Model Properties window, select the Model Item Security page, as shown in figure 7.29.

By selecting the Secure Individual Model Items Independently For This Model check box, you can take control of the permissions at the item level. After checking this box, you need to add a group or user at the root node (AWC in figure 7.29). If a

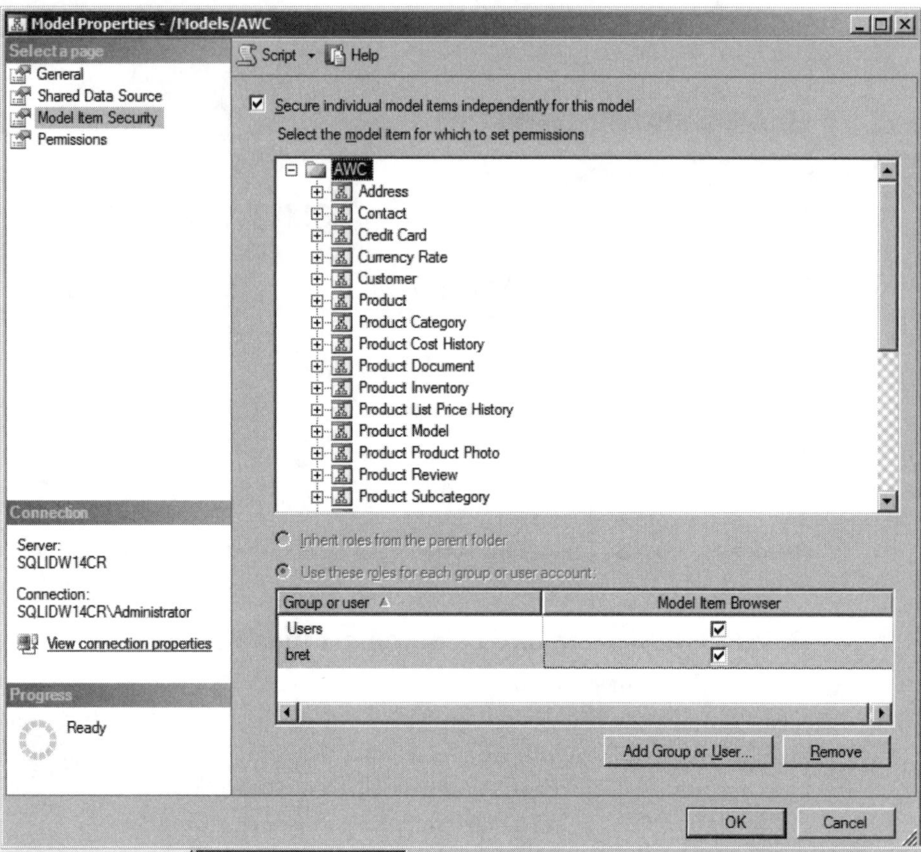

Figure 7.29 The SQL Server Management Studio allows you to manage permissions on entities and fields in your model.

user does not have permission to a particular entity, role, or field, they won't even see this item when creating reports in the Report Builder. The items in the model support inheritance, so if you set permission at the model level these permissions will be defaulted for everything below. With model item security, the Report Server modifies the query that is sent to the data source to exclude any part of the model that is off limits to the user.

Disabling the Report Builder

If you do not want users to be able to download the Report Builder application, you can do this on the server by modifying the system property EnableReportDesignClientDownload. Setting this property to false disables all Report Builder downloads for the Report Server. To set this property, compile and run the following code in a VB .NET application.

Listing 7.1 Setting the EnableReportDesignClientDownload property of the Reporting Service

```
Imports System
Imports System.Web.Services.Protocols
Class Sample
   Public Shared Sub Main()
Dim rs As New ReportingService()
      rs.Credentials = System.Net.CredentialCache.DefaultCredentials
        Dim props(0) As [Property]    <-❶
        Dim setProp As New [Property]
        setProp.Name = " EnableReportDesignClientDownload"    <-❷
        setProp.Value = "False"
        props(0) = setProp
        Try
            rs.SetSystemProperties(props)
        Catch ex As System.Web.Services.Protocols.SoapException
            Console.Write(ex.Detail.InnerXml)
        Catch e as Exception
            Console.Write(e.Message)
        End Try
    End Sub 'Main
End Class 'Sample
```

This code instantiates a ReportingService object so that you can configure its properties through the object model. Next, you set the credentials to the default credentials. You then instantiate a `Property Collection` (`props`) object and a `Property` object (`setProp`) ❶. The method `SetSystemProperties()` expects one parameter that is a collection of `Property` objects, and so you set the `Name` and `Value` of your `setProp` object to `EnableReportDesignClientDownload` and `False`, respectively ❷. Next, you add this `Property` object to the `props` object. Now that you've prepared the objects, you can call the `SetSystemProperties()` method of your `ReportingService` object.

The Report Builder application provides a means of getting to data that was previously not available. Although you can manage a list of users who can download the Report Builder application, some companies may want to ensure that *nobody* can download and run it. If this is the case, you may want to run the code in listing 7.1 to secure the ability to download the Report Builder application.

7.5 SUMMARY

We hope you got a lot out of this chapter. We covered the full spectrum of the Report Builder application, from the developer's role to that of the information worker. We started with an overview of the Report Builder application and discussed the six steps to creating ad hoc reports. These steps covered the roles of both the developer who sets up the environment as well as the end user who creates and works with ad hoc reports. We also covered the tools available for creating and managing report models. Remember that without report models, there is no ad hoc reporting.

The heart and soul of ad hoc reporting is the report model, and we spent the majority of this chapter examining this model. You learned that in order to create a report model, you must first understand the data source and data source views. Once these are set up, you can run the Report Model Wizard to create a report model. This process would be powerful enough if it simply stopped here, but as you learned, after the wizard is finished, you have a number of options for modifying the report model to work as you want. The report model consists of entities, attributes, and roles, each with its own set of properties that you can modify. As a developer, your main goal is to create a report model that will enable your end user to easily create ad hoc reports while still providing as much flexibility as possible to query the data using this model. We also looked at ways that you can organize your entities to make it easier for end users to use your report models.

To help you grasp the full life cycle of ad hoc reporting, we covered the steps needed to set that up (report models), and showed you how to create some simple and advanced ad hoc reports.

You learned that the security model for report models is very flexible and can be managed from a variety of tools. Access to the Report Builder application is managed through role-based security. You learned how to enable or disable the ability for users to access the Report Builder and how you can maintain security for the data once the Report Builder is launched. You saw that by using the SQL Server Management Studio you can manage permissions at the field level. This allows you to control who sees what data in your report models. If used properly, this can be a powerful way to manage the security of the data behind your models.

We could write an entire book on ad hoc reporting with SQL Reporting Services. This chapter covered most, but certainly not all, of the functionality available with the Report Builder. We encourage you to take the knowledge that you gained from reading this chapter and use it to kick-start a deeper focus on report modeling and ad hoc reporting.

PART 2

Managing reports

Once your report is ready, you will need to make it available to your end users. A common requirement posed to enterprisewide reporting frameworks such as Reporting Services is to facilitate report access and management by keeping all report configuration in a single place. To respond to this need, RS captures reports and their related items in a centralized report catalog.

In part 2 we put on our report manager's hat to find out what techniques are available for carrying out the second phase of the report lifecycle—report management. Most of our time is spent discussing how we can leverage the Report Manager web application to perform various management tasks, such as uploading reports, organizing reports in folders, configuring and working with server-side settings, configuring report caching, and so forth.

As a versatile reporting platform, RS provides ways to address various management needs. We explore other management options supported by RS, such as the RS Web service, WMI provider, RS Scripting Host, and specialized utilities.

An important task that every report manager needs to master is securing the report catalog. We look at how the RS role-based security mechanism works and how it can be configured to enforce restricted access to the report catalog. Finally, you learn the way to configure RS code access security to grant the minimum number of permissions that reports with custom code need to execute successfully.

CHAPTER 8

Managing the Reporting Services environment

Reporting Services provides all the tools you need to support the full lifecycle of a report. In a typical enterprise environment, there are usually three groups of people who get involved with each of the three phases of a report's lifecycle:

- Report authors focus on authoring reports using the Report Designer, or business users author reports using the Report Builder.
- Administrators are concerned with managing the report repository.
- Developers report-enable their applications to allow users to request reports on demand or via subscriptions.

In this chapter, we put on our administrators' hats and discuss how we can manage the report environment. As you'll see, Reporting Services provides not one, but several maintenance options for performing various administration tasks. We discuss each option as follows:

- The Report Manager
- The RS Web service
- The Reporting Services WMI Provider
- SQL Server Management Studio
- The Scripting Host
- Other administration utilities

Let's start our tour by looking at how report administrators can leverage the Report Manager web portal to manage the report catalog.

8.1 MANAGING RS WITH THE REPORT MANAGER

As a report administrator, your responsibilities typically include performing various day-to-day tasks to maintain the report catalog. For example, you may want to grant rights to certain users or Windows groups to run a given report.

To reduce the management effort, Reporting Services includes a user-friendly web-based tool called the Report Manager.

The Report Manager serves the following main tasks:

- *Report delivery*—End users can use the Report Manager to request reports on demand or subscribe to reports for delivery.
- *Report management*—You can use the Report Manager to manage all aspects of the report catalog.
- *Report Builder*—As you learned in chapter 7, the Report Manager can be a central place where users launch the Report Builder (the ad hoc report-building client).

In this section we show you how to manage Reporting Services with the Report Manager. First we explore what makes the Report Manager work and learn how to install and configure it. We then spend some time focusing on the settings of the Report Manager. This is where you learn how to manage the My Reports feature as well as jobs and schedules. Once you understand those settings, we look at managing folders and uploading resources. We also describe how to manage linked reports from within the Report Manager.

As you can see, we cover quite a bit in this section, so grab your favorite caffeinated beverage and let's get started with a 10,000-foot view of its architecture.

8.1.1 How the Report Manager works

From an implementation perspective, the Report Manager is simply a web-based front end to the Report Server, as shown in figure 8.1.

From an application standpoint, the Report Manager is implemented as an ASP.NET application, consisting of maintenance pages, styles, images, and other web resources.

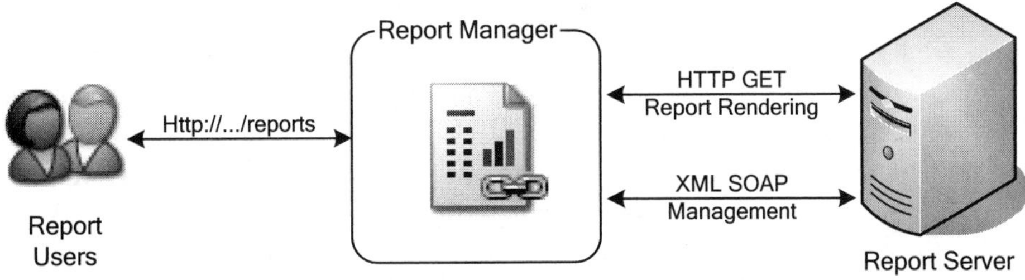

Figure 8.1 The Report Manager is implemented as an ASP.NET application that accesses the Report Server via HTTP-GET and XML SOAP. HTTP-GET requests are used to render reports; XML SOAP requests are used for all other report-management tasks.

In this section we explore how to:

- Configure the Report Manager
- Access the Report Manager
- Use the Report Manager for delivery

Configuring the Report Manager

When you installed Reporting Services the Report Manager was set up for you. The Report Manager's default installation settings are listed in table 8.1.

Table 8.1 The Report Manager's default installation settings

Setting	Value
Virtual Directory	Reports
Physical Folder	`C:\Program Files\Microsoft SQL Server\MSSQL.3\Reporting Services\ReportManager`
URL	`http://<reportserver>/reports`

The Reporting Services Setup program doesn't allow you install the Report Manager separately from the Report Server, which forces you to have both components installed on the same box. This is because deploying the Report Manager on a separate computer requires that you use Kerberos as an authentication protocol so that the user credentials are properly delegated between the Report Manager and the Report Server.

NOTE The Kerberos protocol originated at MIT more than a decade ago. The Windows implementation of Kerberos allows an application to flow an authenticated identity across multiple physical tiers of the application. For more information about how to configure Kerberos, refer to section 8.7.

If enabling Kerberos is not a problem, moving the Report Manager to a separate machine is not difficult. Thanks to the Xcopy ASP.NET deployment, this is as easy as creating a new IIS virtual root and copying all Report Manager files to it. Once you have done this, you should verify that the `ReportServerUrl` setting in the `RSWebApplication` configuration file points to the correct Report Server URL.

The ASP.NET and Report Manager–specific configuration settings are defined in the `web.config` and `RSWebApplication.config` configuration files, respectively. Some of the configuration settings worth mentioning are listed in table 8.2.

Table 8.2 The Report Manager configuration settings

Setting	File	Description
`DefaultTraceSwitch`	`web.config`	Defines the level of tracing information output.
`ReportServerUrl`	`RSWebApplication.config`	Specifies the URL address of the Report Server.
`MaxActiveReqForOneUser`	`RSWebApplication.config`	Limits the number of open HTTP requests by user. Useful for preventing denial-of-service attacks.

The Report Manager uses ASP.NET sessions to maintain folder view preferences, such as showing or hiding folder details. For this reason, you cannot disable the Report Manager ASP.NET session state.

The Report Manager is configured to use Windows-based authentication to authenticate users. We explore Windows-based authentication in detail in chapter 9. In addition, the Report Manager is configured by default to impersonate the user, as you can see by examining the `<identity>` element in the `web.config` configuration file. As a result, all requests to the Report Web Server for both report rendering and management go out under the identity of the Windows user.

Accessing the Report Manager web portal

To access the Report Manager portal, enter its URL address in a browser, which by default is `http://<servername>/reports`, where `<servername>` is the name of the computer where the Report Manager is installed.

> **NOTE** If you installed SQL Server as a named instance, the URL address will need to contain the instance name. The format of the URL for named instances is `http://<servername>/reports$<instance name>`. So if your server name is `devserver` and the SQL instance is `Dev`, then your Report Manager would be accessed by going to `http://devserver/reports$Dev`.

Figure 8.2 shows the Contents tab of Report Manager Home page. Your Contents tab may differ from the one shown in the figure, depending on what custom folders you have created below the Home folder and whether the My Reports feature has been enabled (see section 8.1.2).

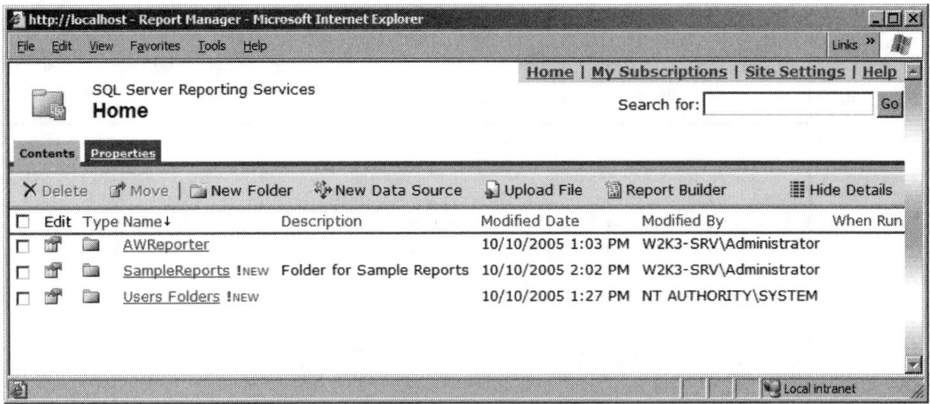

Figure 8.2 The Report Manager portal is used for rendering reports and managing the report catalog.

Users familiar with Microsoft SharePoint will find the Report Manager look and feel similar. The UI interface is very intuitive, so we won't spend much time discussing each individual page. Instead, let's focus on a few topics that warrant more explanation. If you need more information about working with the Report Manager, consult the Reporting Services documentation.

Using the Report Manager for report delivery

The Report Manager can be used as a quick-and-easy report-delivery tool. Organizations that cannot afford or don't need customized reporting applications will appreciate this option.

To render a report using the Report Manager, navigate through the folder structure and click the Report link. Behind the scenes, report rendering is accomplished through client-side URL (HTTP-GET) requests to the Report Server. To accomplish all tasks other than report rendering, the Report Manager calls the RS Web service on the server side using XML SOAP requests. We look into both URL and SOAP requests in more detail in chapter 10.

Now that we've covered the basics of the Report Manager portal, let's explore the Site Settings menu.

8.1.2 Managing Report Server settings

The Site Settings menu of the Report Manager allows you to manage some important Report Server settings and tasks, including role-based security, shared schedules, execution logging, and report history. The Site Settings page is shown in figure 8.3.

The changes that you make on the Site Settings page are saved in the `ConfigurationInfo` table in the Report Configuration Database. Some of the settings are self-explanatory. For example, the Report Execution timeout setting limits the report-execution time to the specified number of seconds.

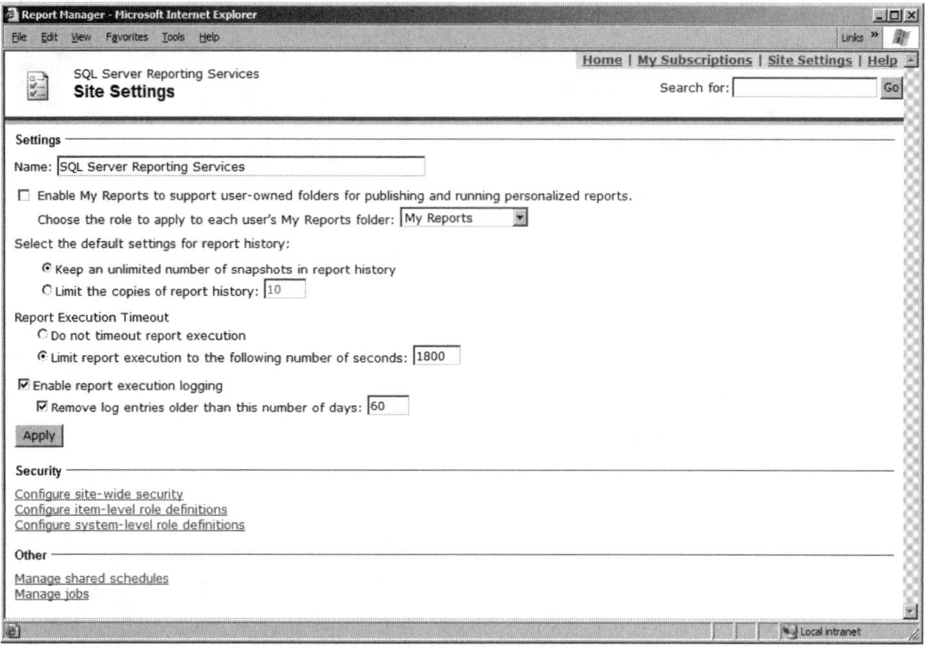

Figure 8.3 Use the Site Settings page to manage server-side settings, to enable the My Reports feature, and to manage shared schedules, jobs, and so on.

We explain how to manage the My Reports, schedule, and job features here, but we postpone discussing role-based security to chapter 9. If you need more information about the system settings, check the "Report Server System Properties" section in the product documentation.

Enabling My Reports

An interesting Reporting Services feature is My Reports. My Reports provides a personal, private workspace for each user. In a typical enterprise environment, you may restrict public access to report folders but grant users restricted rights to upload, manage, and view their own reports in the "sandboxed" My Reports area.

To enable the My Reports feature (it is disabled by default), select the Enable My Reports to Support User-Owned Folders for Publishing and Running Personalized Reports check box.

You can specify which security role will be mapped to My Reports to further restrict the allowable tasks that users can perform. The choices are the Browser, Content Manager, My Reports, Publisher, and Report Builder roles. We postpone discussing these roles to chapter 9. For the time being, note that the default role (My Reports) grants the users rights to create and manage reports, folders, and resources in their private workspace.

When My Reports is enabled, two things happen. First, the Report Manager creates a catalog folder called Users Folders. This folder contains a personal folder for each Windows user. Next, a My Reports link is added to the home page of the Report Manager. To activate My Reports, a report user must click this link, which in turn creates a private catalog folder for this user.

After the personal folder is created, clicking My Reports on the home page navigates the user to her personal folder.

Managing schedules

Using the Report Manager, you can schedule certain report activities to run in an unattended mode once or on a recurring basis. For example, you may need to distribute a report on a regular basis to subscribed users. To accomplish this, you can create a shared schedule to trigger the subscription event.

You can schedule the following activities:

- *Delivering reports through subscriptions ("pushed" reports)*—We look at subscribed report delivery in chapter 12.
- *Generating report snapshots*—We explain what report snapshots are in section 8.1.4.
- *Adding report snapshots to the report history*—We discuss report snapshot history in section 8.1.4.
- *Expiring a cached report copy*—Caching is also explained in section 8.1.4.

Similar to working with data sources, which we covered in chapter 3, you can create two types of schedules:

- *Report-specific schedules*—A report-specific schedule is associated with a single report. You can create a report-specific schedule from the report's Execution property page.
- *Shared schedules*—As its name suggests, a shared report schedule can be shared by reports and subscriptions that need to occur at the same time. Once the shared schedule is created, you can select its name from a drop-down list during the process of scheduling the activity, as we explain in section 8.1.4.

We encourage you to use shared schedules whenever possible because of the following advantages they offer:

- *Centralized maintenance*—Let's say the employees of the Sales department have subscribed to some monthly summary reports to be e-mailed to them on the first day of each month. To simplify report maintenance, you decide to use a shared schedule to initiate the subscribed delivery. If the users later change their mind and request the reports to be delivered on the last day of the month, you need only update the shared schedule.

- *Security*—Similar to a shared data source, a shared schedule is a securable item and can be managed by users who have rights to execute the Manage Shared Schedules task. You learn all about securing items and assigning tasks later in chapter 9.

You create or manage shared schedules using the Manage Shared Schedules link under the Other section of the Site Settings page. This brings you to the Schedule page, as shown in figure 8.4. The SQL Server Agent service must be running to make changes to a schedule.

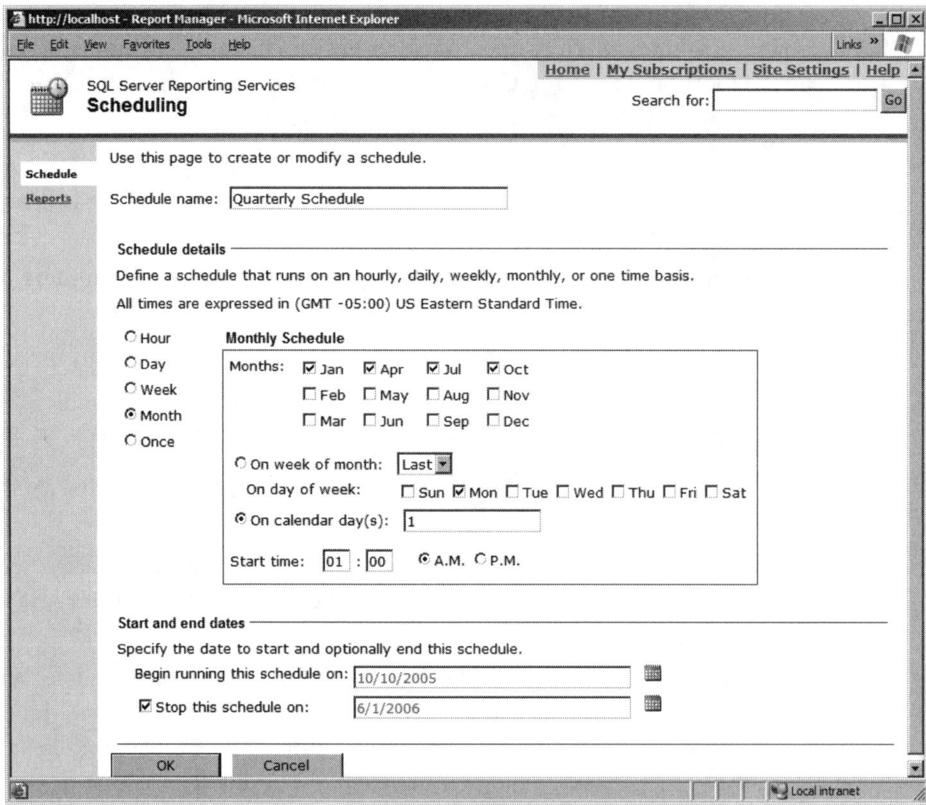

Figure 8.4 Use the Schedule page to specify the shared schedule settings.

In figure 8.4, we have created a schedule that runs on a quarterly basis. Notice that we also have the option to manage the start and end dates for this schedule. To see all reports that depend on the shared schedule, click the Reports link.

NOTE The Start and End Dates section forces you to use the asp.net calendar date picker in order to select dates by disabling the textbox that holds these dates. While this is nice for enforcing valid dates into the textboxes, it is very annoying when you want to choose a date that is more than one year in the future. For example, if you want to select a date that is 18 months in the future, you need to click the *Go to the next month* link 18 times.

The RS Windows service, `ReportingServicesService.exe` (not to be confused with the RS Web service) works with the SQL Server Agent to coordinate the running of scheduled tasks. This is what happens behind the scenes: when a schedule is created, the Report Server creates a SQL Server Agent job and schedules it to run when the event is due. When the time is up, the SQL Server Agent creates a record in the Event table in the Report Server database.

The RS Windows service periodically polls this table for new events. The polling interval can be controlled by the `PollingInterval` setting in the `RSReportServer.config` configuration file. The default value is 10 seconds. In case there is a new event, the Windows service queries the report catalog to get a list of the scheduled tasks that are up. Then, it calls down to the Report Server (directly, not via the web façades) to execute the tasks. Finally, if the schedule is recurring, the Windows service creates a new SQL Server Agent job and schedules it to run according to the specified schedule interval.

As a developer, you can programmatically log an event in the Report Server database by invoking the `FireEvent` SOAP API. This could be useful if you want to disregard the schedule and initiate the execution of a certain task explicitly. For example, as a report administrator, you may have set up the product catalog report to be e-mailed automatically to Internet customers on a monthly basis. However, you may also need to send the report immediately when a new product is entered into the sales database. To meet this objective, you can use a table trigger attached to the Product table to invoke `FireEvent` when a new record is added to this table. We see an example of how this scenario could be implemented in chapter 12.

Managing jobs

Sometimes, you may need to examine the current task activity of the Report Server. For example, users may complain that reports are taking a long time to execute and you need to find out how many report requests are pending.

To see the list of all running jobs, click the Manage Jobs link in the Other section of the Site Settings page. For example, figure 8.5 shows that we are currently executing the Sales By Territory Interactive report.

The Report Server supports two types of running jobs: user jobs and system jobs. A user job is any job that is explicitly initiated by a user, such as all actions that the user can initiate through the Report Manager. These include requesting a report, viewing the report history, subscribing to a report, and so on. A system job is a job running in unattended mode and initiated by the Report Server. System jobs include scheduled snapshots and data-driven subscriptions.

The list of running jobs is retrieved from the `RunningJobs` table in the Report Server database. When the Report Server initiates a new user or system job, it creates

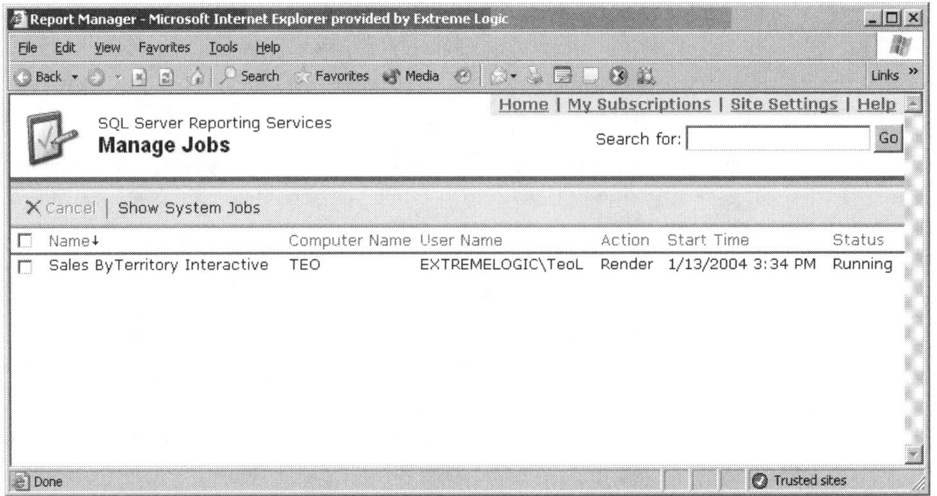

Figure 8.5 Use the Manage Jobs page to see a list of all running user and system jobs.

a record in this table. The RS Windows service periodically scans this table at an interval specified under the `RunningRequestsDbCycle` setting in the `RSReportServer.config` configuration file.

You can attempt to cancel a running job by selecting the job and clicking the Cancel button. This in turns invokes the `CancelJob` web method of the RS Web service, which attempts to terminate the background thread servicing the report request. Canceling a job doesn't guarantee that the job will be immediately terminated. Sometimes, hung jobs may require you to manually restart the Report Server. Because the Report Server's lifetime is controlled by IIS, to restart it you will need to restart IIS.

We've taken a quick look at how to manage a few Report Server settings with the Report Manager. Let's now see how we can use the Report Manager to manage the report catalog.

8.1.3 Managing content

In a typical enterprise environment, report administrators will spend most of their time managing *content.* Content-management tasks include creating folders, uploading resources in these folders, and managing resources. For example, just as you would avoid saving all your files in the root folder of your hard drive, you would stay away from uploading all reports to the Home folder. Instead, from the home page you could use the New Folder button to create subfolders below the Home folder.

Although how you organize folder content on your PC hard drive is a matter of personal preference, the RS folder namespace is publicly accessible. Therefore, as a responsible administrator you need to carefully plan its structure before reports go "live." If you don't, you risk breaking client applications or links that have dependencies on the report folders.

Understanding the folder namespace

Similarly to an OS file system, the Report Manager organizes reports in folders. The RS folder namespace is a hierarchy that contains predefined (Home and My Reports) folders and user-defined folders that the administrator creates. For example, figure 8.2 shows that we have created two folders, AWReporter and SampleReports.

The main purpose of having a folder namespace is to uniquely identify a resource in the report catalog. For example, just as you could have many files named readme.doc on your PC hard drive, you could have many reports named the same in the report catalog. However, you cannot have two reports with the same name uploaded to the same folder.

Although you may find the folder concept similar to the Windows folder structure, note that the folders you create in the Report Manager are virtual and they do not map to physical folders. Instead, the folders and their contents are uploaded to the Report Configuration Database and stored in the report catalog (the `Catalog` table). This table defines a self-referential integrity relationship where each record references its parent. The top folder is predefined and is called Home. When you click a folder link, the Report Manager simply calls down to the RS SOAP API to query the Report Configuration Database and find out which child records are linked to this folder. Using the Report Manager, you can perform the folder tasks listed in table 8.3.

Table 8.3 Management tasks report administrators perform using the Report Manager

Task	Example
Upload content to a folder	Once a new report is created, you have to upload it to the report catalog to make the report globally available.
Move content between folders	Sometimes, you may need to reorganize report content just as you may need to use Windows Explorer to move files from one folder to another.
Create subfolders	Establishing a good hierarchical structure is an important task that every administrator must carefully evaluate. For example, one of the decisions that you must make as early as possible before setting up the report catalog is how the folder namespace should be organized, i.e., per department, application, and so on.
Move folders and all of their content to another folder	The Report Manager allows you to move all the contents of a folder to another folder. For example, a company may go through a reorganization in which some departments are consolidated into one department. Using the Report Manager, you could update the report catalog to reflect the new organizational structure.
Delete folders and all of their content	With the Report Manager you delete resources when they are no longer needed.
Hide folders and resources	To reduce folder clutter, users can exclude resources from the folder view by hiding them.
Modify folder names	Similar to using Windows Explorer, you can rename folders.

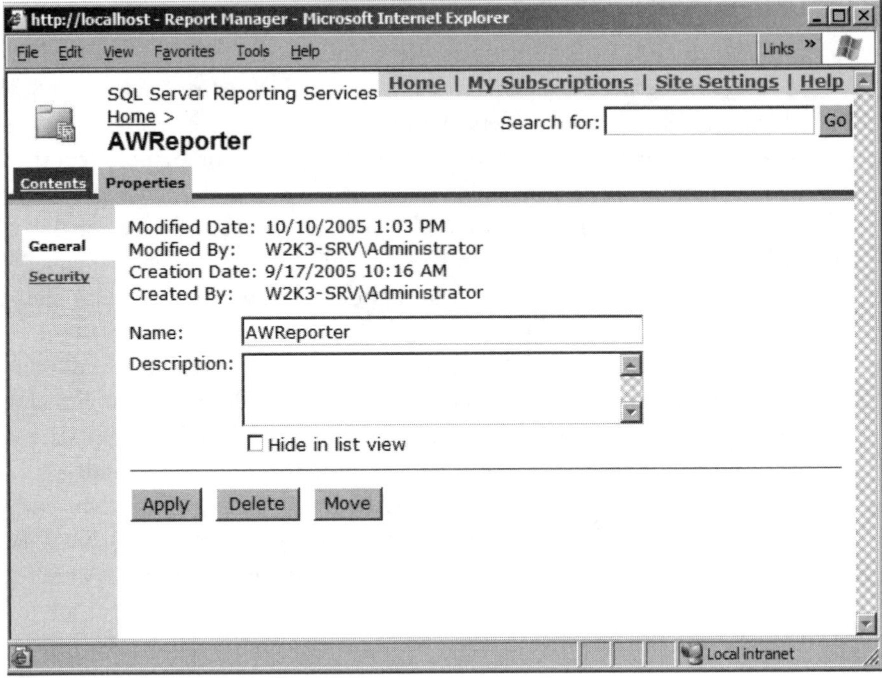

Figure 8.6 Use the folder properties to perform various management tasks, including renaming, deleting, and moving the folder.

To perform these folder tasks, you would access the folder or resource properties and initiate the appropriate action from there. For example, figure 8.6 shows the Properties page of the AWReporter folder that contains our sample reports.

Use the folder's Properties page to perform various management tasks. For example, to delete the folder, click the Delete button.

For some reason, copying folders and resources is not supported. You could upload the files manually as a workaround.

Uploading resources

Once you've established the folder structure, you can upload report content manually using the Upload File link (see figure 8.2). As we mentioned in chapter 2, if the report author has the appropriate security permissions, the Report Designer will create the project folder straight from the VS .NET IDE when the project is deployed. As a part of the deployment process, the Report Designer links the project folder to the root (Home) folder and names it according to the `TargetFolder` setting you specified on the project's properties.

The Report Designer doesn't allow you to create additional folders below the root project folder. However, the Report Manager doesn't expose this restriction. You can create as many nested folders as you like.

There are two common situations when uploading files manually may be necessary: when the report author doesn't have the rights to upload the reports directly from the Report Designer and when the report definition file is authored by an outside party.

What resources can be uploaded to a folder? The Report Server doesn't enforce special rules and allows any file to be uploaded to the report catalog. However, it only makes sense to upload the following resources:

- Report definition (`*.RDL`) files
- Shared data source (`*.RDS`) files
- Image files
- XSL transformation files (`*.XSL`)
- HTML pages

But wait, you might ask, what if the report needs other types of files, for example, an XML file from which to read some settings? Should you upload it to the Report Server catalog so you don't have to specify the absolute or relative file path when you need to load it in XML DOM using custom code?

The answer is, unfortunately, no. Just like any other resource, the file gets serialized and saved to the Report Server database, so it is not physically present in the Report Server virtual root or elsewhere on the file system. For this reason, it makes sense to upload only external resources that Reporting Services supports, which currently include images, XSLT files, and HTML pages.

For example, for the purposes of the AWReporter sample reports, besides the report definition files and the shared data source files, you need to upload to the report catalog the `awc.jpg` logo image file and the `confidential.jpg` image file, as well as the `SalesPromotion.xsl` file that we used to fine-tune the XML output of the Sales Promotion report in chapter 6.

Uploading HTML pages could be useful for reports with navigational features. For example, you may have a report with hyperlinks that display context-sensitive help for different sections of the report. You can put the help content in HTML pages and upload them with the report.

By the way, the file size limit for external files is 4 MB. The 4-MB limit is a browser upload control limitation. You can post larger resources through the SOAP management API.

Managing folders

How should you partition the folder structure so it is well organized and yet simple to maintain? Our advice is to keep it as flat as possible. The advantages of having a flat physical structure are twofold:

- It simplifies the folder maintenance.
- It shortens the report path, which, in turn, makes it easier to request reports programmatically or manually (how do you feel when you have to type in those long URLs in the browser?).

In general, two considerations affect the folder structure: logical partitioning (for example, you may need to organize your reports in such a way that they reflect organizational hierarchy, client applications, and so on) and security.

There may be other factors that affect the folder organization, such as which organizational segment a given Report Server instance serves, how to deal with shared resources, and so forth. Let's look at an example to clarify the last point. To simplify things, let's assume that our hypothetical company, Adventure Works Cycles (AWC), has only one instance of the Report Server installed in its headquarters.

The AWC management has requested the following:

- Reports should be organized logically per department and then per application.
- Cross-department reporting is not permitted.

Given these requirements, figure 8.7 shows what a possible folder structure might look like.

To meet the logical organization requirements, we could create subfolders for each department. Then, we could break the folder namespace down further into subfolders per application. As we see in chapter 9, folders and resources are securable items. To meet the security requirements, we can grant the sales employees permissions to browse the Sales folder but revoke their access to the HR folder.

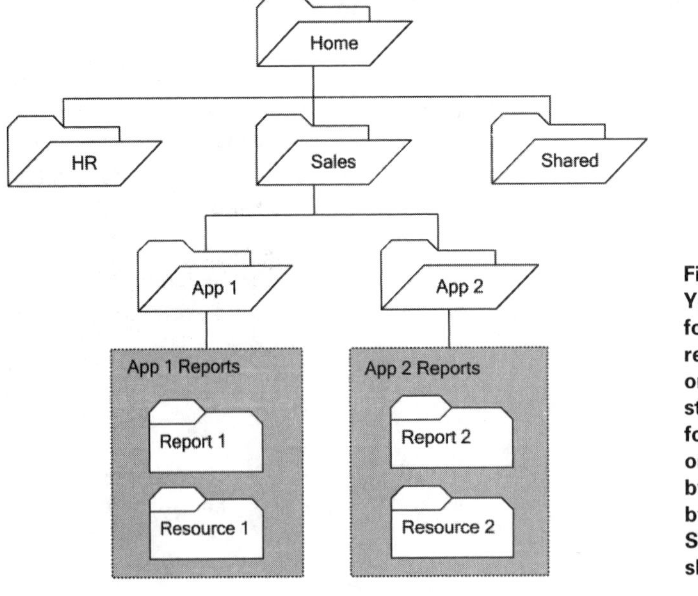

Figure 8.7
You could organize your folder namespace to reflect your company's organizational structure. Here, the folder namespace is organized hierarchically by department and then by application. The Shared folder is for shared resources.

Subject to security permissions, a report in one folder can reference resources from another folder. For example, we can upload the AWC company logo to the Shared folder. Then, we can ensure that all reports reference the logo by setting the image item's Value property to `/Shared/AWC.JPG`.

Those of you familiar with web development may think that to reference a parent folder you can use the `../` specifier. RS simplifies folder navigation by allowing you to reference a folder by its relative path to the root Home folder. For example, reports under the App1 folder can reference Resource 2 under the App2 folder as `/Sales/App2/Resource 2`. When in doubt, make sure that your folder reference matches the value in the `Path` column of the `Catalog` table in the Report Server database.

Managing reports

To manage a published (managed) report, you use the report's Properties page, as shown in figure 8.8. Use the links on the left of the Properties page to manage various report properties.

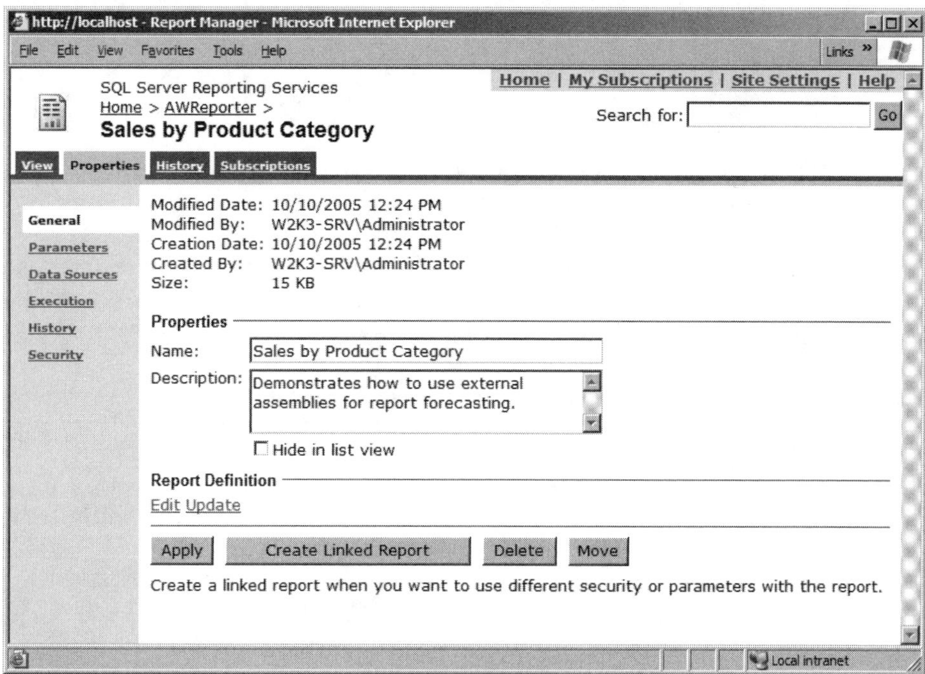

Figure 8.8 Use the report's Properties page to manage the report.

For example, you can use the General link to complete the following tasks:

- Change the report name and description.
- Hide the report from the folder view.

- Download or change the report definition (RDL) file by clicking the Edit and Update links, respectively.
- Create a linked report, as we discuss in section 8.1.5.

To avoid confusion and clutter, you can hide folders or resources by selecting the Hide in List View check box. For example, it is unlikely that you want your users to see shared data source definitions and resources other than the reports in the folder list view. They might confuse these items for reports and attempt to execute them.

No special security permission is required to see a hidden item. The item is simply excluded from the folder view, but the user can see all items by clicking the Show Details button. The Show Details mode also displays the last time the reports were run.

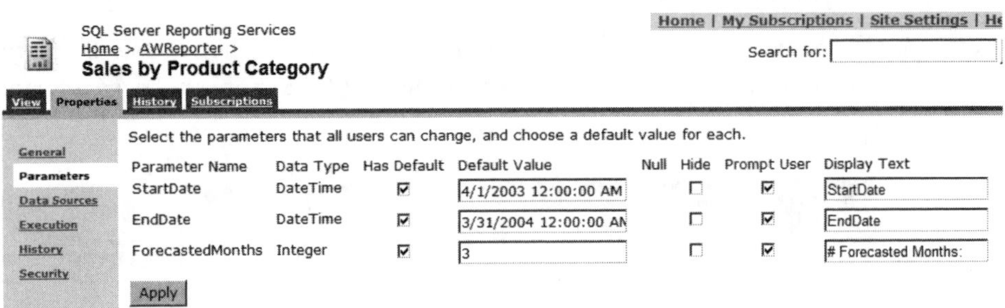

Figure 8.9 Use the Parameters link to manage the report parameters, including the parameter's default value and prompt settings.

Use the Parameters link to manage the report parameters (figure 8.9). Unfortunately, the Parameters page is limited to maintaining existing parameters only. Table 8.4 displays and describes the options for this page.

Table 8.4 Options on the Parameters page

Option	Description
Has Default	Select this check box when you want to specify a default value. If this option is checked, the text in the Default Value textbox will be displayed for this parameter when the report is first displayed.
Default Value	If the Has Default checkbox is selected, the value in this textbox will be displayed for this parameter when the report is first displayed.
Null	Select this check box to specify null as the default value. A null value means that the report runs even if the user does not provide a parameter value. If there is no check box in this column, the parameter does not accept null values. See figure 8.9 for an example of this.
Hide	Select this check box to hide the parameter in the parameter area that appears at the top of the report. The parameter will still appear in subscription definition pages and it can still be specified on a report URL. Hiding the parameter is useful when you want to always run the report with a default value that you specify.

continued on next page

Table 8.4 Options on the Parameters page *(continued)*

Option	Description
Prompt User	Select this check box to display a text box used that prompts users for a parameter value. Clear this check box if you want to run the report in unattended mode (for example, to generate report history or report execution snapshots), if you want to use the same parameter value for all users, or if you do not require user input for the value.
Display Text	Provide a text string that appears next to the parameter text box. This string provides a label or descriptive text. There is no limit on string length. Longer text strings wrap within the space provided.

Use the Data Sources link to manage the report's data source, which could be set up as report-specific or shared. We emphasized the advantages of using shared data sources back in chapter 3.

Use the Execution link to control the report execution by using one of the two mutually exclusive report-caching options: execution and snapshot caching. The report-caching options are rather complex topics that we discuss next.

8.1.4 Managing report execution

As we explained in chapter 1, the Report Server processes reports in two stages: execution and rendering. During the report execution stage, the Report Server retrieves the report data, combines the resulting dataset with the report layout information, and generates the report's intermediate format (IF), which can be cached for fast retrieval. The report administrator can manage report caching via the Execution link of the report's Properties page.

Typically, report data doesn't change that often. For example, to allow client applications to access report data efficiently, an OLAP database could be created exclusively for reporting purposes. In this scenario, report data could be bulk uploaded on a regular basis (e.g., daily) from the OLTP to the OLAP database.

To make report processing more efficient, you can take advantage of the relatively static nature of report data by caching the report's intermediate format. RS supports three forms of caching, as listed in table 8.5.

Note that all options cache the report's intermediate format (IF), not the final rendered output. Having so many caching options may be confusing, so let's discuss each option in more detail.

Report session caching

It turns out that while the last two caching options are user-configurable and can be turned off (disabled by default), report session caching is not. Judging by the questions posted on the RS discussion list, report session caching is confusing for many people. For this reason, we'll explain why report session caching is needed and how it works.

For nonsnapshot reports, the Report Server always caches the report's IF implicitly for the duration of the report session.

Table 8.5 Three forms of caching supported by RS

Caching Option	Purpose	How Does It Work?	Default Setting	How To Configure
Report session caching	Ensures data consistency within a configurable time window (report session) by correlating the client with the cached report IF.	RS executes the report each time a request from a different client arrives and caches the report's IF per client in the `ChunkData` table. For each subsequent request from the same client that includes the session identifier, RS uses the cached IF until the report session expires.	By default, the session duration is 600 seconds.	Cannot be turned completely off. The session duration is controlled by the `SessionTimeout` setting in the `Configuration-Info` table.
Report execution caching	Improves performance by potentially serving all report requests from the same cached IF instance.	RS serves all requests for the same report from a single cached IF instance stored in the `ChunkData` table.	Off	Use the report's Execution properties in the Report Manager.
Snapshot caching	Captures the report execution at a specific point of time, usually on a regular basis.	RS stores the report IF in the `SnapshotData` table and serves all requests from it.	Off	Use the report's Execution properties in the Report Manager.

DEFINITION A *report session* is a configurable time period within which the Report Server can serve subsequent report requests from the same client and for the same report from the cached report IF. A report session is always associated with exactly one client. In this respect, .NET developers can relate report sessions to ASP.NET sessions. However, the Report Server doesn't use ASP.NET sessions at all.

The premise here is that it is likely that the report's consumer may request the same report again within a certain period of time, for example, to export the report to a different format or for report paging. When a report is processed, the Report Server stores its IF in the ReportServerTempDB database and uses the cached copy until the report session expires, as shown in figure 8.10.

The important observation that you can make by looking at figure 8.10 is that with report session caching, the Report Server caches the report's IF per client and the cached report copy is correlated with the client.

Why do we need report sessions? Report session caching ensures data consistency and improves performance; the main reason for having report session caching is to ensure that the report data doesn't change within a given period of time. To understand the need for this, consider the following example. Imagine that you have a presentation and you run a multipage Sales Summary report. Each page displays the sales

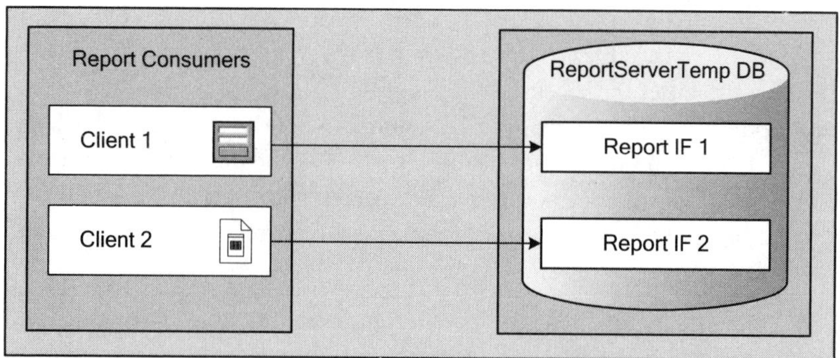

Figure 8.10 With report session caching, the Report Server caches the report's intermediate format as many times as the number of the client applications requesting the same report.

data for a given company branch. When you navigate from one page to another, the browser asks the server to return the next page of the report. Now, let's imagine that while you are paging from branch A to branch B, the sales data for branch A changes. You navigate back to the page that displays the details for branch A, and all of sudden the report shows different numbers. Not a very compelling presentation, right?

Another unfavorable outcome may happen when you try to export the report and you realize later that the exported copy has different data. To ensure data consistency within a configurable period of time, the Report Server always performs report session caching for non-snapshot reports by saving the report's IF in the ReportServer-TempDB database.

Report session caching is also useful for processing reports more efficiently. Let's say you've authored a crosstab report with interactive features such as the Territory Sales Crosstab report we created in chapter 4. The user can expand the report sections to see more data. To process interactive reports more efficiently, the Report Server does not render the whole report at once. Instead, it renders different portions on an as-needed basis.

Finally, because the report session state is stored in the database, it could survive the lifetime of the Report Server application domain. For example, if IIS is restarted, the session state is not lost.

You cannot completely turn off report session caching. However, you can specify the session expiration interval and how the Report Server correlates the report's consumer with the session.

You can manage the report session timeout by changing the value of the `SessionTimeout` setting in the `ConfigurationInfo` table in the Report Server database. Based on our experiments, the minimum value seems to be 60 seconds. The `UseSessionCookies` setting from the same table determines how the report's consumer application will be correlated to the report session. By default, the Report Server will use a session cookie to match the client application with the report session.

If using cookies is not an option when reports are requested by URL, you can configure the Report Server to use cookie-less report sessions by setting `UseSessionCookies` to false. In this case, instead of sending a cookie, the Report Server adds the session identifiers to the report's URL address. This is also called URL *munging*.

When a new report request arrives, the Report Server looks for a session identifier. The Report Server does some decision making to determine whether to serve the report from the report session, if available, or process the report anew. Specifically, the Report Server checks the following:

- Does the report session match the session identifier included in the report request? We see how a client application can specify the session identifier in chapter 9.
- Has the report session expired?
- Are the report parameter values the same as the ones passed with previous report requests?

If the Report Server decides to service the report from the same report session, the session expiration timeout is renewed. For this reason, don't be surprised if the report doesn't show the most current data for subsequent requests. This situation may lead to data inaccuracy because data has become outdated ("stale").

NOTE In general, all caching techniques result in outdated data. As a developer and administrator, you have to carefully evaluate how much "staleness" is acceptable.

As we mentioned, the default report session duration is 10 minutes. If the Report Server decides to use the report session, it will serve the report from the cached copy within the report session duration. But is 10 minutes acceptable? If you configure the session duration to expire too soon, you will lose the performance benefits of caching. If the report is cached for too long, data can get stale.

Sometimes, you may want to force the Report Server to abandon the report session and execute the report anew. As a developer, you can do this in a couple of ways, depending on how the report is requested. If the report's consumer requests the report by URL, you can send the `rs:ClearSessionID` command to the Report Server, as we discuss in chapter 10.

If the report is requested by SOAP, you can programmatically abandon the session by clearing the `SessionId` property of the `SessionHeaderValue` proxy class. If the report's consumer doesn't support cookies, the session ID can be explicitly specified in the request URL or as an argument to the `Render` method call, as we also discuss in chapter 10.

From the end-user perspective, if the report includes the standard toolbar, the end user can click the Refresh Report button (or press Ctrl-F5) to clear the session.

Report execution caching

Optionally, you can turn on report execution caching using the report execution page. To access this page, click the Execution link (see figure 8.8). Report execution caching is another big area of confusion. It is important to note that when report execution caching is enabled, the report's IF is not cached in memory.

Just like report sessions, report execution caching uses the report's IF cached in the ReportServerTempDB database. So what's the difference? While report session caching is correlated with the client, report execution caching is global. In other words, with the latter form of caching, several client applications (or users, for that matter) may access the same cached instance of a given report, as shown in figure 8.11.

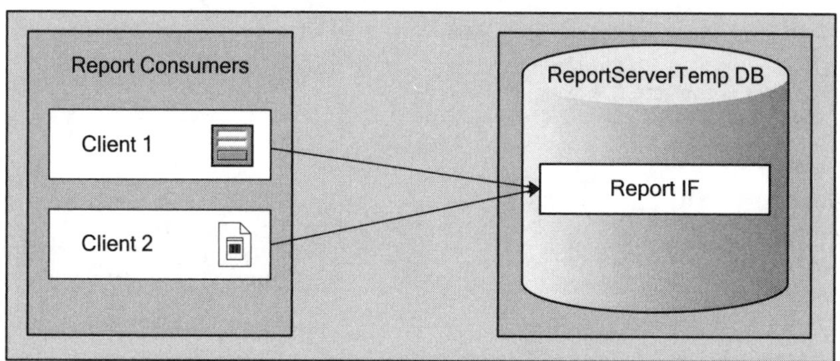

Figure 8.11 With report execution caching, one cached IF instance can be used by more than one client.

How is report execution caching implemented? As we've just seen, with report session caching, when different clients request the same report the Report Server executes the report for each client and caches as many instances of the report's IF in the `ChunkData` table as the number of clients. If report execution caching is on, only one instance of the report's IF is cached in the `ChunkData` table. All subsequent requests will use that instance.

Therefore, while report sessions guarantee data consistency within the duration of the report session, the main goal of report execution caching is better performance. If the report doesn't have parameters, only one instance of the report is cached. Otherwise, several instances of the report are cached, a separate instance for each set of parameters.

The following conditions have to be met to enable report execution caching:

- The report cannot use Windows authentication in expressions or to connect to the database. For example, you cannot use `User.UserID` in your expressions, nor can you use Windows authentication to log in to the database by impersonating the user (the Windows NT Integrated Security option on the data source properties). However, if the data source connection uses Windows Authentication with stored credentials (the Use As Windows Credentials When Connecting to the Data Source option), then the report can be cached in the execution cache.

- The report doesn't prompt the user for database login credentials.

Let's see an example that demonstrates the effect that this form of caching has on the report's execution. Suppose that the AWC management has requested a report that shows the territory sales by quarter. The Territory Sales by Quarter report meets this requirement (figure 8.12).

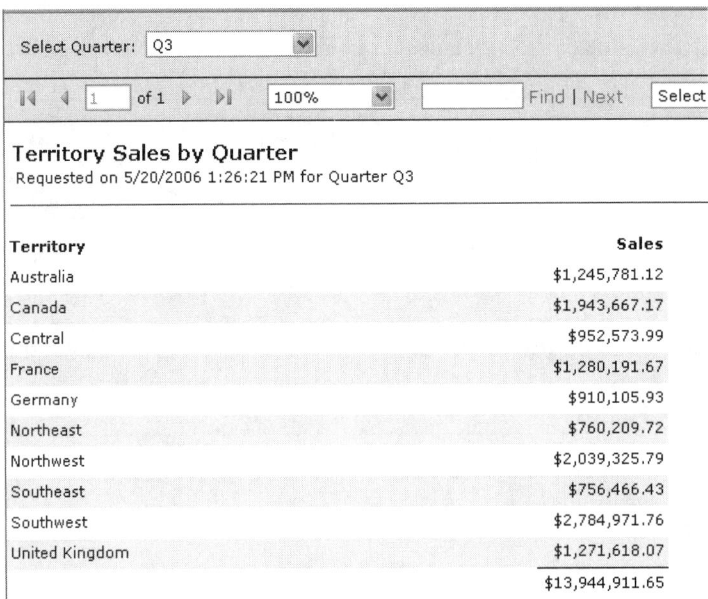

Territory Sales by Quarter

Requested on 5/20/2006 1:26:21 PM for Quarter Q3

Territory	Sales
Australia	$1,245,781.12
Canada	$1,943,667.17
Central	$952,573.99
France	$1,280,191.67
Germany	$910,105.93
Northeast	$760,209.72
Northwest	$2,039,325.79
Southeast	$756,466.43
Southwest	$2,784,971.76
United Kingdom	$1,271,618.07
	$13,944,911.65

Figure 8.12 Once report execution caching is enabled, it doesn't get processed by the Report Server when requested with the same parameters.

The report accepts a parameter so that the user can filter the report data by quarter. For simplicity's sake, we restricted the available parameter values to the 2003 quarters only, with Q1 as the default quarter. To demonstrate how execution caching affects the report's execution, the report shows the report's execution time below the title. If the report is not cached, each time you request the report the execution time changes, which means that the Report Server does indeed process the report.

Because it is likely that data for past quarters will be relatively static, let's change the execution options to cache the report in the execution cache for 10 minutes by using the Execution link in the Report Manager, as shown in figure 8.13.

Now, request the report several times for the same quarter. Notice that the execution time doesn't change, which means the report is effectively cached.

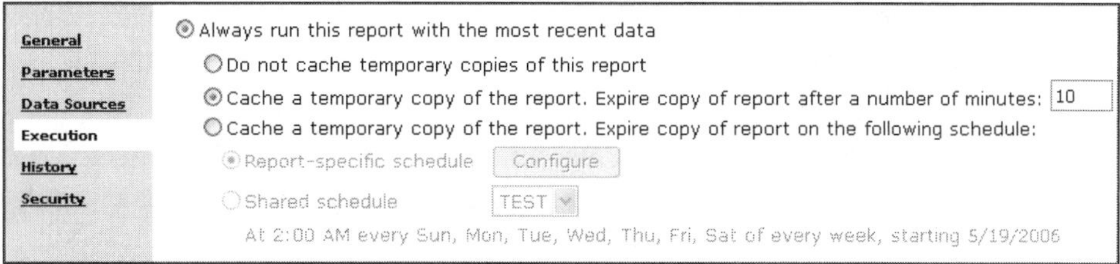

Figure 8.13 Use report execution caching for more efficient report processing.

When the report has parameters, a separate copy of the report is cached for each set of parameters. To see this, change the quarter to Q2 and run the report again. Observe that the execution time changes because the Report Server needs to process the report to reflect the new parameter value. If you run the report again for Q2, the Report Server will use the cached copy for Q2. If you request to see the report for Q1, you'll notice that the cached copy is served. This means that now there are two cached instances for the same report.

When is the cached instance removed from the execution cache? There could be several reasons that cause the Report Server to swap the report out of the cache, including the following:

- The Report Server application domain is restarted, for example, by stopping and starting IIS.
- The cached instance has expired based on the expiration options you specified.
- The cache instance is explicitly invalidated by calling the RS Web service `FlushCache` method.
- The report's execution options have changed.
- Other events have taken place, such as a change to the report definition file and data source.

You can force the Report Server to expire the report's cached instance (if any) on a set schedule. This is useful when you want to ensure that the Report Server will process the report at a specified time. Consider again the Territory Sales by Quarter report; you could set the execution cache to expire at the beginning of every quarter by setting the Quarterly Schedule shared schedule. This ensures that the report requested for the previous quarter reflects the latest changes.

Snapshot caching

The Report Server manages the first two caching options internally, and so you have little control over them. For example, you don't know when the report will be requested for the first time and when the Report Server will start the cache expiration stopwatch. Sometimes, it makes more sense to save report instances at a specific point by configuring the report for snapshot execution. Snapshot caching offers the following advantages:

- It improves the report performance by serving the report from the cached copy in the Report Server database. This could be especially useful for large reports that might take a long time to execute. Such reports can be scheduled to be generated during off-peak hours.
- It allows you to maintain a snapshot history log and compare different snapshot runs of the report.

When a report is configured to be executed as a snapshot, the Report Server saves the report's IF in the Report Configuration Database (the `SnapshotData` table), as shown in figure 8.14.

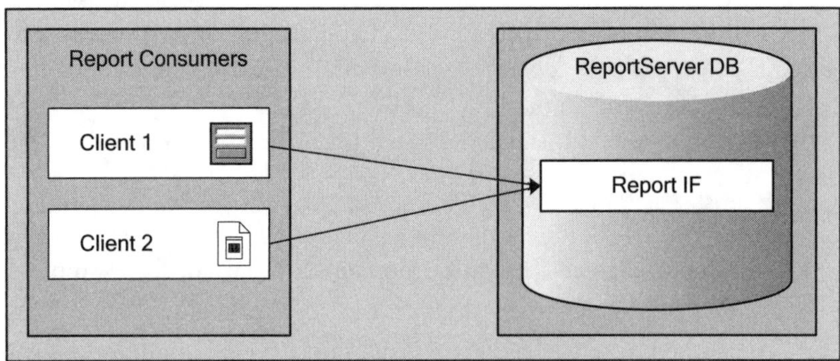

Figure 8.14 With snapshot caching, the Report Server stores the report's IF in the Report Configuration Database.

At this point you may wonder how snapshot caching differs from execution caching. Unlike reports configured to use execution caching, snapshots:

- *Are usually executed in unattended mode*—Typically, snapshots are generated as a result of a time event. However, you can explicitly create a snapshot using the Report Manager portal, or developers can call the `UpdateReportExecution-Snapshot` SOAP API to generate it programmatically.
- *Refresh the report cached copy at a specific point of time*—Unlike with execution caching, you can control exactly when the snapshot cache is refreshed.
- *Require default parameter values in the case of parameter-driven reports*
- *Are not interactive*—Snapshots don't allow the user to change the report parameters if the report is parameter driven.
- *Save the report's IF in the Report Server Configuration database, as opposed to the Report Server Temporary database*

Snapshot caching is subject to the same limitations as execution caching. In addition, because the snapshot execution is unattended, the user cannot set the parameter values if the report accepts parameters. For example, if you schedule the Territory Sales by Quarter report for a snapshot execution, you will see that the Quarter parameter is disabled. If the report is parameter driven, the Report Server will use the parameter default values. In fact, the Report Server will refuse to schedule the report for snapshot execution if default values are not specified for all parameters.

To explain how snapshots can be useful, let's revisit the Territory Sales by Quarter report. Let's assume that once the quarter is up, the data for the previous quarter doesn't change. In addition, we assume that the users want to run the report to see the sales results for the previous quarter only (users can't specify the quarter interactively).

Given the new set of requirements, we can optimize our report by capturing a snapshot of the report on a quarterly basis. As a prerequisite, we need to default the Quarter parameter to a given quarter, for example, Q1. Rather than hardcoding the current quarter value, it would be best to calculate the default value of the current quarter by using an expression. However, in order to keep this example simple, we will just hardcode the default value. Figure 8.15 shows how we can set the snapshot execution using the Report Manager.

Of course, instead of waiting for the current quarter to end, for testing purposes we could see the effect of the snapshot execution sooner by changing the schedule interval to a minute or two. Alternatively, we could manually generate the snapshot by selecting the Create a Snapshot of the Report When the Apply Button Is Selected check box on the report's Execution Properties page and clicking the Apply button. This would create the snapshot immediately. If the Store All Report Execution Snapshots in History option is checked on the History tab, we must remember to cancel the snapshot execution after we finish experimenting to prevent filling up the `History` table.

Once you have finished setting the execution options, run the report. Notice that the report data is filtered by the default quarter and the parameter is disabled. Similar to execution caching, the report's executing time doesn't change and reflects the time when the snapshot was created.

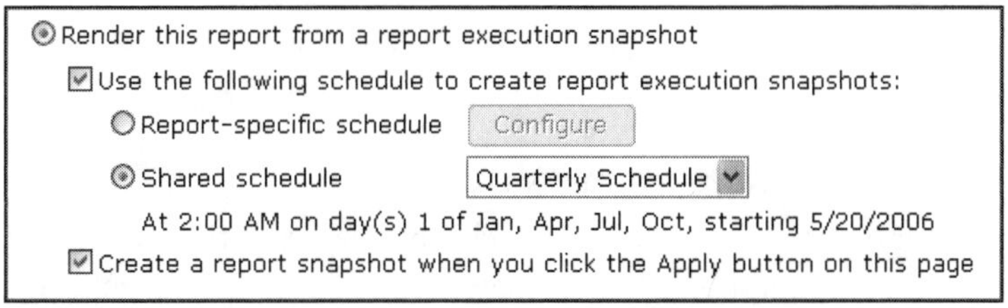

Render this report from a report execution snapshot
Use the following schedule to create report execution snapshots:
Report-specific schedule Configure
Shared schedule Quarterly Schedule
At 2:00 AM on day(s) 1 of Jan, Apr, Jul, Oct, starting 5/20/2006
Create a report snapshot when you click the Apply button on this page

Figure 8.15 You can trigger the snapshot execution from a report-specific or shared schedule.

By default, only one snapshot run is kept in the Report Configuration Database, and it gets replaced each time a new snapshot is generated. You can keep a historical log of the snapshot executions by enabling the snapshot history. This allows you to compare snapshot executions, similar to how Microsoft Project allows you to create and compare project baselines.

For example, in our scenario as the administrator you can decide to keep the snapshot executions for the past four quarters so that management can compare the sales performance from one quarter to the next. You can use the Report History tab (not the Properties tab) to see or delete the snapshot executions.

To change the snapshot history options, click the History link on the Properties tab, as shown in figure 8.16. If the Allow Report History to Be Created Manually check box is selected, a New Snapshot button will appear on the report's History tab that you can use to create snapshots manually. The rest of the options are self-explanatory.

NOTE Figure 8.16 is showing the History Properties; the New Snapshot button will show up by clicking on the History tab at the top of the page.

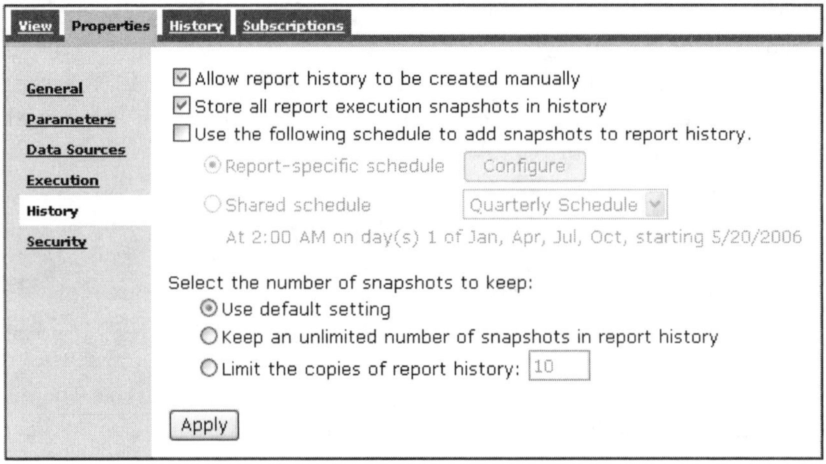

Figure 8.16 Use the History links to manage the snapshot history.

Let's recap our discussion about caching by exploring how all three forms of caching impact the report's execution.

How caching affects the report's execution

The Report Server goes through some decision making to find out whether to serve subsequent report requests from the cached report copy or to generate the report anew. Figure 8.17 depicts a simplified diagram that shows how report caching affects the report's execution phase.

As the diagram in figure 8.17 depicts, the Report Server first checks to see if there is a valid report session associated with the report request. To do so, the Report Server

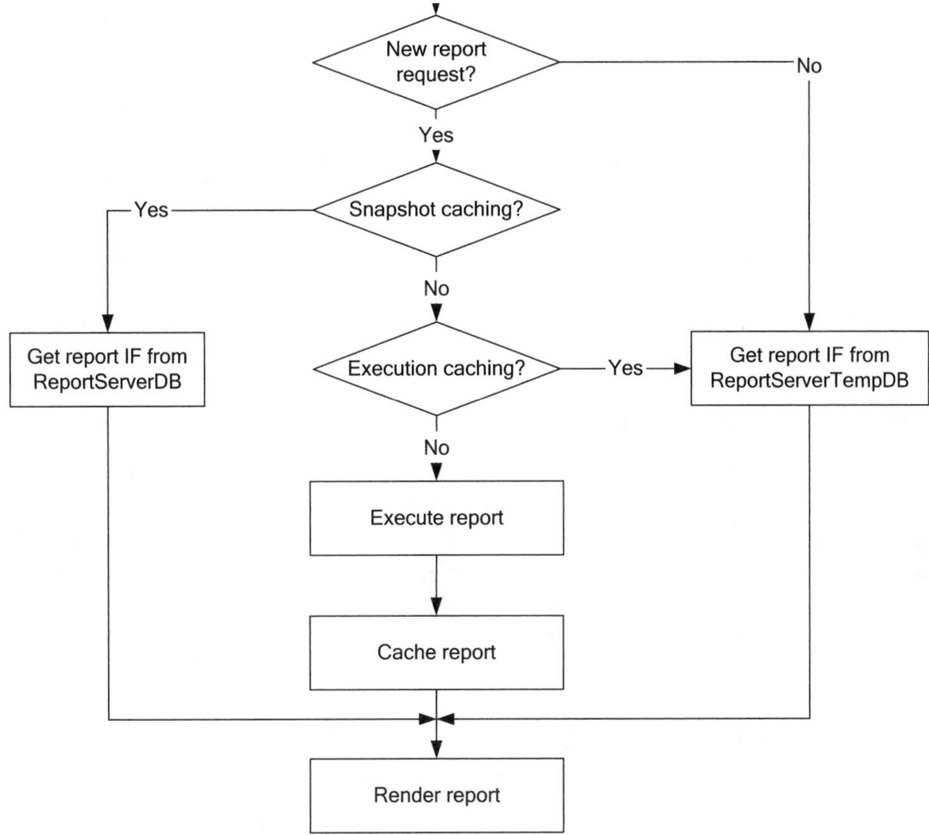

Figure 8.17 RS supports three caching options: report session, execution, and snapshot caching. Report caching may bypass the execution phase completely.

examines the client request for a session identifier and queries the `SessionData` table in the Report Server Temporary database in an attempt to find a match. If there is one, the Report Server serves the report from the report session cache. Otherwise, the Report Server checks the report execution options.

If the report is configured to be executed as a snapshot and a snapshot-cached instance is available, the Report Server uses it. If snapshot caching is turned off, the Report Server checks to see if the report is configured for execution caching. If this is the case, the Report Server serves the report from the execution cache (if the execution cache is available and can be used).

Finally, if the report is not cached or the cached copy cannot be used, the Report Server executes the report and caches it according to its execution settings. If the report is configured for snapshot execution, the Report Server stores the report's IF in the Report Configuration Database. Otherwise, the Report Server saves the report's IF in the Report Server Temporary database.

To recap, the report can be serviced potentially from one of the following three places:

- *Source database*—If the report is requested for the first time or has been invalidated, for example, the report session has timed out.
- *ReportServerTempDB*—If the Report Server decides to reuse the report IF from the report session or execution cache.
- *Report Configuration Database*—For snapshots only, if a snapshot instance has been generated.

It is important that you evaluate when you should cache and what method you should use. Let's switch gears a little and learn how to create linked reports.

8.1.5 Managing linked reports

Reporting Services allows you to create "wrappers" on top of existing reports in the form of *linked* reports. You can think of a linked report as a shortcut to another report. Similar to a file shortcut, a linked report is not a copy of the original report. Instead, it simply points to the original report. You can manage these *linked* reports with the Report Manager. In this section, we describe linked reports, explain why you would create them, and then we see how to manage these in the Report Manager. Let's get started!

Understanding linked reports

Linked reports inherit the following information from the report they are associated with: report definition, report data source, and report datasets. You cannot change these items in a linked report because they are inherited from the base report. However, you can change the following items:

- Role-based security policy
- Parameters
- Properties
- Catalog location

While the parameter default values can be different, and you can change whether or not they are prompted, you can't add parameters to the report, nor can you change their available values.

Why would you ever want to create linked reports? The simple answer is flexibility. Let's see a concrete example to demonstrate how linked reports can be useful.

Implementing linked reports

In the previous section, we set up the Territory Sales by Quarter report for snapshot execution. Although snapshots can be very useful for generating reports according to a schedule, they impose some restrictions, including the fact that the user cannot change the report parameters. However, what if we want the best of both worlds? What if some users would like to see the report for an arbitrary quarter, while others want the report to show the data from the previous quarter only?

One approach would be to clone the Territory Sales by Quarter report. But this would present a maintenance issue. Each time we needed to make changes to the report layout, we would have to remember to propagate the changes to the report copy as well. A more elegant approach is to create a linked report pointing to the original. We can easily accomplish this with the Report Manager by performing a couple of steps:

Step 1 Navigate to the Properties page of the Territory Sales by Quarter report.

Step 2 Click the Create Linked Report button. Enter a name and optionally a description for the linked report, as shown in figure 8.18. You can also change the location of the linked report if you want to place it in a different folder than AWReporter.

By default, the linked report inherits all properties from the original, including the execution properties. To cancel the snapshot execution for the linked report, go to the linked report's Execution tab and select the Render This Report with the Most Recent Data radio button. Once this is done, the users can render the report for any available quarter.

Another practical use for linked reports is security, because the linked report can have a different role-based security policy than the report it is linked to.

As the report administrator, you will most likely rely on the Report Manager portal to interactively manage the RS environment. Some application integration scenarios, however, may require managing RS programmatically. In these cases, you can use the RS Web service.

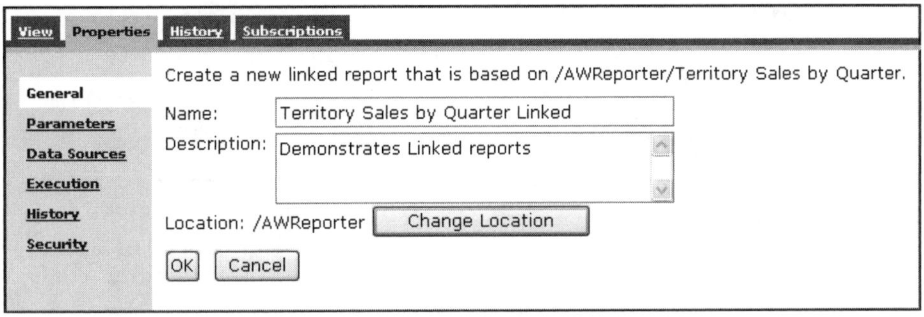

Figure 8.18 You can use a linked report as a shortcut to an existing report.

8.2 MANAGING RS WITH THE WEB SERVICE

As we explained, the Report Manager is just a presentation façade to the Report Server. Behind the scenes, the RS Web service receives SOAP requests from the Report Manager and forwards them to the Report Server. When the Report Manager is not enough, you can build client applications that call the SOAP management API directly. For example, you can create an ad hoc reporting tool that calls down to the RS Web service to upload the generated report definition file to the report catalog.

In this section we take a look at the following:

- Using the Web service management API
- Tracing calls to the SOAP API
- Deploying reports programmatically
- Batching methods together

8.2.1 Using the Web service management API

To allow external applications to manage the report environment, the RS Web service provides a number of web methods, which can be logically grouped in the categories shown in table 8.6.

Table 8.6 Methods for performing various management-related tasks

Category	Purpose	Web method examples
Content Management	Manage site settings, folders, reports and resources	`CreateFolder`, `SetReportDefinition`
Role-Based Security	Manage tasks, roles, and policies	`CreateRole`, `ListTasks`
Data Source	Manage report data sources	`CreateDataSource`, `SetDataSourceContents`
Report Parameters	Manage report parameters	`GetReportParameters`, `SetReportParameters`
Report History	Manage report history	`CreateReportHistorySnapshot`, `ListReportHistory`
Report Scheduling	Manage shared schedules	`CreateSchedule`, `ListSchedules`
Subscribed Delivery	Manage subscriptions	`CreateSubscription`, `ListSubscriptions`
Linked Reports	Manage linked reports	`CreateLinkedReport`, `ListLinkedReports`

The RS Web service also provides a set of web methods for report rendering that we will discuss in chapter 10. For a full list of the Report Server web service methods that the RS Web service provides, see the product documentation.

To become more familiar with these web methods, you can capture all HTTP traffic between the Report Manager and the Report Server using a tracing utility. We'll show you how next.

8.2.2 Tracing calls to the SOAP API

When incorporating RS management capabilities in your applications, you may not know which Web service method you need to call and how to call it. In most cases, you will be able to easily find the web method you need to accomplish a given task programmatically just by looking at its name.

When in doubt, you can use the Report Manager as a learning tool. Because the Report Manager calls down to the RS Web service for all management tasks, you can use a tracing utility (such as SOAP Trace or tcpTrace) to intercept the SOAP traffic between the Report Manager and Report Server.

We will show you how to use the SOAP Trace utility to accomplish this. The steps to use tcpTrace are similar. Both utilities work by capturing the HTTP traffic to a virtual port.

You can download the SOAP Toolkit Version 3 by searching for "SOAP Toolkit Version 3 at `www.microsoft.com`. You can download tcpTrace for free from `www.pocketsoap.com/tcptrace/`.

Using SOAP Trace

For example, let's assume that you need to write a client application that lists all resources located in a given catalog folder. You are not sure which web method to call and which arguments to pass, but you know the Report Manager does this already. You want to find out what happens behind the scenes when you click on a folder in the Report Manager to see the folder content.

As we mentioned, to get started with SOAP Trace, you first need to set up a virtual port to capture the SOAP traffic.

To create a virtual port, change the `ReportServerUrl` setting in the `RSWebApplication.config` file to include a virtual port number such as

```
http://<servername>:8080/ReportServer
```

The `RSWebApplication.config` file is found in the `C:\Program Files\Microsoft SQL Server\MSSQL.3\Reporting Services\ReportManager` directory by default.

Once this is done, you can open the SOAP Trace utility and create a new formatted trace, as shown in figure 8.19.

The settings shown in figure 8.19 assume that the Report Server is installed locally. If this is not the case, then you must replace localhost with the name of the computer on which the Report Server is installed.

Now, open your browser and request the `ReportServerURL`, as specified in `RSWebApplication.config`. At this point, SOAP Trace should capture the SOAP requests that the Report Manager sends to the Report Server. Navigate to the folder in question and explore the SOAP messages captured, as shown in figure 8.20.

Among the captured message calls, you will find a call to the `ListChildren` method that looks promising. A quick look at the documentation confirms that

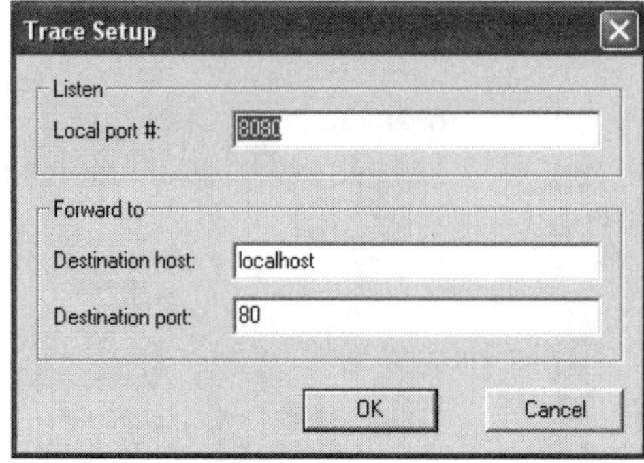

Figure 8.19
Trace the Report Manager to Report Server traffic using the SOAP Trace utility.

`ListChildren` "gets a list of children of a specified folder." As you can see, in this case `ListChildren` passes the name of the folder to the `Item` argument and false to the `Recursive` argument to indicate that it needs a "shallow" traversal, where the resources in the subfolders are excluded.

You can use the tracing technique we've just shown you to watch the entire conversation between the Report Manager and the Report Server and mimic it in your applications. If you need a code sample that demonstrates how you can call the SOAP API to manage programmatically the report catalog, have a look at the RS Catalog Explorer application that comes with RS.

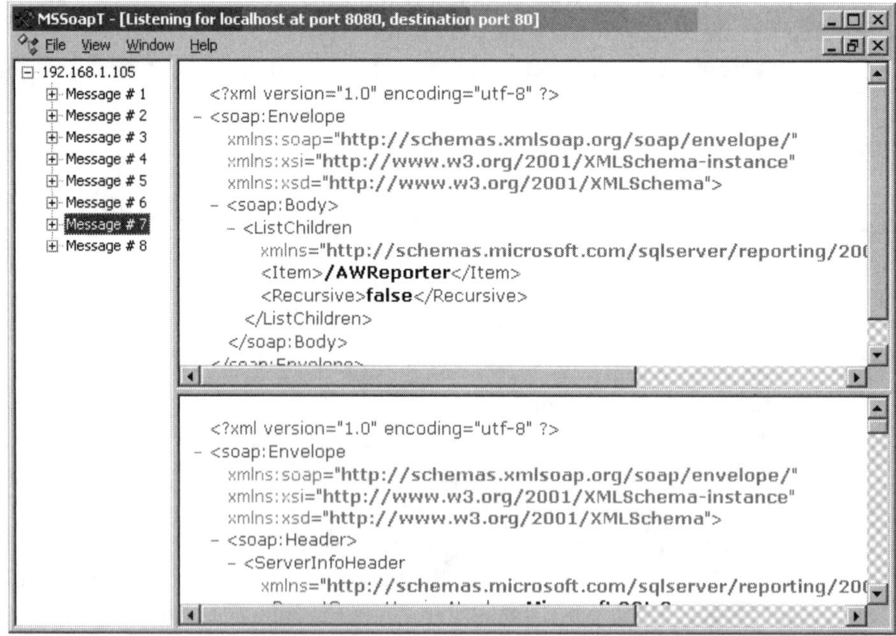

Figure 8.20 Once the Report Manager submits a SOAP request, the SOAP Trace utility will capture it and show the request/response message.

Using the RS Catalog Explorer

The RS team has provided a useful WinForm .NET-based application called the RS Catalog Explorer. You can find the RS Catalog Explorer sample application under the `Samples` folder, which by default is `C:\Program Files\Microsoft SQL Server\90\Samples\Reporting Services\Application Samples\RSExplorer Sample`.

NOTE If you have not installed the SQL Server 2005 samples, you will need to navigate from the Start menu to All Programs > SQL Server 2005 > Documentation and Tutorials > Samples and run the samples installation file.

Just like its web-based counterpart, the Report Manager, the RS Catalog Explorer can be used as a report rendering and management tool. For example, figure 8.21 shows that we used the RS Catalog Explorer to navigate to the AWReporter folder and launch the Employee Sales Freeform with Chart report.

The report properties window displays some report-related properties that you can update, such as the report name. When you do so, RS Catalog Explorer calls the RS

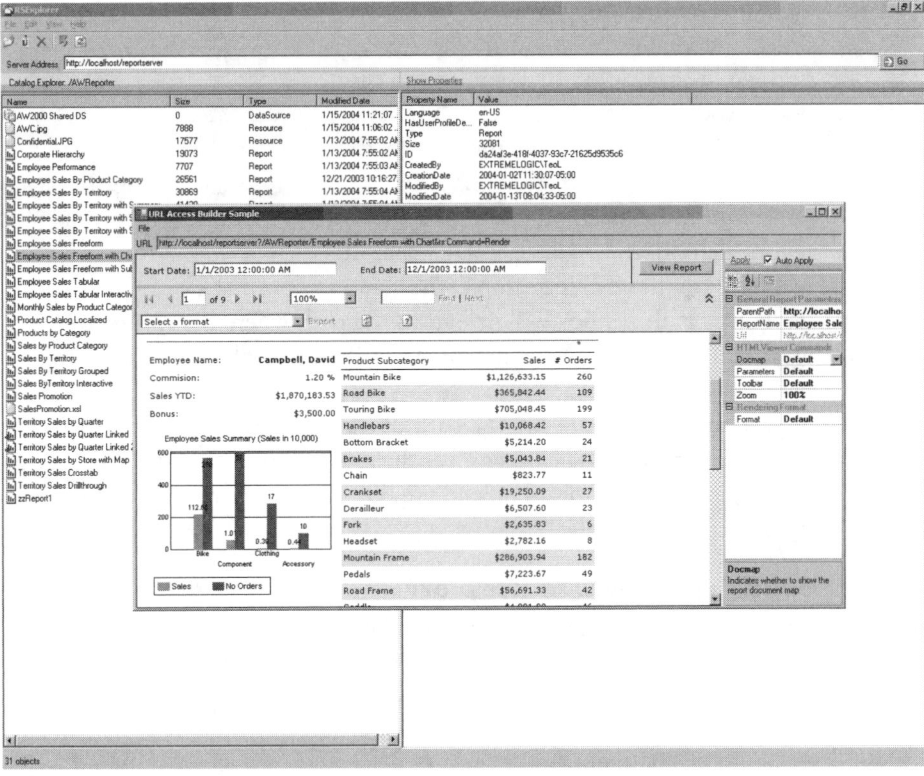

Figure 8.21 You can add management features to your applications, as the RS Catalog Explorer sample demonstrates.

SOAP API to propagate the change to the report catalog. The source code is included in both VB .NET and C#. We highly recommend that you carefully examine this sample, especially if you need to integrate RS with WinForms client applications pre–VS .NET 2005.

Now that you've been introduced to the Report Server management API, let's see how you can use this to perform management tasks.

8.2.3 Deploying reports programmatically

Thanks to the fact that the Report Server exposes its functionality through a series of SOAP APIs, you can easily create client applications to manage the report catalog. Let's write some code to demonstrate how this could be done.

The RDL deployment sample

Back in chapter 2, you saw how to create report definitions programmatically. Now, let's see how easy it is to upload the generated definition to the report catalog to create a new report. You can find the sample under the chapter 8 menu in the AWReporterWin application that comes with this book's code. Once you click on the RDL Deployment menu, you are presented with the options shown in figure 8.22.

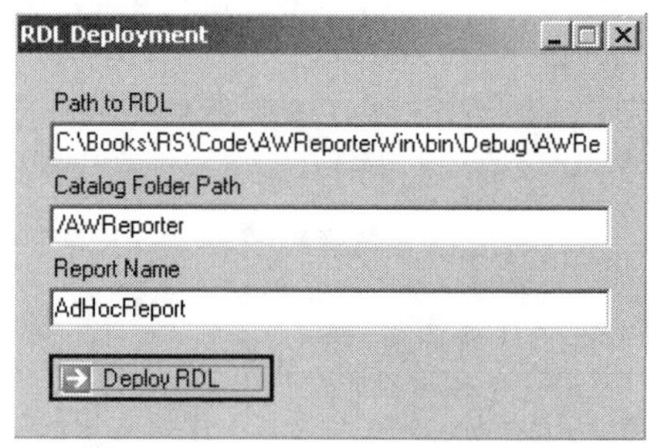

Figure 8.22 The RDL Deployment sample demonstrates how to deploy reports programmatically.

You need to specify the full path to the report definition language (RDL) file. If you have run the AdHoc sample, the Catalog Folder Path textbox will default to the path where the `AWReporter.rdl` file is located. If you don't want to run the AdHoc sample, you'll have to specify a valid path to any RDL file.

You also need to specify the path of the folder where the report will be uploaded to in the RS report catalog, as well as the report name. Once this is done, you can click the Deploy RDL button to upload the file and create the report. Let's now discuss the implementation details.

Setting up the Web service proxy

When accessing XML Web services in managed code, you typically use a proxy class to let the .NET Framework handle all of the SOAP invocation and plumbing details. VS .NET makes it easy to create a Web service proxy class by allowing you to create a web reference to the Web service. In our case, this is what we have to do to establish a web reference to the Reporting Web service:

Step 1 Right-click the References node in the Solution Explorer and choose Add Web Reference. The Add Web Reference dialog box appears.

Step 2 Specify the RS Web service endpoint (the URL to the ReportService-2005.asmx page) in the URL field, for example, http://<servername>/ReportServer/ReportService2005.asmx. If the Report Server is deployed on your local machine, you can click the Web Services on the Local Machine link and choose RS Web Service. VS .NET parses the Web service description and lists all web methods.

Step 3 Specify the Web Reference Name, as shown in figure 8.23. This defines the namespace for the proxy class. For the purposes of the AWReporterWin application, we changed the reference name from localhost to RS. Once you click the Add Reference button, the proxy class will be generated.

To see the proxy class, make sure that the Solution Explorer shows all files (the Show All Files button is activated). Then, you can expand the web reference node. The proxy class name is named Reference.cs if it is a C# project, or Reference.vb in the case of a VB .NET project.

In case you want to trace the SOAP requests going out of the application using a trace utility, you can modify the URL address in the proxy constructor in the proxy class to include a virtual port, for example:

```
this.Url = "http://localhost:8080/ReportServer/ReportService2005.asmx";
```

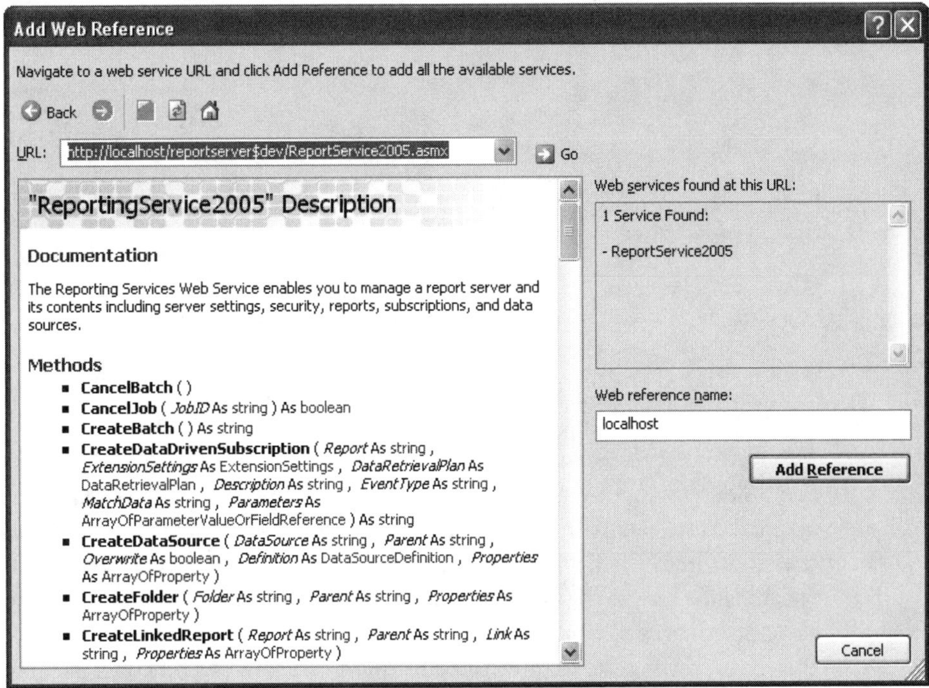

Figure 8.23 Add a web reference to the Report Server Web service.

Then, you can use tcpTrace or SOAP Trace to capture the SOAP traffic, as we discussed earlier. Don't forget to take out the virtual port of the URL when you've finished tracing.

Implementing the sample

To centralize the proxy management in one place, we created the `RsHelpers` wrapper, which encapsulates the proxy instantiation and sets up the authentication credentials. When the application needs the proxy, it gets it from the `RsHelpers.Proxy` accessor.

The actual report deployment takes place in the `DeployRDL` function. Listing 8.1 shows the abbreviated code.

Listing 8.1 Using the RS Web service API to deploy the report definition

```
private void DeployRDL() {
  string[] permissions = {"Create Report"};
  StringBuilder sb = new StringBuilder();
  Byte[] definition = null;
  Warning[] warnings = null;

  if (!RsHelpers.HasPermissions(PermissionType.Item,
           txtFolderPath.Text, permissions)) {
    MessageBox.Show(String.Format("You don't have sufficient
           rights to …"))
    return;
  }

  FileStream stream = File.OpenRead(txtRDLPath.Text);
  definition = new Byte[stream.Length];
  stream.Read(definition, 0, (int) stream.Length);
  stream.Close();

  ReportingService rs = RsHelpers.Proxy;
  warnings = rs.CreateReport(txtReportName.Text,
            txtFolderPath.Text,true, definition, null);
}
```

❶ Checks permissions for creating reports

❷ Loads the report definition

❸ Uploads the report to the report catalog

First, we check to see whether the user has permissions to create reports in the specified folder by calling the `HasPermissions` helper function ❶. This function accepts as arguments the type of the permissions we want to check (item or system), the report item path, and an array of the permissions we want to check. In this case, checking for Create Report rights is sufficient. The `HasPermissions` wrapper calls the `GetPermissions` web method, which returns a string array of all permissions that the user has to a given report item. `HasPermissions` then enumerates through both arrays (requested and granted permissions) and returns true only if all requested permissions are successfully matched.

If the user has the rights to create reports, the report definition is uploaded via a call to the `CreateReport` web method. Next, we load the report definition to a byte array ❷. Then, we invoke `CreateReport` by passing the report name, folder path, and the report definition ❸. We also specify that we want to overwrite the report if it exists. `CreateReport` optionally takes an array of properties you can pass to the last parameter, for example, the report description.

That's it! Once you execute the code, the report will be uploaded to the report catalog and you can use the Report Manager to navigate to it and run it.

Sometimes, when executing a series of interrelated web methods, you want to ensure that all of them will complete successfully or be rolled back in case of a failure. With RS, this can be achieved by encapsulating the web method calls in a batch.

8.2.4 Batching methods together

The RS Web service supports executing management-related web methods within the scope of a single database transaction with a READ COMMITTED isolation level. If any of the batch methods fails, the transaction will be rolled back and all catalog changes will be undone.

For example, let's say that you want to distribute several reports to your customers and these reports are interdependent, such as subreports and related drill-through reports. You want to make sure that the report deployment is an all-or-nothing operation and you don't leave the catalog database in an inconsistent state.

To achieve this you might take advantage of method batching. You can write a simple application or a script that executes all deployment methods in a transactional batch, as follows:

```
try {
  BatchHeader bh = new BatchHeader();
  bh.BatchID = rs.CreateBatch();
  rs.BatchHeaderValue = bh;
  rs.CreateReport ("Report1", …);
  rs.CreateReport ("Report2", …);
  rs.ExecuteBatch();
}
catch (SoapException ex) {
       rs.CancelBatch();
}
```

Developers experienced in writing transaction code will find the batch semantics familiar. When you group web method calls in a batch, the Report Server logs the methods in a Batch table in the Report Server database but doesn't execute them. When the `ExecuteBatch` method is executed, the Report Server creates an explicit transaction and executes all methods within its scope.

If all methods execute successfully, the Report Server commits the database transaction. If the transaction errors out, you can call `CancelBatch` to delete the batch records from the Batch table.

One final note about batching: After you execute or cancel the batch, you need to clear out the batch header after `ExecuteBatch` (or `CancelBatch`); otherwise the proxy will continue to send the header and you will still be operating under a batch.

Using the RS Web service is not the only way to programmatically manage the report catalog. RS also offers a Windows Management Instrumentation (WMI) provider that can be used to manage the settings of multiple RS installations.

8.3 MANAGING RS WITH THE WMI PROVIDER

As useful as the Report Manager is for administering the report environment, it has its limitations. For example, it allows you to manage only the site settings of one Report Server (the one specified in the Report Manager configuration file).

In a typical enterprise environment, however, there may be multiple installed instances of Report Server. For example, you might have one instance serving the reporting needs of customers on the Web and another for intranet use. Or, to scale out, you can have a web farm of report servers. As an administrator, you might need to manage the server settings from a single location. This is exactly the purpose of the RS WMI provider.

8.3.1 Understanding the WMI provider

The WMI provider is built on top of the Windows Management Instrumentation infrastructure baked into the Windows operating system.

> **NOTE** WMI is a system management infrastructure embedded in the Windows OS. It provides an object-oriented interface that developers can use to interact with system management information and the underlying WMI APIs.

With the WMI provider, developers can write code to programmatically access the configurations settings of a given installation instance of the Report Server and Report Manager in an object-oriented way. Specifically, it offers the `MSReportServer_ConfigurationSetting` and `MSReportServerReportManager_ConfigurationSetting` classes.

The first class wraps the Report Server configuration settings stored in the `RSReportServer.config` file. The second represents the Report Manager configuration settings located in the `RSWebApplication.config` file. Consult the documentation for a detailed coverage of the WMI provider functionality.

Let's demonstrate how the WMI provider can be useful. This example was originally written for Reporting Services 2000 before there was a Report Server Configuration Manager. We discuss the Configuration Manager in section 8.4.3. While there isn't much use for this tool in RS 2005, it still provides a great example of how you can work with the WMI Provider. The RS Console is shown in figure 8.24.

Empowered with the RS Console, you can manage the settings of an arbitrary Report Server instance installed in your enterprise by specifying the Report Server name. The RS Console shows you the settings for a given Report Server and allows

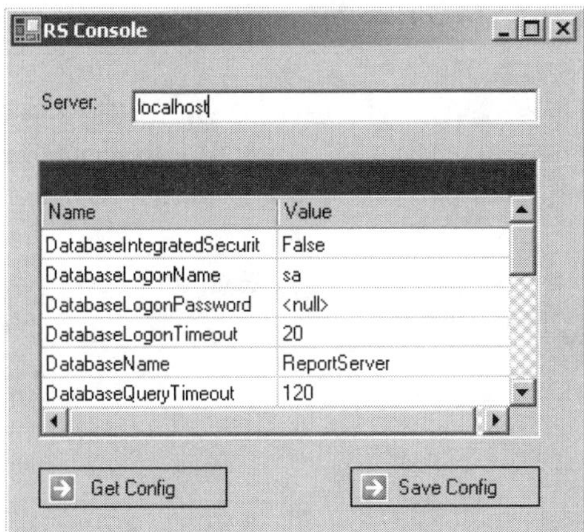

Figure 8.24
Use this sample RS Console to make changes to the RS configuration files of multiple Report Server installations.

you to make changes. This could be particularly useful when you need to change the Report Server database settings. These settings are stored in encrypted format, as you can see by looking at the `RSReportServer.config` file.

For this reason, making changes to the Report Server database settings is not an easy task. In fact, the Report Server provides a utility, `rsconfig.exe`, whose sole purpose is to manage the encrypted database settings. If you are like us, you won't be too excited about working with this command-line utility and messing with switches, which makes the RS Console an even more appealing choice.

8.3.2 Implementing an RS management console

Working with the WMI provider is straightforward. Listing 8.2 shows the abbreviated code of the `GetServerProperties` function, which populates the grid with the configuration settings of the specified server.

Listing 8.2 Getting the server settings

```
private void GetServerProperties()
{
  string WmiNamespace = @"\\" + txtServer.Text +
         @"\root\Microsoft\SqlServer\ReportingServices\v9\Admin";
string WmiRSClass = @"\\" + txtServer.Text +
      @"\root\Microsoft\SqlServer\ReportingServices\" +
     "v9:MSReportServer_ConfigurationSetting";
  ManagementClass serverClass;
  ManagementScope scope;
  scope = new ManagementScope(WmiNamespace);

  scope.Connect();
  serverClass = new ManagementClass(WmiRSClass);       ❶ Instantiates the WMI provider
  serverClass.Get();
  ManagementObjectCollection instances=serverClass.GetInstances();
  IEnumerator enumerator = instances.GetEnumerator();
  bool result = enumerator.MoveNext();
```

```
   m_instance = (ManagementObject)enumerator.Current;

   PropertyDataCollection instProps = m_instance.Properties;
   EntityProperty ds = new EntityProperty ();        <-- ❷ Instantiates a .NET dataset to hold settings
   ds.Property.RowChanged += new
       DataRowChangeEventHandler(this.grdProperties_ChangedEvent);

   foreach(PropertyData prop in instProps)          <-- ❸ Loads the dataset
   {
      ds.Property.AddPropertyRow(prop.Name,
      prop.Value!=null?prop.Value.ToString():"<null>");
   }
   ds.AcceptChanges();
   ds.Property.DefaultView.AllowNew = false;
   ds.Property.DefaultView.AllowDelete = false;
   grdProperties.DataSource = ds.Property;          <-- ❹ Binds the dataset to the grid
}
```

First, we initialize the WMI namespace and class name ❶. Because we are interested in managing the Report Server settings, we use the `MSReportServer_ConfigurationSetting` class. Then, we instantiate the WMI provider and retrieve all Report Server instances installed on the specified server. For simplicity's sake, we default to the first instance.

Next, we get all settings and load them in a grid ❷. For easier data binding and filtering, we decided to create a typed dataset, `EntityProperty`, to hold the settings. The dataset defines a table called `Property` with two columns, `Name` and `Value`. After we instantiate the typed dataset, we hook its `RowChanged` event to an event handler. This event will be triggered when a dataset row is modified, which in turn enables the Save Config button.

Next, we load the dataset with all configuration settings returned by the WMI provider and bind it to the grid control ❸, ❹. As you can see in figure 8.24, the provider decrypts the database authentication settings for us.

Once the grid is loaded, the user can change settings at will. Currently, the WMI provider doesn't support deleting existing settings or creating new ones. The `SaveServerProperties` function writes the changes back to the configuration file, as shown here:

```
private void SaveServerProperties() {
   EntityProperty.PropertyDataTable ds =

   ➥ (EntityProperty.PropertiesDataTable)grdProperties.DataSource;
   DataView view = new DataView(ds);

   view.RowStateFilter = DataViewRowState.ModifiedCurrent;

   PropertyDataCollection instProps = m_instance.Properties;
   for(int i = 0;i < view.Count ;i++) {
```

```
        string name = view[i]["Name"].ToString();
        instProps[name].Value = view[i]["Value"].ToString();
    }
    m_instance.Put();
}
```

Here, we filter out only the changed settings by using a filtered view on top of the typed dataset. Then, we write the changed values back to the WMI provider settings collection. Finally, we call the provider `Put()` method to persist the settings into the configuration file.

Sometimes, writing a full-fledged application to automate maintenance tasks may be overkill. RS provides other options that savvy administrators can add to their belt of management tools, as we discuss in the next section.

8.4 OTHER WAYS TO MANAGE REPORTING SERVICES

RS provides several other options for performing management tasks:

- SQL Management Studio
- Configuration tool
- Executing scripts with the RS script host
- Using specialized management utilities

Let's round out our report management discussion with a high-level overview of these options.

8.4.1 Managing RS with SQL Management Studio

The SQL Server Management Studio (SSMS), as its name implies, is the management tool for all things SQL Server. This of course includes Reporting Services. Those of you who have used SQL Server in the past (SQL 2000 or older) will remember the SQL Server Enterprise Manager. With the launch of SQL Server 2005, SQL Server Enterprise Manager is no more. It has been replaced, thankfully, by SSMS. Figure 8.25 shows the connection options for SSMS. You can connect to and manage much more than just the database engine, as you can see.

Figure 8.25 The new SQL Server Management Studio allows you to connect to and manage more than just the database engine.

Outside of being an all-in-one management environment, SSMS resolves a lot of the

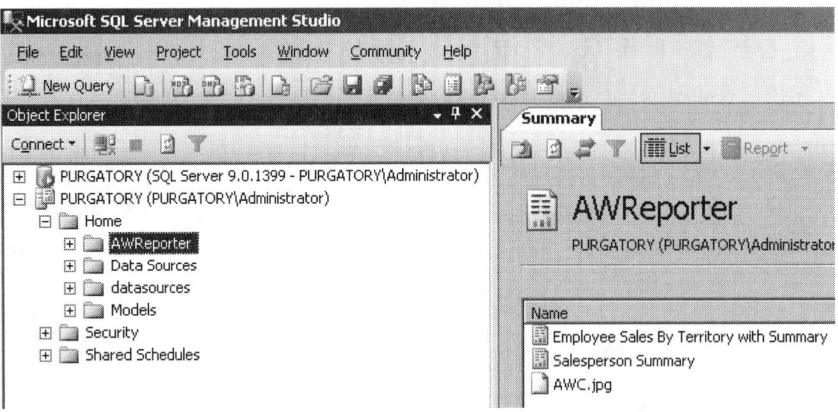

Figure 8.26 SQL Server Management Studio provides you with full management capabilities for RS.

annoyances of the old SQL Server Enterprise Manager, most importantly the modal windows. When you worked with Enterprise Manager and you opened a window to execute some task, you had to wait for the task to finish before you could open another window. SSMS introduces nonmodal windows, which allow you to open a window, start a process, and move on to other windows without affecting the first process. Though there are a few windows that are modal, most of them are not. While this tool does a lot more than help you manage RS, we only focus on how this tool applies to RS. Figure 8.26 shows the SSMS user interface.

You can see that the top level for our reports is `Home` and that all of the folders under Home are what we would see if we navigated to the web-based Report Manager (`http://[servername]/reports`). Also notice that we have a `Security` folder as well as `Shared Schedules`. After further investigation, this seems to be a Windows client version of the Report Manager—which in fact it is. SSMS mirrors the same structure and much of the functionality that is available in the web-based Report Manager. Since SSMS is the tool of choice for the SQL database administrators, they will find themselves right at home in managing the Reporting Services environment.

Now that you have seen the SQL Server Management Studio, let's take a look at some other ways in which you can manage your Reporting Services environment with scripts.

8.4.2 Managing RS with the script host

Traditionally, administrators have relied on scripts to perform routine day-to-day chores. Responding to this common need, RS comes with a script host that can be used to run scripts written in VB .NET. Scripting offers several advantages, including the following:

- It doesn't require advanced development skills.
- Scripts can be easily executed from the command line, batch files, or login scripts.
- Scripts can be easily scheduled to run at specific times.

Exploring RS scripting

RS provides a script host utility (`rs.exe`), which can process and run a script file you pass in. You write RS scripts in VB .NET and you store them as files with the `.RSS` extension. Inside the script you can call any of the RS Web service methods.

The RS script host automatically connects to the requested Report Server, creates a proxy class, and exposes it as a global variable, `rs`. The host accepts command-line switches, which you can use to specify input parameters, including the Report Server URL, the script file, the user credentials to log on to the Report Server, variables, and so on.

Let's now look at a quick example of how scripting with the RS script host can facilitate the management effort. For a detailed discussion of the RS script host, refer to the product documentation.

Scripting with the RS script host

The RS team has provided two sample scripts that demonstrate how you can use scripting to cancel a given running job and publish reports. These scripts should be enough to get you going. For example, we were able to quickly retrofit the `PublishSampleReports` sample and create a useful script to deploy a report. The `RDLDeploy` script uploads a given report definition file to the report catalog. You can find the `DeployRDL.rss` in the chapter 7 folder in the AWReporterWin sample application. To keep things simple, we excluded the role-based security verification.

The bulk of the work is performed by the `PublishReport` function, whose abbreviated code is shown here:

```
Public Sub PublishReport(ByVal reportName As String)
  Dim stream As FileStream = File.OpenRead(filePath)
  definition = New [Byte](stream.Length) {}
  stream.Read(definition, 0, CInt(stream.Length))
  stream.Close()
  warnings = rs.CreateReport(reportName, parentPath, True, _
             definition, Nothing)
End Sub
```

The code should look familiar to you because the `RDLDeploy` sample we discussed in this chapter serves the same purpose. You can execute the `RDLDeploy` script from the command prompt using the following syntax:

```
rs -i RdlDeploy.rss -s http://servername/reportserver -v
filePath=
➥ "C:\Books\RS\Code\AWReporterWin\bin\Debug\AWReporter.rdl" -v
folderPath="AWReporter" -v reportName="AdHocReport"
```

where

-i specifies the input filename
-s specifies the Report Server URL
-v specifies an input variable

In this case, similarly to the `RDLDeploy` sample, we upload the `AWReporter` report definition file to the `AWReporter` catalog folder and name the new report `AdHocReport`.

8.4.3 Using the Reporting Services configuration tool

Reporting Services provides an additional management tool for managing your Reporting Services environment. When you open the Reporting Services Configuration tool, you'll see the following tabs on the left, as shown in figure 8.27:

- Server Status
- Report Server Virtual Directory
- Report Manager Virtual Directory
- Windows Service Identity
- Web Service Identity
- Database Setup
- Encryption Keys
- Initialization
- Email Settings
- Execution Account

Each of these tabs has an icon associated with it that indicates its status (Configured, Not Configured, Optional Configuration, or Recommended Configuration). Let's take a closer look at each of these tabs and learn when and how to use them.

Server Status

The Server Status page shows the SQL Server instance that Reporting Services is running under; for default instances, this will be `MSSQLSERVER`. You can also see the instance ID for RS; with a default installation, this will be MSSQL.3. This is also the directory that contains your Reporting Services–specific files. If you have installed multiple instances of SQL Server, this directory will be different.

By looking at this page you'll also learn whether this instance of RS has been initialized and the status of the service. The only configuration that you can do from this page involves stopping and starting the service. Since this is the default page that the configuration tool displays when opened, it also contains the legend for the icons that show up for each tab on the left.

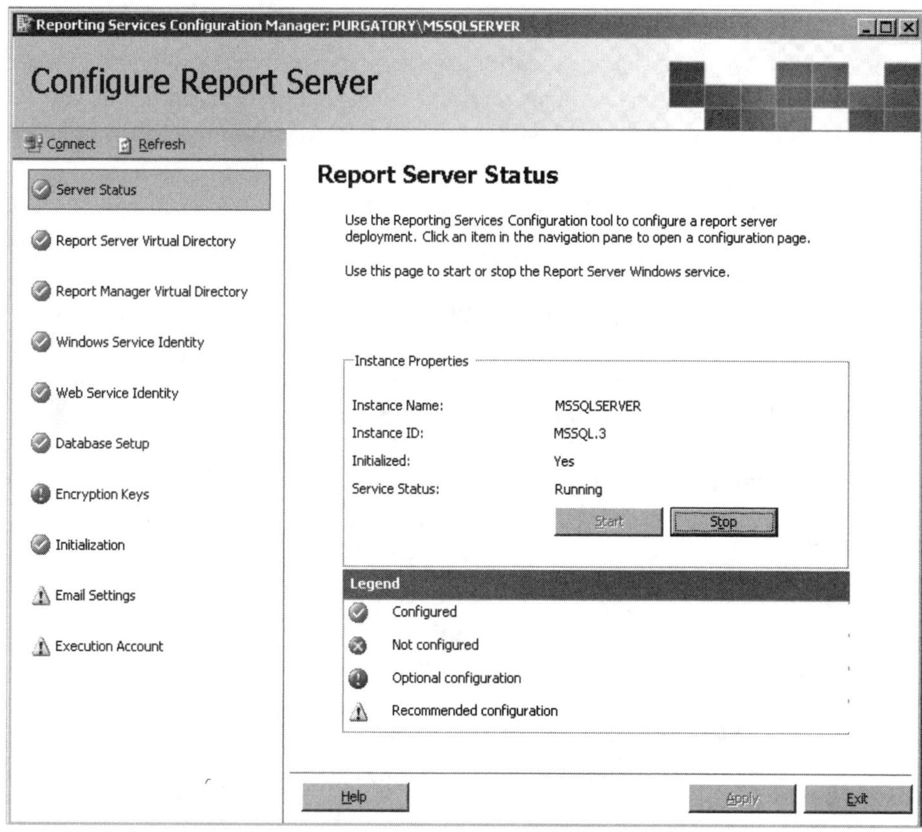

Figure 8.27 Use the configuration tool to manage your RS services, directories, keys, email settings, and more.

Report Server Virtual Directory

The Report Server Virtual Directory page shows the virtual directory that the RS ASP.NET web service runs in. As you learned in chapter 1, the Report Server URL provides access to the SOAP endpoints of the Report Server. You can create a new virtual directory from this page as well as manage your SSL settings and certificate information.

Report Manager Virtual Directory

The Report Manager Virtual Directory page displays the virtual directory that the RS Report Manager runs in. You can also create a new virtual directory from this page.

Windows Service Identity

The Windows Service Identity page defines the service account that is used to run the RS Windows service. This service is configured during setup, but you can modify it from this page if you update the password or want to use a different account.

Web Service Identity

The Web Service Identity page defines the service account that is used to run the RS Web service. Just like its Windows counterpart, this service is configured during setup, but you can modify it from this page if you update the password or want to use a different account. Note that this service cannot be configured if you are using Windows XP or Windows 2000 servers; these operating systems will always use the ASP.NET security identity to run the service.

Database Setup

Since the Report Server is a stateless server, it requires a place for internal storage; for this it uses SQL Server. The Database Setup page allows you to create and configure a connection to a Report Server database. You can connect to an existing database as long as it uses the schema for RS 2005. If you have an RS 2000 database, this page provides an upgrade option that will upgrade it to the 2005 schema.

Encryption Keys

The use and management of symmetric keys for encryption deserves special attention. RS uses this key to encrypt and decrypt sensitive data such as stored credentials and database connection information. We recommend that after installing RS, you use this utility to extract and back up the public encryption key.

What is the purpose of the encryption key? Chances are that you may need to change the account that the RS Windows service (`ReportingServicesService.exe`) runs under. Or, when deploying RS on a web farm environment, you may need to set up a new RS installation that points to an existing report catalog. If the encryption key is different, the Report Server will not initialize. Therefore, it is absolutely crucial that you back up and store the encryption key in a safe place.

Initialization

The Initialization page displays the initialization status of the Report Server. This page allows you to initialize and remove Report Servers. Report Servers that are initialized can store encrypted data on the Report Server.

Email Settings

In chapter 1 you learned that Reporting Services comes with two out-of-the-box delivery extensions: one of them is a File Share extension, which requires no configurations. The other out-of-the-box extension is an e-mail extension, which allows subscribers to have reports delivered to them through e-mail. This extension uses Simple Mail Transport Protocol (SMTP) to deliver the report. You can use the Email Settings page to specify which SMTP server or gateway on your network you want to use for the delivery. Previously, in RS 2000, you had to go into the configuration files and modify the XML directly. Now you have an easier way to manage your SMTP server.

Execution Account

The Execution Account page allows you to set up the account that RS uses to perform unattended operations. You should set up an account with low privileges to perform these operations.

Analyzing the report execution statistics is an essential task that all report administrators worth their salt will need to perform on a regular basis. To assist you in your effort to analyze and troubleshoot report processing, RS performs detailed logging. Let's see how you can use the RS logs to analyze report execution.

8.5 ANALYZING REPORT EXECUTION

Reporting Services maintains a variety of log files that capture the output from the three RS server-side components: the Report Server, the Report Manager, and the RS Windows service. Table 8.7 summarizes these log files.

Table 8.7 Log files maintained by RS

Log	Purpose
The Report Server execution log	Captures report execution statistics useful for auditing purposes.
Trace logs	Stores essential statistics for monitoring and troubleshooting RS.
The Microsoft Windows Event log	Records RS events, such as startup and shutdown events.
Setup logs	Created by the RS Setup program, these logs can be used to troubleshoot setup issues. For more information about these logs, consult the product documentation.

Let's discuss in more detail the first two logging options, starting with the Report Server execution log.

8.5.1 Analyzing the Report Server execution log

By analyzing the historical log, you should be able to answer such questions as "Which are the top requested reports by day, month, and user?" "Which reports didn't execute successfully, and why?" "How long does it take on average for a given report to execute?" You can set the Report Server to store report execution statistics in the `ExecutionLog` table. The execution log is turned on by default and keeps the log data for 60 days. You can modify these settings from the Site Settings menu in the Report Manager.

Retrieving the execution log data

There's really nothing stopping you from querying the `ExecutionLog` table and its related tables directly. But to save you time and effort, the RS team has provided a useful SSIS package and set of reports, which you can find in the SQL Server 2005 samples. From the `C:\Program Files\Microsoft SQL Server\90\Samples\Reporting Services\Report Samples\Server Management Sample Reports` directory, open the `readme_ServerManagementReports.htm` file and follow the setup directions.

Interpreting the execution log data

This SSIS package will assist you in setting up an automatic process to keep your log files in a new database called RSExecutionLog. Once you install and run the package and deploy the Execution Log Sample Reports report project, you will have some useful reports to analyze the execution log data. For example, the Report Execution Summary (figure 8.28) shows you the report activity and top requested reports per day. Glancing at the chart, you can easily see that the Report Server took the most hits on Tuesday during the requested week.

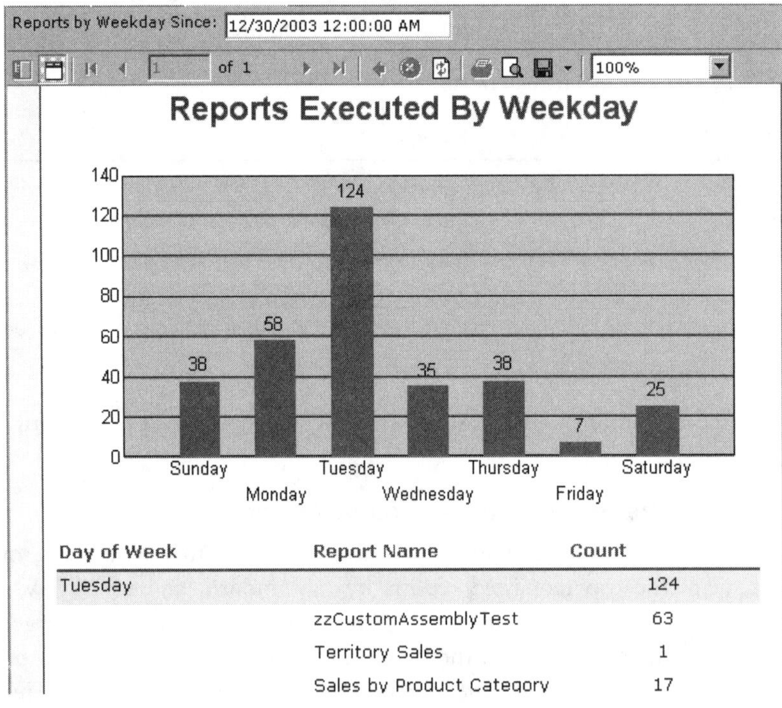

Figure 8.28 Use the Execution Log Sample Reports Project to analyze the statistics captured in the execution log.

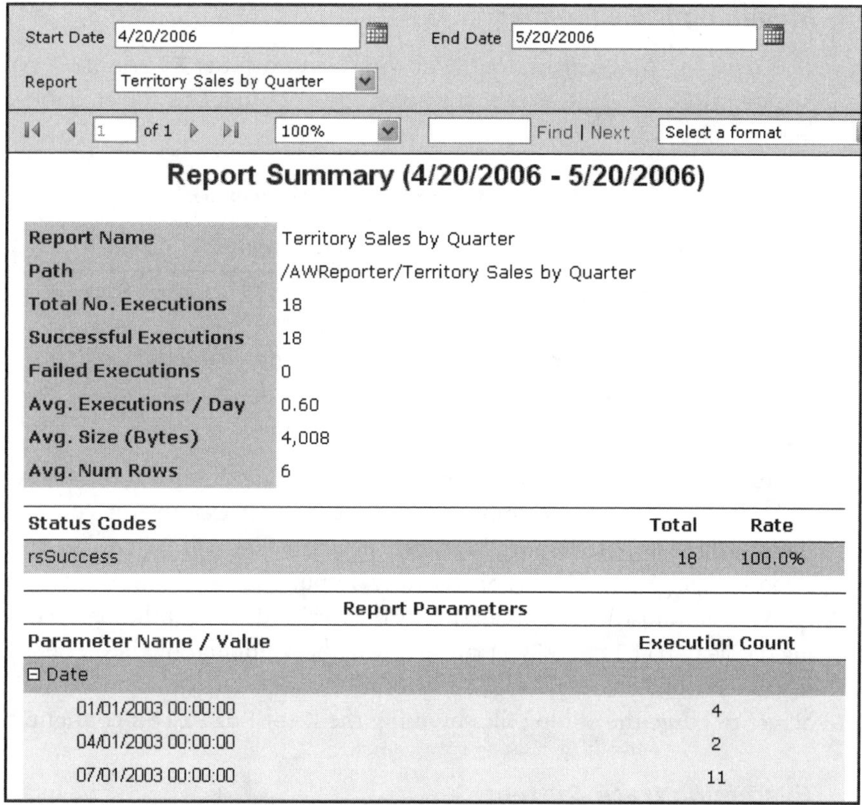

Figure 8.29 The Report Summary report shows that the Territory Sales by Quarter report succeeded 18 times out of 18 times

Another report that can help you troubleshoot specific report executions is called Report Summary and is shown in figure 8.29. Figure 8.29 reveals that the Territory Sales by Quarter report succeeded 18 times out of 18 times. You can also see that this report has only one parameter (Date) and that *07/01/2003 00:00:00* is the most popular choice.

8.5.2 Analyzing trace log files

Each of the RS server-side main components—the Report Server, the Report Manager, and the Windows service—maintains its own trace log file. The information captured in these files conveys vital statistics, which are useful for auditing and troubleshooting the report execution.

For example, by examining the log files you can find out who has accessed the Report Server and what action has been requested.

Managing trace log files

The trace log files can be found in the C:\Program Files\Microsoft SQL Server\MSSQL.3\Reporting Services\LogFiles folder. Table 8.8 outlines their purpose.

Table 8.8 The trace log files, one for each server-side component

Log Filename	Description
ReportServerService_<timestamp>.log	Trace log for the Report Server Windows service and Web service
ReportServerWebApp_<timestamp>.log	Trace log for the Report Manager
ReportServer_<timestamp>.log	Trace log for the Report Server

Reporting Services starts a new log file under two conditions: at the start of a new day and when the server-side component is started. For example, if you restart IIS and then navigate to the Report Manager, new log files will be created to capture the Report Manager and Report Server trace output.

As an administrator, you can specify the level of details for the logged data by adjusting the DefaultTraceSwitch setting in the configuration files. The supported values range from 0 (no tracing) to verbose. In addition, you can instruct the Report Server to purge the old log files by using the KeepForFiles configuration setting.

Examining trace content

The log data is stored in plain text so that you can use your favorite text editor to open and search the logs. For example, this is what the log entry looks like after a user has requested the Sales by Territory report:

```
w3wp!runningrequests!7bc!03/24/2004-22:20:17:: v VERBOSE: User
map'<Users><User><Name>"user identity"</Name><Paths><Path>
http://localhost/ReportServer/reportservice.asmx
</Path><NrReq>1</NrReq></Paths></User></Users>'
w3wp!library!7bc!03/24/2004-22:20:17:: i INFO: Call to GetPermissions:/
AWReporter/Sales By Territory
```

Performing runtime tracing

Sometimes, you may want to watch the tracing output in real time—for example, to see the sequence of events before an exception is thrown. Or you may need to see the tracing output from all three components in one place.

Fortunately, the information captured in the log files is also output to the default trace listener. This allows you to watch the tracing output using tools such as Mark Russinovich's DebugView trace monitor, as shown in figure 8.30.

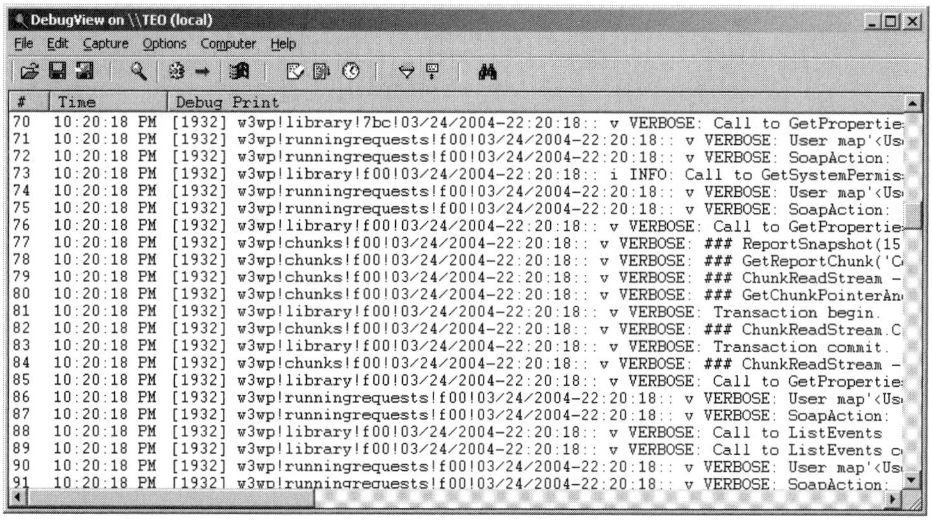

Figure 8.30 Use DebugView to watch the tracing output during runtime.

In this way, not only will you be able to get a consolidated picture of how the different components interact, but you will also be able to watch the tracing statements output by custom code and extensions.

8.6 SUMMARY

In this chapter we showed you how to manage the Report Server environment. Most of the time, you'll rely on the Report Manager or the SQL Server Management Studio to perform day-to-day administration activities, such as managing folders, reports, and resources.

We emphasized the fact that behind the scenes the Report Manager performs management tasks using the RS SOAP APIs. You can call these APIs programmatically in your applications to query and manage the report repository.

If you need to manage multiple Report Servers from a single location, you can use the RS WMI provider. We showed you how this could be done in the RS Console sample.

You learned that the SQL Server Management Studio mirrors much of the administrative features of the Report Manager, thus giving you a comfortable tool to manage Reporting Services items.

You can write script files in VB .NET and execute them with the RS script host. This option doesn't require advanced development skills. Scripts can be easily executed and scheduled to run at specific time.

RS also provides a few management utilities that you can use to perform specific tasks, such as activating a Report Server instance, changing database settings, and saving the encryption keys.

To keep track of report execution, we recommend that you turn on report execution logging and analyze its statistics on a daily basis. To do so, follow the instructions in the `readme_ServerManagementReports.htm` file found with the SQL Server samples.

Our report management journey would not be complete if we didn't discuss security. Securing the Report Server environment is, arguably, the most important aspect of RS management, and chapter 9 teaches you how to do exactly this.

C H A P T E R 9

Securing Reporting Services

Security can no longer be downplayed. Ironically, if you read computer books published in the not-so-distant past, you will usually find the security chapter pushed toward the end of the book, if not in the appendix. It's sort of like, "You will probably never need this stuff, but just in case…" Things have certainly changed! The explosion of viruses and hacker attacks in recent years has pushed security concerns to the forefront of development and application design. To address this issue, the common language runtime (CLR) and .NET Framework include classes that enable developers to write secure code easily.

You won't get far with Reporting Services if you don't have a good grasp of how its security works. In this chapter, you'll gain a strong understanding of how to use role-based security with reporting services. As you'll learn, a system administrator can leverage the role-based security model to secure access to report resources, as well as define the permitted actions that a given user is allowed to perform. We also discuss various strategies for securing reports, such as data filtering, dynamic queries, and data hiding.

Let's begin with an overview of the role-based security model.

9.1 ROLE-BASED SECURITY BASICS

Role-based security is simply a type of authorization process that allows a user to access certain resources and not others. It provides the user with the ability to perform specific tasks, based on the user's "role." You will probably find the RS role-based model similar to the security models of other Microsoft and third-party products or homegrown solutions you have come across in the past.

In this section, we describe the purpose of role-based security and how it works with an authentication model.

9.1.1 The purpose of role-based security

In a nutshell, role-based security provides the necessary infrastructure for the following:

- *User authentication*—During the authentication stage the role-based security model determines who the user is by obtaining her identity from a trusted authority. For example, let's say a user called Terri logs in to her machine as AW\Terri (AW is Terri's login domain) and runs a report. If Windows authentication is used, at the end of the authentication phase the Report Server will know that the identity of the user is AW\Terri.
- *User authorization*—Authorization occurs after authentication and determines what the user can do. Given the previous example, during the authorization process the Report Server would verify whether Terri has sufficient rights to run the report by checking the role-based security policy established for her.

In .NET security terminology, the terms *user* and *principal* are used interchangeably. For example, if you want to obtain the security context of the current user when Windows authentication is used, you can retrieve the current principal from `Thread.CurrentPrincipal`. The `IPrincipal` object returned from the call implements the `IIdentity` interface. You can query `IIdentity.Name` to obtain the user's identity after the user is authenticated.

Once the user's identity is verified, the user can execute tasks or request RS resources subject to the authorization rules set up by the report administrator.

The RS role-based security model serves two purposes:

- It provides the infrastructure to define user roles and assign users to these roles.
- It grants or revokes access to a specific task or resource based on the user's role membership.

9.1.2 Authentication models: using Windows or creating your own

A distinguishing feature of RS role-based security is that it is fully customizable. By default, RS relies on Windows authentication to authenticate users. This configuration will probably meet the security needs of most intranet-based applications. For example, Windows authentication allows the report administrator to leverage the preestablished user and group accounts in Active Directory.

However, when Windows authentication is not an option, developers can replace it with a custom security model in the form of a security extension. For example, using Windows accounts to authenticate web users is often impractical with most Internet-oriented applications. Instead, with this type of application, once the user enters her credentials, the application typically authenticates the user via a database lookup. To add reporting features to such applications, you can write a custom security extension to pass the user's identity to the Report Server. We see how to do just that in chapter 13.

In this chapter, we focus on the RS role-based security model in the context of the default authentication mechanism, which, once again, is Windows authentication.

9.2 WINDOWS AUTHENTICATION: A CLOSER LOOK

For networks running Active Directory, implementing role-based permissions with Windows authentication is simple. How does Reporting Services work with Windows authentication?

The Report Server delegates the security-related tasks to a *security extension.* A security extension is a .NET assembly that handles the authentication and authorization of users or groups in RS. When the Report Server needs to authenticate the user or verify that the user is allowed to perform a given task, it asks the extension to do so.

Because the Report Server web application is configured for Integrated Windows authentication, the security extension gets the Windows identity of the user from Internet Information Services (IIS). IIS authenticates the user and passes the Windows access token to the Report Server.

Although IIS provides several authentication mechanisms, RS supports the Basic and Integrated (NTLM or Kerberos) authentication options only.

NOTE Strictly speaking, although you are discouraged from doing so, you can configure the Report Server virtual root to allow anonymous access. This could be useful in situations when you don't care about the identity of the user; for example, when you want to allow any user to access the Report Server with the same level of permissions. The net effect of enabling anonymous access is that you disable the RS role-based security policy. The reason for this is that the Report Server sees all requests as coming under a single Windows account, which by default is `IUSR_<computer name>`.

Therefore, the role-based security policies cannot be enforced per user, which is a sure recipe for chaos. Note that you still have to establish a security policy for this Anonymous account (or the Windows groups it is a member of) in the Report Server and map it to a role. Because the Report Server will be unable to differentiate the user requests, to be able to manage the report catalog you will need to grant this account system administrator rights. This means that any user will be able to change the Report Server configuration at will. When anonymous access is mandatory, we strongly suggest that you use custom security authentication performed by the application or a custom security extension.

By default, RS is installed in a locked-down mode, and only members of the Windows local administrators group can manage the report environment and run reports. Similar to the Windows NTFS model, to prevent an accidental lockout, this security policy cannot be removed. As a result, Reporting Services will always allow local administrators on the Report Server machine the right to view items and change security policies, even if they're not explicitly defined in a role-based security policy.

To allow other users to request reports or manage RS, you must create additional security policies and add Windows built-in accounts or groups to them. Typically, to simplify the role assignment management, you will organize the Windows user accounts into groups. This will require that you work hand in hand with the network administrator to define the appropriate Windows group memberships and create new groups if needed.

To understand how Windows authentication can be used for securing client applications, consider two common integration scenarios:

- Client-to-Report Server
- Client-to-Façade-to-Report Server

NOTE Another common way to describe the above scenarios is to use the "tier" paradigm. Because the Report Server can be viewed as a separate tier, the first scenario could also be named "three-tiered," while the second could be called "multitiered." You choose.

Let's discuss how security relates to each of these models, starting with the Client-to-Report Server model.

9.2.1 Exploring the Client-to-Report Server model

The Client-to-Report Server scenario is better suited for intranet-based report consumers. With this model, the report consumer, which could be WinForm or web-based, accesses the Report Server on the client side of the application, and the call goes out under the Windows identity of the user. Figure 9.1 depicts the Client-to-Report Server integration approach.

By the way, this is the model that the Report Manager uses for report rendering. When the user clicks the report link inside the Report Manager, an HTTP-GET request is made to the Report Server under the identity of the interactive user.

In figure 9.1 Terri is logged into the AW domain as AW/Terri. Terri then goes to the Report Manager portal to run a report. IIS authenticates Terri as AW/Terri and

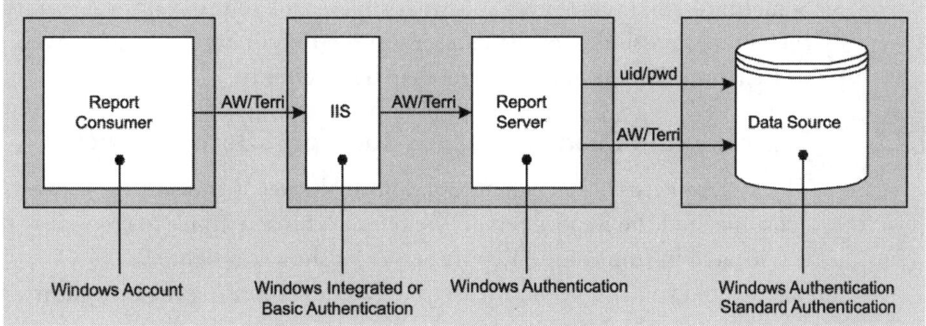

Figure 9.1 The Client-to-Report Server model is most suitable for intranet-based applications and promotes direct access to the Report Server.

passes the security token to the Report Server. Next, the Report Server checks the role-based security policy for Terri and grants or refuses access to the requested report.

Let's assume that Terri is granted permissions to run the report, and the report needs to access a data source to display some data. How the database authenticates the request depends on which data source authentication options have been set for this report, as we discussed in chapter 3. Here are the possible outcomes:

- *Credentials Stored Securely in the Report Server*—If the Use as Windows Credentials When Connecting to the Data Source option is set, the database will use Windows Integrated authentication to authenticate the call using the Windows account credentials the administrator has set up. Otherwise, the data source will use standard authentication. In both cases, the call to the database will go under a designated account (depicted as `uid/pwd` in figure 9.1), which facilitates connection pooling.
- *Windows NT Integrated Security*—If the database is installed on the same machine as the Report Server or on another machine with Kerberos delegation enabled, the call to the database will go out under AW/Terri. If the database is on another machine and Kerberos is not enabled, the remote call will use a `NULL` session and it will fail. As we pointed out in chapter 3, in general you should avoid impersonating the user so you don't lose the benefits of connection pooling.

For the Client-to-Report Server scenario, we recommend the following security configuration:

- Use the default Windows-based authentication coupled with role-based security to enforce restricted access to the Report Server.
- Use the Credentials Stored Securely in the Report Server data source option with Windows or standard authentication for accessing the data source.

Sometimes, this scenario won't be that simple and your integration requirements may rule out the possibility of direct access to the Report Server. In such cases, the Client-to-Façade-to-Report Server model may be a better fit.

9.2.2 Exploring the Client-to-Façade-to-Report Server model

The system gets trickier when an additional layer is introduced between the report consumer and the Report Server. We refer to this as a *façade* to emphasize the fact that it is located in front of the Report Server, as shown in figure 9.2.

Why would you add yet another layer? Besides increasing the complexity, such a layer can serve the following purposes:

- *It may encapsulate the application's business rules*—For example, it may represent the business layer of a WinForm three-tiered application, which could be exposed either as Web services or as a set of .NET remote objects. We discuss this approach in more detail in chapter 10.
- *It may represent the server-side web layer of the report consumer for both intranet and Internet web-based applications*—For example, the Report Manager can be viewed as a façade to the Report Server.
- *It may be needed to isolate the report consumer from the Report Server*—For example, in the business-to-business extranet scenario, it is unlikely that an organization will allow direct access to the Report Server. Instead, a Web service façade could be built to expose some of the RS functionality.
- *It may enforce custom security rules to extend or replace the Report Server role-based security model when the latter is not enough.*

For simplicity's sake, the scenario shown in figure 9.2 assumes that the report consumer runs under the Windows identity of the user. This is the typical case with intranet applications. Things can get more complicated with other implementation approaches. For instance, in the extranet scenario, the report consumers can use client

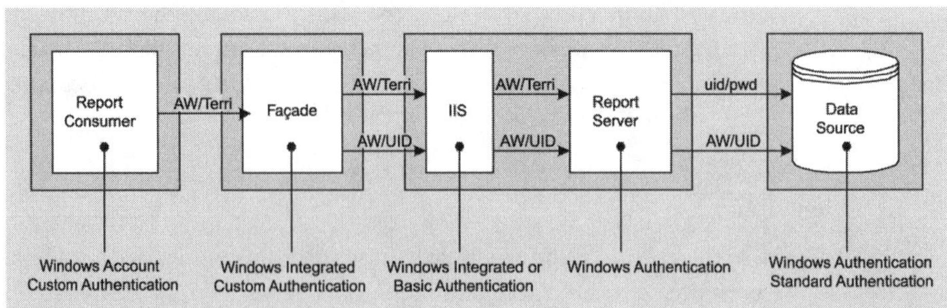

Figure 9.2 In the Client-to-Façade-to-Report Server model, an additional layer is introduced between the report consumer and the Report Server.

certificates for authentication, which can be mapped to Windows accounts. Or, an Internet-based application can use ASP.NET Forms Authentication.

From the Report Server standpoint, how the report consumer is implemented is not important. All the Report Server sees are incoming requests under a given Windows identity. From the report consumer façade standpoint, however, which identity will be passed to the Report Server is very important. Basically, the façade layer has two choices:

- Impersonate the user by passing the user's identity to the Report Server.
- Pass its identity. This model is sometimes referred to as a trusted subsystem.

Impersonating the user

If the façade decides to impersonate the user, the original user's security context and identity will flow to IIS and then to the Report Server. This is the approach the Report Manager takes for submitting SOAP requests to the Report Server on the server side of the application.

To impersonate the user in ASP.NET applications, you can use the `<impersonate>` element in the `web.config` configuration file. You can impersonate the user's identity or use a specific Windows account. If the façade and the Report Server are located on separate machines, you must enable Kerberos authentication to manage the user identity between the Façade and the Report Server because NTLM doesn't support delegation. Then the authentication works as we described in the Client-to-Report Server scenario.

Passing the façade identity

Instead of impersonating the user, the façade can pass its own identity. To accomplish this, you would typically change the identity of the ASP.NET worker process to run under a designated domain account. If you decide to use a local computer account, you'll have to clone this account to the Report Server machine to keep the security gods happy.

As figure 9.2 shows, the ASP.NET worker process runs under a domain account AW/UID, which is passed on to the Report Server. If the façade layer runs under IIS 5 (Windows 2000), this will require that you change the `<processModel>` element in `machine.config`. If IIS 6 is used (Windows 2003), you can change the identity of the application pool to which the application belongs. In addition, you need to add the account that you used for the pool identity to the Windows 2003 IIS_WPG group.

Once the façade identity is set up, you must map it to the appropriate role in the Report Server so that it has proper access to RS resources. If the façade will fulfill report-rendering tasks only, you could create a security policy to grant the façade account Browser role permissions.

While the trusted subsystem approach simplifies the authentication process between the façade and the Report Server, you need to take care of authenticating the end users and authorizing them at the façade layer.

Authenticating the user represents one half of the security equation. After the authentication, the user must be authorized to access a given resource from the report catalog. We explore how to do that next.

9.3 USING ROLE-BASED AUTHORIZATION

Regardless of which authentication model is used, Windows or custom authentication, Reporting Services authorizes requests based on the membership that the user has in one or more RS roles. RS offers a comprehensive role-based security model to authorize user requests. In this section, we discuss the theory behind this model and then demonstrate how you can manage the role-based security infrastructure with the Report Manager and the Report Server Web service.

To understand the RS role-based model and see how its pieces fit together, look at the database diagram shown in figure 9.3. Note that this diagram doesn't exactly match the Report Server physical database model. You'll find only the `Users`, `Roles`, and `Policies` tables in the Report Server database; the rest are fictitious. Where, then, does the Report Server store the rest of the role-based security items? If you examine the actual `Policies` table, you'll notice that it uses proprietary structures to define the role assignment relationship. When the administrator creates a new security policy for a given user to a securable item, a new record is added to the `Policies` table. This record specifies the item that is secured, the user's Windows account, and the role-based security policy stored as an XML fragment.

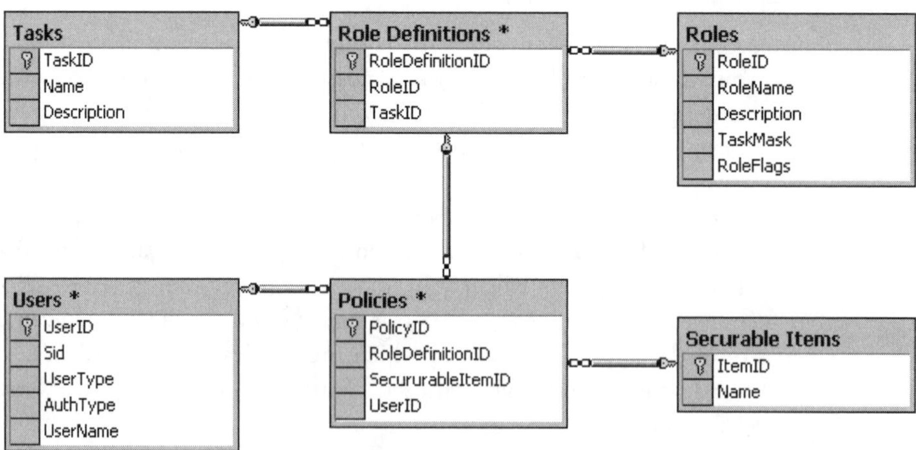

Figure 9.3 Reporting Services comes with a comprehensive role-based security model based on the user's membership in one or more roles.

Note that the diagram in figure 9.3 doesn't exactly match the Report Server physical database model. You will find only the `Users`, `Roles`, and `Policies` tables in the Report Server database; the rest are fictitious. Where, then, does the Report Server store the rest of the role-based security items? If you examine the actual `Policies` table, you will notice that it uses proprietary structures to define the role assignment relationship. When the administrator creates a new security policy for a given user to a securable item, a new record is added to the `Policies` table. This record specifies the item that is secured, the user's Windows account, and the role-based security policy stored as an XML fragment.

Strictly speaking, although not so obvious, tasks in RS are further broken out and consist of entities called *permissions*. However, for simplicity, permissions are not exposed in the Report Manager UI, so you can't see them. The reason for this is that a task is a fixed collection of permissions and can't be changed.

How do you find out what permissions are available with RS? In section 9.5.1 we author a sample report called Show Security Policy, which lists the permissions associated with a given user and report item. To accomplish this, we use the `GetPermissions` SOAP API, which returns a collection of permissions, such as Create Data Source, Create Folder, and so forth.

At this point you may be curious as to how permissions can be used if tasks are fixed entities. RS permissions could be useful if you need to write a custom security extension and you need to deal with permissions—for example, if you want the Report Manager to disable controls according to the security policy associated with the interactive user. We show you how to write a custom security extension in chapter 13.

9.3.1 Understanding tasks

A *task* defines a set of permissions that can be enforced through role-based security. For example, RS defines a task called View Reports, which allows users to run reports.

RS defines two types for tasks:

- System-level tasks
- Item-level tasks

System-level tasks represent maintenance actions, such as Define Roles. Item-level tasks define user permissions—View Reports, View Folders, and so on. Another way to differentiate between these two types is to note that system-level tasks work on global items (which do not have catalog paths), while item-level tasks work on items with paths.

You can find the full list of predefined tasks under the Site Settings menu. Currently, RS doesn't support custom tasks. For this reason, you won't find a `Task` table in the Report Server database. In addition, you cannot map users directly to tasks. Instead, to use a task, you first need to assign it to a role.

9.3.2 Defining roles

As its name suggests, the role-based security infrastructure in RS uses the concept of *roles* to assign a set of permissions to users with the same security requirements. Simply put, a role is a named set of tasks. Currently, RS doesn't support nested roles. For example, you cannot set up a Content Manager role to include the Browser role.

Because the relationship between roles and tasks is many-to-many, the documentation uses the term *role definition* to represent the tasks-to-role membership. For example, RS includes the predefined item-level Browser and Content Manager roles, and both of them include the View Reports task.

NOTE Strictly speaking, Reporting Services implements the roles-to-tasks relationship by a bit-masked value defined in the `TaskMask` column in the `Roles` table. For this reason, the terms *role* and *role definition* are interchangeable. However, we broke it down into two tables to make the concept easier to understand.

Similar to the task types, RS classifies roles in two categories: system roles and item-level roles.

System-level roles

Most applications need an Administrator role that has unrestricted access to the application to perform application-wide maintenance tasks. Reporting Services is no exception. It defines two system roles, as shown in table 9.1.

Table 9.1 Predefined system roles

System-Level Role	Rights
System User	View system properties and shared schedules
System Administrator	System User rights plus the rights to view and modify system role assignments and role definitions

System-level roles can include only system-level tasks. When you install RS, the Setup program maps the Windows local administrators group to the System Administrator role.

Item-level roles

Item-level roles contain item-level tasks. Table 9.2 shows the predefined item-level roles.

Unlike working with tasks, you can define custom system- and item-level roles, as well as modify the predefined roles. Let's say that you don't like the predefined task mapping for the Content Manager role; you don't want members of this role to be able to view reports. You can use the Site Settings menu to either change the role definition or create a new item-level role.

Table 9.2 Predefined item-level roles

Item-Level Role	Rights
Browser	View folders and reports and subscribe to reports
Content Manager	All item-level permissions
My Reports	Publish reports and linked reports; manage folders, reports, and resources in a user's My Reports folder
Publisher	Publish reports and linked reports to the Report Server
Report Builder	Read report definitions, manage subscriptions, view folders, models, reports, and resources.

9.3.3 Understanding securable items

With RS you can secure resources to meet the requirements of your company. For example, say that you don't want your users to be able to view or modify Shared Data Sources. Table 9.3 lists the RS resources that can be secured through role-based security.

Table 9.3 RS-securable resources

Securable resource	Description
Folders	Viewing folders and navigating through the folder hierarchy requires the rights to execute the View Folders task. If the user doesn't have the rights to view a folder, the folder is excluded from the folder view. Requesting the folder explicitly through URL access or Web service results in a security exception. Managing folders requires the Manage Folders task.
Reports	To view a report, the user must have the rights to execute the View Reports task. To manage the report, the user must have the Manage Reports rights.
Shared data sources	The user needs the Manage Reports rights to change the report data source. After that, no special permissions are required to render reports that use a shared data source. To view the shared data source definition, the user must have the View Data Sources permission. To manage it, the rights to execute the Manage Data Sources tasks are required.
Other catalog items	The View Resources permission is required to view an image item. Similarly, View Resources is required to apply an XSL transformation.
Report History	Managing the report snapshot history requires the rights to execute the Manage Report History task.
Subscriptions	Managing user report subscriptions requires the rights to execute the Manage Individual Subscriptions task. Managing report subscriptions of other users requires the rights to execute the Manage All Subscriptions task.
Models	The Models permission is required to create ad hoc reports as discussed in chapter 7. This allows the user to view models in the folder hierarchy, use models as data sources for a report, and run queries against the model to retrieve data.

Tasks and roles are useful only when they are associated with users in order to enforce restricted access to the Report Server. To accomplish this, the administrator defines role-based security policies.

9.3.4 Defining policies

A policy defines the relationship among users, roles, and securable items. In other words, a policy determines the permitted tasks that the user can perform on a given securable item, such as a folder or report. The RS role-based security policy is additive, which means that the user is granted the union of the permitted tasks defined in the roles to which the user is mapped. Let's consider the example shown in figure 9.4.

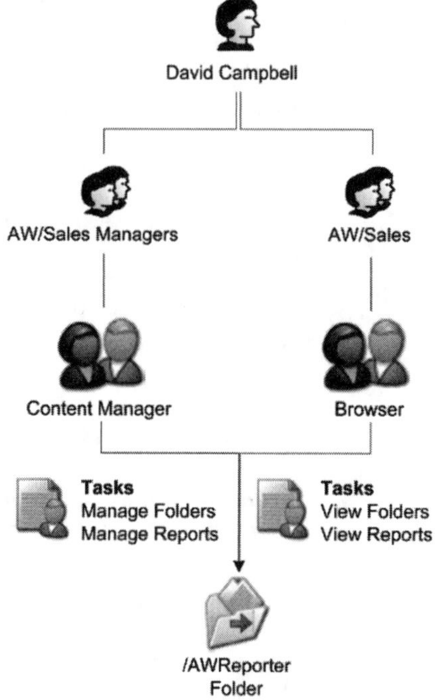

Figure 9.4 The RS role-based security model is additive, and the user is granted the union of the permitted tasks.

In this example, David Campbell is assigned to both the Sales Managers and Sales Windows groups of the AW domain. The RS administrator assigned the Sales Managers group to the Content Manager role when defining the role-based security for the AWReporter folder. The AW Sales group is mapped to the Browser role.

What will be the resultant set of permitted tasks that David Campbell gets? The answer is that he will be able to execute all tasks defined for the Content Manager and Browser roles. If these two roles include the default set of tasks, David will be able to manage the AWReporter folder (create and delete folders, add reports), as well as see all reports and folders in the AWReporter folder.

Overriding security policy inherited from the parent folder

You can enforce role-based security on folders and their contents. By default, the security policy propagates through the children of the parent folder. This is similar to the way Windows access control list (ACL) permissions are inherited from the parent folder by its descendants. However, the inheritance chain can be overridden if the subfolders or resources must have different permissions than their parent.

For example, considering again the scenario shown in figure 9.4, what if the AWReporter folder contains some sensitive reports that only the members of the Sales

Managers group should see? To accomplish this requirement, we can remove the AW/Sales group from the policy list of restricted reports.

What happens when you break the policy inheritance chain at a specific securable item? The Report Server simply assigns a new policy list to this item, which by default gives Content Manager rights to members of the Windows local administrators group.

It is not difficult to understand how the Report Server determines whether the user is permitted to execute a given task on a secured item. First, the Report Server determines whether the item inherits the security policy of its parent. If the security chain is broken at the item level, the Report Server evaluates its policy list to find out which tasks have been assigned to the role(s) the user belongs to. If the security policy is inherited, the Report Server walks recursively up the inheritance chain to find out which of the item ascendants define the security policy.

Simplifying security policy management

To simplify the folder permissions, we suggest that you stick to policy inheritance as much as possible. The approach we recommend is to enforce the minimum set of permissions at the top Home folder. Then, work your way down by adding or taking out permissions on its children on an as-needed basis.

Let's consider a more involved example. Let's say you want to organize your RS folder namespace per department and application, similar to the one shown in figure 9.5.

First, under the Home folder you create department folders, for example, Sales and HR. Then, you create application folders under the department folders, for example, AWReporter for the Sales department to contain all of the sample reports from this book. How can you minimize role-based security maintenance and yet ensure that you enforce a comprehensive level of security? Let's say you don't want users from other departments to be able to browse the Sales folder and see its contents.

Role	Group
Content Manager	AW/Administrators
Browser	AW/Users

Role	Group	Inherited
Content Manager	AW/Administrators	Y
Content Manager	AW/Sales Managers	
Browser	AW/Sales	

Role	Group	Inherited
Content Manager	AW/Administrators	Y
Content Manager	AW/Sales Managers	Y
Browser	AW/Sales	Y

Figure 9.5 You can simplify role-based security management by using policy inheritance.

To simplify the security infrastructure, you can take advantage of the inheritance feature of the role-based security policy. You can allow only AWC domain administrators to manage the full folder namespace by assigning them to the Content Manager role. You can assign all other domain users to the Browser role so they can browse the Home folder. For the Sales folder you can break the folder's inheritance chain. You can remove the Users group from the Browser role and grant the Sales Managers and Sales groups the Content Manager and Browser roles, respectively. You don't have to perform any extra steps if you want the same permissions to propagate to the AWReporter folder.

When the user doesn't have permissions to view a given securable item, the item is excluded from the results of the Web service method call. For example, if the user clicks on the Home folder to see its subfolders, the Report Server will return only the subfolders to which the user has View permissions. Behind the scenes, the Report Manager invokes the `ListChildren` SOAP API, which excludes restricted resources. This makes developing client applications a lot easier because you don't have to filter out the results to enforce restricted access—one less thing to worry about when writing custom applications that target RS.

Now that we've explained the theory behind the RS role-based security model, let's see how we can manage it using the Report Manager.

9.4 MANAGING ROLE-BASED SECURITY WITH THE REPORT MANAGER

It is important to note that when you use the Report Manager to set up a role-based security infrastructure, you are securing not the Report Manager but the Report Server. The policy changes that you make using the Report Manager are persisted in the Report Server database. For this reason, these changes affect all report consumers that use the same instance of the Report Server.

Managing the role-based security infrastructure with the Report Manager is easy. We convince you of this by way of example. In this section, we show you how to secure the resources in the AWReporter folder. Our fictitious scenario is similar to the examples you have already seen in this chapter. Using the Report Manager, you are going to complete the following tasks:

- Create a few Windows user accounts and assign them to Windows groups
- Assign the Windows groups to predefined and custom roles
- Enforce a role-based security policy on the AWReporter folder and its resources

To make this example more realistic, let's define the new accounts and groups to correspond with the AWC organizational structure. Back in chapter 5, you created a Corporate Hierarchy report that you can use to get started, as shown in figure 9.6.

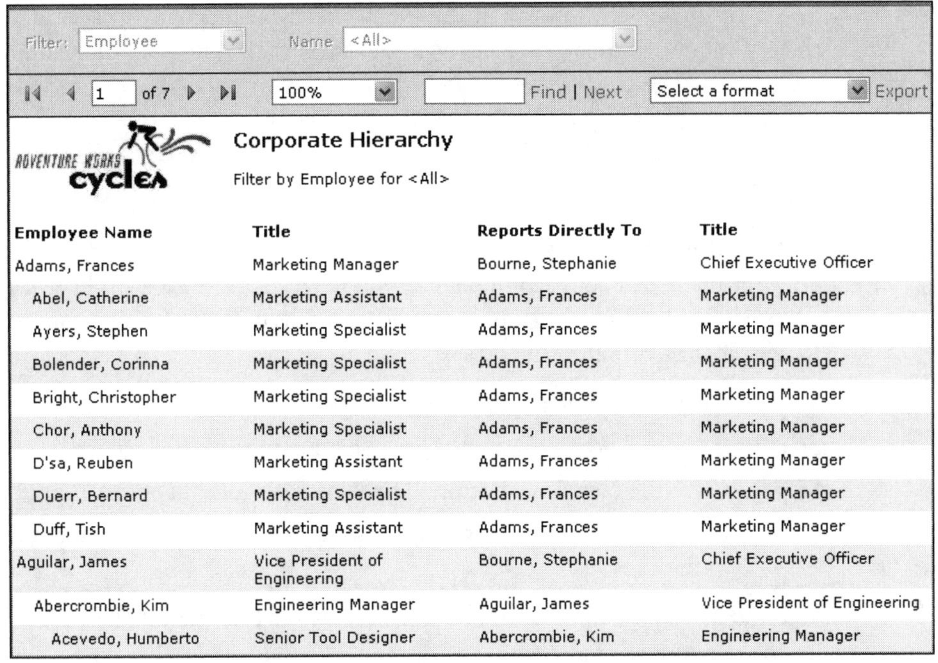

Corporate Hierarchy

Filter by Employee for <All>

Employee Name	Title	Reports Directly To	Title
Adams, Frances	Marketing Manager	Bourne, Stephanie	Chief Executive Officer
Abel, Catherine	Marketing Assistant	Adams, Frances	Marketing Manager
Ayers, Stephen	Marketing Specialist	Adams, Frances	Marketing Manager
Bolender, Corinna	Marketing Specialist	Adams, Frances	Marketing Manager
Bright, Christopher	Marketing Specialist	Adams, Frances	Marketing Manager
Chor, Anthony	Marketing Specialist	Adams, Frances	Marketing Manager
D'sa, Reuben	Marketing Assistant	Adams, Frances	Marketing Manager
Duerr, Bernard	Marketing Specialist	Adams, Frances	Marketing Manager
Duff, Tish	Marketing Assistant	Adams, Frances	Marketing Manager
Aguilar, James	Vice President of Engineering	Bourne, Stephanie	Chief Executive Officer
Abercrombie, Kim	Engineering Manager	Aguilar, James	Vice President of Engineering
Acevedo, Humberto	Senior Tool Designer	Abercrombie, Kim	Engineering Manager

Figure 9.6 Use the Corporate Hierarchy report to see the AWC organizational structure.

Your security requirements are as follows:

- Only the members of the Sales Managers and Sales groups can access the AWReporter folder.
- The members of the Sales Managers group have unrestricted access to the AWReporter folder.
- The members of the Sales group are able to run reports only.
- The AWC network administrator can manage the AWReporter folder and its resources but cannot view any reports in this folder.

9.4.1 Creating Windows user accounts and groups

The `HumanResources.Employee` table in the AdventureWorks database can give you the necessary details to set up the Windows accounts, as shown in table 9.4.

Table 9.4 Test accounts and groups needed to run the role-based security sample

Username	Login ID	Password	Description	Windows group
Michael Blythe	Michael9	Michael9	Sales Manager	AW Sales Managers, Users
David Campbell	David8	David8	Sales Representative	AW Sales, Users
Ashvini Sharma	Ashvini0	Ashvini0	Network Administrator	AW Sales Admin, Users

To set up these accounts, open the Computer Management console and create the three Windows groups (AW Sales Managers, AW Sales, and AW Sales Admin) listed in table 9.4. In the process of doing so, don't forget to uncheck the User Must Change Password at Next Logon check box.

Then, create the three Windows user accounts (Michael9, David8, and Ashvini0) and assign them to the appropriate groups.

9.4.2 Creating custom roles

To meet the last of your requirements, you need to create a new role because none of the predefined roles includes only management tasks. To create a custom role with the Report Manager, follow these steps:

Step 1 Click the Site Settings menu.

Step 2 Click the Configure Item-Level Role Definitions link.

Step 3 Click the New Role button. The New Role screen appears (figure 9.7).

Step 4 Name the new role Sales Admin and assign to it all management tasks shown in figure 9.7.

You now have a custom role that you can use to define the role-based security policy for the network administrator.

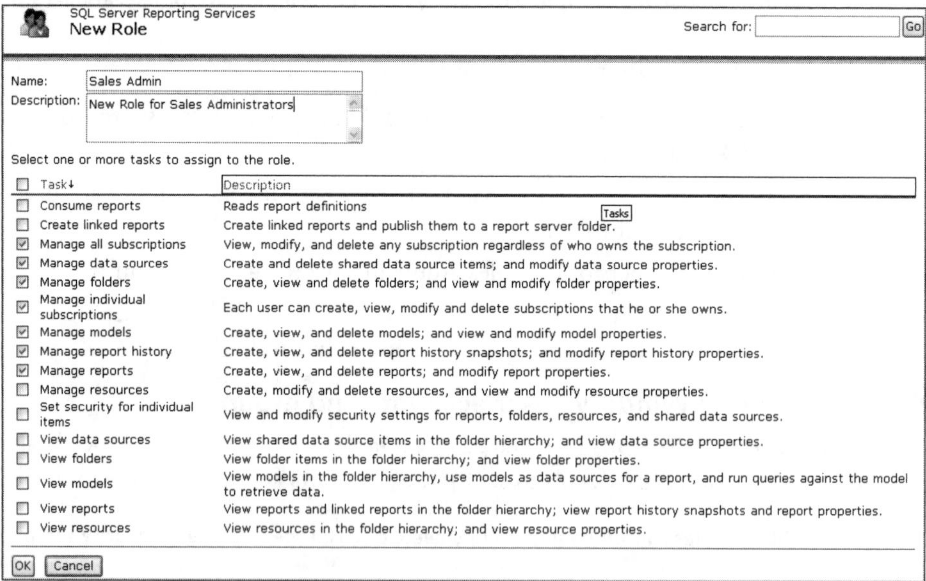

Figure 9.7 With RS you can create a custom role that includes one or more predefined tasks.

9.4.3 Defining security policies

Next, let's enforce restricted access to the AWReporter folder. Using the Report Manager, navigate to the AWReporter folder and click the Security tab on the folder's Properties page. If you haven't made any changes to the default security policy, you will see a single button named Edit Item Security. When you click it, you see the confirmation prompt shown in figure 9.8.

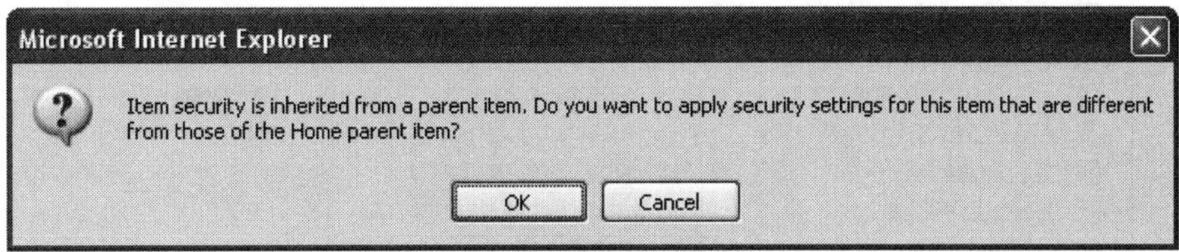

Figure 9.8 When the security policy inherited from the item parent is not a good fit, you can override it. You will see this warning message when breaking the inherited security for an item.

Click OK to confirm your intention to override the security policy inherited from the Home folder. The user interface changes and now shows two buttons (figure 9.9).

The default security policy allows only local administrators to access this folder by granting them permissions to execute all tasks of the Content Manager role. Let's now define three additional security policies that will grant different levels of access to the AWReporter folder for the Sales Managers, Sales, and Sales Admin Windows groups.

Let's start with granting the members of the Sales Managers group the Content Manager rights to the AWReporter folder. Click New Role Assignment to create a new security policy, as shown in figure 9.10.

Create two more role assignments to assign the members of the AW Sales group to the Browser role and the members of the AW Sales Admin group to the Sales Admin role. When you return to the Security tab, your screen should look like the one shown in figure 9.11.

You've finished! You can test the role-based security policies by logging onto Windows as each of the three users. For example, if you log on as Ashvini0, you will be able to manage the AWReporter folder and its resources, but you won't be able to run any of the reports. When you click the report's link, the Report Manager will not render the report. Instead, the report's Properties page will be open.

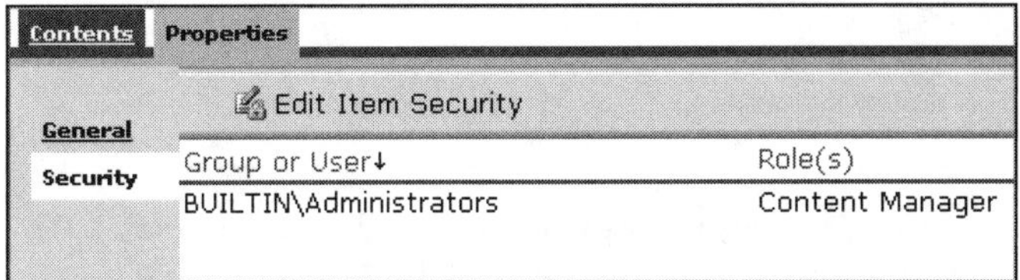

Figure 9.9 Use the report's Security tab to create new role-based security policies.

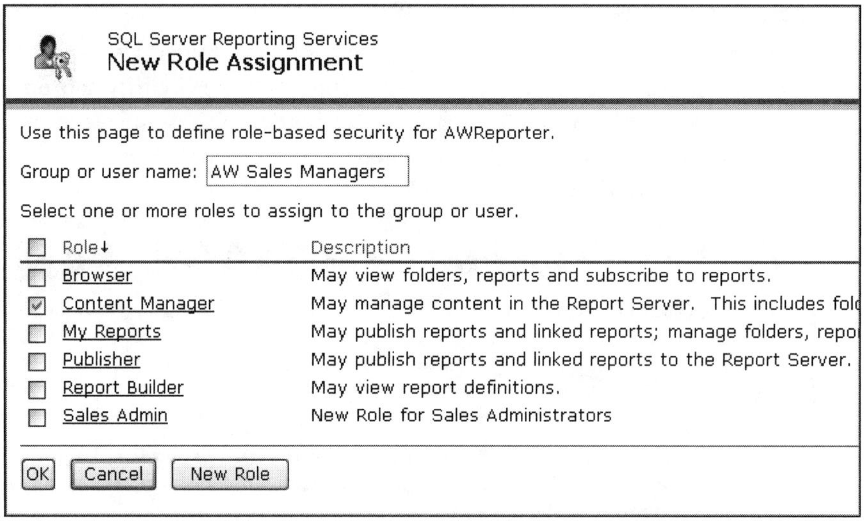

Figure 9.10 You create a new role-based security policy by assigning Windows user or group accounts to roles.

But wait, you say, what if you need to enforce a more restrictive policy on specific resources? For example, what if you want to prevent the members of the AW Sales group from running the Sales by Territory report? To accomplish this, you can enforce a report-specific security policy by overriding the AWReporter folder policy. To do so, you can click the Edit Item Security button found on the Security tab of the report's Properties page. When you do this, you are presented again with the confirmation prompt shown in figure 9.8, asking whether you really want to break the security policy inheritance.

Once you confirm your intention, you can delete the AW Sales group from the policy list, which, in turn, prevents its group members from rendering the report. If you later change your mind, you can always restore the policy inheritance by clicking the Revert to Parent Security button.

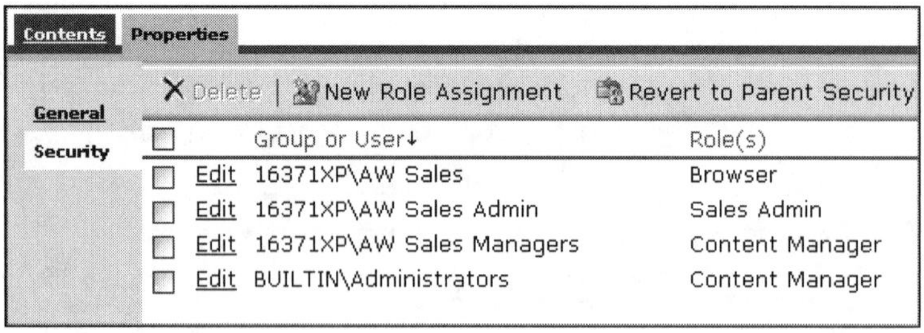

Figure 9.11 Based on your security requirements, you may need to create several security policies to provide restricted access to the report based on the users' role membership.

As we explained in chapter 8, the Report Manager is just a user-friendly application layer on top of the Report Server. The Report Manager calls down to the RS Web service to perform all management tasks behind the scenes. In a similar way, you can manage programmatically the RS role-based security in your applications by invoking the Web service's security-related methods, as we discuss next.

9.5 MANAGING ROLE-BASED SECURITY WITH THE WEB SERVICE

As we discussed in chapter 8, the RS Web service provides a series of security-related methods that you can use to manage programmatically all aspects of the role-based security infrastructure. When the Report Manager is not enough, you can create custom applications (or reports) that call the security API directly.

For example, as an administrator, you may be interested in authoring a report that lists the permissions a given user has to all resources within a given folder. Or, you may have defined resource-specific security policies already, and you need a report that shows you where the role assignment takes place.

In this section we show you how to use the RS Web service to determine role-based security policies, call security-related methods, and implement "pseudo" report events.

9.5.1 Determining role-based security policies

Requirements like the ones discussed in the previous section go beyond the Report Manager feature set. However, with a little bit of programming effort, you can author such reports easily by directly calling the Web service authorization APIs. In figure 9.12 we see the Show Security Policy report, which fulfills your requirements.

The Show Security Policy report takes as parameters the user's Windows login name and password, as well as the Report Server Web service URL. If the Item Name parameter is left NULL, the report will show which permissions the user has to all securable resources. For example, figure 9.12 shows that we wanted the report to indicate which permissions Ashvini has to the resources located in the AWReporter folder.

Alternatively, as the administrator you can enter the name of a resource (in the Item Name parameter) to filter the report for a single resource. That way, you see the security policy defined for this item only.

TIP In the real world you will rarely know the user's password. If you don't need the user's permission set but only want to see the user's roles, then you can use the approach suggested by Tudor Trufinesco, a Microsoft engineer from the RS team. You can use an account with Admin rights to call `GetPolicies` on all the items in the catalog and find out which ones are not inherited. Then you can display or parse the XML policy in the report.

Let's look at how this report is implemented.

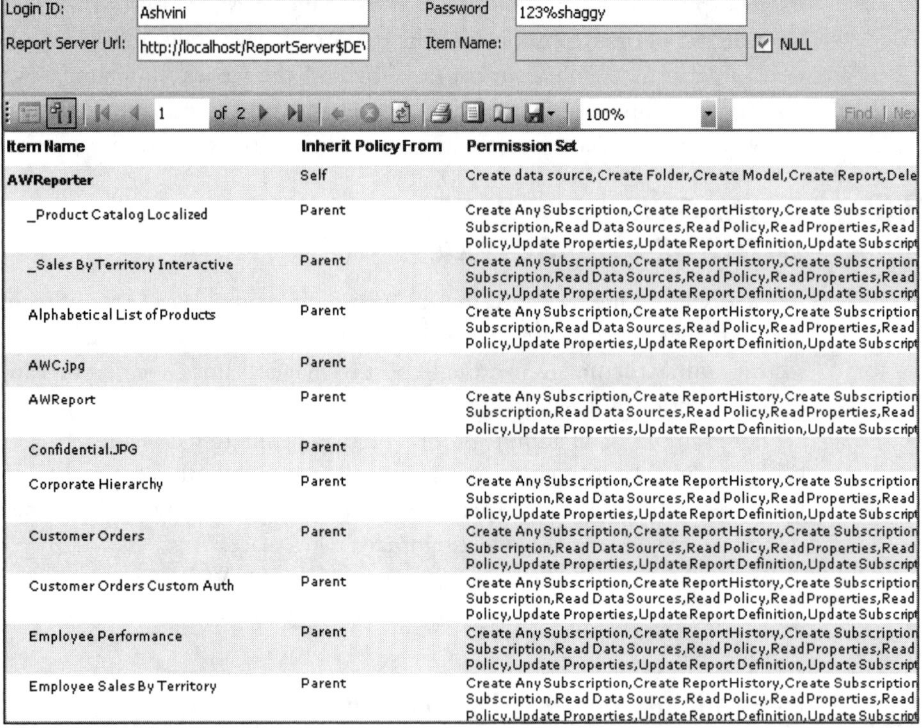

Login ID: Ashvini | Password 123%shaggy
Report Server Url: http://localhost/ReportServer$DE\ | Item Name: | NULL

Item Name	Inherit Policy From	Permission Set
AWReporter	Self	Create data source,Create Folder,Create Model,Create Report,Dele
_Product Catalog Localized	Parent	Create Any Subscription,Create ReportHistory,Create Subscription Subscription,Read Data Sources,Read Policy,Read Properties,Read Policy,Update Properties,Update Report Definition,Update Subscript
_Sales By Territory Interactive	Parent	Create Any Subscription,Create ReportHistory,Create Subscription Subscription,Read Data Sources,Read Policy,Read Properties,Read Policy,Update Properties,Update Report Definition,Update Subscript
Alphabetical List of Products	Parent	Create Any Subscription,Create ReportHistory,Create Subscription Subscription,Read Data Sources,Read Policy,Read Properties,Read Policy,Update Properties,Update Report Definition,Update Subscript
AWC.jpg	Parent	
AWReport	Parent	Create Any Subscription,Create ReportHistory,Create Subscription Subscription,Read Data Sources,Read Policy,Read Properties,Read Policy,Update Properties,Update Report Definition,Update Subscript
Confidential.JPG	Parent	
Corporate Hierarchy	Parent	Create Any Subscription,Create ReportHistory,Create Subscription Subscription,Read Data Sources,Read Policy,Read Properties,Read Policy,Update Properties,Update Report Definition,Update Subscript
Customer Orders	Parent	Create Any Subscription,Create ReportHistory,Create Subscription Subscription,Read Data Sources,Read Policy,Read Properties,Read Policy,Update Properties,Update Report Definition,Update Subscript
Customer Orders Custom Auth	Parent	Create Any Subscription,Create ReportHistory,Create Subscription Subscription,Read Data Sources,Read Policy,Read Properties,Read Policy,Update Properties,Update Report Definition,Update Subscript
Employee Performance	Parent	Create Any Subscription,Create ReportHistory,Create Subscription Subscription,Read Data Sources,Read Policy,Read Properties,Read Policy,Update Properties,Update Report Definition,Update Subscript
Employee Sales By Territory	Parent	Create Any Subscription,Create ReportHistory,Create Subscription Subscription,Read Data Sources,Read Policy,Read Properties,Read Policy,Update Properties,Update Report Definition,Update Subscript

Figure 9.12 You can query and manage the role-based security infrastructure by calling the RS Web service in your applications and reports.

9.5.2 Calling security-related Web service methods

Implementing the Show Security Policy report is straightforward. The report takes advantage of the self-referential integrity defined in the `Catalog` table in the Report Server database and the RS recursive hierarchy-reporting feature, which we discussed back in chapter 5. The report traverses recursively the Report Server folder namespace and checks the type of the item. If the item is a folder, the item name is shown in bold. For each securable item, the report shows the name of the parent from which the security policy is inherited, as well as the set of permissions that the user has to this item.

To obtain this information, the Show Security Policy report calls down to the `AwRsLibrary` custom assembly. Specifically, it calls the `PolicyInheritedFrom` method to get the inheritance information and the `GetPermissions` method to get the list of allowed permissions. Listing 9.1 shows the abbreviated custom code.

Listing 9.1 The Show Security Policy custom code

```
public string SetProxy (string uid, string pwd, string rsUrl) {
  m_rs = new ReportingService2005();
  m_rs.Url = rsUrl;
  m_uid = uid;
  m_pwd = pwd;
  return "None";
}

public string GetPermissions(string itemPath) {
  string result = null;

  m_rs.Credentials = new NetworkCredential(m_uid, m_pwd);
  String[] permissions = m_rs.GetPermissions( itemPath );   <-- Gets permissions associated with the resource
  System.Array.Sort(permissions);
  result = String.Join(",", permissions);

 return result;
}

public string PolicyInheritedFrom( string itemPath) {
  bool inheritParent;
  string rolePath = itemPath;
  m_rs.Credentials = System.Net.CredentialCache.DefaultCredentials;

  m_rs.GetPolicies(rolePath, out inheritParent);   <-- Gets role-based policies recursively for report items
  while (inheritParent) {
   rolePath = GetParentPath(rolePath);
   m_rs.GetPolicies(rolePath, out inheritParent);
  }
  return FormatPath(itemPath, rolePath);
}
```

The `GetPermissions` method calls the RS Web service's `GetPermissions` web method under the context of the user whose security policy you need to check. The method returns a string array of the allowed permissions, which you sort and flatten to a string.

The `PolicyInheritedFrom` method invokes the `GetPolicies` web method to find out which ascendant in the catalog hierarchy defines the security policy for each item displayed in the table region. To accomplish this, `PolicyInheritedFrom` calls `GetPolicies` recursively until `inheritParent` is false. Finally, it evaluates the item path and returns one of the following values:

- *Self*—If the item defines its own policy
- *Parent*—If the security policy is inherited from the item parent
- *Home*—If the item inherits the root folder security policy
- In all other cases, the path to the ascendant item that defines the security policy

Besides showing how you can use the security-related Web service API, this example also demonstrates how you can implement "pseudo" events in your reports.

9.5.3 Implementing "pseudo" report events

To initialize the Web service proxy and some class-level variables inside the custom code, you use an expression for the Body `BorderStyle` property. Placing code here will ensure that the `SetProxy` method is called only once and before the other two custom methods. Use the following expression for the `BorderStyle` property of the Report Body band:

```
=Code.m_Library.SetProxy(Parameters!Uid.Value,
➥ Parameters!Pwd.Value, Parameters!Url.Value)
```

Strictly speaking, you could have made the class stateless by passing the user credentials to the `GetPermissions` method, but we wanted to demonstrate how you can execute custom methods in a specific order.

This expression will be executed before the expressions in the table region, and it can be safely used to initialize the custom code state. Because you are calling instance methods in the custom assembly, you reference the assembly in the Report Properties dialog box, as shown in figure 9.13.

Before testing the report, don't forget to follow the steps for deploying the `RsLibrary` assembly and elevating its code access security to the Report Designer and Report Server folders, as we discussed in chapter 6.

So far, you've seen how to enforce secured access to the Report Server catalog based on the user's role membership. As we explained in chapter 6, developers can expand the report capabilities by using custom code. When this happens, you, as an

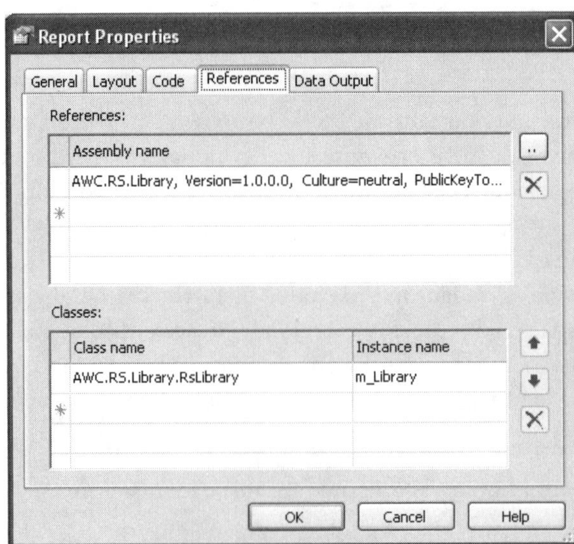

Figure 9.13 Referencing assemblies in the Report Properties dialog box allows you to call these assemblies from your reports.

administrator, need to know how to properly configure the RS code access security. This topic is covered in appendix B.

Let's round out this chapter with a look at some techniques for securing reports with reporting services.

9.6 TECHNIQUES FOR ADVANCED SECURITY ISSUES

If everything we've discussed so far has been mind-boggling, here is what we would like for you to take from this chapter. Your specific application needs dictate which authentication options you'll use. However, as with almost any architecture design, you should carefully weigh the different implementation approaches and make a trade-off between flexibility and simplicity.

Unless you are architecting an enterprise-wide reporting services infrastructure, don't try to make your security implementation too sophisticated. Try to take advantage of the RS role-based security model as much as possible. Some of the questions that you should ask yourself are

- What is the application architectural model? WinForm or web-based? Intranet, extranet, or intranet?
- How strict are the security requirements? How sensitive is the report information?
- How granular does the security policy level need to be? For example, do you have to enforce restricted access at the report level, or do you need a more granular level of security? Do you need to secure some portion of the data inside the report?
- Can you use Windows-based authentication?
- To simplify the role-based security setup with Windows-based authentication, can you group the accounts into Windows groups?

Sometimes, you may find the RS role-based security model too coarse. Such will be the case when you need to secure sensitive data inside the report, or what we refer to as "horizontal security."

Take, for instance, the Employee Sales Freeform report you created in chapter 4. This report shows sensitive data, such as salesperson performance, bonus, and commission. What if you want each salesperson to be restricted to seeing their own sales data without being able to request the report for other sales representatives? Further, what if you want only the members of a certain Windows group, such as Sales Managers, to be able to see the sales data for the sales representatives of whom the manager is in charge?

In such cases, you need to take extra steps to supplement the role-based security model or, in more extreme cases, to replace it altogether. Let's consider some techniques that you can use to provide a more granular level of security policy.

9.6.1 Filtering data

This technique involves filtering the sensitive data at the data source or by using dataset filters. Let's say you want to restrict a salesperson to view his sales performance data only when requesting the Employee Sales Freeform report. Let's assume also that the `HumanResources.Employee` table in the database defines a column for the user login ID, which is exactly the case with `the HumanResources.Employee` table in the AdventureWorks database. It defines a `LoginID` column, which you can use to filter the available values for the `Employee` parameter. Save the modified version of the report as Employee Sales Freeform Secured.

In this example, we demonstrate data filtering at the data source. To implement this, replace the dataset query of the `Employee` parameter with the following statement:

```
SELECT    s.SalesPersonID, c.LastName + N','
           + c.FirstName AS EmployeeName, e.LoginID
FROM      Sales.SalesPerson s
      INNER JOIN HumanResources.Employee e ON
      e.EmployeeID = s.SalesPersonID
      INNER JOIN  Person.Contact c ON
      c.ContactID = e.EmployeeId
WHERE     LoginID = @LoginID
ORDER BY   EmployeeName
```

The `LoginID` parameter is defined as dataset specific, as shown in figure 9.14.

As we discussed in chapter 5, the `User.UserID` property returns the Windows login ID if the default Windows-based authentication is used. Therefore, after the lookup dataset is filtered, the user will see his name only in the `Employee` parameter drop-down list. In fact, in this scenario, you can go one step further and take out the `Employee` parameter entirely.

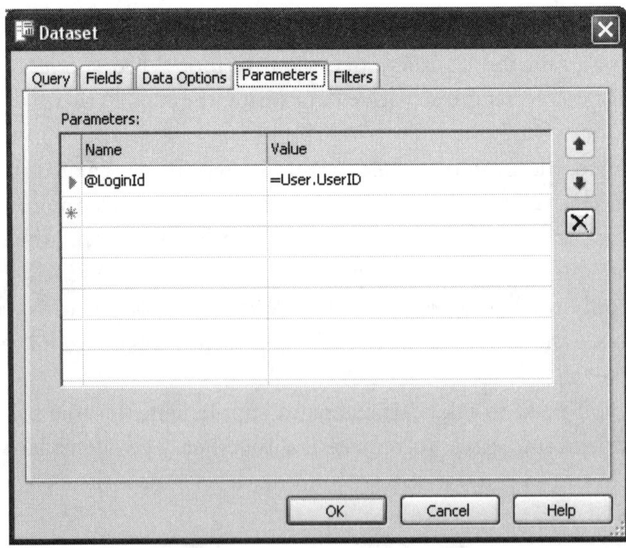

Figure 9.14 By setting a dataset parameter to the value of User.UserID, you can filter the results of your query.

NOTE The AdventureWorks database uses `adventure-works` as a domain name in the `LoginID` column of the `HumanResources.Employee` table. To test the Employee Sales Freeform Secured report, replace the domain name with your login domain name or your computer name, if the Report Server is installed locally.

For example, assuming that you created the test accounts shown in table 9.4 as local computer accounts and the Report Server is installed locally, make sure that you replace the domain name in the `LoginID` column with the name of your computer, that is, `<mycomputer-name>\Michael9`. Then, to test the report, you can either log in locally or establish a remote connection to your computer from another box using the test account credentials.

9.6.2 Using dynamic dataset queries

A variation of the data-filtering technique is to use dynamic queries, where a stored procedure or an expression determines what data will be fetched based on the user's identity.

Let's consider a more complicated scenario than those already discussed. This time say you want to factor in the user's Windows group membership. For example, you want to allow members of the Sales Managers Windows group to be able to select any salesperson. However, you still want to allow members of the Sales Windows group to be able to see their sales data only.

Determining the user's Windows group membership

With a little bit of embedded custom code, implementing these more complex requirements is straightforward. You could write a simple function to tell you whether the user is a member of a given Windows group. A possible implementation of such a function is the `IsInRole` function:

```
Function IsInRole(ByVal roleName as String) As Boolean
    Dim myPrincipal As WindowsPrincipal =
      New WindowsPrincipal(WindowsIdentity.GetCurrent())

    Return myPrincipal.IsInRole(roleName)
End Function
```

You can find this function as embedded code in the Employee Sales Freeform Secured report sample. The `IsInRole` function calls the `WindowsPrincipal.IsInRole` method and returns true if the user is a member of the passed role, or false otherwise.

Implementing the dataset query

The next step is trivial. You can pass the Boolean flag to the parameter (or report) dataset stored procedure, which can filter the data accordingly. If the user is a sales manager, the stored procedure will return all salespersons, just as the original version of this report (Employee Sales Freeform) does. Otherwise, the `Employee` parameter will contain only the name of the user.

Of course, if needed, you can call the `GetPolicies` method of the RS Web service to find out to which role(s) this user or Windows group has been mapped. You saw an example of how to call this method in the Show Security Policy report. The `GetPolicies` method returns an array of `Policy` objects, which represents the security policies associated with a given item, as shown in figure 9.15.

To see the definition of the policy object, step through the `PolicyInheritedFrom` method in the `AwRsLibrary` assembly, and once you've invoked the `GetPolicies` SOAP API, display the policies collection in the Object Browser (Ctrl-Alt-J).

Once you know the user's association with a given Windows group, you can find out what role the user is mapped to by enumerating the report's security policy.

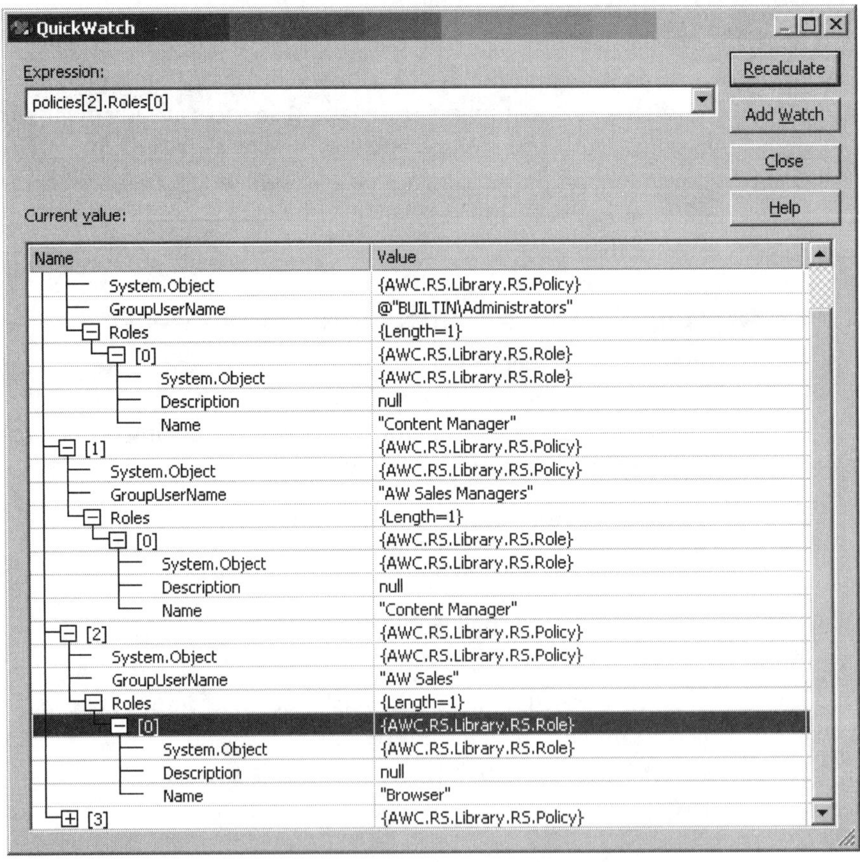

Figure 9.15 The GetPolicies SOAP API returns an array of Policy objects.

9.6.3 Hiding data

Sometimes you might need a technique to hide some report elements. For example, let's say you have a report that shows the employee's salary, and only users of the HR department can see it. Similar to the Dynamic Queries technique, you can determine whether the report user is a member of the HR group.

Then you can use an expression for the salary item's visibility to hide it if the user is not a member. For example:

```
= Not Code.IsInRole("HR")
```

9.6.4 Implementing custom security models

Occasionally, RS role-based security is not sufficient and you need to replace it with your own solution. There are two main scenarios that may call for a custom security implementation.

First, the application may need to check some business rules before granting the user the rights to view a report. For example, let's say you have a report that shows the consolidated sales data from all the company's branches. The users can see the report only after all branches have submitted their data. In a typical three-tier model, this rule will be evaluated in the application business layer.

In this scenario, the business layer can serve as a façade to the Report Server. The added benefit of this approach is that it simplifies the role-based security maintenance, as we discussed in the Client-to-Façade-to-Report Server scenario. Instead of impersonating the user, the request to the Report Server could go out under the Windows account of the business layer's process identity. If this is the case, the report administrator is concerned with setting up the appropriate security for this account only.

Second, the Report Server security model needs to be integrated with the application security model. The application may already have a custom security implementation in place. For example, the application might use the Windows 2003 Authorization Manager to implement secured access to areas of the application based on predefined roles. Supporting two role-based security models may present a challenge for the report administrator. In this case, the application will be responsible for enforcing restricted access to the Report Server.

9.6.5 Enforcing a secured connection to the Report Server

Sometimes a report might contain sensitive information, such as a customer's credit card number. This is especially true when reports are requested over the Internet. In this case, the report data must be encrypted when it is transmitted between the Report Server and the report consumer to prevent hackers from sniffing the data. For implementing secure data transfer, you can use Secure Sockets Layer (SSL).

With RS, the report administrator can configure which Report Server operations require an SSL connection by using the `SecureConnectionLevel` setting in the `RSReportServer.config` file. The allowable range of values is between zero (no SSL required) and three (all access to the Report Server must be encrypted). For example, let's say you want to enforce that all reports must be viewed over an SSL connection. To accomplish this, you can elevate `SecureConnectionLevel` to two. It is important to note that if a secured connection is enforced, the Report Server will demand that both the HTTP-GET and SOAP types of requests use SSL. Because the RS folders do not correspond to physical folders, you cannot enforce SSL on a per-folder or report basis. It is an all-or-nothing proposition.

Sometimes, you may need to enable SSL selectively. For example, an organization might need an encrypted connection for web reporting only. One possible solution would be to use separate Report Servers—one to serve Internet customers with a secure SSL connection and another for internal reporting needs. For more information about the `SecureConnectionLevel` setting, refer to the product documentation.

9.7 SUMMARY

As a report administrator, you shouldn't take report security lightly. Reports often contain sensitive data that must be safeguarded. You can use the RS role-based security model to restrict user access to RS resources based on the Windows identity of the user. To set up a comprehensive role-based security infrastructure, you define policies that spell out which tasks a given user or group is permitted to execute on a given resource.

The Report Manager makes managing role-based security easy. Alternatively, you can manipulate the role-based model programmatically by calling the Web service security management APIs.

Finally, to implement a more granular security level to the report data, you can use several techniques, including data filtering, dynamic queries, and data hiding. When they are not enough, you can implement custom security techniques, some of which we discuss in subsequent chapters.

With part 2 now under your belt, you should feel comfortable managing Reporting Services. Now it is time to learn about the third phase of the report lifecycle: report delivery. In the next chapter, we examine how on-demand delivery works.

PART 3

Delivering reports

Often, your reporting requirements call for integrating Reporting Services with custom applications. The focus of part 3 is the third and final phase of the report life-cycle—report delivery. Here, we implement various reporting solutions to demonstrate how you can integrate RS with different application scenarios.

We start by exploring the two access options available with RS: URL and Web service. You learn how these options compare in the context of different deployment needs, such as intranet, Internet, and extranet applications.

In this part we implement an end-to-end code sample that demonstrates how you can report-enable a WinForm application. We also discuss various techniques for requesting RS reports on the client and server sides of a web application. You will learn how to use the new ReportViewer controls to easily integrate Reporting Services reports into your .NET applications.

We round out this part by exploring the second option that RS offers for distributing reports—through subscriptions.

CHAPTER 10

On-demand report delivery

Once a report is deployed to the report catalog and configured properly, it is ready to fulfill its ultimate purpose: delivery of requested information to the end users. In this chapter we examine on-demand report delivery, in which the user takes an explicit action to view a report. In chapter 12, you learn about subscribed report delivery, in which reports are "pushed" to the user.

We discuss the controls that you can use to add reports to your .NET 2.0 applications in chapter 11, but this chapter focuses on the core architectural *access options* that make these controls work. By the time you finish reading this chapter, you'll know how consumers can use these access options to submit report requests to the Report Server.

Let's start with a look at how on-demand report delivery works.

10.1 HOW RS PROVIDES ON-DEMAND REPORT DELIVERY

Let's say you have authored a set of reports and deployed them to the report catalog. Now you want to provide users with a way to request reports on demand. You could use the Report Manager (you saw how to use the Report Manager as a quick-and-easy report-rendering tool in chapter 8), but that might not always provide the functionality you are looking for. Although useful, the Report Manager will sometimes be insufficient to fully meet your report delivery needs, as in the following use cases:

- *You need to integrate RS with custom applications*—Many application scenarios call for report-enabling existing or new applications. In most cases, these scenarios rule out using the Report Manager because the application will be responsible for supplying the details of the report request, such as the parameter values, export format, and so on.
- *Your reporting needs go beyond the Report Manager feature set*—For example, you may need to validate the report parameters before the user submits the report request. As we mentioned in chapter 3, the standard report toolbar that the Report Server generates when reports are requested by URL provides limited parameter validation capabilities.
- *You do not have access to a Report Server*—For example, you may have field agents that need to run reports based on data from their local machines.

In these cases, a more flexible approach to report-enabling is to integrate the Report Server with your custom applications. Integrating the Report Server with your application requires that you use one of the following access options:

- *URL access*—The request is submitted via the HTTP-GET protocol.
- *Web service access* —The request is submitted via the SOAP protocol.

Figure 10.1 depicts these two integration options. The figure shows the two options that can be used to access reports from the Report Server.

NOTE In the next chapter we discuss the ReportViewer controls. Don't confuse the ReportViewer controls with these access methods. The ReportViewer controls are not an additional access method; rather, they simply use one or both of these options to consume reports from the Report Server and make the access methods transparent to the developer who is using them.

A key benefit to integrating reports into your applications is that your end users do not have to pull up a separate application or browser to view these reports. This provides a smooth experience for the users of your application.

In the rest of this chapter, we describe URL-based report access and Web service–based report access. We investigate the various properties of these methods as well as show you how to implement the methods through example.

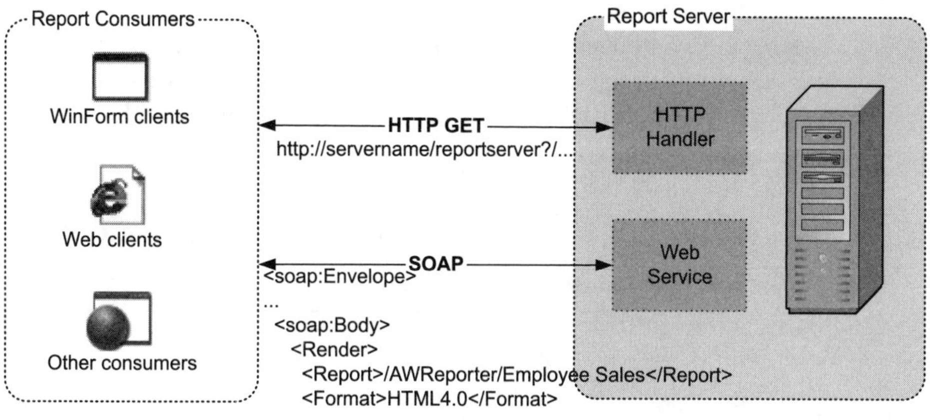

Figure 10.1 The Report Server supports two access options: URL and SOAP.

10.2 URL-BASED REPORT ACCESS

A report consumer can request a resource from the Report Server by submitting an HTTP-GET request that specifies the resource URL. For example, you can request the Sales by Territory report in the browser by navigating to the following URL:

```
http://localhost/reportserver?/AWReporter/Sales By Territory
```

The Report Server's entry point for HTTP-GET requests is the `ReportService-HttpHandler` HTTP handler. The handler intercepts HTTP-GET requests, parses them, and forwards them to the Report Server for processing.

NOTE If your reporting requirements rule out URL access, you can set up the Report Server to reject incoming HTTP-GET requests by commenting out the `<httpHandlers>` section in the Report Server `web.config` file.

As a developer, you can use different techniques in your applications to programmatically request reports by URL. At its simplest, a WinForm-based client could allow the end user to request a report by clicking a hyperlink. For example, a .NET-based WinForm application could use a LinkLabel control with the report's hyperlink embedded in the control's label. When static hyperlinks cannot be used, a WinForm client can shell out to the browser or use the Microsoft WebBrowser ActiveX control to render the report, as we demonstrate in section 10.3.

The web-based reporting model of RS integrates well with browser-based applications. You have already seen an example of a web-based application that requests reports by URL: the Report Manager.

Finally, both WinForm applications and web-based applications can leverage other techniques to meet more exotic integration requirements. For example, you may need to implement an application that crawls and parses the report's content similarly to the way web robots and crawlers, such as Google and Yahoo, index web content. To accomplish this requirement, a legacy WinForm client can use the XMLHTTP component on the client side or the ServerXMLHTTP component on the server side of the application to programmatically submit web requests and "scrape" the received report payload. Both components are included with Internet Explorer. A .NET-based client can accomplish the same thing by using the `System.Net.WebRequest` object. Table 10.1 summarizes these techniques.

Table 10.1 Techniques for integrating report consumers with the Report Server by URL

Application type	Implementation approaches
WinForm	LinkLabel buttons pointing to the URL address of the report; Microsoft Web Browser ActiveX Control; shell to the browser
Web-based	Client-side report generation: all anchor-capable elements, such as hyperlinks, images, and frames; server-side report generation; HTML fragments; Response.Write
Both	XMLHTTP; ServerXMLHTTP (native code); WebRequest (managed code)

To report-enable your applications by URL, you need to learn the URL syntax supported by the Report Server.

10.2.1 Understanding URL syntax

The URL access option uses a typical HTTP-GET syntax, where additional arguments can be passed as query parameters, as follows:

```
http://<ComputerName>/<ReportServerVroot>?[/<ResourcePath>]
➥ &prefix:param=value[&prefix:param=value]...n]
```

Table 10.2 lists the supported URL arguments.

Table 10.2 URL arguments for HTTP-GET requests

Argument	Description	Example
`ComputerName`	Specifies the name of the computer hosting the Report Server.	`localhost`
`ReportServerVroot`	Specifies the Report Server's virtual root name.	`ReportServer`
`ResourcePath`	Specifies the catalog path to the resource relative to the root (Home) folder. Cannot be longer than 260 characters.	`/AWReporter/Sales By Territory`
`prefix`	Specifies the command type. Can be one of the following values: `rs`—For commands targeting the Report Server `rc`—For commands targeting the HTML Viewer `dsu` and `dsp`—For specifying the username and password when the The Credentials Supplied by the User Running the Report data source option is used. `blank`—A report parameter is assumed.	`http://localhost/reportserver?/AWReporter/Sales By Territory Interactive&Year=2006&Territory=1&rs:Command=Render`

continued on next page

Table 10.2 URL arguments for HTTP-GET requests *(continued)*

Argument	Description	Example
`param`	Specifies the name of the command or parameter.	See the previous example, where `Year` and `Territory` are report parameters,

The URL syntax is not case sensitive. Note the question mark that prefixes the `ResourcePath` argument. It is easy to miss (we've done it many times), but if you omit it, the URL request will fail.

Notice that when you submit URL requests from the browser, the browser URL-escapes the string. For example, / is encoded as `%2f`. You don't have to do this explicitly when you define static hyperlinks or submit URL requests programmatically, because the browser (or the Web Browser ActiveX control) handles this automatically for you.

Now that you're familiar with the URL syntax, let's see how to request RS resources by URL.

10.2.2 Requesting resources by URL

With RS you are not limited to requesting just reports. Instead, you can ask the Report Server to return any resource stored in the report catalog, such as folders and data sources. For example, you may have a web page that needs to show the Adventure Works Cycles (AWC) logo, which is stored as an image file in the report catalog. To accomplish this, you can set the image source to the URL address of the image item, as shown here:

```
<IMG SRC="http://localhost/ReportServer?/AWReporter/AWC.jpg"/>
```

NOTE We are far from advocating that you use the report catalog as a document repository—it should be used only to store report-related items.

The response that the Report Server sends back depends on the type of requested resource.

Requesting folders

Just as you would use Windows Explorer to see the files a given folder contains, you may want to see the contents of an RS folder. To see the folder contents using the URL access options, use the syntax

```
http://<ComputerName>/ReportServer?/<FolderPath>
```

where `<FolderPath>` is the path to the folder in the report catalog.

Optionally, for faster performance, you can tell the Report Server that you mean to view the folder contents by using the `ListChildren` command. If you don't use this command, the Report Server has to determine the type of the resource being requested and uses the default command.

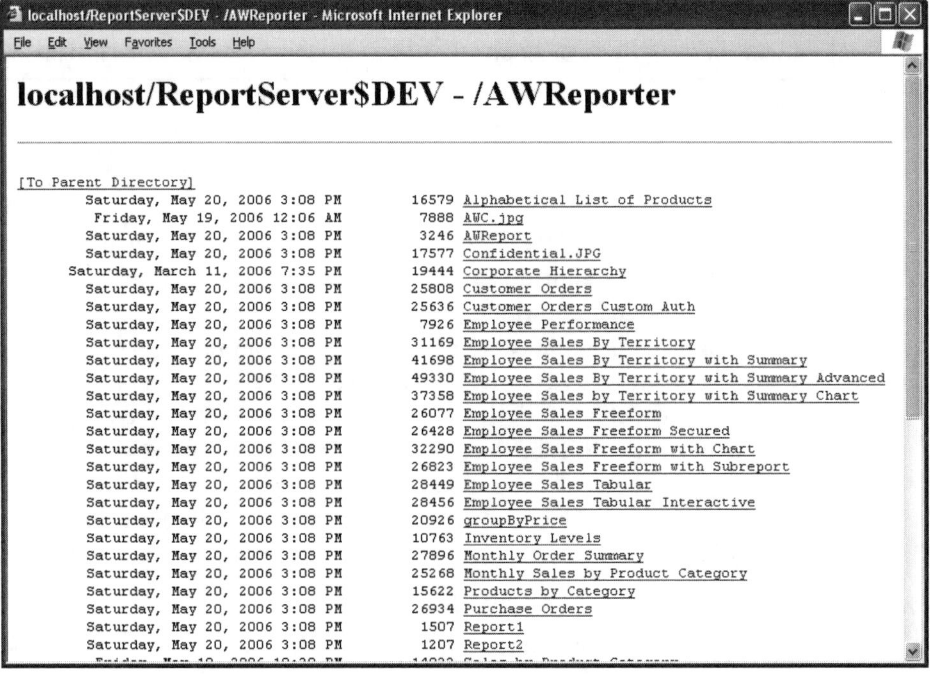

Figure 10.2 You request the AWReporter folder resources by URL.

For example, to view the contents of the AWReporter folder, use the following syntax:

```
http://localhost/ReportServer?/AWReporter&rs:Command=ListChildren
```

If a folder is requested, the Report Server renders the folder's contents, as shown in figure 10.2.

When you request a folder, the names of the resources contained in that folder appear as hyperlinks. When the link points to another folder, the user can click the hyperlink to drill down further in the folder namespace. Otherwise, the hyperlink will render the resource. As with the Report Manager, the Report Server will show only resources that the user has the rights to view (at minimum, Browser rights are required to view a resource).

Requesting data sources

Although we do not recommend this for security reasons, you can allow users to view the definition of a shared data source using the following syntax:

```
http://<ComputerName>/ReportServer?/<FolderPath>/
   <DataSourceName>
```

where `<FolderPath>` is the folder path of the folder where the shared data source resides and `<DataSourceName>` is the name of the shared data source. Optionally, as a performance enhancement technique, you can let the Report Server know that you indeed mean to view the data source definition by using the `GetDataSource-Contents` command, as follows:

```
http://localhost/ReportServer?/AWReporter/AW Shared DS&
rs:Command=GetDataSourceContents
```

This request asks for the contents of the AW Shared DS shared data source. When a shared data source is requested, the Report Server will stream its definition in XML, as shown here:

```
<DataSourceDefinition>
  <Extension>SQL</Extension>
  <ConnectString>data source=.;…</ConnectString>
  <!-The rest of the data source definition-
 </DataSourceDefinition>
```

Even though the password is not returned, you should avoid allowing users to see the data source definition for security reasons. To prevent users from doing so, exclude the View Data Sources task from their security policy, as we discussed in chapter 9.

Requesting other resources

If a report is requested, the Report Server renders the report in the specified format. We discuss this in detail in section 10.2.3.

If an image is requested, the image will be rendered in the browser. For other resource requests, the Report Server will stream the file content to the browser.

In most cases, your applications will request reports by URL. To custom-tailor the report output, you can use a variety of commands, which we discuss in section 10.2.4. First, though, let's take a closer look at how to request a report.

10.2.3 Requesting reports by URL

When requesting reports, at minimum you need to specify the report path and the name of the report, for example:

```
http://localhost/reportserver?/AWReporter/Sales By Territory
```

Here, we are requesting the Sales by Territory report located in the AWReporter folder. As we mentioned in section 10.2.1, you can also optionally pass other arguments to control the report processing (see table 10.2).

One of the most common uses of the URL arguments is to pass parameter values when requesting parameterized reports.

Passing report parameters

To request a report that takes parameters, you append them to the URL string in the form of query parameters. For example, the URL string to request the Sales by Territory Interactive report for the year 2004 and Northwest is:

```
http://localhost/reportserver?/AWReporter/Sales By Territory
Interactive&Year=2004&Territory=1
```

There are a few rules worth mentioning when requesting parameterized reports, as follows:

- *Default values*—If the parameter has a default value and you want to use it when requesting the report, you don't have to pass the parameter value explicitly.
- *Parameters with labels and values*—If the parameter is defined with a label and a value, the value must be passed. The previous example adheres to this rule by using the value of the `Territory` parameter (1), not its label (Northwest).
- *Missing parameter value*—If you don't pass the parameter value in the URL request and the parameter doesn't have a default value, the Report Server will react to this condition differently, depending on the export format requested. If HTML is requested and the report toolbar is not suppressed, the Report Server will generate the parameter area of the report toolbar so that the user can enter the report parameters. In all other cases, an exception will be thrown.
- *Parameter validation*—The parameter validation and type casting are performed on the server side. If a parameter doesn't validate successfully, the Report Server throws an exception, for example:

  ```
  The value provided for the report parameter 'Territory'
  is not valid for its type. (rsReportParameterTypeMismatch).
  ```

The Report Server doesn't set any specific HTTP response codes when reporting errors. Instead, the error string is shown in the browser. Therefore, you cannot programmatically react to error conditions when requesting reports via URL.

10.2.4 Working with report commands

The Report Server recognizes several commands that you can specify by using the `rs` argument, such as commands for exporting reports and requesting report history snapshots.

For a full list of all supported commands, refer to the product documentation.

Rendering commands

For better performance, you can explicitly tell the Report Server that you mean to render a *report* by using the `rs:Command=Render` argument, for example:

```
http://localhost/reportserver?/AWReporter/Sales By Territory&
rs:Command=Render
```

If you don't specify this argument, the Report Server will incur a slight performance hit to find out what type of resource you are requesting.

Exporting commands

Another useful command that you will frequently need is the `Format` command, which lets you export reports in a given format. For example, to export the Sales by Territory report as PDF, you can send the following URL to the Report Server:

```
http://localhost/ReportServer?/AWReporter/Sales By Territory&
rs:Command=Render&rs:Format=PDF
```

When the Report Server receives a request to export a report, it renders the report in the specified format and streams it back to the report consumer. It notifies the consumer about the export format by using the ContentType header. For example, the previous request will produce an HTTP response with a content type of `application/pdf`. If the request is initiated within a browser, the browser will pop up the all-too-familiar prompt to ask the user whether to open or save the streamed content.

If the export format is not explicitly specified, the report is rendered in HTML. If the Report Server can determine the type of browser (if the Accept HTTP header is specified), it renders the report in HTML 4.0 for up-level browsers (e.g., Internet Explorer 4.*x* and later) or HTML 3.2 otherwise.

All export formats support additional parameters that can be passed to control their output. The documentation refers to these parameters as *device settings*. For example, let's say you want to export a report as an image in a format other than the default image format, which happens to be TIFF. You can achieve this by using the `OutputFormat` device setting, as follows:

```
http://localhost/ReportServer?/AWReporter/Sales By Territory&
rs:Command=Render&rs:Format=IMAGE&rc:OutputFormat=JPEG
```

Another useful device setting is `HTMLFragment`, which you can use to render a report as an HTML fragment (without the `HTML`, `HEAD`, and `BODY` `HTML` tags), as follows:

```
http://localhost/ReportServer?/AWReporter/Sales By Territory&
rs:Command=Render&rc:HTMLFragment=true&rc:Toolbar=false
```

For a full list of supported device settings, see the product documentation.

Snapshot history commands

As you'll recall from chapter 8, a report can be executed and cached as a snapshot on a regular basis. The Report Server can be configured to save the snapshot runs in the snapshot history.

You can use the `Snapshot` command to request a specific snapshot run from the report history, based on the date it was generated, for example:

```
http://localhost/ReportServer?/AWReporter/Territory Sales
by Quarter&rs:Snapshot=2004-01-16T02:28:01
```

The `Snapshot` command accepts as a parameter value the date and time when the snapshot was generated. The snapshot time has to be converted to GMT.

Commands for interactive features

One of the most valuable aspects of URL access is that it supports all of the interactive features that we discussed in chapters 4 and 5. There are a few commands that you can use to control these interactive features.

For example, in chapter 4 we authored a report (`Employee Sales Tabular Interactive.rdl`) that demonstrated visible-on-demand sections. Specifically, the Product Subcategory sections are hidden when the report is initially requested but can be expanded by clicking the plus sign (+).

Instead of hiding all items, sometimes you may need to show a certain section expanded. To accomplish this, you can use the `ShowHideToggle` command, for example:

```
http://localhost/reportserver?/AWReporter/Employee Sales Tabular
Interactive&StartDate=1/1/2003&EndDate=12/1/2003&Employee=-1
&rs:Format=HTML4.0&rs:Command=Render&rs:ShowHideToggle=29
```

The net effect of using the `ShowHideToggle` command in this example is that the first Product Subcategory section (the one for Tsoflias, Lynn) will be expanded when the report is requested. As its names suggests, `ShowHideToggle` toggles the section visibility with each subsequent request (if the item is hidden, it will be expanded, and vice versa).

How do you get the section identifier? Unfortunately, there is currently no way to programmatically find out what the section identifiers are. Instead, you need to look at the source of the rendered report. Each expandable section is assigned an ID number when the report is requested. The section identifiers are formatted as `ID="<section identifier">`.

The inability to determine the section identifiers in advance makes the commands that target interactive features by section identifiers (`ShowHideToggle` for expandable sections, `BookmarkID` to jump to a report bookmark, and `DocMapID` to scroll to a particular document map section) of limited use to developers.

Managing report sessions

As we explained in chapter 8, to ensure data consistency and optimize report performance, the Report Server uses report sessions. When the Report Server creates a session for a given report, it caches the report's intermediate format (IF) in the Report Server Temporary Database (ReportServerTempDB) for a configurable period of time.

By default, to correlate the report consumer with the session, the Report Server uses cookies. If cookies are used to track sessions, you don't have to do anything special from a programming standpoint to manage sessions. The Report Server will automatically generate a cookie for each report session and add it to the HTTP response header. The cookie will then ping-pong between the browser and the Report Server with each subsequent report request.

For example, the following trace excerpt shows the cookie's HTTP header after we requested several reports using the same instance of the browser:

```
Cookie:%2fAWReporter%2fSales+By+Territory+Interactive=
52vl3e55bfox0zisan0rsqjy; %2fAWReporter%2fzzTest=
gbsyl4mapuz0m555spbbdsje; %2fAWReporter%2fCorporate+Hierarchy=
gqn5cn5543bjmy45bak5al55;
```

Sometimes the report session caching may get in the way. For example, you may need to view the report with the most recent data. As we learned in chapter 8, you cannot turn off report session caching. However, you can use either of the following approaches to clear the report session so that the report is processed anew:

- If the standard report toolbar is not suppressed, you can click the Refresh Report button (not the browser's Refresh button) or press Ctrl-F5. When you do this, the HTML Viewer intercepts the request and sends the `ClearSession` command (`rs:ClearSession=true`) to the Report Server to clear the report session. The Report Server will then process the report again.
- Send the `ClearSession` command explicitly as a part of the URL request.

Refreshing the report in the browser (by pressing F5) doesn't clear the session. This means that if the report session is valid (hasn't expired, has the same set of parameters, and so on), the Report Server will serve the report from the same report session.

For browsers that are configured to not support cookies, you can use cookie-less report sessions by setting the `UseSessionCookies` setting in the `ConfigurationInfo` table in the RS Configuration Database to false. In this case, instead of sending a cookie, the Report Server adds a parameter to the URL to identify the session.

One of the main advantages of requesting reports by URL is the handy report toolbar that the Report Server generates by default, as we discuss next.

10.2.5 Working with the HTML Viewer

When a report is requested by URL and rendered in HTML, the Report Server generates a useful toolbar, called the HTML Viewer, at the top of the report, as shown in figure 10.3.

With the breadth of features that this toolbar provides, you can really appreciate the effort that the RS team has gone to on your behalf. It is a mini-application by itself! The RS documentation refers to the HTML framework that hosts both the toolbar and the report as the HTML Viewer.

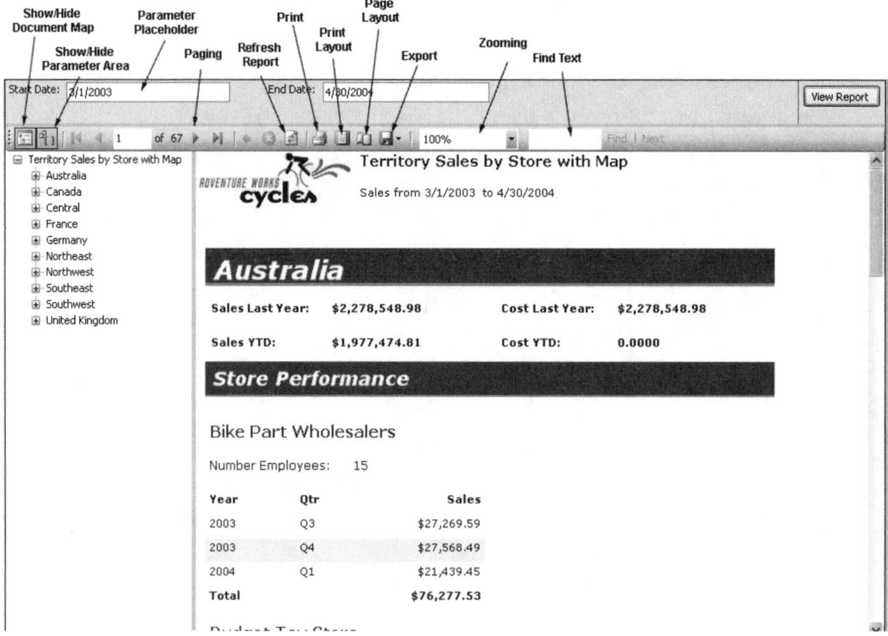

Figure 10.3 When reports are rendered via URL, the Report Server generates the HTML Viewer toolbar.

HTML Viewer features

You will find the HTML Viewer very similar to the report toolbar, which the Report Designer generates in report preview mode. Table 10.3 outlines the interactive features supported by the HTML Viewer.

Table 10.3 Interactive features supported by the HTML Viewer

Feature	Description
Show/hide Document Map	Toggles the document map's visibility for reports with document maps.
Parameter placeholders	Generates parameter placeholders for parameterized reports. For example, the screenshot in figure 10.3 shows that the Territory Sales by Store with Map report takes two parameters, Start Date and End Date. If a parameter has a list of available values, the HTML Viewer will automatically generate a drop-down list. If a parameter has a default value, its placeholder will be set accordingly. Only parameters that are set to prompt the user are shown.
Zooming	Zooms the report in or out.
Finding text	For example, as figure 10.3 shows, after we performed a search for the word *Bike*, if a match is found, the browser scrolls and highlights the match. For multipage reports, clicking Next to search subsequent pages causes the HTML Viewer to submit additional requests to the Report Server.

continued on next page

Table 10.3 Interactive features supported by the HTML Viewer *(continued)*

Feature	Description
Exporting	Exports the report to all of the formats supported by the Report Server, e.g., PDF.
Refresh Report	Refreshes the report by resubmitting the URL request and clears the report session.
Online help	Navigates to the HTML Viewer online help.
Client side printing	Prints the report without the need to export first.

The HTML Viewer is also somewhat customizable. As a part of the URL report request, you can include HTML Viewer–specific commands to customize certain aspects of the HTML Viewer.

Customizing the HTML Viewer

The Report Server supports a series of commands that are specifically targeted to the HTML Viewer. These commands can be classified in two categories:

- Commands for controlling the visibility of the toolbar or its items
- Commands for performing an action, for example, zoom at a specified level, go to a specified page, and so on

With so many URL commands available, you may find it difficult to construct the right syntax of the URL report request. You may be tempted to try URL request tracing of the requests submitted by the HTML Viewer, similar to the technique you saw in chapter 8 for tracing SOAP calls. Unfortunately, we haven't been very successful in our attempts to set a virtual port in SOAP Trace or tcpTrace that we can use for tracing URL requests, either from the Report Manager or from the browser. The problem stems from the fact that when the Report Server renders the HTML page for the report, it defaults to the computer name where the Report Server is installed. For this reason, you can capture the first URL request by redirecting it to a virtual port, such as `http://servername:8080/reports...`, but rendering the report subsequently by clicking the View Report button from the report toolbar will bypass the virtual port.

As you can see by looking at the HTML source of the page, the reason for this is that the action URL of the form that includes the report's rendered presentation doesn't include the port number. As a workaround, you can examine the IIS web logs to find out what URL requests have been sent by the browser.

An example of the first category of commands is the `Toolbar` command. You can use this command to request that the report toolbar not be rendered at all, as follows:

```
http://localhost/reportserver?/AWReporter/
Sales by Territory&rc:Toolbar=false
```

Or, let's say you want to instruct the Report Server not to render the toolbar parameter area. This could be useful when you embed the parameters programmatically in the report URL and you don't want the user to see the report parameter area at all. You can accomplish this by using the `Parameters` command.

For example, the following command will render Sales by Territory report and will exclude the parameter section from the HTML Viewer toolbar:

```
http://localhost/reportserver?/AWReporter/
Sales by Territory Interactive&Year=2004&Territory=1&rc:Parameters=false
```

An example of an action command is `Zoom`. Use this command to zoom the report in or out before it is rendered. The following URL request zooms the report to its page width:

```
http://localhost/reportserver?/AWReporter/
Sales by Territory Interactive&Year=2004&Territory=1&rc:Zoom=Page Width
```

For a full list of all HTML Viewer–targeted commands, see the product documentation.

HTML Viewer limitations

The HTML Viewer saves you a lot of effort when integrating applications with RS. It is one of the biggest selling points for choosing the URL access option to render reports. However, it may also be its Achilles' heel. Why? You see, outside the supported commands, the HTML Viewer is not customizable. The area that takes the most criticism and requests for enhancements is the parameters section.

For example, what if you want to implement your custom parameter validation? Or, what if you want to validate the parameters on the client side before the report is submitted? All of these are valid questions and concerns, but currently they go beyond the HTML Viewer feature set.

You can expect Microsoft to make the HTML Viewer more flexible and customizable in the future. For example, there are plans that the toolbar will support custom validation by the virtue of ASP.NET user controls in the next release. Until that time, however, you have to take the HTML Viewer as it is or provide your own custom application front end to replace it.

Now that we've covered the theory behind URL access, let's see a code sample that demonstrates how a client application can be integrated with the Report Server by URL.

10.3 URL ACCESS IN ACTION

To demonstrate how both a WinForm-based report consumer and a Web-based report consumer can leverage the URL access option to request reports, let's look at a couple of sample applications from the source code available with this book.

10.3.1 URL Access with WinForms: AccessOptions

The code sample for this section can be launched from the chapter 10 menu in the AWReporterWin project.

This one-form sample application actually uses both access options (URL and SOAP), but for the purposes of our discussion in this section, we describe only the URL access option. We cover the SOAP access methods that this sample code uses later in section 10.5.

This code sample demonstrates two possible implementation approaches to integrate a WinForm-based report consumer with Reporting Services by URL:

- Using the Microsoft WebBrowser ActiveX control
- Shelling out to the browser

We kept the code simple on purpose. For now, the design goals for the AccessOptions application are to show you the minimum steps needed to access reports using the URL access option. Figure 10.4 shows the AccessOptions form.

To run a report by URL, the user has to specify the Report Server URL, the report path, and the export format. In the case of parameterized reports, the user must also enter all parameters (name and value) in the Parameters grid, that do not have default values specified.

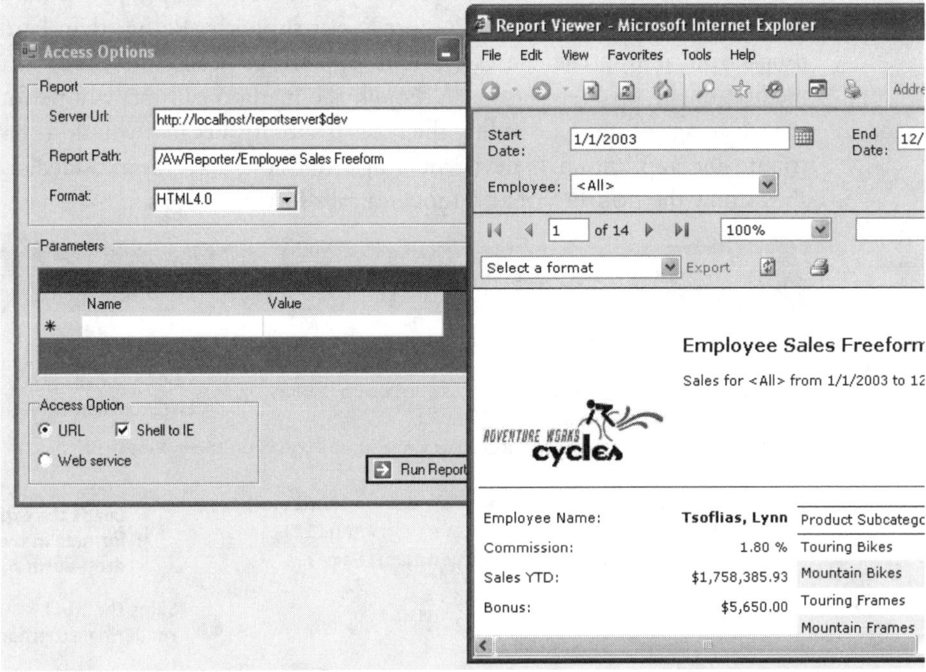

Figure 10.4 The AccessOptions application demonstrates how a WinForm application can request reports via URL or the RS Web service (SOAP).

Let's first see how this code sample integrates with the Report Server by URL. Then in section 10.5 you'll learn how to do this by using the RS Web service.

Using the Microsoft WebBrowser ActiveX control

To request reports by URL, a WinForm application can leverage the Microsoft Web Browser ActiveX control to embed the report inside a form. One possibility where embedding the report can be useful is when your requirements call for implementing a Report Search form. Once the user selects a report, you may want to display the report inside the search form instead of navigating to a new form.

If you haven't used the Microsoft WebBrowser control in the past, you will be happy to find that it allows you to add browsing, document viewing, and data downloading capabilities to your applications. Because the WebBrowser control is COM-based, this approach is also suitable for classic Windows-based applications, for example, Visual Basic 6 clients.

The WebBrowser control is found in the Common Controls section of the Windows Application Project toolbox in Visual Studio 2005. If you need more information about this control, check the "Resources" section at the end of this book.

Loading the export formats

When the AccessOptions form is loaded, the Format drop-down is populated with the rendering formats that the Report Server supports. Rather than hardcoding the drop-down items, the AccessOptions application calls the `ListExtensions` method of the RS Web service. Although the method call incurs a performance hit, the advantage of not hardcoding the list is flexibility, because you don't have to redistribute the application if new rendering extensions have been added. Listing 10.1 shows how the `LoadFormats` function calls ListExtensions.

Listing 10.1 Using the ListExtensions SOAP API to populate the drop-down list with export formats

```
private void LoadFormats()
{
  ReportingService2005 rs = RsHelpers.Proxy;
  Extension[] extensions = null;
  extensions = rs.ListExtensions(ExtensionTypeEnum.Render);

  foreach (Extension extension in extensions) {
     if (extension.Name.ToLower()!="null")
     cmbFormat.Items.Add(extension.Name);
   }
   cmbFormat.SelectedText = "HTML4.0";
}
```

Calls the ListExtensions API

Loads the export formats in the drop-down

❶ Skips the NULL rendering extension

Because this method is executed when the form loads, be sure to update the Report Server URL, which defaults to localhost, before running the sample. The `ListExtension` method returns an array of all supported rendering extensions as specified in the `RSReportServer.config` file. Each rendering extension is exposed as of type `Extension`.

Note that the code specifically ignores the NULL rendering extension ❶. This extension is not a rendering extension per se because it doesn't render reports in any specific format. Instead, it is useful for prepopulating the report session cache for subscribed report delivery, as we explain in more detail in chapter 12. Because this is a "dummy" extension and cannot be used for report rendering, we skip it.

For the sake of simplicity, we don't retrieve the list of report parameters from the RS Web service, nor do we validate the parameters in any way. For the purposes of this example, the user is responsible for setting up the parameters correctly. To show the parameters in the grid, we use a typed dataset, EntityParameter, which we bind to the grid.

Requesting the report

Once the user has filled in the report parameters (if any), we are ready to request the report by calling the `RunByURL` function, whose abbreviated code is shown in listing 10.2.

Listing 10.2 The Microsoft WebBrowser control, which WinForm clients can use to place the report inside a form

```
private void RunByURL()
 {
  StringBuilder urlBuilder = new StringBuilder();
  urlBuilder.Append(txtServer.Text);
  urlBuilder.Append ("?");
  urlBuilder.Append (txtReportPath.Text);
  EntityParameter.ParametersDataTable table =
     EntityParameter.ParametersDataTable)grdParams.DataSource;
  foreach (EntityParameter.ParametersRow row in table.Rows){
    urlBuilder.Append (String.Format("&{0}={1}",
       row.Name, row.Value));
  }
  urlBuilder.Append (@"&rs:Format=" + cmbFormat.Text);
  urlBuilder.Append (@"&rs:Command=Render");

  ReportBrowser reportBrowser = new ReportBrowser();
  reportBrowser.RenderReport(urlBuilder.ToString());
  reportBrowser.Show();
 }
```

Constructs the report URL

Appends the report parameters

Uses the ReportBrowser form

First, the code crafts the report URL programmatically according to the URL syntax rules that we discussed in section 10.2. We set up the report path, followed by the report parameters and the specified export format.

Once the URL string is constructed, we instantiate the ReportBrowser form to render the report using the Microsoft WebBrowser control. Inside the ReportBrowser form, we call the Microsoft WebBrowser control's `Navigate` method and pass the report URL:

```
public void RenderReport(string url){
  Object optional = System.Reflection.Missing.Value;
  webBrowser.Navigate(url, ref optional, ref optional,
  ref optional,ref optional);
}
```

At this point the report is displayed. If there are any errors, they are shown in the WebBrowser control.

Shelling out to the browser

Sometimes you may just need a quick way to show the report in the browser by navigating to the report's URL address. You can do this by simply shelling out the report request to the browser. To accomplish this task, .NET developers can use the `Process.Start` method to start the application associated with a file extension.

When the Shell to IE option is selected on the AccessOptions form, once the report URL is ready, displaying the report in the browser takes one line of code:

```
Process.Start ("IExplore", url).
```

When you don't need to embed the report in a form, you should consider shelling out to the browser as a more lightweight implementation approach of requesting a report by URL.

Now that we have seen how to integrate the Report Server in our WinForm applications, let's examine some practical web-reporting techniques. We refer collectively to our web samples as the Adventure Works Web Reporter, or AWReporterWeb for short.

10.3.2 URL Access with WebForms: AWReporterWeb

Once you've authored your report in RS, there are myriad ways to get it to your web-based users. From an implementation standpoint, you can organize the web reporting techniques into two categories: client-side reporting techniques and server-side reporting techniques. This breakdown reflects the location from which the report request originates.

In the case of client-side reporting, the report request is initiated on the client side of the application, for example, by clicking a hyperlink on a page rendered in the browser. Most of the techniques in this category follow the Client-to-Report Server pattern and request reports by URL.

In the latter case, the report is requested and rendered on the server side of the application, for example, by using ASP.NET server-side code. In general, the techniques under this category follow the Client-to-Façade-to-Report Server approach and request reports by SOAP.

The AWReporterWeb code examples can be found under the `Chapter10` folder in the AWReporterWeb project. Once you request the `default.aspx` page, you are presented with the drop-down main menu, as shown in figure 10.5.

The main menu is implemented as a drop-down menu. The client-side reporting samples can be initiated from the client-side Reporting menu, while the server-side reporting samples can be launched from the server-side Reporting menu.

NOTE We used Peter Bromberg's excellent ASP.NET menu sample to easily integrate his menu control with our web application. The menu items are specified in the `menu.xml` file. The menu control loads the menu definition and applies an XSLT transformation to render the menu in DHTML.

For more implementation details about the menu control, check the "Resources" section at the end of this book.

Let's now discuss the AWReporterWeb client-side reporting samples in the order in which they appear on the menu.

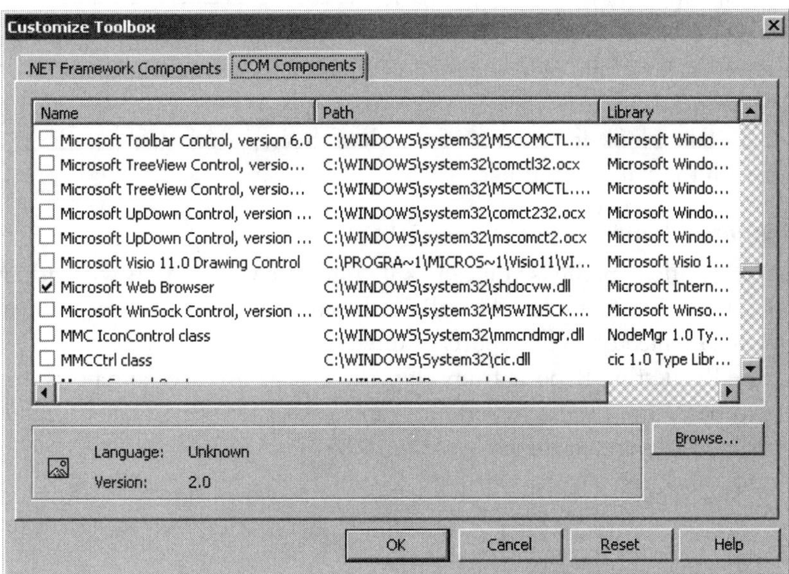

Figure 10.5 The main menu of the AWReporterWeb project displays two menus: one for the client-side reporting samples and one for the server-side reporting samples. To see the server-side menu items, hover your mouse cursor on top of the Server-side Reporting menu.

Requesting reports from hyperlinks

A very simple technique that allows users to request a report from a web-based application is to provide a hyperlink that points to a URL report address. In this section, we discuss three techniques for using hyperlinks to access reports:

- In its simplest implementation, you can use *static* hyperlinks to run reports. A static hyperlink contains a hardcoded URL report address.
- Or you can use *dynamic* hyperlinks to run reports. Unlike a static hyperlink, which contains a fixed address, a *dynamic* hyperlink contains a URL report address that is generated on the fly on the client side of the web application.
- Finally, you can also use *server-side generated* hyperlinks, in which the hyperlinks are generated on the server side of the web application.

The AWReporterWeb project employs all three types of hyperlinks. The Requesting Reports from Hyperlinks (`Hyperlinks.aspx`) page shown in figure 10.6 allows users to click a report name to open the report. You can't tell which hyperlink technique is used just by looking at the figure, but we cover each technique in the following sections.

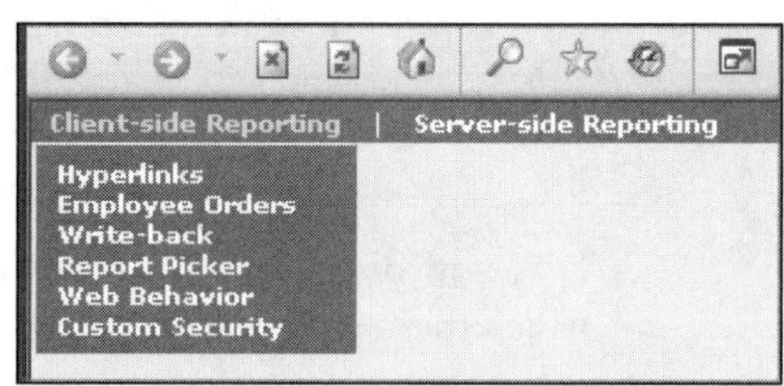

Figure 10.6 You can use static and dynamic hyperlinks to requests reports by URL.

Let's take a look at the syntax for each of the hyperlinks listed in figure 10.6. We'll start with the static hyperlinks.

Technique 1: using static hyperlinks

By using static hyperlinks you can easily integrate your reports with other web-based applications. For example, a SharePoint-based web portal can have web parts that use static hyperlinks to render reports of interest.

The Requesting Reports from Hyperlinks page lists several reports that you navigate to based on a static hyperlink. Table 10.4 shows the syntax for the first three hyperlinked reports in the list (see figure 10.6):

- The Sales by Territory report URL generates the Sales by Territory report in the default format, which is HTML4.0 for up-level browsers or HTML3.2 for down-level browsers.
- The Employee Sales Freeform report URL demonstrates how to request a parameterized report from a hyperlink.
- The Sales by Territory with Chart report URL demonstrates how to embed Report Server commands and device settings into a static hyperlink.

Table 10.4 Syntax for URL access

Report name	Hyperlink syntax
Sales by Territory	`http://localhost/reportserver?/AWReporter/Sales by Territory`
Employee Sales Freeform	`http://localhost/reportserver?/AWReporter/Employee Sales Freeform&StartDate=1/1/2003 12:00:00 AM&EndDate=12/1/2003 12:00:00 AM&Employee=-1`
Sales by Territory with Chart	`http://localhost/reportserver?/AWReporter/Employee Sales Freeform with Chart&StartDate=1/1/2003 12:00:00 AM&EndDate=12/1/2003 12:00:00 AM&rs:Format=PDF&rs:Command=Render`

Although the static hyperlink approach excels in simplicity, it falls short in terms of customization and security. For example, when using static hyperlinks, you have little control over the appearance of the browser window. At most, you can request the report to be rendered in a new instance of the browser or a particular frame by setting the hyperlink's target property to `_blank`. Using static hyperlinks may also present a security risk because the user can see and change the report's URL at will to request another report or modify the report's parameters.

Fortunately, with RS you are not limited to using only static hyperlinks. Often, your application requirements may rule out hardcoding the report's URL address in the hyperlink. In such cases, you can dynamically construct the link on the client or server side of the application.

Technique 2: using dynamic hyperlinks

Dynamic hyperlinks can be useful when you need to custom-tailor the browser window and hide the report request's details by using familiar client-side web techniques.

For example, the Territory Sales Drillthrough report URL demonstrates how you can use JavaScript code to customize the browser window:

```
<A onclick='window.open("http://localhost/reportserver?/
➥ AWReporter/Territory Sales Drillthrough&

➥ StartDate=1/1/2003 12:00:00 AM&

➥ EndDate=12/1/2003 12:00:00 AM&

➥ rs:Command=Render", "_blank",

➥ "location=no,toolbar=no,left=100,top=100,height=600,width=800")'>
```

The `onclick` JavaScript handler displays the report in a customized browser window, as shown in figure 10.7.

To hide the report's URL from the end user, the window doesn't have a toolbar or address bar. In addition, the JavaScript code sizes and positions the window explicitly. This approach may offer a good compromise between simplicity and security for intranet-based applications.

Requesting Reports from Hyperlinks

Report Name	Description
Sales by Territory	As simple as it can get. No parameters, no devices settings, just the report please
Employee Sales Freeform	Requesting a report that takes parameters.
Sales by Territory with Chart	Specifying the report format and device settings.
Territory Sales Drillthrough	Custom-tailored report window.
Territory Sales Crosstab	With user-specified parameters.

Figure 10.7 Use dynamic hyperlinks when you need to customize the browser window.

The Territory Sales Crosstab report URL extends the dynamic hyperlink technique by allowing the user to enter the report's parameters and then encapsulates the report request in a client-side JavaScript function, as shown in figure 10.8. In this example, the `onclick` event handler attached to the hyperlink toggles the visibility of the parameter section. Once the parameters are entered, the user can request the report by clicking the Run Report button.

The button event handler invokes the `requestReport` client-side function and passes the start and end date parameters as arguments:

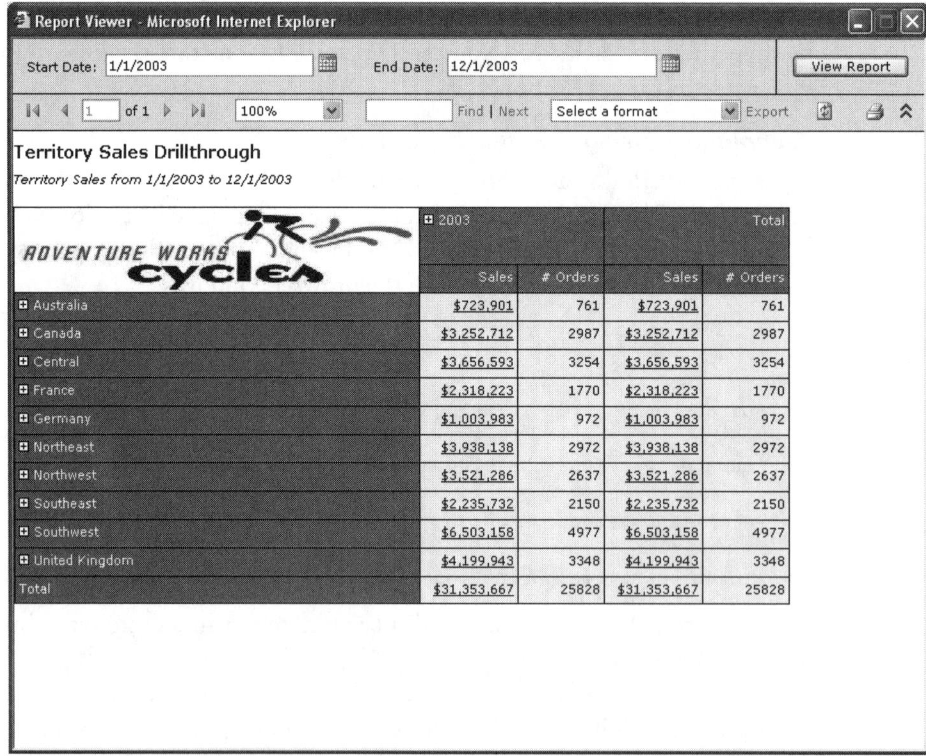

	2003		Total	
	Sales	# Orders	Sales	# Orders
Australia	$723,901	761	$723,901	761
Canada	$3,252,712	2987	$3,252,712	2987
Central	$3,656,593	3254	$3,656,593	3254
France	$2,318,223	1770	$2,318,223	1770
Germany	$1,003,983	972	$1,003,983	972
Northeast	$3,938,138	2972	$3,938,138	2972
Northwest	$3,521,286	2637	$3,521,286	2637
Southeast	$2,235,732	2150	$2,235,732	2150
Southwest	$6,503,158	4977	$6,503,158	4977
United Kingdom	$4,199,943	3348	$4,199,943	3348
Total	$31,353,667	25828	$31,353,667	25828

Figure 10.8 You can use client-side JavaScript to generate the report's hyperlink.

```
function requestReport(startDate, endDate) {
  window.open("http://localhost/reportserver?/
      AWReporter/Territory Sales
      Crosstab&StartDate=" + startDate + "&EndDate=" + endDate+
      "&rs:Command=Render", "_blank", "location=no,toolbar=no,
       left=100, top=100, height=600,width=800")
}
```

The `reportRequest` function renders the report in a customized browser window, as was done for the Territory Sales Drillthrough report (figure 10.7).

Technique 3: using server-side generated hyperlinks

Most web-based applications require some server-side preprocessing before the page is rendered. For example, it is a common requirement to generate HTML tables on the server side of the application that include clickable hyperlinks to bring the user to another page or report that shows more details.

To see how to integrate a report's hyperlinks with a server-side-generated ASP.NET grid, click the Employee Orders link from the main menu of AWReporterWeb. The Salesperson Orders (`EmployeeOrders.aspx`) page is shown in figure 10.9.

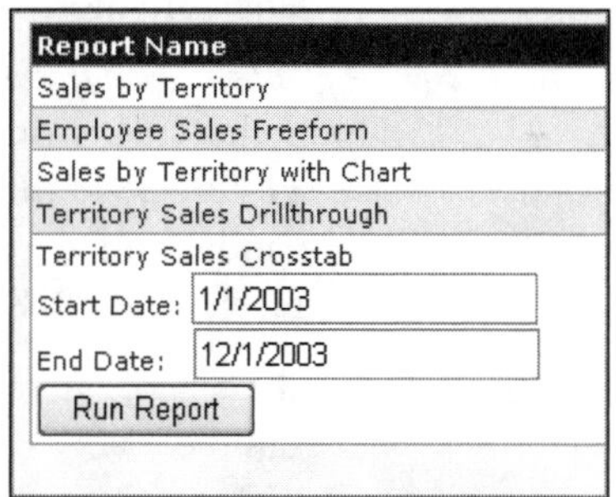

Figure 10.9 Report hyperlinks can be generated on the server side.

The `EmployeeOrders.aspx` page retrieves the sales order information from the AdventureWorks database using a data reader. The user can click the Details hyperlink to see the order details. This action displays the Sales Order Details report, which happens to be one of the Reporting Services sample reports.

The hyperlink passes the order number from the same grid row as the report parameter. This is accomplished by defining the `Details` column as a grid template column:

```
<asp:TemplateColumn HeaderText="Details">
  <ItemTemplate>
   <a href="#" onclick="javascript:requestReport
     ('<%#DataBinder.Eval(Container.DataItem,"SalesOrderNumber")
    %>');">Details</a>
  </ItemTemplate>
</asp:TemplateColumn>
```

For those of you not familiar with the ASP.NET data-binding model, the odd-looking `DataBinder` expression retrieves the `SalesOrderNumber` field from the underlying data reader row and injects it into the page. As a result, when the page is rendered, the `onclick` event for the first record will be set to something like this:

```
onclick="javascript:requestReport('SO5812');"
```

The `requestReport` JavaScript client-side function submits the report request as we've just seen.

We have now covered the techniques for requesting reports through the use of hyperlinks. Let's take a look at how you request reports by using HTTP-POST.

Submitting report requests with HTTP-POST

All of the examples so far in this chapter have used HTTP-GET to submit the report request to the Report Server on the client side of the application. The important difference between HTTP-GET and HTTP-POST is that the request details are not passed in the URL; therefore they are not seen in the address toolbar of the browser. Sometimes, using HTTP-POST as a web protocol may be a better choice because of the following advantages it has over HTTP-GET:

- *The report URL address is less exposed than with HTTP-GET*—The report request details are more hidden from prying eyes and cannot be easily changed.
- *Unlimited parameter length*—Many browsers impose limitations on the length of the URL string in the case of the HTTP-GET protocol. In contrast, with HTTP-POST, the length of the request parameters (report parameters, commands, and device settings) is unlimited, because the name/value pairs are transferred in the request's HTTP header, not in the URL.

Let's take a look at requesting reports by using HTTP-POST in our AWReporterWeb example.

To view a report requested by HTTP-POST, click the Report Picker link from the main menu of the AWReporterWeb. The Report Picker page is shown in figure 10.10.

Salesperson Orders

Salesperson: Abbas Syed

Order Date	Order #	Store	Sub Total	Details
9/1/2003	SO53485	Nationwide Supply	$77,513.42	Details
9/1/2003	SO53492	Liquidation Sales	$22,751.11	Details
9/1/2003	SO53502	Popular Bike Lines	$41,030.55	Details
9/1/2003	SO53554	Inexpensive Parts Shop	$4,112.38	Details
9/1/2003	SO53588	Online Bike Catalog	$67.76	Details
9/1/2003	SO53594	Twin Cycles	$1,326.26	Details
11/1/2003	SO57059	Uncompromising Quality Co	$3,433.06	Details
12/1/2003	SO58915	Bike Part Wholesalers	$32,866.56	Details
12/1/2003	SO59045	Twin Cycles	$4,307.75	Details

Figure 10.10 Use HTTP-POST to hide the URL address details and unlimited parameter length.

NOTE Because the Report Picker and the samples that follow use the credentials of the interactive user to invoke the RS SOAP API, make sure that the AWReporterWeb application is configured for Integrated Windows security and that Anonymous access is disabled.

The Reports drop-down is set to post back the page automatically. When the report selection changes, the page posts back to itself to retrieve and display the report parameters.

The page gets the report parameters on the server side by invoking the `GetReportParameters` RS web method; then the page loops through the report parameters and loads them into a `DataTable` object. Finally, the page binds the parameter table to the Parameter grid control. The grid's `Value` column is implemented as a template column similar to that in the Sales Orders sample report.

To request the report via HTTP-POST on the client side of the application, the page defines a second form that includes a few hidden fields to capture the report request's details and post them back to the Report Server:

```
<FORM id="frmRender" action="http://localhost/reportserver?"
          method="post" target="report">
  <INPUT type="hidden" value="Render" name="rs:Command">
  <INPUT type="hidden" value="HTML4.0" name="rs:Format">
  <INPUT type="hidden" value="_blank" name="rc:LinkTarget">
</FORM>
```

The hidden fields serve as placeholders for Report Server commands and device settings.

As part of submitting the report request via HTTP-POST, we need to send the parameter values. We discuss how that's done next.

Handling parameters

Handling the report parameters is tricky because a report could have an arbitrary number of parameters. For this reason, you need to generate the parameters' placeholders dynamically. This is done inside the `runReport` client-side JavaScript function, as shown in listing 10.3.

Listing 10.3 Submitting a report via HTTP-POST

```
var reportServerUrl = null;
function runReport()  {
  frmRender.action = reportServerUrl +          <-- 1 Generates the action target of the form
       frmReports.drpReports.value;
  frmRender.Format.value = frmReports.drpExport.value;

  var parameters = frmReports.txtParameter;     <-- 2 Gets a reference to the parameter textboxes
  var paramUrl ="";
  var oldParameters = frmRender.Parameter;
  if (oldParameters!=undefined) {
   var count = parameters.length
   for (i=0;i<count;i++) {
    oldParameter = oldParameters[i];
```

```
    frmRender.removeChild(oldParameter);
    i--;count--;
   } // end for
  } // end if
                                          ❸ Generates hidden fields
                                             for report parameters
  if (parameters.length>0) {     <-┘
    for (i=0;i<parameters.length;i++) {
      var newParam = document.createElement("INPUT");
      newParam.type = "hidden";
      newParam.id = "Parameter";
      newParam.name = parameters[i].name;
      newParam.value = parameters[i].value;
     frmRender.appendChild(newParam);
   } // end for
  } // end if

  window.open("about:blank", "report",
    "location=yes,toolbar=no,left=100,
    top=100,height=600,width=800")

  frmRender.submit();        <-┐ Submits the form
}                              ❹ via HTTP-POST
```

The `runReport` function is invoked from the `onclick` event of the Run Report hyperlink. First, you set the form's action to the report's URL ❶. Next, you set the hidden field, `Format`, to the selected export format. Next, you remove the parameters from the previous report run ❷. Then, you loop through all parameter textbox controls in the grid ❸. For each parameter, you create a new hidden input element and set its name and value. To render the report, you create a new named browser window. Finally, you submit `frmRender` to the Report Server ❹ and display the report in a custom-tailored browser window.

Now that you have seen examples of requesting reports from the client side of your applications, let's explore how you might do your requests from the server side of your applications using SOAP.

10.4 WEB SERVICE-BASED REPORT ACCESS

Requesting reports on demand via SOAP calls to the RS Web service is your second option for accessing reports from the Report Server. The entry point for SOAP requests is the `ReportService2005.asmx` page. We covered the RS Web Service in full detail in chapter 8.

Here are some application scenarios that might require that you use this integration option:

- *When you need to come up with a hybrid approach that encompasses both the URL and Web service access options*—For example, you may need to implement both report rendering and management features in your applications, similar to the feature set supported by the Report Manager. While your application could request reports by URL, only the Web service supports the management API.

- *When direct access to the Report Server is not an option*—For example, an Intranet-oriented application may rule out direct access to Report Server for security reasons.
- *When a distributed application needs to validate the report request against some business rules before the request is handed out to the Report Server*—This calls for server-side report generation, which rules out the URL access option.
- *When you need to generate one or more reports in unattended mode*—The AWC Campaigner example that we look at in section 10.5.2 demonstrates this scenario.

The widespread adoption of SOAP facilitates integrating Reporting Services with many types of report consumers and platforms. Because SOAP has been embraced as an industry standard for communication with Web services, most platforms provide programmatic ways for handling SOAP messages and invoking web methods. For example, a web-based application running on UNIX can send a SOAP request to the RS Web service and then generate the report on the server side of the application.

Table 10.5 outlines some common techniques that developers writing Microsoft-centric applications can use to integrate their applications with the RS Web service.

Table 10.5 Techniques to integrate report consumers with the RS Web Service

Client type	Application example	Implementation approaches
WinForm	.NET-based applications Legacy applications written in Visual Basic 6.0	Web service proxy (.NET) Microsoft SOAP Toolkit (legacy applications, e.g., Visual Basic 6.0)
Web-based	.NET-based applications Other web-based applications	Web service proxy (.NET) to submit the report request on the server side Microsoft Web service behavior for Internet Explorer to submit the report request on the client side

Invoking the Report Server SOAP API is easy with .NET clients (both WinForm and web-based) because .NET provides native support for calling Web services. .NET developers are for the most part abstracted from the SOAP message complexities when using Visual Studio .NET. As we saw in chapter 8, in VS .NET you can establish a web reference to the Web service. Once this is done, invoking the RS Web service is not much different than invoking a local object. We see a code sample that demonstrates requesting a report by SOAP in section 10.4.1.

Legacy clients, for example, Visual Basic 6.0 clients, can integrate with the RS Web service by using the Microsoft SOAP toolkit (see section 10.5). Finally, other types of clients can use whatever infrastructure the programming language and platform support for Web service calls.

Next, let's see how a report consumer can request reports with SOAP.

10.4.1 Requesting reports with SOAP

As we saw in chapter 8, the RS Web service provides a series of methods that you can use to query and manage the report catalog. It also provides methods related to report rendering and execution. The pivotal method is the `Render` method, which you can use to render reports on demand. It takes several arguments that you have to set before invoking the method, such as an array of parameters for parameterized reports, the export format, specific device settings, and so on.

If the method succeeds, it returns the report payload as a byte array. In most cases, this means that an extra step is needed on your part, as the developer, to render the report to the user. For example, this may involve saving the byte array to a file and shelling out to it.

Invoking the Render method

To understand how you can call the `Render` method, let's return to the Access-Options application we used in section 10.3. This time we will see how we can request the report with SOAP. To do so, select the second radio button called Web Service.

When you click the Run Report button, AccessOptions invokes `RunByWS` function, whose abbreviated code is shown in listing 10.4.

Listing 10.4 Calling the Render Report SOAP API

```
private void RunByWS()
 {
   ReportingService2005 rs = RsHelpers.Proxy;
   rs.Url = txtServer.Text + @"/ReportService2005.asmx";
   byte[] result = null;
   string reportPath = txtReportPath.Text;
   string historyID = null;
   string format = cmbFormat.Text;
   string devInfo = null;
   DataSourceCredentials[] credentials = null;
   string showHideToggle = null;
   string encoding;
   string mimeType;
   Warning[] warnings = null;
   ParameterValue[] reportHistoryParameters = null;
   string[] streamIDs = null;
   ParameterValue[] proxyParameters = null;

   EntityParameter.ParametersDataTable userParameters =        ❶
    (EntityParameter.ParametersDataTable)grdParams.DataSource;

   if (userParameters.Rows.Count > 0)  proxyParameters = new
            ParameterValue[userParameters.Rows.Count];

   for (int i = 0; i<userParameters.Rows.Count;i++) {        ❷
      proxyParameters[i] = new ParameterValue();
```

❶ Gets the parameters from the data grid

❷ Prepares the parameter array

```
        proxyParameters[i].Name = userParameters[i].Name;
        proxyParameters[i].Value = userParameters[i].Value;
    }
                                  Calls the Web service to render the report ❸
  result = rs.Render(reportPath, format, historyID, devInfo,      <┘
           proxyParameters, credentials, showHideToggle,
           out encoding, out mimeType,
           out reportHistoryParameters,
           out warnings, out streamIDs);

  string filePath = Util.GetFileForReport(reportPath,
    cmbFormat.Text);    <-❹ Gets the file path for saving report payload
  FileStream stream = File.Create( filePath, result.Length);     <-❺
  stream.Write( result, 0, result.Length );                    Persists
  stream.Close();                                              the report
  Process.Start(filePath);    <-❻ Shells out to the application   payload to
}                                                              a file
```

One of the benefits of using the RS Web service is that it allows you to request the report in an object-oriented way. First, you obtain a reference to the Web service proxy by calling the `RsHelpers.Proxy` utility function. This function also takes care of setting the proxy credentials. Next, you set up the Web service URL to the `ReportService.asmx` end point. Then, you initialize the `Render` arguments to their default values.

The `Render` method is an all-encompassing method for report rendering. For example, by setting appropriate arguments, you can request a cached report from the snapshot history. You saw how to do this in section 10.2.4. For now, let's ignore the report history parameters as well as the device settings.

To specify the report parameters for parameterized reports, you load an array of the `ParameterValue` structures ❶, ❷, then, you call the `Render` method ❸ to request the report.

Finally, you need to take an extra step for showing the report. When a report is requested by URL, the browser does this automatically for you. However, when requesting reports via SOAP, you are on your own. To display the report, you save the report payload to a file with the appropriate extension. For example, if the report is requested in HTML, the file extension is `.HTML`; if it is IMAGE, then the extension is `.TIF` (the default image format), and so on.

You save the report file in the Application Data folder under the user called Document and in the Setting folder ❹, ❺. To get the file path and name right, you use a simple `GetFileForReport` helper function that takes the report name and export format and returns the full path to the file.

Once the file is saved, you shell out to it using `Process.Start` ❻. This will start the application associated with the file extension to load the file and display the report.

Dealing with errors

Unlike the URL access option, using SOAP allows you to deal gracefully with error conditions. The Report Server exposes exceptions as SOAP faults. The common language runtime (CLR) subsequently maps them to a .NET exception of type `System.Web.Services.Protocols.SoapException`. This allows developers to code defensively using `Try…Catch` blocks, as the following example shows:

```
try {
…Invoke a web method
}
catch (SoapException ex){
   // RS exception
   switch (ex.Detail["ErrorCode"].InnerText)
  {
    case "rsReportParameterValueNotSet":
       Util.ShowErrorMessage("The report parameters do not
           match.\n" + ex.Detail.InnerText); return;
    case "rsItemNotFound":
       Util.ShowErrorMessage("Wrong report name."); return;
    default: throw;
 }
}
catch (System.Exception ex)  {
  // something else is wrong
}
```

The bulk of the exception information is exposed as an XML string under the `Detail` property of the `SoapException` class. For this reason, you can get to the error code using the `SoapException.Detail` property and to the error message itself using the `Detail.InnerText` or `Detail.InnerXml` (to get as XML) property. For a full list of the RS error codes, see the product documentation.

As you have begun to see, requesting reports by SOAP is more involved than the URL option. Another area that requires additional effort on your part is rendering reports that include images.

10.4.2 Rendering images

When you export such reports to multistream exporting formats, such as all HTML flavors besides MIME HTML (MHTML), the report images and charts are not rendered by default. The reason for this odd behavior is that when the web browser renders an HTML page, it spawns additional requests to the web server to download the images included in the page. This presents an issue for dynamically generated images, such as charts.

To address this dilemma, when generating the report, the Report Server serializes the images in the report session cache associated with the report. Unfortunately, in the case of rendering reports by SOAP, the image URLs don't include the session identifier of the report session that the Report Server has created for the report. As a result, the Report Server is unable to match the request with the report session, and the image download request fails. Even if the session identifier were included in the image URL, it would be of little help because direct access to the Report Server is usually not an option when requesting reports by SOAP.

Handling images for exported-to-HTML reports could be quite a hassle. Currently, there are three workarounds for this problem:

- For external images, use the `HTMLFragment` setting.
- Download the images explicitly using the `RenderStream` method.
- Use cookie-less report sessions. In this case, the image URLs will have the session ID on them.

Let's look at the first two options in more detail.

Rendering external images

As you recall from chapter 4, you can use the image report item to reference external images by specifying their relative path in the report catalog. This is what we did to display the AWC company logo in our reports. One option to display external images when requesting reports via SOAP is to render the report as an HTML fragment by setting the HTMLFragment Device Info setting to true.

When this setting is used, the web server will include the `SessionID` in the image URL string. Then the HTTP-GET request to the Report Server that the browser will spawn to download the image will succeed. This is as simple as it gets but requires direct HTTP access from the browser to the Report Server. Besides, it doesn't work with chart reports because the Report Server generates the chart images dynamically.

Let's see if we can derive to a "universal" image-handling solution that works for all types of images and integration scenarios.

Downloading the images explicitly

For intranet-oriented applications you can explicitly download and save the report images using the `RenderStream` web method. This approach involves two implementation steps:

- Setting the `StreamRoot` device setting to a location where the images will be downloaded
- Enumerating through the image streams and downloading the images explicitly

Rendering images by using the `RenderStream` method is simple. You can set the `StreamRoot` device setting to a common folder on the user's hard drive, for example, the Documents and Settings folder. This is the approach we demonstrate in the Access Options sample, as shown in listing 10.5.

Listing 10.5 Downloading the images explicitly by using the RenderStream API

```
devInf="<DeviceInfo><StreamRoot>" + Application.UserAppDataPath+
        "/</StreamRoot></DeviceInfo>";

result = rs.Render(...) // render the report

// render the images when report is exported to HTML
if ("html" == format.Substring(0, 4).ToLower()){
   foreach (string streamID in streamIDs)   {
     byte [] image = rs.RenderStream(reportPath, format,
       streamID, null, null, proxyParameters,
       out optionalString, out optionalString);

   FileStream stream=File.OpenWrite(Application.UserAppDataPath
        + Path.DirectorySeparatorChar + streamID);
   stream.Write(image, 0, image.Length);
   stream.Close();
  }
}
```

❶ Specifies the download location

❷ Handles images when exporting to HTML

❸ Gets the image payload

❹ Downloads the image to a folder

First, you use the `StreamRoot` device ❶ setting to set the image URLs to point to the user's application folder. Then, you render the report. When the Report Server processes the report, it will see the `StreamRoot` setting and will adjust the report image URLs accordingly. In our example, the image URL will be set like so:

```
file:///C:/Documents and Settings/<user>
➥ /Application Data/AWC/Win/1.0.0.0/<streamID>
```

The last argument of the `Render` method takes a `StreamIds` ❷ argument in the form of a string array. When the `Render` method returns, the array will be loaded with the stream identifiers of all report images and charts that the report includes. You may think that the stream identifiers correspond to the report item identifiers as defined in the Report Server catalog, but such is not the case. The Report Server assigns them during report processing.

NOTE The Report Server prefixes the chart stream identifiers with C_. You can take advantage of this naming convention if you want to render only the chart images.

Next, you loop through all image identifiers and download the images by calling the `RenderStream` web method ❸. One thing that we want to bring to your attention is that you must pass the report parameters when calling the `RenderStream` method for parameterized reports so that the Report Server can correlate the report request with the right report session. If you don't, you will get the "Stream could not be found" exception.

When `RenderStream` returns ❹, you save the image as a binary file to the folder specified by the `StreamRoot` device setting.

So, as you've seen, using `RenderStream` to render report images is not that difficult. Unfortunately, this approach is often impractical with web-based applications, as we discuss next.

Proposing a universal image handler approach

Dealing with images gets trickier for web-based applications. In this case, you don't have access to the user's local environment to save the image files. Instead, your only option is to download the images to a globally accessible file store.

For intranet-based applications, you can set the `StreamRoot` device setting to a network file share. Needless to say, you must take care of deleting the image files on a regular basis to avoid filling up the server.

What about Internet-based applications? In this case, storing files on a network share is not an option because it won't be accessible to your web users. You may think that you can get around this predicament by setting `StreamRoot` to a virtual root on your web server. Unfortunately, this doesn't always work. To understand the problem, consider the following example.

Let's say your application's virtual folder is AWReporterWeb and that it has a subfolder called temp. If you set `StreamRoot` to

```
http://<servername>/AwReporterWeb/temp
```

the image URLs will be adjusted to

```
http://<servername>/AwReporterWeb/temp/<streamID>
```

where `streamID` is the image identifier.

There's one last and important consideration about the `RenderStream` method. The `Render` and `RenderStream` calls need to share the same report session. Handling report sessions with SOAP access requires more programming effort on your part, as we discuss next.

10.4.3 Handling report sessions

Recall our discussion in chapter 8 that when a new non-snapshot report request arrives, the Report Server caches the report's IF in the RS Temporary Database in the form of a report session.

NOTE Ensuring data consistency by using report sessions is more of a concern with URL access than with SOAP. When the report is requested via SOAP, the whole report payload is streamed back to the client. This means that you will get all pages of a multipage report, and no additional requests to the Report Server are necessary when the user pages from one page to the next. On the other hand, when the report is request by URL, only the first page is rendered. Navigating to another page initiates a new URL request. That said, you might still want to consider leveraging report sessions with SOAP as a performance-enhancement technique.

Unlike the automatic report session management that the browser provides when the report is rendered by URL, you have to take care of correlating the report sessions yourself when requesting the report by SOAP. The reason for this is that the Web service proxy keeps only one session identifier, so each subsequent report request overrides the report session identifier set by the previous request.

There are two cases when you may need to take care of handling the report sessions by yourself:

- *Rendering the report images via calls to* `RenderStream`—Note that this is needed only if the session identifier is overridden by another report request. Typically, you will download the report images via calls to `RenderStream` *immediately* after the report is rendered. If this is the case, you don't have to handle report sessions explicitly because the proxy will already have the session identifier associated with the report.
- *Optimizing the Report Server's performance*—As we explained in chapter 8, if the Report Server can correlate the report request with a session, it will bypass the execution phase and use the cached copy. As you see in chapter 14, report session caching can boost the Report Server's performance considerably. If the report data is not volatile and some data "staleness" is tolerable, we recommend that you leverage report session caching.

To understand how to handle report sessions when requesting reports via SOAP, you need to know how the Web service proxy stores the session identifiers.

How SOAP access handles report sessions

When the report is requested via SOAP, the Report Server exposes the report session–related properties under the `SessionHeader` proxy class. The `SessionId` member of this class returns the report session identifier that matches the `SessionID` primary key in the `SessionData` table from the ReportServerTempDB database. You can check the `IsNewExecution` property to find out whether the call to the `Render` method has resulted in a new execution. If `IsNewExecution` is false, the Report Server has served the report request from an already existing report session.

The Report Server overwrites the `SessionID` member after each call to the `Render` method. Therefore, if you are not proactive, two subsequent report requests will share the same sessions only if they ask for the same report (assuming that the parameter set is the same).

For example, let's say you run report A, then report B, and then report A again. When report B is rendered, its session identifier will overwrite the previous session identifier, which means that you will lose report A's session identifier. When report A is run again, even if the parameter set is the same, its execution will create a new report session and `IsNewExecution` will return true.

Therefore, if you need to leverage report sessions, you need to write some code to store the report session identifiers and correlate them with the requested reports. Next we'll discuss a possible implementation approach that does this.

Correlating the report request with a report session

You could keep the reports-to-session association in a collection of some kind. For example, a hashtable collection, as shown in listing 10.6, can do this by storing the report names and session identifiers as name-value pairs.

Listing 10.6 Correlating the report request with the report session

```
Hashtable sessionCollection = new Hashtable();
rs.Render("reportA"....);
sessionCollection.Add("reportA", rs.SessionId);
rs.Render("reportB ");
sessionCollection.Add("reportB ", rs.SessionId);
// need to call report A again
SessionHeader sessionHeader = new SessionHeader();
sessionHeader.SessionId=sessionCollection["reportA"].ToString();
rs.SessionHeaderValue=sessionHeader;
rs.Render("reportA"....);
```

Each time you render a report you retrieve the session identifier from the Web service proxy and stuff it into the hashtable collection. When the same report needs to be rendered again, you set the proxy's `SessionId` accordingly.

Now that you've learned the SOAP access basics, let's see how SOAP affects the interactive features of your reports.

SOAP and report interactive features

One important limitation that you will inevitably discover when requesting reports by SOAP is that most interactive features, such as drilldown, drill-through, document maps, toggled visibility, and document maps, rely on URL access.

For example, request the Sales by Territory Crosstab report using the Access-Options application. As you recall from chapter 4, this report allows the end user to drill down by expanding row or column groups. At first glance, when this report is requested by SOAP, it appears that the drilldown interactive feature is unaffected. Don't be fooled, though! This feature relies on direct access to the Report Server by URL.

The way this works is that when the interactive feature is requested by the end user (in this case by clicking the + indicator) the HTML Viewer framework fires an HTTP-GET request to the Report Server to refresh the report. Once again, in order for the request to succeed, the Report Server must be directly accessible by HTTP-GET. In many cases, this presents a problem because you would typically choose SOAP over HTTP-GET when direct access to the Report Server by URL is not an option, for example, to generate reports on the server side of an Internet web-based application.

As a developer, there is nothing you can do to change this behavior and avoid using HTTP-GET for interactive features. This poses an interesting dilemma, which may further complicate your decision-making process when you are pondering which access option to choose. How important are the report's interactive features to your end users? If interactivity is a must, then your choice is predetermined and it is URL access. Of course, we are not excluding the possibility of a hybrid approach in which the report is rendered initially by SOAP but URL access is used to support the interactive features.

But what about security if URL access is the only option? This is an especially valid question for Internet-oriented web applications. The good news is that you can have the best of both worlds: URL access to provide a rich user experience and a comprehensive level of security that doesn't rely on Windows authentication. To accomplish the second objective, you may need to write a custom security extension to replace the default RS Windows-based security mechanism.

At this point you are probably ready to throw SOAP out the window. After all, it is more difficult to implement and cannot be used for reports with interactive features. Not so fast! As you see next, requesting reports by SOAP can actually be very useful.

10.5 WEB SERVICE ACCESS (SOAP) IN ACTION

While URL access is more suitable for interactive applications when the user can initiate the report request explicitly, it falls short when the report needs to be generated in an unattended mode, such as for automating the report generation as a result of an event. For example, in a business-to-business situation, a vendor may need to pull a report on a regular basis to find out the customer's inventory level. If the inventory level falls below a certain threshold, the vendor system can send a notification to the manufacturing department.

Thanks to its object-oriented nature, when reports need to be generated in an unattended mode, SOAP may be a better choice than URL. Let's examine a simple code demo to emphasize this point.

10.5.1 Generating report requests with SOAP on the client side

There are at least two good reasons for generating reports via SOAP with web-based applications:

- *URL access to the Report Server is not allowed*—For example, security requirements may force the report administrator to disallow requesting reports via HTTP-GET or POST. As we mentioned in chapter 9, you can do this by removing the `ReportServiceHttpHandler` declaration from the Report Server's `web.config` file.
- *"Pseudo" web-based rich clients*—The web application can be designed to behave like a WinForm stateful application, where the data retrieval and rendering are

done entirely on the client side, for example, by using XSL transformations. This approach has been popular with "fat" DHTML clients that don't post their pages back to the web server.

To submit the report request via SOAP on the client side of a web-based application, you can use the Microsoft WebService behavior.

Calling web methods with the Microsoft WebService behavior

If your target browser is Internet Explorer, you can use the Microsoft WebService behavior to call web methods on the client side of the application using your favorite scripting language. To learn more about the WebService behavior, see the "Resources" section at the end of this book.

The Web Behavior sample builds on the Report Picker sample to demonstrate how reports can be requested via SOAP. At first look, the `WebBehavior.aspx` page appears identical to the `ReportPicker.aspx` page. However, the client-side reporting model is very different. Now, when the report request is submitted, the page doesn't post to itself. Instead, it invokes the RS Web service to request the report via SOAP and render it on the client side of the application.

Once you've downloaded the WebService behavior file (`webservice.htc`) from the Microsoft web site, configure it as follows.

First, create a `DIV` element to expose the WebService behavior as a DHTML element:

```
<div id="proxy" style="BEHAVIOR: url(webservice.htc)"></div>
```

Next, change the page body element to invoke the JavaScript `init()` function so that you can initialize the behavior to point to the RS Web service by calling the `useService` method:

```
<body onload="init()">
function init() {
   proxy.useService("http://localhost/reportserver/
      reportservice.asmx?WSDL","RS");
}
```

The second argument of the `useService` method allows you to specify a friendly name for the Web service.

After you've configured the Web service behavior file, you're ready to make the actual request for your report.

Requesting reports

Listing 10.7 shows the implementation details for requesting a report using the WebService behavior.

Listing 10.7 JavaScript functions for requesting reports

```
function runReport() {
  var optional;
  var objCall = proxy.createCallOptions();
  objCall.funcName = "Render";
  objCall.params = new Array();
  objCall.params.Report = frmReports.drpReports.value;
  objCall.params.Format = "XML";
  objCall.params.HistoryID = optional;
  var parameters = frmReports.txtParameter;
  if (parameters.length>0)
    objCall.params.Parameters = getParameters(parameters)

  proxy.RS.callService (fnHandler, objCall);
}

function parameter()  {
  this.Name = null;
  this.Value = null;
  return true;
}

function getParameters(parameters)  {
  reportParams = new Array();
  for (i=0;i<parameters.length;i++) {
    var newParam = new parameter();
    newParam.Name = parameters[i].name;
    newParam.Value = parameters[i].value;
    reportParams[i] = newParam;
  }
  return reportParams;
}

function fnHandler(res)  {
  if (!res.error) {
    var decodedResult = decode(res.value.Result);
    OpenReport (decodedResult);
  }
  else alert(res.errorDetail.string);
}
```

❶ Prepares the report request

❷ Sets the report parameters

❸ Defines the report parameter

❹ Enumerates the report parameters

❺ Decodes results

❻ Calls the OpenReport function

Clicking the Run Report hyperlink triggers a call to the `runReport` JavaScript function.

You start by defining your report request to the `Render` web method ❶. We decided it was best to hardcode the report format as XML so that you could save the report's payload as a disk file. To accomplish this, use the `FileSystemObject` object, which currently doesn't provide the ability to save binary data to a file.

NOTE You may need to adjust the browser's security settings to prevent client-side JavaScript errors when using `FileSystemObject`.

Next you populate the report parameters ❷ by calling the `getParameters` function ❹, which loops through the parameter elements on the page and adds them to an array object.

Because the `Render` method defines the parameter argument as of the `ParameterValue` type, you need to define a JavaScript structure that matches the `ParameterValue` layout. This is exactly what the `parameter()` function ❸ does.

Next, you call the `Render` method asynchronously and pass a pointer to the `fnHandler` callback function ❺, which is called automatically when the web method returns something. If the call completes successfully, you decode the results from Base64 encoding.

Finally, you call the `OpenReport` function ❻ to save the report's payload to a text file and shell out to the browser so that you can see the file's contents.

While intranet-based applications can generally enjoy the simplicity and the rich feature set of the Client-to-Report Server reporting model, other scenarios require server-side report generation via the Client-to-Façade-to-Report Server pattern. The next section shows you how you can do just that.

10.5.2 An automation solution: AW Campaigner

Back in chapter 6 we demonstrated how to export the Sales Promotion report to an RSS-compliant XML format. When there is a new campaign, the report's author could run the report by passing the offer identifier, export the report to the XML, and update the RSS blog file manually.

Let's enhance this example by implementing the AW Campaigner solution for automating the whole process. To fulfill the new requirements, our implementation approach involves these steps:

Step 1 Create a table trigger that will fire when a campaign record is inserted into the `Sales.SpecialOffer` table and invoke the stored procedure.

Step 2 Create a SQL Server stored procedure that will invoke a custom Web service façade.

Step 3 Create a Web service façade that will run the report and update the RSS file.

Figure 10.11 shows the sequence diagram of our solution.

The AW Campaigner process is initiated when a record is inserted into the `Sales.SpecialOffer` table. This causes the `trgSpecialOffer` trigger to fire. The trigger calls the `spUpdateRssFeed` stored procedure. The stored procedure in turn invokes our `StartCampaign` web method of the Campaigner Web service.

The Campaigner Web service then requests the Sales Promotion report via SOAP. It asks the report to be exported as XML. Finally, the Campaigner Web service updates the RSS blog file.

The source code of the Campaigner Web service can be found under the `Chapter10` folder in the AWReporterWeb web project, while the stored procedure and trigger script files are included in the Database project.

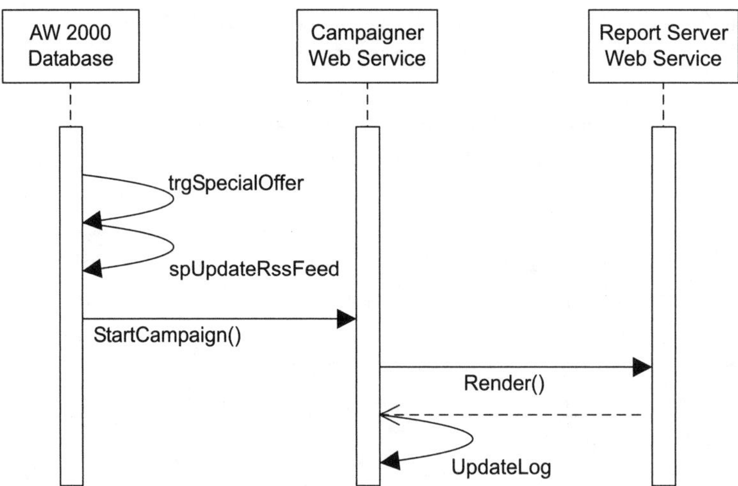

Figure 10.11 The AW Campaigner Web service sequence diagram shows that a table-level trigger initiates the blog file update process.

First we explore the details of how to start the campaign process, and then we explain how each component is implemented. We round out our discussion by showing you how to set up security for the AW Campaigner.

Triggering the process

The campaign process starts when a new offer record is inserted into the `SpecialOffer` table. The `trgSpecialOffer` trigger is implemented as an `AFTER INSERT` trigger on the `Sales.SpecialOffer` table, as shown in listing 10.8.

Listing 10.8 The trgSpecialOffer trigger

```
CREATE TRIGGER trgSpecialOffer ON [Sales].[SpecialOffer]
AFTER INSERT
AS

/* Get the new special offer id. */
DECLARE  @SpecialOfferID int
SELECT   @SpecialOfferID = SpecialOfferID
FROM     inserted

DECLARE  @Result varchar(8000)
EXEC     spUpdateRssFeed @SpecialOfferID, @Result OUT
```

The trigger gets the identifier of the record from the inserted table and calls the `spUpdateRssFeed` stored procedure, passing the special offer identifier to it.

One thing to watch for when you work with triggers is that all database operations inside the trigger are performed within the scope of an implicit transaction. This bit me quite badly at first. I wondered why the web method call inside the spUpdate-RssFeed stored procedure never succeeded. Upon further investigation, I realized that the trigger locks the new record. When the Sales Promotion report tries to read it, the SELECT statement gets deadlocked and the web method call inside spUpdateRssFeed eventually times out.

To solve this issue, I added the NOLOCK table hint in the report query. The NOLOCK table hint permits the report to read "dirty" data that has not yet been committed. For the purposes of the Campaigner scenario, this is fine, because the trigger is defined as AFTER INSERT, which means that the record has been inserted successfully. In other cases, however, you have to take into account the fact that the update operation may fail, in which case the database changes will get rolled back.

Invoking the Campaigner Web service

The main role of the spUpdateRssFeed stored procedure is to invoke the AW Campaigner web service. The abbreviated spUpdateRssFeed stored procedure code (excluding the error-handling logic) is shown in listing 10.9.

Listing 10.9 The spUpdateRssFeed stored procedure, which uses the XMLHTTP component to invoke the Campaigner Web service

```
CREATE  PROCEDURE spUpdateRssFeed( @SpecialOfferID  int,
        @Response varchar(8000) out)
AS
DECLARE
  @Url varchar(1000)
 ,@obj   int
 ,@hr   int
 ,@status int
 ,@msg varchar(255)

   set   @Url =
➥ 'http://localhost/AWReporterWeb/Chapter10/Campaigner.asmx/
➥ StartCampaign?CampaignID='
➥ + CAST(@SpecialOfferID AS VARCHAR(10))
   exec @hr = sp_OACreate 'MSXML2.ServerXMLHttp', @obj out
   exec @hr = sp_OAMethod @obj, 'Open', NULL, 'GET', @Url, false
   exec @hr = sp_OAMethod @obj, 'send'
   exec @hr = sp_OAGetProperty @obj, 'status', @status OUT
   exec @hr = sp_OAGetProperty @obj, 'responseText', @response OUT
   exec @hr = sp_OADestroy @obj
   return
```

The stored procedure uses the XMLHTTP component included with the Microsoft XML Parser (MSXML) to invoke the Campaigner Web service. (If you need more background information about this technology, see the "Resources" section at the end of this book.)

Once the XMLHTTP object is instantiated, you invoke the `StartCampaign` method of the Campaigner Web service and pass the new record identifier.

Implementing the Campaigner Web service

The `StartCampaign` web method renders the Sales Promotion report as XML for the given special offer identifier. You have already seen how to request a report by SOAP in the Access Options sample.

Next, `StartCampaign` calls the `AddSpecialOffer` method. This method uses XML DOM to load the XML report payload. To do this, you use a memory stream to wrap the payload array and load the `XmlDocument` from it:

```
MemoryStream stream = new MemoryStream(specialOffer);
XmlDocument specialOfferDoc = new XmlDocument();
specialOfferDoc.Load(stream);
```

Finally, `StartCampaign` updates the RSS blog file (`AWCSpecialDeals.xml`). This is the file that the RSS newsreaders need to reference when subscribing to the AWC feed. The `StartCampaign` method simply appends the XML definition of the new special offer item to the end of the file. This should be enough to trigger a new item notification in the newsreader.

Securing AW Campaigner

Setting up security for the Campaigner sample warrants more explanation. In real life, it is likely that its three components (the SQL Server database, Campaigner Web service, and Report Server) will be located on separate machines. Table 10.6 shows the Windows authentication setup that we used for testing.

Table 10.6 Setting up Windows authentication

Component	Authentication	Identity
SQL Server	Standard or Windows Integrated	Local system
AWReporterWeb (Campaigner Web service)	Anonymous access (rights to write to `AWCSpecialDeals.xml`)	Application pool identity changed to a domain account (or member of Users for local machine testing)
Report Server	Windows Integrated	The Campaigner application pool identity mapped to the Browser role for the Sales Promotion report and `SalesPromotion.xslt`

In this test environment, the SQL Server runs under the context of the Local System account. Because this is a local account, its identity cannot cross the machine boundary when the web method invocation occurs. For this reason, you have at least two choices for authenticating the SQL Server call to the Campaigner Web service:

- Change the SQL Server process identity to a domain account or a local account that is duplicated on the machine where the Campaigner Web service is installed (this has the same name and password).
- Set up the AWReporterWeb vroot to allow anonymous access.

For testing purposes, we'll adopt the latter approach, but in real life you should carefully consider the ramifications of using Anonymous access. When Anonymous access is enabled, IIS authenticates all users using a low-privileged Windows account (IUSR_computername by default), which is a member of the Guest Windows group. All requests to access local resources go under the identity of this account. In this case, the `StartCampaign` method needs to write to the blog file. For this reason, you need to grant the Anonymous account write permissions to this file. Alternatively, you can change the Anonymous identity to an account that has an elevated set of permissions.

Finally, you need to take care of setting the identity of the cross-machine call from the Campaigner Web service to the Report Server. Here, again you have two options:

- *Impersonating the user*—Assuming that Anonymous access is enabled, this means that we will pass the identity of the Anonymous account to the Report Server. Again, in order for the cross-machine call to succeed between the Campaigner machine and the Report Server machine, this account has to be a domain account or a duplicated local account, which exists on both machines.
- *Using the trusted subsystem approach by passing the Campaigner Web service identity to the Report Server*—You can change the identity of the ASP.NET worker process on the machine where the Campaigner Web service is running to a domain account.

In both cases, you have to set up a role-based security policy in the Report Server to grant the Campaigner account sufficient rights to view the Sales Promotion report and `SalesPromotion.xsl` file.

Now that you have a good high-level overview of both access options available for requesting reports, let's wrap up our discussion by comparing these options.

10.6 Evaluating URL and Web Service Access Options

Choosing the right integration scenario for report-enabling your applications can be challenging. You need to make a careful decision between the ease of use in the case of URL access and the flexibility offered by the RS Web service. Here are some of the questions that you need to ask yourself:

- *Is this an intranet or Internet-oriented application?*—While both access options can be used with intranet-oriented applications, unless you use a custom security extension, Internet reporting in most cases will require requesting reports by SOAP.

- *Can the Report Server be accessed directly by the client application?*—If the answer is no (for security, or other reasons), then SOAP is the only choice.
- *Does the report request need to be validated before it is handed out to the Report Server?*—If business rules need to be validated before the report request is authorized, SOAP may be the better choice.
- *How will the report parameters be handled?*—If the HTML Viewer fits the bill, it would be naive not to take advantage of URL access.

In general, we recommend that you evaluate URL access first and *only* if it doesn't meet your integration requirements should you settle on Web service access. As you've seen in this chapter, there are good reasons to keep things simple, and simplicity is the biggest strength of URL access.

Let's enumerate the pros and cons of each option in more detail to help you with the decision-making process.

10.6.1 Evaluating URL access

In general, URL access is best suited for interactive, intranet-oriented applications where the report request can originate on the client side of the application.

Pros of URL access

The advantages of this approach are as follows:

- *Simplicity*—Compared to requesting reports by SOAP, URL access is far easier. No postprocessing steps are required to render the report payload. The browser handles report sessions automatically. In case of HTML reports, you don't have to worry about downloading the image files. If you are using SOAP, taking care of the report images and charts could be a hassle, especially for Internet-based reports.
- *Relatively easy to integrate with client applications*—Due to the venerable history of the HTTP protocol, most development tools and platforms can handle HTTP-GET requests and responses.
- *No client footprint*—Usually, there will be nothing that you need to install to integrate a client application with RS by URL. It could be as easy as embedding the report's URL in a hyperlink. For example, you can have a SharePoint Web part that references a report by URL.
- *Interactive features*—You can leverage URL access to provide a rich user experience by adding interactive features to your reports, such as drilldown, toggled visibility, document maps, navigational features, and the HTML Viewer. When a report with interactive features is requested in HTML, the Report Server embeds the request-specific details, such as the parameter values, in the report page. When the interactive feature is requested by the end user, for example to perform a drilldown, the report spawns an HTTP-GET request to the Report Server to refresh itself.

- *Performance*—The performance advantages of URL access are several. First, the report payload is smaller compared to requesting a report by SOAP. When the report is requested by URL, the Report Server doesn't have to serialize the report payload to a byte array before sending it to the consumer. Second, URL access doesn't require any preprocessing by the report consumer to render the report. By contrast, if you request the report from the Web service, in most cases you will need to save the report payload to a disk file and shell out to it so that the user can see it. Finally, report sessions are handled automatically by the browser, which can speed up subsequent requests to render the same report.

Cons of URL access

The disadvantages of this approach are as follows:

- *Restricted to report rendering*—You can only render reports using URL access to the Report Server. For all other tasks, you will need to use the RS Web service.
- *Not object-oriented*—Crafting these query parameters can be difficult! However, you can get around it by creating a wrapper, which will generate the right URL syntax for you. For example, the RS Catalog Explorer demonstrates this approach by using a helper class, called `URLAccessBuilder`.
- *Not suitable for server-side report rendering*—The URL access option is more suitable for interactive applications that generate reports on the client side. For example, you cannot programmatically catch exceptions and react to error conditions. In addition, requesting reports by URL requires direct access to the Report Server. This could be an issue in cases where there is a façade between the consumer and the Report Server and you need to validate business rules, provide custom security, or abstract the Report Server.
- *URL length limitations*—Many browsers impose restrictions on the maximum length of the URL address. For example, Internet Explorer has a maximum URL length of 2 KB (2,048 characters). This makes passing large data structures as report parameters impossible. For instance, you won't be able to pass application datasets as a report parameter from a WinForm front end to a report. Although the custom dataset extension (which we create in chapter 13) allows you to report off application datasets, the serialized dataset payload may often exceed 2 KB. As a workaround to this limitation, you can use HTTP-POST.

10.6.2 Evaluating Web service access

On the other hand, the Web service access option may be more suitable for generating reports on the server side of the application.

Pros of Web service access

Here are the advantages:

- *Broad set of features*—Unlike the URL access option, the RS Web service is not limited to report rendering. It exposes the full functionality of the Report Server as a series of web methods.
- *An industry standard for exchanging messages between heterogeneous platforms*—This increases the RS client base to applications running on other platforms.
- *Object-oriented access*—Requesting a report via SOAP is as easy as instantiating the Web service proxy and calling its methods. In addition, the Report Server exposes exceptions as SOAP faults, which allows developers to code defensively.
- *Flexible invocation*—As you've seen, interfacing with the Web service doesn't require user interaction.

Cons of Web service access

And here are the disadvantages:

- *HTML Viewer not available*—Unlike the URL option, a report rendered via SOAP doesn't include the HTML Viewer toolbar. For this reason, development effort will typically be required up front for interactive client applications—for example, to get the report parameters, export format, and so on.
- *Interactive features rely on URL access*—In general, you'll find that requesting reports from the Web service gives you a reduced interactive feature set. For example, although interactive features, such as drilldown, hyperlinks, and document maps, are available when reports are rendered via SOAP, they rely on URL access to the Report Server. This could be a problem if the Report Server is behind a façade and direct HTTP-GET access to the Report Server is impossible.
- *More involved report rendering*—Extra steps are required for report rendering and maintaining report sessions.
- *Slower performance*—Report serialization results in an increased report payload. The percentage of increase varies based on the export format and the report itself, but experiments show an added overhead of about 20–30 percent. This could be an issue with low-speed connections between the client and the Report Server.

10.6.3 Choosing an integration approach

So, where does this chapter's discussion leave you in terms of integrating client applications with Reporting Services? You saw that two access options are available when adding on-demand reporting capabilities to client applications: URL and SOAP. How would you choose between them? In some cases, the application requirements dictate the access option and you won't have much choice. For example, the AW Campaigner requirements mandate the use of the RS Web service for report rendering in unattended mode.

In other cases, you have to carefully weigh the pros and cons of each option before deciding which one will be better suited for your particular situation. Once again, we recommend that you consider the URL access option first. It supports all interactive features, and it is easier to integrate with client applications.

The main advantages of using the Web service are its flexible invocation options and extensive set of web methods. However, introducing additional layers and using SOAP for report rendering will often necessitate extra development effort and compromises in the interactive feature set.

One excellent approach would be to take the best of both worlds by using URL for report rendering and SOAP for everything else. There may be other factors that might influence your decision, including the type of the application (WinForm or web-based) and restrictions that the application's requirements might impose. For this reason, we revisit this topic in subsequent chapters and make more specific recommendations as we examine various application scenarios.

10.7 SUMMARY

In this chapter we examined the core architectural options that the Report Server offers for integrating with client applications.

First, we discussed the URL access option. We explored its syntax and discussed the HTML Viewer, which is available only with this option. Then we saw a practical example, the AccessOptions application, which demonstrated how a WinForm-based application could submit a report request by URL.

Second, we examined the RS Web service access option. You saw how you can address some of its complexities, such as handling report sessions and images. Again, we looked at the AccessOptions application to find out how a client application could leverage this option to request reports by SOAP.

Finally, we rounded off our discussion by comparing both integration options. We pointed out that URL access is the fastest and easiest way to request reports and that it supports all of a report's interactive features. For these reasons, we recommend that you consider URL access first when choosing an integration approach for report-enabling your applications.

However, URL access may not be a good fit with more involved integration scenarios, such as when you need to generate reports in an unattended mode, as we demonstrated in the AW Campaigner code sample. In this case, consider integrating your applications with the RS Web service by SOAP.

In the next chapter, you'll be introduced to the ReportViewer controls, which are available with the 2.0 version of the .NET Framework. Use these controls to integrate Reporting Services reports into your Windows or Web applications that use the .NET 2.0 framework. Although they use both the URL and SOAP methods under the hood, they do not require a strong understanding of either the URL or SOAP methods. The ReportViewer controls let developers focus on more important things than coding to render reports in their applications.

CHAPTER 11

Mastering the ReportViewer controls

ReportViewer controls are part of Visual Studio 2005 and, when used, are guaranteed to change the way you integrate RS reports into your applications. The ReportViewer controls are built into the toolbox of Visual Studio 2005 and don't require any downloads or additional installation. When you want to place an RS report in your windows or web application, you can simply drag the control into the design environment, configure the control with properties for your report, and run your application. It's that easy. Why dedicate an entire chapter to these controls if it's that easy, you may ask? Let's just say it *can* be that easy, but as with any of the .NET controls, there are many ways to configure and tweak them to meet your needs.

In this chapter you learn how these controls work. We examine the different modes of these controls, and explain when you'll want to use each mode. You also see how these controls can be used to integrate the reports that have been deployed to the Report Server (in remote mode), as well as how these controls can be used to render reports into your applications without the use of a Report Server (in local mode). In addition, we explore how to implement custom validation of your report parameters and how to convert your Report Server reports so that they can be used in an environment that is disconnected from a Report Server. Finally, we discuss deploying applications that use the ReportViewer controls and what you need to do for your deployments to be successful.

Let's get started by learning how these controls work.

11.1 HOW THE .NET REPORTVIEWER CONTROLS WORK

In chapter 10 we covered the architecture for pulling reports out of the Report Server. While that information is very important for the report developer, .NET application developers won't need this level of understanding to add reports to their applications using the ReportViewer controls. Because the ReportViewer controls mask the RS architecture from application developers, developers can add existing reports to their applications without having a strong background in Reporting Services.

Using these controls should be your method of choice when integrating RS reports into your Visual Studio 2005 Windows and web applications for two reasons:

- Ease of use
- The ability to completely manage the report properties through these controls

Using the ReportViewer controls allows you to spend more time focusing on the business logic of your applications and less time integrating reports into your applications.

Let's look first at how the ReportViewer controls work for web applications versus Windows applications.

11.1.1 Controls for web and Windows applications

There is a ReportViewer control for both Windows and web applications. Depending on the type of application you are working with, the Visual Studio toolbox will contain the appropriate control. While at first glance these controls seem to be identical, there are actually a few subtle differences between them. Table 11.1 showcases these differences.

Table 11.1 Differences between the Windows and web ReportViewer controls

ReportViewer control feature	Web	Windows
Presentation	Uses HTML formatting to display a report.	Uses a Graphical Device Interface (GDI) to provide a visual experience that is consistent with Windows user interface styles.
Processing	Local report processing can be configured for asynchronous processing.	Local report processing is always performed as an asynchronous process.

continued on next page

Table 11.1 Differences between the Windows and web ReportViewer controls *(continued)*

ReportViewer control feature	Web	Windows
Printing	Printing reports from the web server control uses an ActiveX print control if the report is processed on a remote server. If you want to print a locally processed report from the web server control, you can export the report to another output format before you print.	Printing reports from the Windows Forms control uses the print functionality of the operating system.
Deployment	The deployment strategy for reports hosted in the Web server control in an ASP.NET application must take session state and web farm configuration into account. If you are using the web server control to process a report on a remote Report Server, you must consider how to authenticate application users to access the server and any external data sources that provide data to reports.	If you are deploying the ReportViewer with a Windows application, you will need to use the bootstrap features in Visual Studio to be sure that ReportViewer is installed on the client machine along with your application. See section 11.6 of this chapter for more information.

The ReportViewer controls each have two processing modes: remote and local. Let's take a closer look at these modes so that you'll know when to use each mode and also understand the differences as well as limitations of each.

11.1.2 Choosing remote or local mode

The ReportViewer controls can process and render a report with or without Report Server access. If you have server access (and this is more common), you choose *remote* mode. Remote mode allows the application developer to select a Report Server and path to a report as well as control most of the properties and features of RS by changing properties of this control. We explore these properties in section 11.1.3.

In some cases, you might not want to access the Report Server, or you may not have access to it, so you choose *local* mode. Local mode provides some additional options that take Reporting Services to the next level from its original version. You are no longer tied to the Report Server, which means that you can create reports that run from local data sources in a disconnected environment. Local mode also enables you to use objects and Web services as data sources for your reports. This opens a whole new world of reporting for you.

Regardless of the processing mode, ReportViewer-generated reports look and function in a very similar way. To help you better appreciate the differences between processing modes, table 11.2 lists several ReportViewer features and how these features are affected by the mode used.

Table 11.2 Differences between remote and local modes

ReportViewer control feature	Remote mode	Local mode
RDL Management	Report definition (RDL) is supplied and rendered by the Report Server.	The RDL is supplied by the host application instead of being retrieved from a Report Server.
Report Engine	Uses the Report Server engine.	Uses the same engine as the Report Server but is embedded into the application.
DataSet	Supplies the data as SQL Server DataSet.	Supplies the data as an ADO.NET DataTable to the report engine.
Export Formats	Full Export options (see chapter 1).	Only exports to Excel or PDF format.
Report Creation	Report Creation is done in the Business Intelligence Development Studio with the Reporting Services project.	Report creation is integrated into the Windows application VS 2005 project instead of having a separate Reporting Services project.

Before you see each processing mode in action, let's learn about some of the ReportViewer properties that you'll encounter most often.

11.1.3 Managing properties of the ReportViewer controls

Both modes of the ReportViewer controls share a number of common properties that can be set. For example, you might want to change the color for the links in the toolbar (`LinkActiveColor` and `LinkActiveHoverColor`) or the height and width of the ReportViewer (`Height` and `Width`). Another common configuration is to hide or show the toolbar itself by using the `ShowToolbar` property. We explore this in more detail in section 11.2.2.

Table 11.3 lists the properties you will use most of the time. Two of the properties that we cover in our examples later in this chapter are the `ShowToolbar` and the `ShowContextMenu` properties.

Table 11.3 does not contain the complete list of properties; for that, see the SQL Server Books Online documentation or search for "ReportViewer Controls (Visual Studio)" in the Visual Studio product documentation. The best way to understand how these properties affect the ReportViewer controls is through example. In the next section, we walk you through an example of using the ReportViewer in remote mode, and we also configure many of the properties that are shown in table 11.3.

Table 11.3 Commonly used properties of the ReportViewer controls

Member	Description
`ProcessingMode`	Gets or sets the processing mode for the control. Possible values are `Remote` and `Local`.
`DocumentMapWidth`	Gets or sets the document map width in pixels.
`LinkActiveColor`	Gets or sets the active color for links in the toolbar. Note that this does not have any effect on links in your reports.
`LinkActiveHoverColor`	Gets or sets the hover color for links in the toolbar. Note that this does not have any effect on any links in your reports.
`LinkDisabledColor`	Gets or sets the color for disabled links in the toolbar. Note that this does not have any effect on any links in your reports.
`PromptAreaCollapsed`	Gets or sets a Boolean value that determines whether the parameter area is initially collapsed or expanded. You must specify a default value for all parameters if you are going to set this to true. If you do not specify default values, you will receive an error similar to the following: *The 'Customer Name' parameter is missing a value.*
`ShowParameterPrompts`	Gets or sets a Boolean value that determines whether the parameter area is shown in the control. You must specify a default value for all parameters if you are going to set this property to false. If you do not specify default values, you will receive an error similar to the following: *The 'Customer Name' parameter is missing a value.*
`ShowToolbar`	Gets or sets a Boolean value that enables or disables the HTML Viewer toolbar. If you are disabling the toolbar as a means to limit the end user's functionality for Windows applications, you should also set the `ShowContextMenu` to false.
`ShowContextMenu`	Gets or sets a Boolean value that enables or disables the context menu for the ReportViewer control. This property is only available in the Windows ReportViewer control. The context menu will expose many of the features in the toolbar such as print, export, zoom, and page properties.
`ShowProgress`	Gets or sets a Boolean value that determines whether a progress animation is shown while waiting for the report to render.
`Height` and `Width`	These properties allow you to get or set the `height` and `width` properties of the ReportViewer control. For the Windows control you need to specify this value as number of pixels (without adding px at the end of the number). For the web control you can use both pixels or percentages for the width column. While the `width` property works well with both pixels and percentages, the `height` property does not seem to function well with percentages.

11.2 USING REPORTVIEWER IN REMOTE MODE

As we stated earlier, using the ReportViewer controls in remote mode forces you to pull the reports directly from the Report Server. This means that the reports have already been created and deployed to the Report Server and you use the ReportViewer controls in remote mode to get the reports and render them into your applications.

In this section, you see some examples of using the ReportViewer control to pull data from objects. Also, we cover some of the many properties of the ReportViewer controls and explore some real-world examples. For these walkthrough examples, we encourage you to create your own Windows or web projects and use the code provided with the book as a reference. You'll find the code samples in the chapter 11 folder in the AWReporterWin and AWReporterWeb projects.

11.2.1 Creating, configuring, and running the control

In this section you learn how to create and configure the ReportViewer controls in remote mode by doing the following:

- Create a Windows Form and add the ReportViewer to it.
- Configure the properties of the ReportViewer.
- Run the Windows Form and view the Sales By Territory report from part 1 in the ReportViewer.

Adding the ReportViewer control to a Windows Form

The example code for this section is in the chapter 11 folder of the AWReporterWin project. We recommend you create your own Windows application project for this walkthrough. Once you have a project to work with, follow these steps:

Step 1 Create a Windows Form project and name it **ReportViewerRemote.cs**. If you created a new project for this walkthrough, you can use the default form in the project named Form1.cs and rename it to **ReportViewerRemote.cs**. You can find the ReportViewer control within the data controls of the toolbox (see figure 11.1).

Step 2 Drag and drop this control onto the Windows Form.

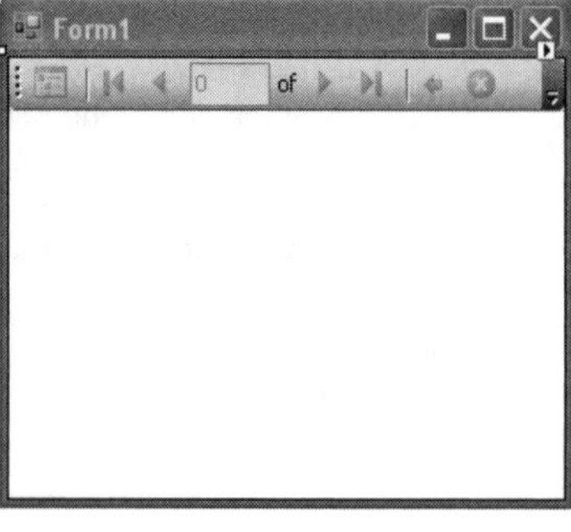

Figure 11.1 The ReportViewer Control is shown here in a Windows Form.

Configuring the ReportViewer control

Now you need to enter all of the required information to integrate an RS report into a Windows application. Follow these steps:

Step 1 Set the size properties and dock the control to the form. For this example you want to set the size properties to about 600 pixels wide by 450 pixels high. When the ReportViewer control is dropped onto the form, the smart tag window appears. Dock the ReportViewer control to your form by clicking on the *dock to parent form...* link in the smart tag window. If you don't see the smart tag window, you can get to it by selecting the ReportViewer control and clicking on the small arrow icon, as shown in figure 11.1.

Step 2 Set the control properties. First, expose the properties by selecting the control and viewing the properties window for the control. Let's set the `ShowZoomControl` property to false, as shown in figure 11.2. You can see that there are a number of items in the toolbar that can be shown or hidden when the report is rendered. We work with these properties a little later on, but for now let's switch our attention to configuring the control to process the Sales By Territory Interactive report that you created in chapter 4.

Step 3 Configure the control. To view configuration properties, click on the smart tag icon found in the upper right of the control. Since we are exploring the remote mode of the ReportViewer, select `<Server Report>` from the `Choose Report` field.

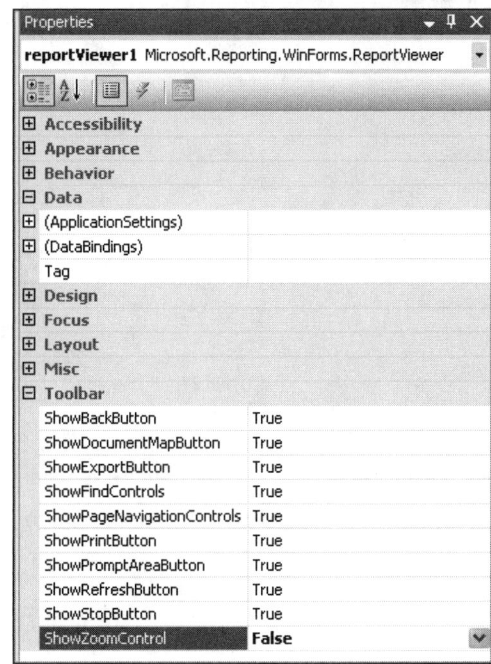

Figure 11.2
You can hide or show toolbar buttons by modifying properties of the ReportViewer control.

NOTE Choosing `<Server Report>` automatically sets the `ProcessingMode` property to `Remote`. We could have simply gone through the property settings to configure this control, but the smart tags settings are an easier way to accomplish our goal.

Step 4 Enter a valid Report Server URL and report path (shown in figure 11.3). Be sure to include the full path for the report starting with a slash (/). Also be sure to leave the extension off the report name. For this example, the report path should be **/AWReporter/Sales By Territory**.

Figure 11.3 The smart tag window exposes a great starting point for configuring the ReportViewer control.

Running and viewing your report

You are now ready to see the results of your work. When you run the application, you should see the report shown in figure 11.4.

Let's take a look at how you might customize the ReportViewer.

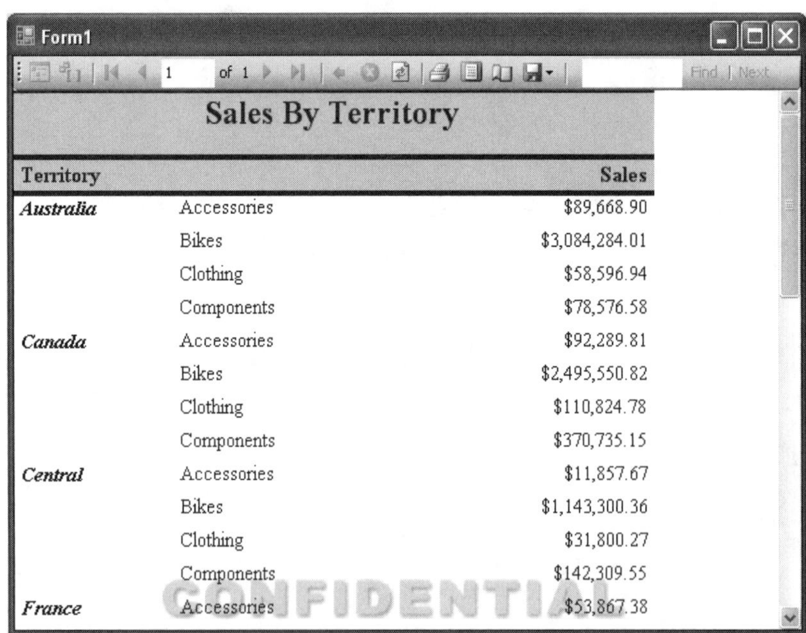

Territory		Sales
Australia	Accessories	$89,668.90
	Bikes	$3,084,284.01
	Clothing	$58,596.94
	Components	$78,576.58
Canada	Accessories	$92,289.81
	Bikes	$2,495,550.82
	Clothing	$110,824.78
	Components	$370,735.15
Central	Accessories	$11,857.67
	Bikes	$1,143,300.36
	Clothing	$31,800.27
	Components	$142,309.55
France	Accessories	$53,867.38

Figure 11.4 In the Sales By Territory report, the Zoom functionality is hidden from the toolbar.

11.2.2 Additional customizations for the ReportViewer control

Let's say you don't want your end users to see the HTML toolbar. Maybe you have your own toolbar in your application, or maybe you just don't want your users to have the functionality provided in the HTML toolbar. Simply set the `ShowToolbar` property to false from the ReportViewer control property window (figure 11.2). The toolbar is shown right above the report title in figure 11.4.

If you are trying to disable functionality from the end user, hiding the toolbar won't enforce this. Users can simply right-click on the rendered report to show the context menu, which exposes the toolbar functionality. To truly disable all toolbox functionality, you need to either set both `ShowToolbar` and `ShowContextMenu` to false or set the properties for the functionality that you want to disable.

What if you want to disable some of the functionality, but not all of it? In this hypothetical situation, you don't want your users to be able to export or print this particular report, but you do want them to have the ability to zoom in and out. Therefore, you need to expose the toolbar, but to disable the export or print functionality, you have to set `ShowExportButton` and `ShowPrintButton` to false. Not only will the control hide the buttons, but if users right-click on the control they won't see the option to export or print.

Using remote mode allows you to add the reports that you created and deployed to your Report Server in part 1 of this book. Using this mode is the easiest and quickest way to add existing reports to your applications. After reading this section, you should be armed with the knowledge needed to integrate, configure, and customize existing reports into your .NET 2.0 applications.

NOTE Even though there are separate controls for Windows applications versus web applications, it is important to understand that the differences are minor. If we had demonstrated this in an ASP.NET web application, you would have seen that all of the steps are virtually the same.

In the next section, we examine the other side of the ReportViewer controls: local mode.

11.3 USING REPORTVIEWER IN LOCAL MODE

The local mode of the ReportViewer controls provides rich reporting without the use of a Report Server by embedding the report definition inside the application. This is a great way to use Reporting Services when you can't access a Report Server.

To use local mode, you first have to create a report using Visual Studio 2005 from within your Windows or web application project. This is different from remote mode, in which you used reports that were created using the Report Designer and deployed to a Report Server. This means that with local mode you cannot natively use reports that you have already created and deployed to your Report Server.

Report Server (remote mode) reports have an `.rdl` extension whereas local reports used by the ReportViewer controls use the `.rdlc` extension. Later in section 11.5.1 you learn how to convert your RDL files for use with local mode.

In this section, you learn how to create the RDLC from your Windows or web applications by creating local reports from a variety of data sources. Let's start off by using the ReportViewer control to get information from a database.

As before, for this walkthrough example you can reference the sample code in the Chapter 11 folder of the AWReporterWin project.

11.3.1 Creating a local report with a database as the data source

As stated earlier, in local mode the report file is created as an RDLC file instead of an RDL file. A second difference is that the report is created from within your application projects instead of a separate Reporting Services project. For the most part, everything else will feel the same as it did with remote mode, but there are some minor differences. We showcase many of these differences in our examples.

For this hypothetical situation, you've been asked to make the AWC employee directory available to field sales agents who don't typically have access to the AWC network. Let's assume that there is a process built that replicates or syncs the data from the AWC database to a database on the sales agent's local machine.

NOTE We chose to run this from the same local database that the other examples run from. In a real-world scenario, the client computer would likely be running SQL Express and would also not have an exact replica of the original database. To simplify the code setup for this book, we simply pretend this is a separate database.

Step 1 Create a new Windows Form and call it **ReportViewerLocal.cs**. Stretch the form, add the ReportViewer, and anchor the control just as you did in the ReportViewer remote example earlier. Instead of choosing `<Server Report>` from the `Choose Report` property of the smart tag window (figure 11.3), click the *design new report* link. This creates a new RDLC file and opens it up in your project. On the left side of your design window you should see a Data Sources tab; if not, you can add it by selecting Data > Show Data Sources from the top menu. You can also toggle the Data Sources view by pressing Shift-Alt-D.

Step 2 Create a data source for your report by right-clicking in the Data Sources section or by selecting Data > Add New Data Source from the top menu. This opens the Data Source Configuration Wizard, as shown in figure 11.5.

Step 3 Select Database and click the Next button. The next screen lets you choose your data connection by either selecting an existing connection or creating a new connection. Let's set this data source up for our AdventureWorks database.

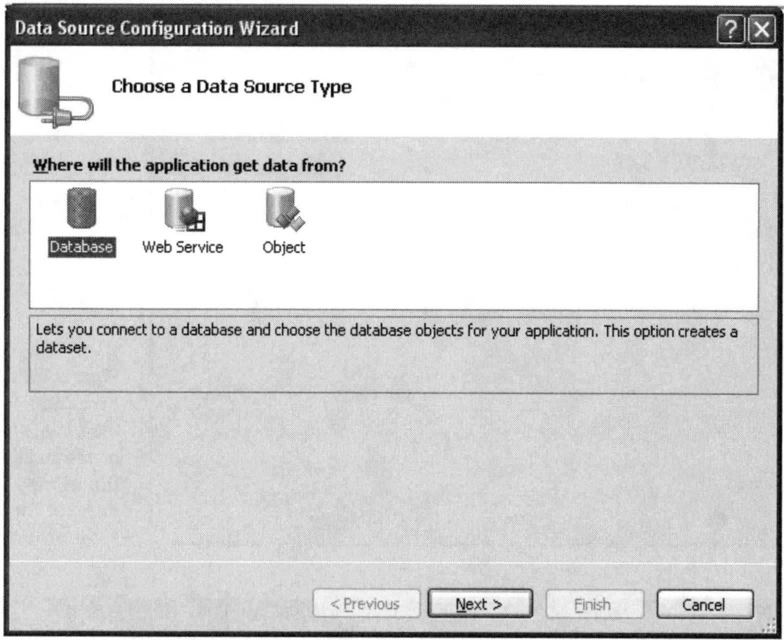

Figure 11.5 The Data Source Configuration Wizard allows you to create data sources from a database, Web service, or an object.

Step 4 Once you've set up the data connection and clicked the Next button, you'll see a screen that prompts you to name your dataset and choose which database objects you want to include. Figure 11.6 shows the high level of the available database objects. For this example, name your dataset **EmployeeDirectory** and select a database view to retrieve the data. To use the database view, you must expand the views by clicking on the plus sign and then select the `vEmployee(HumanResources)` view. Then click Finish. Figure 11.7 shows the design environment after you've created the dataset for your report. Notice that `EmployeeDirectory` is created as an XSD file in your project, which allows you to reuse this dataset in other reports, forms, or code if needed.

Step 5 Because reports are created in the Business Intelligence Development Studio environment, you should be comfortable creating your report from this point on. For this report we created a simple table report with six columns:

- Name
- Job Title
- Phone
- Email
- City
- State

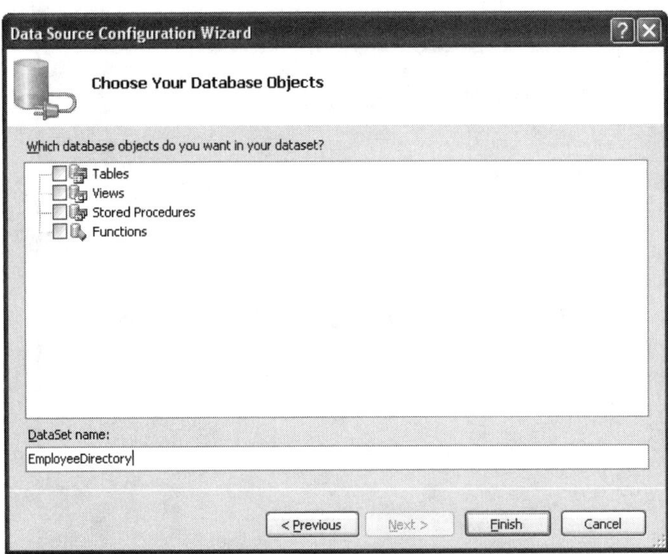

Figure 11.6
You can add tables, views, stored procedures, and functions to your dataset for use in local reports.

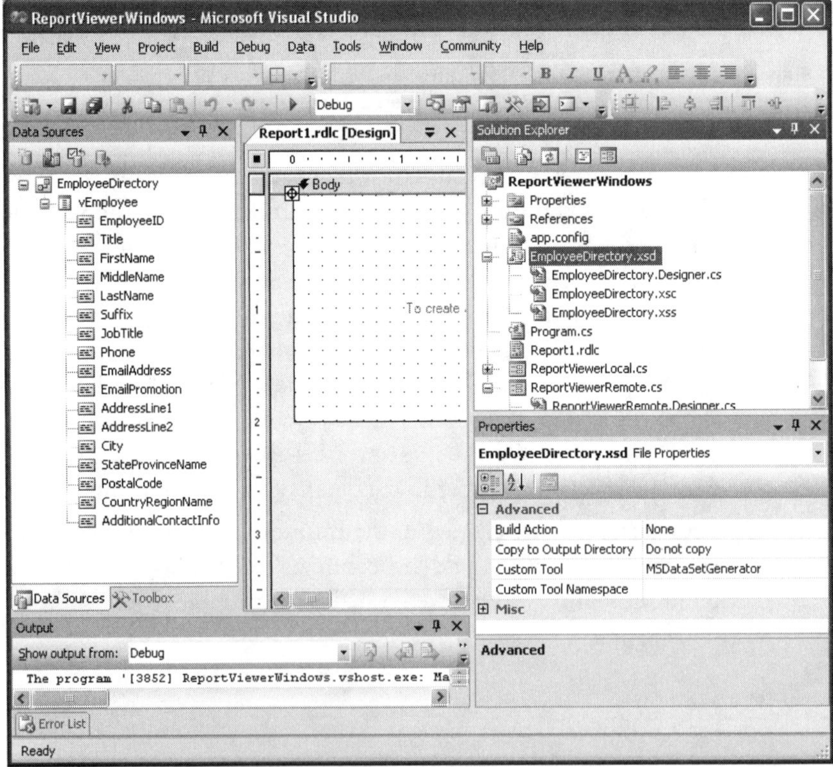

Figure 11.7 The dataset EmployeeDirectory shows up in the Data Sources section as well as in your project code as an XSD file.

NOTE For more information on creating tabular reports, see part 1 of this book.

One problem with creating local reports is that you can't preview the report in the Visual Studio IDE as you could if you were designing in a Reporting Services project. To preview your report you will need to complete step 5. For now, apply any formatting and save this report.

Step 6 Now we'll add the report to the form. First, open the `ReportViewerLocal` Windows Form, and in the smart tag window, select the report that you created to add it to the form. Figure 11.8 shows the ReportViewer task's smart tag window after you've created a local report in your project.

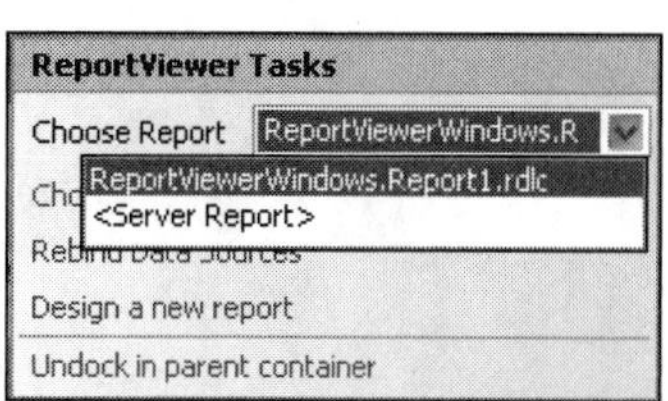

Figure 11.8 The ReportViewer lets you choose the local reports.

You have now created your first local report, which you can run without using a Report Server. If you doubt that this report is *completely* local, try stopping the SQL Server Reporting Services service and rerunning the report.

11.3.2 Creating a local report with an object as the data source

You are not limited to getting data directly from a database. Using local mode, you can get data for your reports from your .NET business objects or data objects. In fact, you may not have to do any special coding to your business objects in order to use them. Let's take a look. The chapter 11 folder in the AWReporterWin project contains a sample of a business object that gets all of the products and aggregates the sales by category and subcategory. First we will go through the objects that have been created for this example.

Business object code

The `Product.cs` file has two classes: `Product` and `ProductInformation`. Listing 11.1 shows the code for the `Product` class.

Listing 11.1 AWC.Reporter.Win product object

```
namespace AWC.Reporter.Win
{
    public class Product
    {

        private string productName;
        public string ProductName
        {
            get{return productName;}
            set { this.productName = value; }
        }
```

```
        private string productCategory;
        public string ProductCategory
        {
            get { return productCategory; }
            set { this.productCategory = value; }
        }
        private string productSubCategory;
        public string ProductSubCategory
        {
            get { return productSubCategory; }
            set { this.productSubCategory = value; }
        }

        private decimal productSales;
        public decimal ProductSales
        {
            get { return productSales; }
            set { this.productSales = value; }
        }
    }
```

The `Product` class contains four properties: `ProductName`, `CategoryName`, `SubCategoryName`, and `ProductSales`. You'll use this object when you set up your dataset for your report. Listing 11.2 shows the code for the `ProductInformation` class.

Listing 11.2 The ProductInformation object, which uses .NET generics to return a list of product objects

```
public class ProductInformation
 {
     public static List<Product> GetProducts()           <-- ❶ Returns generic list of Product objects
     {
         SqlDataReader rdr = null;
         SqlCommand cmd = null;
         SqlConnection conn = new SqlConnection
            (global::AWC.Reporter.Win.Properties.Settings.
            ➥ Default.AdventureWorksConnectionString);
         List<Product> ProductList = new List<Product>();   <-- ❷ Instantiates a new Generic object
         try
         {
             conn.Open();
             cmd = new SqlCommand("spGetProductSalesByCategory",conn);
             cmd.CommandType = CommandType.StoredProcedure;
             rdr = cmd.ExecuteReader();         <-- ❸ Puts returned dataset into SqlDataReader
             Product prod = null;
             while (rdr.Read())
             {
                 prod = new Product();
                 prod.ProductName = rdr.GetString
                 (rdr.GetOrdinal("ProductName"));
```

```
                prod.ProductCategory = rdr.GetString
                (rdr.GetOrdinal("ProductCategory"));
                prod.ProductSubCategory = rdr.GetString
                (rdr.GetOrdinal("ProductSubCategory"));
                prod.ProductSales = rdr.GetDecimal
                (rdr.GetOrdinal("Sales"));
                ProductList.Add(prod);      <-- 4 Adds product objects to
            }                                     generic ProductList object
        }
        catch( SqlException ex)
        {
            throw ex;
        }
        finally
        {
            conn.Close();
        }
        return ProductList;      <-- 5 Returns list of product
    }                                  objects to caller
}
```

The code here is pretty straightforward. The ProductImport object has a static class called GetProducts() ❶. You've created this as a static method so that you can simply call this method without having to instantiate the object first. Note that this method returns a new type of object that is available in the 2.0 version of the .NET Framework. This <List>Product states that you will return a list of objects, but not just any type of object. The only type of object that you'll be able to put in this list is a Product object. This is not a requirement for your objects to work with Reporting Services, but it does provide a level of safety that was not available by using an ArrayList, for example. (For more information on .NET generics, see the "Resources" section at the end of this book.) The first thing this method does is set up the objects that you'll use to connect to the database. You also instantiate a new generic list (ProductList) that contains your product objects ❷. This ProductList object is the object that you'll return to the caller. You open a connection to the database and put the result set into a SqlDataReader object ❸. Once you have your data, you loop through each row of data in your SqlDataReader. Within this loop you set the properties of your Product object and then add the Product object to your list ❹. Once the loop is finished, you simply return your list to the caller ❺.

Adding and configuring the ReportViewer to use a business object data source

As in our previous examples, begin by creating a new Windows Form and this time name it **ReportViewerLocalObject.cs**. Next, stretch the form to an appropriate size for your report and add a ReportViewer control. From the ReportViewer task smart

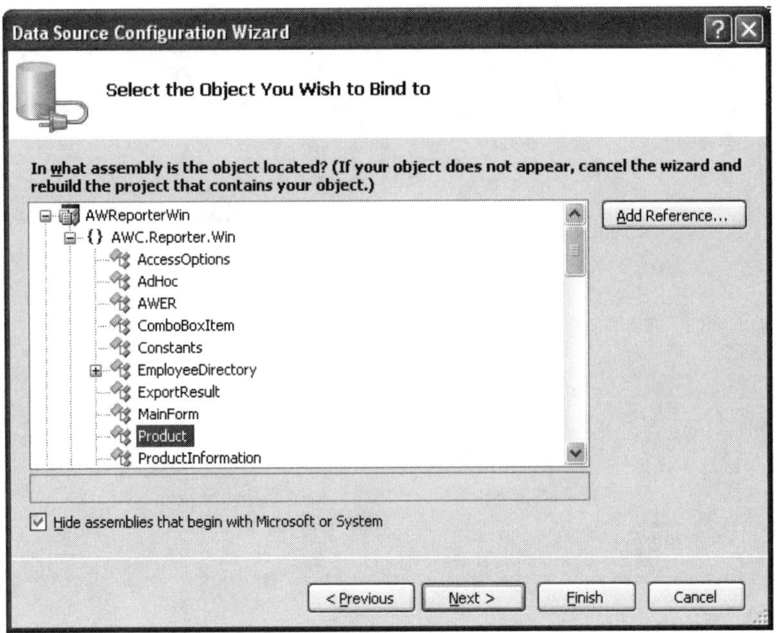

Figure 11.9 The Product object is found in the AWC.Reporter.Win namespace.

tag window, choose Design a New Report. From the Data menu select Add New Data Source to open the Data Source Configuration Wizard. Select Object as the Data Source type and click Next.

This brings up a screen that lets you select an object from assemblies on your machine as well as objects in your project. Expand the AWReporterWin project and the `AWC.Reporter.Win` namespace, as shown in figure 11.9.

Once you click Next you see a screen that displays the objects that will be added. Click Finish to complete the wizard. You should see the new `Product` object in the Data Sources Explorer, as shown in figure 11.10.

Now you're ready for the next step: creating the report.

Creating the report using business object fields

Creating a report using fields from a business object is similar to what you've done in previous chapters using database fields from a dataset. Figure 11.11 shows the report that we created by simply dragging the dataset fields onto a table entity.

As long as the properties (fields) are at the top level, you will be able to drag them just as you can with the database datasets. If you have nested objects, you have to set the path to the property by editing the expression at the field level. We show an example of this later on.

You are now ready to add your object-based report to your Windows Form. From the ReportViewer smart tag window, select the report that you just created. This not

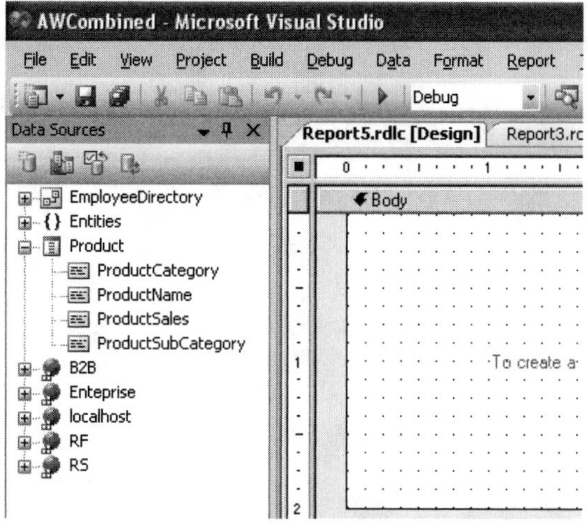

Figure 11.10 The Product object appears in the Data Sources panel.

only adds the report to the ReportViewer but also adds a `BindingSource` object to your code. In the `Load` event of your ReportViewer on the Windows Form, add one line of code:

```
this.ProductBindingSource.DataSource =
➥ ProductInformation.GetProducts();
```

This code will set the data source of your `BindingSource` object to the return value of the `GetProducts()` method of your `ProductInformation` object. Remember that `GetProducts()` was a static method—that's why you can simply call this method and you don't need to instantiate the object first. This method returns a list of `Product` objects.

NOTE The `ProductBindingSource` was created when you added the report to your ReportViewer, and since it is dynamically named, it may not be named `ProductBindingSource`.

Assuming you added the color and format to your report, after you run it your report should look similar to figure 11.12.

You've now learned how to build a simple business object and use it to create a report using the local mode of the ReportViewer control. You can now build on this example and configure a suite of business objects that makes creating reports a breeze.

Product Category	Product Sub Category	Product Name	Product Sales
=Fields!ProductCategory.Value			=Sum(Fields!ProductSales.Value)
	=Fields!ProductSubCategory.		=Sum(Fields!ProductSales.Value)
		=Fields!ProductName.Value	=Fields!ProductSales.Value

Figure 11.11 The Product Sales Report is shown here in the Visual Studio Designer.

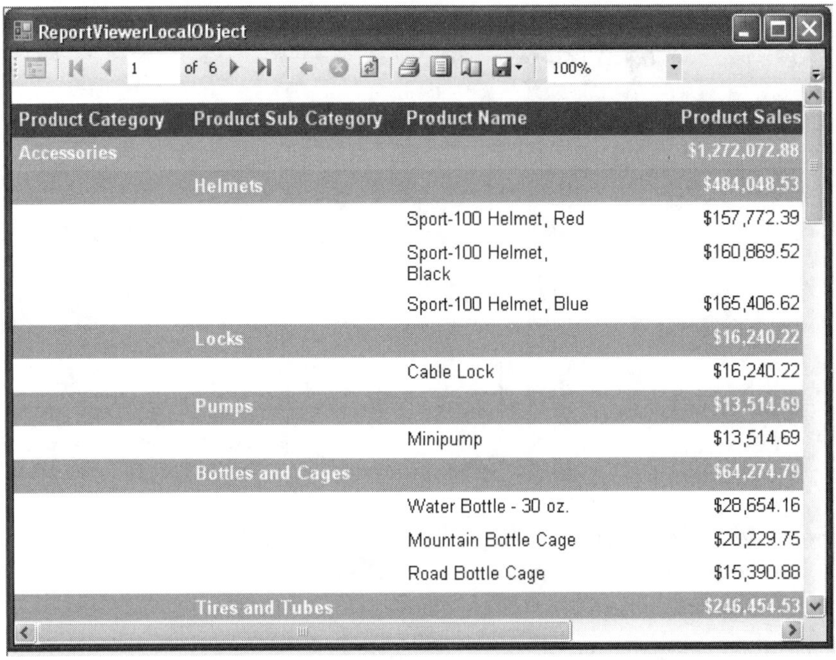

ReportViewerLocalObject

Product Category	Product Sub Category	Product Name	Product Sales
Accessories			$1,272,072.88
	Helmets		$484,048.53
		Sport-100 Helmet, Red	$157,772.39
		Sport-100 Helmet, Black	$160,869.52
		Sport-100 Helmet, Blue	$165,406.62
	Locks		$16,240.22
		Cable Lock	$16,240.22
	Pumps		$13,514.69
		Minipump	$13,514.69
	Bottles and Cages		$64,274.79
		Water Bottle - 30 oz.	$28,654.16
		Mountain Bottle Cage	$20,229.75
		Road Bottle Cage	$15,390.88
	Tires and Tubes		$246,454.53

Figure 11.12 The Product Sales Report appears in the Visual Studio Designer.

Finally, we take a look at an example of implementing custom validation of report parameters with the ReportViewer controls.

11.4 CUSTOM VALIDATION WITH THE REPORTVIEWER CONTROL

The ReportViewer control adds a toolbar that provides navigation, search, export, and print functionality so that you can work with reports in a deployed application. This toolbar exposes the report parameters that you add to your reports. As you learned in chapters 3 and 10, you don't have a lot of control over parameter validation outside of simple checks. This means that by using the toolbar, you are unable to perform advanced validation of your report parameters. Let's explore one method of using custom validation of report parameters by hiding the toolbar and creating your own parameters section.

One common situation that we have run into is having to validate begin and end dates that feed the report query. Let's say that you need to make sure that the begin date is earlier than the end date for your parameters. You can implement this functionality in the following steps:

1. Create a parameters section on your WinForm and add some controls to capture date information.
2. Create event methods.
3. Write validation code.

The code for this section can be found in the `ReportViewerRemote.cs` file in the code samples provided with this book.

11.4.1 Creating a parameters section

First you must make room for your new parameters section. In section 11.2 you added a ReportViewer control to your WinForm. In this WinForm you'll move the ReportViewer control down so that you have about an inch available at the top of the form.

After you create space for the parameters section, you can start dragging labels, date-time pickers, textboxes, and buttons on the form, as shown in figure 11.3. Use the information listed in table 11.4 to add eight controls. Be sure to name the controls appropriately to match the source code.

Table 11.4 Adding controls for custom parameter validation with the ReportViewer

Name	Type	Value
`lblBeginDate`	Label	Begin Date
`lblEndDate`	Label	End Date
`lblForcasted`	Label	# of Forecasted Months
`dtBeginDate`	DateTimePicker	
`dtEndDate`	DateTimePicker	
`txtForcasted`	Textbox	
`btnRunReport`	Button	Run Report
`lblError`	Label	

When you are done, the form should look like figure 11.13. Notice that the Begin Date, End Date, and # of Forecasted Months parameters are located outside of the ReportViewer control.

Now that you have created the controls, you need to create a couple of event methods.

11.4.2 Creating event methods

The first event method you'll create is the event for when your Windows Form is invoked. This event method, `ReportViewerRemote_Load()`, shown in listing 11.3, provides you with a place to set the properties of the ReportViewer control at runtime.

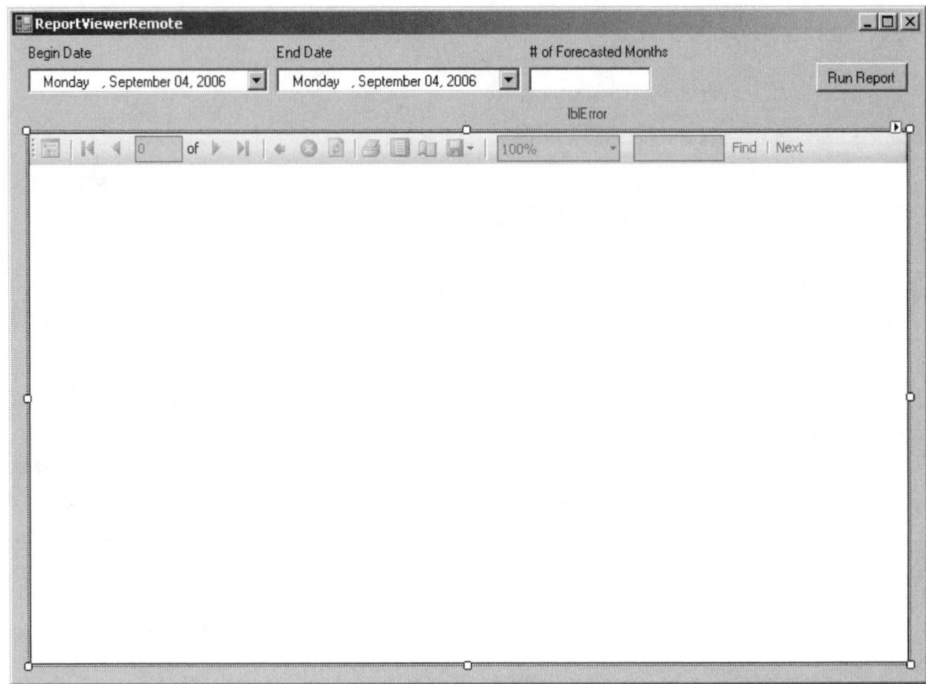

Figure 11.13 The anchor property of the ReportViewer control allows you to anchor this control to your form.

Listing 11.3 The ReportViewerRemote_Load method

```
private void ReportViewerRemote_Load(object sender, EventArgs e)
{
  lblError.Text = "";
  reportViewer1.ShowParameterPrompts = false;
  reportViewer1.Visible = false;
}
```

The `ReportViewerRemote_Load` event method does the following three things:

- It clears the error label to ensure that this label is instantiated as blank.
- It sets the `ShowParameterPrompts` property to false. This hides the `HTMLViewer` parameters section, as you wouldn't want this exposed to the user.
- It sets the visibility of the ReportViewer control to false. You want to hide the control until you've validated and collected all of the required parameters.

The second event method that you'll create will be for the action of clicking the Run Report button that you added to the form, as shown in listing 11.4. This provides you with a place to manage the validation of your parameter controls.

Listing 11.4 The button1_Click() method

```
private void button1_Click(object sender, EventArgs e)
{
  if (IsValid())
  {
    lblError.Text = "";                           Creates and populates
    //Set Parameter Values                        ReportParameter objects
    ReportParameter param1 = new ReportParameter("StartDate",
      ➥ dtBeginDate.Value.ToString());
    ReportParameter param2 = new ReportParameter("EndDate",
      ➥ dtEndDate.Value.ToString());
    ReportParameter param3 =
➥   new ReportParameter("ForecastedMonths", txtForcasted.Text.ToString());
    this.reportViewer1.ServerReport.SetParameters
➥   (new ReportParameter[] { param1,
      ➥ param2, param3 });    <-- Adds ReportParameters to report
    reportViewer1.Visible = true;
    reportViewer1.RefreshReport();    <-- Refreshes ReportViewer control
  }
  else
  {
    reportViewer1.Visible = false;    <-- Hides display of report
  }
}
```

The method shown in listing 11.4 first checks the validity of the entered parameters by calling the `IsValid()` method. (We cover the `IsValid()` method later in this section.) If the parameters entered on your form are valid, then the code creates and populates the `ReportParameter` objects and adds these objects to your ReportViewer control. If the user entered parameters that are not valid, you set the visibility of the ReportViewer control to false.

You can easily create these event methods from the design view of your report by using one of two techniques. The first approach consists of the following three steps:

1. Go to the property tabs for the form and the button.
2. Click the Event icon in the property toolbar (indicated by arrow 1 in figure 11.14).
3. Double-click the text area of the `Load` event for the `ReportViewerRemote` form (indicated by arrow 2 in figure 11.14). Do the same for the `Click` event of the `btnRunReport` properties. This will create the event handler bindings as well as a skeleton method for your code. You can type in (or copy) your code at this point

The second technique for creating event methods is to copy the code from listings 11.3 and 11.4 into the code-behind page and then choose the pasted methods from the `Load` and `Click` drop-down lists in the property window.

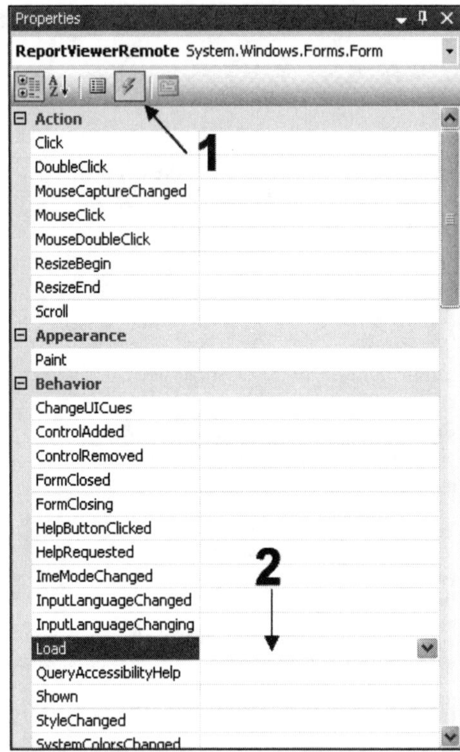

Figure 11.14
From the Events mode of the properties window, you can select existing methods for various behaviors from the drop-down list, or create an empty method by double-clicking on the drop-down itself.

In order for these methods to work, you need to add the `Microsoft.Reporting.WinForms` namespace to the `ReportViewerRemote.cs` file with the following line of code:

```
using Microsoft.Reporting.WinForms;
```

After you've created and correctly bound the event methods, the next step is to create the `IsValid()` method that will handle your custom validation for the report parameters.

11.4.3 Write validation code

As you saw earlier, the `button_1_Click()` method calls the `IsValid()` method shown in listing 11.5 to check the validity of the entered parameters.

Listing 11.5 The IsValid method

```
private bool IsValid()
{
    if (dtBeginDate.Value > dtEndDate.Value)
    {
        lblError.Text = _
"Begin Date must be earlier than the End Date.";
        return false;
```

```
    }
    if (txtForecasted.Text.Length == 0)
    {
        lblError.Text = _
"You must enter a value for # of Forecasted Months.";
        return false;
    }
    return true;
}
```

The `IsValid()` method returns a Boolean that tells you whether the parameters are valid. If they are valid, the code in the `button1_Click` method sets the parameters by creating three `ReportParameter` objects: `param1`, `param2`, and `param3`. The `ReportParameter` object belongs to the `Microsoft.Reporting.WinForms` namespace that you added earlier. These three `ReportParameter` objects are holders for the valid parameter values and are added to the ReportViewer through the `SetParameters()` call.

You then set the `visible` property of the ReportViewer control to true and refresh the control. You must call the `RefreshReport` method to render the report.

This was a simple example of doing custom parameter validation with the ReportViewer control. We hope this will give you a jump-start on creating powerful reports with full control of parameter validation in your Windows applications.

In the next section, you learn how to use this control to add reporting to your applications when you don't have access to a Report Server.

11.5 CONVERTING REPORT FILES

As you'll recall, the local mode of the ReportViewer control uses the `.rdlc` file extension when it creates the report definition file. Reporting Services now offers you the ability to convert a local report file (`.rdlc`) to a Report Server file (`.rdl`), and vice versa. In this section, you'll see working examples in each direction. But, you may ask, when would this type of file conversion be necessary?

Let's say you created a report that was deployed to the Report Server. Now you have a Windows application that will be working with a local set of the data and will not be able to access the Report Server. This would be a good time to convert the Report Server file (`.rdl`) into a local report file (`.rdlc`).

NOTE Only SQL Server 2005 RDL files can be converted into RDLC files. If you want to convert a SQL Server 2000 RDL file, you must first upgrade it to SQL Server 2005.

Conversely, say you had some local report files that you wanted to deploy to the Report Server to take advantage of some of the features that are only available with Report Server reports, such as subscriptions or caching. In this case, you'd convert the local report file (`.rdlc`) to a Report Server file (`.rdl`).

NOTE Both the ReportViewer control and the Report Server use the same Report Definition Language schema to generate their respective report files, but the RDLC file does not contain a `<Query>` element. Even if it did, the ReportViewer would ignore it since it gets its data from the dataset defined from within the ReportViewer.

Let's explore some examples of converting these files.

11.5.1 Converting RDL files into RDLC files

For this example let's take the Sales By Territory report (`Sales By Territory.rdl`) from chapter 4 and convert it to work in the local mode of the ReportViewer. The sample project, AWConvertRDLToRDLC, is available with the source code for this book. In this section we go through the steps listed in table 11.5 to re-create this project.

Table 11.5 Steps to convert RDL files into RDLC files

Task	Description
1	Set up the RDLC file.
2	Create a new project.
3	Create a DataSet for your project.
4	Add a ReportViewer control to your form.
5	Add an RDLC file to the project.
6	Choose the report and data source for your report.
7	Configure additional properties.

As you'll see, the conversion process is pretty straightforward.

Setting up the RDLC file

The first step in converting your file is renaming it. Find the `Sales By Territory.rdl` file, copy it into a temporary location, and rename it to **Sales By Territory.rdlc**. You'll come back to this file a little later in the process.

Creating a new project

To keep the deployment simple, create a new project for this conversion. Open Visual Studio 2005, and select File > New > Project. Create a new Windows Form application and give it a name. When the project opens, you'll be presented with the default form (`Form1.cs`). For this example, let's keep this name (of course, in the real world you'd provide a more meaningful name).

Creating the dataset for your project

This step is where the "trick" comes in. In order for our RDLC file to work properly without having to modify the report code, you need to be sure that the dataset matches the dataset that was specified for the Report Server version of the file. To do this, create a dataset and use the same SQL query that you used originally. The steps to create a dataset are as follows:

Step 1 Choose Project > Add New Item to open a screen similar to the one shown in figure 11.15. Name this new dataset **SalesByTerritory** and click Add.

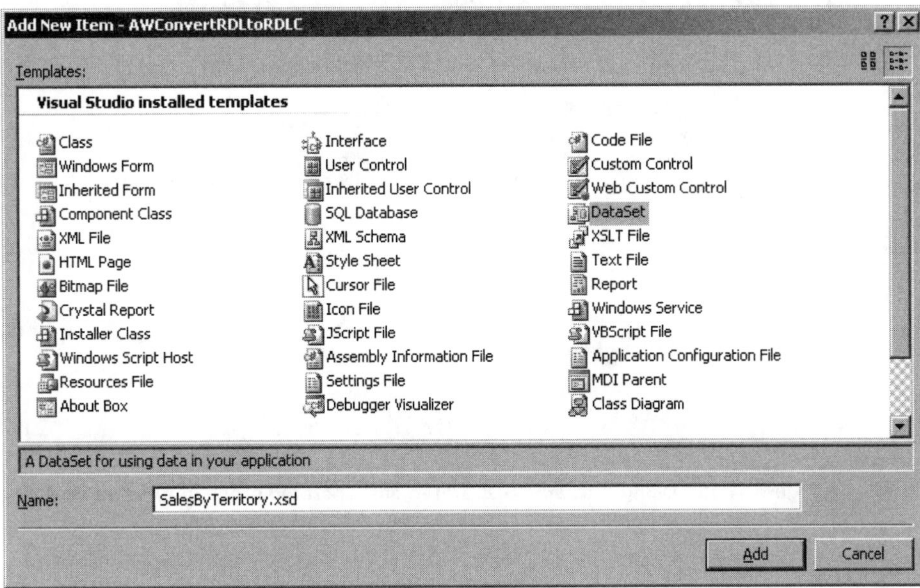

Figure 11.15 Create a dataset for a local ReportViewer report.

Step 2 With the `SalesByTerritory.xsd` file open in Visual Studio, drag a TableAdapter from the toolbox and drop it in right on the page. Doing this launches the TableAdapter Configuration Wizard.

Step 3 In the first wizard screen, set up a proper connection string and click Next.

Step 4 The second screen prompts you to name the connection. For this example keep the default.

Step 5 The next screen offers some choices for configuring how the TableAdapter will access the database. For this example, you want to use a SQL statement, so select that option and click Next.

Step 6 On the next screen (figure 11.16), enter the exact SQL statement that you used in the original report, and then click Next.

You can find this SQL statement in the example project; it's titled `SalesByTerritory.sql`. Or, you could copy this statement from the original project code. Copy and paste the SQL statement into the available space and click Next.

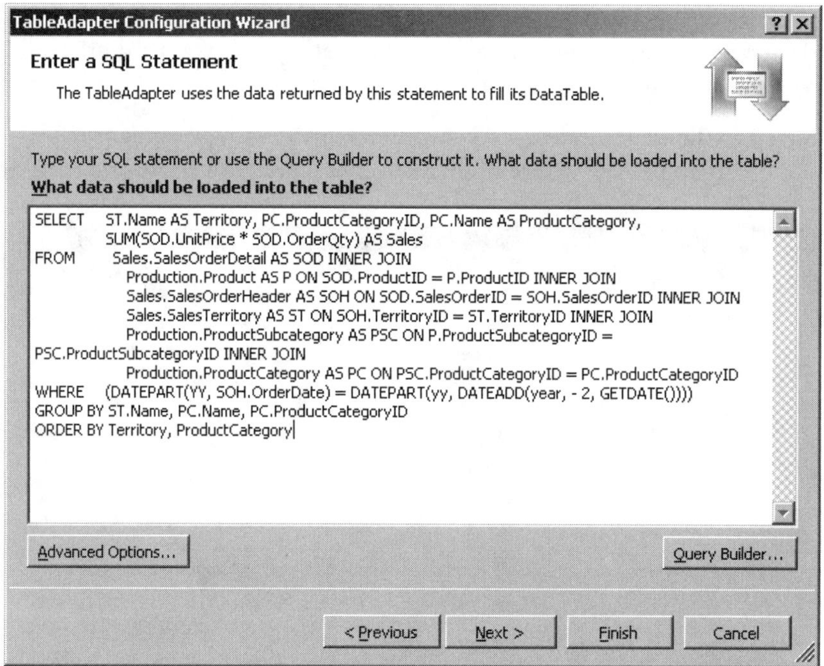

Figure 11.16 Using the same SQL statement (or stored procedure) helps keep the conversion simple.

Step 7 On the next screen, Choose Methods to Generate, keep the defaults and click Finish.

You have now finished creating your dataset. Let's move on and add the RDLC file to your project.

Adding the RDLC file to your project

From the Project menu, select Add Existing Item. Browse to the `Sales By Territory.rdlc` file that you created earlier and add it to your project.

Adding a ReportViewer control to your form

Next, open the `Form1.cs` file and stretch the form out so that there is room for your ReportViewer control. For this report, 530 pixels wide by 432 pixels high should be fine. Next, drag a ReportViewer control onto the form.

Choosing the report and data source

In the smart tag window, select the report that you added to your project and then click the *Choose Data Sources* link. Open the Data Source Instance drop-down list and you should see something similar to figure 11.17.

Figure 11.17 Once you have created a matching data source, you can add this to your local report

It is very important that you navigate all the way down to and click on DataTable1. If you choose SalesByTerritory you won't get an error, but you'll find that your report won't render. At this point for many report conversions, you would be done. However, we selected this report to work with in order to show you some additional properties that you'll need to set in certain circumstances.

Configuring additional properties

The Sales By Territory report uses an external image for the logo. Therefore, you need to modify two properties:

- `EnableExternalImages`—Set this property to true.
- `EnforceConstraints`—Set this property of the dataset to false.

If you don't modify these properties the report won't render in the ReportViewer control. Listing 11.6 shows these properties set in the `Form1_load` method.

Listing 11.6 The Load event of the form

```
private void Form1_Load(object sender, EventArgs e)
 {
    salesByTerritory.EnforceConstraints = false;
    reportViewer1.LocalReport.EnableExternalImages = true;
    this.dataTable1TableAdapter.Fill(
    ➥ this.salesByTerritory.DataTable1);
    this.reportViewer1.RefreshReport();
 }
```

You are now ready to see the finished product. Simply run the application and the ReportViewer will show you your newly converted report. To prove that this local report is not dependent on the Report Server, try stopping the ReportServer service (ReportingServicesService.exe) and running the application.

11.5.2 Converting RDLC files into RDL files

You may find yourself wanting to convert a local client report file (`.rdlc`) into an `.rdl` file so that you can deploy it to the Report Server and take advantage of server features such as caching, scheduling, or snapshots. Let's take the report that you created in section 11.3.1 and convert it into a format that you can deploy to the Report Server. This is a simple three-step process.

Step 1 Copy the RDLC file from the file system into a temporary directory and rename it with an `.rdl` extension. If you didn't rename the RDLC file from the example earlier, it is called `Report1.rdlc`.

Step 2 From an RS Project in Visual Studio, add the file from step 1 to the project by right-clicking on the Project menu, selecting Add Existing Item, and navigating to and adding the file you renamed in step 1.

Step 3 When the file has been imported, open it in the designer, select the Data tab, and click the Edit (...) button, as shown in figure 11.18. Update the connection information to point to the database that you want (AdventureWorks) and you are done. You can now click the Run (!) button and verify that the dataset can be retrieved.

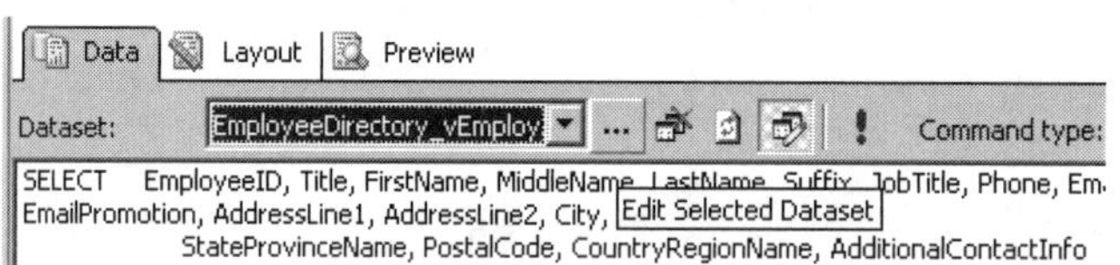

Figure 11.18 You will need to configure the dataset connection when converting RDLC files to RDL files.

You've now converted a local report file (`.rdlc`) to a Report Server file (`.rdl`) and vice versa. There are pros and cons for using local mode or remote mode with the ReportViewer. After absorbing the content in this section, switching between modes will seem simple.

You're now ready to investigate what you need to do to successfully deploy applications that use the ReportViewer controls.

11.6 DEPLOYING APPLICATIONS THAT USE REPORTVIEWER CONTROLS

Deployment requirements vary depending on what type of control (web or Windows) you are working with and what mode (remote or local) you use. Quite simply, you need to run the ReportViewer redistributable file (`ReportViewer.exe`) in the environment where the ReportViewer will execute. This section discusses the ReportViewer-specific requirements for deploying your web and Windows applications.

11.6.1 Redistributing the ReportViewer controls

Microsoft has provided a redistributable, self-extracting component called `ReportViewer.exe` that includes an MSI file along with other files required for a proper installation. This redistributable file can be found at `C:\Program Files\Microsoft Visual Studio 8\SDK\v2.0\BootStrapper\Packages\ReportViewer\ReportViewer.exe`.

When you run this redistributable component, the files listed in table 11.6 are copied to the Global Assembly Cache folder on the deployment computer.

Table 11.6 Files installed by the ReportViewer redistributable component

File	Description
`Microsoft.ReportViewer.WebForms`	ReportViewer control for ASP.NET pages.
`Microsoft.ReportViewer.WinForms`	ReportViewer control for Windows applications.
`Microsoft.ReportViewer.Common`	Both the Windows forms and Web server control use this for the main reporting functionality that is common in these controls.
`Microsoft.ReportViewer.ProcessingObjectModel`	This exposes the report object model to allow expressions in the report definition and access it programmatically at runtime.

11.6.2 ReportViewer deployment for Windows applications

For Windows applications, be sure to include the controls as application prerequisites so that they can be automatically installed with your application.

You choose prerequisites in the Prerequisites dialog box. To open this dialog box:

1 Select your Windows project in the Solution Explorer and then select Properties.
2 From the Properties window, select the Publish tab to open the Publish page.
3 From the Publish page, select Prerequisites.

Figure 11.19 shows the Prerequisites dialog box.

Simply select the Microsoft Visual Studio 2005 ReportViewer check box and click OK. Now when your application is installed, a check is performed by the installation

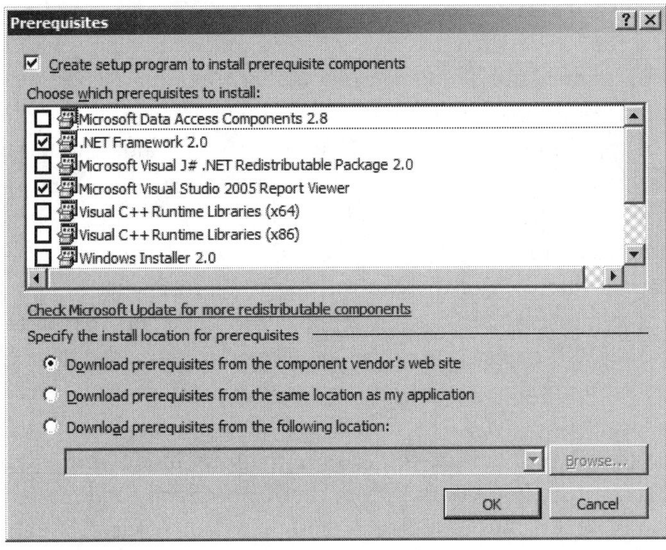

Figure 11.19 Setting the ReportViewer redistributable component will allow the bootstrapping application to automate the installation of the ReportViewer controls for Windows applications.

to see if the ReportViewer is already installed. If it is not installed, the Setup program installs it.

11.6.3 ReportViewer deployment for web applications

If you are using the ReportViewer controls in a web application, be sure that the web server has the ReportViewer controls loaded. If you have installed Visual Studio on your web server, you won't need to take any further action. Typically, though, Visual Studio is not installed on a web server unless it is a development server. In most cases, then, you have to run the redistributable file (`ReportViewer.exe`) on your web server.

11.6.4 Using the ReportViewer web server control in a web farm

You must take some additional steps if you're deploying an ASP.NET application in a web farm to ensure that view state is maintained across the farm. You'll have to modify your web application's `Web.config` file by setting the `machineKey` element. Setting the `machineKey` element forces all nodes in the web farm to use the same process identity. This is an important step to ensure that the interactive features such as drill-through will work properly.

For more information on setting the `machineKey` element, see the Microsoft .NET Framework 2.0 documentation.

11.7 SUMMARY

We covered a lot of material in this chapter and hope you have realized that your life has been made much easier with the ReportViewer control. No more adding browser controls to your Windows applications; no more adding iFrames to your web pages...

We started out with an overview of the ReportViewer control and how it works. We learned that the ReportViewer is a very handy control available with the 2.0 version of the .NET framework. The nice thing is that there is a ReportViewer control for both Windows and web applications. While there are two different controls for the two types of applications, the design UI, properties, and look and feel are virtually identical. This makes it easy for developers to switch between Windows and web applications with ease when it comes to adding Reporting Services reports. We spent a little time comparing the differences between the two controls.

We also learned that each of the controls has two processing modes: remote and local. The remote mode is used to pull reports from a Report Server and integrate them into the .NET 2.0 applications. This allows you to take advantage of the server features such as subscriptions, history, and centralized management. This works great for your applications where you have a dedicated access to a Report Server. If you do not have access to a Report Server, you can use the local mode of the ReportViewer. This means you can "unplug" yourself from the Report Server and create reports that access data from databases, business objects, and even Web services. We compared the difference between these two modes by looking at how several features of the ReportViewer are affected by each mode. We rounded out our overview by looking at many of the properties available with the ReportViewer, and you saw when and why you might want to modify these properties.

We walked through an example of how to do custom validation with the report parameters by using the ReportViewer control. This works for both the Windows and web control and also works for both modes of these controls. Specifically, we showed you how to hide the parameters section and create your own parameter so that you can have full control of the validation and placement of your parameter controls. We modified our application to validate two date fields and ensure that the first date was chronological before the second date.

You learned in the first chapters of this book that Report Server reports that are deployed to the Report Server use the `.rdl` file extension for the report files. In this chapter we introduced a new type of report file: the local (client) report file, which uses the `.rdlc` extension. The `.rdlc` file extension is used by the local mode of the ReportViewer. You learned that both of these files hold XML defined by the same RDL schema. Since there will certainly be a need for some organizations to share reports between these formats, we found it worthwhile to spend some time showing how you can convert one format into the other.

Finally, we looked at the deployment of applications that use the ReportViewer control. You must be sure that the environment that the ReportViewer will execute in has been prepared before running the ReportViewer. You can accomplish this with a redistributable file called `ReportViewer.exe`. This is pretty simple for web applications. We covered the details of how to include the redistributable file with the application prerequisites so that they will be automatically installed with your application.

It is our hope that you learned enough from this chapter to start using the ReportViewer control in your .NET 2.0 applications. You'll see that using these controls is very simple and will save you and your organization a lot of time in integrating reports into your code.

CHAPTER 12

Subscribed report delivery

In this fast-paced information age, we all know the value of having access to accurate, relevant, and up-to-the-minute data. Most of us enjoy various subscription-based services, such as magazine or e-mail subscribed delivery. Regardless of the type of information being delivered, these services share the same common model; the subscriber initiates the subscription service for a given period of time. The service provider delivers the service either on a regular basis or as a result of an event.

In chapter 10 we provided an overview of how RS provides on-demand delivery, and we showed how to implement on-demand reporting features for various types of client applications. With on-demand report delivery, the interactive user explicitly initiates the report request.

In this chapter, we discuss the second report delivery scenario supported by Reporting Services, where the reports are "pushed" to the user automatically by the Report Server. As you will see, RS offers a flexible and extensible subscription-based reporting model, suitable for both Internet and intranet-based reporting solutions.

Our discussion covers the following main topics:

- Overview of the subscribed report delivery process
- Creating standard subscriptions

- Creating data-driven subscriptions
- Triggering the subscribed report delivery process programmatically

12.1 UNDERSTANDING SUBSCRIBED REPORT DELIVERY

I love subscription-based information delivery! As I type this chapter, several subscription-based applications are running on my computer. Microsoft Outlook lets me know when a new e-mail arrives. My favorite RSS aggregator, IntraVNews, notifies me when my feeds are updated. The Microsoft Messenger Alerts service interrupts me every now and then to tell me how much value my favorite stocks have lost during the course of the day's trading session.

The subscription-based delivery model is great because I don't have to poll the information sources to find out when data has changed. Instead, as long as I am subscribed, information is delivered to me. This saves me a lot of time and, as the famous adage says, time is money.

How does all this translate to reporting? There are many reporting scenarios that may call for delivering reports via subscription, as we discuss next.

12.1.1 Subscription-based reporting scenarios

You can use subscribed report delivery to meet various reporting requirements, including the following:

- *"Pushing" reports to users on a regular basis*—There could be many valid reasons why an organization might want to implement automatic report delivery. For example, a sales manager may want his subordinates to receive an employee performance report on a quarterly basis. The company's CEO may require that the company sales report be sent to the top managers periodically. A financial institution may want to distribute the monthly statement report to its customers.
- *Generating reports when the underlying data changes*—For example, an organization may want to e-mail the updated product catalog report when a new product is introduced.
- *Offloading long-running reports*—Some reports may take substantial time and resources to be processed. Such reports could be scheduled to be generated during off-peak hours.
- *Report archiving*—You may need to periodically archive reports to a network share for auditing purposes.

Now that you've seen some popular subscription possibilities, let's discuss how the RS subscribed delivery process works.

12.1.2 The subscriber-publisher design pattern

The RS subscribed delivery model follows the subscriber-publisher (also called *observer*) design pattern. This pattern is very popular with many modern programming frameworks. For example, one of the main reasons for the immense success of Microsoft Windows is its event-driven architecture. Figure 12.1 shows how you can use the subscriber-publisher programming model in your applications.

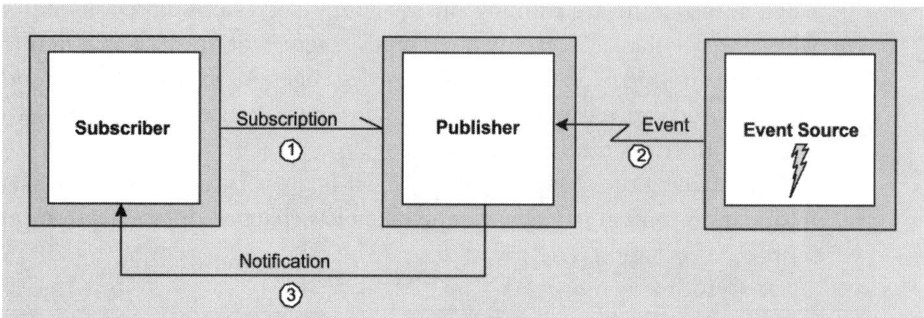

Figure 12.1 In the subscriber-publisher model, the client (subscriber) subscribes to one or more events. When the event occurs, the publisher notifies the subscriber.

The process is initiated by the *subscriber* ① when it informs the *publisher* of its intent to be notified when a certain *event* of interest takes place.

When the event occurs ②, the publisher notifies the subscriber ③ about the event's occurrence.

The publisher typically runs in unattended mode, such as a background service listening to incoming events. For example, as I type on my laptop keyboard, each keystroke generates a hardware interrupt request. The CPU intercepts the request and generates a software interrupt. The event traverses the operating system and application layers to output the character on the screen. In this example, you can view the keystroke as an event source, the CPU as a publisher, and the OS and application layers as subscribers.

Let's now see how the subscriber-publisher pattern applies to the RS subscription-based delivery mechanism.

12.1.3 How the RS subscription-based model works

In a nutshell, when a report is scheduled for subscribed delivery, report processing is triggered as a result of an event, such as a timing event from a schedule. The generated report is then delivered asynchronously to its subscribers, as shown in figure 12.2.

With RS, here's how the subscriber-publisher pattern applies: the subscriber is typically the report's end user who subscribes himself or other users on their behalf. For example, a manager could subscribe herself and her subordinates to receive a report. The publisher is the Report Server, and the event source is the SQL Server Agent.

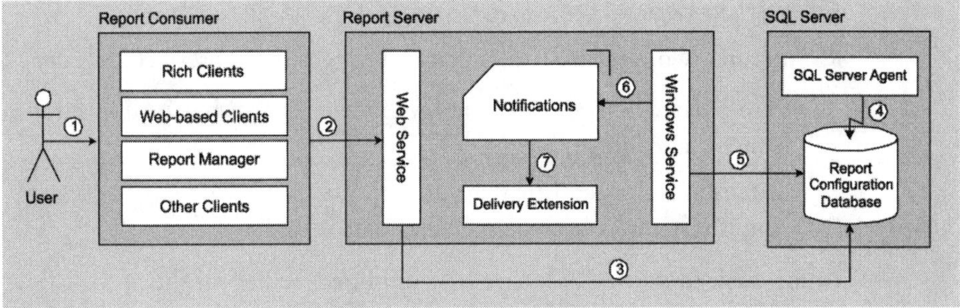

Figure 12.2 With the subscription-based report delivery model, the report processing is triggered by an event and the generated report is delivered asynchronously to its subscribers.

To better understand the process flow, we could break down subscribed report delivery into two phases:

- Creating the report subscription interactively by the user
- Processing and delivering the report asynchronously

In the sections that follow, we refer back to figure 12.2 to explain each phase.

Creating report subscriptions

While we are not excluding the possibility of more sophisticated ways to generate subscriptions, such as by applications running in unattended mode, typically the user will create the subscription interactively by using a client application, which we call a report consumer. For example, the user could access ① the Report Manager to initiate the subscription process.

Once user has entered the subscription details, the report consumer invokes ② one of the `CreateSubscriptionXXX` RS Web service SOAP APIs to save ③ the subscription details in the Report Catalog and schedule the subscription.

NOTE Some of you may need to create subscriptions programmatically using the SOAP API. The documentation has good examples of how this could be done for both subscription types supported by RS. For this reason, we decided not to include a code sample to demonstrate this concept. If the documentation samples are not enough, you can use the tracing technique we showed you in chapter 8 to find out how the Report Manager uses the Web service API to create and schedule subscriptions.

At this point, the Report Server has saved the subscription details in the Subscriptions table in the report catalog, and control is returned to the report consumer. This step concludes the interactive, synchronous part of the subscription process.

Executing report subscriptions

RS supports two kinds of events that can trigger the subscribed delivery:

- Time-based events, such as events generated by a subscription-specific or shared schedule
- Snapshot refreshes (for snapshot reports only), where the subscription processing is initiated when the snapshot data is updated

Going back to figure 12.2, here is a simplified version of the process flow for executing subscriptions. Once the subscription event is up, the SQL Agent job inserts ④ a record into the `Event` table. As you saw in chapter 8, the Reporting Services Windows Service (`ReportingServicesService.exe`) scans this table on a regular basis to see if any new events have been published. As you probably recall, the polling interval can be configured by adjusting the `PollingInterval` setting in the `RSReportServer.config` configuration file.

In case there is a new event, the Reporting Services Windows Service picks it up ⑤ and handles the event. Specifically, for a time-based subscription this means creating a notification record in the `Notifications` table. The Windows Service polls the `Notifications` table periodically. When it discovers a new entry, the Windows Service creates ⑥ a *notification object*. If the subscription is data driven (more on this in section 12.2.2), the Windows Service creates as many notifications as the number of recipients.

Next, the Report Server instantiates the *delivery extension* associated with the subscription and passes ⑦ the notification object to it.

DEFINITION *Delivery extensions* are .NET assemblies that implement the Reporting Services delivery extension API. Delivery extensions are able to receive notifications from the Report Server and distribute reports to various destinations. Out of the box, RS comes with two delivery extensions for e-mail and file share delivery. Developers can write custom delivery extensions to distribute reports to other destinations, as we demonstrate in chapter 13.

Finally, the delivery extension distributes the report to its final destination—for example, by sending an e-mail to the recipient in the case of e-mail delivery or saving the report's payload to a network share for file share delivery.

As you've just seen, the second phase of subscribed report delivery is executed entirely in unattended mode. Therefore, subscribed reports are subject to the same limitations as report snapshots, which we discussed in chapter 8. Specifically, these limitations are as follows:

- The identity of the interactive user is not available during the report's processing stage.
- Report parameter values must be specified when the subscription is created.
- Stored data source credentials must be used for database authentication.

Let's explain each of these limitations in more detail.

First, the user-specific information is not available when reports are delivered via subscriptions. Specifically, this means that it is not possible to access the properties of the `User` global collection, for example, to get the user's identity or the language identifier. Failure to abide by this rule results in the following error message when an attempt is made to create a new subscription:

```
Subscriptions cannot be created because the credentials used to
run the report are not stored, the report is using user-defined
parameter values, or if a linked report, the link is no longer
valid.
```

Second, because the report is generated in unattended mode, the report parameter values have to be known by the time the report is processed. Look at the signatures of both subscription-related web methods, `CreateSubscription` and `CreateDataDrivenSubscription`, and you notice that they take a `Parameters` array of type `ParameterValue`, which you can use to fill in and pass the report parameters. If you use the Report Manager to create the subscription, notice that it generates parameter placeholders for each parameter on the Subscriptions page.

> **NOTE** If a user creates a subscription with a certain parameter, and then you set the report to snapshot execution but choose a new parameter value, if the subscription is run, it will be deactivated. Deactivating the subscription provides an indication that the report has been modified. To reactivate the subscription, the user needs to open and then save the subscription.

If the parameter has a default value, you can use it if you don't want to specify the value explicitly.

Finally, stored credentials must be used for authenticating against the data source, because subscriptions are processed in an unattended mode and it is not possible to supply the credentials interactively.

Having discussed subscribed report delivery at a high level, let's now see how the end user can configure and manage subscriptions using the Report Manager.

12.2 CONFIGURING SUBSCRIBED REPORT DELIVERY

Subject to security permissions, with RS each end user can use the Report Manager web portal to subscribe to a report of interest. For example, a sales manager can subscribe to receive the Territory Sales Crosstab report that we authored in chapter 4 on a regular basis, for example, each quarter.

To create a new subscription, the user must specify the following:

- The report that the subscription will be attached to; a subscription is always associated with exactly one user and one report.
- The subscription type, for example, standard or data driven; we discuss the supported subscription types in section 12.2.2.

- The delivery extension type, for example, e-mail or file share delivery.
- The event that will trigger the subscription, such as a timing event based on a schedule.
- The report parameter values for parameterized non-snapshot reports.

Although the process of creating subscriptions looks involved, the Report Manager makes it easy, as you see next.

12.2.1 Creating a new subscription

In the typical scenario, enterprise users access the Report Manager portal to create and manage the subscriptions they own, as shown in figure 12.3.

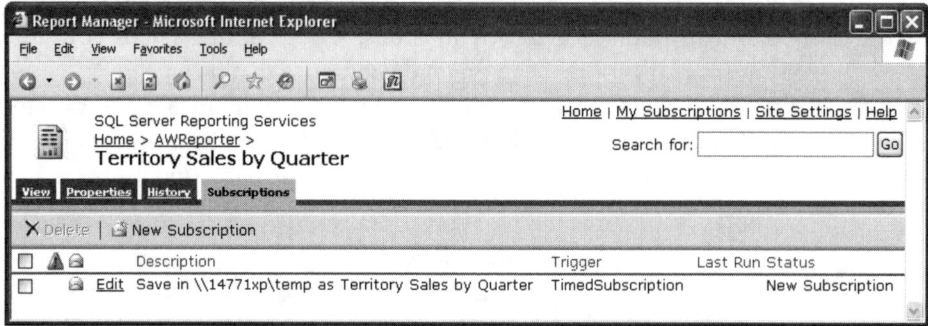

Figure 12.3 End users can use the Report Manager to create subscriptions.

To create a new standard subscription with the Report Manager, the end user performs the following steps:

Step 1 Navigate to the report the user wants to subscribe to.

Step 2 Click the New Subscription button found on the View and Subscriptions tabs.

Step 3 Enter the subscription details.

These steps require that the user is in a role with the `Manage Individual Subscriptions` task assigned to it. Refer to section 9.3 of chapter 9 to review configuring the tasks assigned to roles.

Some delivery extensions may call for a more involved setup process. For example, most organizations will be cautious about letting users send reports via e-mail to an arbitrary list of recipients. For this reason, the Report Server is set up by default to require a two-phase setup process for configuring e-mail subscriptions, as follows:

- *Creating the subscription*—This phase can be performed by individual users and requires only the Manage Individual Subscription task. During this phase the Report Manager prevents the user from entering the recipients' addresses by disabling the To field and hiding the Cc (Carbon copy) and Bcc (Blind carbon copy) fields.

- *Finalizing the subscription*—By default, only users with rights to execute the Manage All Subscriptions task can enter the recipients' addresses.

NOTE The availability of the e-mail address fields (To, Cc, and Bcc) is controlled by the `SendEmailToUserAlias` setting in the Report Server configuration file (`RSReportServer.config`). If this setting is True (the default), only users who have rights to the Manage All Subscriptions task can change these fields. If the setting is False, these fields are enabled for any user who has rights to the Manage Individual Subscriptions task. For better security, we suggest that you leave this setting set to True so that you can control the e-mail recipient list.

Let's now discuss what types of subscriptions are natively supported by Reporting Services.

12.2.2 Choosing the subscription type

With RS you can create two types of subscriptions:

- *Standard subscriptions*—With this type of subscription, the subscription configuration details are fixed and must be known at the time the subscription is set up.
- *Data-driven subscriptions*—With data-driven subscriptions, many aspects of the subscription can be dynamic. For example, a data-driven e-mail subscription can retrieve the list of recipients from a database. The Report Server retrieves them from a data store when the subscription is processed.

These two types correspond to the `CreateSubscription` and `CreateDataDrivenSubscription` SOAP APIs, respectively. Let's find out how to create and manage both types of subscriptions.

Setting up standard subscriptions

The configuration details of standard subscriptions, such as the report's export format, list of recipients, and so forth, are static. For example, with standard e-mail subscriptions you enter a fixed list of e-mail recipients by specifying each recipient's e-mail address. Standard subscriptions require only rights to the Manage Individual Subscriptions task, which the predefined Browser role already includes.

To create a standard subscription using the Report Manager, the end user follows these steps:

Step 1 Navigate to the report of interest.

Step 2 Click the Subscriptions tab, as shown in figure 12.4.

Step 3 Click New Subscription.

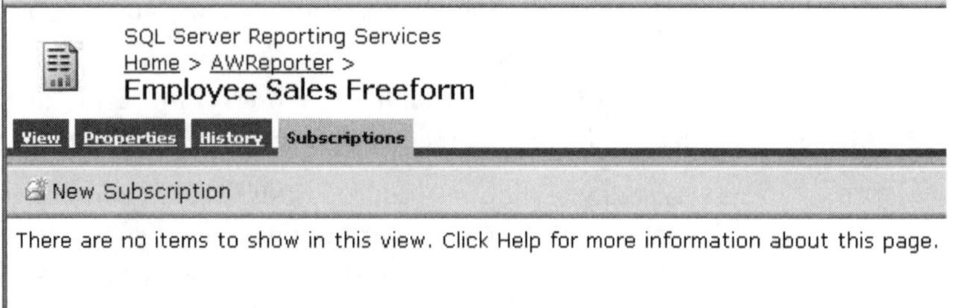

Figure 12.4 To create a standard subscription with the Report Manager, click the New Subscription button found on the report's Subscriptions tab.

Clicking New Subscription opens the Report Delivery Options screen. The options on this screen vary depending on the selected delivery extension; you see an example in section 12.3.

You use standard subscriptions when the subscription details for all recipients are the same. For example, you may want to push a report by e-mail to a small list of recipients. All recipients will receive the report in a single format, such as PDF. No personalization is necessary, meaning you don't have to greet the recipient by first name. In this case, a standard e-mail subscription is a good choice.

Sometimes your requirements may call for more flexible subscription options, such as when you want to allow the recipients to specify their preferred report format. In this case, you can use data-driven subscriptions.

Setting up data-driven subscriptions

As its name suggests, data-driven subscriptions permit certain subscription properties to be retrieved from the database during runtime, including:

- The list of recipients
- The report rendering format
- The report parameters
- Extension-specific properties, such as Priority and Subject for reports delivered via e-mail

As you can probably imagine, data-driven subscriptions offer a lot of flexibility by allowing you to customize the report's content and destination. Here are some scenarios where data-driven subscriptions could be useful:

- An organization can e-mail the product catalog report to its customers who have placed orders in the past six months.
- Reports can be personalized by synchronizing the report parameters with the results from the subscription query. For instance, an Order History report could greet the user by his name.

- An organization could permit the report's users to customize certain aspects of the report delivery during the subscription process. For example, a customer could be given an option to specify the preferred report format, such as MHTML or PDF, during the subscription process.

Data-driven subscriptions mandate having rights to the Manage All Subscriptions task. If the role-based security policy of the interactive user includes this task, then the New Data-driven Subscription button is visible in the Report Manager interface, as shown in figure 12.4.

Data-driven subscriptions require a data store that holds the subscriber's data. As a part of setting up a data-driven subscription, you need to specify a database query to retrieve the recipient list. This query could be one of the following:

- A non-parameterized SQL `SELECT` statement that retrieves the recipient list from a database table or view, for example:

  ```
  select * from recipients where type='individual'
  ```

- A stored procedure call prefixed with `EXEC`, for example:

  ```
  EXEC spGetRecipients 1, '2006',…
  ```

You cannot use input parameters for this query; however, you can use the results from this query to determine the delivery extension settings in the next step.

The statement must produce a rowset with as many rows as the number of recipients. The Report Manager Subscription Wizard facilitates the query setup process, as shown in figure 12.5.

In this case, we omitted the `EXEC` command from the stored procedure call, which resulted in an error when Validate was clicked. The validation logic checks to determine whether the query is syntactically correct by parsing and sending the query to the data source. It doesn't validate whether the returned data is semantically correct or whether the call has resulted in an empty dataset.

The Subscription Wizard is kind enough to list the delivery extension's publicly available properties. You can use fields from the query to set these properties, as you see in a data-driven subscription example in section 12.3.3. During runtime, the Report Server executes the query to get the list of recipients. For each recipient row, the Report Server sets the data-driven properties of the delivery extension and asks the extension to distribute the report.

Developers writing custom delivery extensions appreciate the data-driven subscription model because querying the database and setting up the subscription properties are responsibilities of the Report Server, not the extension. This allows developers to focus only on implementing the delivery logic by shifting the task of generating the list of recipients to the Report Server. Once the delivery extension is ready, it can be used as both a standard and a data-driven extension. You learn how this can be done in chapter 13.

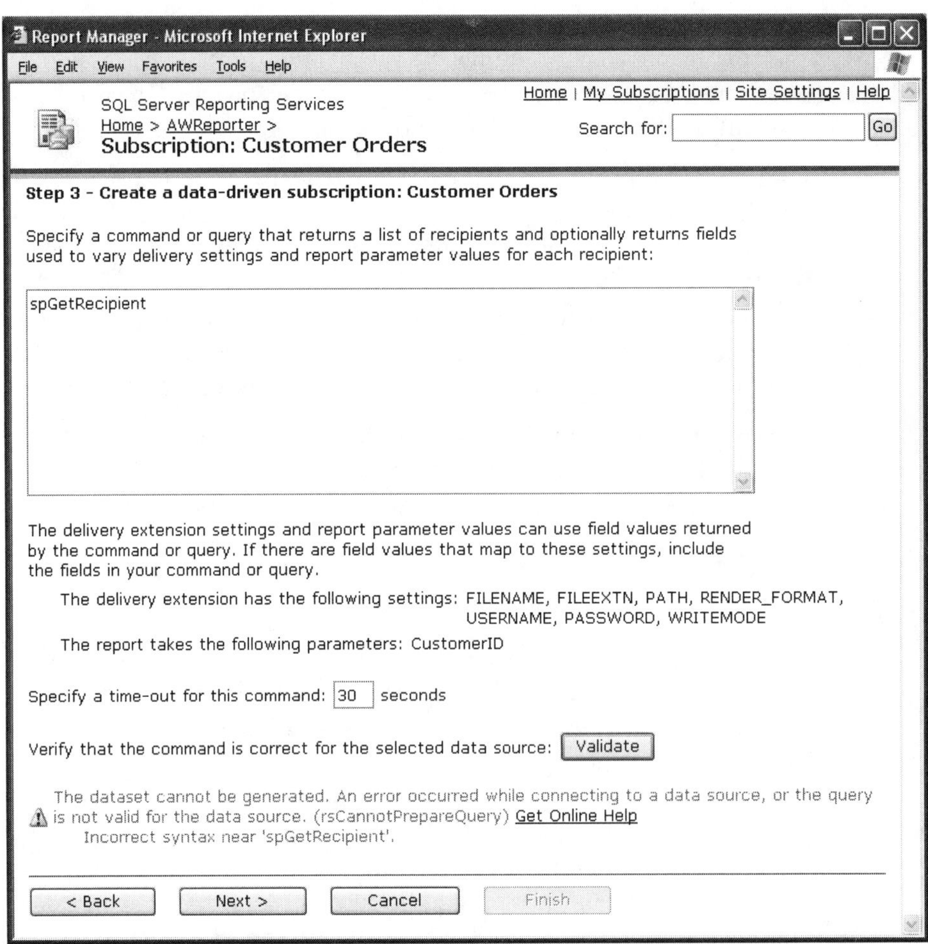

Figure 12.5 The Report Manager Subscription Wizard makes setting up the subscription query easy.

12.2.3 Configuring delivery extensions

As a part of the subscription configuration process, you select the extension responsible for delivering the report to its final destination. If you use the Report Manager, you define the subscription-delivery extension association using the Report Delivery Options page (see figure 12.7 later in this chapter), which is the first page shown after you click either New Subscription or New Data-Driven Subscription.

Out of the box, RS comes with two extensions to address two of the most common delivery scenarios:

- *E-mail delivery extension*—Sends reports to one or more recipients via e-mail
- *File share delivery extension*—Persists reports as disk files to a target folder, such as a network share

When these two extensions are not enough, you can extend RS by plugging in custom extensions. We show how to accomplish this by creating a Web service delivery extension in chapter 13, which can be used to send reports to a Web service.

When you set up your subscription, you may wonder why none of the HTML-based export flavors appear in the Format drop-down list. This can be explained by the fact that all HTML formats except MHTML are multistream rendering formats and require additional trips to the Report Server to fetch the report's images.

Although a delivery extension can render the report's image streams on the server, "shredding" the report in this way may be unacceptable. For example, in the case of e-mail report delivery, using an HTML-based format may result in several mail attachments: one for the report body and one for each report image. Therefore, if you need to send reports in HTML format, consider the MHTML export option, which embeds the images inside the report's payload.

Configuring the e-mail delivery extension

Delivering reports successfully via the e-mail delivery extension requires a preconfigured and functioning mail server.

NOTE Windows 2000 and 2003 include SMTP services that you can use to send e-mail. Windows 2003 also comes with a POP3 service that you can leverage to receive e-mail in your applications if they need this functionality. For more information about how to set up these services, refer to your operating system documentation.

Once the e-mail server is ready, you need to configure the Report Server to use it for e-mail delivery. To accomplish this, change the e-mail extension settings found under the `<Report Server Email>` element in the `RSReportServer.config` configuration file. The RS documentation explains the role of these settings in detail, so we won't discuss them here.

TIP Many organizations use Microsoft Exchange Server as an e-mail server. If you want to use an existing Exchange Server for e-mail report delivery, here's how to configure the Report Server. First, find the fully qualified domain name (FQDN) of the Exchange Server. One way to accomplish this, besides harassing the network administrator, is to look at the message header of any of the e-mail messages received in your Outlook Inbox. To do so, open a received e-mail and select Options from the View menu. In the Internet Headers textbox you see something like this:

```
Microsoft Mail Internet Headers Version 2.0
Received: from <exchange server FQDN> ([xxx.xx.xxx.xxx]) by
<exchange Server FQDN > with Microsoft SMTPSVC(xxx.xx.xxx.xxx);
   Sat, 13 Mar 2006 11:44:49 -0600
```

In my case, the first Exchange Server FQDN gave me the fully qualified name of the Exchange Server responsible for servicing the outgoing e-mail in my domain.

Sometimes the FQDN of the Exchange Server that you will get from the message headers may point to an incoming mail server that may not necessarily be the server responsible for outbound mail messages. Check with your network administrator to verify whether this is the case. In addition, an outbound Exchange Server may require authentication to avoid relaying.

NOTE Once you get the name of the Exchange Server, you can change the `SMTPServer` setting in `RSReportServer.config` to point to that Exchange Server. In my case, changing this setting and setting the "From" e-mail account were sufficient to send reports via e-mail successfully.

It is important to note that the RS e-mail extension doesn't verify the status of the e-mail delivery. For example, the Report Server has no way of knowing whether the e-mail delivery to a given recipient address has failed. Developers who have written code in the past to send e-mail programmatically should be able to relate to this limitation easily.

As far as the Report Server is concerned, the execution of the subscribed delivery task is successful as long as the e-mail is relayed successfully to the mail server. Therefore, you must work with the mail server's administrator to ensure that the report has indeed been delivered successfully to all subscribers.

Configuring the file share delivery extension

Configuring file share delivery is easy. As a part of the subscription process, you specify the file share location and credentials in order to access the file share.

The file share path must be specified in Uniform Naming Convention (UNC) format. The UNC format requires the following syntax:

```
\\<computername>\<sharename>
```

Make sure that the shared folder exists because the file delivery extension doesn't create the folder, so the delivery process will fail otherwise.

You also need to enter the credentials (username and password) of the Windows account that will be used to access the file share. Once the subscription is configured, it can be managed via the Report Manager UI.

12.2.4 Managing subscriptions

As the report administrator, you configure the role-based security policies that dictate which rights a given user has for managing report subscriptions. For example, typically end users have rights to manage the subscriptions they own, while you are responsible for managing all subscriptions.

Using My Subscriptions

End users who have rights to the Manage Individual Subscriptions task can view and use the options on the Report Manager's My Subscriptions page. This page lists the subscriptions they own, as shown in figure 12.6.

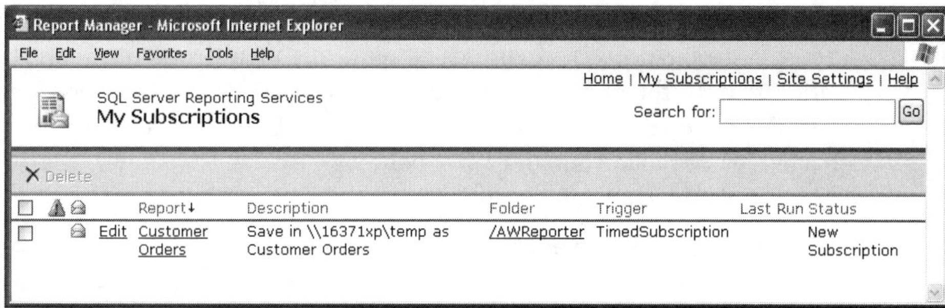

Figure 12.6 Users can use the My Subscriptions page to manage the subscriptions they own. Here, the user is subscribed to the Sales by Territory report.

The My Subscriptions page is similar to the screen linked to the Subscriptions tab, but it doesn't give the user an option to create new subscriptions. Using My Subscriptions or the Subscriptions tab from the report properties allow users to:

- Make changes to an existing subscription
- See the last date and time when the subscription was run
- Verify the subscription status
- Delete the subscription

Managing all subscriptions

Users with rights to the Manage All Subscriptions task can manage the subscriptions they own plus those of other users. The Report Manager doesn't include a screen that shows a single view of all subscriptions. Instead, you need to drill down to individual reports to see the subscriptions associated with each report.

For example, to see all time-based subscriptions, follow these steps:

Step 1 Click the Manage Shared Schedules link from the Site Settings menu.

Step 2 Select the schedule of interest.

Step 3 View the reports linked to that schedule.

Step 4 Click the Subscriptions tab for each report to get to the subscriptions associated with that report.

As a workaround, if you want to see all subscriptions, you can create a database view that links the `Subscriptions`, `Catalog`, and `Users` tables to return the report and usernames.

You can prevent individual users from creating subscriptions by setting up a new role that doesn't include the Manage Individual Subscriptions task and assigning users to this role. Alternatively, assuming that the users belong to the Browser role, you can exclude the Manage Individual Subscriptions task from this role.

Sometimes you may want to prevent users from selecting specific delivery options. For example, strict security requirements may disallow sending reports via e-mail. You can disable delivery extensions by removing their definitions from the configuration files. In the previous scenario, to prevent the Report Manager from showing the Report Server Email delivery option in the Deliver By drop-down list, simply remove or comment out the corresponding element from the `RSWebApplication.config` configuration file.

NOTE Removing a delivery extension from the `RSWebApplication.config` file only prevents this extension from showing in the Report Manager UI. You can still use the SOAP subscription-related APIs to create subscriptions associated with the excluded extension. If you want to prevent users from creating subscriptions with a given delivery extension, remove it from the `RSReportServer.config` file.

Now that we've covered the theory behind subscribed report delivery, let's put it into action to address some common subscription-based needs.

12.3 SUBSCRIBED REPORT DELIVERY IN ACTION

In this section, we implement the following examples:

- A standard e-mail subscription
- A standard file-based subscription
- A data-driven e-mail subscription
- Triggering a subscription programmatically

12.3.1 "Pushing" reports via standard e-mail subscriptions

In our fictitious scenario, the AWC North American Sales Manager, Michael Blythe, will subscribe his subordinates to receive the Employee Sales Freeform with Chart report, which you created in chapter 4. Let's assume that Michael has rights to execute the Manage Individual Subscriptions task included by default in the Browser role. To simulate this scenario, you could reuse Michael's Windows account that you created in chapter 9. If you decide to do so, remember to grant this account Browser permissions to the AWReporter folder.

To make things more interesting, let's also assume that Michael doesn't have rights to the Manage All Subscriptions task and that `SendEmailToUserAlias` is set to True (the default value). As a result, the e-mail address fields (To, Cc, and Bcc) will appear disabled for Michael. Therefore, you will need to finalize the subscription that was initiated by Michael by entering the recipients' e-mail addresses.

Creating a standard e-mail subscription

Start by logging into Windows with Michael's login credentials. Next, perform the following steps:

Step 1 Use your favorite browser to open the Report Manager web application.

Step 2 Navigate to the Employee Sales Freeform with Chart report.

Step 3 Select New Subscription from the View or Subscriptions tab. This initiates the process of creating a new subscription, as shown in figure 12.7.

As you can see, the Report Manager adjusts the user interface to reflect the fact that Michael doesn't have rights to execute the Manage All Subscriptions task. Specifically, the following changes are made:

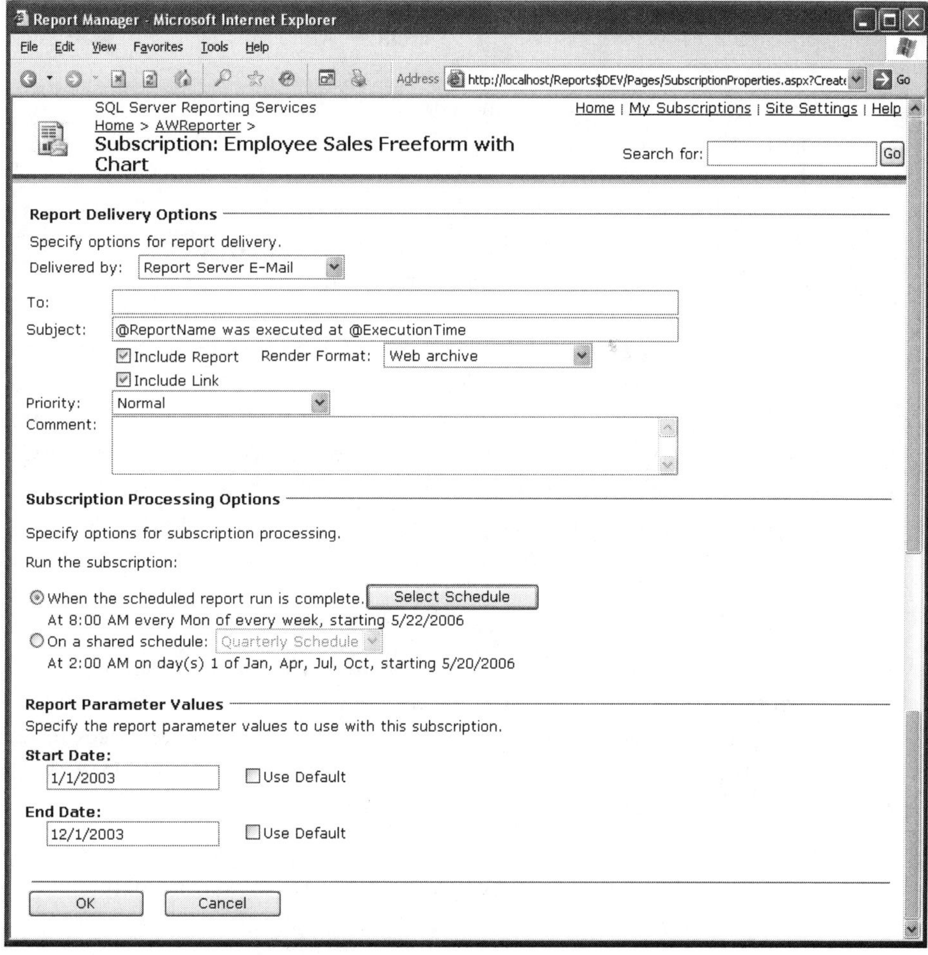

Figure 12.7 Use the Report Manager to create an individual e-mail subscription.

- The To field is disabled, so Michael can't enter the recipients' e-mail addresses.
- The Cc, Bcc, and Reply-To fields are missing.
- The screen doesn't give the user an option to run the subscription on a shared schedule.

Some of the available fields deserve more attention. The default Subject field has two predefined variable placeholders, `@ReportName` and `@ExecutionTime`. During runtime, the Report Server will replace them with their counterparts from the Global object collection, `ReportName` and `ExecutionTime`. While you may think that you can use the rest of the `Global` variables, for example, `TotalPages` or `ReportServerUrl`, this is not the case. Why? We don't know. A good case could be made to support parameter values, results from a call to custom code, and so on.

Checking the Include Report check box will embed the report in the e-mail when the export format is a Web archive (MHTML) or else it will enclose it as an e-mail attachment.

If selected, the Include Link check box will add the report's URL to the body of the e-mail. This could be useful when you want to let the user conveniently request the report to see the latest data.

The Priority field reflects the status under which the e-mail will be sent. For example, if the subscription is created with a high priority, Microsoft Outlook will show an exclamation mark in the Importance field.

Finally, for parameter-driven reports, the Report Manager generates placeholders for each report parameter. For nonsnapshot reports, the user can enter the parameter values or opt to use the default values.

Although Michael can create a subscription-specific schedule to trigger the subscribed delivery, he won't get very far. The e-mail server will error out when trying to resolve the recipients' addresses. In short, the security-conscious user interface of Report Manager is good enough to log the subscription request, but not to execute it successfully. Doing so requires intervention by you, the report administrator.

Finalizing the e-mail subscription

Let's now assume that Michael has notified you of his intention to distribute the report to a fixed number of sales representatives. At this point, ensure that you are logged in as the administrator, navigate to the report, and override Michael's subscription, as shown in figure 12.8. In our scenario, you would enter the e-mail addresses of Michael's subordinates.

> **TIP** You will probably recall that in chapter 5 we authored the Corporate Hierarchy report. You can create similar reports to find out who reports to whom.

The e-mail addresses shown in figure 12.8 are taken from the AdventuresWorks database and are fictitious. To test the example successfully, you may want to enter valid

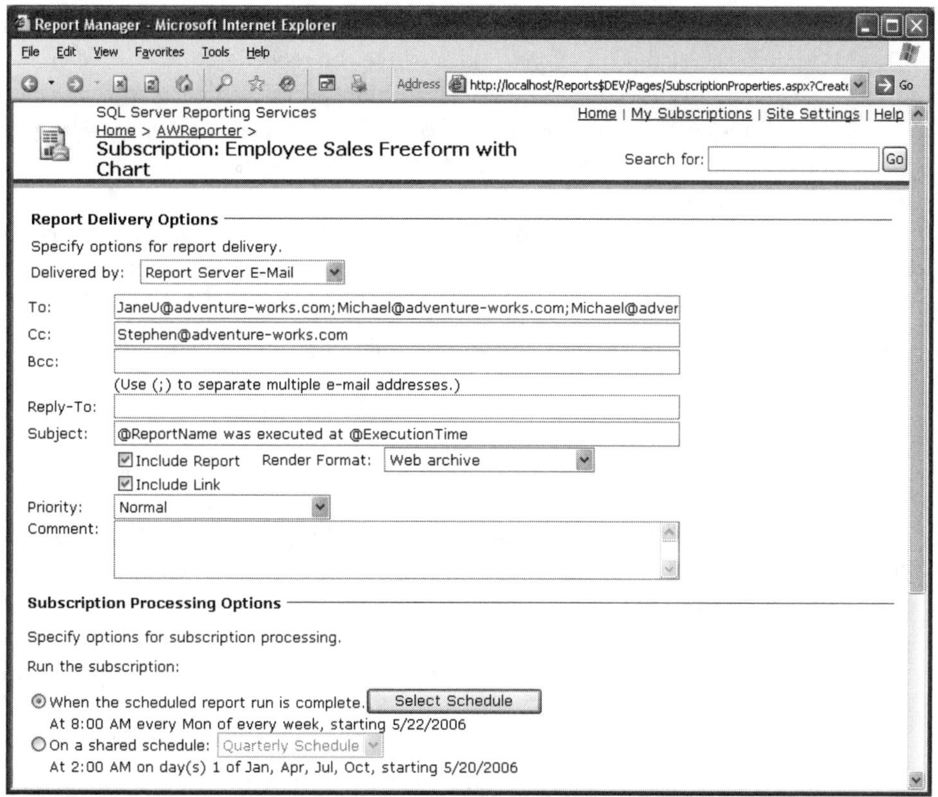

Figure 12.8 As report administrator, you can finalize the report subscription by entering the recipients' addresses.

e-mail addresses in the To field. In addition, you may want to change the schedule duration to a shorter interval, such as every five minutes. Don't forget to stop the schedule or dissociate the report from it when you have finished experimenting to prevent filling up your e-mail box.

That's it! At this point the standard e-mail subscription is scheduled and ready for execution. When the schedule is up, the Report Server generates the Employee Sales Freeform with Chart report and mails it to the specified recipients.

12.3.2 Archiving reports to a file share

In this scenario, you archive the Territory Sales by Quarter report that you authored in chapter 8 each time its underlying data is refreshed. As you probably recall, you configured this report to be executed as a snapshot that is refreshed on a quarterly basis. You set the snapshot execution process to be triggered by a shared schedule.

This time you'll extend this example by creating a subscription that runs each time the snapshot is refreshed. The subscription exports the report in PDF and uses the file share delivery extension to save the report as a file to a network share.

Setting up the target folder

Start by choosing the target folder where the report archive will be created. The file share delivery extension doesn't create the specified folder if it doesn't exist, so you need to specify an existing folder. For the purposes of this demo, choose to export the report to the `C:\Reports` folder. In real life, you would probably want to use a globally accessible network share. As we've discussed, the target folder must be specified in the Uniform Naming Convention (UNC) format that includes the computer's network name. In our example, the UNC format for `C:\Reports` is `\\<computername>\C$\Reports`.

NOTE In our case we use an administrative share (indicated by the `$` sign). In real life, you should use network shares that are off the root of the server, for example, `<computername>\Reports`.

As we've said, to create file share subscriptions, the user must have rights to the Manage Individual Subscriptions task. Unlike working with e-mail subscriptions, however, the Report Manager doesn't enforce any additional security rules. Therefore, users with rights to the Manage Individual Subscriptions task will be able to configure execution-ready file share subscriptions.

You may wonder why file share subscriptions are more relaxed in terms of security. The reason for this laissez faire approach is that file share delivery is naturally more restricted than e-mail delivery because the report cannot be exported outside the organization's boundaries. In addition, access to UNC shares can be controlled by other means, such as using Windows access control lists (ACLs).

Configuring file share delivery

Once you've decided on the target folder, follow these steps to configure the Territory Sales by Quarter report for file-share delivery:

Step 1 Using the Report Manager, navigate to the Territory Sales by Quarter report.

Step 2 Verify that the report is scheduled for a snapshot execution by checking the Execution tab's properties. If it isn't, follow the directions in chapter 8 to configure the report for snapshot execution that is triggered by the shared Quarterly Schedule.

Step 3 Click the New Subscription button on the View or Subscriptions tab. Configure the file share delivery as shown in figure 12.9.

To export the report to a target folder, use the Report Server File Share delivery option, which delegates the report distribution to the file share extension. To append the export format extension, select the Add a File Extension When the File Is Created check box. This allows the user to double-click on the file and load the report in the application that is associated with the file extension, for example, Adobe Acrobat for files with the .PDF extension.

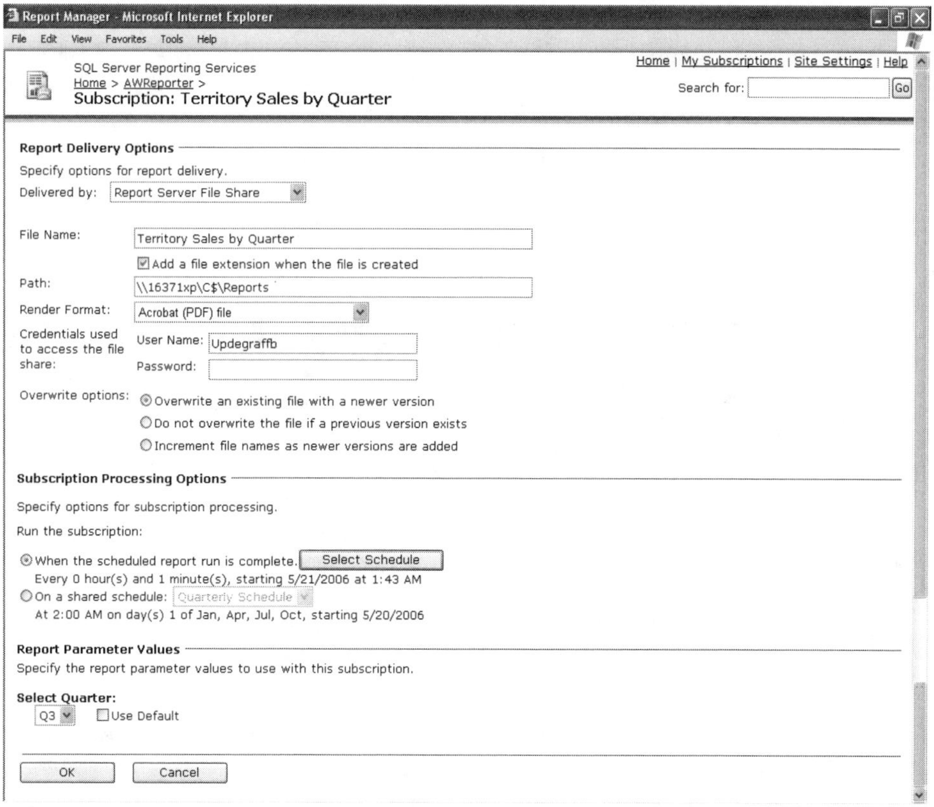

Figure 12.9 **To configure a file share subscription for report archiving, specify the file share path in UNC and the account credentials.**

In my case, the share UNC path is \\16371xp\c$\reports because my computer is named 16371xp. The export format is set to Adobe Acrobat (PDF). The file share extension requires you to specify the credentials of a Windows account that has write access to the target folder. The overwrite options are self-explanatory.

To trigger the subscription when the report snapshot is refreshed, choose the When the Report Content Is Refreshed option. This option is available only for snapshot reports.

Parameter limitations

Finally, note that the parameter placeholders are disabled. As we discussed in chapter 8, once the snapshot parameter values have been defined, they cannot be changed prior to the report's execution. In our case, this means that the report will filter the report data for the third quarter.

Remember to change the parameter value on the report's Parameters tab before the next quarterly execution. Of course, you could avoid having to do this by changing the report to filter the underlying data using the system date instead of using a report parameter.

Observing the subscription results

Once you've defined the file share subscription, you're ready to put it into action.

Instead of waiting for the next quarter, let's change the Quarterly shared schedule interval to five minutes. Then, switch to the Territory Sales by Quarter report's Subscriptions tab, as shown in figure 12.10.

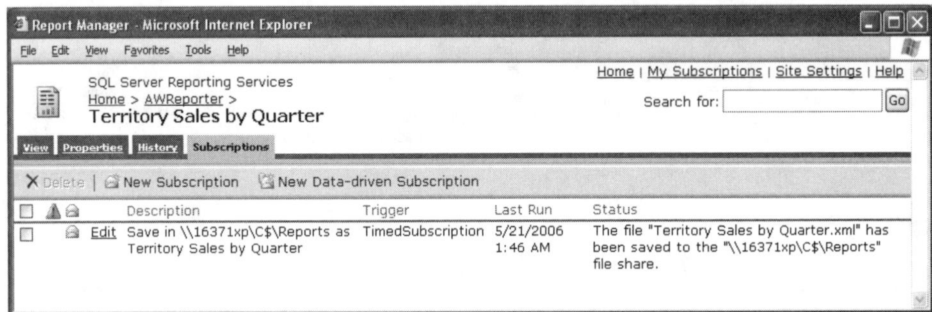

Figure 12.10 Use the Subscriptions tab to observe the subscription run.

Note that the Trigger column shows `SnapshotUpdated` to signify that the subscription will be triggered by a snapshot refresh.

Once the schedule is up, the Report Server processes the report and asks the file share extension to deliver the report. As a result, the report is saved to the specified target folder.

12.3.3 Sending reports to a data-driven list of recipients

While distributing reports to a fixed list of recipients may be useful for intranet-oriented reports, it may be impractical when reports need to be delivered to web-based subscribers. For example, imagine that Adventure Works Cycles (AWC) would like to send the Product Catalog report to its web customers on a regular basis. Hardcoding hundreds and thousands of customers' e-mail addresses would present a maintenance challenge.

In addition, a common requirement for Internet-oriented applications is to support report personalization features and customize the report to meet the specific requirements of the user. For example, it is unlikely that all customers would like to receive the Product Catalog report exported in the same format. Instead, a better approach is to allow the subscribers to specify the export format, such as PDF or HTML. All of these requirements call for a more flexible subscribed delivery option.

On the provider side, many organizations may want to implement custom delivery rules to filter out the list of recipients who will receive the report. For example, to fight the recent proliferation of spam e-mail, government regulations in the United States dictate that all commercial e-mail must allow the subscribers to be able to opt out at will from e-mail distribution lists.

Another common scenario that requires validating business rules is when an organization wants to deliver reports only to recipients who meet specific criteria. For example, AWC may want to distribute the product catalog report only to subscribers who have placed orders in the past six months.

To address needs such as these, RS supports data-driven subscriptions. In this section, you implement a data-driven e-mail subscription to meet the following design goals:

- Create a data store to capture the subscribers' data. In real life, the AWC customers would typically use a web-based front end to opt in for subscribed report delivery. The data store could also save the customers' subscription preferences.
- Configure an e-mail data-driven subscription to send the Customer Order History report to all subscribers. As you'll probably recall, you created this report in chapter 11 to show the orders placed by the customer in the past.
- Allow the report's recipients to customize the report by specifying the export format and e-mail priority.

Creating the subscriber data store

The AdventureWorks database model supports several types of customers, including individuals, stores, and retail. The individuals' profile data is captured in the `Individual` table. If you look at the definition of this table you will see that, among other things, it stores the customers' names and e-mail addresses, which makes this table suitable for a recipient data store. Unfortunately, the AdventureWorks data is not consistent. Specifically, the orders placed by individuals don't have matching records in the `Individual` table.

To fix this, you need to add customer records to the `Individual` table with identifiers matching the `CustomerID` column in the `SalesOrderHeader` table. To make your life easier, we've provided a SQL script that you can run to insert a few customer records. The script is called `Recipients.sql` and it is located in the `Database.dbp` project. If you want to test the e-mail delivery end to end, be sure to change the customers' e-mail addresses to valid e-mail addresses.

To simulate an opt-in distribution list, we created a database view, called Recipients, which you can find in the `Views.sql` script located in the same project. The view simply filters out data in the `Sales.Individual` table to return only the customers whom we've added using the `Recipients.sql` script. In real life, instead of a view, you may want to use a stored procedure to implement additional business rules. Figure 12.11 shows what the subscriber data looks like as returned by the view.

To implement the view, we decided to reuse the `CreditCardNumber` and `EmailPromotion` columns from the `Individual` table to store the report format

CustomerID	FirstName	LastName	EmailAddress	Format	Priority
21768	Ryan	Lewis	rlewis@adventure-works.com	MHTML	LOW
28389	Miguel	Thomas	mthomas@adventure-works.com	PDF	NORMAL
25863	Nicholas	Thompson	nthompson@adventure-works.com	IMAGE	HIGH
14501	Ariana	Ramirez	aramirez@adventure-works.com	PDF	LOW
11003	Maya	Hill	mhill@adventure-works.com	MHTML	NORMAL

Figure 12.11 Create a view to serve as a subscriber data source.

and e-mail priority data, respectively. We did so to avoid adding columns to the `Individual` table.

Once you've created the view, don't forget to grant permissions to it for the database login that the AW Shared DS data source uses to log in to the AdventureWorks database.

Configuring the e-mail data-driven extension

Now it is time to create the subscription. Open the Report Manager portal and navigate to the Customer Orders report. Click the Subscriptions tab and choose New Data-Driven Subscription to launch the Data-Driven Subscription Wizard. For our example, choose to distribute the report via e-mail (figure 12.12). In addition, specify that the subscriber data store will be queried using a shared data source; you'll specify that data source in the next step. Click Next.

Because you chose the shared data source option in Step 1, you need to tell the wizard where it is located, as shown in figure 12.13. In this example, select the

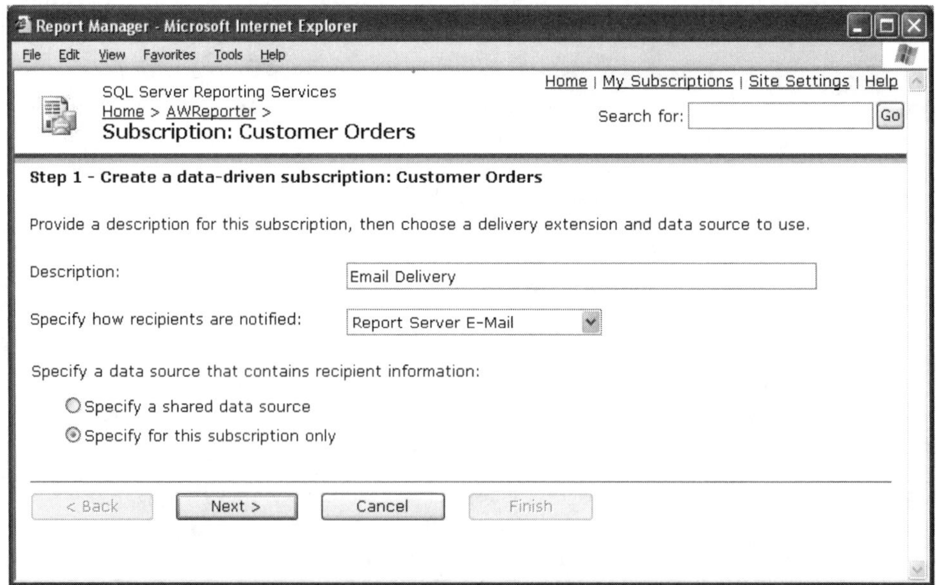

Figure 12.12 The first step of the Data-Driven Subscription Wizard allows you to name your subscription and choose the subscription type.

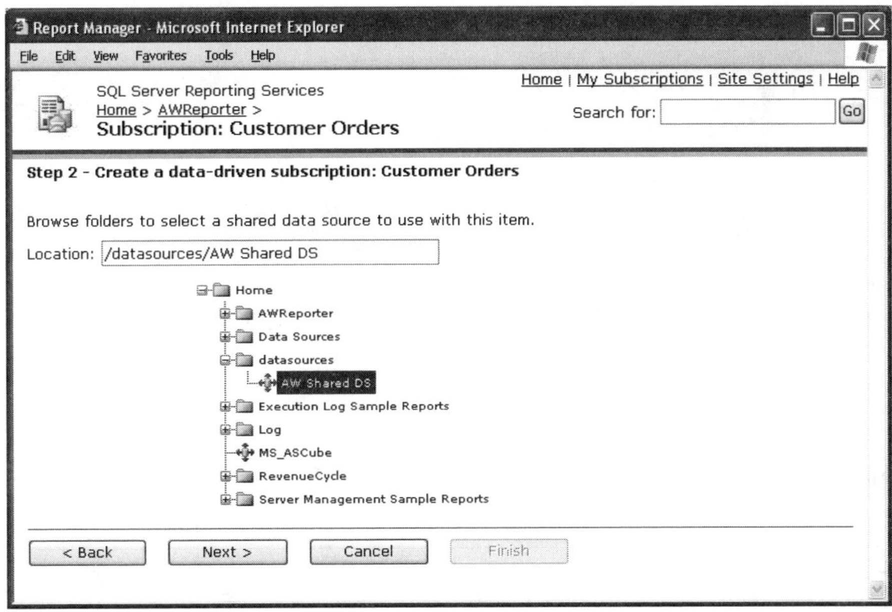

Figure 12.13 In Step 2 of the wizard, specify the data source that will be used to get the subscriber data.

AW Shared DS data source because the Recipient view is located in the Adventure-Works database.

Next, you need to set up the query that will return the list of recipients, as shown in figure 12.14. To follow along with our example, select all records from the Recipient view.

The next step is the most important: setting up the data-driven subscription. Here, you map the recipients' addresses and optionally other extension-specific properties to the query fields, as shown in figure 12.15. Set the extension properties as shown in table 12.1.

As you can see, data-driven subscriptions provide a lot of flexibility to customize the report's execution. Any delivery extension property can be set to get its value from the recipients' rowset. In our scenario, your web customers could specify the report's format and e-mail priority.

In the next step, you must take care of the report parameters, as shown in figure 12.16. The Customer Orders report takes a single parameter, `CustomerID`. To synchronize the report with the recipients' rowset, link this parameter to the `CustomerID` column returned by the query.

Finally, let's set this subscription to be triggered on a quarterly basis by using the predefined Quarterly Schedule, as shown in figure 12.17.

That's it! You've managed to set up an automated data-driven report delivery in six easy steps. You can apply a similar approach to implement an e-mail campaigner

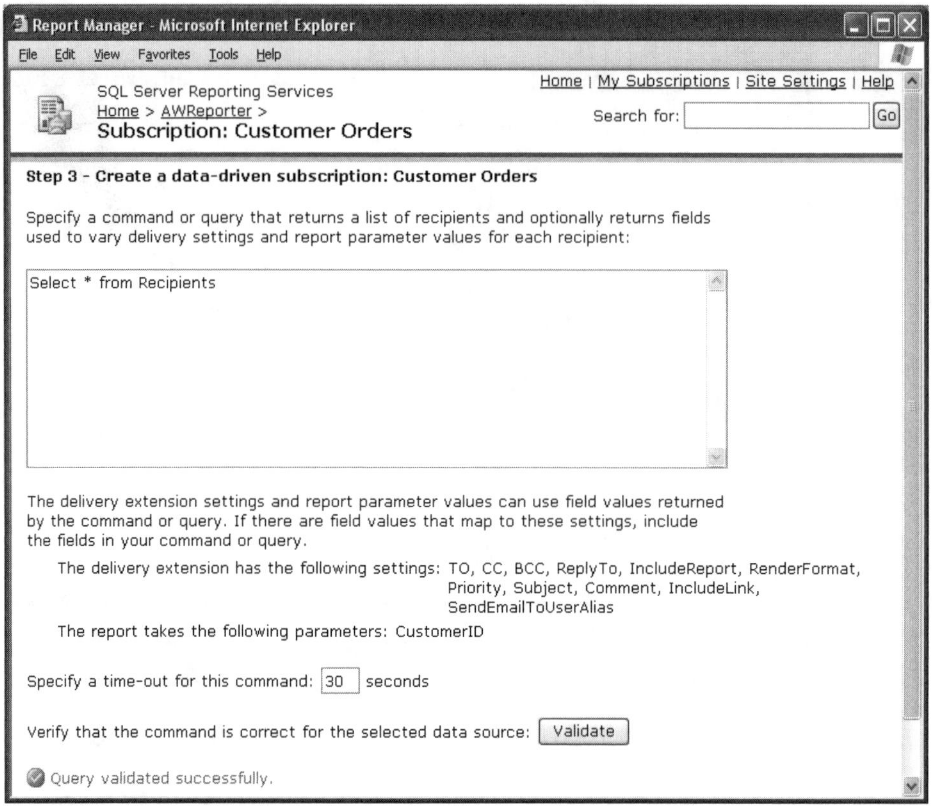

Figure 12.14 In Step 3 of the data-driven subscription wizard, specify the query statement used to return the recipient list.

Figure 12.15 In Step 4 of the data-driven subscription wizard, specify the delivery extension settings.

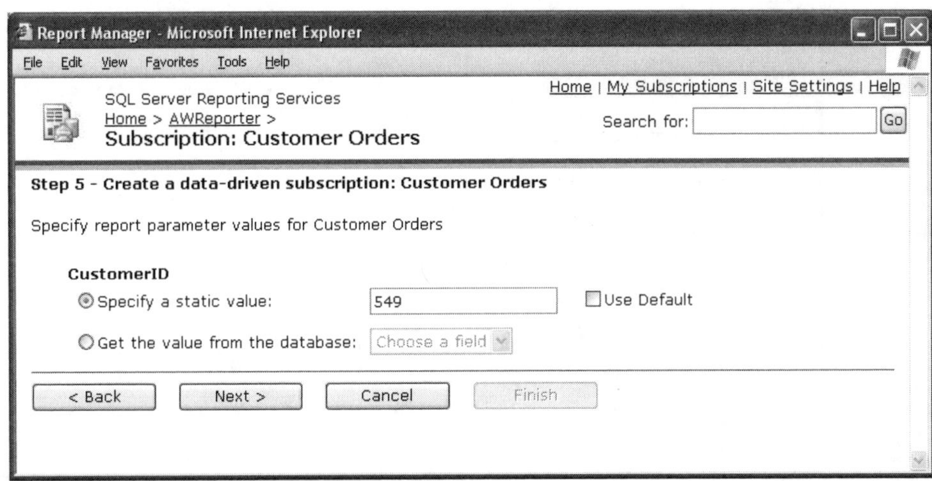

Figure 12.16 In Step 5 of the wizard, filter the customer orders per recipient. Do this by setting the CustomerID report parameter to the CustomerID column from the recipients' rowset.

Table 12.1 Mapping extension properties to query fields

Extension Property	Setting	Comment
To	EmailAddress (database field)	Data-driven from the recipient query.
Cc	No Value	We won't cc the e-mail to another recipient.
Bcc	No Value	We won't bcc the e-mail to another recipient.
Reply-To	No Value	There is no need to specify an explicit return address.
Include Report	True	The report will be embedded when the report format is MHTML or attached otherwise.
Render Format	Format (database field)	Data-driven from the recipient query.
Priority	Priority (database field)	Data-driven from the recipient query.
Subject	@ReportName was executed at @ExecutionTime	Will be replaced automatically by the Report Server to read "Customer Order was executed at <the time when the schedule is triggered>".
Comment	No Value	There is no need for comments.
Include Link	False	Web-based recipients won't normally have URL access to the Report Server, so there is no need to give them an option to request the report by URL

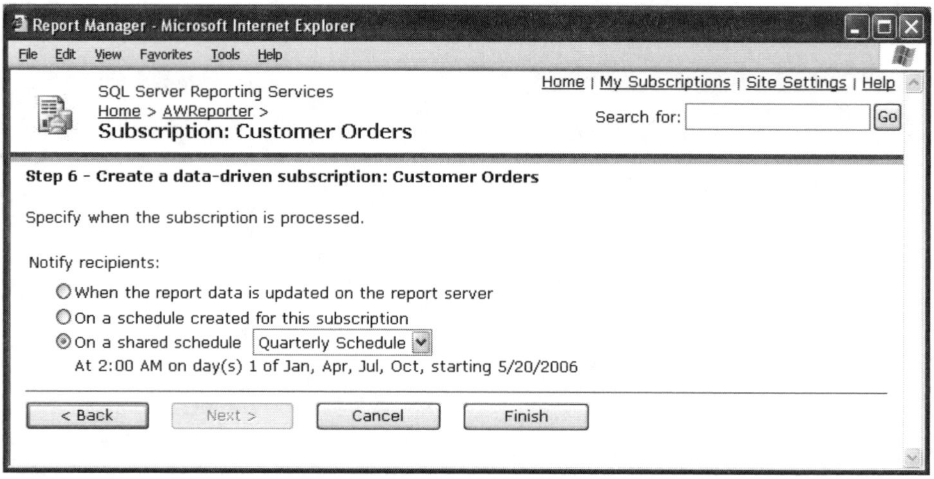

Figure 12.17 In Step 6 of the wizard, specify how the data-driven subscription will be triggered.

service to send the product catalog by e-mail to a list of subscribers when there is a new product promotion. Or a spam service? (Just kidding to see if you are still here!) You can further enhance this scenario to add more personalization features. For example, you could easily modify the Customer Orders report to greet the user by name.

You can use any delivery extension with data-driven subscriptions. For example, with file share subscriptions, the recipient's data source could keep the target folders where the reports need to be saved.

With RS you are not limited to triggering your subscriptions on a fixed schedule. Instead, you can programmatically fire subscriptions, as we discuss next.

12.3.4 Triggering subscriptions programmatically

While running subscriptions at a reoccurring scheduled interval can be very useful, sometimes you may need to programmatically trigger the subscribed delivery process.

For example, say you have scheduled an e-mail delivery of the Adventure Works product catalog to a list of subscribers on a quarterly basis. However, the company management has requested the report to also be distributed when a new product is added to the catalog. How would you implement this?

Publishing events programatically

One option to trigger a subscription programmatically is to reset the subscription schedule to run when a new product is added. Although this will work, it requires manual intervention. Ideally, what you need is the ability to automate the process by being able to programatically fire the subscription event. Can you do this with RS? You bet.

The RS Web service already includes a web method for this task. It is called `FireEvent`, and it has the following signature:

```
public void FireEvent(string EventType,  string EventData);
```

It is one of the event types listed under the `EventProcessing` element in the `RSReportServer.config` configuration file. The event data is the identifier of the item that triggered the event and can be of the following values:

- For subscriptions based on shared schedules, the `EventData` is the schedule identifier, as specified in the `ScheduleID` column in the `Schedule` table.
- For subscriptions with private schedules, the `EventData` corresponds to the subscription identifier, which is the value of the `SubscriptionID` column from the `Subscriptions` table.

In a nutshell, triggering the subscription programmatically involves inserting an event record into the `Event` table in the Report Server database. There's nothing stopping you from writing a table trigger on the Adventure Works `Product` table to insert a new record in the `Event` table when a new product has been added, but the recommended way is to use the `FireEvent` API.

TIP If you decide to log the event directly into the `Event` table, you may wonder how to get the event type and data. One way to obtain them is to wait for the subscription schedule to run, and then query the `Event` table in the Report Server catalog. To avoid racing with the Reporting Services Windows Service to determine who will get to the logged event first, you can stop the Reporting Services Windows Service.

Among other things, when the `FireEvent` API is used, the Report Server could verify that the call is permitted as configured by the administrator's role-based security policy. Only callers who have rights to execute the Generate Events system-level task are trusted to fire events programmatically, as shown in figure 12.18.

Interestingly, by default the System Administrator role doesn't include this task. Therefore, as a prerequisite for running our sample successfully, you need to grant the `FireEvent` caller the Generate Events task.

Implementing the solution

Once the security policy is set up, you are ready to implement the code sample. Table 12.2 lists the task map of the solution.

Similarly to the Campaigner example discussed in chapter 10, you use a table trigger to call a web method, which in turn calls the `FireEvent` API. Why don't you call the `FireEvent` method directly from the trigger? If you did this, it would require hardcoding the event type and data inside the trigger, which is something that you should avoid. Instead, you write a new web method, called `FireSubscription`

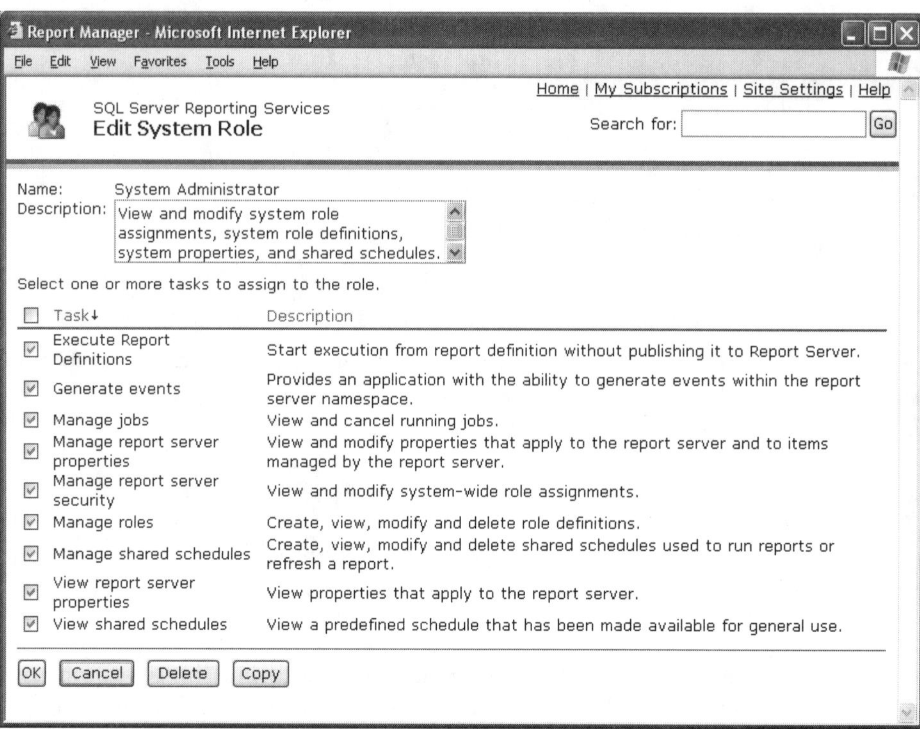

Figure 12.18 Calling FireEvents requires the Generate Events task.

Table 12.2 The task map for programmatically firing a subscription

Component	Task	Description
Table Trigger	Create `INSERT` table trigger.	Write an `ON INSERT` table trigger attached to the `Product` table that will fire when a new product is added.
	Call the web method `FireSubscription`.	Inside the trigger, call a custom web method called `FireSubscription`. Pass the report and user identity with which the subscription is associated.
Web method `Fire-Subscription`	Call `ListSubscriptions`.	Get the list of subscriptions associated with the report-user combination.
	Call `GetDataDriven-SubscriptionProperties`.	Retrieve the subscription properties to get to the event details.
	Call `FireEvent`.	Call `FireEvent` to publish the event programmatically.

(found in the Campaigner Web service source code under the Chapter09 folder in the AWReporterWeb project). The `FireSubscription` source code is shown in listing 12.1.

Listing 12.1 Triggering a subscription programmatically using the FireEvent API

```
[WebMethod]
public void FireSubscription(string reportPath, string userName)  {
  ReportingService2005 rs = new ReportingService2005();
  rs.Credentials=System.Net.CredentialCache.DefaultCredentials;

  DataRetrievalPlan dataRetrievalPlan = null;
  ExtensionSettings extSettings;
  string desc;
  ActiveState active;
  string status;
  string eventType;
  string matchData;
  Subscription[] subscriptions = null;
  ParameterValueOrFieldReference[] extensionParams = null;

  subscriptions = rs.ListSubscriptions(reportPath, userName);   <-- Gets the list of subscriptions

  if ( subscriptions != null )  {   <-- Gets the subscription properties
rs.GetDataDrivenSubscriptionProperties(
  subscriptions[0].SubscriptionID,
  out extSettings,  out dataRetrievalPlan, out desc, out active,
  out status, out eventType, out matchData,
  out extensionParams );

      rs.FireEvent(eventType, matchData);   <-- Fires the event
  }
}
```

To make the `FireSubscription` method more generic, pass the report path of the report that needs to be delivered as well as the owner's name in the format `DOMAIN\USERNAME`. The latter argument is needed because, as you probably recall, a subscription is associated with exactly one user and one report.

The call to the `ListSubscription` web method returns a list of subscriptions associated with the requested report-user combination. For the sake of simplicity, default to the first subscription. If you need to support reports that have more than one subscription per given user, you may want to pass the subscription identifier as a third argument to `FireSubscription`.

Next, you get the subscription properties by calling the `GetDataDrivenSubscriptionProperties` web method. This is needed to get the event type and data before the call to `FireEvent`. Because there are two types of subscriptions, standard and data-driven, the RS Web service API includes two web methods: `GetSubscriptionProperties` and `GetDataDrivenSubscriptionProperties`.

In this example, assume that you need to trigger a data-driven subscription. Once the `GetDataDrivenSubscriptionProperties` call executes successfully, the event type and data are exposed under the `eventType` and `matchData` arguments, respectively. Finally, you call the `FireEvent` method to log the event that will trigger the subscription processing.

The only piece left to implement is the `INSERT` trigger attached to the `Products` table. This trigger will invoke the `FireSubscription` method when a new product is added to the `Products` table in the AdventureWorks database. It will be very similar to the `trgSpecialOffer` trigger discussed in chapter 10, so let's leave its implementation details to you.

12.4 SUMMARY

In this chapter we explored the second option for distributing reports with Reporting Services—via subscriptions. Coupled with requesting reports on demand, subscribed report delivery should address the most common distribution requirements for making the reports available to your users.

Once you've read this chapter along with chapter 8, you should know when and how to use both delivery options appropriately. When the report's requirements call for immediate synchronous access to the report, the on-demand option could be a better fit. Alternatively, when a report needs to be executed on a regular basis in unattended mode, it can be scheduled and "pushed" to recipients via subscribed delivery.

With subscribed report delivery, users can subscribe to reports that are distributed to them or other destinations as a result of an event. RS supports standard and data-driven subscriptions. Standard subscription options are fixed, while data-driven subscription options can be set during runtime when the subscription is executed.

We put these concepts into practice by implementing various examples. We showed how you can create standard e-mail and file share delivery subscriptions. Then, we demonstrated how data-driven subscriptions work to deliver reports to a data-driven list of recipients. Finally, you saw how developers can programmatically trigger subscriptions using the `FireEvent` API.

By now, you would probably agree that RS offers a lot of flexibility in all three phases of the report's lifecycle: authoring, management, and delivery. But, as flexible as it is, there will be cases in which RS may not fit all reporting needs out of the box.

In such cases, you will probably appreciate the extensible nature of the RS architecture that allows developers to plug in programming logic in the form of custom extensions, as we discuss in chapter 13.

PART 4

Advanced reporting

One of the most appealing features of Reporting Services is that it can be easily extended by writing custom add-ons in the form of extensions. Part 4 discusses the implementation details of three custom extensions that you can use to extend the RS features.

You'll learn how to author a dataset data extension to report off ADO.NET datasets. You'll also see how to distribute reports to Web services by means of a custom delivery extension. In addition, we'll show you how to replace the RS Windows-based security model with a custom security extension.

Aside from being feature-rich, your reporting solutions must also perform and scale well under increased user loads. To ensure that these objectives are met, you need to know how to evaluate the Report Server performance and capacity before "going live" in a production environment. In this part, you'll learn how to establish performance goals, how to create test scripts with the Application Center Test, and how to stress-load your Report Server installation.

CHAPTER 13

Extending Reporting Services

An important characteristic of every enterprise-oriented framework, such as Reporting Services, is that it has to be easily extensible. Simply put, *extensibility* relates to the system's ability to accommodate new features that are built out of old ones. When a software platform is extensible, it allows developers to customize it to meet their specific needs. For example, when your reporting requirements rule out Windows-based security, RS allows you to replace it with custom security models.

One of the most prominent and appealing aspects of RS is its modular architecture, which is designed for extensibility. You've already witnessed this in chapter 6 when you saw how to supercharge your reports by writing custom code. In this chapter, we explore additional ways to take advantage of the unique extensibility model of RS by writing custom extensions. Specifically, we develop the following extensions:

- A dataset data extension to report off ADO.NET datasets
- A Web service delivery extension to distribute reports to Web services
- A security extension to implement custom authentication and authorization

By the time you finish reading this chapter, you should have enough knowledge to develop, install, and manage custom extensions. First, though, let's discuss the essential concepts that you need to know to effectively leverage the extensibility features of RS.

13.1 UNDERSTANDING REPORTING SERVICES EXTENSIBILITY

You can extend RS by plugging in custom extensions written in .NET code. To do that, you need to be familiar with the concept of *interface-based* programming. Based on our experience, many developers find working with interfaces difficult to grasp.

For this reason, let's make a little detour at the beginning of this chapter and explain the basic concepts and benefits of this style of programming. First we provide you with an understanding of interface-based programming and then focus on working with interface inheritance.

By no means will our discussion attempt to afford exhaustive coverage of these topics. If you need more information, refer to the .NET product documentation, which includes many technical articles on object-oriented programming.

13.1.1 Interface-based programming

Suppose that you are an architect on the Microsoft RS team and you are responsible for designing a flexible model for plugging in delivery extensions. As you saw in chapter 12, RS comes with two delivery extensions out of the box: e-mail and file share extensions. As useful as these extensions are, it is unlikely that they will meet all subscription-based distribution requirements. For example, what if an organization wants to automate the report-printing process by sending reports directly to a printer? Instead of enduring the Herculean effort of creating and supporting all possible delivery scenarios out there, you prudently decide to let customers author and plug in their own extensions.

What implementation pattern will you choose? Obviously, you must establish some standardization to which other developers will have to conform. Once you've come up with an easy-to-follow standard pattern, you could use generic code logic to load and execute custom extensions. As a seasoned architect, you set the following high-level design goals for the envisioned extensibility model:

- It must allow developers to write and plug in their own extensions.
- It shouldn't require an intimate knowledge of how the extension is implemented, or what it does for that matter. In other words, as long as the extension adheres to the standard, it can be treated as a "black box."
- It should be as robust as possible. For example, the model should be able to determine at runtime whether a given custom extension follows the standard design pattern and, if it doesn't, the Report Server will not attempt to load it.

Let's now discuss how to implement these requirements. To enforce a common standard for report delivery, you can lay out the following rules:

- Each custom extension type must expose a method that the Report Server will invoke to distribute the report.
- This method must have at least one argument that the Report Server will use to pass the report notification object.

Given the above specifications, figure 13.1 shows how two custom delivery extensions could be implemented.

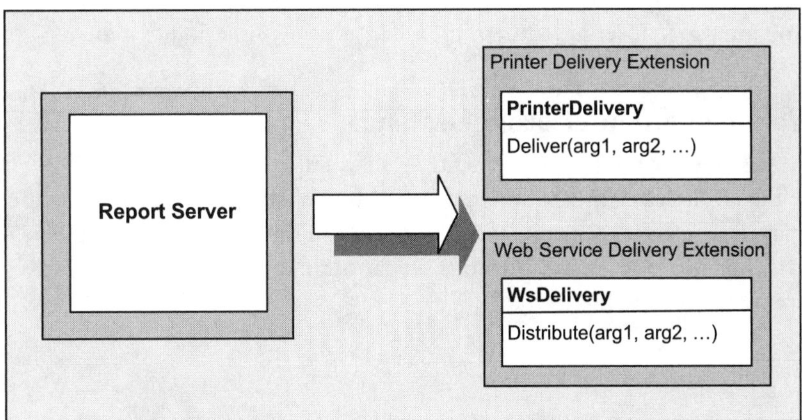

Figure 13.1 Without interfaces, it is difficult to achieve standardization. For example, this figure shows two possible implementation approaches to implement custom delivery extensions. Because they don't follow a single standard, it is difficult for the Report Server to integrate them.

Let's say that the first extension supports report delivery to a printer, similar to the sample that comes with RS, while the second can be used to distribute reports to a Web service. In the first case, you've decided to encapsulate the delivery logic in a method called `Deliver`, while in the latter, in a method called `Distribute`.

Once the custom extensions are registered with the Report Server, you can define subscriptions that use these extensions, as we discussed in chapter 12. During runtime, the Report Server will instantiate the appropriate extension and delegate the report delivery to it. Everything looks great! Or does it?

Upon further inspection, several issues surface:

- *Method names*—First, the Report Server has to know beforehand not only the type name of the extension but also the name of the method responsible for the report delivery. One possible workaround would be to save the method name in the configuration file too, but this would present a maintenance issue. Another solution would be to change the specification and stipulate that all delivery methods must have the same name, for example, *Deliver.* However, this approach is not easily enforceable, especially by people who are as opinionated and strong-willed as developers tend to be.

- *Signatures*—Second, the Report Server won't be able to easily inspect the signature of the delivery method in advance to check to see if it follows the specification. For example, what if the developer has neglected to specify an argument for the notification object? This will certainly result in a runtime exception.
- *Invoking methods*—Finally, there is no easy way for the Report Server to invoke the delivery method.

These issues can be easily overcome by using *interface inheritance*. In object-oriented programming, interface inheritance is a type of inheritance wherein one or more classes share a set of messages.

13.1.2 Working with interface inheritance

At this point, you may be curious as to what an *interface* really is. We can loosely define an interface as a set of methods, properties, and events that define an object's characteristics and behavior. You define an interface similarly to the way you define a class. For example, in the previous scenario, this is what the delivery extension interface may look like in C#:

```
interface IDeliveryExtension {
  void Deliver (Notification notification);
}
```

By convention, the interface name is prefixed with a capital *I*. Note that an interface contains only the method's signatures, not their implementation. In addition, unlike working with objects, an interface cannot be instantiated. In fact, the whole purpose of having an interface is to inherit from it, as shown in figure 13.2.

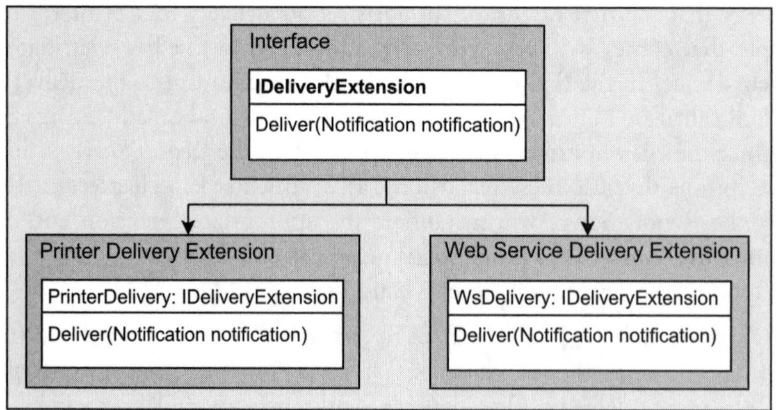

Figure 13.2 Use interface inheritance to enforce a specification. Now both extensions follow the same standard. The Report Server can load them by using the factory design pattern.

Now both extension classes inherit from the `IDeliveryExtension` interface, which in C# is denoted by the colon (:). When a class inherits from an interface, we say that the class *implements* this interface.

Interface inheritance offers the following benefits:

- Standardization
- Dynamic type discovery
- Polymorphism
- Multiple inheritance

Achieving standardization by using interfaces

Once a class inherits from an interface, it must implement all methods included in the interface definition. In addition, the implementation of the method names and signatures must match those defined in the interface. The compiler enforces these rules during code compilation.

Therefore, to enforce a common standard, you can change your specification to stipulate that all custom extensions must inherit from the `IDelivery` interface. This means that all custom extensions will expose a method called `Deliver`, which takes exactly one parameter of the type Notification, as required by the definition of the interface.

Dynamic type discovery

But what if the developer forgets to inherit the custom extension class from your interface? After all, a standard is only good when it is followed. You see, the second advantage of using interface inheritance, as well as object inheritance for that matter, is that the caller can easily discover whether an object implements a given interface during runtime. For example, you can write the following code in the Report Server to find out if the custom extension indeed adheres to your specification:

```
// instantiate the custom extension using Factory design pattern.
if (typeof(customExtension) is IDeliveryExtension)
  // do something with the extension
else
  throw new Exception("This custom extension doesn't
       implement IDeliveryInterface");
```

Here, you use the C# type of operator (the VB .NET equivalent is TypeOf) to check whether the extension class implements the required interface after the custom extension object is instantiated. If this is not the case, you can react to this condition by throwing an exception.

Polymorphism

Interface inheritance allows you to use another powerful object-oriented technique called *polymorphism*. It allows the caller to treat different objects in the same way. Let's say that you implemented two pluggable report adapters that inherited from a common IReportAdapter interface. Then, you use the factory design pattern to instantiate the requested adapter and cast its reference to IReportAdapter.

In this situation, polymorphism helps to expand the earlier example and work with the custom extension objects in this way:

```
// instantiate the custom extension using Factory design pattern.
if (typeof(customExtension) is IDeliveryExtension)
  // cast to IDeliveryExtension to call Deliver
  ((IDeliveryExtension) customExtension).Deliver(notification);
else
  throw new Exception("This custom extension doesn't
    implement IDeliveryInterface");
```

Once you make sure that the extension object is of the right type, you can cast to its base interface and call the Deliver method. As you can see, if you use interface inheritance, the caller can easily discover the type of the object during runtime and treat all objects that implement the required interface in the same way.

Implementing multiple interfaces

Finally, unlike class inheritance, with interface inheritance you can implement as many interfaces as you'd like. For example, to introduce a common standard that all custom delivery extensions will follow when retrieving the configuration information, we could use this interface:

```
interface IExtension  {
  void SetConfiguration(string);
}
```

Once a custom extension implements the IExtension interface, the Report Server can call its SetConfiguration method to pass the extension's configuration settings that can be defined in the Report Server configuration file. This looks like a cool feature, so let's enhance our printer delivery extension to implement both the IDeliveryExtension and IExtension interfaces, as follows:

```
public class WebServiceDeliveryProvider : IDeliveryExtension, IExtension {
    public void Deliver (Notification notification)  {…}
    public void SetConfiguration (string configSettings)  {…}
}
```

Note that, in most cases, the Report Server makes multiple interface inheritance unnecessary because the more "specialized" interfaces inherit from the IExtension interface. This means that all custom extensions indirectly inherit from IExtension.

Now that you have a good grasp of interface inheritance, you are ready to extend the RS features by writing custom data, delivery, rendering, and security extensions.

13.1.3 Extending RS with interface inheritance

To make your life easier, Microsoft has encapsulated all RS-related interface definitions into a single `Microsoft.ReportingServices.Interfaces` library. Figure 13.3 shows the publicly available type definitions included in this library.

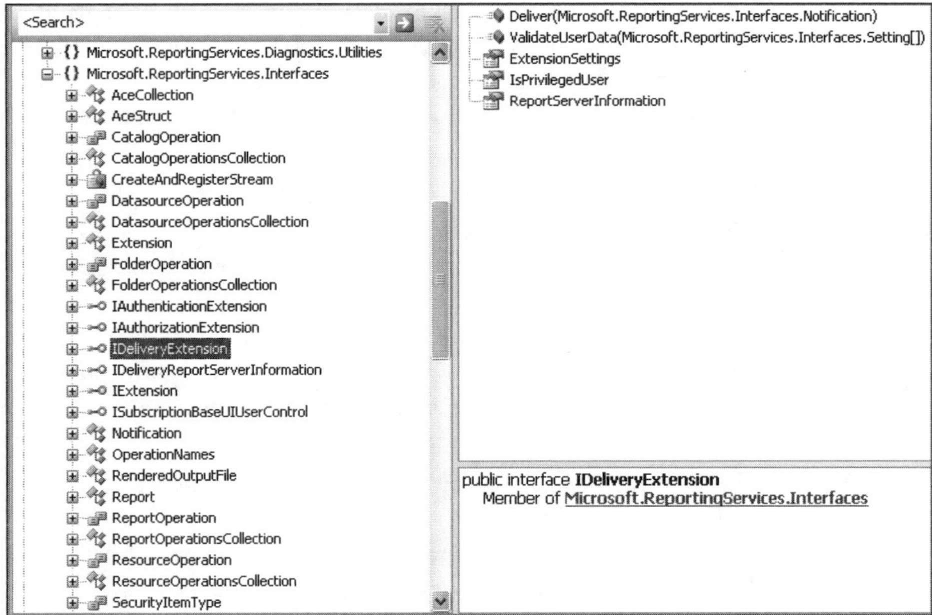

Figure 13.3 The Microsoft.ReportingServices.Interfaces library includes all interface definitions.

Therefore, as a prerequisite for writing a custom extension, in your project you need to set up a reference to this library, which can be found in both the Report Server binary folder (`C:\Program Files\Microsoft SQL Server\MSSQL.3\Reporting Services\ReportServer\Bin`) and the Report Manager binary folder (`C:\Program Files\Microsoft SQL Server\MSSQL.3\Reporting Services\ReportManager\Bin`).

For your convenience, we have encapsulated all custom extensions in this chapter into a single project called AWC.RS.Extensions. This setup also simplifies configuring the code access security for the custom extensions because you need to grant full trust permission to this assembly only. This project also includes our versions of both the Report Server and Report Manager configuration files to help you configure the sample extensions properly.

Now, let's put interface-based programming into action by creating our first custom extension.

13.2 REPORTING WITH A CUSTOM DATASET DATA EXTENSION

Knowing that RS can retrieve its data from virtually any database, why would you want to write a custom data extension? One good reason would be to report off custom data structures, such as ADO.NET datasets and XML documents. Reporting Services does support binding and reporting off application ADO.NET datasets through the use of the ReportViewer control. However, if you are not using the ReportViewer control, you can write a custom data extension to expose an ADO.NET dataset as a report's data source.

There are at least two approaches to implementing this process:

- *The custom extension calls an external .NET assembly to get the dataset*—This is the approach that the product documentation demonstrates. The advantage is better performance because the dataset doesn't have to cross process boundaries. However, this comes at the expense of flexibility. For example, this approach cannot be easily retrofitted to support the situation in which a three-tier application needs to report off datasets returned from the data tier layer. In addition, the application cannot preprocess the dataset before the report is generated.
- *The application passes the copy of the dataset that has been serialized to XML to the Report Server*—This approach allows a report consumer's application to obtain a dataset during runtime, for example, from a data layer, and "bind" it to a report. This is the design pattern that our dataset extension will follow.

Figure 13.4 depicts a typical integration scenario for requesting a report that uses the custom dataset extension.

The report consumer will typically obtain the dataset from the application data layer. Then, the report consumer will serialize the dataset to XML and request the report by passing the serialized dataset copy as a report parameter. Assuming that the report is configured to use the custom dataset extension, the Report Server will

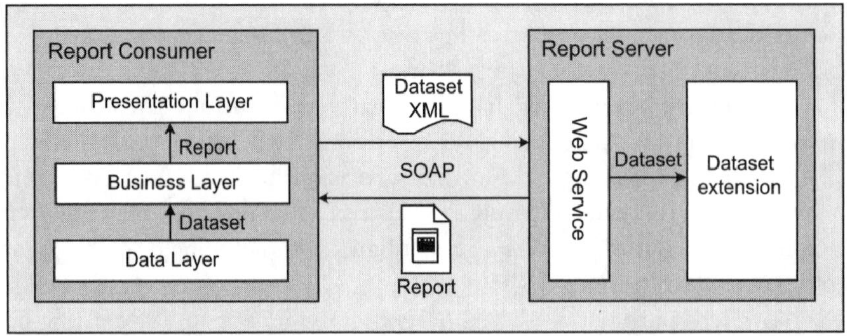

Figure 13.4 A report consumer can use a custom dataset extension to report off application datasets.

ask the extension to provide the report data. To do this, the extension reconstructs the dataset and exposes its data through a well-defined set of interfaces. During the report-processing phase, the report draws its data from the dataset. Finally, the generated report is sent back to the report consumer.

An alternative usage scenario could be reporting off datasets that are persisted as XML files. In such a case, the application is responsible for saving the dataset to a file and passing the file's location as a report parameter.

We break this section into four parts:

1 Identifying design goals and trade-offs
2 Authoring dataset-bound reports
3 Implementing the custom dataset extension
4 Debugging dataset extensions

Let's get started by focusing on what our design goals are and identify some of the trade-offs for this custom extension.

13.2.1 Identifying design goals and trade-offs

The high-level design goals for our custom dataset data extension are as follows:

- *The custom dataset extension should be integrated seamlessly with the RS data architecture*—From the report design point of view, the use of datasets should be transparent to the report's author.
- *Dataset table columns should be exposed as fields in the Report Designer to facilitate the familiar drag-and-drop technique for laying out the report*—For this reason, the custom dataset extension promotes the use of XML schemas and typed datasets during the report's design phase.
- *The dataset data extension should support reporting off an arbitrary table from a multitable dataset*—This will provide options and not limit the extension to using a dataset with only one table.
- *The dataset data extension should support reporting from serialized datasets, as well as datasets saved to XML files*—The latter option could be useful for reports with interactive features.

NOTE Adding interactive features to dataset-bound reports presents an unusual challenge. As we explained in chapter 10, these features rely on HTTP-GET, which cannot be used with large parameters. As a workaround, consider saving the dataset as an XML file and passing the file path as a report parameter.

Our implementation of the custom extension will be subject to the following trade-offs:

- *Performance overhead is incurred from serializing and marshaling the dataset between the application and the Report Server*—When a .NET dataset crosses the application's domain boundary, the .NET Framework automatically serializes it to XML. The dataset is subsequently deserialized into the receiving application's domain (the Report Server process).

- *Data relations are not supported*—An ADO.NET dataset can include several tables joined with data relations. Unfortunately, ADO.NET datasets currently don't support SQL-like `SELECT` statements to fetch data from joined tables. As a result, supporting queries from multiple tables linked with data relationships could become rather involved. If this is a definite requirement, you may try to extend the sample by implementing row filtering, for example, by using the `GetChildRows` method of the `DataRow` object. That said, note that the report's author can configure your extension and specify which table from a multitable dataset will be used for reporting.
- *Requesting a dataset-bound report via HTTP-GET is impractical*—Due to the query parameter's size limitation of the HTTP-GET protocol, the report consumer would typically use SOAP for passing the serialized dataset copy to the Report Server. If URL access is the preferred option, you have two choices. First, you could use HTTP-POST to pass the ADO.NET dataset. As we mentioned in chapter 10, HTTP-POST enjoys almost unlimited parameter length because the parameter name/value pairs are transferred in the request's HTTP header instead of in the form of a URL query string. The Report Picker code sample that we discussed in chapter 10 demonstrated how a web application can leverage HTTP-POST to request reports. Another option for getting around the HTTP-GET request limitations is to save the dataset to a file on the server side of the application and pass the file path as a report parameter.

Now, let's see how to use the custom dataset extension to report off application datasets. Inside the AWReporter BI project, you'll find the TestDS report that we'll use to demonstrate creating dataset-bound reports.

13.2.2 Authoring dataset-bound reports

Before using the custom dataset extension to create dataset-bound reports, you need to configure it properly. We included detailed setup instructions in the README file found under the `DataExtensions\Dataset` folder in the AWC.RS.Extensions project.

Once the extension is set up, you can follow the task map shown in table 13.1 to author a dataset-bound report.

As noted in the table, the first task for creating a dataset-bound report is to define the schema.

Table 13.1 **The task map for creating a dataset-bound report**

Phase	Task
Create the dataset schema.	Create a typed dataset. Alternatively, infer the schema from a persisted-to-file dataset.
Set up the report dataset.	Create a private data source. Set up the query parameters. Retrieve the dataset fields. Configure the `DataSource` report-level parameter.
Lay out the report.	Use the Report Designer's Layout tab to drag and drop dataset fields.
Test the report.	Use the Report Designer's Preview tab to test the report.
Deploy the report.	Use VS .NET or the Report Manager to deploy the report to the Report Server.
Request the report.	Request the report programmatically on demand via SOAP.

Creating the dataset schema

Although there's nothing stopping you from hardcoding the dataset field names inside report items, a better approach is to expose the dataset schema in the Report Designer. Once this is done, the report's author can drag and drop dataset fields to the report canvas, as she would do when working with extensions natively supported by RS.

With the custom dataset extension, you can expose the dataset schema in one of the following ways:

- *Create a typed dataset*—With VS .NET, you can create typed datasets easily. The end result is a file with the `.xsd` extension. The Test Harness application includes a typed dataset called `EntitySalesOrder.xsd`. It was created by using the SQL Data Adapter component found on the Data tab of the VS .NET toolbox.
- *Infer the schema from a persisted dataset*—The custom extension can be configured to infer the dataset schema from a dataset that has been saved to a file. For example, the Test Harness application includes the `DatasetSalesOrder.xml` file, which contains the XML presentation of a dataset. The file could include only the schema, only the data, or both the dataset schema and the data. The custom extension uses the `ReadXml` method of the dataset to load the dataset and infer its schema.

Now that we have the dataset schema, we are ready to author the dataset-bound report.

Setting the report dataset

Let's start by setting up a new private data source that points to the dataset schema file. Begin by creating a new report. Flip to the Report Designer Data tab and create a new dataset.

Creating a private data source

Start by adding a new report to your project. From the Data tab in the Report Designer choose New Dataset from the Dataset prompt. This opens the Dataset dialog box. On the Query tab, select New Data Source from the Data Source prompt. This will open the Data Source configuration window and allow you to create a new data source, as shown in figure 13.5.

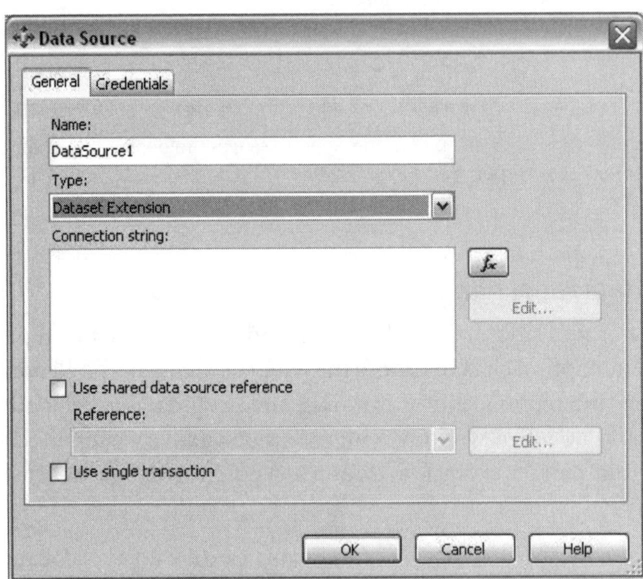

Figure 13.5 Use the dataset extension to set up the report's data source.

If the dataset extension is configured properly, it will be listed in the Type drop-down list. Set the data source type to Dataset Extension.

Leave the Connection String blank, because the dataset extension doesn't establish a database connection. Remember, the report's data will be encapsulated inside the dataset that will be passed as a report parameter. The Credentials tab is also not applicable in this case because the extension doesn't establish a database connection. To move past the Report Wizard validation, choose the Windows Authentication (Integrated Security) option on the Credentials tab.

Back in the Dataset dialog box, in the Query String text area of the Query tab, enter the name of the dataset table from which you want to report, as shown in figure 13.6.

> **NOTE** If the Dataset dialog box does not open as shown in figure 13.6, then click the ellipsis (...) button to the right of the DataSet selection drop-down list.

A dataset can have multiple tables. In case there is only one table or you want to default to the first table, you can enter **Nothing** as a query string. Initially, we were planning to default to the first table in case the query text was left blank, but the

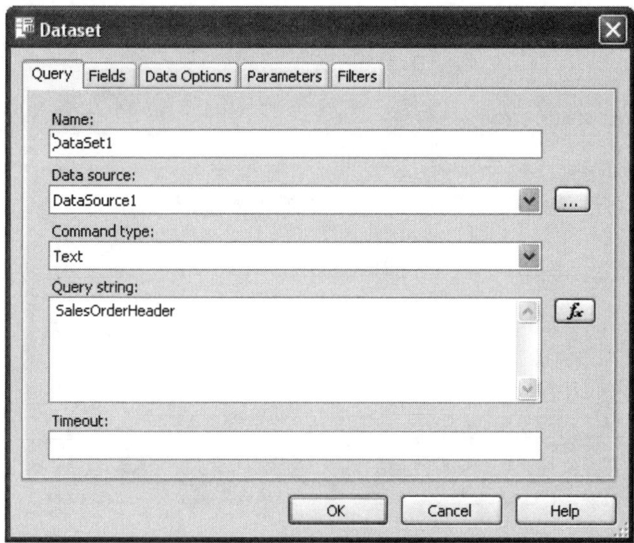

Figure 13.6
Set the query string to the dataset table used for reporting.

Report Designer insisted that we specify a query string. For the purposes of the TestDS report, enter **SalesOrderHeader** (or **Nothing**) as the query text because this is the name of the first (and only) dataset table.

Setting up the query parameters

Now, you're ready to set up the query parameters. Because the query string you just entered is not a valid SQL statement, you need to switch to the Generic Query Designer. Now, run the query by clicking the exclamation (!) button. The Generic Query Designer will ask the data extension to parse the query text and return a list of query parameters.

The custom dataset extension is wired to prompt for a parameter named `DataSource`. When designing the report, you need to set this parameter to the path pointing to the dataset schema file. During runtime, you will use this parameter to pass the serialized copy of the dataset or the path to the persisted dataset file.

As shown in figure 13.7, enter the full path to the `EntitySalesOrder.xsd` typed dataset file as a parameter value.

Retrieving the dataset fields

Now, click OK so that the data extension can parse the dataset schema and return the fields of the requested table, as shown in figure 13.8.

TIP You may wonder why the Generic Query Designer doesn't show any data after you click the ! button. The reason for this is that a typed dataset schema contains only the dataset's definition, not its data. However, if you use a dataset that has been saved to a file instead of only its schema, then the Generic Query Designer will show the table records in the query pane.

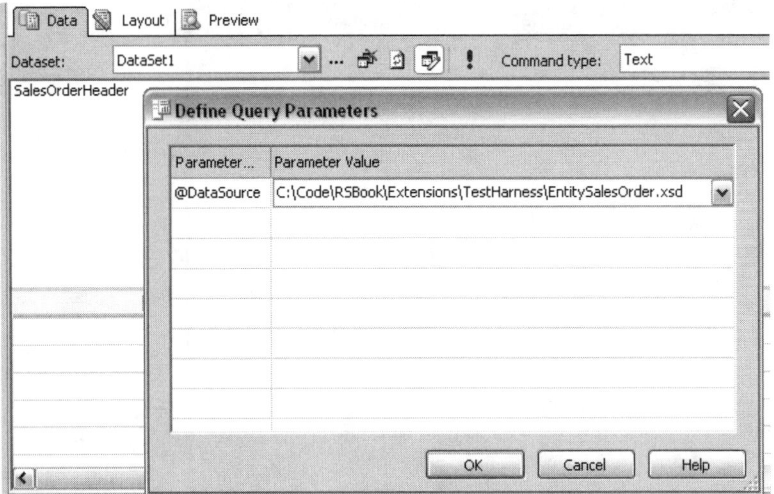

Figure 13.7 You set up the DataSource parameter by entering the file path to the dataset schema file

At this point, the Fields toolbar should show all table columns, as defined in the dataset schema. In addition, the Parameter tab of dataset properties should include the `DataSource` parameter.

Configuring the DataSource report-level parameter

Next, you need to verify that the `DataSource` parameter is linked to the `DataSource` report-level parameter, as shown in figure 13.9.

This is perhaps the most crucial step of the dataset-driven report-authoring process. As we noted earlier, during runtime the report consumer will pass the dataset as a report-level parameter. By linking the `DataSource` report-level parameter to its query counterpart, we ensure that the dataset will indeed be passed to the dataset extension. If your report needs more parameters, you can define them using the Report Parameters dialog box.

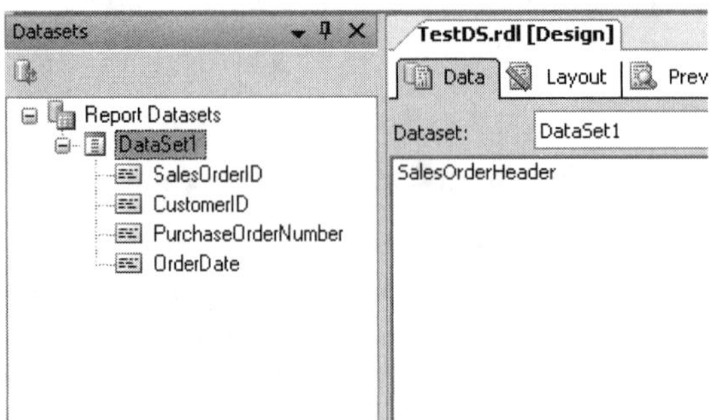

Figure 13.8 The dataset extension will parse the dataset schema and retrieve a list of table fields

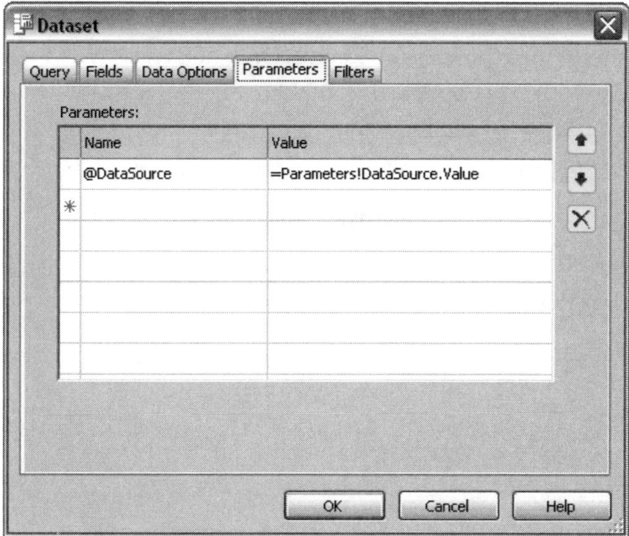

Figure 13.9 Verify that the DataSource parameter is linked to the DataSource report-level parameter.

Laying out the report

Now that the report dataset is set up, you can proceed to laying out the report itself using the familiar drag-and-drop approach. Switch to the Report Designer's Layout tab and lay out the report as you normally would. For example, figure 13.10 shows that we used a table region to create a tabular report. Then we dragged and dropped some dataset fields into the table region.

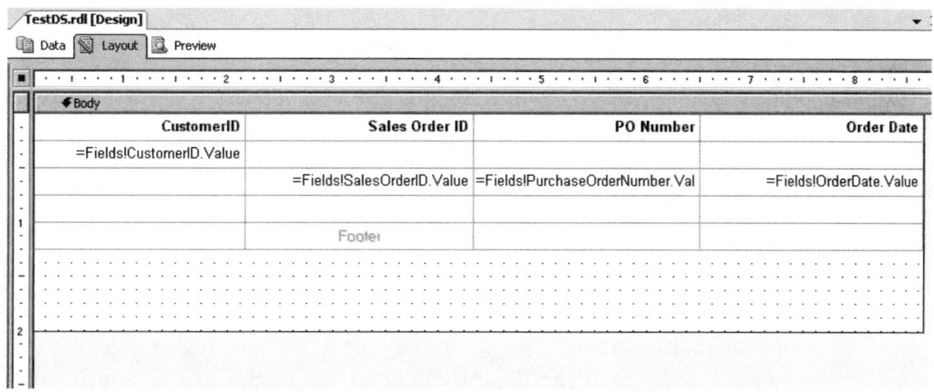

Figure 13.10 You can use the Report Designer's Layout tab to lay out the report.

Testing the report

To successfully preview the report in the Report Designer, you have to feed it data by setting the report's `DataSource` parameter. During design time, you may find it more convenient to use one of the following techniques:

- Copy and paste an XML snippet from the dataset's serialized copy.
- Specify the path to the dataset that was saved to disk.

For example, figure 13.11 shows that we used the first approach and entered the following XML string as the `DataSource` value:

```
 <SalesOrderHeader>
  <SalesOrderID>5001</SalesOrderID>
  <CustomerID>304</CustomerID>
  <PurchaseOrderNumber>PO29199294</PurchaseOrderNumber>
  <OrderDate>2003-09-01</OrderDate>
</SalesOrderHeader>
```

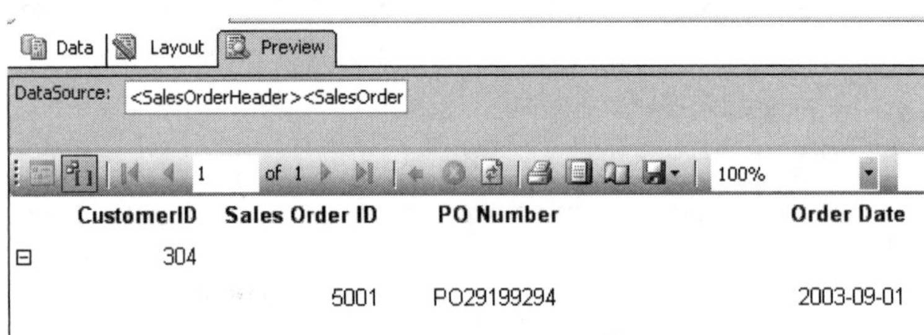

Figure 13.11 You can use an XML snippet as a report's data source during design time.

Once you have finished with the report, you can deploy it to the Report Server so that it is available for delivery.

Deploying the report

As you know by now, the easiest way to deploy the report (if you have Content Manager permissions to the Report Server repository) is to deploy it straight from the Visual Studio IDE by right-clicking the report file and choosing the Deploy command from the context menu.

Alternatively, you can deploy the report manually by uploading its report definition file using the Report Manager web application.

Requesting the report

When requesting a dataset-bound report, the client application must set the `DataSource` parameter as follows:

- If the report is accessed by SOAP, the application can pass the serialized dataset or the path to the dataset file (if the application has persisted the dataset beforehand).
- Due to the size limitations of the HTTP-GET query string, passing a large dataset as a query parameter is not possible. For this reason, this protocol will seldom be used to request dataset-bound reports. As noted before, if the URL method must be used, the report consumer can save the dataset to a file and pass the file path to the `DataSource` parameter. Otherwise, the report consumer can leverage HTTP-POST.

The implementation pattern that a client application will typically follow when requesting a dataset-bound report by SOAP is shown in listing 13.1.

Listing 13.1 Passing a dataset to Reporting Services

```
ReportingService2005 rs = new ReportingService2005();
// Set the Render method arguments
ParameterValue[] proxyParameters = new ParameterValue[1];   <-- 1 Creates a parameter placeholder

DataSet ds = new DataSet();   <-- 2 Gets the dataset
sqlDataAdapter.Fill(ds);
proxyParameters[0] = new ParameterValue();
proxyParameters[0].Name = "DataSource";
proxyParameters[0].Value = entitySalesOrder.GetXml();   <-- 3 Passes the dataset's serialized-to-XML copy
result = rs.Render(...);
```

First, you create at least one parameter placeholder ❶ for the `DataSource` parameter. In this case, the application uses a plain-vanilla dataset ❷. However, there's nothing stopping you from using typed datasets if your application's design supports them.

Next, the application serializes the dataset to XML and passes the serialized copy under the `DataSource` parameter ❸.

To facilitate the TestDS report testing, we enclose a simple WinForm-based client that takes the Report Server's URL and report path and uses similar code to request the report by SOAP.

Now that you've seen how to use the custom dataset extension to create dataset-bound reports, let's discuss its implementation.

13.2.3 Implementing the custom dataset extension

Armed with the `FsiDataExtension` source code (included with the RS samples) and the RS product documentation, you'll find the process of implementing the custom dataset extension straightforward.

Custom dataset extension types

Table 13.2 lists the types used to implement the custom dataset extension. At first, you may find dealing with so many interfaces mind-boggling. Your requirements may call for implementing many of these interface methods as simple passthroughs.

Table 13.2 Types used to implement the custom dataset extension

Type	Inherit from	Purpose	Implemented?
`DsConnectionWrapper`	`IDbConnection, IDbConnection-Extension, IExtension`	Responsible for establishing a database connection	No
`DsTransaction`	`IDbTransaction`	Enlists the database commands in the data source transaction	No
`DsCommand`	`IDbCommand, IDbCommandAnalysis`	Responsible for handling the report query string	Yes
`DsDataParameter`	`IDataParameter`	Represents a query parameter	Yes
`DsDataParameter-Collection`	`ArrayList, IDataParameter-Collection`	Holds a collection of query parameters	Yes
`DsDataReader`	`IDataReader`	Handles the access to the dataset data	Yes

Runtime conversation map

Figure 13.12 shows a simplified version of the conversation map between the Report Server and the custom extension during runtime. First, the Report Server instructs the dataset extension to establish a database connection by passing the connection string to it. Then, the Report Server asks the Connection object to return a reference of type `IDbCommand`.

Next, the Report Server calls the `IDbCommand.CreateParameter` method as many times as the number of parameters in the report query. The `Command` object responds by returning an object of type `IDataParameter` for each parameter.

NOTE The Report Server will pass only the query parameter to the data extension and not the report-level parameters. If a report-level parameter is not linked to the query parameter, it won't be passed. An important consequence of this rule is that you can't get a reference to the report-level parameters inside the dataset extension if they are not linked to the query parameters.

Because each parameter is of a common base type, the Report Server knows how to set it up. After the parameter is initialized, the Report Server invokes the `IData-ParameterCollection.Add` method so that you can append this parameter to the parameter collection. Once the parameters have been taken care of, the Report

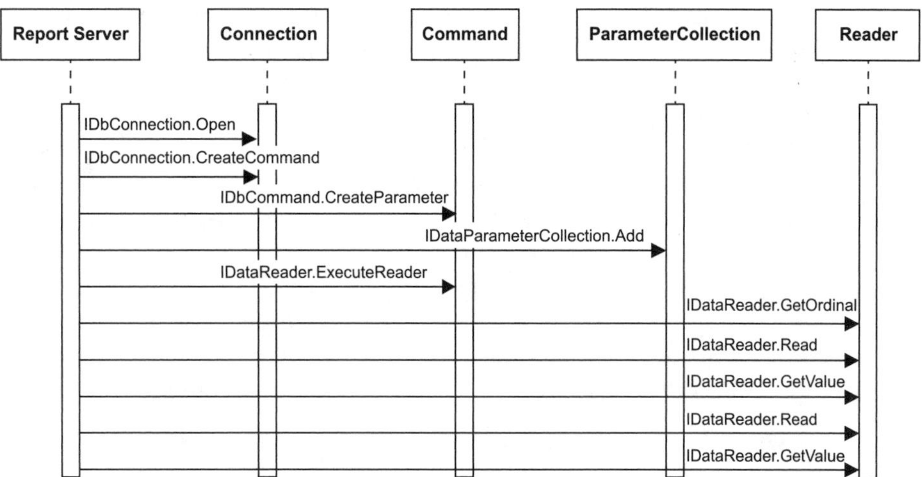

Figure 13.12 This is a sequence diagram of custom dataset extension processing. The Report Server calls the implemented interface methods to configure the extension and retrieve the data.

Server calls the `ExecuteReader` method of the `Command` object to get a reference to an object of type `IDataReader`.

For each report dataset field, the Report Server calls the `IDataReader.GetOrdinal` to get the positional index of each field in the reader's field collection. This is needed because later the Report Server will ask for the value of the field by its positional index. Once the fields are matched, the Report Server asks the reader repeatedly to advance to the next row of the rowset until the end of the rowset is reached. For each field, the Report Server calls the `IDataReader.GetValue` method to retrieve the field's value.

Now that we've discussed the high-level interaction between the Report Server and the extension, let's talk about some implementation sketches.

Implementing IDbConnection

You can relate the `IDbConnection` interface to the ADO.NET connection wrappers, for example, `SqlConnection`. The main purpose of this object is to establish a database connection to the data source, if this is needed. As noted earlier, in our case we have nothing to connect to because all data is either passed as a dataset during runtime or is retrieved from a dataset file.

If you do need to connect to a data source, you use the `IDbConnection.Open` method to establish a database connection. Prior to calling this method, the Report Server calls the `IDbConnectionExtension` public properties to pass the user's credentials that you set on the Data Source Credentials property. Strictly speaking, in our example, you didn't have to implement the `IDbConnectionExtension` interface at all, but we set up the example to do this so that you could see the sequence of events when you step through the extension code.

Implementing IDbCommand

The main tasks of the object that implements the `IDbCommand` interface are to populate the query parameters and to execute the report query, and then return a reference to a data reader object that allows the caller to process the results.

In this respect, you can relate the `IDbCommand` interface to the ADO.NET Command objects, such as `SqlCommand`. The Report Server passes the query text prior to executing the `ExecuteReader` method. In our example, the query text represents the name of the table off of which you want to report. Then, `ExecuteReader` instantiates the reader object and calls `LoadDataset` to retrieve the rowset.

Implementing IDataReader

This step is where the crux of the data retrieval and processing logic is. Similar to the ADO.NET `IDataReader`, an object that implements this interface is responsible for providing a means to read the rowset in a forward-only fashion. The bulk of the data retrieval and manipulation logic (exception handling excluded) is shown in listing 13.2.

Listing 13.2 Retrieving the rowset

```
internal void LoadDataset()   {
  string dataSource = null;
  DsDataParameter parameter = m_parameters.GetByName(Util.DATA_SOURCE)
                              as DsDataParameter;       <-- 1 Gets DataSource parameter
  dataSource = parameter.Value.ToString();
  m_dataset = GetDataSet(dataSource);
  if (m_cmdText.Trim().ToLower()=="nothing")          <-- 4 References requested table
    m_datatable = m_dataset.Tables[0];
  else {
    m_datatable = m_dataset.Tables[m_cmdText];
  }
  m_ie = m_datatable.Rows.GetEnumerator();         <-- 5 Sets up row enumerator
}
private DataSet GetDataSet(string dataSource)    {
  DataSet dataset = new DataSet();
  if (dataSource.IndexOf("<")>=0) {
    StringReader reader = new StringReader(dataSource);      <-- 2 Contains serialized copy of dataset
    dataset.ReadXml(reader);
  }
  else {
    FileIOPermission permission = new      <-- 3 Contains path to persisted-to-file dataset
    FileIOPermission(FileIOPermissionAccess.Read, dataSource);
    permission.Assert();
    dataset.ReadXml(dataSource);
  }
  return dataset;
}
```

First, you attempt to find a parameter named `DataSource` ❶. As you probably recall, the value passed to this parameter can be one of the following: the serialized-to-XML dataset copy or a file path to the persisted-to-file dataset. `GetDataSet` determines what the value of the `DataSource` represents by inspecting its payload. In the first case, you deserialize the dataset from its XML payload ❷. In the latter, you read the dataset's content from the file ❸. Note that you are specifically demanding a read permission to the physical file. Regardless of the fact that the code access policy of the dataset extension assembly is configured for Full Trust rights, Code Access Security (CAS) is layered on top of the OS security. For this reason, if you decide to use persisted datasets, make sure you grant the ASP.NET worker process identity at least read permissions to their files.

Once the dataset is successfully deserialized, you reference the table specified by the query text ❹. Finally, you save the row enumerator to a class-level variable ❺ to save its state between subsequent calls to `IDataReader.Read`.

13.2.4 Debugging dataset extensions

The easiest way to debug a custom dataset extension is to follow these steps:

Step 1 Add the custom dataset extension project to your Business Intelligence (BI) solution in VS .NET.

Step 2 Set the `StartItem` setting of your BI project to the name of the report that uses the extension.

Step 3 Set breakpoints in the data extension code.

Step 4 Run the report in Debug mode (press F5). Once you click the ViewReport button, your breakpoints should be hit.

As you'll probably agree, authoring custom data extensions is not that difficult. Once you get used to interface-based programming, you'll find writing different types of extensions similar. Let's now see how you can create custom delivery extensions.

13.3 DISTRIBUTING REPORTS TO WEB SERVICES USING CUSTOM DELIVERY EXTENSIONS

In chapter 10 we discussed how RS could be used in the B2B scenario. We talked about an Inventory Level report as a Web service that the Adventure Works Cycles (AWC) partners could use to request the report on demand. Instead of "pulling" the report, you'll now implement a mechanism that will allow AWC to "push" the report to the vendor's Web service on a regular basis through subscribed report delivery. Figure 13.13 depicts the high-level architectural view of this solution.

In this hypothetical scenario, the report's administrator could configure one or more reports for subscribed delivery to the vendor's Web service. As part of the subscription setup process, the report's administrator will specify the following Web service particulars:

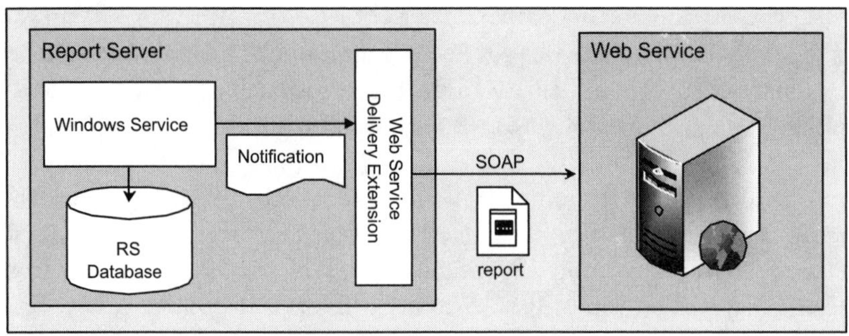

Figure 13.13 You can use a custom delivery extension to distribute reports to a Web service.

- The endpoint URL
- The Web service name (type name)
- The web method name responsible for receiving the report's payload

As figure 13.13 shows, once the subscription is triggered, the Report Server instantiates your extension and passes the notification object to it. Next, the custom delivery extension asks the Report Server to render the report and serializes the report's payload to an XML document. Finally, the custom extension dynamically invokes the Web service and passes the report's payload to the web method.

13.3.1 Design goals and trade-offs

The high-level design goals for your custom delivery extension are as follows:

- *The custom delivery extension should plug seamlessly into the presentation layer of the Report Manager*—To accomplish this requirement, the extension implements an intuitive user interface to help the end user configure the extension.
- *The custom delivery extension must validate the user's input on the client and server sides*—This will allow this extension to work from both web forms and from custom applications.
- *The custom delivery extension should support dynamic binding to the Web service by constructing the web service proxy during runtime*—This will allow the extension to send the report to an arbitrary Web service.

Your implementation of the custom delivery extension will be subject to the following trade-offs:

- *The custom extension will pass the report's payload (exported as XML) to the first argument of the web method*—Therefore, the target web method must be parameterized, and the first argument must be a string data type. Enhancing the custom delivery extension to fit your specific Web service requirements should be simple.

- *Currently, the extension doesn't provide a user interface for configuring the export format; it renders the report as XML before passing it to the Web service*—Enhancing the custom delivery extension to let the user choose the export format should be easy. For example, as with the e-mail and file share extensions, the custom extension web control could include a drop-down list that is populated with the results from a call to the `ListExtensions` SOAP API, as you saw in chapter 10.

Now that you have a high-level understanding of what the custom delivery extension does, let's see how to put it into action.

13.3.2 Using the custom delivery extension

Before using the custom delivery extension to distribute reports to Web services, you need to configure it properly. We included detailed setup instructions in the README file found under the `DeliveryExtensions\WebService` folder in the AWC.RS.Extensions project.

Once the custom delivery extension is configured, you can use the Report Manager to create a report subscription that uses the extension. We've already shown how to do this in chapter 12, so we'll discuss only the custom delivery extension specifics.

After you've decided on the subscription type, either a standard or data-driven subscription, you choose a delivery extension, as shown in figure 13.14.

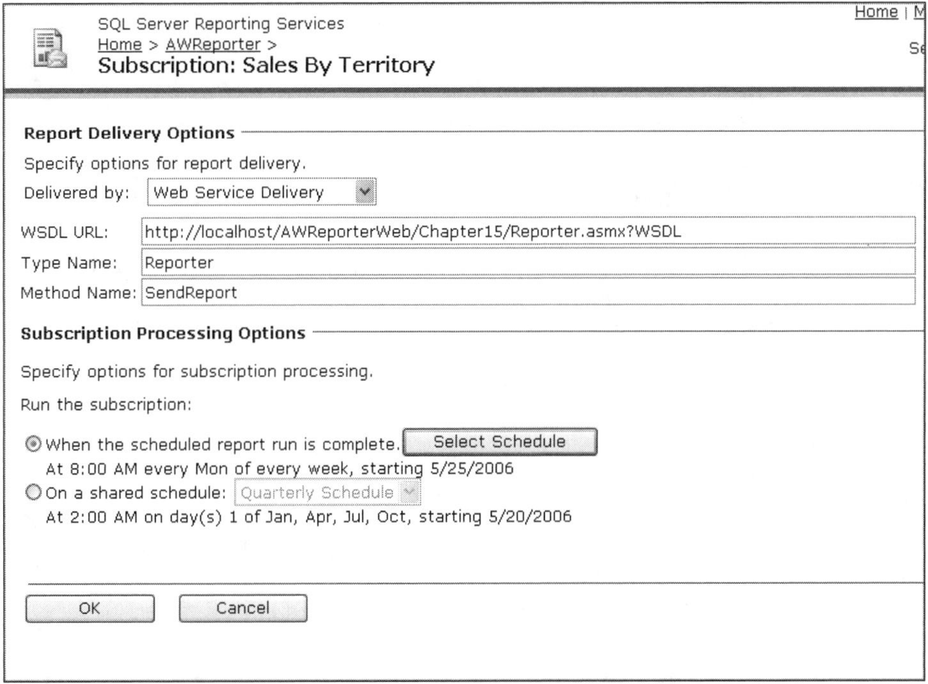

Figure 13.14 To use the custom Web service delivery extension, select it from the Delivered By drop-down list in the Report Manager UI.

If the custom delivery extension is registered properly, it will appear in the Delivered By drop-down as Web Service Delivery. In case you are wondering where this name comes from, it is returned by our implementation of the `IExtension.LocalizedName` property inside the extension's source code. As its names suggests, this property lets the developer localize the extension name based on the user's language settings.

The user interface of the custom delivery extension consists of three text placeholders for the Web service description language URL, its type, and its method name. The default settings are retrieved from the `RSReportServer.config` configuration file but can be overwritten by the user.

13.3.3 Implementing the custom delivery extension

To understand how the custom Web service extension works, it may be beneficial to break its functionality into two stages:

- Design time, when the extension is hosted in the Report Manager and used for setting up the subscription
- Runtime, when the Report Server asks the extension to deliver the report

To mirror the above stages, we've separated the extension logic into two source files: `WebServiceDeliveryUIControl`, which encapsulates the extension UI, and `WebServiceDeliveryProvider`, which hosts the runtime functionality.

Implementing the user interface

The Report Manager will ask your extension to render itself as a part of the subscription setup process. From an implementation standpoint, this requires writing a custom web control that is implemented in the `WebServiceDeliveryUIControl` class.

This control implements the `ISubscriptionBaseUIUserControl` interface, which in turn inherits from `IExtension`. Figure 13.15 shows a simplified version of the conversation map between the Report Manager and the custom delivery extension during design time.

When the Web service delivery extension is selected on the Subscription setup page, the Report Manager instantiates the WebServiceDeliveryUIControl web control and calls the `IExtension.SetConfiguration` method first. When you register a custom delivery extension, you can optionally specify configuration settings in both the Report Server and Report Manager configuration files. As noted earlier, you use the Report Server settings to specify the default Web service specifics. You can also use the Report Manager's configuration file to define any UI-related settings. In our example, the custom delivery extension doesn't need any UI-specific settings. For this reason, the `SetConfiguration` call passes an empty string.

Next, the Report Manager sites the control that invokes the control's `Init` method. At this point, the web control is supposed to render itself. This boils down to creating three textbox controls and some validation controls to validate the user-entered values on the client side. Because the web control has access to all of the

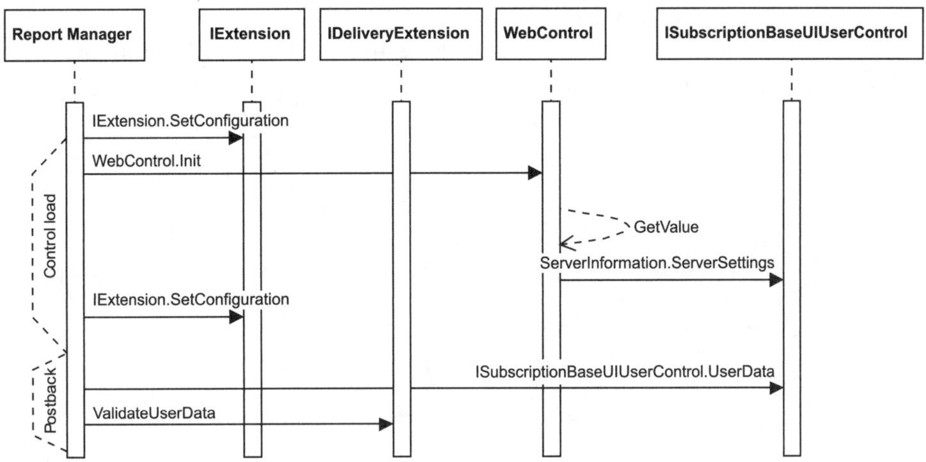

Figure 13.15 This diagram shows the conversation map between the Report Manager and the custom delivery extension.

ASP.NET functionality, you can use any ASP.NET-compatible control for the user interface. For example, if you decide to expand the extension to allow the user to specify the report's format, you can use a drop-down control that contains the supported export formats.

Each control gets its default value by calling the `GetValue` private member. To retrieve the configuration settings defined in `RSReportServer.config`, `GetValue` accesses the `ISubscriptionBaseUIUserControl.ReportServerInformation.ServerSettings`. This call triggers the invocation of `IExtension.SetConfiguration` by the Report Manager to pass the server-side configuration settings in XML. The `ServerSide` property exposes them as an array of `Settings` objects. The code iterates through this array to find the setting that corresponds to the textbox. At this point, the web control is rendered on the screen.

Once the user posts the page back to the server, the Report Manager calls the `ISubscriptionBaseUIUserControl.UserData` property to pass the user-entered values. Finally, the Report Manager calls `IDeliveryExtension.ValidateUserData` to give the control a chance to inspect the user-entered values and throws an exception if they are not valid.

If everything is fine, the Report Manager calls to the Report Server Web service API to persist the subscription configuration in the Report Server database.

Implementing the runtime functionality

The runtime interaction is much simpler. When the subscription is triggered, the Report Server first calls `IExtension.SetConfiguration` to pass the user-entered extension-specific values. Then, the Report Server prepares a notification object and invokes the `Deliver` method.

In the case of a data-driven subscription, the Report Server invokes `IDeliveryExtension.Deliver` for each recipient. The notification object encapsulates everything the extension needs to deliver the reports and notifies the Report Server about the delivery status.

First, the code retrieves the user-entered values from the `Notification.UserData` property. Then, it calls the `DeliverReport` method, which is where the bulk of the custom delivery logic resides, as shown in listing 13.3.

Listing 13.3 Implementing the report delivery

```
private void DeliverReport(Notification notification,
               SubscriptionData data) {
  StringWriter stringWriter = null;
  m_files = notification.Report.Render("XML", @"<DeviceInfo/>");   <-- ❶ Renders the report

  if (m_files[0].Data.Length > 0) {
   byte[] reportPayload = new byte[m_files[0].Data.Length];   <-- ❷ Gets the first stream
   m_files[0].Data.Position = 0;
   m_files[0].Data.Read(reportPayload, 0, reportPayload.Length);
   m_files[0].Data.Flush();
   string payload = Convert.ToBase64String(reportPayload);
   StringBuilder stringBuilder = new StringBuilder();
   stringWriter = new StringWriter(stringBuilder);
   XmlTextWriter writer = new XmlTextWriter(stringWriter);
   writer.Formatting = Formatting.Indented;
   writer.WriteStartElement("Report");
   writer.WriteElementString("ReportPayload", payload);
   writer.WriteEndElement();
                                                      ❸ Processes the report's payload
   DynamicWebServiceProxy ws = new DynamicWebServiceProxy();
   ws.WSDL = data.WSDL;
   ws.TypeName = data.typeName;
   ws.MethodName = data.methodName;
   ws.AddParameter(stringBuilder.ToString());
   string result = ws.InvokeCall() as string;
                                                      ❹ Sends payload to the Web service
   if (result==null) throw new Exception(...);
  }

  notification.Status=String.Format("Report delivered to {0}",
                  data.WSDL);   <-- Notifies the Report Server status
 }
```

First, the code instructs the Report Server to render the report in XML ❶. As listing 13.3 shows, rendering the report is as simple as calling the `Notification.Report.Render` method. It really can't be simpler!

Once the report is rendered, its payload is exposed as one or more streams ❷. As we noted in chapter 12, if you request the report in one of the HTML multistream rendering formats (all HTML formats except MHTML), the first stream will include the report's payload, while the subsequent streams will include the report's images. Single-stream rendering formats will always produce only one stream with the images embedded in it. Because you are rendering the report in XML, you can get the entire report results from the first stream.

Next, you create a simple XML document to contain the Base64-encoded version of the report's payload ❸, so that it can be sent over the Web to the target Web service.

Finally, you send the XML payload to the target Web service ❹.

Delivering the report to a Web service

Now for the fun part! As we've mentioned, our custom delivery extension supports sending the report's payload to an arbitrary Web service. This presents an implementation challenge, though. Because the Web service's endpoint is not known until runtime, you cannot "early bind" to it by establishing a web reference. Instead, you need to generate the Web service proxy dynamically.

How should you go about implementing this? Before I decided to write my own dynamic Web service invocation using `CodeDom`, it dawned on me that someone else might have already done this. Indeed, a quick Google search confirmed my hypothesis.

It turned out that there is already a great Dynamic Web Service invocation library, `DynWSLib`, written by Christian Weyer (see the "Resources" section at the end of this book). As the author says, "Given the URL to the Web Service WSDL file, the type and method name, `DynWSLib` uses `CodeDom` to generate the proxy. For better performance, `DynWSLib` caches the generated proxy library as a file in the system temp folder." A quick `DynWSLib` test convinced me that this is exactly what I needed to dynamically invoke an arbitrary web method.

As you can see in listing 13.3, you instantiate `DynWSLib` and pass the user-entered WSDL URL, type, and method name. Next, you pass the report's payload as a parameter to the proxy. Finally, you invoke the web method. Under the `Chapter13` folder in the AWReporterWeb project, you'll find a simple Web service, `Reporter.asmx`, which the default extension configuration settings point to. It simply gets the report's payload and outputs it using `Trace.WriteLine`.

Note that you won't get far testing the custom extension if you don't adjust the code access security policy for both the `AWC.RS.Extensions` and `DynWS-Library` assemblies to full trust. In addition, you need to grant Full Trust rights to the cached Web service proxy library. This presents a challenge because `DynWSLib` generates a unique name for the temporary file for each Web service. You must grant Full Trust rights to all assemblies in that folder, as the setup instructions for the custom delivery extension explain.

NOTE For some obscure reason that I wasn't able to figure out, the system `Temp` folder appears to be treated differently by the RS code access security policy.

Despite the fact that I assigned Full Trust rights to folder and its contents (by using the * wildcard), I wasn't able to get past code access security. I was getting a target invocation exception. Strangely, switching to another folder seemed to keep the CAS gods happy. Therefore, as a workaround, you may want to change the `DynWSLib` source code to save the temporary file to another folder, for example, `C:\Temp`. Let me know if you find a way to get CAS working with the system `Temp` folder.

13.3.4 Debugging custom delivery extensions

Debugging a custom delivery extension is tricky because it isn't loaded when the report is generated, so using the dataset extension debugging approach won't work. Because a custom delivery extension could be invoked from both the Report Manager and the Report Server Windows service, the debug instructions vary.

Design time debugging

During design time, the Report Manager process invokes the custom extension. To be able to debug your custom extension, start the Report Manager and manually attach to its process from the Debug > Attach to Process menu in VS .NET, as shown in figure 13.16.

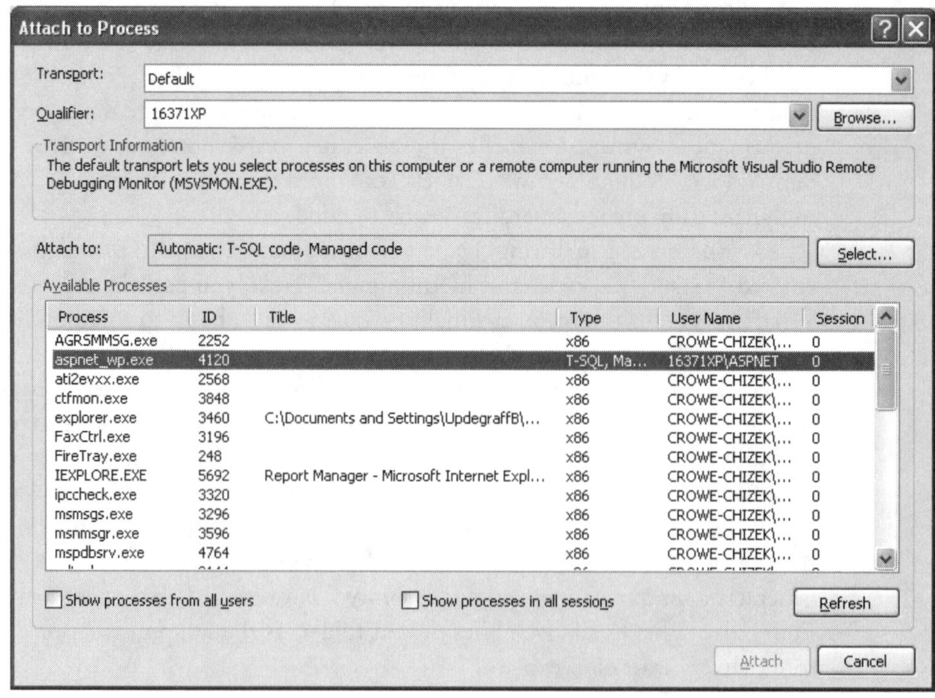

Figure 13.16 To debug your custom extension during design time, attach to the Report Manager process.

In our example, we used Windows XP as the operating system, so we attached to the `aspnet_wp.exe` worker process (if you are using Windows 2000, use the same process). If you use Windows 2003, you'll need to attach to the IIS worker process, `w3wp.exe`. Finally, to step through the extension code, create a new subscription in the Report Manager that uses your extension, or edit an existing one. At this point, your breakpoints should be hit.

Runtime debugging

To debug a custom delivery extension during runtime, for instance, when the subscription is triggered by a schedule, follow the design time debugging steps shown previously, but this time attach to the Report Server's Windows Service process (`ReportingServicesService.exe`), as shown in figure 13.17.

This should come as no surprise to you, if you recall that it is the Report Server's Windows service that monitors the report catalog for the event's occurrence and initiates the subscribed report delivery. For this reason, the delivery extension is loaded during runtime in the `ReportingServicesService.exe` process.

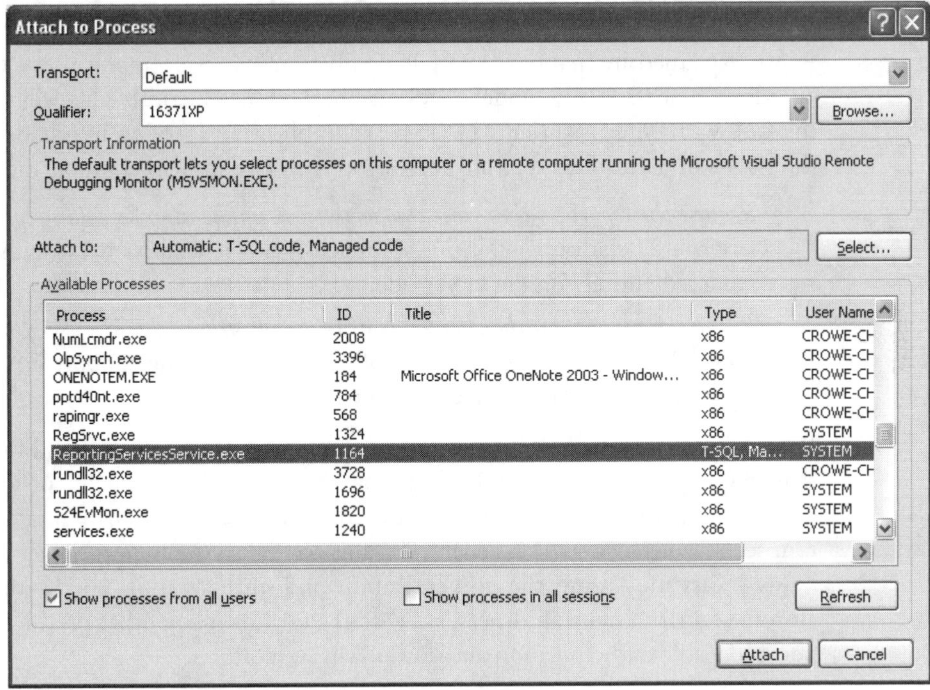

Figure 13.17 To debug a custom delivery extension during runtime, attach to the ReportingServicesService.exe Windows Service process.

TIP I've found that the easiest way to trigger the subscription execution for debugging purposes is to base the subscription on a schedule that's configured to run once. To use this approach, stop the `ReportingServicesService.exe` Windows service and wait until the event record is inserted into the `Event` table in the Report Server database. Then, start the Windows service and attach your extension to its process, as explained previously. To trigger the subscription's execution, paste the event record in the `Event` table. The next time the Windows service polls this table, it will pick up the event and run your extension.

There is an issue associated with debugging custom delivery extensions in successfully calling the `Notification.Render` method to render the report. To do this you need to be logged in to your login domain controller. If you are logged in using a disconnected session, the call results in the following exception:

```
Report Server has encountered a configuration error;
more details in the log files, AuthzInitializeContextFromSid:
Win32 error: 1053
```

13.4 IMPLEMENTING CUSTOM SECURITY

As we explained in chapters 9 and 10, with some types of applications, the default Windows-based security model of RS may become impractical. This will typically be the case with Internet-oriented web-based applications serving hundreds and often thousands of users. This typically leaves you with two implementation choices:

- *Request the report on the server-side of the web application by calling to the RS Web service*—The advantage of this approach is better security because the report is rendered entirely on the server side.
- *Request the report on the client-side of the application by URL*—As you know by now, URL access offers a number of benefits, including support for all interactive features, the HTML Viewer toolbar, and so forth.

Requesting reports by URL with Internet-oriented applications almost always requires that you replace the default RS Windows-based security model. Fortunately, the extensible RS architecture allows you to replace the default security model with custom security extensions. This enables you to configure the Report Server for Anonymous access and route the authentication and authorization checks through the custom security extension. I personally don't know of many other products that support pluggable authentication and authorization modules.

TIP If you haven't done this already, before going any further, read the "Using Forms Authentication in Reporting Services" white paper listed in the resources at the end of this book. This article, as well as the accompanying code sample, will give you the essential knowledge that every developer must have before implementing custom security extensions with RS.

Using custom security with Internet-oriented applications can be a good option for these reasons:

- *The application can request reports by URL on the client side by directly accessing the Report Server*—For example, a web page can include a View My Reports hyperlink with the URL address of the report.
- *The Report Server can discriminate among web users*—For example, an online hotel portal can assign users to Silver, Gold, and Platinum roles and give users different levels of access based on their user membership. In this respect, custom security is no different than the default Windows-based security model.

Figure 13.18 depicts how your applications can leverage a custom security extension to implement your own authentication and authorization rules.

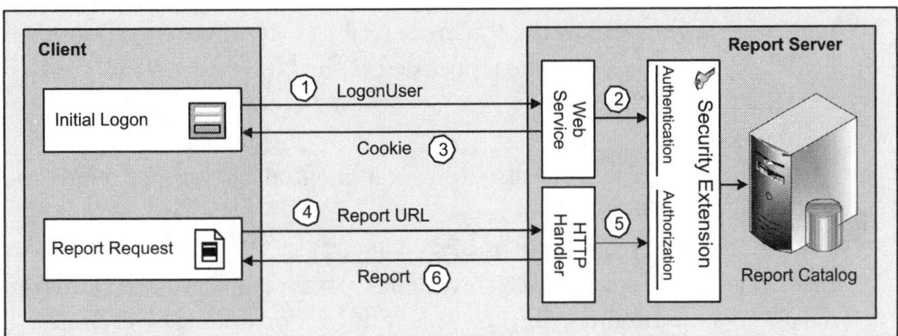

Figure 13.18 You can use a security extension for custom authentication and authorization.

Although the RS custom security architecture is most suitable for and works best with web-based applications, any type of application can take advantage of it, including WinForm clients and Web services.

NOTE Bending the custom security model to work with non-web clients boils down to writing additional code for storing the session cookie returned by the `LogonUser` method and sending it back with each request to the Report Server. This requires that you overwrite the RS Web service proxy. For more information, check the LogonUser documentation.

.NET developers familiar with the ASP.NET Forms Authentication will probably find the RS custom security model to be familiar. Here is the sequence flow (shown in figure 13.18) between the client and the Report Server, configured to use a custom security extension:

The client application displays a login form to prompt the user for credentials, such as the username and password. In the case of ASP.NET applications, Forms Authentication can be used to redirect the user to the login form automatically. Once the user's credentials are collected, the application invokes ① the `LogonUser` RS web method to log the user on to RS. For example, a web application that leverages Forms Authentication can call the `LogonUser` SOAP API once the user is authenticated in the logon page.

Next, the Report Server asks ② the custom security extension to authenticate the user. How the custom security extension does this is of no concern to the Report Server. Typically, with a large number of users, a database store will be used to store the user's profile and credentials.

If the user is successfully authenticated, the `LogonUser` method returns ③ a ticket in the form of a session cookie, which the Report Server expects to find in subsequent calls from the client. When a browser is used as a client, the session cookie will be automatically passed back when a URL request is made to render a report. When other types of clients are used, you need to take an extra step to pass the cookie explicitly with the call to the Report Server.

The client submits ④ the report request by URL to the Report Server.

The Report Server asks ⑤ the custom security extension to authorize the user request.

If the request is successfully authorized, the Report Server generates the report and sends ⑥ it back to the client.

Although the sequence depicted in figure 13.18 specifically refers to requesting reports, any type of action against the report catalog is subject to custom authorization checks. For example, if the client is the Report Manager, each time the user initiates a new action from the portal, the Report Server calls the custom authentication to authorize it.

NOTE Before you jump onto the custom security bandwagon, carefully evaluate the implications of doing so, including the following:

- *RS doesn't support a mixed-security mode*—As a consequence, once you switch to custom security, you won't be able to use Windows-based security anymore, even for administrator access to the Report Server.
- *You may need to implement features that you take for granted when Windows authentication is used*—For example, if you need to assign users to groups for easier maintenance, you will have to roll off your own group membership infrastructure. You may consider using the Microsoft Authorization Manager when your requirements call for a more involved application security model.
- *Because the report consumers will access the Report Server directly, you may need to secure the connection to the Report Server using SSL*—This is especially important for Internet-oriented applications. If you don't, a hacker may sniff the network traffic and intercept the login credentials.
- *Configuring RS for custom security is an involved process that requires a number of steps to set up the Report Server and Report Manager*—Going

back to Windows-based security and "undoing" all steps could be quite a hassle, so make sure that you know what you're getting yourself into.

Because in most cases the main purpose of using custom security is to allow reports to be requested by URL, you may have to take extra steps to protect the data. For example, you will need to ensure that a customer can see only her order history data by filtering the orders at the data source.

There may be other trade-offs applicable to your particular situation.

Now that you've seen at a high level how custom security works, let's examine its implementation details.

13.4.1 Design goals and trade-offs

Here is our hypothetical scenario. AWC wants to implement a report that lets web-based customers log in and view their order history. You've created a report called Customer Orders Custom Auth. To ensure secure access to the Report Server, you use a custom security extension to authenticate and authorize the report requests. Here are the high-level requirements for this solution:

- Allow customers to access reports by URL.
- Enforce restricted access to the Report Server by implementing a custom security extension.
- Authenticate users against a user profile store. In this case, the profile store will be represented by the `Individuals` table in the AdventureWorks database.
- Implement horizontal data filtering at the data source based on the user's identity to ensure that a customer can see only her own orders.
- Implement the necessary infrastructure to provide administrator-level access to the Report Server using a designated admin account.
- Support assigning customers to groups for easier maintenance. Creating role-based security policies for hundreds and thousands of web customers is impractical. Instead, a better approach is to assign customers to groups; for example, Individual or Store groups, to reflect the existing customer types in the AdventureWorks database.

The implementation will be subject to the following trade-offs:

- *To keep the solution as lightweight as possible, you won't require the customer to enter a password*—Needless to say, in real life, you should provide authentication that's as robust as possible. The Microsoft custom security sample shows you some practical techniques for using strong passwords. Once again, consider using SSL to secure the connection to the Report Server.
- *For the sake of simplicity, you won't provide the database infrastructure needed to support organizing customers in groups*—Instead, you will use the customer's identifier as a username and a hardcoded group name called Individual. During

the authorization stage, you check the name and, if it is a valid number, you assume that the customer belongs to the Individual group. In real life, your authorization logic typically makes a database call to determine the level of access the user has based on his group membership.

- *Unlike with the Microsoft custom security sample, you won't be implementing a login form to log the user into the Report Server in case the session has expired or the user has bypassed the application authentication*—Having too many login screens might be confusing for the user and could present a security risk. Instead, this design pattern promotes a single logon to both the application and the Report Server, which will be the responsibility of the application. In cases where the user requests an RS resource without being authenticated or the RS cookie session has expired, you display an error page and prompt the user to log in again to the web application.

Now, let's see how this solution works from an end-user perspective.

13.4.2 Intranet reporting with custom security

Let's assume that AWC customers have been already registered and their profile data is captured in the `Individual` table. The first step that you as the report administrator need to take is to grant the users access to view the appropriate reports.

Setting up role-based security policies

This step should look familiar to you. You use the Report Manager portal to create role-based security policies for AWC customers. In real life, the Report Manager portal won't be configured for Internet access, and only a few privileged users are assigned as administrators. Ideally, you should be able to configure the Report Manager with Windows-based security for user authentication, while the Report Server could be configured with custom security.

However, as we've mentioned, currently RS doesn't support a mixed security model. For this reason, once we switch to custom security, we need to take care of authenticating the user's access to the Report Manager, as well as the Report Server. Therefore, once the user accesses the Report Manager, the authentication screen shown in figure 13.19 is displayed.

Report Manager Login

User ID: rstester

Logon

Figure 13.19 The authentication screen enforces secured access to the Report Manager portal

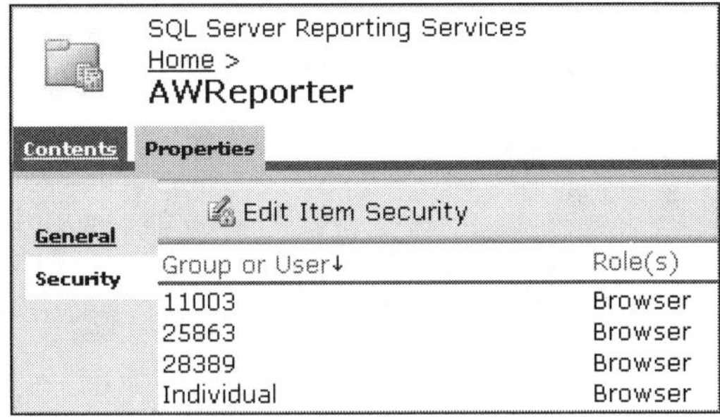

Figure 13.20
You can set up the security policies for your non-Active Directory users and groups with the Report Manager.

If you have followed the setup instructions (`readme.htm`) in the source code folder, there will be a predefined admin account, rstester, which you can use to log into the Report Manager portal.

Next, you must grant rights to those web customers who will be able to access the Customer Orders Custom Auth report. The custom security extension supports creating role-based security policies using individual and group accounts. For the purposes of this demo, let's grant Browser role rights for the Home and AWReporter folders to the accounts shown in figure 13.20.

In figure 13.20 we've created one group-based security policy (the Individual group) and three individual security policies that correspond to three of the customer identifiers created by the `Recipients.sql` script (see the README file for setup instructions). The Individual-based security policies are for demonstration only. Even if you don't set them up, all customers listed in the `Individual` table will be authenticated successfully because they belong to the Individual group. When creating a new security policy, the Report Server asks the custom security extension to validate the user, so make sure that the customer identifiers you use exist in the `Individual` table.

Requesting reports

Once the security policies have been set up, customers can request reports using the AWReporterWeb web application by navigating to the default page. To simulate this, expand the client-side Reporting menu and choose Custom Security. If the application is set up correctly to use Forms Authentication, at this point you should see the Adventure Works Portal Login form, as shown in figure 13.21.

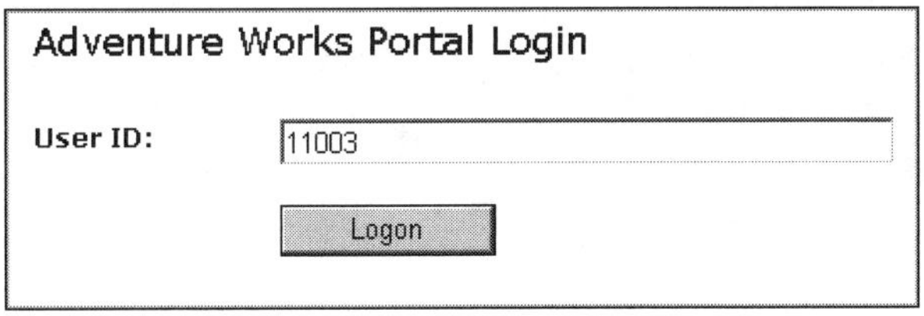

Figure 13.21
To request a report, the customer has to be authenticated by the application.

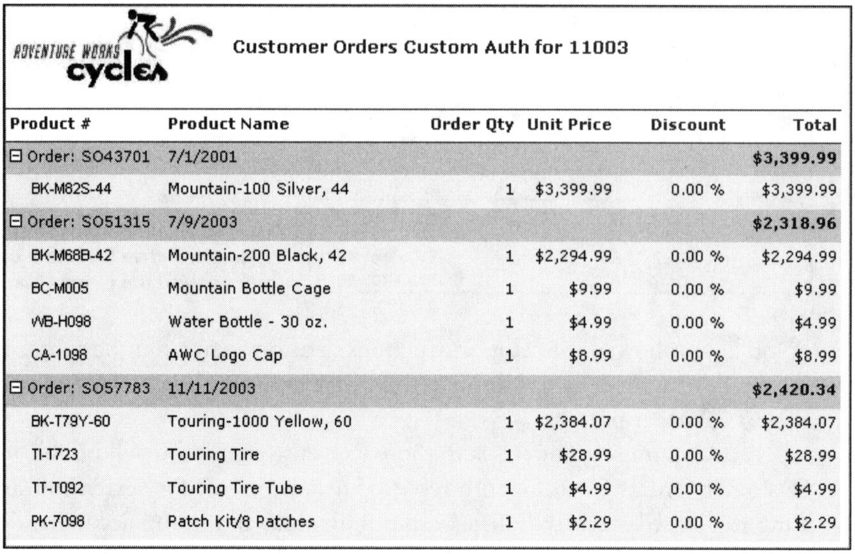

ADVENTURE WORKS cycles — Customer Orders Custom Auth for 11003

Product #	Product Name	Order Qty	Unit Price	Discount	Total
⊟ Order: SO43701	7/1/2001				**$3,399.99**
BK-M82S-44	Mountain-100 Silver, 44	1	$3,399.99	0.00 %	$3,399.99
⊟ Order: SO51315	7/9/2003				**$2,318.96**
BK-M68B-42	Mountain-200 Black, 42	1	$2,294.99	0.00 %	$2,294.99
BC-M005	Mountain Bottle Cage	1	$9.99	0.00 %	$9.99
WB-H098	Water Bottle - 30 oz.	1	$4.99	0.00 %	$4.99
CA-1098	AWC Logo Cap	1	$8.99	0.00 %	$8.99
⊟ Order: SO57783	11/11/2003				**$2,420.34**
BK-T79Y-60	Touring-1000 Yellow, 60	1	$2,384.07	0.00 %	$2,384.07
TI-T723	Touring Tire	1	$28.99	0.00 %	$28.99
TT-T092	Touring Tire Tube	1	$4.99	0.00 %	$4.99
PK-7098	Patch Kit/8 Patches	1	$2.29	0.00 %	$2.29

Figure 13.22 With custom security, web users can request reports by URL.

The Custom Security menu points to the MyOrders page located under the Chapter13 folder. Because this page is defined in the application's configuration file as secured, the ASP.NET Forms Authentication security framework automatically navigates to the designated login page, `Login.aspx`. Once the customer posts to the page, it calls the `LogonUser` method to pass the customer's credentials to the Report Server.

Next, the MyOrders page is displayed. This page features a URL link to the Customer Orders Custom Auth report. Using the link, the user can see his order history by requesting the report by URL, as shown in figure 13.22.

This report filters the data based on the identity of the authenticated user. In our case, we set the user's identity to match the customer's identifier. In this way, we enforce at the data source the security-related business rule that customers can see only their own orders.

Having seen how this demo works, let's delve into the technical details to find out how it is implemented.

13.4.3 Implementing the custom security extension

You can find the custom security extension code under the `SecurityExtensions` folder in the AWC.RS.Extensions project. Detailed setup instructions can be found in the README file located in this folder. Because setting up the custom extension requires changing almost all configuration files, we copied our version of the Report Server and Report Manager configuration files to the `ConfigurationFiles/CustomSecurity` folder.

The custom security extension was built on the Microsoft sample extension. Once again, read the white paper if you feel that you need more background information.

Custom security extension types

Table 13.3 lists the most significant security extension components and their purpose.

Table 13.3 Security extension components

Source file	Inherit from	Purpose
`AuthenticationExtension`	`IAuthentication-Extension`	Include custom authentication implementation
`Authorization`	`IAuthorization-Extension`	Include custom authorization implementation
Logon page	`System.Web.UI.Page`	The login page for authenticating the user if direct browsing of the report catalog is permitted. Our implementation simply returns an error message.
UILogon page	`System.Web.UI.Page`	The login page for authenticating the user for access to the Report Manager

Our custom authentication logic is encapsulated in the `Authentication-Extension` class, which implements the `IAuthenticationExtension` interface. It includes code for validating the user against the user profile's database store.

The `Authorization` class implements the `IAuthorizationExtension` interface. Its main task is to authorize the user's actions against the predefined role-based security policy. The `Authorization` class includes several overloaded versions of `CheckAccess` that will be called by the Report Server. Which version of `CheckAccess` will be called depends on the type of action attempted.

Why do we need two login pages? The UILogon page is meant to authenticate the user when the user tries to access the Report Manager portal, as shown in figure 13.19. The second login screen, Logon, is used to authenticate the user when she tries to browse the report catalog. As we've said, in this example, you don't allow bypassing the application's authentication and hitting the Report Server directly, so the implementation of this page is very simple. It prompts the user to log in again by clicking a hyperlink that will bring her to the application's login screen.

Let's now see how the custom security extension works by looking at the processes of authentication and authorization in detail.

Runtime conversation map

As we explained in chapter 9, when implementing custom security models, you need to differentiate between the processes of authentication and authorization. During the authentication phase, you determine the identity of the user, while the authorization phase is concerned with verifying the user's rights to the requested resource. Figure 13.23 shows the simplified sequence of events for both phases.

As figure 13.23 depicts, authentication must take place before the request is authorized. After a successful authentication handshake, the Report Server sends the

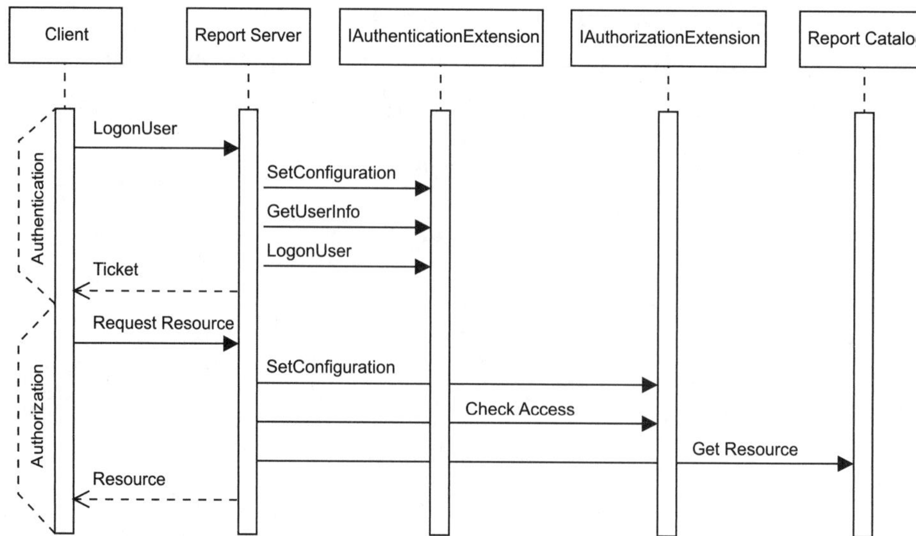

Figure 13.23 As this map shows, authentication must take place before the request is authorized.

application a ticket in the form of a session cookie. The Report Server automatically checks this cookie during subsequent requests to the Report Server catalog. If the cookie is not found or it is invalidated, the Report Server displays the Logon page.

NOTE Although you can use the same settings in the Report Server `web.config` file to configure the cookie (name, expiration, and so on) as you would when using ASP.NET Forms Authentication, the two cookies are not compatible. In other words, if you have a web application that needs to support both ASP.NET Forms Authentication and custom security, you will end up with two cookies—one generated by the ASP.NET Forms Authentication APIs and another generated by the Report Server when the `LogonUser` API is called. As a consequence, you will typically need to synchronize both cookies to expire at the same time by using the same timeout setting in the configuration files.

If the cookie is valid, authorization takes place. Here, the request is validated against the predefined role-based security policy you set up. Your custom authorization logic has the final say when the request is authorized successfully. This adds a lot of flexibility because developers can implement custom rules to validate the request, as you will see shortly.

Implementing custom authentication

From the client perspective, the first task that the application has to do to grant the user access to the Report Server is to call the RS `LogonUser` web method and pass the user's credentials.

NOTE The RS documentation states that the `LogonUser` method should be called over a secured (SSL) connection. While you must definitely consider securing the connection to the Report Server with your real-life applications, you don't need SSL when calling this method.

Another consideration to watch for, which bit me at the beginning, is that when using the Report Manager with custom security, you need to enter the portal's URL exactly as specified under the `ReportServerUrl` element in the `RSWebApplication.config` Report Manager configuration file. If you don't do this, for example, if you use localhost as a server name, you will get an exception and custom security won't work. However, you can request reports using localhost.

After the `LogonUser` call, the Report Server invokes the `IAuthenticationExtension` methods in the sequence shown in figure 13.23.

First, the Report Server invokes the `IAuthenticationExtension.SetConfiguration` method to give the authentication extension a chance to configure itself by passing the configuration XML fragment from the `RSReportServer.config` configuration file. In our example, the configuration section includes the connection string to the user's profile store as well as the credentials that the report administrator can use to log in to the Report Manager. The premise here is that, in real life, you will typically keep the administrator's credentials and the user's profile store separate. Of course, there's nothing stopping you from putting the administrator's credentials in the user's profile store if your application's design calls for it.

Once the extension is initialized, the Report Server calls `GetUserInfo` to obtain the user's identity. This method is also called with each request to the Report Server. Set the user identity as follows:

```
userIdentity = HttpContext.Current.User.Identity;
```

When the user is not yet authenticated (`IAuthenticationExtension.LogonUser` is not yet called), the Report Server sets the user's identity to a temporary user. The `userIdentity` object passed as an `out` argument to `GetUserInfo` is of the type `System.Security.Principal.IIdentity` interface, so it can be set to any valid object that implements this interface.

NOTE I was initially tempted to implement the user-to-group membership assignment in `GetUserInfo`. My envisioned approach was to check the user's profile store and assign the user to one or multiple roles as you could do when using ASP.NET Forms Authentication, for example:

```
// check the group membership and assign user to the Individual
role
HttpContext.Current.User = new GenericPrincipal (userIdentity,
         new string[] { "Invididual" });
```

Then, my plan called for verifying the user group in `CheckAccess` by using the `IPrincipal.IsInRole()` method and authorizing the user based on the group membership. Unfortunately, while this approach will work, `GetUserInfo` is called repeatedly within a single request, and performing a database lookup each time may very well hinder the application's performance. For this reason, I abandoned my original plan in favor of performing the database lookup in the `CheckAccess` overloads, as suggested by a Microsoft engineer from the RS group.

After several `SetConfiguration` and `GetUserInfo` calls, the Report Server eventually calls the `LogonUser` method to ask you to validate the user's credentials. The Report Server conveniently passes the username and password that were sent in the `LogonUser` web method call. This implementation of `LogonUser` performs a database lookup against the `Individual` table in an attempt to find a customer identifier that matches the username. If this is the case, you consider the user valid and set the method's return value to true.

Note that the Report Server calls `IAuthentication.LogonUser` only once during the lifetime of the user's session as a result of the call to the `LogonUser` web method. As we've noted earlier, if the user is authenticated successfully, the Report Server will issue a ticket in the form of a cookie that will be checked automatically with each request to determine if authentication has already taken place. The cookie's details are specified in the Report Server's `web.config` configuration file. Set the cookie to expire after one hour, as shown here:

```
<authentication mode="Forms">
  <forms loginUrl="logon.aspx" name="sqlAuthCookie"
     timeout="60" slidingExpiration="true" path="/">
  </forms>
</authentication>
```

ASP.NET developers familiar with the ASP.NET Forms Authentication model will find this syntax familiar. For example, you can use the same declaration attributes to configure the RS custom authentication.

You may wonder how the Report Server validates the username when the administrator creates a new role-based security policy using the Report Manager portal. When an attempt is made to change the role-based security policy of a given item in the report catalog, the Report Server calls `IAuthenticationExtension.IsValidPrincipalName` (not shown in the sequence diagram). The Report Server will pass only the username (not the password) and ask your authentication extension to verify that the username is valid.

You can view the call to IsValidPrincipalName as a safeguard against the possibility that some malicious code could try to exploit the RS role-based security policy to gain access to the report catalog. Interestingly, the Report Server calls IAuthenticationExtension.IsValidPrincipalName for each user or group assigned to the catalog item. If a match is not found, an exception is raised and the attempt to change the role-based security policy won't succeed.

Implementing custom authorization

Once authenticated, our custom authorization model needs to verify that the user has adequate rights to perform the attempted action. How involved this gets will depend on your security requirements. In the simplest case, you won't have to change the authorization code included in the Microsoft sample at all. Its authorization implementation checks to see whether the user has permissions to perform the requested action. If you don't need to support assigning users to groups, the sample authorization implementation will most likely suffice for your needs.

Similarly to the authentication model, the authorization process starts when the Report Server calls IAuthorizationExtension.SetConfiguration to give your custom authorization extension a chance to configure itself using the setting in the configuration file. In our example, the configuration section includes only the administrator's name. This is needed because you want to bypass the authorization check if the user has admin rights.

Depending on the type of attempted action, the Report Server will call different CheckAccess overloads. For example, if a report is requested, the Report Server will call the following overload:

```
public bool CheckAccess(string userName, IntPtr userToken,
          byte[] secDesc, ReportOperation requiredOperation)
```

If the report includes images, the Report Server will also call the CheckAccess overload that takes ResourceOperation as the last argument:

```
// Overload for Report operations
public bool CheckAccess( string userName, IntPtr userToken,
      byte[] secDesc, ReportOperation requiredOperation) {

   if (0 == String.Compare(userName, m_adminUserName, true,
        CultureInfo.CurrentCulture)) return true;

   IPrincipal user = HttpContext.Current.User;
   if (Util.IsNumeric(userName)) userName = "individual";

   AceCollection acl = DeserializeAcl(secDesc);
   foreach(AceStruct ace in acl)    {
     if (0 == String.Compare(userName, ace.PrincipalName,
             true, CultureInfo.CurrentCulture) { )
       foreach(ReportOperation aclOp in   ace.ReportOperations)
          if (aclOp == requiredOperation) return true;
```

Allows unrestricted access for administrator

Assigns user to group

Determines user's access to resource

```
        }
    }
    return false;
}
```

All CheckAccess variations take as an argument the security descriptor of the requested item in the form of a serialized array. In your CheckAccess implementation, you can deserialize the item's security descriptor in the form of an AceCollection class to find out which role-based security policies have been defined for this item. The Report Server passes all role-based security policies defined for the requested catalog item, not just the ones defined for the interactive user. It simply tells you, "Here are all role-based policies defined in the report catalog for this item." This is great because it can dramatically simplify your authorization implementation, as you see in the next section. It is important to note that your authentication extension can take the stand and have a final say before the Report Server grants or revokes access to the requested resource. Our default implementation is to loop through the role-based policies and find out whether the user has been associated at all with the requested resource. If this is the case, the code verifies whether the user indeed has rights to the requested operation.

NOTE If you change the CheckAccess overloads you may need to change also the implementation of the IAuthorizationExtension.GetPermissions method. GetPermissions returns the list of permissions available to a given user and it is only called by the Report Manager. Although the sequence diagram on figure 13.23 doesn't show it, the Report Manager calls AuthorizationExtension.GetPermissions to adjust its UI based on the security policy defined for the logged-on user.

Assigning users to groups

But wait—do you have to create a role-based policy for each user? Just imagine the nightmare that would follow if you had to maintain hundreds and thousands of role-based security policies with large sites that support many registered users, such as AWC. In such cases, groups provide a practical solution for implementing more granular security assignments because rights are granted to groups, not individual users.

Can groups be used with custom security? You bet, provided that you are willing to write some code. Currently, the Report Server doesn't have any notion about assigning users into application groups. Although you may implement a custom infrastructure to support assigning users to one or more application groups, for example, database-driven or based on the Authorization Manager, the Report Server doesn't have the means to differentiate users and groups. However, because it will pass all security policies defined to the requested item to the CheckAccess overloads, you can easily perform additional lookups to resolve the user-role relationship. For example, if the user is not explicitly granted permissions to request reports, you can find out which roles she belongs to and iterate through the `AceCollection` collection to find out whether these roles have been given the rights to do so.

There are at least two approaches for supporting group assignments. As we mentioned before, assigning the user to groups in `GetUserInfo` is impractical because it is called many times within each request. One approach is to use a custom HTTP handler, similar to the one we discuss shortly, to perform the database lookup based on the user's identity; create a new `GenericPrincipal` object; and assign the groups (roles) to that user. The advantage of this approach is that it centralizes the group assignments in one place. In addition, it allows the developer to use `IPrincipal.IsInRole` to simplify the authorization checks. The disadvantage is that it requires a custom HTTP handler. Microsoft doesn't officially support using HTTP handlers to extend RS.

Another approach is to use the `CheckAccess` overloads for additional authorization rules, such as group membership. This is the approach we decided to implement for both report and resource authorization checks. We kept our implementation simple on purpose. The code checks only to see if the username is a valid number, because the custom identifiers are numeric. If this is the case, we reset the username to Individual. In other words, we assume that the user can belong to only one group. Then, we leave the rest of the authorization logic to find out if a principal named Individual has been assigned the rights to request the resource.

If you want, you could extend our sample by allowing accounts defined in the `Store` table to log into the Adventure Works portal. You could assign these accounts to a group called Store, which could have a different level of access to the report catalog. Your application requirements may call for assigning users to multiple groups. Thanks to the fact that the authorization checks are performed in the custom security extension, you can make them as flexible and sophisticated as needed.

13.4.4 Debugging the custom security extension

Debugging the custom security extension is easy when you follow these steps:

Step 1 Request the `MyOrders.aspx` page from the AWReporterWeb application. This will start the aspnet_wp (w3wp in IIS6) process. Or you can open the Internet Information Services (IIS) management console and browse the `ReportService2005.asmx` page.

Step 2 Open the AWC.RS.Extensions project and set your breakpoints.

Step 3 From the Debug menu in VS .NET select Attach to Process, find the aspnet_wp (w3wp) process, and attach to it.

Step 4 Log in using the Login form in AWReporterWeb. At this point, the call to the `LogonUser` web method will be made, and the breakpoints in your custom authentication extension should be hit.

Step 5 Click the My Order History link found in the `MyOrders.aspx` page. This will request the Customer Orders report. At this point, the breakpoints in your custom authorization extension should be hit.

13.5 SUMMARY

Having read this chapter, you should view Reporting Services as a reporting framework that you can use to create versatile reporting solutions. No matter how hard Microsoft works to enhance RS, it will not be able to meet all possible integration requirements. In cases such as these, you need to take the road less traveled and customize RS to meet your particular needs.

Thanks to the extensible architecture of RS, .NET developers can easily extend or replace RS's "canned" features by writing add-ons in the form of custom extensions. In this chapter, we showed you how you can do just that by enhancing the RS data processing, delivery, and security features.

To demonstrate how you can extend the RS data processing features, we authored a custom dataset extension that you can use to report off ADO.NET datasets. Also, to explain how you can distribute your reports in flexible ways, we created a custom delivery extension. You can use it to send reports to Web services.

When Windows-based security is not a good fit, you can replace it by writing a custom security extension. We did this to show how custom security extensions can be leveraged in the Internet reporting scenario.

Finally, although we didn't demonstrate it, to export reports to formats not supported by RS, you can write custom rendering extensions.

Another important and often-neglected requirement posed to enterprise-oriented applications is that they need to perform and scale well under heavy loads. The next chapter discusses practical techniques you can use to ensure that your report-enabled solutions are well prepared to meet the anticipated request loads.

C H A P T E R 1 4

Performance and scalability

To realize the full potential of a report-enabled application, developers must meet the users' demands, which typically consist of quality of service, quality of content, and efficient access to the application's resources. So far, this book has shown you how applications integrated with RS can meet the first two objectives.

In this chapter, we discuss how you can ensure that your reporting solutions also perform and scale well to meet increased user loads. To guarantee that these objectives are met, you must learn how to evaluate the application's performance and capacity before "going live" in a production environment. The specific areas of focus in this chapter are as follows:

- Explaining the capacity-planning process
- Establishing a performance goal
- Stress-testing the Report Server
- Identifying performance bottlenecks
- Optimizing the application's performance

Although this chapter specifically targets evaluating the Report Server's performance and scalability, you can use the same principles to plan the capacity requirements of other web-based applications.

14.1 UNDERSTANDING CAPACITY PLANNING

Reading the messages posted on the Reporting Services discussion list, we frequently come across questions related to RS scalability and performance. Usually people ask, "Is Reporting Services capable of supporting *x* number of users?" or "What are the recommended hardware and software specifications to handle high loads?"

Answering questions like these is not easy. It is difficult to predict how variables in application design, database schema, user behavior, and architecture will combine to affect the application's performance. Because no exact formulas can be given, the burden of ensuring that your reporting solutions will meet the anticipated load is shifted to you. This is known as *capacity planning*. Microsoft has done its job by giving you a platform that can scale up and out. Your job is to prove that your reporting solutions meet your specific performance and capacity requirements. In this section, we explore some basic capacity-planning concepts and look at the specific stages involved in applying capacity planning.

14.1.1 Capacity-planning fundamentals

Conducting a capacity-planning study is not difficult. While discussing this subject in detail is beyond the scope of this book, our goal is to give you the essential knowledge and techniques needed to get you started. If you need more information, refer to the "Resources" section at the end of this book.

Let's start by examining some essential capacity-planning concepts.

Performance vs. scalability

The terms *performance* and *scalability* are often used interchangeably, but an important distinction exists. Performance usually measures how fast the application's code executes; scalability is concerned with how the application responds under increased user loads.

An application that scales well usually performs well. The reverse is not necessarily true. An application may exhibit excellent performance with a small number of users but may grind to a halt in a high-volume environment. Take, for example, Microsoft Access database applications. When serving a handful of clients, this type of application performs well. However, due to the file-based nature of the Access Jet engine database, the application's performance deteriorates quickly as the number of users increases. In this respect, the application is not scalable.

When conducting a capacity-planning study of Reporting Services, you are trying to understand how the Report Server responds at various user load levels. In general, you want to measure the *latency*, *throughput*, and *utilization* of the Report Server by simulating simultaneous report requests by virtual users. Ideally, you find that your Report Server site exhibits low latency, high throughput, and low utilization.

Understanding latency

Latency is the delay experienced between the time when the client makes a report request and the Report Server receives the report's payload. Latency is typically measured in terms of seconds or milliseconds. Some stress-testing tools, such as the Visual Studio .NET Application Center Test, use the *time to last byte* (TTLB) metric to represent latency. The request-response trip delay depends on two major latency factors: network and application latencies. *Network* latency characterizes the time spent to move data through the wire. *Application* latency refers to the delay incurred to process the report request on the server side. Figure 14.1 depicts how the application and network latencies impact the overall report request's round-trip in a typical on-demand reporting solution.

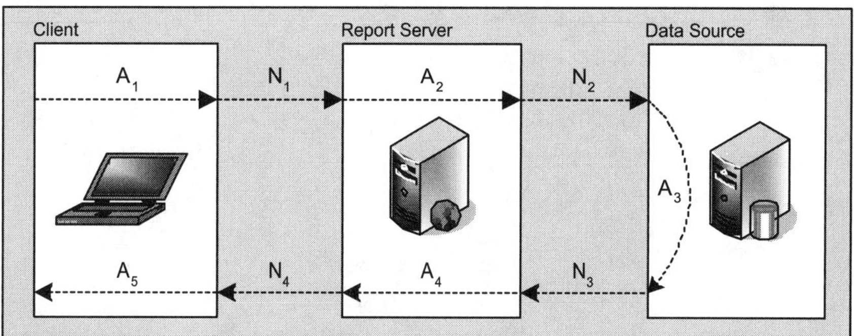

Figure 14.1 The report's request-response trip incurs network and application latencies.

As shown in figure 14.1, the total latency time from the point of requesting the report to rendering it on the screen can be calculated with the following formula:

`Total latency (response time) = (A1+A2+A3+A4+A5) + (N1+N2+N3+N4)`, where `An` represents application latencies and `Nn` stands for network latencies, as explained in table 14.1. The report request's round-trip incurs application and network latencies. To improve the performance and scalability of your reporting environment, you need to find ways to minimize these latencies.

How much the network delays impact the report request's total latency depends to a great extent on the type of the reporting application and your deployment scenario. For example, with intranet-based reporting applications deployed on a 100Mb corporate network, network latency may not be an issue at all. However, it may become a constraining factor with Internet-oriented solutions, where slow dial-up connections are still prevalent.

Table 14.1 Application and network latencies

Latency	Reason
A_1	Prepare the report request on the client, e.g., validate the report request, prepare the report parameters, etc.
A_2	Process the report request.
A_3	Process the report query.
A_4	Generate the report.
A_5	Render the report, e.g., in the case of a SOAP call save the report's payload to a file and shell out to it.
N_1, N_4	Network delays between the client and the Report Server.
N_2, N_3	Network delays between the Report Server and the database server.

One way to reduce the network delays on the trip from the Report Server back to the client is to minimize the network traffic by requesting reports by URL instead of SOAP. As we discussed in chapter 10, the latter access option adds about 20–30 percent overhead for serializing the report's payload to a binary array.

Minimizing the application's latencies is often more of an art than a science. With custom applications, you would typically use code profilers to determine which code sections take up the most time and seek ways to optimize them. Of course, with RS, this is not an option because you don't have access to its source code. Instead, you need to focus on optimization techniques within your reach. For example, as we discussed in chapter 8, you can use several report-caching techniques to minimize the report's processing time. If caching doesn't conflict with your particular reporting requirements, we recommend that you use it abundantly. For instance, the easiest way to reduce the time spent on the Report Server to generate a report is not to generate it at all but to serve it from a cached copy.

Another potential area that may negatively affect the latency of the server-side application is the time required to process the report query. If you determine that the database is a constraining factor, you can use query profilers, such as the Microsoft SQL Server Query Analyzer, to find out how you can optimize your report queries. Alternatively, you can use the report's execution log (see section 14.2.1) to determine how much time the Report Server has spent on processing the query and executing and rendering the report.

"How can I get a latency breakdown of the request-response round-trip?" we hear you ask. We've used a third-party tool, Compuware Application Expert (which is now packaged with ApplicationVantage), to address similar questions with our performance-related projects. To use this tool, you first need to capture the network traffic of the request-response round-trip using network-tracing tools, such as the Microsoft Network Monitor. For the best results, you may want to obtain network traces from all nodes involved in your reporting solution, such as the client application, the Report Server, and the database server where the report data resides.

Once you have captured the network traffic, you can import it into the Application Expert to get a conversation map showing you the network and application latencies. This tool also supports what-if analysis. Let's say you need to find out how a 56K dial-up connection will impact the report's response time. Application Expert includes a predictor component that uses sophisticated algorithms to extrapolate the latency map for factoring in various network connection speeds.

Understanding throughput

In the context of planning the capacity of your RS environment, the term *throughput* is the number of report requests that the Report Server can process within a given unit of time. No matter how scalable a given application is, its throughput-versus-load graph will eventually reach its peak, as shown in figure 14.2.

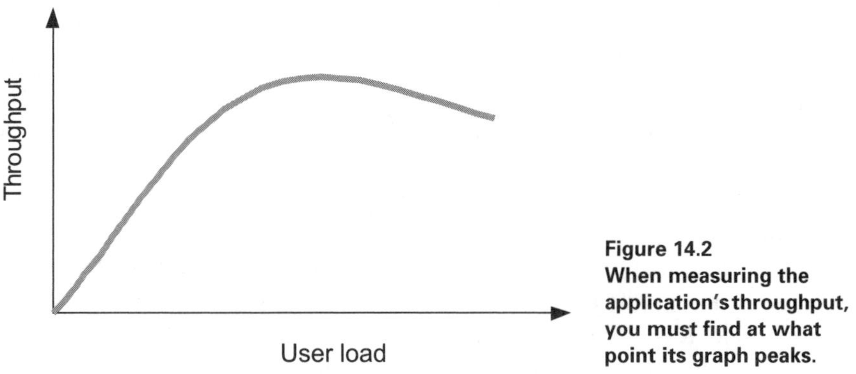

Figure 14.2
When measuring the application's throughput, you must find at what point its graph peaks.

In this respect, you can visualize your reporting application as a highway. When traffic is light, vehicles move quickly. However, as most big-city dwellers can relate, once all highway lines are saturated, traffic jams follow and throughput decreases. Therefore, when you evaluate the capacity of a given RS installation, you apply increasing loads to the Report Server to find out the point of maximum throughput.

How do you measure the application's throughput? Often, people want to know how many concurrent users a given web application, in this case the Report Server, can handle. Trying to quantify the application's throughput using concurrent users could be highly inaccurate for a couple of reasons.

First, it is not clear within what time frame the users are considered to be concurrent. Second, "concurrent users" is an ambiguous term that may mean different things to different people. For example, many people use this term to refer to the number of users logged on to the application. But should a user who has logged on to the Report Manager to request five reports and then has gone on a one-hour lunch break be considered a concurrent user?

Instead, you typically measure throughput in *requests per second* (RPS) or *pages per second* (PPS). What's the difference between the two? Readers experienced with web development will probably recall that rendering one page in a browser can result in several round-trips to the server. For example, when you request a report that includes images in HTML, the browser will spawn additional requests to fetch the images. Therefore, a page is more granular than a request because one page (report) may require several requests.

NOTE For the purposes of stress-testing the Report Server, you need to differentiate between requests and pages only when the report is requested in a multistream format. The multistream formats supported natively by the Report Server are all HTML options except MHTML. Because browsers tend to cache images, you may find it easier to ignore the image requests, especially with high-speed networks.

But wait, all reports are not created equal, right? Although some may take seconds to render, others may need significant processing resources. What, then, does a request really mean, and how can you use it to represent various reports? These are excellent questions that deserve more attention. The short answer is that there isn't an exact rule to correlate requests with the actual reports. Let's go back to our highway example to clarify this.

Imagine that you need to measure the highway throughput for a given period of time. One way to do this is to count how many vehicles of different types, such as tractor-trailers, minivans, cars, and so on, have gone down the highway during the time period in question. The advantage of this approach is its accuracy. On the negative side, it is more involved because it is difficult to work with multiple units. For example, how many cars can be substituted for a tractor-trailer? What car models are we talking about? As they say, the devil is in the details. To simplify things, you can introduce an abstraction metric called a "vehicle" that you would use to represent an average vehicle on the highway. This simplifies your task considerably because now you are not concerned with the type of vehicles. In fact, you can use automatic counting equipment to count the vehicles for you.

In a similar way, you can use requests per second to represent the number of successfully completed report requests that the Report Server can handle within a second. Instead of requests per second, you may prefer to use other metrics. For example, another common stress-testing metric is the number of virtual users that the application can handle before its utilization exceeds the specific threshold values. Note, though, that this approach is more involved to set up because you need to simulate the users' request patterns. For instance, once the user has requested the report, she will typically analyze it or print it before requesting another report. When using virtual users, you need to examine the report's execution history and factor in the user's think time. Another disadvantage of this method is that it may require a significant number of test client machines to "saturate" the web server.

If you want, you can conduct two sets of tests to use both approaches—requests per second and virtual users. Ideally, in this case, your test findings should match.

Understanding utilization

While determining the maximum load that the Report Server can handle is useful, often you need to find out how your report-enabled applications can scale better to meet your performance goal. In other words, an essential objective of every capacity-planning study is to find what performance bottlenecks cause the throughput graph to decline, as shown in figure 14.2.

You can determine resource constraints by examining the *utilization* of your system. You typically do this by monitoring a set of performance counters. Specifically, you must monitor the utilization of the following resources at minimum:

- CPU
- Memory
- Database server

Table 14.2 lists the most frequently used Windows performance counters to track the utilization of these resources.

Table 14.2 Windows performance counters that you can use to monitor the Report Server's usage

Resource	Performance Counter	Purpose
CPU	Processor(_Total)\% Processor Time	Represents the average CPU utilization. The average CPU utilization on any processor should not exceed 60–70%.
CPU	Process(aspnet_wp)\% Processor Time (or Process(w3wp)\% Processor Time for Windows 2003)	The percentage of the CPU utilization spent in the ASP.NET worker thread
SQL Server	Process(sqlservr)\% Processor Time	The percentage of the CPU utilization consumed by SQL Server
Memory	Memory\Available Bytes	The amount of available RAM memory in bytes

RS comes with its own performance counters that you can use to track the utilization of the RS Web service and Windows Service. For more information about RS-related counters, see the product documentation.

Let's turn now to the actual process of capacity planning.

14.1.2 The capacity-planning process

A successful capacity-planning study necessitates a guided process that shouldn't be much different than the software development methodology in general. The capacity-planning process consists of several stages, as shown in figure 14.3.

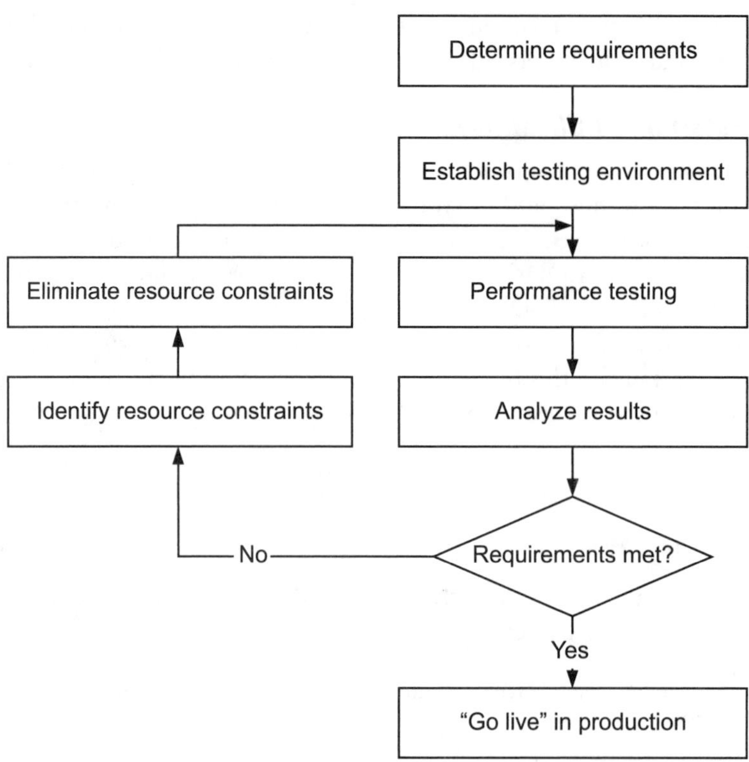

Figure 14.3 The capacity-planning process consists of several stages and may include more than one iteration until the performance goals are met.

As you can see, the capacity-planning process is an iterative one. At the end of each iteration, you compare the performance results against preestablished performance goals. If our objectives are not met, you need to find out why and think of ways to improve the system's scalability.

Let's discuss each of the stages in more detail.

Determining requirements

This is, arguably, the most important stage of the capacity-planning effort. As with any software project, you shouldn't underestimate the importance of getting and documenting the application's performance requirements. My overall impression is that developers tend to ignore establishing performance goals for their applications. In most cases, the result of this optimistic approach is poor scalability, which necessitates total redesign of the application.

NOTE I was once involved in a large-scale web-based project. My first task was to find out why the application was performing poorly. After stress-testing the system, I found out that it couldn't handle more than one request per second! For a web-based application this was clearly unacceptable. After a long and painstaking process of running tests against each application tier, I found several performance bottlenecks. The most significant were related to the poor throughput when requesting data from the mainframe database. In addition, I discovered that, enamored with XML, the application developers had used XML DOM manipulations and XSL transformations abundantly in each tier of the application. The application was moving ever-growing XML payloads between the web server and the browser. XSL transformations were used on the client side to render the presentation screens.

"Fixing" the application to scale better wasn't easy. It had to be totally redesigned and rewritten in ASP.NET. After several iterations, the application finally met the performance goals and was deployed to the high-volume production environment. The moral of this story is that you must plan for performance as early as possible in the application's lifecycle.

After you determine the application's performance requirements, you need to quantify them in performance metrics. For applications integrated with RS, these metrics could include the following:

- *Requests per second*—This is the total number of report requests that the web server (or cluster) can handle.
- *Utilization counters*—For example, the average CPU utilization of any of the web server's processors should stay below 70 percent, the memory consumption shouldn't top 80 percent, and so on.
- *Response time*—The industry standard response time for web-based applications is no more than 10 seconds measured from the time the request is made until the page is rendered to the browser or the response is received from the web server. This is a reasonable latency time for report rendering as well.
- *Application availability*—For example, your reporting requirements may call for 99.9 percent availability. Aside from scalability, this is one of the main reasons to use a cluster or web servers, as we discuss in section 14.2.6.

While the last three of the above-mentioned metrics are easy to formulate, establishing a throughput benchmark may require more effort. Basically, to accomplish this you can use the following two approaches:

- *Empirical*—If RS is deployed and running in a production environment, this will be the preferred method because it is more realistic and accurate. This method involves analyzing the report's execution log to gather some statistics about the application's usage. This is the method that we demonstrate shortly.
- *Theoretical*—If production data is not available, you can derive the throughput metrics by calculating the envisioned load. For example, say you determine that your user base will consist of 5,000 users and each user may request up to 100 reports per day. Assuming that the report requests are distributed evenly

throughout the day, this means that the Report Server needs to handle about six requests per second (`(5,000 x 100)/(24 x 3600) = 6 requests/sec.`).

The performance goal you establish at the end of the "Determining requirements" phase will serve as a benchmark against which you will measure the actual performance and determine whether additional performance optimization work is required.

Establishing a testing environment

This stage typically involves the following steps:

- *Understanding the application architecture*—In general, you need to have an intimate knowledge about the architecture of the reporting application. This necessitates working hand-in-hand with the application's developers and report authors throughout the entire capacity-planning effort.
- *Setting up the testing environment*—You should get a dedicated test server with hardware and software specifications matching as closely as possible the production server setup. Otherwise, your test results will be skewed.
- *Creating test use cases*—In a typical web application, you should create test use cases that you will later script and stress test. For example, you may come up with a use case called User Login that involves two web pages: the home page and the login page. For reporting applications, you could identify a representative set of reports that need to be tested. You can analyze the RS Execution Log to find out the most requested reports.
- *Preparing test scripts*—This is where you will put on your developer's hat and create test scripts using your favorite stress-testing tool. You will use the scripts to apply an ever-increasing load to the Report Server to determine its maximum throughput.

Once the test environment is set up, it is time to find out whether your specific RS installation can stand up to the test and deliver what is expected of it.

Performance testing

This is our favorite sit-and-watch stage. Most stress tools are designed to simulate multiple users submitting requests via HTTP-GET or HTTP-POST. For example, Microsoft Application Compatibility Toolkit (ACT) can be used to generate customizable loads and offers a rich set of reporting features for analyzing performance data.

The main objective of this stage is to produce the graph shown previously in figure 14.2. Our favorite method to accomplish this is to increase the number of the Application Center Test's virtual users (connections) by a factor of 2; for example, 1, 2, 4, 8, and so on. Eventually, the web server utilization will max out. At this point, you will know the maximum throughout that your particular RS installation can handle expressed in requests per second.

Next, you compare these results against the previously established performance benchmark. If the results meet or exceed your expectations, you can congratulate yourself. Otherwise, you need to cancel your vacation and go back to the drawing board and identify the performance bottlenecks.

Identifying performance bottlenecks

A bottleneck is a resource constraint, either hardware or software, that prevents performance from improving. As noted earlier, you determine the performance bottlenecks at a high level by examining the performance counters. Identifying performance bottlenecks is not always easy, but here are some tips you may find useful:

- Often, with web-based applications such as Reporting Services, the web server processor will become the first resource constraint. The Processor: % Processor Time/Total is the best counter for viewing processor saturation. If the processors are running between 90 and 100 percent, then they are most likely the bottleneck.
- If there is heavy disk activity, then the memory is likely to be the bottleneck. The Memory: Available Bytes performance counter can tell you how much physical memory is remaining and available for use.
- If the database server's processor is highly utilized, this is an indication that the database may be a resource constraint. In the case of the SQL Server, check the Process(sqlservr)\% Processor Time counter to find out whether this is the case.
- If the ASP.NET Applications/Requests Queued counter fluctuates considerably during the test run, and the processor utilization remains low, this is an indication that the report is most likely calling custom code that is receiving more calls than it can handle.
- If none of these resources is a problem, yet the requests/second still do not increase despite the increased load, then the network card bandwidth should be examined. The best counter to use to examine the network card saturation bottlenecks is Network Interface: Bytes Total/sec. The bytes/sec should be less than 40 percent of the total available bandwidth.

Once you identify the resource contention area, you can focus on finding ways to eliminate it.

Eliminating performance bottlenecks

There are a number of performance-enhancing techniques you can try based on your particular situation. For example, if the CPU utilization is high, you may want to consider using report execution or session caching. As we discussed in chapter 10, when reports are requested via URL, report sessions are handled automatically. With SOAP access, you have to go an extra step to correlate the report with the session.

Another potential area that may lead to a high CPU utilization is if your reports use resource-intensive custom code. If you suspect this to be the case, you can use third-party profilers, such as the Compuware DevPartner, to find which portions of your code are the most processor-intensive.

If your report queries process vast volumes of data, you may want to explore options to decrease the amount of data displayed. For example, consider implementing web-style paging to display one page of a report at a time with a handful of records. Finally, when performance-optimization techniques don't yield results, you can add more processing power by scaling RS up and out.

Now that we've covered both the fundamentals and process of capacity planning, let's see how you might apply it in practice.

14.2 CAPACITY PLANNING FOR REPORTING SERVICES IN ACTION

Here is our hypothetical scenario that will drive the capacity-planning effort for Adventure Works. As we've mentioned on several occasions throughout this book, Adventure Works Cycles (AWC) is blessed with success. The company is expanding by acquiring some of its competitors. As a part of this process, the IT management needs to plan for growth. You've been tasked with determining whether the reporting infrastructure can handle an increased load that is expected to be 10 times greater than before. To estimate the impact, you decide to perform a capacity-planning study by following the steps we just discussed.

You can find the ACT scripts we used in this chapter included in the book's source code under the Performance Testing folder.

14.2.1 Determining requirements

In this stage you determine the capacity-planning requirements and establish a performance goal. The bulk of the effort will be spent on quantifying the anticipated load in requests per second (reports per second). In our hypothetical scenario, RS has already been deployed and is running in production. Therefore, as a first step, you need to analyze the RS Execution Log to find out the following:

- How many report requests has the Report Server handled for a given period?
- How were these requests distributed?

Once you answer these questions, you can easily extrapolate the increased load.

Determining the number of report requests

By far, the easiest way to find out how many reports the Report Server has handled within a given period of time is to analyze the report's execution log.

NOTE If you are evaluating web-based applications other than Report Server, you can determine the number of report requests by examining the web server logs. There are many third-party commercial and free tools you can use to analyze web server log files. For example, for our real-world projects we have used the Analog log analyzer with a great deal of success. Among the several analyzers that we've tried in the past, we've found the Analog's output to be the most accurate. The tool is also free of charge. If you need glitzier and more convincing presentation formats than those produced by Analog, you may want to try another free tool, ReportMagic. See the "Resources" section to find out how to obtain Analog and ReportMagic.

As we discussed in chapter 8, RS stores important execution statistics in the `ExecutionLog` table in the RS Configuration Database (ReportServer). We also said that to convert the statistics to a format that is easy to understand, you can use the Execution Log DTS package (RSExecutionLog_Update.dts) included with the RS Setup CD. This package extracts the report's execution log data, transforms it, and uploads it to a separate SQL Server database called RSExecutionLog.

The data captured in the RSExecutionLog database includes a wealth of information associated with the report's execution, as well as vital performance-related metrics. For example, the `ExecutionLogs` table in the RSExecutionLog database includes report response times as well as times spent in retrieving data (the `TimeDataRetrieval` column) and in executing (the `TimeProcessing` column) and rendering (the `TimeRendering` column) the report. For this reason, the report's execution log should be your first resource when troubleshooting performance issues with your reports.

Finding out the number of reports handled by the Report Server from the report's execution log is a matter of running the following simple query against the `ExecutionLogs` table:

```
SELECT COUNT(*) AS ReportCount
FROM   ExecutionLog INNER JOIN
       [Catalog] ON ExecutionLog.ReportId = [Catalog].ItemId
WHERE  [Type] = 2 /*reports only*/
AND    TimeStart BETWEEN <start date> AND <end date>
```

where `<start date>` and `<end date>` specify the time period you are interested in.

If you are running the Report Server in a web farm environment and you need to find out how many reports a particular node in the cluster has handled, you can filter the query further by the `MachineKey` column.

To derive the number of requests per second, a weekly time period should be sufficient. Let's say that after you run this query you determine that for a given week your Report Server handled 2,000 reports. This number includes both on-demand (user) and subscribed (system) report requests.

You need to account for the extra load incurred by the web server to handle images for multistream rending formats, Report Manager pages, and so on. To be on the safe side, increase this number by 50 percent. As a result, you come up with the estimate that, for that week, the Report Server handled about 3,000 report requests.

If the web server where RS is installed hosts other web applications, you must account for their load as well. As you've already guessed, determining the Report Server's load, as well as that of any other type of application, is not an exact science but rather an educated guess.

Determining request distribution statistics

One more thing you need to account for is the fact that it is unlikely that all requests were distributed evenly during the day. For example, typically more requests are submitted within normal working hours. To find out the request distribution statistics, use the `ReportsExecutedByHour.rdl` chart report, which you can find included with the book's source code (in the Performance Testing folder).

The Reports Executed By Hour chart report accepts a start date parameter and breaks down the report's execution statistics per hour for all report requests handled after that date, as shown in figure 14.4.

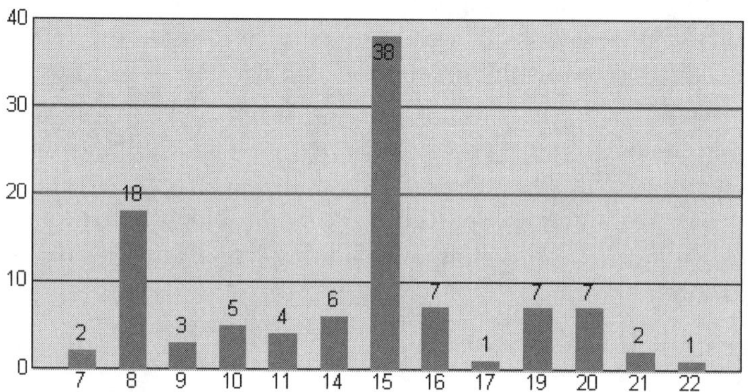

Figure 14.4 To account for the load distribution pattern, use the Reports Executed By Hour sample report.

Examining the distribution chart shown in figure 14.4, we determined that all of the activity for the given week occurred within the period 7 a.m.–10 p.m.

> **NOTE** As attentive readers will probably point out, the report count shown in the chart report doesn't total to our hypothetical metric of 2,000 report requests. This is because we ran the report against our local report execution log, which, of course, doesn't represent a real-world production environment.

Therefore, within that week, the web report server has handled about 0.07 requests per second (`3,000/(13 hrs. x 3600 sec.`). As you can tell, our web server hasn't been very busy, but your production load will likely be many times that number.

As the new capacity requirements state, your web server is expected to handle a tenfold increase in load in the future. This means that the anticipated load will be about 0.7 requests per second (`0.07 requests per sec. x 10`). Finally, let's account for the unexpected, such as holiday seasons, end-of-quarter activity, and so on, by tossing in another 50 percent increase. This means that your throughput performance goal will be about *one request per second.*

As we've discussed before, besides throughput, there are other important performance metrics to consider. Table 14.3 lists all performance goals for the AWC scenario.

Table 14.3 Performance goals for the AWC scenario

Metric	Goal
Latency	Less than 10 seconds to render a report
Throughput	1 request/sec.
Utilization (CPU)	Less than 70% on average
Utilization (memory)	Less than 80%

Now that you've established your performance goals, you can continue with the next phase of the capacity-planning effort: setting up the testing environment.

14.2.2 Setting up the testing environment

The prerequisite for successfully executing this phase is setting up the machines used for testing. You should have dedicated machines for the client and the test server. You will use the client machine to run the ACT tests, while the server will host RS. Once again, the server configuration should match the production server setup as closely as possible to avoid skewing the results. On the other hand, you don't need a beefed-up client because it will spend most of its time waiting for the server to respond.

Table 14.4 lists the configuration details of the client and server machines that we used for testing. Both the Report Server and SQL Server were installed on the server machine.

Table 14.4 The configuration specifications of the test machines

	Client	Server
Make	Dell Dimension 4550	Compaq Evo N610c
OS	Windows Server 2003	Windows Server 2003
CPU Speed	2.5GHz	2.5GHz
RAM	512MB	1GB

As you can see, our server configuration is somewhat modest. We recommend that you consider a more powerful server machine, for example, a two-way server with several gigabytes of RAM.

Creating use cases

Creating use cases for testing reports usually involves identifying a good representative set of reports that will be stress-tested. Again, the easiest way to accomplish this is to examine the RS execution log. Although there isn't a precise formula for determining a good representative set, scripting the top 10 reports is sufficient in most cases. To find the most popular reports, you can create a query that retrieves this information from the Execution Logs and Reports table, as shown here:

```
SELECT   TOP 10 COUNT([Catalog].Name) AS ReportCount,
         [Catalog].Name AS ReportName
FROM     ExecutionLog INNER JOIN
         [Catalog] ON ExecutionLog.ReportID=[Catalog].ItemID
WHERE    [Catalog].[Type]= 2
GROUP BY [Catalog].Name, [Catalog].[Type]
ORDER BY COUNT([Catalog].Name) DESC
```

For the sake of simplicity and for the purposes of our hypothetical capacity-planning study, let's limit the number of scripted reports to three, as follows:

- Employee Sales Summary
- Territory Sales Drillthrough
- Purchase Orders

In addition, let's assume that the types of requests for these reports are divided equally between URL and SOAP access.

TIP If you need to do so, you can account for disproportional request access distributions (URL versus SOAP) programmatically in your test scripts. One reason why you may want to do so is to simulate as closely as possible your production environment, for example, to account for the increased size of the report's payload in the case of SOAP. Unfortunately, the report's execution log doesn't capture the type of request access. However, you can examine the IIS log files to find out the URL-to-SOAP access ratio. For example, let's say that after analyzing the IIS logs you find that only 10 percent of the report requests have been submitted via the RS Web service (SOAP) and the rest via URL (HTTP-GET). You can simulate these distribution statistics by adding scripting logic to fire a SOAP request after nine HTTP-GET requests.

Having identified the reports to be tested, it is time to use your favorite stress-testing tool to craft a script that will be used to simulate the request load.

Creating test scripts

To stress-test the Report Server, we created an ACT script that you can find in the AWReporter.act Application Center Test project. Although ACT doesn't have ambitions to be a high-level stress-testing package, it is our tool of choice because of the following advantages it has to offer:

- *Flexibility*—We've used ACT on several real-life projects and found it to be very flexible. Because you can write tests using your preferred scripting language, you can do with ACT anything that can be done with scripting, such as manipulating files using the File System Object, reading environment variables, logging, and so on.
- *Ease of use*—Many stress-testing tools require that you use C++ or proprietary language derivatives for scripting. Most Visual Basic or Java programmers will find themselves instantly at home using VBScript or JScript languages.
- *Excellent reporting capabilities*—ACT provides some great reporting on the results of your tests.
- *Cost*—ACT is bundled with Visual Studio .NET.

NOTE At the time of the writing of this chapter Microsoft is working on a new and improved version of Application Center. Visit the Application Center website at `www.microsoft.com/applicationcenter/default.mspx` for current details.

Of course, ACT is far from perfect. One feature that we hope a future release will bring is tighter integration with the VS .NET IDE environment for easier debugging. Another welcome addition would be the ability to write scripts in managed code instead of using script languages.

The best way to get started creating scripts is to use the New Test Wizard's autorecord feature. This starts an instance of the Internet Explorer browser so that you can request the desired report by URL. Then, you can examine the produced script and customize it to meet your particular needs.

Most Visual Basic programmers will find our report-testing script easy to understand. The only area that deserves more attention is generating SOAP requests, as shown in listing 14.1.

Listing 14.1 Generating SOAP report requests with the Application Center Test project

```
Sub SendRequestSoap(payloadFile)
  Set oRequest = Test.CreateRequest
  oRequest.Path = "/ReportServer/ReportService2005.asmx"   <-- Sets the path to Web service
  oRequest.Verb = "POST"
  oRequest.HTTPVersion = "HTTP/1.1"
  set oHeaders = oRequest.Headers
  oHeaders.RemoveAll
  oHeaders.Add "Accept", "image/gif, image/x-xbitmap, …"
  oHeaders.Add "Accept-Language", "en-us"
  oHeaders.Add "User-Agent", "…"
  oHeaders.Add "Host", "(automatic)"
  oHeaders.Add "Content-Length", "(automatic)"
  oHeaders.Add "Content-Type", "text/xml; charset=utf-8"   <-- Sets the request content type
  RemoveCookies()   <-- Removes all browser cookies
```

```
  oHeaders.Add "SOAPAction", _
        "http://schemas/.../reportingservices/Render"   ◁─ Sets the SOAP action
  oRequest.Body = GetXMLRequest(payloadFile)   ◁─ Gets the report's payload

  Set oResponse = g_oConnection.Send(oRequest)
  CheckResponse oResponse, payloadFile
End Sub
```

SOAP requests can become rather verbose, so embedding them in the script page may be impractical. Instead, you can follow these steps to facilitate submitting report requests to the RS Web service:

Step 1 Use the AccessOptions sample (chapter 10) and your favorite tracing tool to capture the SOAP report request's payload.

Step 2 Save the payload to a disk file.

Step 3 To submit a report request, read the contents of the file using the file system object and set the request body.

This is exactly the design pattern that `SendRequestSoap` follows. It accepts the full path to the report request file. First, the code creates a report request using the ACT object model. Next, it sets the request path to point to the RS Web service endpoint. Because the Report Server relies on Windows authentication, you need to change the HTTP version from the default 1.0 to 1.1. When this is done, ACT will handle the authentication handshake between the browser and the server automatically.

Next, you need to set the required HTTP headers. You start by clearing the browser's cookies collection. For URL requests, this is done to prevent the automatic report session caching that the Report Server automatically performs behind the scenes. While in real life you should use caching techniques abundantly, we wanted to avoid report sessions so they won't skew the results. As we've said, when requesting reports via SOAP, this is not required because you have to set explicitly the session identifier anyway.

The code continues by defining the SOAP `action` attribute, which is mandatory for SOAP-based calls. Then, you call the `GetXmlRequest` helper function to read the report's payload from the file and set the request body accordingly. Once the request is submitted, you check the response code to find out whether the request has resulted in an exception and, if so, log the exception accordingly.

TIP Dealing with SOAP exceptions is easy if you follow this tip. When a SOAP exception is thrown, the Report Server will set the response code to indicate that an error condition has occurred. However, the actual exception message is in the SOAP response's payload and it won't be logged by default. To find out more about what went wrong, you can intercept the ACT request using a tracing tool, such as MSSoapT or tcpTrace. To redirect the request to the virtual port, you will need to change the `RS_PORT` constant in the ACT script accordingly, for example, to 8080. Now, you can run the script to fire a single request and look at the SOAP response's payload to get to the exception message. Alternatively, you can use DebugView to trace the Report Server's output.

Once the script is ready, you can run it and verify that it runs successfully. In our script, we implemented a logging feature that you can use to examine the status of the request by setting the `g_iDebugMode` variable to 1. When you have finished debugging the script, don't forget to reset it to 0 to avoid additional performance overhead and filling up your hard drive.

14.2.3 Performance testing

Let's put our test script into action to find out how scalable our web server is. To accomplish this, you need to apply an ever-increasing load to the web server until its throughput graph peaks. Let's start by defining only one virtual user using the script properties, as shown in figure 14.5.

Don't forget to specify some time for warming up the web server. After a certain period of inactivity, the Report Server's web application will time out and shut down. By warming up the web server, you ensure that the initialization tasks don't skew your results.

Now comes the fun part! Run the script and enjoy the show, as figure 14.6 depicts.

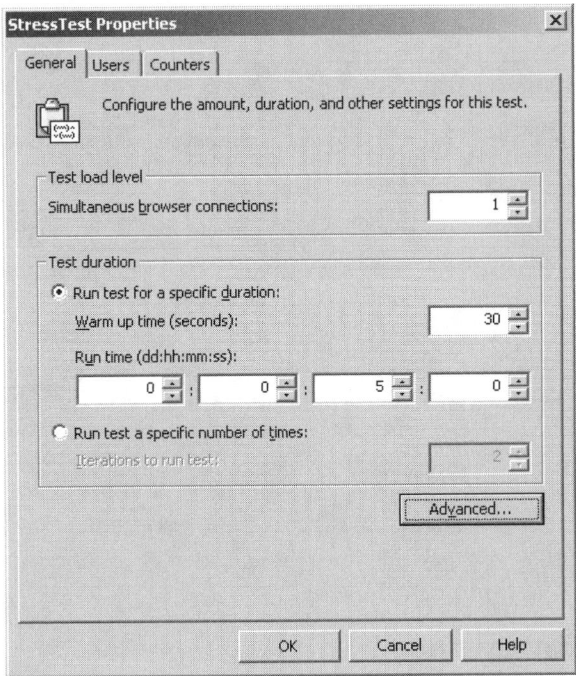

Figure 14.5 Determining the throughput graph's peak requires that you gradually apply an ever-increasing load to the web server by incrementing the number of simultaneous browser connections.

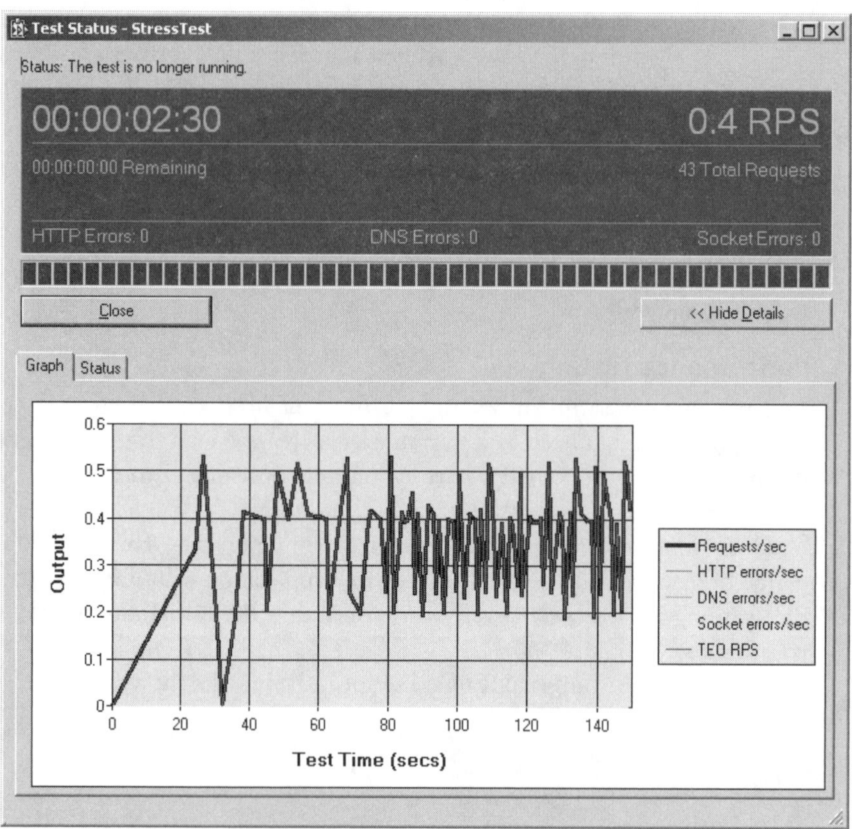

Figure 14.6 While the script is running, ACT displays performance metrics in the Test Status window.

NOTE ACT runs scripts under a designated Windows user account called ACTUser. Based on our experience, the default permissions assigned to this account are insufficient to execute scripts successfully. You will know that this is the case when you receive an "Access Denied" error when you start the script. If this happens, elevate the ACTUser account's permissions, for example, by assigning it to the local Administrators group.

You may want to configure the script to run for at least five minutes to get stable statistics. When a script is run, ACT displays valuable metrics in the Status area. The most interesting measure of these is perhaps the Requests Per Second (RPS) indicator, which reflects the throughput capacity. Note, though, that this indicator is updated on a regular basis, and it may not reflect the final RPS result.

14.2.4 Analyzing performance results

Once the script is run, you may want to analyze its execution by examining the ACT Overview Summary report, as shown in figure 14.7.

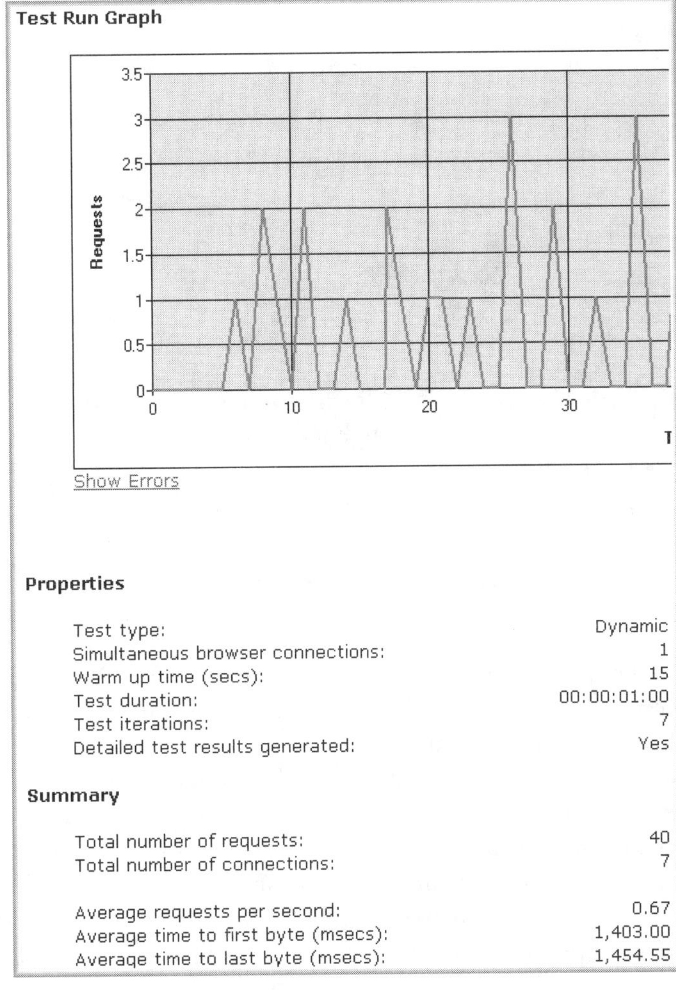

Figure 14.7 Analyze the script results with the Overview Summary report.

In figure 14.7, you can see that the web server has processed 40 requests and the RPS ratio is 0.67 with one virtual user. In addition, the Average Time to Last Byte (TTLB) metric tells us that ACT has received the complete report payload within about 1.5 seconds.

Another interesting report is the Requests: Summary report shown in figure 14.8. Using this report, you can see how both report access options, SOAP and URL, stack up against each other. For example, when requesting the Employee Sales Freeform report, you can see that accessing the report via SOAP adds about 20 percent more overhead to the report's payload. This stems from the fact that when a report is requested by SOAP, the report's payload is serialized to a binary array.

Surprisingly, despite the increased payload, requesting reports via SOAP is somewhat faster than URL access, as you can see by looking at the Time to Last Byte

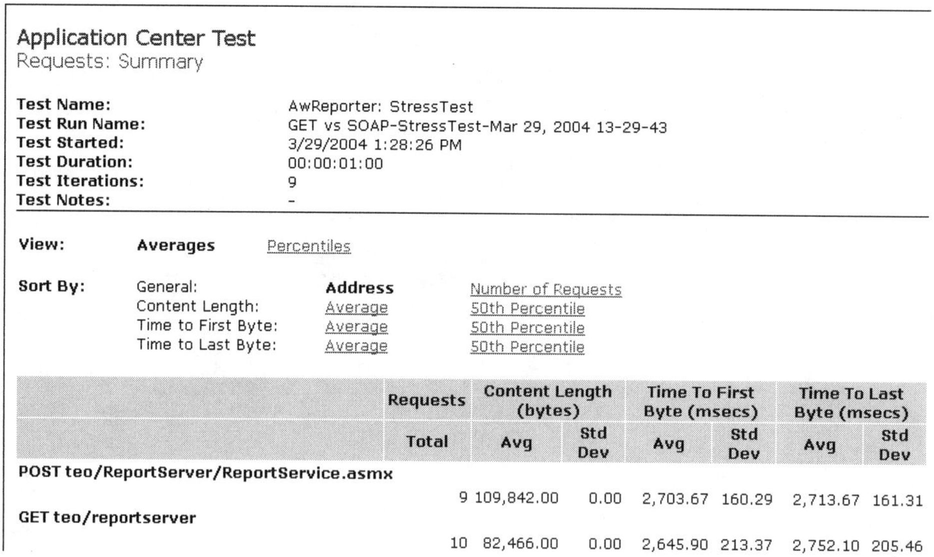

Application Center Test
Requests: Summary

Test Name: AwReporter: StressTest
Test Run Name: GET vs SOAP-StressTest-Mar 29, 2004 13-29-43
Test Started: 3/29/2004 1:28:26 PM
Test Duration: 00:00:01:00
Test Iterations: 9
Test Notes: -

View: **Averages** Percentiles

Sort By:
General: **Address** Number of Requests
Content Length: Average 50th Percentile
Time to First Byte: Average 50th Percentile
Time to Last Byte: Average 50th Percentile

	Requests	Content Length (bytes)		Time To First Byte (msecs)		Time To Last Byte (msecs)	
	Total	Avg	Std Dev	Avg	Std Dev	Avg	Std Dev
POST teo/ReportServer/ReportService.asmx	9	109,842.00	0.00	2,703.67	160.29	2,713.67	161.31
GET teo/reportserver	10	82,466.00	0.00	2,645.90	213.37	2,752.10	205.46

Figure 14.8 To compare SOAP versus URL access statistics, use the Requests: Summary report.

(TTLB) column. For high-speed 100Mbit networks, such as our LAN, the SOAP overhead should be negligible. However, it may be a constraining factor for low-speed networks, such as 56K dial-up connections.

Now run a few more iterations by increasing the number of connections by a factor of 2. When you do this, ACT creates additional threads to simulate concurrent users. ACT may not create as many threads as the number of connections. Instead, it is intelligent enough to adjust the thread pool on an as-needed basis. For example, if the web server doesn't return responses quickly, new threads won't be created.

You don't have to plot the throughput graph manually because ACT does this for you. In our case, for the six report requests we scripted, the server throughput graph maxed out with about five simultaneous users, as shown in figure 14.9.

Before you jump to conclusions, note that the point of this chapter is not to show how scalable (or not scalable, for that matter) Reporting Services is. Instead, its goal is to teach you how to conduct a comprehensive capacity-planning study to determine whether your particular reporting environment meets the anticipated load. As we've said, there are many hardware- and software-related factors that will affect the server throughput, so your results may be completely different from ours.

Analyzing the throughput graph, you conclude that the results don't meet your performance goal. Specifically, the maximum requests/sec. ratio of 0.7 is less than the benchmark—one request/sec. Therefore, you need to identify the source of the performance bottleneck.

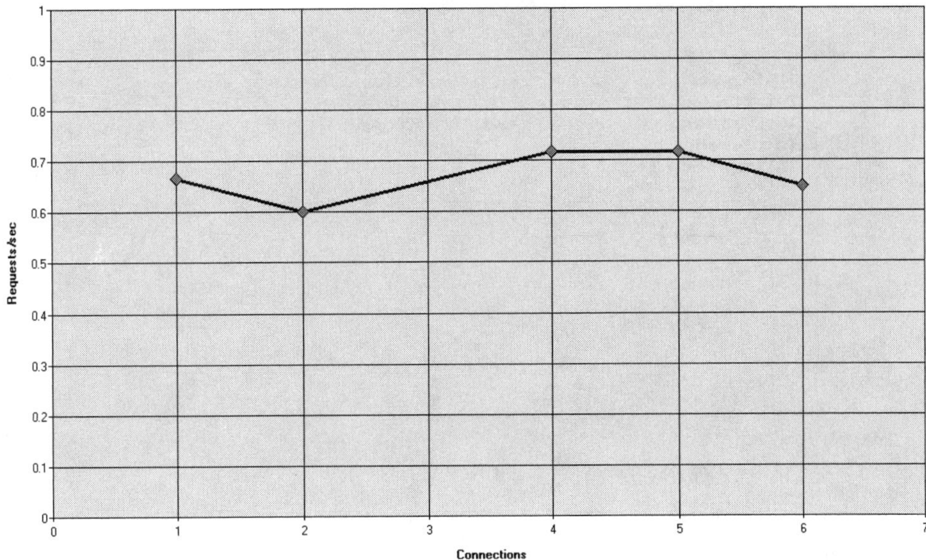

Figure 14.9 This throughput graph depicts requests/sec. versus browser connections.

14.2.5 Identifying resource constraints

You can use the ACT Performance Counters report, shown in figure 14.10, to identify the resource constraints at a high level.

A quick look at this report reveals the following:

- Even with one connection, the average CPU utilization of 75 percent is above the targeted threshold of 70 percent.
- The memory is not a constraint.
- The processor time spent on carrying out SQL Server activities (not shown in figure 14.10) is low; therefore, the database is not a constraint either.

As we expected, due to the processor-intensive report-generation activities, CPU utilization is a major resource constraint. Analyzing the results from the successive runs reveals that the CPU utilization reaches 85 percent when the throughput graph peaks at five concurrent users. Therefore, you need to find ways to eliminate this performance bottleneck.

Application Center Test
Overview: Performance Counters

Test Name:	AwReporter: StressTest
Test Run Name:	report-StressTest-Mar 28, 2004 17-35-22
Test Started:	3/28/2004 5:34:04 PM
Test Duration:	00:00:01:00
Test Iterations:	7
Test Notes:	-

\\TEO\Process\% Processor Time\w3wp

Minimum:	39.68
Maximum:	46.76
Average:	42.88
25th Percentile	42.53
50th Percentile	42.58
75th Percentile	45.02

\\TEO\Processor\% Processor Time_Total

Minimum:	70.59
Maximum:	77.39
Average:	73.61
25th Percentile	73.45
50th Percentile	73.61
75th Percentile	75.67

Figure 14.10 Use the ACT Performance Counters report to identify high-level performance bottlenecks.

14.2.6 Eliminating resource constraints

When CPU utilization is a constraining factor, you basically have two ways to increase the web server's throughput: 1) optimize report performance or 2) add more processing power by scaling up or out.

These two approaches are not mutually exclusive. The best approach is to optimize the application's performance before scaling up or out.

Optimizing report performance

With custom applications, determining the code bottlenecks requires meticulous and painstaking profiling using code profilers. When doing so, a useful approach is to follow the method of the biggest returns. In a nutshell, this entails identifying the 10 slowest code areas and seeking ways to optimize them. However, with off-the-shelf applications such as Reporting Services, this is not an option, unless your reports make extensive use of custom code. Instead, you can try other ways to take some of the burden off the CPU, such as using different forms for report caching.

Let's see how report execution caching affects server utilization by changing the execution options for all three scripted reports. As we discussed in chapter 8, this option causes the Report Server to cache the report's intermediate format in the database and to serve subsequent requests from the cached copy. Figure 14.11 shows what the new throughput graph looks like when you rerun the tests after turning on report execution caching.

Not bad for a few seconds of work! All of a sudden, you can now scale to 15 requests per second. But don't get us wrong. We're not advocating that you fire the Report Manager and turn on report execution caching for all reports. For example, if a report needs to display the most recent data, it may not be a good candidate for caching. But definitely do consider all three forms of report caching—report execution caching, snapshots, and report sessions—as performance-enhancement techniques.

Scaling up

Sometimes, there may not be much you can do to improve the web server's performance. If this is the case, you can scale Reporting Services up (vertical scalability) and out (horizontal scalability).

> **NOTE** Microsoft has released a white paper about RS performance and scalability. The white paper includes performance tests comparing scaling up and out approaches. This document is meant to help customers understand the

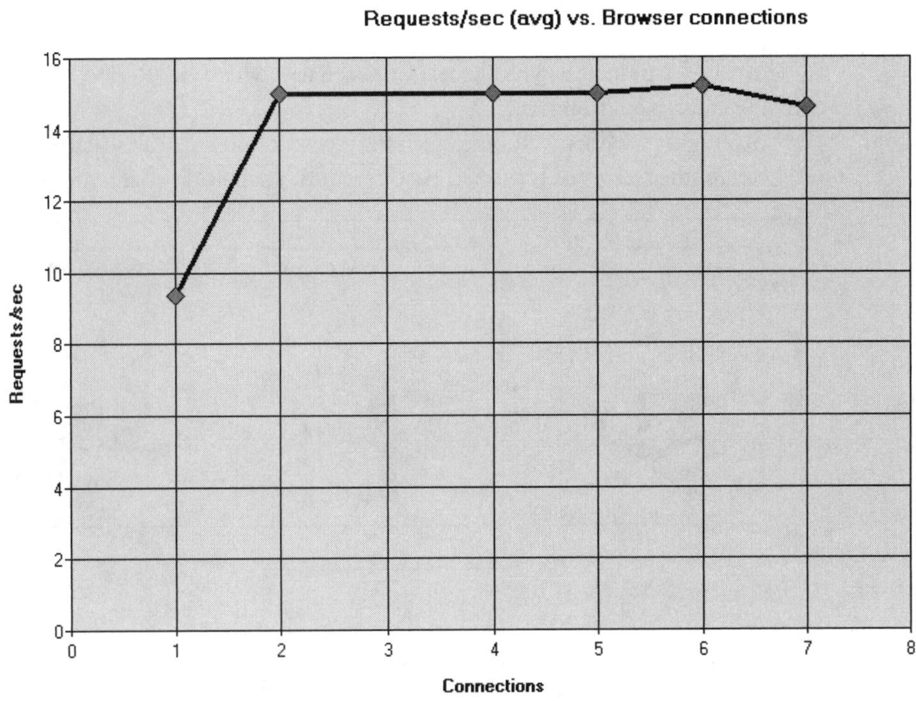

Figure 14.11 Using report caching is the easiest way to increase the Report Server's scalability.

scalability characteristics of RS and determine hardware and software requirements needed to support planned deployments.

You scale RS up by beefing up your server hardware, that is, by adding memory or CPU power. The memory capacity recommended by Microsoft for a production report server is 4GB of RAM.

When scaling up by adding more processors, you shouldn't expect linear scalability. For example, adding a second CPU may result in a 60 percent increase in performance, while adding a third CPU may result in only 30 percent more.

When scaling up becomes counterproductive, you can scale out RS by deploying it in a web farm environment.

Scaling out

You scale out RS by distributing the processing load across multiple report servers. Scaling out offers the following advantages:

- Allows you to incrementally add (or remove) resources as needed
- Makes it possible to balance heavy workloads across multiple servers configured in a web farm environment
- Offers fault tolerance, because even if one of the clustered servers fails, the rest of the cluster is unaffected

Figure 14.12 depicts a typical scale-out scenario where the Report Server is deployed in a web farm environment.

Scaling out works well because it results in almost linear scalability to the point where another resource is pushed past its limits, such as database, memory, or network

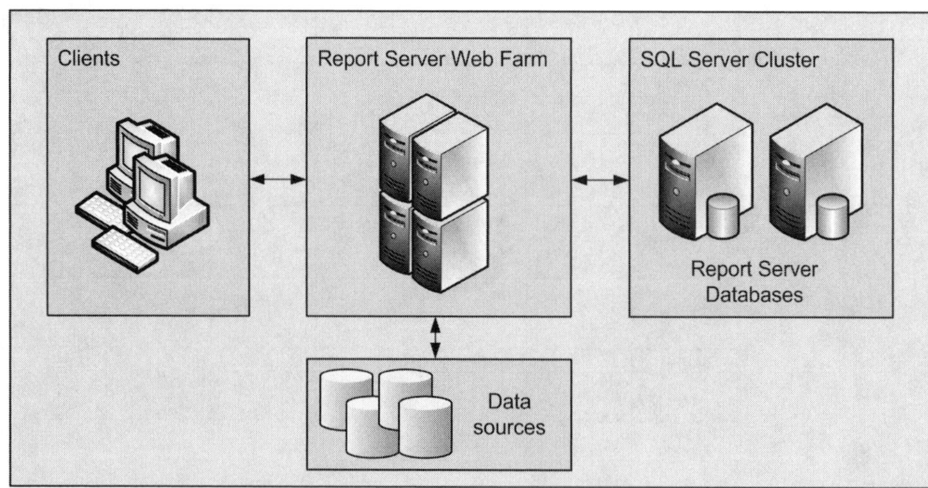

Figure 14.12 A typical enterprise deployment model uses a cluster of Report Servers and clustered Report Server databases.

utilization. In general, even if only one web server meets your performance objectives, we suggest that you pair it with a second server for fault-tolerance reasons.

The Reporting Services Enterprise and Developer editions support scaling out. When you scale out RS, multiple report servers share a single Report Server database (or a cluster of Report Server databases). When the RS Setup program detects that the Report Server database already exists, it assumes a web farm deployment and doesn't create the Report Server database.

For more information about setting up RS, read appendix A. For more information about configuring RS in a clustered web farm environment, read the "SQL Server Reporting Services Deployment Guide" document and the "Installing Reporting Services" section of the RS product documentation (see the "Resources" section at the end of this book).

14.3 SUMMARY

Thanks to its web-oriented stateless architecture, RS is well positioned to meet the high-volume reporting requirements of today's enterprises. This chapter has given you the necessary skills to find out whether your specific reporting infrastructure will meet your capacity needs.

Specifically, we discussed the capacity-planning process and learned how to establish performance goals. Next, we showed how you can stress-test the Report Server with the Visual Studio .NET Application Center Test.

Finally, we looked at ways to identify performance bottlenecks and increase the Report Server's capacity by scaling up and out.

Well, we are at the end of the RS journey! We've traveled a long and, we hope, enjoyable road to see how Reporting Services can help you author, manage, and integrate reports with your applications. We trust you have found this product to be a well-rounded, comprehensive reporting platform.

APPENDIX A

Installing SQL Server Reporting Services

For those of you who have installed SQL Server Reporting Services 2000, you will notice that the installation is different. First of all, SQL Server Reporting Services 2005 must be installed from the SQL Server media, and is not available as a separate installation. Also, the installation has been made much simpler. This appendix covers the installation of SQL Server Reporting Services. We won't go into detail about setting up other services such as Analysis Services, Integration Services, or Notification Services.

Let's start by examining the software requirements.

A.1 SOFTWARE REQUIREMENTS

Before you install SQL Server Reporting Services, make sure that you have the correct software setup. The following operating systems are supported by SQL Server Reporting Services 2005:

- Microsoft Windows Server 2000
- Microsoft Windows Server 2003
- Microsoft Windows XP Professional

In addition to the correct operating system, the server must have IIS 5.0 or greater installed and must be configured to use the Microsoft .NET Framework version 2.0 or later.

A.2 INSTALLING SQL SERVER REPORTING SERVICES

This section covers the preinstallation setup and installation steps for Reporting Services. After reading through these steps, you should have a good understanding of how to set up and configure Reporting Services to meet your needs.

A.2.1 Setting up the service account

Later in the installation setup, you will be asked to enter a service account for running the SQL Server Reporting Services service. You will need to set up this user before starting the wizard. To set up a local service account, follow these steps:

1. Open the Computer Management console.
2. Expand the Local Users and Groups node.
3. Right-click the Users folder and select New User.
4. Enter a username, description, and a strong password.
5. Clear the User Must Change Password at Next Logon check box and select the User Cannot Change Password check box.
6. Click Create.

A.2.2 Starting the setup wizard

To start the installation of Reporting Services, follow these steps:

1. Start the setup wizard from the installation CD.
2. Once you run Setup, the first screen you will be presented with is the End User License Agreement. Once you review the agreement, select the I Accept The Licensing Terms and Conditions check box, and click Next.
3. Review the required components from the Installing Prerequisites screen and click Install. At this point the SQL Server wizard will scan your computer's configuration. This step may take a few minutes. When it has finished successfully, click Next.
4. On the SQL Server Installation Welcome screen, click Next. The wizard will then do a system configuration check on your computer. If all checks are successful, the setup will continue. Otherwise you will need to fix any listed problems. Click Next.
5. On the Registration Information screen, enter your name and optionally your company. Then enter your 25-character Product Key and click Next.

A.2.3 Installing the components

The Components to Install screen is where you will select the components (or services) that you want to install. Figure A.1 shows the features that you should choose if you want to follow along with the examples provided in this book.

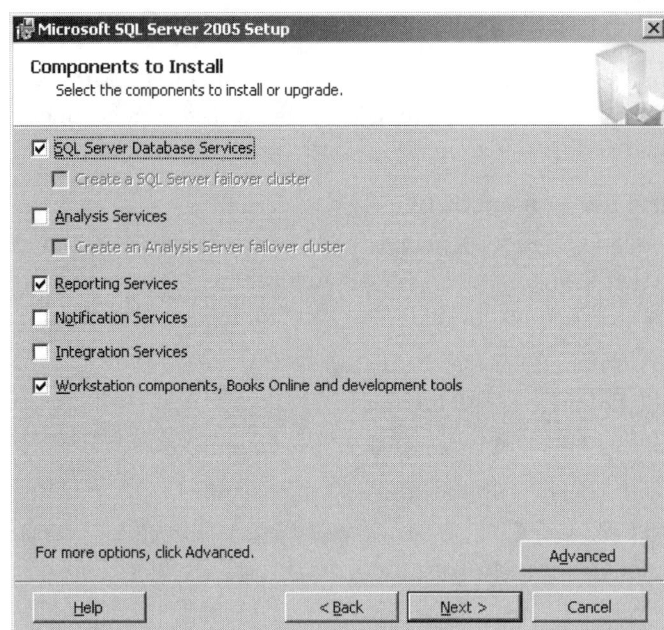

Figure A.1 The Components to Install screen lets you choose the components that you want for your installation.

This example assumes that you do not already have SQL Server installed. If you do you will not need to select the SQL Server Database Services check box.

1. Click the check boxes as shown in figure A.1.
2. You will see the Feature Selection screen displayed. Click the plus sign next to the Documentation, Samples, and Sample Databases. Then click the arrow next to Sample Databases and select Entire Feature Will Be Installed on Local Hard Drive. Then click the arrow next to Sample Code and Applications and select Entire Feature Will Be Installed on Local Hard Drive (figure A.2). Once you have selected the features, click Next.

   NOTE The Reporting Services samples and Adventure Works database is not installed by default. You will need the AdventureWorks database for the code samples and walkthroughs in this book.

3. The next screen is the Instance Name screen (figure A.3). If you have not installed SQL Server yet, you can select the Default instance; otherwise you will need to enter an instance name for this installation. Either select the Default instance option and click Next or select Named instance, enter a name, and click Next.

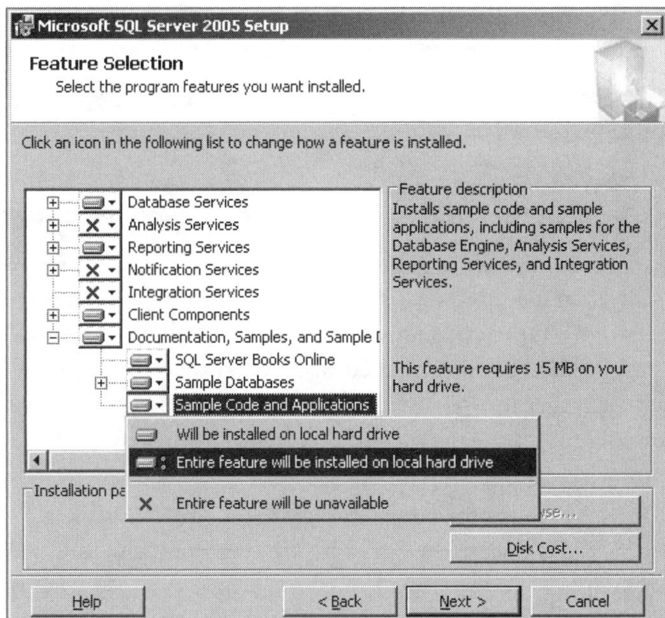

Figure A.2
You can choose the features of each component that you want installed on your local hard drive.

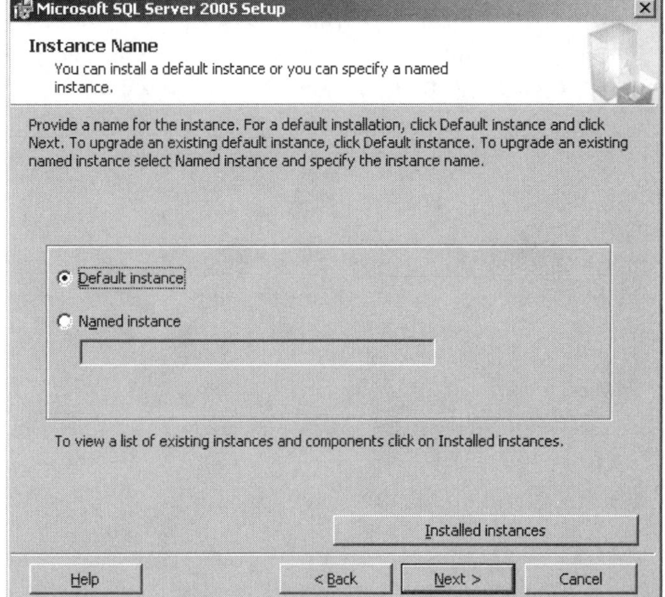

Figure A.3
The instance Name screen allows you to name the instance for this installation of SQL Server.

NOTE If you name the instance **TestInstance** you will need to change the URL for the Report Manager and the Report Web Service

from `http://localhost/reports` and `http://localhost/reportserver` to

`http://localhost/reports$TestInstance` and `http://localhost/reportserver$TestInstance`, respectively.

4 If the wizard finds any existing components on the machine, it will prompt you to select an upgrade option. In figure A.4 some components are already installed. To avoid upgrading this instance of SQL Server and Reporting Services, be sure to create a new Named instance in the previous step. It is worth mentioning here that it is possible to have installations of SQL Server 2000 and SQL Server 2005 on the same machine. It is also possible to have RS 2000 running side by side with RS 2005.

5 Choose a service account for your services to run under, as shown in figure A.5. You should create this service account before running the wizard.

6 If you are installing the Database Services, the next two screens will ask you to enter the authentication mode for connecting to SQL Server and the collation settings. Complete these screens and click Next.

7 The next screen (figure A.6) provides the choice of installing with the Default settings or installing without configuring the server. Choose Install the Default Configuration and click Next. If you want to change the default settings or if

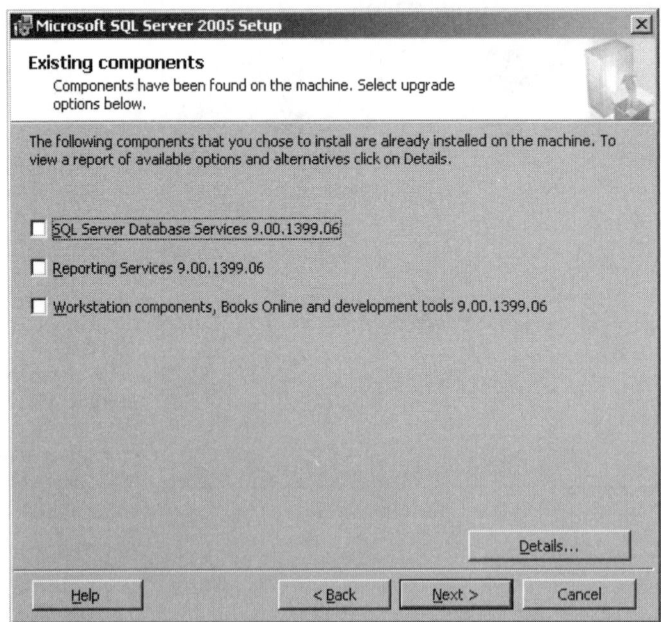

Figure A.4
If you have previous versions of components, the wizard will prompt you to upgrade them.

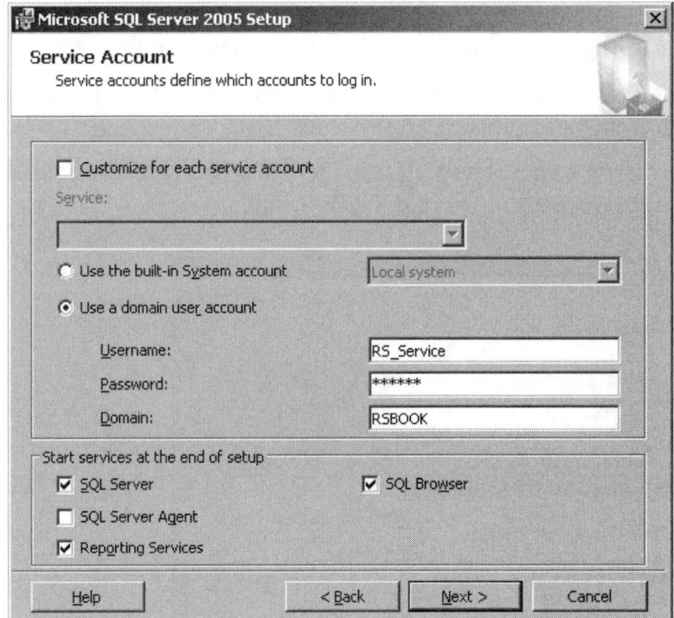

Figure A.5
You should have a dedicated service account to run the services.

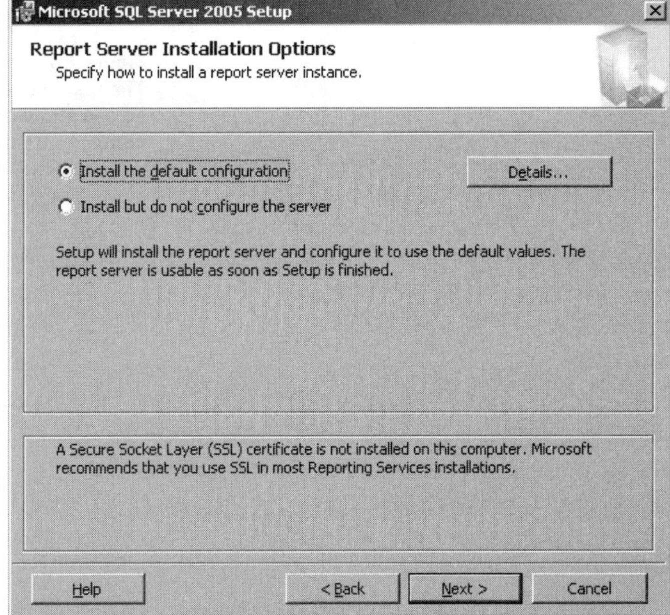

Figure A.6
The Report Server Installation Options allow you to choose how you want to configure Reporting Services.

you select Install But Do Not Configure the Server, you can use the Reporting Services Configuration tool that is described in chapter 8.

8 The next screen asks you to select whether you want information sent to Microsoft in the event that an error occurs. Make your selection and click Next.

9 The last wizard screen (figure A.7) is the Ready to Install screen, which shows you the components you selected. Click Install.

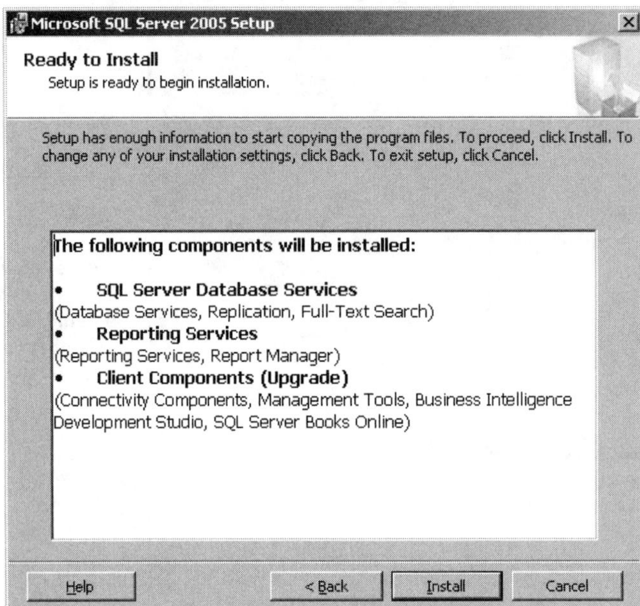

Figure A.7
The Ready to Install screen shows you the components that you are installing.

A P P E N D I X B

Understanding .NET code access security

Code access security is security that has no knowledge of the individual user and deals solely with the permissions management of your custom code. It can be used to "sandbox" custom code by taking advantage of the code access security infrastructure baked into the .NET CLR.

In chapters 6 and 13 you learned that you can execute virtually any piece of code from Reporting Services. The Report Server is an ASP.NET application that can execute custom code through the `Code` element of the report definition language. This includes calling existing assemblies as well as custom assemblies. Because of this tremendous flexibility, you need to be careful when managing security around this execution. With code access security, a user may have access to specific resources, but if the code the user executes is not trusted, access to the resource will be denied.

Because RS is written entirely in .NET-managed code, it can take full advantage of the code access security infrastructure built into the .NET CLR. To understand how you can manage the RS code access security model, you first need to learn how it works. By no means will we attempt to provide thorough coverage on this topic, which could easily fill a whole book.

B.1 CODE ACCESS SECURITY BASICS

As long as you don't plan to extend RS with custom code, you can live a happy and oblivious life without worrying about RS code access security (CAS). In fact, even if you decide to use custom code, for example, to call code in an external assembly or to create a custom data extension, you may find that in most cases the default CAS settings defined in the Report Server configuration files fulfill your needs. If this is the case, the only code access–related management task you need to learn is how to register the custom assemblies with the Report Server and Report Designer. You saw how to do this in chapter 6.

Sometimes, however, you may need to adjust the default code access policy. Usually, this will happen when the custom assembly needs more rights than the default permissions granted by the Report Server. You will know that this is the case when the Report Server complains with a `SecurityException` error. As a responsible administrator, you should learn how to solve this issue by giving the failing assembly the minimum set of permissions it needs to execute successfully. If you elevate the code access security too much, you open security holes that could be exploited by malicious code.

CAS is one of the most valuable, and arguably most misunderstood, services that the .NET Common Language Runtime (CLR) provides. In a nutshell, this security model grants permissions to code, not users. This is important because even if the Report Server runs under a highly privileged account, the CLR will sandbox custom code to restrict the actions it can execute. For example, the default RS code access security policy prevents custom code from writing to the Windows file system.

Let's turn now to common code access terminology.

B.2 UNDERSTANDING CODE ACCESS TERMINOLOGY

When RS loads an assembly, the .NET CLR goes through some decision making to determine what the assembly can do. As a part of this process, the CLR gathers some information about the assembly, which is called *evidence*. The assembly evidence is then passed to the CLR *code access security policy* for evaluation. Finally, the assembly is given a set of *permissions*, as shown in figure B.1.

Let's now discuss evidence, code access security, and permissions in more detail.

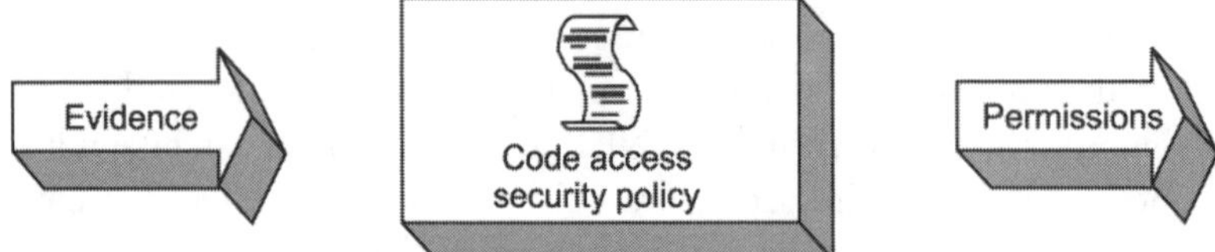

Figure B.1 The CLR code access security policy takes the assembly evidence as input and produces a permission set as output.

B.2.1 Exploring evidence

The assembly evidence provides the CAS policy with the following information about the assembly:

- The assembly origin, which tells the CLR where the assembly is loaded from, including the site, URL, zone, and application directory
- For strongly named assemblies, the assembly author information, which includes the assembly's strong name and publisher information

For example, as we saw in chapter 6, the Sales by Product Category report uses custom code located in the `AWC.RS.Library.dll` assembly. When RS processes the report, it gathers the following evidence about the assembly:

- *Zone*—MyComputer, because the code is loaded from the local file system
- *URL*—`file://C:\Program Files\Microsoft SQL Server\MSSQL\Reporting Services\ReportServer\bin\AWC.RS.Library.dll`

Because the assembly is not strongly named, there will be no evidence about its publisher and strong name.

Once the assembly evidence is obtained, this evidence is evaluated based on the security policy configured by the administrator.

B.2.2 Understanding code access security policies

The administrator can set up the security policy at the hierarchical levels listed in table B.1.

Table B.1 Code access security policy levels

Security level	Purpose
Enterprise	Applies to all machines that are part of an Active Directory installation.
Machine	Specifies the machine-wide policy settings.
User	Spells out the user-specific policy settings.
AppDomain	Includes settings specific to the application host domain. In case of RS, this is the Report Server host domain.

The first three security policy levels are defined in configuration files under the `C:\WINDOWS\Microsoft.NET\Framework\<version number>\CONFIG` folder. An application can override these settings by using an application-specific configuration file to scope the policy at the application level (more on this in a moment).

The recommended way to make changes to .NET configuration policy files is to use the CasPol utility or the .NET Configuration management console (shown in figure B.2).

The fourth policy level, AppDomain, is not shown in the .NET Configuration console and must be set programmatically. An application can use the AppDomain

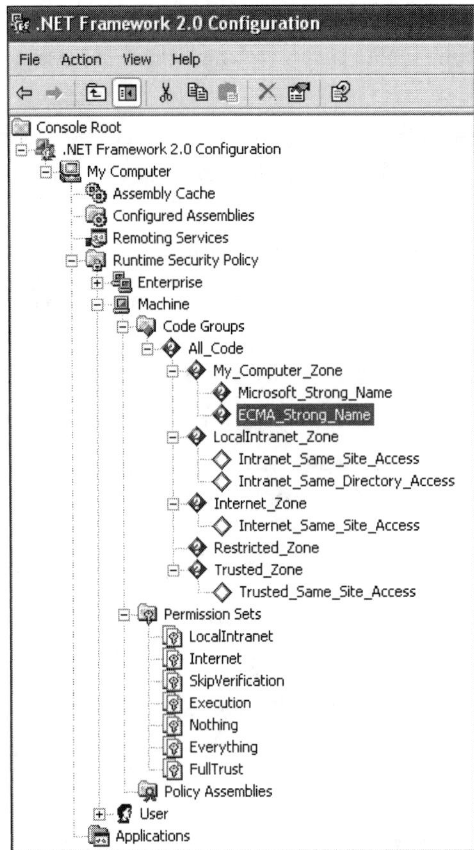

Figure B.2
To manage the .NET code access security policy, use the .NET Configuration console.

policy level to dynamically sandbox the .NET code by further restricting the set of permissions granted by the other three policy levels.

To use the AppDomain policy level, an application creates a separate application domain and calls `AppDomain.SetAppDomainPolicy`. The security policy configuration file can be loaded via a call to `SecurityManager.PolicyLevelFromFile`.

B.2.3 Overriding code access security policy

Now you know why the Enterprise, Machine, and User policies don't seem to apply to the RS code access security model. When the Report Server is initialized, it reads the `securityPolicy` element from the Report Server `web.config` file to determine the name of the configuration file that contains the CAS policies. By using the AppDomain policy level, the Report Server overrides the three levels with the policy settings from this file.

NOTE Although we highly discourage you from doing so, you can entirely bypass the Report Server CAS policy by commenting out the `securityPolicy` element. The net effect of doing so is reverting to the CAS policies defined in the .NET configuration files that you can manage using the .NET Configuration management console.

When the CLR evaluates the security policies, it starts from the enterprise-level policy and works its way down to determine the intersection of the permissions grants. Each policy level consists of three elements: a code group hierarchy, a list of predefined permission sets, and a list of fully trusted assemblies at this policy level.

Defining code groups

Policy levels can be further broken down into code groups. Most code groups are instances of `System.Security.Policy.UnionCodeGroup`. The CLR runtime comes with a number of predefined code groups. Four of them—Local Intranet, Internet, Restricted, and Trusted—correspond to Internet Explorer security zones. In fact, one of the easiest ways to elevate (or decrease) the allowed permissions in these zones is to use the Internet Explorer security-related settings. From the RS point of view, the only zone of interest is the MyComputer zone, because all custom code is loaded from the local file system.

To filter out the allowable permissions, each code group has a membership condition. For example, if you look at the properties of the My Computer code group, you will see that it defines a Zone membership condition, which applies the security policy to assemblies from the MyComputer zone only and assigns the `FullTrust` named permission set to it. As a result, if an assembly is evaluated as belonging to this code group and no further restrictions are imposed, its code can execute unrestricted.

To further restrict the security policy, each code group can contain nested code groups. When the CLR evaluates the code group membership of a given assembly, it traverses the code group hierarchy to find the right match for the assembly.

Using permission sets

Each code group can have a predefined set of permissions, also known as a *named permission set*. You can think of permission sets as equivalent to the role definition concept we discussed in the role-based security section. Similarly, you can relate the code access permissions to role tasks.

For example, figure B.3 shows the predefined permissions for the Execution permission set. To bring up this dialog box, click the Execution permission set in the .NET Configuration console (see figure B.2); then right-click the Security permission item in the right pane and choose View Permission from the context menu.

As you can see, the only allowable permission here is to execute code. This means that if a custom assembly needs to write to a file under the default Execution permission set, the method call will fail with a security exception.

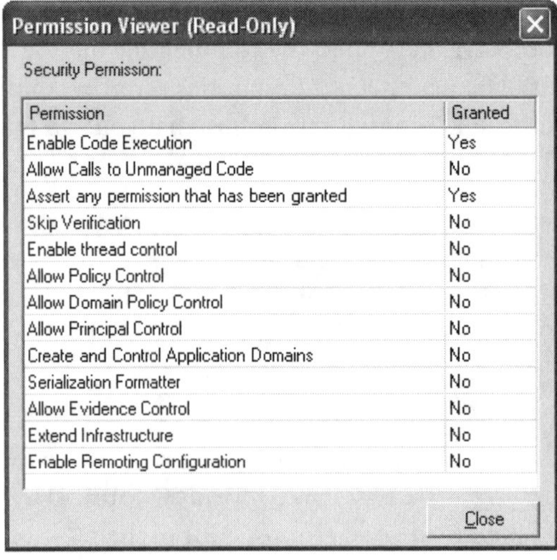

Figure B.3
By default, the Report Server is configured to grant custom code Execution rights only.

Most permission sets are instances of the `System.Security.NamedPermissionSet` class. The predefined permission sets cannot be modified. Instead, if they don't meet your security needs, you can create new permission sets. You may find this process similar to working with the RS role-based security model when you create new roles that include different sets of tasks.

B.3 EXPLORING THE RS DEFAULT SECURITY POLICY

How does our code access discussion relate to RS? As we mentioned, any custom code executed under the Report Server and Report Designer (in the Preview window) is subject to CAS restrictions. Not all custom code is created equal, though. To determine which permissions need to be assigned to the executing code, the Report Server categorizes the code by mapping it to a specific code access security policy.

In this section we will:

- Define the default code access permissions
- Explain the configuration files

B.3.1 Defining default code access permissions

RS defines default code access security policies for each category of custom code, as shown in table B.2.

For example, looking at table B.2, you can see that if a report calls external code in a custom assembly, code in this assembly will be assigned the Execution permission set by default. This is fine if this assembly is self-contained and doesn't access external resources that require a more restrictive set of permissions, for example, writing to

Table B.2 RS default code access security policies

Code category	Membership condition	Permission set
Report Server native assemblies	Strong name	Full Trust
Custom extensions	MyComputer zone	Require Full Trust
Expressions	MyComputer zone	Execution
Custom assemblies	MyComputer zone	Execution

files, opening database connections, and so on. If it does, then you need to adjust its code access policy accordingly.

B.3.2 Understanding configuration files

The default RS security policy is defined in policy configuration files. RS has three policy configuration files, one per each component, as shown in table B.3.

Table B.3 Policy configuration files

Component	Configuration file	Path
Report Server	`rssrvpolicy.config`	`C:\Program Files\Microsoft SQL Server\MSSQL.3\Reporting Services\ReportServer`
Report Manager	`rsmgrpolicy.config`	`C:\Program Files\Microsoft SQL Server\MSSQL.3\Reporting Services\ReportManager`
Report Designer	`rspreviewpolicy.config`	`C:\Program Files\Microsoft Visual Studio 8\Common7\IDE\PrivateAssemblies`

Why do you need to enforce CAS policy for the Report Designer? As you recall from our discussion in chapter 2, the Report Designer gives you the option to run the report in the Preview window. You can use the Preview window to simulate the Report Server environment by cloning its code access settings to the `rspreviewpolicy.config` configuration file. When you run the report (by pressing F5), the Report Host will read and apply these settings to sandbox the custom code that the report uses.

The Preview window mode allows the author of the report to change the CAS policy locally, and once the custom code executes properly, to propagate the configuration changes to the Report Server policy file. Note that previewing reports using the Report Designer's Preview tab bypasses the Report Designer's security policy and grants the Full Trust permission set to custom assemblies. Once again, to see the effect of the policy settings from the `rspreviewpolicy.config` configuration file, preview the report in the Preview window by running the report in Debug mode (press F5).

B.4 MANAGING RS CODE ACCESS SECURITY

The report administrator can easily adjust the CAS policies by making changes to the appropriate configuration files. For example, let's say our custom assembly, `MyAssembly`, requires the ability to read from the file `C:\MyFile.xml`. Because the default code access policy gives custom assemblies only Execution rights, when the assembly attempts to read from the file, it will fail.

As an administrator, you can rectify this situation in two ways. The first one is easier and not recommended. You can modify the Report Server policy file to give all custom assemblies Full Trust execution rights by making the following changes to `rssrv-policy.config` (and `rspreviewpolicy.config` for testing purposes):

```
<CodeGroup class="FirstMatchCodeGroup" version="1"
  PermissionSetName="FullTrust" Description="This code group
  grants MyComputer code Execution permission. ">
```

The important change here is that instead of Execution rights, now all custom code will be given Full Trust rights. Of course, the net effect of doing this will be kissing code access security good-bye for custom code execution. Therefore, you should resist the temptation to take the easy way and open security holes.

B.4.1 Defining custom permission sets and code groups

When you need to elevate the CAS policy, the recommended approach is to grant permissions on an as-needed basis. First, you can define a named permission set that includes the `FileIOPermission` permission to read from the file, as follows:

```
<PermissionSet class="NamedPermissionSet"
   version="1"
   Name="MyFilePermissionSet"
   Description="Grant access to read from myfile.xml.">
    <IPermission class="FileIOPermission"
       version="1"
       Read="C:\MyFile.xml"/>
</PermissionSet>
```

Once the permission set is defined, you can then create code groups to associate custom assemblies with the named permission set. For example, the code group definition might look like this:

```
 <CodeGroup class="UnionCodeGroup"
   version="1"
   PermissionSetName="MyFilePermissionSet"
   Name="MyAssemblyCodeGroup"
   Description="A code group specifically created for
   myassembly.dll">
   <IMembershipCondition class="UrlMembershipCondition"
      version="1"
      Url="C:\Program Files\Microsoft SQL Server\MSSQL.3\Reporting
      Services\ReportServer\bin\myassembly.dll"/>
</CodeGroup>
```

Note also that the CAS security is layered on top of the OS security. Therefore, in addition to the CAS settings, you need to grant the appropriate ACL permissions to any files that the custom assembly needs. In this case, the custom assembly requires at least Read permissions to `MyFile.xml`. To satisfy this requirement, open the file (or its containing folder) properties and grant the Report Server process account (by default, ASP.NET with IIS 5 or Network Service with IIS 6) Read permissions to this file.

How do you know which code access permissions a given assembly requires? Well, if the assembly developer has taken the effort to declare the required permissions using attributes, you can use the .NET Framework Permissions View tool, `Permview.exe`. Most often, though, you will find that this is not the case and you will have to rely on other sources, such as the product documentation or your peers from newsgroups. This entails the trial-and-error approach, which can be painful.

NOTE We struggled quite a bit to find out why the `OpenForecast` assembly, which we discussed in chapter 6, was failing to execute regardless of the fact that it was given Full Trust permission rights. We went through all possible permutations but to no avail. The strange thing was that neither `OpenForecast` nor its caller was accessing external resources. We went to the trouble of converting it to C# only to realize that the C# version was executing properly. Finally, we resorted to using `System.Diagnostics.Trace.WriteLine` to find out at what point the code was failing. Using the DbgView utility we were able to pinpoint the security violation to an overridden implementation of the `toString` method inside the Open-Source DataSet structure. Our code was calling this method to output the observed and forecasted values. Removing the tracing calls fixed the problem. The exact reason for the security violation was beyond us, but the moral of this story is this. If giving your custom code Full Trust permissions doesn't help, you should start exploring your code to find out at what point it fails. Once you manage to identify the offending line, the next step will be to find out which code access security permissions it requires. As a last resort, if nothing else works, you could bypass the Report Server CAS policy by commenting out the `securityPolicy` element in `web.config`, as we noted earlier. Before you decide to do this, however, make sure that you have a convincing story when you are asked to stand before the CAS court.

Currently, to the best of our knowledge, there is no tool to help you troubleshoot code access security problems. In future versions of the .NET Framework we'd like to see clearer error descriptions when a security exception is thrown. At least the exception message should spell out the name of the failing permission and the offending line of code. Our experience is that often this information is missing.

B.4.2 Granting custom assemblies Full Trust rights

Back in chapter 6 we said that `AWC.RS.Library` and `OpenForecast` assemblies require Full Trust permissions to execute successfully. Let's see what changes are required to accomplish this. The assemblies don't require any custom permission sets. To elevate the CAS policy for both assemblies from Execution to Full Trust, we need to add the following lines to the Report Designer (`rspreviewpolicy.config`) and Report Server (`rssrvpolicy.config`) security configuration files:

```
<CodeGroup
        class="UnionCodeGroup"
        version="1"
        PermissionSetName="FullTrust"
        Name="SharePoint_Server_Strong_Name"
    />
</CodeGroup>
<CodeGroup class="UnionCodeGroup" version="1"
   PermissionSetName="FullTrust" Name="AWCLibrary">
   <IMembershipCondition class="UrlMembershipCondition" version="1"
   Url="C:\Program Files\Microsoft SQL Server\MSSQL.3\Reporting
   Services\ReportServer\bin\AWC.RS.Library.dll"/>
</CodeGroup>
<CodeGroup class="UnionCodeGroup" version="1"
   PermissionSetName="FullTrust" Name="OpenForecast">
  <IMembershipCondition class="UrlMembershipCondition" version="1"
  Url="C:\Program Files\Microsoft SQL Server\MSSQL.3\Reporting
  Services\ReportServer\bin\OpenForecast.dll"/>
</CodeGroup>
```

Grants Full Trust to AWC.RS.Library.dll

Grants Full Trust to OpenForecast.dll

It is important to note that when elevating the code access rights for custom code, you need to do so for all custom assemblies where this code resides, because CLR will check the entire call stack. This is why we specifically granted full rights to both the `AWC.RS.Library` and `OpenForecast` assemblies.

B.4.3 Dealing with unmanaged resources

Sometimes, granting your custom code the Full Trust permission set may not be enough. This may be the case when you need to deal with unmanaged resources.

For example, you could have authored a custom dataset extension that opens a database connection through the .NET `System.Data.SqlClient.SqlConnection` managed wrapper to a SQL Server database. A database connection is an unmanaged resource, and your custom code requires explicit permissions to execute unmanaged code. Specifically, you declare a new permission set, as shown here:

```
 <PermissionSet class="NamedPermissionSet"  version="1"
                Unrestricted="true" Name="MyPermission">
  <IPermission
      class="SecurityPermission"
      version="1"
      Flags="UnmanagedCode" />
</PermissionSet>
```

Then you assert the permission needed in your custom code before accessing the unmanaged resource:

```
SqlClientPermission permission = new
            SqlClientPermission(PermissionState.Unrestricted);
try {
    permission.Assert(); // Assert security permission!
    SqlConnection con = new SqlConnection("...");
    con.Open();
    //do something with the connection
}
```

When the custom code is called from a report expression, you need to always assert the permission because the code access security checks walk up each stack frame and expect permissions at each level. The default CAS policy grants report expressions Execution rights only, so the security check will fail. `Assert` will short-circuit the stack walk at the current frame.

The MSDN documentation specifically states which permissions are needed by certain method calls. For example, in the case of the `SqlConnection` class, the documentation says, "SqlConnection makes security demands using the SqlClientPermission object." The `CodeAccessSecurityPermission.Assert` method call instructs CLR to grant your code the requested permission, regardless of the fact that its callers might not have rights to this permission.

For more information about code access security considerations, check out the security chapter in the product documentation.

resources

Here we provide additional resources and links to dive more deeply into specific topics from this book. The resources are organized by chapter and direct you to more information beyond the text of this book.

CHAPTER 1

- Microsoft RS website (www.microsoft.com/sql/technologies/reporting/default.mspx)—First stop for the latest on RS.
- Microsoft Business Intelligence Platform website (www.microsoft.com/sql/evaluation/BI/default.asp)—The Microsoft BI portal home page.
- A Guide to Developing and Running Connected Systems with Indigo (http://msdn.microsoft.com/msdnmag/issues/04/01/Indigo/)—In section 1.3 I emphasized the role of the RS service-oriented programming model. Read Don Box's article for more information about SOA.

CHAPTER 2

- Report Definition Language Specification (www.microsoft.com/sql/technologies/reporting/rdlspec.mspx)—Report Definition Language (RDL) is an XML-based schema for defining reports.
- Cizer's home page (www.cizer.com)—Cizer Software specializes in Microsoft-platform database reporting solutions.
- Hitachi's RDL Generator (www.hitachiconsulting.com/page.cfm?ID=pdfRepository&pdfId=251)—Hitachi Consulting provides services for converting Crystal Reports into the Reporting Services RDL format.
- Report Services Partners (www.microsoft.com/sql/technologies/reporting/partners.mspx)—A list of partner solutions that expand the benefits of SQL Server Reporting Services.

CHAPTER 3

- Connecting to a Data Source Using ADO.NET (`http://msdn.microsoft.com/library/default.asp?url=/library/en-us/cpguide/html/cpconConnectionPoolingForSQLServerNETDataProvider.asp`)—A chapter from the VS .NET documentation that discusses database connection pooling.
- Designing Data Tier Components and Passing Data Through Tiers (`http://msdn.microsoft.com/library/default.asp?url=/library/en-us/dnbda/html/BOAGag.asp`)—A good best practices read from the MSDN .NET Architecture Center that might be interesting for .NET developers. Learn how to best expose your data to Microsoft .NET applications and how to implement an effective strategy for passing data between the tiers in a distributed application.

CHAPTER 4

- The Dundas Software website (`www.dundas.com`)—Dundas is the creator of the charting features in Reporting Services. They also provide a wealth of charting products and add-ons for Reporting Services.

CHAPTER 5

- Globalizing and Localizing Applications (`http://msdn2.microsoft.com/en-us/library/1021kkz0.aspx`)—A chapter from the Visual Studio .NET documentation that introduces you to the internationalization features built into .NET.

CHAPTER 6

- The OpenForecast website (`http://openforecast.sourceforge.net/`)—OpenForecast is a package of general-purpose forecasting models written in Java that can be applied to any data series.
- Microsoft Java Language Conversion Assistant (`http://msdn.microsoft.com/vstudio/downloads/tools/jlca/default.aspx`)—Converts Java-language code to C#.
- Mark Russinovich's DebugView tool (`www.sysinternals.com/Utilities/DebugView.html`)—DebugView is an application that lets you monitor debug output on your local system or any computer on the network that you can reach via TCP/IP.
- What Is RSS? (`www.xml.com/pub/a/2002/12/18/dive-into-xml.html`)—A good introduction to RSS.
- Lutz Roeder's .NET Reflector (`www.aisto.com/roeder/dotnet/`)—Similar to the VS .NET Object Browser, Reflector is a class browser for .NET components.

CHAPTER 7

- Introduction to ClickOnce Deployment (`http://msdn.microsoft.com/vbasic/learning/clickonce/`)—ClickOnce is a deployment technology that allows you to create self-updating Windows-based applications that can be installed and run with minimal user interaction.

- Working with Snapshot Isolation (http://msdn2.microsoft.com/en-us/library/ms130975.aspx)—New with SQL Server 2005, Snapshot Isolation is intended to enhance concurrency for online transaction processing (OLTP) applications.
- User-Schema Separation (http://msdn2.microsoft.com/en-us/library/ms190387.aspx)—An explanation of the changes in User and Schema in SQL Server 2005.

CHAPTER 8

- SOAP Toolkit version 3.0 (http://msdn.microsoft.com/webservices/webservices/building/soaptk/default.aspx)—Download the SOAP Toolkit, which includes the SOAP Trace utility, from the Microsoft MSDN download center.
- TcpTrace (www.pocketsoap.com/tcptrace/)—A great utility that captures the TCP traffic between a client and a server.
- How To: Implement Kerberos Delegation for Windows 2000 (http://msdn.microsoft.com/library/default.asp?url=/library/en-us/dnnetsec/html/SecNet-HT05.asp)—This article lists the steps required to configure Kerberos authentication.

CHAPTER 9

- Microsoft Security Development Center (http://msdn.microsoft.com/security/)—Tons of excellent information to help you secure your applications, including entire books.
- Building Secure ASP.NET Applications: Authentication, Authorization, and Secure Communication (http://msdn.microsoft.com/library/en-us/dnnetsec/html/secnetlpMSDN.asp)—This guide presents a practical, scenario-driven approach to designing and building secure ASP.NET applications.

CHAPTER 10

- WebBrowser Control Overviews and Tutorials (http://msdn.microsoft.com/workshop/browser/webbrowser/browser_control_ovw_entry.asp)—Provides an overview and tutorial articles for the Microsoft WebBrowser control.
- Microsoft XML Parser (MSXML) (http://msdn.microsoft.com/library/default.asp?url=/library/en-us/xmlsdk/html/7e831db8-9d0a-43ff-87e9-11382721eb99.asp)—The MSXML Software Development Kit (SDK) provides conceptual and reference information for developers using MSXML.
- Building Secure ASP.NET Applications: Authentication, Authorization, and Secure Communication (http://msdn.microsoft.com/library/default.asp?url=/library/en-us/dnnetsec/html/secnetlpmsdn.asp)—This guide presents a practical, scenario-driven approach to designing and building secure ASP.NET applications.

- Web Services Enhancements (WSE) 1.0 SP1 for Microsoft .NET (`www.microsoft.com/downloads/details.aspx?FamilyId=06255A94-2635-4D29-A90C-28B282993A41&displaylang=en`)—Web Services Enhancements for Microsoft .NET (WSE) is an add-on to Microsoft Visual Studio .NET and the Microsoft .NET Framework, providing developers with the latest advanced Web services capabilities to keep pace with the evolving Web services protocol specifications, such as WS-Security, WS-Routing, WS-Attachments, and DIME specifications.
- Generic ASP.NET XML/XSL DHTML Menu ServerControl (`www.gotdotnet.com/Community/UserSamples/Details.aspx?SampleGuid=175796d4-d08b-4130-8bbf-8d1a7fa94d85`)—Generic ServerControl takes your custom XML, XSL, JavaScript, and CSS files and renders your DHTML drop-down or other menu. A sample implementation is included along with the article and documentation.
- About the WebService Behavior (`msdn.microsoft.com/workshop/author/webservice/overview.asp`)—The WebService behavior enables client-side script to invoke remote methods exposed by Web services, or other web servers, that support the SOAP and Web Services Description Language (WSDL) 1.1.

CHAPTER 11

- Web.config Settings for ReportViewer (`http://msdn2.microsoft.com/en-us/library/ms251661.aspx`)—There are several settings and options that can be configured in the `web.config` file for the ReportViewer control.
- Converting RDL and RDLC Files (`http://msdn2.microsoft.com/en-us/library/ms252109.aspx`)—If you use both the ReportViewer controls and Microsoft SQL Server 2005 Reporting Services, you can reuse the reports that you create in both reporting technologies.

CHAPTER 12

- SMTP (Simple Mail Transfer Protocol) Server (`http://msdn.microsoft.com/library/default.asp?url=/library/en-us/smtpevt/html/5c031f56-29bf-4fcb-abf6-3eab6789a5bf.asp`)—Learn how to configure an e-mail server using the Windows 2003 SMTP and POP3 services.
- Delivering Reports Through Subscriptions (`http://msdn2.microsoft.com/en-us/library/ms159762.aspx`)—SQL Server Reporting Services distributes reports through subscriptions. Reporting Services provides two ways to deliver reports: you can send reports through e-mail, or you can deliver reports to a file share on the file system. When you create a subscription, you specify which delivery mode to use.

CHAPTER 13

- Custom Dataset Data Extension for Microsoft Reporting Services (`www.gotdotnet.com/Community/UserSamples/Details.aspx?SampleGuid=B8468707-56EF-4864-AC51-D83FC3273FE5`)—My custom dataset extension uploaded to the GotDotNet site.

- Christian Weyer's Dynamic XML Web Services Invocation sample (www.gotdotnet.com/Community/UserSamples/Details.aspx?SampleGuid=e9c2f46f-449b-4344-b796-7d8b63a2f954)—Dynamically creates a proxy from the Web service WSDL file.
- "Authentication in Reporting Services" white paper on MSDN (http://msdn2.microsoft.com/en-us/library/ms152899.aspx)—A must-read for implementing custom security extensions.
- Securely Implement Request Processing, Filtering, and Content Redirection with HTTP Pipelines in ASP.NET (http://msdn.microsoft.com/msdnmag/issues/02/09/http-pipelines/)—A great article by Tim Ewald and Keith Brown that introduces you to the architecture of the ASP.NET pipeline and shows you how to create your own HTTP modules and handlers.
- The SoftArtisans OfficeWriter (http://officewriter.softartisans.com/officewriter-250.aspx)—Reporting Services reports can now be designed directly in Microsoft Word and Excel; business users can thus avoid report design tools that may be unfamiliar to them.

CHAPTER 14

- *Performance Testing Microsoft .NET Web Applications* (www.amazon.com/exec/obidos/tg/detail/-/0735615381/qid=1080272077/sr=8-1/ref=sr_8_xs_ap_i1_xgl14/104-6183135-6491931?v=glance&s=books&n=507846)—Direct from a Microsoft team that has analyzed hundreds of web-based and .NET-based applications, this book shows developers how to plan and execute performance tests, configure profile tools, analyze data from Microsoft Internet Information Services, analyze transaction costs, and more.
- The "Performance" chapter from the Visual Studio .NET documentation (http://msdn.microsoft.com/library/default.asp?url=/library/en-us/vsent7/html/vxconperformanceoverview.asp)—Discusses how to write efficient and scalable .NET applications.
- The Compuware Application Expert tool (www.compuware.com/products/vantage/appexpert.htm)—An excellent tool that you can use to find out how changes in network bandwidth, latency, load, and TCP window size affect the application's response time.
- The Analog analyzer (www.analog.cx)—Analog is a tool that is good for measuring the usage on your web server. It tells you which pages are most popular, from which countries people are visiting, from which sites they tried to follow broken links, and all sorts of other helpful information.
- ReportMagic for Analog (www.reportmagic.org)—By harnessing the power of Analog and building readable, compelling reports, Report Magic can help you and the rest of your organization understand how your website is used.

APPENDIX A

- Installing SQL Server Reporting Services (http://msdn2.microsoft.com/en-us/library/ms143736.aspx)—This article provides an overview of installing and configuring Reporting Services.

APPENDIX B

- Code Access Security (http://msdn.microsoft.com/library/en-us/cpguide/html/cpconcodeaccesssecurity.asp)—From the *.NET Framework Developer's Guide.*
- Introducing Code Access Security in Reporting Services (http://msdn2.microsoft.com/fr-fr/library/ms154658.aspx)—This article outlines the new code access security policies of Microsoft SQL Server 2000 Reporting Services.
- The Security Infrastructure of the CLR Provides Evidence, Policy, Permissions, and Enforcement Services (http://msdn.microsoft.com/msdnmag/issues/02/09/SecurityinNET/)—In this article, Don Box explains how code access security works in the CLR.
- Security in .NET: Enforce Code Access Rights with the Common Language Runtime (http://msdn.microsoft.com/msdnmag/issues/01/02/CAS/)—Keith Brown's article on the same topic.

index

Symbols

A

B

C

D

E

F

G

H

I

J

K

Q

R

S

T

X

Z

Windows Explorer